CONTEMPORARY THOUGHT ON
NINETEENTH CENTURY SOCIALISM

CONTEMPORARY THOUGHT ON NINETEENTH CENTURY SOCIALISM

General Editors
Peter Gurney and Kevin Morgan

Volume I
Owenism

Edited by
Ophélie Siméon

LONDON AND NEW YORK

First published 2021
by Routledge
2 Park Square, Milton Park, Abingdon, Oxon OX14 4RN

and by Routledge
52 Vanderbilt Avenue, New York, NY 10017

Routledge is an imprint of the Taylor & Francis Group, an informa business

© 2021 selection and editorial matter, Ophélie Siméon; individual owners retain copyright in their own material.

The right of Ophélie Siméon to be identified as the author of the editorial material, and of the authors for their individual chapters, has been asserted in accordance with sections 77 and 78 of the Copyright, Designs and Patents Act 1988.

All rights reserved. No part of this book may be reprinted or reproduced or utilised in any form or by any electronic, mechanical, or other means, now known or hereafter invented, including photocopying and recording, or in any information storage or retrieval system, without permission in writing from the publishers.

Trademark notice: Product or corporate names may be trademarks or registered trademarks, and are used only for identification and explanation without intent to infringe.

British Library Cataloguing-in-Publication Data
A catalogue record for this book is available from the British Library

Library of Congress Cataloging-in-Publication Data
A catalog record for this book has been requested

ISBN: 978-1-138-49019-2 (set)
eISBN: 978-1-351-03570-5 (set)
ISBN: 978-1-138-32104-5 (volume I)
eISBN: 978-0-429-45237-6 (volume I)

Typeset in Times New Roman
by Apex CoVantage, LLC

Publisher's Note
References within each chapter are as they appear in the original complete work

CONTENTS

Preface   xxxi

General introduction: socialism before the age of party   1
PETER GURNEY AND KEVIN MORGAN

Volume I   Owenism
EDITED BY OPHÉLIE SIMÉON

Introduction   13
OPHÉLIE SIMÉON

PART 1
Work as it was and how it might be   27

1   "An Address to the Superintendents of Manufactories, and to those Individuals generally, who, by giving Employment to an aggregated Population, may easily adopt the Means to form the Sentiments and Manners of such a Population", in *A New View of Society, or, Essays on the Formation of the Human Character: Preparatory to the Development of a Plan for Gradually Ameliorating the Condition of Mankind*, III (London: printed for Longman, Hurst, Rees, Orme, and Brown, [1814] 1816), 71–77.   29
ROBERT OWEN

2   "Evidence of Robert Owen on his New Lanark Experiment", in *Report of Minutes of Evidence, taken before the Select Committee on the State of Children employed in the Manufactories of the United Kingdom* (London: Hansard, 1816), 20–28.   33
HOUSE OF COMMONS

CONTENTS

3   "Letter, dated July 25 and 16, 1817, containing a Further Development of the Plan contained in the Report to the Committee of the Association for the Relief of the Manufacturing and Labouring Poor, with Answers and Objections" (1817), in *A Supplementary Appendix to the First Volume of The Life of Robert Owen, Containing a Series of Reports, Addresses, Memorials, and Other Documents, Referred to in That Volume. 1803–1820* (London: Effingham Wilson, 1858) Appendix I.2, 65–78.   38
ROBERT OWEN

4   *Remarks on the Practicability of Mr. Robert Owen's Plan to Improve the Condition of the Lower Classes* (London: S. Leigh, 1819), 25–28.   43
PHILANTHROPOS [JOHN MINTER MORGAN]

5   "On the Causes of the Distress Prevalent in Great Britain", in *Report of the Committee appointed at a Meeting of Journeymen, Chiefly Printers, to take into Consideration Certain Propositions, Submitted to Them by Mr. George Mudie, Having for their Object a System of Social Arrangement, Calculated to Effect Essential Improvements in the Condition of the Working Classes* (London: The Medallic Cabinet, 1821), 4–5.   45
GEORGE MUDIE

6   "Rights of Industry. Founding of the National Regeneration Society in Favour of the Eight-Hour Day", *Crisis*, 7 December 1833, 117.   48
JOSHUA MILNE

7   "Master v. Slave. On Paid Labour in Communities", *New Moral World*, 2 February 1839, 228–229.   51
BENJAMIN WARDEN

PART 2
Visions of the future   55

8   *Address Delivered to the Inhabitants of New Lanark, on January 1st, 1816, on the Opening of the Institution Established for the Formation of Character* (London: Hatchard, 1816).   57
ROBERT OWEN

CONTENTS

9   "Prospectus", *Economist*, 19 January 1821, viii–xii.   79
GEORGE MUDIE

10   *The Revolt of the Bees* (London: printed for Longman, Rees, Orme, Browne and Greene [1826] 1839), 22–27.   86
JOHN MINTER MORGAN

11   "The Social System, Chapter V [continued], Constitutions, Laws and Regulations of a Community", *New Harmony Gazette*, 21 February 1827.   89
ROBERT OWEN

12   "One of 'the People'", "To the Wealth-Producing Classes of England", *Magazine of Useful Knowledge and Co-operative Miscellany*, n°1, January 1830, 7–10.   96
WILLIAM LOVETT

13   "To the Socialists of Great Britain. Letter from Tytherly Community", *New Moral World*, 30 November 1839, 920–922.   100
GEORGE FLEMING

PART 3
Concepts of political change   105

14   *A New View of Society, or, Essays on the Formation of the Human Character: Preparatory to the Development of a Plan for Gradually Ameliorating the Condition of Mankind* (London: printed for Longman, Hurst, Rees, Orme and Brown, 1816), Fourth Essay, 143–170.   107
ROBERT OWEN

15   "Motion Respecting Mr. Owen's Plan", *Parliamentary Debates* (London: Hansard), 16 December 1819.   119
HOUSE OF COMMONS

16   *Lectures on an Entire New State of Society: Comprehending an Analysis of British Society, Relative to the Production and Distribution of Wealth, the Formation of Character, and Government, Domestic and Foreign* (London: J. Brooks, 1830) III, 42–45.   141
ROBERT OWEN

CONTENTS

17 *An Address, Delivered to the Members of the New Mechanics' Institution, Manchester, on Friday Evening, March 25, 1831: On the Necessity of an Extension of Moral and Political Instruction among the Working Classes* (Manchester: W. Strange, 1831).   143
ROWLAND DETROSIER

18 *The First Trumpet. An Address to the Disciples of Robert Owen, on the Importance and Necessity of Speedily Accomplishing a Bond of Union of Mutual Interest, for Gradually carrying into Operation the New Science of Society* (London: J. Brooks, 1832).   156
WILLIAM CAMERON

19 "Liverpool - First Public Social Festival and Ball", letter to the editor of the *Liverpool Chronicle*, 29 November 1838, reprinted in the *New Moral World*, 1 December 1838, 91.   174
JOHN FINCH

20 "Progress of Moral Reform. Mr. Campbell's Missionary Tour", *New Moral World*, 30 March 1839, 362.   177
ALEXANDER CAMPBELL

PART 4
Political economy   179

21 *Report to the County of Lanark, of a Plan for Relieving Public Distress* (Glasgow: Wardlaw & Cunninghame [1820] 1821), 1–7.   181
ROBERT OWEN

22 *Labour Defended against the Claims of Capital or the Unproductiveness of Capital Proved with Reference to the Present Combinations Amongst Journeymen* (London: Knight and Lacey, 1825), 83–92.   187
THOMAS HODGSKIN

23 *Labor Rewarded. The Claims of Labor and Capital Conciliated: or, How to Secure to Labor the Whole Products of its Exertions. By One of the Idle Classes* (London: printed for Hunt and Clarke, 1827), 75–88.   191
WILLIAM THOMPSON

CONTENTS

24 "Laws of the Birmingham Co-operative Society, and Trading Fund Association", in *An Address Delivered at the Opening of the Birmingham Cooperative Society* (Birmingham: printed for W. Plastans, and published by the Society, 1828), 27–32.   203
WILLIAM PARE

25 "Sketch of a Commercial Constitution", in *The Social System: a Treatise on the Principle of Exchange* (Edinburgh: William Tait, 1831), 30–39.   210
JOHN GRAY

26 *Gazette of the Exchange Bazaars, and Practical Guide to the Rapid Establishment of the Public Prosperity*, 20 October 1832, n°5.   215
GEORGE MUDIE

27 "An Outline of a Social Movement", in *Labour's Wrongs and Labour's Remedy; or, The Age of Might and the Age of Right* (Leeds: David Green, 1839), 154–176.   219
JOHN FRANCIS BRAY

PART 5
Ways of organising   237

28 "Articles of Agreement of the Establishment at Orbiston", *Register for the First Society of Adherents to Divine Revelation, at Orbiston*, n°1, 10 November 1825.   239

29 "Proceedings of the London Co-operative Society. An Address Delivered before the Society, on New Year's-Day", *Co-operative Magazine and Monthly Herald*, n°2, February 1826, 54–59.   242

30 "Rules and Regulations of the Equitable Labour Exchange, Gray's Inn Road, London, for the Purpose of Relieving the Productive Classes from Poverty, by their Own Industry, and for the Mutual Exchange of Labour for Equal Value of Labour", *Crisis*, n°27, 8 September 1832, 105–106.   248

31 "Incipient Community" in *Proceedings of the Third Cooperative Congress, held in London* (London: W. Strange, 1832), 85–95.   254

CONTENTS

32 *Rules and Regulations of the Grand National Consolidated Trades' Union of Great Britain and Ireland: instituted for the Purpose of More Effectually Enabling the Working Classes to Secure, Protect, and Establish the Rights of Industry* (London: Harjette and Saville, 1834). 266

33 "Progress of Social Reform", *New Moral World*, 6 August 1843, 46–47. 274

34 Universal Community of Rational Religionists, *The Constitution and Laws of the Rational Society: as Agreed to at the Annual Congress, held at Harmony Hall, Hants., May 10, 1843* (London: printed and published for the Society by W. Johnston, 1843). 277

PART 6
Democracy and the State 291

35 *An Address to the Working Classes* (1819), reprinted in *A Supplementary Appendix to the First Volume of the Life of Robert Owen* . . . (London: Effingham Wilson, 1858), 225–231. 295
ROBERT OWEN

36 *Fanny Wright Unmasked by her Own Pen. Explanatory Notes, Respecting the Nature and Objects of the Institution of Nashoba, and of the Principles Upon Which It is Founded, Addressed to the Friends of Human Improvement, in All Countries and of All Nations* (New York: printed for the purchasers [1827] 1830). 302
FRANCES WRIGHT

37 "Mr. Owen's Memorial to the Republic of Mexico, and a Narrative of the Proceedings Thereon", in *Robert Owen's Opening Speech, and His Reply to the Rev. Alex. Campbell* . . . (Cincinnati: published for R. Owen, 1829), 184–190. 317
ROBERT OWEN

38 *An Address to the Working Classes on the Reform Bill* (London: W. Strange, 1831), 13–16. 322
WILLIAM CARPENTER

CONTENTS

39 *Poor Man's Guardian*, 14 January 1832, 245–246. 328
    HENRY HETHERINGTON

40 *Model Republic: a Monthly Journal of Politics, Literature, and Theology*, n°1, 1 January 1843, 1–4. 332
    JAMES NAPIER BAILEY

41 "Meeting of Congress, Friday, May 10, 1844", *New Moral World*, 8 June 1844, 402–404. 336

PART 7
The new religion and the old 341

42 *Economist*, n°51, 2 March 1821, 399–408. 343
    "PHILADELPHUS" [BENJAMIN SCOTT JONES]

43 *The Religious Creed of the New System* (Edinburgh: printed by D. Schaw, 1824), 3–6. 351
    ABRAM COMBE

44 "Address Delivered at the Annual Congress of the Association of All Classes of All Nations, held in Manchester, from the 10th to the 30th of May, 1837", in *Six Lectures Delivered in Manchester previously to the Discussion between Mr. Robert Owen and the Rev. J.H. Roebuck* (Manchester: A. Heywood, 1837), 102–112. 355
    ROBERT OWEN

45 "Policy versus Principle. To the Socialists of England. Letter V", *Oracle of Reason; Or, Philosophy Vindicated*, n°11, 5 March 1842, 89–91. 363
    CHARLES SOUTHWELL

46 *Religion Superseded, or the Moral Code of Nature Sufficient for the Guidance of Man* (London: Watson, 1844). 369
    EMMA MARTIN

47 "Account of an Owenite Nuptial Ceremony", *New Moral World*, 29 March 1845, 319. 382
    "T.B."

xi

CONTENTS

PART 8
Gender, sexuality and family relations   385

48   "Conclusion, in which some Thoughts on Female Education are Offered", in *An Astronomical Catechism, Or, Dialogues Between a Mother and her Daughter* (London: printed for and sold by the author, 1818), 345–359.   387
CATHERINE VALE WHITWELL

49   *Appeal to One Half of the Human Race, Women, Against the Pretensions of the Other Half, Men: to Retain in Political, and Thence in Civil and Domestic Slavery; in Reply to a Paragraph of Mr. Mill's Celebrated "Article on Government"* (London: Longman, Hurst, Rees, Orme, Brown and Green, 1825), 198–206.   395
WILLIAM THOMPSON AND ANNA DOYLE WHEELER

50   "Rights of Women. A Lecture delivered by Mrs. Wheeler, last year, in a Chapel near Finsbury Square", *British Co-operator*, 1830, 12–15.   401
ANNA DOYLE WHEELER

51   *Moral Physiology; or, A Brief and Plain Treatise on the Population Question* (New York: Wright and Owen, 1830), 13–18.   406
ROBERT DALE OWEN

52   "To Robert Owen, Esq.", *Crisis*, 22 June 1833, 189–190.   410
"CONCORDIA"

53   *Lectures on the Marriages of the Priesthood of the old Immoral World, Delivered in the year 1835, before the passing of the new Marriage Act* (Leeds: J. Hobson [1835] 1840), 3–14.   414
ROBERT OWEN

54   "On the Necessary Co-operation of Both Sexes for Human Advancement", *New Moral World*, 26 August 1843, 65.   423
"M.A.S."

PART 9
War, peace and internationalism 427

55 "Memorial of Robert Owen, of New Lanark, in Scotland, to the Allied Powers Assembled in Congress, at Aix-la-Chapelle, on Behalf of the Working Classes, 1818", reprinted in *Manifesto of Robert Owen*... (London: Effingham Wilson, 1840), 31–41. 429
ROBERT OWEN

56 Constitution of the Blue Spring Community for the Promotion of Science and Industry (1826). 440

57 "Ralahine (Ireland); or Human Improvement and Human Happiness", Letters I–IV, *New Moral World*, 31 March–21 April 1838. 446
JOHN FINCH

58 "Proceedings of Congress, Saturday, May 16, 1840", *New Moral World*, 13 June 1840, 1314–1316. 457

59 *Report to a Meeting of Intending Emigrants: Comprehending a Practical Plan for Founding Co-operative Colonies of United Interests in the North-Western Territories of the United States* (London: W. Ostell, 1843), 2–10. 465
THOMAS HUNT

60 "Progress of Social Reform on the Continent. N° II. Germany and Switzerland", *New Moral World*, 18 November 1843, 161–162. 470
FRIEDRICH ENGELS

61 "Meeting of English and Foreign Communists", *New Moral World*, 28 September 1844, 109–111. 477

Bibliography 492

Volume II Socialism and Co-operation in Britain, 1850–1918
EDITED BY PETER GURNEY

Introduction: socialism and co-operation in Britain, 1850–1918 1
PETER GURNEY

CONTENTS

PART 1
Redefining socialism 21

1   "Labour and the Poor", *Fraser's Magazine*, January 1850, 13–18. 23
    J.M. LUDLOW

2   *Report of the 2nd Co-operative Conference held at Manchester ... 1853* (London: E. Lumley, 1853), 3–7. 28
    E.V. NEALE

3   *Life and Last days of Robert Owen, of New Lanark* (London: Holyoake & Co., 1859), 17–24. 33
    G.J. HOLYOAKE

4   "Industrial Co-operation", *Fortnightly Review*, January 1866, 479–488, 491–493, 497–499. 40
    FREDERIC HARRISON

5   "The Land! The Land!", *Co-operative News*, 5 October 1872, 505–506. 53
    WILLIAM PARE

6   "Co-operative Villages – Co-operation and Communism", *Co-operative News*, 12 February 1876; 19 February 1876, 81, 93. 58
    GEORGE DAWSON

7   "Modern English Communism", *Co-operative News*, 25 August 1877, 448. 65
    W.H.C.

8   "Advanced Co-operation, the Socialism of England", *English Socialism* (Manchester: Abel Heywood, 1879), 1–7. 71
    HENRY TRAVIS

PART 2
Political economy 77

9   *The Economic Advantages of Co-operation Substantiated. A letter addressed to the Rev. Norman Macleod, D.D., proving the truth of the large profits from co-operative economy, as stated at the*

CONTENTS

Glasgow meeting of the Association for the Promotion of Social Science (Leeds: David Green, 1860), 12–18, 21–23, 25–26, 29–30.   79
JOHN HOLMES

10   "Land, Free Trade, and Reciprocity", *Co-operator*, 4 December 1869, 836–837.   85
JOHN PARKER

11   *The Logic of Co-operation* (Manchester: Co-op Printing Society, 1873), 6–11.   89
G.J. HOLYOAKE

12   "Suggestions for Carrying out the Proposals for the Education of Co-operators", *Co-operative News*, 4 November 1882, 743–744.   94
BEN JONES

13   *Inaugural address delivered at the twenty-first annual Co-operative Congress . . . 1889* (Manchester: Central Co-operative Board, 1889), 3–5, 7–13, 28–30.   99
ALFRED MARSHALL

14   *The Marriage of Labour and Capital* (London: The Labour Association, 1896), 1–3, 6–8.   106
HODGSON PRATT

15   Resolution and Discussion on Trusts, *The 35th Annual Co-operative Congress, 1903* (Manchester: Co-op Union, 1903), 345–347.   111

PART 3
Class, democracy and the State   115

16   "Discussion at Halifax", *Notes to the People*, Vol. 2, 1852, 793–806, 823–829.   117
ERNEST JONES AND LLOYD JONES

17   *Co-operation v. Socialism: Being a Report of a Debate between Mr H. H. Champion and Mr Ben Jones* (Manchester: Central Co-op Board, 1887), 6–23.   148

CONTENTS

18 *Trade Unionism, Co-operation, and Social Democracy* (London: Twentieth Century Press, 1892), 10–16.   158
HARRY QUELCH

19 *Co-operation is Reasonable Socialism* (Manchester: Co-op Union, 1894), 1–8.   165
W.T. CARTER

20 *The Co-operative Movement in Great Britain* (London: Swan Sonnenschein, 3rd edn, 1895), 224–241.   172
BEATRICE WEBB

21 "Trade Unionism and Co-operation", in Edward Carpenter (ed), *Forecasts of the Coming Century* (Manchester: Labour Press, 1897), 31–36, 40.   181
TOM MANN

22 *Co-operative News*, 29 April 1905, 493.   186
PHILIP SNOWDEN

23 "The Conflict of Capitalism and Democracy", *CWS Annual* (Manchester: CWS, 1910), 191–192, 196–198, 201–218.   189
PERCY REDFERN

24 *Justice*, 10 May 1913, 7.   208
JOHN MACLEAN

PART 4
Utopianism and the religion of co-operation   211

25 J.T.W. Mitchell's presidential address, *The 24th Annual Co-operative Congress, 1892* (Manchester: Co-op Union, 1892), 6–8.   213
J.T.W. MITCHELL

26 *Co-operative Production* (Oxford: Oxford University Press, 1894), 730–732, 809–815.   222
BEN JONES

CONTENTS

27 *Co-operation as a Democratic Force: Being a Sermon Preached before the Delegates at the Co-operative Congress, Huddersfield on June 9th, 1895, in Fitzwilliam Street Unitarian Church* (London: The Labour Association, 1895), 1–7. 229
    RAMSDEN BALMFORTH

28 "The 'Community Idea'", *Millgate Monthly*, November 1908, 87–91. 236
    CATHERINE WEBB

29 *Co-operation for All* (Manchester: Co-op Union, 1914), 115–124. 243
    PERCY REDFERN

PART 5
Gender and consumer organising 251

30 "Vice President's Address", Miss Greenwood on women's position, *Report of the 17th Annual Congress of Delegates from Co-operative Societies . . . 1885* (Manchester: Co-op Union, 1885), 71–72. 253

31 *The Marcroft Family and the Inner Circle of Human Life* (Rochdale: E. Wrigley & Sons Ltd., 1888), 50–52. 256
    WILLIAM MARCROFT

32 *The Relations between Co-operation and Socialistic Aspirations* (Manchester: Co-op Union, 1890), 12–13. 259
    MARGARET LLEWELYN DAVIES

33 *The Women's Guild and Store Life* (London: 1892), 1–8. 266
    CATHERINE WEBB

34 *The Women's Co-operative Guild, 1883–1904* (Kirkby Lonsdale: WCG, 1904), 141–147, 161–163. 273
    MARGARET LLEWELYN DAVIES

35 "The Efforts of Women in the Co-operative Movement", *Bolton Co-operative Record*, January 1916, 8–9. 279
    SARAH REDDISH

PART 6
Internationalism, empire and war 283

36 *International Co-operation and the Constitution of the International Co-operative Alliance* (London: Co-op Printing Society, 1895), 1–8. 285
EDWARD OWEN GREENING

37 *Wheatsheaf*, October 1902, 52–53. 291
ÉDOUARD DE BOYVE

38 T.W. Allen's speech, *The 40th Annual Co-operative Congress, 1908* (Manchester: Co-op Union, 1908), 359–360. 295
T.W. ALLEN

39 "Co-operation and Socialism", *Co-operative News*, 14 January 1911, 46–47. 298
HANS MÜLLER

40 "Mr W. Lander's Visit to West Africa", *Bolton Co-operative Record*, November 1914, 3–4. 302
WILLIAM LANDER

41 W.J. Douse's presidential address, *The 47th Annual Co-operative Congress, 1915* (Manchester: Co-op Union, 1915), 54–55. 306
W.J. DOUSE

PART 7
The sense of the past 309

42 "History of the Rochdale Pioneers", *Daily News*, 6 July 1857. 311
G.J. HOLYOAKE

43 *Our Story: The Co-operative Movement* (Manchester: Co-op Union, 1903), 7–28. 317
ISA NICHOLSON

44 "The Great Miners' Lock-out. £67,000 Withdrawn from the Society, 1893", in *The Coronation History of the Barnsley*

CONTENTS

British Co-operative Society Limited. 1862–1902 (Manchester: Co-operative Wholesale Society, 1903), 93–99.   325

45   "Industrial Accrington: Historical Sketch of its Development", in *A History of Fifty Years of Progress of Accrington and Church Industrial Co-operative Society Ltd., 1860–1910* (Manchester: Co-op Newspaper Society, 1910), 194–205, 208.   329
JASMES HASLAM

46   *The Men who Fought for us in the "Hungry Forties": a Tale of Pioneers and Beginnings* (Manchester: Co-operative Newspaper Society, 1914), 58–74, 167–172   337
ALLEN CLARKE

47   "An Irish Utopia", in *Labour in Ireland. Labour in Irish History. The Re-conquest of Ireland* (Dublin: Maunsel & Co., 1917), 129–144.   349
JAMES CONNOLLY

Bibliography   357

Volume III   Fabians, the ILP and the Labour Party
EDITED BY PETER LAMB

Introduction: the birth of British parliamentary socialism   1
PETER LAMB

PART 1
Work as it was and how it might be   15

1   *Land Lessons for Town Folk* (London: Clarion, 1896), 1–12.   17
WILLIAM JAMESON

2   "Dealing with the Unemployed: A Hint from the Past", *Nineteenth Century*, December, 1904, 1–14.   30
J. KEIR HARDIE

3   *The Right to Work* (London: Independent Labour Party, c. 1908), 3–15.   44
H. RUSSELL SMART

CONTENTS

PART 2
Visions of the future   59

4   *The Progress of Socialism: A Lecture* (London: Modern Press, William Reeves and Freethought Publishing Company, c. 1888), 3–18.   61
SIDNEY WEBB

5   *The Claims and Progress of Labour Representation* (Newcastle-on-Tyne: Labour Literature Society [North England], c. 1894), 3–16.   75
FRED HAMMILL

6   "The Need for a Labour Party", in *Britain for the British* (London: Clarion Press, 1902), 148–155.   90
ROBERT BLATCHFORD

7   *The Individual under Socialism: A Lecture* (London: ILP, c. 1908), 3–14.   96
PHILIP SNOWDEN

PART 3
Concepts of political change   109

8   *What Socialism Means: A Call to the Unconverted – A Lecture Delivered for the Fabian Society*, 3rd ed (London: William Reeves, c. 1888), 2.   111
SIDNEY WEBB

9   *What Socialism Is* (London: Fabian Society, 1890), 1–3.   113
FABIAN SOCIETY

10   Poster for *Socialism!: The First of a Course of Four Lectures Will be Given in the Co-operative Hall, High Street, on Tuesday, Nov. 4, 1890 by Sidney Webb*, 1890.   118
SIDNEY WEBB

11   *On the Importance of Right Methods in Teaching Socialism: A Paper Read to the Manchester and District Fabian Society, February 10th*, 1891 (Manchester: R.J. Derfel, 1891), 1–15.   120
R.J. DERFEL

CONTENTS

12 What is Socialism? A Discussion between Mrs. Annie Besant
    and Mr W. J. Nairn (Glasgow: SDF, 1892), 1–8.   130
    ANNIE BESANT AND W.J. NAIRN

PART 4
Political economy   137

13 *Miners' Eight Hours Bill. Speech by J. Keir Hardie, MP, in the
    House of Commons*, reprinted from *The Labour Leader*
    (London: John Penny, 1902).   139
    KEIR HARDIE

14 *The New Unemployed Bill of the Labour Party* (London:
    Independent Labour Party, c. 1907), 3–15.   142
    J. RAMSAY MACDONALD

15 *Socialism and Agriculture* (London: Independent Labour Party
    1908), 3–15.   155
    RICHARD HIGGS

PART 5
Ways of organising   169

16 *Manifesto of the Joint Committee of Socialist Bodies* (London:
    Twentieth Century Press, 1893), 1–8.   171
    JOINT COMMITTEE OF SOCIALIST BODIES

17 *Why We Are Independent* (London: Labour Representation
    Committee, 1903), 1–4.   177
    LABOUR REPRESENTATION COMMITTEE

18 *Why is the L.R.C. Independent?* (London: Labour Representation
    Committee, c. 1905).   183
    LABOUR REPRESENTATION COMMITTEE

19 *Labour and Politics: Why Trade Unionists Should Support the
    Labour Party* (London: Labour Party, c. 1907).   187
    LABOUR PARTY

20 *The Party Pledge and the Osborne Judgement* (Manchester: The National Press Ltd, 1910), 1–16.   192
KEIR HARDIE

PART 6
Democracy and the State   209

21 *The Law and Trade Union Funds. A Plea for "Ante-Taff Vale"* (London: Independent Labour Party, 1903), 3–15.   211
J. RAMSAY MACDONALD

22 *The Women's Suffrage Controversy* (London: Adult Suffrage Society, 1905), 1–4.   222
MARGARET BONDFIELD

23 *The Citizenship of Women: A Plea for Women's Suffrage*, third edition (London: Independent Labour Party, 1906), 5–15.   227
KEIR HARDIE

PART 7
The new religion and the old   239

24 *A Socialist's View of Religion and the Churches* (London: Clarion, 1896), 1–16.   241
TOM MANN

25 *The New Religion*, 2nd edition (London: Clarion, 1897), 1–12.   254
ROBERT BLATCHFORD

PART 8
Gender, sexuality and family relations   265

26 *Women and the Factory Acts* (London: Fabian Society, 1896), 3–15.   267
BEATRICE WEBB

27 *Socialism and the Family* (London: A.C. Fifield, 1906), 43–60.   281
H.G. WELLS

28 *Will Socialism Destroy the Home?* (London: Independent Labour Party, c. 1907), 1–14.   288
H.G. WELLS

CONTENTS

29 *Socialism and the Home* (London: Independent Labour Party, c. 1909), 1–11. 296
    KATHARINE BRUCE GLASIER

30 *The New Children's Charter* (London: Independent Labour Party and Fabian Society, 1912), 3, 6–20. 307
    C.M. LLOYD

PART 9
War, peace and internationalism 321

31 *Hands Across the Sea: Labour's Pleas for International Peace* (Manchester: The National Labour Press, c. 1910), 1–16. 323
    G.H. PERRIS

32 *A Labour Case Against Conscription* (Manchester: National Labour Press, c. 1913), 3–14. 339
    HARRY DUBERY

33 *The Origins of the Great War* (London: Union of Democratic Control, 1914), 3–17. 350
    HENRY NOEL BRAILSFORD

    Bibliography 363

Volume IV Anglo-Marxists
EDITED BY KEVIN MORGAN

   Introduction: the Anglo-Marxists 1
   KEVIN MORGAN

PART 1
The idea of socialism 17

1 *Socialism Made Plain. Being the Social and Political Manifesto of the Democratic Federation* (Democratic Federation, 1883) 19

2 "The Manifesto of the *Socialist League*", *Commonweal*, February 1885, 1–2. 24

xxiii

CONTENTS

3 "Anarchism", *Justice*, 8, 22, 29 November and
   6 December 1884.   29
   CHARLOTTE WILSON

4 "Why Not?", *Justice*, 12 April 1884.   38
   WILLIAM MORRIS

5 *The Man with the Red Flag* (London: Twentieth Century
   Press, 1886), 3–12.   42
   JOHN BURNS

6 "How I became a Socialist", *Justice*, 30 June 1894.   51
   WALTER CRANE

7 *Social Democracy or Democratic Socialism* (Social
   Democratic Federation: Salford District Council, 1895),
   3–6, 15–16.   55
   H.W. HOBART

8 "Social-democrat or socialist?", *Social Democrat*,
   August 1897, 228–231.   59
   H.M. HYNDMAN

9 *Socialism and Art* (Social Democratic Federation, 1907), 5–16.   65
   JACK C. SQUIRE

PART 2
Concepts of political change   75

10 "How the Change Came" from *News from Nowhere*, chapter 17,
   reprinted in *Commonweal*, 17, 24 and 31 May 1890.   77
   WILLIAM MORRIS

11 *An Anti-Statist, Communist Manifesto*, International
   Revolutionary Library, 1887, 2–22.   86
   JOSEPH LANE

12 *The Co-Partnership Snare* (Twentieth Century Press,
   c. 1913), 1–3, 14–16.   101
   HARRY QUELCH

CONTENTS

13   "Social-Democrats and the Administration of the Poor Law", *Social Democrat*, January 1897, 14–18.   106
GEORGE LANSBURY

14   "Long Live Syndicalism!", *The Syndicalist*, May 1912.   112
EDWARD CARPENTER

PART 3
Political economy   115

15   "The Iron Law of Wages", *Justice*, 15 March 1884, 3.   117
H.M. HYNDMAN

16   *Socialism and Slavery* (1884), Social Democratic Federation (London: Twentieth Century Press, 1899 edn), 3–15.   120
H.M. HYNDMAN

17   *Useful Work Versus Useless Toil* (1885), Hammersmith Socialist Society, 1893 edn, 3–12, 19.   132
WILLIAM MORRIS

18   "The Reward of 'Genius'", *Commonweal*, 25 September 1886, 205–206.   142
WILLIAM MORRIS

19   "The Great Money Trick" from *The Ragged Trousered Philanthropists* (1914), ch. 21.   146
ROBERT TRESSELL

PART 4
Work and social conditions   155

20   *What a Compulsory Eight-hour Day Means to the Workers* (London: Modern Press, 1886).   157
TOM MANN

21   *Unemployment: Its Causes and Consequences* (London: Twentieth Century Press, 1906), 5–16.   168
COUNTESS OF WARWICK

CONTENTS

22 *Prison Reform from a Social-Democratic Point of View* (London: Twentieth Century Press, 1909), 1–14.   177
DORA B. MONTEFIORE

23 *Social-Democracy and the Housing Problem* (London: Twentieth Century Press, 1900), 3–4, 6–7, 22–24.   189
F.O. PICKARD-CAMBRIDGE

PART 5
Ways of organising   197

24 "Organised Labour. The Duty of the Trades Unions in Relation to Socialism", *Commonweal*, 14, 21 and 28 August 1886.   199
THOMAS BINNING

25 "Social Democracy and Industrial Organisation", *Social Democrat*, 15 April 1910.   211
HARRY QUELCH

26 "Prepare for Action", *Industrial Syndicalist*, July 1910, 31–54.   216
TOM MANN

27 "Leadermania", *Justice*, 13 November 1897, 2.   229
T. HUNTER

PART 6
Democracy and the state   235

28 "The Will of the Majority", in *The Ethics of Socialism* (London: Swan Sonnenschein, 1889), 120–128.   237
ERNEST BELFORT BAX

29 "Workmen's Jubilee Ode", *Social Democrat*, February 1897.   243
HENRY SALT

30 "After the Jubilee", *Justice*, 16 October 1897, 2.   246

31 "The 'Monstrous Regiment' of Womanhood", in *Essays in Socialism New and Old* (London: Grant Richards, 1906), 276–279, 282–294.   248
ERNEST BELFORT BAX

CONTENTS

32 "Why I Am Opposed to Female Suffrage", *Social Democrat*, April 1909. 257
DORA MONTEFIORE

PART 7
The new religion and the old 263

33 "The Socialist Conception of Ethics", in *A New Catechism of Socialism* (London: Twentieth Century Press, 1902), 22–30. 265
E. BELFORT BAX AND H. QUELCH

34 "A Christmas Sermon which the Bishop of London has been asked to Preach in Westminster Abbey on Sunday, December 25", *Justice*, 24 December 1887, 4. 273
HERBERT BURROWS

35 *Socialism and the Survival of the Fittest* (London: Twentieth Century Press [c. 1891], third edition, 1910), 1–17. 277
J. CONNELL

36 *Was Jesus a Socialist?* ([1891], Huddersfield: Worker Office, c. 1908), 1–15. 294
JAMES LEATHAM

37 "Simplification of Life", in *England's Ideal* (Swan Sonnenschein, Lowrey & Co, 1887), 79–99. 309
EDWARD CARPENTER

PART 8
Gender, sexuality, family and personal relations 323

38 "The Commercial Hearth", *Commonweal*, 8 May 1886, 42 and 15 May 1886, 50. 325
ERNEST BELFORT BAX

39 *Some Words to Socialist Women*, Social Democratic Party Women's Committee (London: Twentieth Century Press, 1908), 5–16. 333
DORA B. MONTEFIORE

40	*The Future of Woman* (London: Twentieth Century Press, 1909), 1–14. HERBERT BURROWS	345
41	*Socialism and Eugenics* (London: Twentieth Century Press, 1911), 1–15. GEORGE WHITEHEAD	359

PART 9
War, peace and internationalism — 375

42	*Manifesto of the Socialist League on the Soudan War*, Socialist League, 1885.	377
43	*The Imperial Kailyard. Being a Biting Satire on English Colonisation* (London: Twentieth Century Press, 1896), 3–15. R.B. CUNNINGHAME GRAHAM	381
44	*The Approaching Catastrophe in India* (London: Twentieth Century Press, 1897), 3–16. H.M. HYNDMAN	389
45	"Socialism and Colonial Development", *Social Democrat*, July 1898, 208–211. JOHN R. WIDDUP	406
46	*Social-Democracy and the Armed Nation* (London: Twentieth Century Press, 1900), 3–14, 16. HARRY QUELCH	412
47	*Anti-militarism from the workers' point of view: why every working man and woman should be an anti-militarist*, Workers' Anti-Militarist Committee, 1913, 1–7. DORA MONTEFIORE	424
48	"A Continental Revolution", *Forward*, 15 August 1914, 38–42. JAMES CONNOLLY	431

CONTENTS

PART 10
The sense of the past — 435

49 "George Julian Harney: A Straggler of 1848", *Social Democrat*, January 1897, 3–8. — 437
EDWARD AVELING

50 "Bloody Niggers", *Social Democrat*, April 1897, 104–109. — 444
R.B. CUNNINGHAME GRAHAM

51 "Why is Socialism in England at a Discount?", *Social Democrat*, March 1898, 69–74 and April 1898, 112–117. — 451
THEODORE ROTHSTEIN

52 *The First of May: The International Labour Day* (1900) (London: Twentieth Century Press, 1904), 3–16. — 464
H.W. LEE

Bibliography — 478

PREFACE

"The most encouraging fact about revolutionary activity is that, although it always fails, it always continues. The vision of a world of free and equal human beings . . . never materialises, but the belief in it never dies out". The words are George Orwell's, introducing a compilation of British political writings from the sixteenth to the twentieth centuries. *Contemporary Thought on Nineteenth Century Socialism* is a project devoted to one of the most fascinating, prolific and politically consequential phases in this longer tradition. Not all the authors selected would have described themselves as revolutionary. Most did, however, subscribe to some or other vision of that "state of brotherhood" or classless society which Orwell identified with socialism. The overall scope of the project is described in the general introduction at the start of Volume I. Though no treatment can be fully comprehensive, we believe that the four volumes together do reflect the richness and diversity of socialist thinking in one of the principal countries (along with France) in which it originated. From Robert Owen in 1814 to James Connolly on the outbreak of the First World War, the volumes document precisely a century of socialist activity. Many times it may have ebbed away or been diverted into other channels, but without belief in its basic ideals ever dying out.

Each volume is organised around a series of thematic headings, loosely adapted to its contents. Within this broad approach, each volume editor has had complete discretion regarding the selection of materials and the overall scope of each volume. Many of the texts are reproduced in full, others are substantial extracts. Each chapter comprises the selected text prefaced by an editorial introduction providing context, evaluation and a clarification of references that may now be obscure. At the beginning of each volume there is also an introductory overview by the editor.

There has been no modernisation of spellings or other editorial conventions. Offensive or taboo terms remain as in the original text, and the use of the universal male pronoun (like Orwell's state of brotherhood) is reproduced without comment unless it is that of the original author. Where notes from the original text are reproduced, these will be found within each chapter with the document they derive from. Where editorial notes are provided, these are collected at the end of that part of the volume.

PREFACE

The sources of the texts reproduced include the British Library, Hathi Trust, British Library of Political and Economic Science and the Co-operative Archive. The great majority of the documents in Volumes III–IV have been reproduced from originals in the Working Class Movement Library in Manchester, which has one of the finest collections in the world of print materials relating to British nineteenth-century socialism. Our thanks and grateful acknowledgements to all of these.

P.G.
K.M.

GENERAL INTRODUCTION
Socialism before the age of party

Peter Gurney and Kevin Morgan

Socialism was a movement and a body of ideas long before it became a party. The boundaries of this movement were fluid. It ebbed and flowed over time. It had no single organisational focus, no commonly accepted programme, no seer or recognised founder, least of all a single leader as some said Ferdinand Lassalle briefly was in Germany. Nevertheless, it is easy to describe it as a movement because socialists themselves described it that way; and as they so identified themselves, they had some clear sense of who the socialists were, and who were not. "At last, I am a socialist!", recorded one famous convert in her journal in 1890.[1] Not every socialist had to cross William Morris's "river of fire" to get there. But for a great many socialists there was this sense of something to be crossed, as fluid as it may have been, and of socialism as both the answer to the challenge of their times and the future that would supersede them.

As the modern socialist movement took shape from the 1880s, there were multiple attempts to celebrate its origins, plot its course over time and conjure up the sense of the past that defined its world-view almost as much as its sense of the future. Socialists were disputatious of their very nature. There could no more have been a single narrative of their history than a single guiding text or leader's portrait image. Socialism was pluralistic, and socialisms (plural) has some force as the looser term that acknowledges what were sometimes fundamental differences. Nevertheless, it is striking how far socialists of different persuasions had some common notion of the movement's limits, both temporal and political. They also had a surprisingly distinct sense of who and what belonged, and who did not. The Fabian socialist Sidney Webb, the marxists William Morris and Belfort Bax, the future Labour Party leader Ramsay MacDonald: all provided accounts in which socialism was both the general direction in which society as a whole was necessarily heading and the movement of those who sought to guide it there.

All acknowledged continental forbears, from Henri de Saint-Simon and Charles Fourier to Karl Marx and Friedrich Engels. Most found space for Thomas Spence (1750–1814), whose lecture on land reform, *The Real Rights of Man* (1775) was one of the first historical documents to be reissued as the socialist movement revived in the late nineteenth century. Nevertheless, in its own collective memory socialism was a movement that first appeared in Britain around the end of the Napoleonic

Wars and proceeded thereafter in two distinct, somewhat loosely connected phases. In leading the way in the first phase, socialism's most important early advocate was Robert Owen and the first true organised movement of socialists was the Owenites. The mass Chartist movement of the 1830s–50s could not itself be described as socialist, but contained a socialist current within it that was most commonly associated with James Bronterre O'Brien and regarded by later socialists as Chartism's most forward-looking section. With Chartism's protracted decline after the crisis year of 1848, socialism as a self-conscious movement of opinion more or less ceased to exist. According to its later advocates, the socialist leaven was still at work, but at work in more labyrinthine ways, through movements that were not themselves avowedly socialist. When a new wave of socialist societies were formed in the 1880s and 90s, these were at once boldly modern in their self-perception and conscious of a longer lineage that had never completely died away.

What made socialism possible from the early nineteenth century, initially to conceptualise and talk about, later to organise and think of as a movement? It had not always been possible: we have to go back to the Diggers in the 1640s to get something close, and the experiment on St George's Hill was limited and soon extinguished. It was the long revolution in ideas usually referred to and simplified as the Enlightenment that made socialism thinkable in a modern sense. The development of the notion of "society" as something existing in its own right and not merely an agglomeration of individuals was crucial, as was fuller appreciation of different kinds of "societies". Critics of early industrial capitalism frequently conjured up images of "organic societies" that were supposed to have existed in the past as a way of berating the present. Classical political economy in which a labour theory of value played a key role also constituted a fecund source of critical ideas and did not serve only as rationalisations for a rising bourgeoisie.[2] Natural rights' arguments culminating in Tom Paine's *Rights of Man* was another necessary foundation for the full flowering of socialist ideology in the 1820s, especially the second part Paine published in 1792 that contained a blueprint for a "welfare state".[3] Most important was the continuing influence of Christianity: the legacy of religious dissent stretched back to the 1640s and although the observation that the British labour movement owed more to Methodism than Marx is a cliché it is no less true for that. The desire for working-class independence of thought and action was essential for the spread of nonconformity. Methodism was not a symptomatic expression of the "chiliasm of despair" either. Individual moral improvement was a vital aspect of both socialism and working-class association more generally from the very outset, not merely a sign of "bourgeois" indoctrination.[4] Christianity had traditionally helped keep the majority down, certainly, but it also provided much of the language and mental furniture that enabled a far-reaching critique of capitalism: Spence imagined the general strike as a "Jubilee"; Chartists called it the "Sacred Month".

The noun "socialist" first appeared in English in the *Co-operative Magazine and Monthly Herald* in 1827 to describe Owen's communitarian schemes. The diffusion of the term was slow and the next example is not found until six years later, when it was used in the *Poor Man's Guardian*, the most important newspaper in the so-called war of the unstamped press. "Socialism" itself did not appear until 1837.[5] It developed in opposition to another early nineteenth century neologism, "individualism", which stressed the primacy of abstract individuals in the whole social and economic order, against the claims of society.[6] Significantly, before Owenism and Chartism collapsed as mass movements in the late 1840s, the key word "socialism" was used synonymously with "communism" and "co-operation". Capitalist development did not make socialism inevitable in any straightforward sense during this early phase, though its revolutionary effects did create fertile ground, especially in the new urban environments, for the dissemination of radical ideas and the growth of radical organisations.

Popular literacy was central: the tools of literacy and socialist criticism were inextricably intertwined and conversion to socialism depended always on reading and sometimes on writing texts. The (usually male) artisan autodidact poring over his books and teaching himself Latin and Greek classics by candlelight is a stock image and easily overdone, but it captures important elements. George Jacob Holyoake who quit the engineering workshop to pursue a life as a "propagandist" and who was employed for a time as a "Social Missionary" by the Owenite movement in the early 1840s, actively cultivated the outsider identity that public profession of socialist belief frequently conferred. As with plebeian intellectuals generally, his autodidacticism was not a lonely affair, however. He knew very well that reading and writing were social acts and he did what he could to share the skills he had acquired: his *Practical Grammar* published in 1844 had run to eight editions by 1870, the *Spectator* noting that it was "written in the conjoint style of *Punch* and an Ultra-Radical setting the world to rights".[7] Education and persuasion were regarded as the best means of achieving the New Moral World by this as well as later generations of socialists. Even those Owenites and Chartists who employed the most combative language and contemplated the necessity for armed confrontation believed that education was the real key to social and economic transformation. Organic intellectuals such as Holyoake spoke to a wide audience: recent studies have demonstrated the reach of literacy skills before the coming of a national state controlled system of education in the late nineteenth century, which found various rich expressions, from pauper letters to poor law authorities to working-class writing in the popular press and a veritable explosion of working-class autobiography.[8]

Although Chartism should not be understood as a socialist movement in either embryo or disguise, the socialist current within it was influential and did not run in a confined channel. Indeed, many socialists called themselves Chartists and vice versa, not only figures such as Holyoake and William Lovett who have often been labelled moderates but also revolutionary firebrands such as Bronterre O'Brien and George Julian Harney. For sure, Chartism was deeply rooted in earlier movements for political reform and its leaders often employed the language of constitutionalism to attack "Old Corruption" – what William Cobbett (no socialist but a fierce critic of capitalism) called "the Thing". But this aspect has been much overplayed by historians during recent decades with damaging results: the threat posed by Chartism to the emerging economic and social order has been obscured, including the reach of socialist ideas. Robert Owen may have had an empty space in his head where most people had political responses but many others whose outlook had been shaped by his work thought deeply about political power and often used a much more threatening, overtly democratic discourse. O'Brien's nickname as "the schoolmaster of Chartism" was significant surely, gained after his work as editor of the *Poor Man's Guardian* that was established by the radical London printer Henry Hetherington, another Owenite-Chartist.

Clearly, Owenites as well as Chartists thought politically, and they were also frequently far more practical than Owen was, establishing hundreds of co-operative stores as well as scores of local organisations in towns and cities across the country from the 1820s. In these branches, women and men drawn mainly from the artisan stratum of the working class built an alternative culture from below, one that was democratic and family-centred. Such people were as passionate about individual moral change as they were about collective transformation, enthusiastically taking up a host of alternative practices and ideas, including phrenology, temperance and vegetarianism.[9] Henceforth, making a new culture was a distinctive feature of the socialist project in Britain.[10] George Orwell's dismissive swipe at socialist faddists in the 1930s was merely yet another iteration of a common jibe that can be traced back to the Owenite phase, via later figures in the same tradition such as Edward Carpenter. The emphasis on practical change was invariably mixed with a great deal of utopian longing, within Chartism as well as Owenism. Another socialist democrat, the radical printer Thomas Frost, wanted nothing more than to quit the Old Immoral World in the early 1840s. He tried unsuccessfully to establish a community himself, attempted to join Owen's settlement at Queenwood, again with no luck, and contemplated enlisting in the Concordists that had set up a community at Ham Common. Their regime of strict vegetarianism, teetotalism and sexual abstinence proved too much even for Frost, who went on to edit the *Communist Chronicle* for John Goodwyn Barmby, the individual responsible for introducing the term "communism" to England from France after a visit to Paris in 1840. Barmby established a Communist Church on his return that attempted to combine communism with Christianity, much to the dismay of most Owenite socialists. Like many other radicals, Frost liked to call himself "a Chartist and something more", a description he used both at the time and throughout later life.[11]

After mid-century, with radicals scattered and liberal free trade in triumphant mode, anti-capitalist utopianism understandably became more difficult to sustain. It was not fully extinguished, however. Historians used to accept uncritically the views of the "Red Republican" Chartist Ernest Jones who, like his mentor Karl Marx, considered consumer co-operation that attracted so much working-class energy from this time as dominated by those motivated mainly by narrow material gain made possible by the success of shopkeeping. This was a simplistic reading: Owenites and Chartists were instrumental in establishing many local co-operative societies, including the Rochdale Society of Equitable Pioneers in 1844, which has often been regarded, erroneously, as originator of the modern movement. The press helped transmit the socialist legacy, first through the pages of Henry Pitman's *Co-operator* during the 1860s, then by means of a national weekly established in 1871 by a growing movement, the *Co-operative News and Journal of Associated Industry*. These publications featured many articles by old Owenites such as William Pare, Henry Travis and J.C. Farn and also reported continuing if isolated attempts at community life. Co-operators in the second half of the nineteenth century were as keen on building an alternative culture as socialists had been in the first, this time around the social nexus of the store. Hence, they invested a percentage of the "surplus" (not profit) from trade on education, including formal classes and an extensive network of libraries and newsrooms, and also sought to cater to the desire for sociality and fellowship among members, organising tea parties, soirees, excursions, exhibitions, festivals and so on. The culture building associated with socialists that rallied round Robert Blatchford's weekly *Clarion* newspaper was writ large in the co-operative movement: here was the British equivalent to the alternative culture constructed by the Social Democratic Party of Germany before the First World War.

The influence of Christian socialism was also important after 1850, as a group of clerics and bourgeois intellectuals concerned about class polarisation sought to Christianise economy and society. E.V. Neale and J.M. Ludlow in particular worked to remove some of the legal disabilities that were constraining co-operation, though not without trying to impose a straightjacket of their own. They much preferred co-operatives to trade unions, as the former they believed tended to harmonise relations between capital and labour, helping to render class conflict redundant. Although it is unlikely that this group had much influence on the majority of co-operators in the industrial north – the co-operative movement's heartland – Christian Socialist involvement did facilitate better communication across classes. The widely read text, *Progress of the Working Class*, published in 1867 by Ludlow and the ex-fustian cutter and Owenite "Social Missionary", Patrick Lloyd Jones, illustrated this dialogue. As the title suggested, the work painted an optimistic picture, once workers had rejected visionary schemes. Admitting that the influence of Owenite socialists had been "far from inconsiderable" in manufacturing districts, Ludlow and Jones went on to assert that "their views as to 'community of property' were regarded by themselves as matters for private experiment rather than general acceptance".[12] This rejection of the Owenite past and emphasis on class harmony helped leaders such as Holyoake form alliances with sympathetic members of the liberal middle class, including John Bright, J.S. Mill and William Gladstone. Those modern historians keen to highlight the popular bases and tenacity of liberalism have made much of such links, which were undoubtedly significant, though they also conceal a great deal.[13]

Socialism as an ethic and ideal of social organisation was nevertheless a presence that is continuously discernible across the later decades of the nineteenth century. If ever a text summed up the spirit of an age, it was John Stuart Mill's *On Liberty* (1859), which according to A.V. Dicey provided its thousands of admiring disciples, of whom he was one, with the "final and conclusive demonstration of the absolute truth of individualism".[14] Nevertheless, under Harriet Taylor's influence

Mill was much attracted to socialism – co-operators often drew attention to the fact – and when he died in 1873 he was working on a study of socialism of which only a handful of chapters were ever completed. The scope of his study was international, and Mill had no doubt that it was on the continent that "anti-property doctrines" were now most actively promulgated. Nevertheless, he also opined that "even in England the more prominent and active leaders of the working classes are usually in their private creed Socialists of one order or another, though . . . better aware than their continental brethren that great and permanent changes in the fundamental ideas of mankind are not to be accomplished by a *coup de main*".[15] Nearly forty years later, the Fabian socialists Sidney and Beatrice Webb would write that in Britain as elsewhere there was "far more Socialism than there are Socialists", and it was a basic precept of the Fabians that across the nineteenth century this socialism that did not call itself socialism had been relentlessly advancing. What better evidence than Mill himself, who in his autobiography had described his "ideal of ultimate improvement" as one that could only be rightly classed as socialist. In the Fabian view looking back, the first edition of Mill's *Principles of Political Economy* (1848) had marked the boundary of the old individualist economics, and every other one that followed the further advance of socialism.[16]

Socialism, however, could not yet be described as a political movement. In the articles they wrote in 1913, the Webbs wrote of socialism, not just as an aspiration or trend of thought, but as the revolt against oppression which gave the socialist movement "its halo of martyrdom, its unrecorded lives of silent heroism, its comradeship in privation and endurance and the strenuous unpaid work of millions of members". It was socialism in this sense that marked its reappearance in Britain from the 1880s. Honour was paid to surviving Chartists like the "straggler" Harney.[17] Owen and O'Brien were regarded as forbears; some even looked to the coming together of the co-operators and political socialists as the "two distinct bodies of social reformers" whose founding father Owen was.[18] In the founding texts of Britain's socialist revival of the 1880s the sense of this inheritance was strongly marked. In H.M. Hyndman's *England for All* (1881) and *Historical Basis of Socialism in England* (1883), the very titles gave it away. Nevertheless, even Hyndman, while delicately avoiding any direct reference to Marx, was conscious from the start that the socialism he now embraced signified the assimilation into the long course of English history of what he called "theories now gaining ground all over the Continent".[19]

Socialism as a body of ideas had never been confined within national boundaries. It was, moreover, on British soil and among British workers that the idea of an international labour organisation first took root. Already, the Chartist William Lovett has been described as the "first working man of modern times with an international outlook".[20] When Marx in 1864 took the lead in establishing the International Workingmen's Association, this too was launched from London with trade unionists like George Odger amongst its most important advocates. In the inaugural address which he wrote for it, Marx not only invoked the political economy of labour, but also described the "great social experiments" of the co-operative movement as the greatest victory it had yet recorded.[21] Even so, the socialist ideal did not yet provide a sufficient basis for such a movement. Marx's address did not refer to it. Following the defeat of the Paris Commune of 1871, British trade unionists were among the first to make their exit as the International disintegrated. The theories gaining ground elsewhere now took the shape of national parties: Marx in 1878 mentioned those of Germany, Switzerland, Denmark, Portugal, Italy, Belgium, Holland and North America.[22] Beginning with Hyndman and the Democratic Federation (later the Social Democratic Federation or SDF), socialists in Britain set about forming their own additions to the list. Hyndman described it as the dawn of a revolutionary epoch in which the ideas of Fourier, Owen and Marx were everywhere in Europe being "taken down from the closet of the Utopian investigator into the street".[23] From Belgium had come the initiatives for the international socialist congresses held at Ghent in 1877 and Chur in 1881. The idea of the International was in the air and in 1889 it for the first time took the relatively stable organisational form that came to be known as the Second International. All of Britain's principal socialist bodies affiliated as a matter of course. In 1904, even the Labour Party was admitted on the basis that it practised the class war even if it did not preach it. Co-operators for their part practised as well as preached internationalism before the First World War, more so than did trade unionists. They felt an affinity between their ambitions and the Owenite goal of universal brotherhood. The picture is complicated, however, by the fact that some bourgeois supporters saw in international co-operation a bulwark against international socialism in the 1890s, and that the British co-operative movement itself was deeply implicated in the growth of empire owing to its expanding trading operations.

An age of organisation might be thought to have simplified the search for socialist ideas and the places where these were documented. In reality, it was in many ways harder than ever. As a figurehead for socialism, Hyndman was at once indefatigable and disinterested and at the same time flamboyantly self-opinionated and erratic in his judgment. Like the organisation which he founded, he was also a Londoner by origin and affinity, and counted it among the principal weaknesses of Chartism that it had had so little impact on that crucible of any conceivable revolution which was the capital.[24] Though Hyndman could hardly have borne the sole responsibility, he was at least a symbol of the failure to establish in Britain any single socialist organisation enjoying a clear ascendancy over its rivals. The Fabian Society, founded in 1884, was as strongly rooted in the capital as the marxist groupings of the SDF and breakaway Socialist League. Nevertheless, the Fabians for the time being rejected the very premise of a separate socialist party. Instead, they saw their role as one of guiding forward the tendencies to socialism they believed to be at work in all parts of British society, and more particularly those parts committed to some notion of social progress. Following some years later in 1893, the Independent Labour Party (ILP) combined the SDF's approach to popular campaigning with the pragmatic constitutionalism of the Fabians, but from a basis in Britain's industrial heartlands in which the SDF and Fabians had alike been deficient. According to the proceedings of its second annual conference in 1894, a proposal that the ILP have its headquarters in the capital was received "with laughter".[25]

Socialists were therefore scattered across a range of organisations. They moved through them and between them and not infrequently, in a spirit of inclusiveness or indecision, belonged to two or more of them simultaneously. Others gave voice to socialist ideas without becoming a member of any of them, and sometimes did so within the socialist press itself. Even party organs did not for the most part have the exclusive character of the fortress parties of the continent.[26] With the extension of a basic education, the size of Britain's reading public had increased significantly since the years of the Owenites and Chartists. Socialism had to mark its territory as part of the "long revolution" whose more conspicuous manifestations included the explosion of a mass-circulation commercial press. Socialists continued to have faith in education and the power of the printed word. They addressed each other through the "graphosphere" that for decades to come would remain such a characteristic feature of the international left.[27] Nevertheless, the limitations of a purely factional press were impossible to overlook in a country like Britain in which it faced such an uphill battle. Moreover, for Labour's emerging political class, commercial journalism was one of the few obvious ways of underwriting a political career, as the ILPers Hardie, MacDonald and Snowden would all at some point demonstrate.

Socialism in consequence was not a respecter of boundaries. From the penny dreadfuls to respectable weeklies and monthlies of no particular socialist bias, there were sometimes opportunities for socialists to reach a wider public and even get paid for it. At the same time, there were justified warnings from the outset that a socialist press could never achieve a mass circulation without making some provision for the diversion and entertainment of its readers in the manner now identified with Fleet Street. If this were the criterion, then the most influential socialist of the day was not Hardie, MacDonald or Hyndman but Robert Blatchford. Blatchford had no stable party affiliation. He had an instinct for socialist unity and a sort of openhearted and hedonistic irreverence that aroused considerable mistrust among some ILP leaders in particular. Nevertheless, through the *Clarion* and pamphlets like *Merrie England*, Blatchford by common consent made more converts to the socialist cause than any of his contemporaries.

It was not just that there was more socialism than socialists. For those who would seek to document them, it is also a matter of some delicacy to determine just who the socialists were. "The Fabian Society consists of socialists", declared the society's "Basis" without apparent ambiguity. Nevertheless, the society freely admitted Liberals and even Tories, while Sidney Webb worked closely with collectivist "progressives" on the London County Council. The "new liberalism" of the day was clearly not a section of the socialist movement. Nevertheless, it did clearly influence the policies of the first Labour governments, and did so moreover through the direct agency of the former Liberals who sat within them. In the case of the anarchists, there was almost a reverse of this converging movement, and a clearer delineation of a movement of activists and ideas that could not simply be assimilated within the broader socialist movement. Nevertheless, as the example of Charlotte Wilson shows in these volumes, in the early years of the socialist revival the connections could hardly have been closer.

The concept of the labour movement meant a further blurring of boundaries. Entering into wider currency in the early 1890s, this implied some notion of solidarity and shared objectives extending to any or all of the movements of co-operators, trade unionists and political socialists. In all three cases there remained instincts of fierce independence and often mutual antagonism or mistrust. There was certainly no common programme or consensus on either ends or means. Nevertheless, there was a sufficient basis for the labour alliance strategy which from 1900 saw the ILP and Fabian Society combine with the mass of non-socialist trade unionists to form the Labour Representation Committee, which later became the Labour Party. Activists of more militant outlook saw the unions themselves as possible instruments of social transformation, and lingering notions of a general strike re-emerged as a central strategic objective for the syndicalists of the immediate pre-1914 period.

The co-operative movement was also caught up in the widening of horizons and quickening anticipation of a new social order. Crucially, its liberal middle-class sympathisers were in this period increasingly marginalised. The movement sloughed off patrons and asserted its independence as a working-class organisation. Outsiders like the Russian anarchist Peter Kropotkin embraced co-operation as a total alternative to capitalism, a system of mutual aid writ large, while insiders often described it as "practical socialism", regardless of whether all its members acknowledged this or not. Although they were wary of equating socialism with co-operation – owing to the rise of "state socialism" – influential figures like the chairman of the English Co-operative Wholesale Society, J.T.W. Mitchell, believed that the movement would eventually supplant capitalism entirely. So too did other leaders of the wholesaling operations such as William Maxwell of the Scottish Co-operative Wholesale Society, whose uncle had been an Owenite. The discourse these co-operators articulated was neo-Owenite in its ambition, although now community building had to take place within the existing urban environment.

From the 1890s in particular, co-operators used a new term, "Co-operative Commonwealth", to describe their ultimate goal. This was a term they shared with socialists from Walter Crane to Keir Hardie. Its most famous exponent was the Danish-American Laurence Gronlund, who had used it to describe the statist ideals of the German socialist school which the great majority of co-operators would not have recognised as their own. Many of them also remained suspicious of the politics of class and class struggle, preferring instead the peaceful mode of social and economic transformation effected by co-operation. The break with liberalism was therefore protracted, made more difficult by the fact that for co-operators the state was more often regarded as a source of anxiety rather than salvation. Co-operators' views on this shifted over time as consumption became more overtly politicised from the turn of the century, a trend that greatly accelerated during the First World War. Increasingly, boundaries between the co-operative and socialist movement became more porous: co-operators permeated socialist bodies and vice versa, just as activists within Chartism and Owenism had worked together generations before.

In the spring of 1905, Ramsay MacDonald launched the Socialist Library for the ILP. His reasoning in doing so was that Britain's socialist literature, as compared with those of other European countries, was mainly ephemeral in nature and devoid of any endeavour to deal in a more substantial way with the social, economic, political and ethical aspects of socialism. One of the principal objects of the series was therefore to introduce readers to those writings in other European languages which MacDonald held to have a less ephemeral character. It is indeed difficult to overstate how far socialism as a political ideal now represented an engagement with movements and ideas that sought to link up in a common cause that overreached national boundaries. From their earliest publications in the 1880s, the SDF and its successors had consistently aimed at providing its readers with both texts and reports of events originating overseas. So renowned a figure as Eleanor Marx figures chiefly in the socialist press as a translator and compiler of reports on the socialist movement internationally. Gronlund's *Co-operative Commonwealth* was among those foreign texts now largely forgotten that exercised an enormous influence at this time. For the generation of the early 1900s, the productions of Charles H. Kerr & Co of Chicago were a crucial element in the library of the self-educating worker turning to marxism. The Bostonian Edward Bellamy's *Looking Backward* was also read by as many British socialists as any but a handful of home-produced writings of comparable scope. Only the Fabian Society tracts, which MacDonald had presumably had in his sights, were determinedly resistant to any taint of external influence.

The documents collected here are for the most part of just that ephemeral character that MacDonald seemed to rate so lowly. This is partly because texts and authors deemed to be of more enduring interest tend to be more familiar and easily accessible to readers. Doubtless to MacDonald's posthumous chagrin, it is also true that his and others' more substantial writings have not in practice proved any less ephemeral than their slighter productions of the moment. The documents are not intended as a socialist canon, or even as an alternative to one, but as a representation of a movement and tradition which, for all their divergences, were always interested in ideas as a way of understanding the world and collectively acting upon that understanding. With a few exceptions, the documents are restricted to original texts by British socialists and co-operators mostly published independently or under socialist auspices in the broader sense. The international character of many of these publications is therefore registered only through the British interlocutors in a wider debate: so that Bellamy's *Looking Backward*, for example, appears here only indirectly through the extract of William Morris's counter-utopia *News From Nowhere*. Though the best-known socialists like Morris are not excluded, they appear here in the context of the wider movements of which they were part, including even the most ephemeral of their productions where these give insight into the political culture of which they are the surviving traces.

It has become commonplace to refer to the short twentieth century inaugurated by the outbreak of war in 1914. Eric Hobsbawm, among the most eminent of those to have done so, also referred to it as an age of extremes. Within the context of the movements represented in these volumes, it may also be considered as an age of party. In 1918, the Labour Party for the first time became a national mass membership party with a programme and constitution that included the socialist commitment of its famous Clause IV. Two years later, Britain's marxist parties, sects and fragments mostly sunk their identity in the Communist Party of Great Britain, formed as a section of the new Communist International. The ILP and smaller left parties found themselves relentlessly squeezed. The anarchist movement for a period almost disappeared. Co-operation went from strength to strength but with its political horizons narrowed. Even the Fabian Society, though continuing its work even today, seemed so closely identified with the Labour Party as to lose its identity within it. With Labour on the one side and the CPGB on the other, some historians have described the effect of a synchronised pincer movement that forced into the shadows the myriad variants of left-wing politics that had hitherto coexisted and cross-fertilised each other. Ethical, feminist, revolutionary and anti-statist socialisms have all been portrayed as the victims of this so-called double close of the warring leviathans.

This is an over-simplification and should not be taken at face value. Each generation has its own complexity and historical agency and cannot just be used as a backdrop for those that followed or came before. In any case, observers of these movements continued to remark upon what the Austrian secretary of the reborn Second International described as the "very English" trait of disorganisation. With all these caveats, it is nevertheless the case that socialists in Britain were entering into a new age of party. The ideas they expressed were structured by party loyalties and subject to party disciplines in a way only dimly prefigured before the war. They were informed by research departments or the first of the new breed of academic socialists who before the 1920s were an exclusively continental phenomenon. Going far beyond the communists' ranks, many were also drawn by Soviet communism, and its purported realisation of socialist ideals would necessarily figure prominently in any collection of socialist documents after 1917. Whatever the undoubted continuities that existed, the period of the First World War was therefore a political watershed and marked the onset of a new set of debates, institutions and party alignments, and new languages to describe them. Though it begins here a little later than in some other historical contexts, the long nineteenth century that is covered in these volumes has a logic and a rationale that did not survive the larger crisis that centred on the years of the First World War.

Notes

1 Beatrice Webb, 1950 ed. *My Apprenticeship*. London: Longman & Green Co, 348–349.
2 William Stafford, 1987. *Socialism, Radicalism and Nostalgia: Social Criticism in Britain, 1775–1830*. Cambridge: Cambridge University Press, 31–90; Noel Thompson, 1984. *The People's Science: The Popular Political Economy of Exploitation and Crisis, 1816–34*. Cambridge: Cambridge University Press.
3 See Mark Philp, 1989. *Paine*. Oxford: Oxford University Press.

4 E.P. Thompson,1963. *The Making of the English Working Class*. London: Gollancz; J.A. Jaffe, 1989. "The 'Chiliasm of Despair' Reconsidered: Revivalism and Working-Class Agitation in County Durham". *Journal of British Studies* 28 (1): 23–42; Tom Scriven, 2017. *Popular Virtue. Continuity and Change in Radical Moral Politics, 1820–70*. Manchester: Manchester University Press.
5 A.E. Bestor, 1948. "The Evolution of the Socialist Vocabulary". *Journal of the History of Ideas* 9 (3): 277–278.
6 See Raymond Williams, 1983. *Keywords: a vocabulary of culture and society*. Oxford: Oxford University Press, 164–165.
7 Sophia Collett, 1855. *George Jacob Holyoake and Modern Atheism*. London: Trübner & Co, 15.
8 David Vincent, 1989. *Literacy and Popular Culture: England, 1750–1914*. Cambridge: Cambridge University Press; Jonathan Rose, 2001. *The Intellectual Life of the British Working Classes*. New Haven: Yale University Press; Steven King, 2019. *Writing the Lives of the English Poor, 1750s–1830s*. Montreal: McGill-Queens University Press.
9 Eileen Yeo, 1971. "Robert Owen and Radical Culture". In *Robert Owen, Prophet of the Poor: Essays in the Honour of the Two Hundredth Anniversary of His Birth*, edited by Sidney Pollard and John Salt. London: Macmillan.
10 Chris Waters, 1990. *British Socialists and the Politics of Popular Culture, 1884–1914*. Manchester: Manchester University Press.
11 Bestor, "The Evolution of the Socialist Vocabulary", 280; Thomas Frost, 1880. *Forty Years Recollections, Literary and Political*. London: Sampson Low, 41–49, 54–60.
12 J.M. Ludlow and Patrick Lloyd Jones, 1867. *The Progress of the Working Class, 1832–1867*. London: Alexander Strahan, 296–297.
13 See especially Eugenio Biagini, 1990. *Liberty, Retrenchment and Reform: Popular Liberalism in the Age of Gladstone, 1860–1880*. Cambridge: Cambridge University Press.
14 A.V. Dicey, 1905. *Law and Public Opinion in the Nineteenth Century*. Cited by Stefan Collini, 1991. *Public Moralists: Political Thought and Intellectual Life in Britain*. Oxford: Oxford University Press, 326–327.
15 John Stuart Mill ed. W.D. Bliss, 1891. *Socialism: A Collection of his Writings on Socialism, with Chapters on Democracy, the Right of Property in Land and the Enfranchisement of Women*. New York: Humboldt.
16 Sidney and Beatrice Webb, "What is socialism?", *New Statesman*, 1 April 1913, 13; Sidney Webb, 1889. "Historic". In *Fabian Essays in Socialism,* ed. G. Bernard Shaw. London: Walter Scott, 58.
17 See Vol. IV, Part 10, Chapter 49, below.
18 Beatrice Potter (Webb), 1930 edn. *The Co-operative Movement in Great Britain*. London: Allen & Unwin, 240.
19 H.M. Hyndman, 1881. *England for All*. London: Gilbert & Rivington, 6.
20 Lewis L. Lorwin, 1929. *Labor and Internationalism*. New York: Macmillan, 17.
21 The address is reproduced in G.M. Stekloff, 1927. *History of the First International*. Martin Lawrence, 439–449.
22 Franz Mehring, 1936. *Karl Marx: The Story of his Life*. London: Allen & Unwin, 483.
23 Henry Hyndman, "The dawn of a revolutionary epoch", *The Nineteenth Century*, Jan. 1881: 2.
24 Henry Hyndman, "The Revolution of Today", *Today*, Jan. 1884: 23.
25 Independent Labour Party second national conference *Report*, February 1894, 10–11.
26 Kevin Morgan, 2006. *Labour Legends and Moscow Gold: Bolshevism and the British Left part 1*. London: Lawrence & Wishart, ch. 4.
27 See Régis Debray, "Socialism: A Life-Cycle", *New Left Review* 46 (July–August 2007): 5–28.

INTRODUCTION

Ophélie Siméon

As the "Father of British Socialism", Robert Owen (1771–1858) has often come across as a paradox. Though he was born into modest circumstances, his aspiration to raise the condition of the working classes was not informed by traditional radicalism, but by his life experience as a self-made factory owner. Additionally, while he successfully federated his supporters from the late 1820s onwards, the first British socialist movement – also known as Owenism – had already collapsed by 1845. Owen is also associated with Karl Marx and Friedrich Engels's *Communist Manifesto*, which disparaged his philosophies as an idealistic, "utopian" forerunner to their own, "scientific" socialism ([1848] 1992, 34–37). Notwithstanding, in a later text, Engels conceded that despite Owenism's millenarian overtones, "every social movement, every real advance in England on behalf of the workers links itself to the name of Robert Owen" ([1880] 1970, 95). As a result, "The enigma – and charm – of Owen, which so attracted his contemporaries, casts its spell on succeeding generations of reformers. [. . .] A good part of the English socialist tradition is in fact a series of reinterpretations of enigmatic figures from the past. For each age there is a new view of Mr. Owen" (Harrison 1971, 1).

Long seen as merely "utopian", early socialism is now studied as a strand of economic and political thought in its own right. Following on from J.F.C. Harrison's (1969) seminal study of Owenism in Britain and the United States, Gareth Stedman Jones (1983), Maxine Berg (1980), Jonathan Beecher (1986) and Gregory Claeys (1987; 1989) broke away from earlier, dominant teleological approaches. In doing so, they acknowledged the works of Charles Fourier, Henri de Saint-Simon and Robert Owen by setting them within their own time, and in their own terms. More specifically, these studies explored how socialism emerged in early nineteenth-century Europe as a response to the challenges of the new industrial age and the threat of rising distress in the midst of unprecedented abundance. In contrast to classical political economy, socialist thought denounced the economic status quo and refused to rationalise the depreciation of labour (Thompson 1984, 21; Claeys 1987). Furthermore, the early socialists were not content with the piecemeal nature of traditional methods of social relief, and sought to design universal reform schemes in a bid to provide a definitive answer to the social question. Far from being "utopian" in the negative sense of the word, i.e. a mere fiction or chimera, this vision leaned on Enlightenment-era rationalism and the subsequent belief in limitless human perfectibility. The force of imagination was used to conjure up a better future, but the new world was to be built here and now, through brick-and-mortar experiments, not in a distant future. Acknowledging the overlap of millenarian discourses and pragmatic methods has therefore challenged the classical distinction between "utopian" and "scientific" socialism.

Aside from the renewed focus on early socialist thought, recent research has also provided a complementary social history perspective, in the vein of Eileen Yeo's (1971) pathbreaking account of radical culture in the Owenite movement. In dealing with grassroots initiatives, beliefs and activism, studies by Simon Gunn, Robert J. Morris, Katrina Navickas and others have shown that in crafting a political vision for the future, the often overlooked minutiae of everyday life matters just as much the epic of well-known political events (Gunn and Morris 2001; Navickas 2016, 12–13).

This book is informed by and builds on these renewed approaches in the history of early socialism. Blending political, economic, intellectual and social history, it showcases the richness and diversity of the Owenite movement. Spanning from Robert Owen's first seminal works in 1813–1816 to the late 1840s, it encompasses political allegiances, genders and epochs.

This volume therefore draws on an unprecedented wide variety of sources that have never before been brought together and that are not easily accessible. The formats include books, pamphlets, archival sources and newspaper articles – and a variety of often overlapping voices – from Chartists to early co-operators, secularists, non-British Owenites and proponents of women's rights. The sheer range of Owenite ventures – intentional communities, co-operatives, labour exchanges, Halls of Science and experiments in popular education – are all covered. This mapping of the Owenite movement draws out the identification of its shared, core principles and values: internationalism, co-operation, concepts of political change, and above all, the ideal of community.

Robert Owen: from philanthropy to socialism (1771–1825)

Robert Owen was born on 14 May 1771 in Newtown, Wales, the youngest but one of seven children. His father, Robert Senior, was a saddler, ironmonger and churchwarden, while his mother, Anne, came from an impoverished gentry family. At the age of ten, after a short stint at the local school where, according to his own account, he showed great proficiency, Owen was sent to work with a Lincolnshire master clothier (Owen 1857–1858, 42; Donnachie 1998). By 1788, the young Welshman had relocated to Manchester, then already the capital of Britain's booming textile sector. The next few years were marked by his rapid upward social mobility. After working for a firm of drapers, Owen set up his own business as a spinning-machine builder and yarn dealer. In 1792, he was appointed under-manager at Peter Drinkwater's Piccadilly factory, one of the biggest Mancunian spinning mills. Four years later, at the age of twenty-five, he established his own firm, the Chorlton Twist Company, thus becoming part of Britain's industrial elite. Unlike most of his fellow factory owners, he had also established a reputation as a progressive employer, with a strong interest in poor relief, no doubt helped by his own humble beginnings. The 1790s saw him join both the prestigious Manchester Literary and Philosophical Society, one of the country's biggest learned societies, and the Manchester Board of Health, a group of local philanthropists determined to improve the conditions of factory workers, and which would later play a key role in the passing of the 1802 Health and Morals of Apprentices Act (Chaloner 1954; Innes 2002).

In 1798, while on a business trip to Glasgow, Robert Owen met his future wife, Anne Caroline Dale. Her father, David, had established the factory village of New Lanark as a joint venture with Richard Arkwright in 1785, and he had already found national fame as a progressive entrepreneur and philanthropist. On Anne Caroline's advice, Owen called at New Lanark on 15 June 1798 where he made acquaintance with her father. At first glance, it would seem that the two men had little in common. Dale was a staunch Evangelical Dissenter and a Tory, while Owen harboured deist opinions and less conservative political views. Yet both had been born into modest circumstances and they shared an interest in charitable management. It soon became obvious that the founder of New Lanark, already in his old age, was looking to sell, but struggled to find potential buyers who were as keen as he was. In his own words, he hoped to find successors willing to "unite the things which [. . .] have been thought impossible to go on together, the prosperity of the works and the health, morals [. . .] of the people" (Dale 1792, cited in Currie 1831, 132). Owen, in comparison, seemed like a suitable candidate, as his Manchester years had convinced him that benevolent management of the workers' material, moral and intellectual environment held the key to the social and economic upheavals of the new industrial age (Siméon 2017, 1). David Dale thus sold New Lanark in September 1799 to Owen, who married Anne Caroline Dale the very same month. The young entrepreneur was officially appointed mill manager on the first of January 1800.

Though Owen believed that industrialisation and the advent of the factory system held tremendous economic promise, he also feared that they had widened social divisions – between employer and worker, town and country, men and women – thus posing an unprecedented threat on the nation's peace and long-term prosperity. His proposed solution was essentially deterministic. As a deist, he thought that individual character was not predetermined by the stain of original sin, but that it was formed by a combination of environmental factors defined as "whatever you see, or feel, or know to exist around you" (1824). This "doctrine of circumstances" was in his eyes the most fundamental law of nature, and therefore the only rule upon which to build effective social reform. This he called a "science of society", or "social system" (Owen 1826–1827). To eradicate the vices of society, it was necessary to create an environment where the nefarious impact of industrialisation could be mitigated, thus reconciling the potential of the new economic order with an ancestral sense of community. In keeping with Enlightenment thinking, Owen wished to turn the chaotic world in which he lived into a state of order, and was also deeply confident in the perfectibility of human beings. He accordingly placed particular importance on education and experimentation as vehicles of social change. Lastly, Owen believed that the rich and powerful had a moral duty to provide for their dependents' welfare; as symbols of the new industrial age, factories were seen as the ideal testing ground, and his budding theories were thus tried out at New Lanark.

He had to endure a difficult start. While David Dale had been a mostly absentee proprietor, Robert Owen, Anne Caroline and their seven children took up residence at Braxfield House, a manor adjoining the factory village. This enabled closer surveillance of the workforce, but many employees resented the new director's management style. Owen also faced great hostility from his Mancunian business partners, who did not share his enthusiasm for factory reform. This, in addition to Owen's carelessness in money matters,[1] meant that he was unable to put his plan to the test until a decade later. Indeed, in 1813, he secured backing from a group of new associates which included Jeremy Bentham and the Quaker philanthropists William Allen, Joseph Fox and John Walker (Siméon 2017, 45). Thanks to this new latitude, Owen progressively reduced the day's work to ten hours. With the Institute for the Formation of Character (IFC) that he inaugurated in 1816, he also developed the Dale-era infant, day and evening schools well beyond the educational practices of the time, without sacrificing the factory's profitability. Thanks to his new business partners, Owen also gained entry into London's reformist circles, and this encouraged him to write his first major political treatise, *A New View of Society*.[2]

Published between 1813 and 1816, the four-volume book first arranged into a coherent whole the pillars of Owen's thought: determinism, education as the means and end of true change, and the superiority of community life as a form of social organisation. Most of these ideas were quite certainly formed in the 1790s when Owen came into contact with Manchester's enlightened and philanthropic circles; however, the details of his intellectual journey remain a mystery. Throughout his public career, Owen strategically insisted that his system was entirely derived from personal experience, thus setting himself apart from classic social and political thinkers, whom he saw as "mere closet theorists" ([1820] 1991, 271). Even though these claims were sincere, Owen also deliberately used his empiricist conception to establish himself – the low-born, self-taught reformer and philanthropist – as a *bona fide* social scientist in the learned and influential spheres of his day. In this way, his autobiography offers scant evidence of his formative readings, with the notable exception of *Treatise on the Wealth, Power and Resources of the British Empire* by Patrick Colquhoun (1814), whose blend of statistical data and social observation was reminiscent of his own works. Historians have nevertheless rightly pointed out that Owen's ideas, interests and methods were profoundly informed by late-Enlightenment thought, which he applied to the tide of rising industrialisation (Harrison 1969, 7–33; O'Brien and Quinault

1993). More specifically, many have remarked upon Owen's indebtedness to William Godwin. In the years 1812–1813, while writing his *New View of Society*, Owen spent most of that time in London, where he met Godwin at least fifty times according to the latter's diary (1788–1836). While its characteristically terse tone reveals nothing of the nature of these conversations, Godwin's influence, especially his deterministic theory of character formation and his support for popular education as an agent of social change, can be felt throughout Owen's *New View* (Harrison 1969, 84–85; Seed 1982, 4; Siméon 2017, 24).

In keeping with Owen's wish to build a "science of society", the seemingly positive results of the New Lanark experiment were given pride of place in *A New View of Society* (1813–1816). As the book became immensely successful, this pragmatic stance brought legitimacy to Owen's growing forays into factory and social reform. New Lanark became a popular tourist attraction for reformers, philanthropists and curious travellers generally, with the schools receiving special attention. Though the village was run along paternalistic, not socialist lines, the experiment foreshadowed some of Owenism's later developments, including the will to embrace all-encompassing reform schemes. Owen's willingness to join the national debate was encouraged by the fact that he had now attracted a small group of middle- and upper-class supporters that included the Duke of Kent (father of the future Queen Victoria), Sir Robert Peel the Elder, Whig MP William Champion de Crespigny, Henry Brougham and Alexander Hamilton of Dalzell, a Scottish radical and improving landowner. Beyond their political differences, Owen and his allies shared an interest in philanthropic endeavour, and a fear that rampant, unchecked industrialisation might wreak havoc on the United Kingdom's social fabric. Moreover, Owen knew that the success of his plans depended on his ability to secure backing from "those who have influence in the affairs of men" ([1813–1816] 1991, 10). This, however, he was unable to achieve, a fact that fuelled his transition from philanthropy to socialism in the years 1815–1820.

In the context of Britain's post-Waterloo crisis, Owen became active in two reform campaigns. In 1815, with the support of Robert Peel, he drafted a bill advocating the regulation of child labour in textile factories, as a means to amend the 1802 Health and Morals of Apprentices Act. That same year, Owen also championed the creation of "Villages of Co-operation" as an improvement upon the Old Poor Law system. Partly modelled on New Lanark, these communities on the land were meant to combine industrial and agricultural work to counter both rampant unemployment and the rural exodus that had soared in the wake of the enclosure movement. Both projects were met with great hostility. Owen's communitarian schemes, especially, were criticised by Tories and Radicals alike, who saw it respectively as a misguided utopia, and as an instance of enlightened despotism (Malthus [1798] 1817, vol. 2: 40–48, 395–99; Cobbett 1817; Siméon 2014, 22).

Owen's public response showed a shift in his intellectual approach. In August 1817, during a series of public speeches at the City of London Tavern, he expressed his conviction that all established institutions – be it organised religion, private property, and traditional, outdoor relief schemes – encouraged unnecessary divisions, thereby standing in the way of progress. "Villages of Co-operation" were now advocated, not only as a remedy to the woes of the labouring classes, but as the foundation of the ultimate regeneration and emancipation of mankind. With increasingly universalist and prophetic overtones, what had originated as a scheme for unemployment relief turned, in just a few years, into a blueprint for the reorganisation of society on a communitarian basis. This "Plan", as Owen's reform schemes were now colloquially known, was further refined in the *Report to the County of Lanark* (1820), a book which cemented Owen's move away from classical philanthropy. Calling for communities to usher in a "New Moral World", he now rejected all traditional means of political action, private property and the search for profit as an end in itself, advocating instead a fair wage system benefiting producers, not capitalists and their middlemen. This set of principles, which Owen called "social science" or "science of society" would be popularised by his followers under the name of "socialism" from the late 1820s onwards (Claeys 1986).

Starting in 1817, support within and outside New Lanark declined dramatically. In 1823, disagreeing with Owen's religious scepticism, his Quaker partners fired most of the IFC's teaching staff and increased the amount of Bible study classes. Tired of being considered objects of curiosity, Owen's labour force also campaigned to have New Lanark closed to the public, and their demands were finally met in March 1824 (Owen 1824). Finally, Owen's radicalisation had put a strain on his marriage, as his wife disagreed both with her husband's "Plan" and with his freethinking opinions. Family rifts came into full view in 1824, when Owen brought his business career to an end and set out to establish his now fully-formed communitarian plans. Those were put to the test one year later, when he and the Scottish-American reformer William Maclure acquired the village of New Harmony (Indiana, USA) from Wilhelm Rapp, a German-American Pietist pastor. Owen moved to North America with his four sons Robert Dale, William, Richard and David Dale, while Anne Caroline remained in Scotland with their daughters Mary, Anne and Jane (though only Mary shared her mother's disagreement with Owen's notions). Anne Caroline Owen passed away in 1832, without seemingly having resumed contact with her estranged husband (Siméon 2017, 128).

Early Owenism (1820–1834): co-operators and trade unionists

The word "socialist" first appeared in print in the July 1827 issue of the *Co-operative Magazine and Monthly Herald*,[3] in relation to Owen's communitarian schemes. "Socialism" and "Owenism" thus became synonymous in Britain until 1848, when the movement started to collapse after the rise of Chartism and Communism. The origins of Owenism can be traced to the early 1820s, following the publication of the *Report to the County of Lanark*. Especially after his anti-religious diatribe of 1817, many of Owen's former allies, his business partners included, had turned their backs on him. The Duke of Kent's death in 1820 was another dent in Owen's reputation, as he had now lost one of his most powerful allies. In 1822, Owen founded a subscription group to establish a "Village of Co-operation" at Motherwell, near New Lanark, but he failed to attract support from aristocratic and middle-class backers. Even among those who respected Owen's philanthropic endeavours, like Henry Brougham and William de Crespigny, few were ready to align with his more "visionary" notions.

Yet at the same time, Owen's ideas began to find favour among a new band of mostly working-class disciples. Starting in 1821, the first attempts to establish such "Villages of Co-operation" were pioneered by Abram Combe's Edinburgh Practical Society and George Mudie's Co-operative and Economical Society at Spa Fields, London. In 1825, after their respective experiments had failed, both men joined forces with Archibald Hamilton to create a community in Orbiston (Lanarkshire). Though these early ventures were short-lived, interest in the "social system" grew in British radical circles while Owen was still residing in America. Some early middle- and upper-class followers, like Archibald Hamilton, William Thompson and Anna Doyle Wheeler, had remained faithful to the "new views", but the bulk of new supporters now hailed from the skilled, artisan classes across the country's main industrial regions, especially London, the Scottish Lowlands and the North of England. Ideological variation was considerable, and major rifts gradually emerged around three main issues: the compatibility between the "new views" and religion, the means to achieve community and working-class agency, especially in the context of the Great Reform Act, 1832.

Nevertheless, the likes of Christian Socialist John Minter Morgan, feminist Anna Doyle Wheeler and future Chartist William Lovett somewhat found common ground in Owen's thought. First of all, there was a broad consensus over his insistence that workers alone had the right to control production, trading relationships and the wage system, a stance known as his "labour theory of value", which he had first developed in the *Report to the County of Lanark*. This critique of capitalism and classical political economy was expanded upon in the writings of early supporters like George Mudie and William Thompson, who gained tremendous popularity within the emerging Owenite movement. Second, in contrast to earlier strands of radicalism, the Owenites eschewed agrarian conceptions of community building. Though farming was an essential part of their reform plans, in the vein of Owen's 1817 "Villages of Co-operation", they insisted that only a rational use of machinery would harness the economic potential of the labouring classes, thus securing the fruits of abundance for all (Claeys 1987, 148; Chase 1988, 139; Langdon 2000, 12).

Lastly, Owen's emphasis on community resonated with long-established working-class traditions of mutuality and self-help (Harrison 1969, 50; Kumar 1990, 12). In 1769, the earliest recorded consumer co-operative was established in Scotland by the Fenwick Weavers' Society, a local corporation. To create an additional stream of revenue and guarantee relief in times of need, they pooled part of their funds to buy food in bulk and sell it to members and outsiders alike at a fair price

INTRODUCTION

(Fenwick Weavers' Society Records, 1761–1873). Similar initiatives followed throughout the late eighteenth- and early nineteenth centuries, notably with the founding of co-operative corn mills at Woolwich, Chatham and in Yorkshire (Harrison 1969, 254–255). Under the aegis of Abram Combe and George Mudie, the first Owenite associations had formed with the belief that workers needed to take matters into their own hands if they were to achieve "the complete emancipation of the labouring class from the tyranny of capital and monopoly" (*To Unionists* 1834, 13, cited in Taylor 1983, 93). Due to the failure of the Orbiston and Spa Fields communities, and faced with a lack of resources and political connections, subsequent groups like the London Co-operative Society (LCS) took cues from the earliest grassroots initiatives and gradually opted to invest in consumer and producer co-operatives. Setting up shop would circumvent the lack of capital and political connections that had plagued earlier ventures, as profits would be redirected to the funding of intentional communities instead of going to capitalists and middlemen. The strategy proved highly successful. In 1827, the LCS established its own outlet, the London Co-operative Trading Association. By 1830, nearly 300 of such institutions had been founded throughout the United Kingdom, with branches in London, Manchester, Glasgow, Belfast and elsewhere. Nearly a dozen publications, including the LCS-edited *Co-operative Magazine and Monthly Herald* (1826–1830) attested to the growing popularity of Socialist ideals.[4]

Meanwhile, attempts to bring the same "science of society" to the United States of America failed to materialise. Upon his arrival in the New World, Owen embarked on a lecture tour to promote his views that culminated with two addresses given to the President and Members of Congress in early 1825. Following this wave of enthusiasm, a motley crew of some 800 reformers, freethinkers, radicals, millenarians and scientists flocked to New Harmony (Claeys 1991, xvi). Most had trouble adapting to community life, due to a lack of farming skills and to disagreements with Owen's leadership, and the venture folded in less than three years. Several other Owenite communities were founded in the United States and Canada over the same period, but all met with a similar fate.[5] Owen left for Europe in 1828 but travelled back to North America in November of the same year, hoping to establish a community in Texas, then part of the newly independent state of Mexico. When that project failed, he returned to Britain for good in 1829.

Now settled in London, Owen found himself the *de facto* leader of a budding workers' movement with links to radical and trade unionist circles (Claeys 1982, 170). At first, he treated his new band of disciples with contempt, as he felt that co-operative shops were but a pale imitation of his all-encompassing "science of society". Retail co-operatives, in particular, amounted in his eyes to "a mere pawnbroker's shop" unless they were submitted to the broader ideals of community life (*Proceedings of the Sixth Co-operative Congress*, 8 October 1833, cited in Royle 1998, 54). But after witnessing the growing popularity of co-operation as a vehicle for his communitarian schemes, Owen agreed to take part in the movement that bore his name, federating it and steering it closer to his own universalist principles. (Lovett [1876] 1967, 35; Taylor 1983, 93–94).

Owenism was officially launched in May 1831, when the First Co-operative Congress brought together the delegates from 250 co-operative societies who publicly declared their support for Owen's social system. Following a resolution from the First Birmingham Co-operative Society, they agreed to pool their action and resources on a national scale to establish a community which would prove by the virtue of example the truth of their co-operative ideals (*Carpenter's Political Letters and Pamphlets*, 30 April 1831, cited in Langdon 2000, 37). The following year, Owen formed his own co-operative workshop and store, the National Equitable Labour Exchange, which was located on the premises of the movement's headquarters off Gray's Inn Road, London. Labour exchanges had been launched in London and Birmingham by three of his disciples, William Pare, William King and James Tucker, and several of these institutions were created in Britain in the years 1832–1833.

But by now, Owen was turning his attention towards the growing trades' union movement, which had been on the rise following the repeal of the Combination Acts in 1825. Having witnessed rising support for his ideas among unionists, he now believed that syndicalism would usher in a "New Moral World" more effectively than co-operative trading alone. Ideally, a union of all trades under Socialist principles would help create a comprehensive system of political and economic co-operation that would supersede the present system based on unrestrained competition and individual interest (Siméon 2018, 23). The Co-operative Congress approved this change in strategy in November 1833, and the Grand National Consolidated Trades' Union (GNCTU) was founded in February 1834. Launched in 1833, the *Crisis, and National Co-operative Trades' Union Gazette*, became the official Owenite newspaper, and reported on the progress of social reform. But just like earlier community experiments, these attempts at political and economic co-operation were short-lived. Plagued by economic difficulties, Owen's Labour Exchange closed down in 1834 after only two years in operation. Despite widespread popular support, the GNCTU also collapsed that same year due to a combination of infighting, organisational inadequacies and political repression in the wake of the trial and deportation of the Tolpuddle Martyrs, who had been affiliated with the union. This added to the general feeling of frustration that pervaded working-class politics in the wake of the Reform Act 1832. Deeming that working men were as yet too uneducated to be given the vote, Owen had favoured co-operation and unionism in part as alternatives to an extended franchise. Unsurprisingly, the demise of early Owenite institutions was mirrored by a surge of support for universal male suffrage, while future Chartist leaders like William Lovett and Henry Hetherington gradually distanced themselves from Owen's top-down leadership.

Late Owenism (1834–1845): the age of communities

In spite of these obstacles, the Owenite movement managed to reinvent itself over the next decade. For most early British socialists, the collapse of specific institutions did not hinder their faith in community and Owenism as a whole (Harrison

1969, 218). As a result, co-operative trading did not die out, as shown most notably by the establishment of the Rochdale Society of Equitable Pioneers in 1843. Throughout the 1830s and early 1840s, isolated efforts in community formation had been initiated in Devon (1826–1827), at Ralahine (County Clare, Ireland, 1831–1833), Manea Fen (Cambridgeshire, 1838–1840) and Pant Glas (Merionethshire, 1840), but they were all short-lived due to a lack of funding and backing from Owen himself, who saw them as renegade ventures (Siméon 2017, 144).

From 1835 onwards, however, Owen launched a wide-ranging initiative meant to finally realise his "Plan". In his eyes, the time was ripe for a return to the essence of his "new views" – the founding of large-scale "Villages of Co-operation", and a renewed focus on communitarian ideals.

This change was mirrored by an institutional shift. Whereas the early Owenite movement was characterised by "a loose network of cooperatives and trade union branches" (Taylor 1983, 120), its new incarnation was much more formalised. During the Co-operative Congress of May 1835, Owen announced the creation of a new umbrella organisation, the Association of all Classes of All Nations (AACAN). Aside from this new central body, a subscription scheme, the National Community Friendly Society, was established two years later to promote the foundation of intentional communities. The two were merged in 1842 to become the Universal Community Society of Rational Religionists, also known as the "Rational Society" for short. Throughout the later stage of the Owenite movement, the main body of activism was divided into local branches, including one that Owen personally supervised from his new headquarters in Charlotte Street, London. Under the authority of a national executive, the Central Board, over which Owen presided between 1835 and 1845, local socialist activity took place within a network of schools, libraries and meeting halls known as "Social Institutions" in the 1830s and "Halls of Science" in the following decade. Owen also launched a new publication, the *New Moral World*, whose title called unequivocally for a return to the source of his ideals. Socialist propaganda was in full swing. In London, Owen gave weekly talks, while in the provinces, a group of lecturers appointed by the Central Board and known as the "Social Missionaries" toured the country to extol the virtues of the social system and its application. The earlier annual Co-operative gatherings were replaced by Socialist Congresses. They welcomed the delegates from the branches, voted resolutions and provided a platform for debate, thus becoming the "nerve centre of the Owenite movement" (Harrison 1969, 268).

By 1840, the Owenite movement had a total of fifty branches, located mostly in traditional centres of working-class political activity like London, Birmingham, the North of England and Glasgow, as well as one outpost in New York. The *New Moral World* had reached a weekly circulation of 40,000 copies. (Claeys 1991, xx; Royle 1998, 65).

This widespread popular support and flurry of activity culminated in 1839 with the foundation of the movement's official community at Queenwood, Hampshire. The new venture was established on an estate belonging to Sir Isaac Lyon

Goldsmid (1778–1859), a London banker and personal friend of Owen's. From the onset, the community was presented as the only authentic attempt to establish a "Village of Co-operation", as it was essentially Owen's brainchild, and not a grassroots initiative. However, the Queenwood experiment was plagued by internal strife, and these would eventually bring the Owenite movement to its knees.

Queenwood's residents were mostly working-class Owenite families recruited from the local branches. The community's plebeian government greatly displeased Owen, who still held on to the belief, first expressed in his *New View of Society*, that the "New Moral World" could only be ushered in through support from the rich and powerful. With the economic downturn of the 1830s, and due to the Owenites' general lack of farming experience, the community was in a dire financial situation. Frustrated with this lack of progress, many Owenites opted for emigration to the United States, and took part in the Fourierist-led communitarian revival of the 1840s (Claeys 1991, xvi). This helped Owen gain control of the operations. In 1842, he took up residence at Queenwood, and set out to oversee daily operations with the help of an executive committee of middle-class patrons established one year prior, the Home Colonisation Society (Harrison 1969, 172; Taylor 1983, 234; Royle 1998, 191). But this autocratic chairmanship, which was essentially a return to New Lanark's paternalistic rule, did nothing to appease existing tensions. Refusing to use existing farmhouses on the Queenwood estate, and adamant that the building of the "New Moral World" had to start *ex nihilo*, Owen ordered the building of a new community centre known as Harmony Hall, whose grandeur was meant to facilitate the conversion of mankind to his social system. By 1841, expenses had risen to the extravagant sum of £30,000, thus sinking the Rational Society's funds. Harmony Hall became known among Socialists as a "monument of ill-timed magnificence" (Holyoake 1844, 10) and a symbol of Owen's benevolent despotism. In protest, most of the branches refused to pay the £50 subscription to the community fund, preferring to pool their resources towards local activism instead.

Tensions turned into open warfare in May 1844, when Congress delegates voted to oust Owen as Queenwood's governor and replace him with a working-class executive led by the Manchester socialist John Buxton, who promised to implement democratic governance and complete community of goods and property. Though the decision raised many hopes, the new regime never managed to overturn Owen's financial mismanagement. The would-be flagship community filed for bankruptcy in 1845, effectively tolling the death knell of Owenism as an organised political movement.

The Owenite legacy

In spite of the Queenwood debacle, Owen remained politically active throughout his life. In 1845, he revisited the United States; three years later, he travelled to Paris in the wake of the 1848 revolution to promote his ideas among the French provisional government. Even in his later years, he worked relentlessly on a variety of publications while giving numerous lectures. In Owen's eyes, the demise of Britain's first socialist movement did not negate the truth of his "social system", but had merely shown that his ideas had never been properly put to the test. This long-lasting confidence was shared by a small retinue of admirers that included long-term supporters like Henry Travis, William Pare and John Finch. But in the context of Chartism and secularism, Owen's condescending attitude towards working-class politics, his refusal to compromise and his conversion to spiritualism in 1853 greatly damaged his reputation. By the 1850s, he had retired to the market town of Sevenoaks in Kent, and only travelled occasionally to address a dwindling number of disciples. In 1858, feeling that his end was near, he expressed a desire to travel to his birthplace of Newtown (Wales), which he had not visited in nearly seventy years. It was there that he passed away on 17 November 1858, at the age of eighty-seven, with his eldest son Robert Dale by his side (Claeys 1991, xxii–iii; Siméon 2017, 153).

Owen's political legacy has endured in spite of all his contradictions. Many of his principles remained relevant according to later Socialists and co-operators, thus gradually entering the canon of the British left. Not only did Owen's former supporters take part in the Chartist movement; some, like George Jacob Holyoake and William Pare, played a pivotal role in the co-operative revival of the 1860s, while others continued to promote the cause of popular education. In the 1880s, the Fabian Society rediscovered Owen's thinking and introduced it to a new audience, one which would later form the Labour Party. With his emphasis on character formation and peaceful reform, Owen offered a welcome alternative to Marxian class struggle, and was furthermore deemed representative of a typically British ideal of political moderation (Potter Webb 1899, 15–16). His community spirit was deemed worthy of attention, though its field of application was no longer the ill-fated "Village of Co-operation", but the democratic nation-state (Jones 1983, 146; Chase 2007, 250; Siméon 2017, 154).

Subsequently, this reasoning has helped cement Owen's reputation as the "Father of British Socialism", a badge of honour that he retains to this day. This is particularly true for the modern co-operative movement which, more than any other British socialist platform, traces its ancestry back to Robert Owen, through his impact on early worker-owned stores and the later Rochdale Society of Equitable Pioneers. In 1994, the first monument to Owen was inaugurated outside the Co-operative Wholesale Society headquarters in Manchester, and most of Owen's correspondence is now held on the same premises as part of the National Co-operative Archive (Donnachie and Hewitt 1993, 184; Davis and O'Hagan 2014, 194). In many ways, modern co-operators have perpetuated modes of action that are reminiscent to those favoured by their nineteenth-century forebears, a minutiae of initiatives often "at the edges (. . .) of national policy making" whether they be experiments in popular education, circulating libraries, social enterprises, or the variety of co-operative ventures, ranging from retail schemes to voluntary work and local politics (Davis and O'Hagan 2014, 181; Siméon 2017, 156).

INTRODUCTION

Owen's social system reached a wide audience in his days because it resonated with the realities of working-class lives. Starting with the New Lanark experiment, the "science of society" touched upon virtually every aspect of the common people's existence: from industrial relations to gender roles, from family life to the need to strike a balance between work and leisure. In the words of William Thompson (1824, 427), Owen's "Villages of Co-operation" formed "one grand moral as well as economical experiment", at once universal and highly concrete; one from which Owenites drew inspiration to advance political and economic reform while seeking more immediate solutions to their quest for "bread, knowledge and freedom" (Lovett [1876] 1967; Claeys 1989, 197; Siméon 2017, 158–159).

The significance of Owenism for the history of working-class politics and socialism in general is therefore immense, as it helped the early British socialism movement acquire its political identity as an alternative to unchecked capitalism and rampant individualism. In spite of internal tension, the movement's tight-knit social framework was construed as an antidote to the perceived vanishing of social bonds in the new industrial age. It also looked forward to a time when progress would not depend on divisive government-led reforms and party politics, but on the advent of a new form of bottom-up social organisation based on the principle of voluntary association. At a time when the working classes were still largely excluded from parliamentary politics, Owenism generated a community of ideas and a *modus operandi* for radicals in Britain, as well as abroad to a much lesser extent (see Part 9). Institutions such as co-operatives, labour exchanges, unions, Halls of Science and intentional communities emerged from that locus, often from grassroots initiatives. Despite continuous arguments over the nature and speed of political reform and the room for working-class agency, active participation in these institutions was largely accepted as a valuable experiment in alternative forms of democracy. This was not through the exertion of voting rights, but via the application of community ideals and practices in the political and economic realms (Siméon 2017, 159).

Some aspects of Robert Owen's "social system" may sound idealistic to a twenty-first century audience, especially his unwavering belief that it would bring a conclusive solution to the evils and injustices of his day. Nor does his authoritarianism sit well with modern notions of democracy. But in view of the established continuities between Owen and the future British socialist movement, considering him as no more than a misguided visionary is no longer acceptable. That the issues he tackled are still considered relevant today points to the enduring quality, in many respects, of his "science of society". Owenism may have been utopian, but only insofar as it posited the quest for a better life as a condition of individual and collective progress, even for the labouring poor. If imagination is indeed an instrument of critique, then the early socialist vision of the future was firmly embedded in the empirical realities of modern capitalist society (Ricœur 1985; Claeys 2011; Levitas 2013; Siméon 2017, 160).

Notes

1. In October 1810, Owen bought New Lanark from the Chorlton Twist Company with the help of new business partners. Among them were Robert Dennistoun and Alexander Campbell of Hallyhards, the sons-in-law of Archibald Campbell of Jura, a prominent Highland laird and David Dale's cousin by marriage. In 1806, shortly before Dale's death, Campbell of Jura secretly lent Owen £20,000 to invest at New Lanark, but the money was mostly spent on planning a new school building – possibly the future Institute for the Formation of Character. By 1812, expenses amounted to £30,000. Having discovered Owen's arrangement with their father-in-law, Dennistoun and Campbell of Hallyhards dissolved the New Lanark partnership on 30 June 1812. Owen was sued and dismissed. Though he managed to buy New Lanark back from the Campbells thanks to new backers (who included Quaker philanthropist William Allen and Jeremy Bentham), Owen only escaped bankruptcy thanks to the intervention of his sisters-in-law, Jane and Mary Dale. The operation sank much of the Dale inheritance, and probably played an important part in the deterioration of Robert and Anne Caroline Owen's marriage. The Campbell debt was not fully settled until November 1822 (Robertson 1969; Siméon 2017, 52–53).
2. Earlier works included *Observations on the Cotton Trade* (1803) and the privately circulated *Statement Regarding the New Lanark Establishment* (1812).
3. Also known as the *London Co-operative Magazine*.
4. Other titles included the *Belfast Co-operative Advocate* (1830), the *Lancashire and Yorkshire Co-operator* (1831–1832) and the *Weekly Free Press* (1825–1830).
5. In addition to New Harmony, Owenite communities were established in Indiana (Blue Spring, 1826–1827), Ohio (Kendal, 1826–1829; Yellow Springs, 1825–1826); Pennsylvania (Valley Forge, 1826), upstate New York (Haverstraw, 1826; Forestville, 1825–1826) and Tennessee (Nashoba, 1825–1830). See Part 6, Chapter 36, for an account of the Nashoba community, and Part 9, Chapter 56, for the Constitution of the Blue Spring Community.

Part 1

WORK AS IT WAS AND HOW IT MIGHT BE

Robert Owen's "science of society" was primarily informed by his early experience as a reform-minded industrialist. In the 1790s, his involvement with both the Manchester Literary and Philosophical Society and the Manchester Board of Health had brought him into contact with liberal and dissenting circles, as well as with the practice and rhetoric of philanthropy (Fraser 1937–38; Siméon 2017, 22). This formed the basis of his critical assessment of industrialisation and its impact on the lives and work of the labouring classes, a critique which would later be encompassed in his general scheme of social regeneration on a communitarian basis.

Owen's analysis of the factory system rested on both moral and economic considerations. Though he conceded that "the main pillar and prop of the political greatness and prosperity of our country is a manufacture which, as it is now carried on, is destructive to the health, morals, and social comforts of the mass of the people engaged in it" (Owen 1815, 16), he was not rejecting the new industrial age *per se* but its irrational management. Though Owen ultimately endorsed the establishment of rural communities to solve the dual issues of unemployment and pauperism, his system was by no means a purely nostalgic, agrarian alternative to modern industrialisation. His book *A New View of Society* (1813–1816) consequently explored the following paradox: even though the rise of machines and the new division of labour were meant to ensure the wealth of nations and improve human condition, the factory system had failed thus far to guarantee a fair redistribution of profit in the interest of the common good. On the contrary, the new industrial age had fostered a selfish, individualistic and greedy spirit of competition that had left behind the impoverished working classes – despite their pivotal role as the main producers of wealth. For Owen, this immoral organisation of work posed a threat to the very fabric of society, as it negated the ancestral sense of community and co-operation that prevailed, according to Owen, in the old world of rural settlements. In the context of both the post-war crisis especially and the growing obsolescence of the Old Poor Law system, bettering the condition of the poor was a matter of national urgency, and the first necessary step before all other social reforms could be implemented (Chapter 1).

Like Owen, his disciples claimed that well-managed technical change was the key to social and economic progress. In doing so, they stood in contrast to Whig laissez-faire political economy, as well as to the view held by many Tories and Radicals that machinery was the main oppressor of mankind. At the same time, they rejected essentialist perceptions of poverty, and countered that the plight of the working classes was the result of unfortunate circumstances, rather than any ontological flaw (Claeys 1987, 24–26; Siméon 2017, 20). Though Owenism was ultimately a critique of capitalism, the aim was not to abandon machinery and modern modes of production, but to humanise them and harness their potential through a range of proposed reforms in a variety of fields – including industrial relations (Chapters 1–5), changes in the wage system (Chapter 7), factory reform (Chapter 2) and campaigns for the eight-hour working day (Chapter 6).

1
"AN ADDRESS TO THE SUPERINTENDENTS OF MANUFACTORIES, AND TO THOSE INDIVIDUALS GENERALLY, WHO, BY GIVING EMPLOYMENT TO AN AGGREGATED POPULATION, MAY EASILY ADOPT THE MEANS TO FORM THE SENTIMENTS AND MANNERS OF SUCH A POPULATION", IN *A NEW VIEW OF SOCIETY, OR, ESSAYS ON THE FORMATION OF THE HUMAN CHARACTER: PREPARATORY TO THE DEVELOPMENT OF A PLAN FOR GRADUALLY AMELIORATING THE CONDITION OF MANKIND*, III (LONDON: PRINTED FOR LONGMAN, HURST, REES, ORME, AND BROWN, [1814] 1816), 71–77.

Robert Owen

[The years 1813–1814 were pivotal in Owen's political career. After having garnered the support of progressive business partners like William Allen, Jeremy Bentham and John Walker, he found the confidence to publicise his social system with his *New View of Society, or Essays on the Formation of Character*

(1813–1816). The first two essays in the book outlined Owen's deterministic philosophies, while the third and fourth explored ways to put these principles into practice. In the preface to the third essay, Owen urged his fellow master-manufacturers to imitate the regime of benevolent, paternalistic governance he had set up at New Lanark since the year 1800. Refusing to objectify factory workers as mere "hands", as was common at the time in accordance with Malthusian principles, Owen envisaged the union of man and machine in a joint quest for social and economic progress, thereby refusing to separate his duties as a businessman and as a citizen (Bestor [1950] 2018; Siméon 2017, 21).]

Address prefixed to Third Essay

To the superintendents of manufactories, and to those individuals generally, who, by giving employment to an aggregated population, may easily adopt the means to form the sentiments and manners of such a population.

Like you, I am a manufacturer for pecuniary profit. But having for many years acted on principles the revers in many respects of those in which you have been instructed, and having found my procedure beneficial to others and to myself, even in a pecuniary point of view, I am anxious to explain such valuable principles, that you and those under your influence may equally partake of their advantages.

In two Essays, already published, I have developed some of these principles, and in the following pages you will find still more of them explained, with some detail of their application to practice under the peculiar circumstances in which I took the direction of the New Lanark Mills and Establishment.

By those details you will find that from the commencement of my management I viewed the population, with the mechanism and every other part of the establishment, as a system composed of many parts, and which it was my duty and interest so to combine, as that every hand, as well as every spring, lever, and wheel, should effectually co-operate to produce the greatest pecuniary gain to the proprietors.

Many of you have long experienced in your manufacturing operations the advantages of substantial, well-contrived, and well-executed machinery.

Experience has also shown you the difference of the results between mechanism which is neat, clean, well-arranged, and always in a high state of repair; and that which is allowed to be dirty, in disorder, without the means of preventing unnecessary friction, and which therefore becomes, and works, much out of repair.

In the first case the whole economy and management are good; every operation proceeds with ease, order, and success. In the last, the reverse must follow, and a scene be presented of counteraction, confusion, and dissatisfaction among all the agents and instruments interested or occupied in the general process, which cannot fail to create great loss.

If, then, due care as to the state of your inanimate machines can produce such beneficial results, what may not be expected if you devote equal attention to your vital machines, which are far more wonderfully constructed?

When you shall acquire a right knowledge of these, of their curious mechanism, of their self-adjusting powers; when the proper mainspring shall be applied to their varied movements you will become conscious of their real value, and you will readily be induced to turn your thoughts more frequently from your inanimate to your living machines; you will discover that the latter may be easily trained and directed to procure a large increase of pecuniary gain, while you may also derive from them high and substantial gratification.

Will you then continue to expend large sums of money to procure the best devised mechanism of wood, brass, or iron; to retain it in perfect repair; to provide the best substance for the prevention of unnecessary friction, and to save it from falling into premature decay? — Will you also devote years of intense application to understand the connection of the various parts of these lifeless machines, to improve their effective powers, and to calculate with mathematical precision all their minute and combined movements? — And when in these transactions you estimate time by minutes, and the money expended for the chance of increased gain by fractions, will you not afford some of your attention to consider whether a portion of your time and capital would not be more advantageously applied to improve your living machines? From experience which cannot deceive me, I venture to assure you, that your time and money so applied, if directed by a true knowledge of the subject, would return you, not five, ten, or fifteen per cent for your capital so expended, but often fifty, and in many cases a hundred per cent.

I have expended much time and capital upon improvements of the living machinery; and it will soon appear that time and the money so expended in the manufactory at New Lanark, even while such improvements are in progress only, and but half their beneficial effects attained, are now producing a return exceeding fifty per cent, and will shortly create profits equal to cent per cent on the original capital expended in them.

Indeed, after experience of the beneficial effects from due care and attention to the mechanical implements, it became easy to a reflecting mind to conclude at once, that at least equal advantages would arise from the application of similar care and attention to the living instruments. And when it was perceived that inanimate mechanism was greatly improved by being made firm and substantial; that it was the essence of economy to keep it neat, clean, regularly supplied with the best substance to prevent unnecessary friction, and by proper provision for the purpose to preserve it in good repair, it was natural to conclude that the more delicate, complex, living mechanism would be equally improved by being trained to strength and activity and that it would also prove true economy to keep it neat and clean; to treat it with kindness, that its mental movements might not experience too much irritating friction; to endeavour by every means to make it more perfect; to supply it regularly with a sufficient quantity of wholesome food and other necessaries of life, that the body might be preserved in good working condition, and prevented from being out of repair, or falling prematurely to decay.

These anticipations are proved by experience to be just.

Since the general introduction of inanimate mechanism into British manufactories, man, with few exceptions, has been treated as a secondary and inferior machine; and far more attention has been given to perfect the raw materials of wood and metals than those of body and mind. Give but due reflection to the subject, and you will find that man, even as an instrument for the creation of wealth, may be still greatly improved.

But, my friends, a far more interesting and gratifying consideration remains. Adopt the means which ere long shall be rendered obvious to every understanding, and you may not only partially improve those living instruments, but learn how to impart to them such excellence as shall make them infinitely surpass those of the present and all former times.

Here, then, is an object which truly deserves your attention; and, instead of devoting all your faculties to invent improved inanimate mechanism, let your thoughts be, at least in part, directed to discover how to combine the more excellent materials of body and mind which, by a well-devised experiment, will be found capable of progressive improvement.

Thus seeing with the clearness of noonday light, thus convinced with the certainty of conviction itself, let us not perpetuate the really unnecessary evils which our present practices inflict on this large proportion of our fellow subjects. Should your pecuniary interests somewhat suffer by adopting the line of conduct now urged, many of you are so wealthy that the expense of founding and continuing at your respective establishments the institutions necessary to improve your animate machines would not be felt, but when you may have ocular demonstration, that, instead of any pecuniary loss, a well-directed attention to form the character and increase the comforts of those who are so entirely at your mercy, will essentially add to your gains, prosperity, and happiness, no reasons, except those founded on ignorance of your self-interest, can in future prevent you from bestowing your chief care on the living machines which you employ. And by so doing you will prevent an accumulation of human misery, of which it is now difficult to form an adequate conception.

That you may be convinced of this most valuable truth, which due reflection will show you is founded on the evidence of unerring facts, is the sincere wish of

THE AUTHOR

2

"EVIDENCE OF ROBERT OWEN ON HIS NEW LANARK EXPERIMENT", IN *REPORT OF MINUTES OF EVIDENCE, TAKEN BEFORE THE SELECT COMMITTEE ON THE STATE OF CHILDREN EMPLOYED IN THE MANUFACTORIES OF THE UNITED KINGDOM* (LONDON: HANSARD, 1816), 20–28.

House of Commons

[Robert Owen's growing involvement in factory reform campaigns from 1815 onwards was the logical follow-up to his *New View of Society*. Wishing to put his New Lanark policies to the test, he drafted a bill that he addressed to the House of Commons in June 1815. His proposals, which were meant to amend the Health and Morals Apprentices Act 1802, were submitted in 1816 to a Select Committee chaired by Robert Peel MP. Owen advised to extend the previous legislation to all child factory workers, not just labourers in cotton mills. He also advocated a series of radical labour regulations, directly inspired by his most ambitious measures at New Lanark, which he had introduced on 1 January, 1816. These included a ban on child labour before the age of ten, a ten and three-quarters hours working day and extensive educational provisions thanks to the inauguration of the Institute for the Formation of Character (see Part 2, Chapter 8). While giving evidence before the Select Committee, Owen provided a detailed account of daily life at New Lanark to prove the soundness of his principles (Siméon 2017, 87–89; Innes 2002, 233). Owen's views on factory reform were pioneering, and many of his proposals, notably the case for compulsory education and reduced working hours, were included in the 1833 and subsequent Factory Acts. Yet his bill and evidence put before the 1816 Select Committee were met with great hostility by politicians, both Whigs and Tories, and fellow manufacturers alike, at a time when philanthropy was largely seen as an individual, leisurely pursuit beyond the reach of state intervention (Claeys 1989, 207). Despite Peel's support, a watered-down version of the bill was voted in 1819 with the Cotton Mills and Factories Act (59 Geo. III c66), thus heightening Owen's frustration and encouraging him to adopt a more radical approach to social reform.]

Jovis, 25 die Aprilis, 1816.
SIR ROBERT PEEL, Baronet, in The Chair. [. . .]
Mr. *Robert Owen*, called in, and Examined.

What is your situation in life? — I am principal proprietor and sole acting partner of the establishment at New Lanark, in Scotland.

How many persons, Young and old, are immediately supported by the New Lanark manufactory and establishment? — About 2,300: Upon the first of January last the numbers were 2,297, I believe.

To how many out of that number do you give employment? — [. . .] upon the average about sixteen or seventeen hundred.

The remainder of the 2,300 are the wives and children? — Children too young, and persons too old, of the same families; some of the wives are employed [. . .]

At what age do you take children into your mills? — At ten and upwards

What are your regular hours of labour per day, exclusive of meal times? — Ten hours and three quarters

What time do you allow for meals? — Three quarters of an hour for dinner, and half an hour for breakfast.

Then your full time of work per day is twelve hours, out of which time you allow the mills to cease work for an hour and a quarter? — Yes.

Why do you not employ children at an earlier age? — Because I consider it would be injurious to the children, and not beneficial to the proprietors.

What reason have you to suppose it is injurious to the children to be employed in regular manufactories at an earlier age? — The evidence of very strong facts.

What are those facts? — Seventeen years ago, a number of individuals, with myself, purchased the New Lanark establishment from the late Mr. Dale of Glasgow: At that period I found there were 500 children, who had been taken from poor-houses, chiefly in Edinburgh, and these children were generally from the age of five and six, to seven and eight; they were so taken because Mr. Dale could not, I learned afterward, obtain them at a more advanced period of life; if he did not take them at those ages, he could not obtain them at all. The hours of work at that time were thirteen, inclusive of meal times, and an hour and a half was allowed for meals. I very soon discovered that, although those children were extremely well fed, well clothed, well lodged, and very great care taken of them when out of the mills, their growth and their minds were materially injured by being employed at those ages within the cotton mills for eleven hours and a half per day. It is true that those children, in consequence of being so well fed and clothed and lodged, looked fresh, and to a superficial observer, healthy in their countenances; yet their limbs were very generally deformed, their growth was stunted, and, although one of the best schoolmasters upon the old plan was engaged to instruct those children regularly every night, in general they made but a very slow progress, even in learning the common alphabet. Those appearances strongly impressed themselves upon my mind to proceed solely from the number of hours they were employed [. . .] because in every other respect, they were as well taken care of, and as well looked after, as any children could be. Those were some, and perhaps they may be considered by the Committee sufficient, facts to induce me to suppose that the children were injured by being taken into the mills at this early age, and employed for so many hours; therefore, as soon as I had it in my power, I adopted regulations to put an end to a system which appeared to me to be so injurious.

In consequence then of your conviction that children are injured by being employed the usual daily hours in manufactories, when under ten years of age, you have for some time refused to receive children into your works till they are ten years of age? — Yes.

Do you think the age of ten to be the best period for the admission of children into full and constant employment for ten or eleven hours per day, within woollen, cotton, or other mills or manufactories? — I do not.

What other period would you recommend for this admission to full work? — Twelve years.

How then would you employ them from ten to the age of twelve? — For the two years preceding, to be partially instructed; to be instructed one half the day, and the other half to be initiated into the manufactories by parties employing two sets of children in the day [. . .].

If such be your opinion, how happen you not to have acted upon it? — Had the works been entirely my own, I should have acted upon that principle some time ago, but being connected with other gentlemen, I deem it necessary in practice not to deviate so much from the common regulations of the country as I otherwise would have done; and, besides, it required some time to prepare the population for so material a change from that to which they had been previously accustomed.

In your opinion, what parties would be benefited by such a regulation? — The children, the proprietors of manufactories, and the country. [. . .]

Do you think ten hours and three quarters a day the proper time for children to be employed in manufactories?— I do not.

What time would you recommend? — About ten hours of actual employment, or, at the most, 10 hours and a half.

Do you think, if such an arrangement were made in regard to the number of hours, the manufacturers would suffer any loss in consequence? — My conviction is, that no party would suffer in consequence of it [. . .] either with reference to the home or the foreign trade.

What benefits do you contemplate from this limitation of time? — A very considerable improvement in the health of the operatives, both young and old; a very considerable improvement in the instruction of the rising generation; and a very considerable diminution in the poor rates of the country.

In fact, have you, during the time that the hours were longer, found any sensible difference in those three respects that you have mentioned? — I have found, from our last regulations, which only took place upon the 1st of January last, that that there has been a very sensible difference in the general health and spirit of the whole mass of the population so employed, so much so, that they feel strongly the change which has taken place [. . .].

Do you give instruction to any part of your population? — Yes.

What part? — To the children from three years old, upwards; and to every other part of the population that choose to receive it.

Will you state the particulars? — There is a preparatory school, into which all the children, from the age of three to six, are admitted at the option of the parents; there is a second school, in which all the children of the population, from six to ten, are admitted; and if any of the parents, from being more easy in their circumstances, and setting a higher value upon instruction, wish to continue their children at school for one, two, three, or four years longer, they are at liberty to do so; they are never asked to take the children from the school to the works.

Will you state who supports the schools? — The schools are supported immediately at the expense of the establishment; they are indeed literally and truly supported by the people themselves.

Will you explain how that is? — New Lanark was a new settlement formed by Mr. Dale; the part of the country in which these works were erected was very thinly inhabited; and the Scottish peasantry generally were disinclined to work in cotton mills; it was necessary that great efforts should therefore be made to collect a new population in such a situation, and such population was collected before the usual and customary means for conveniently supplying a population with food were formed, the work people were therefore obliged to buy their food and other articles at a very high price, and under many great disadvantages; to counterbalance this inconvenience, a store was opened at the establishment, into which provisions of the best quality, and clothes of the most useful kind, were introduced, to be sold at the option of the people, at a price sufficient to cover prime-cost and charges, and to cover the accidents of such a business, it being understood [. . .] that whatever profits arose from this establishment, those profits should be employed for the general benefit of the work people themselves; and these school establishments have been supported, as well as other things, by the surplus profits, because in consequence of the pretty general moral habits of the people, there have been very few losses by bad debts, and although they have been supplied considerably under the price of provisions in the neighbourhood, yet the surplus profits have in all cases been sufficient to bear the expense of these school establishments; therefore, they have literally been supported by the people themselves.

What effects have experienced from these plans of instruction? — The best possible. It perhaps may be useful, as there are many gentlemen present who are interested in these questions, and who may not have had the experience I have had, to state, that when these schools were opened, it was not considered sufficient that attention should be paid merely to instructing the children in what are called the common rudiments of learning, that is, in reading, writing, arithmetic, and the girls also in sewing, but it was deemed of much greater importance, that attention should be given by the masters to form the moral habits of the children, and their dispositions; and in consequence, the moral habits of the children have been improved in such a manner that from the 1st of January last to the time I left the establishment, about a week ago, out of two hundred and about twenty children, who are in school in the day, and three hundred and eighty or ninety, who are in school at night, there has not been occasion to punish one single individual; and as the school is arranged upon such principles as are calculated to give the children a good deal of exercise and some amusement, the children are more willing and more desirous of attending the school, and the occupations which they are engaged in there, than of going to their ordinary play: the most unpleasant time they have in the week is the Saturday afternoon, which is necessarily a holiday, in consequence of the schools, in which they are taught, being washed and cleaned on that day. I have found other and very important advantages, in a pecuniary view, from this arrangement and these plans. In consequence of the individuals observing that real attention is given to their comforts and to their improvements, they are willing to work at much lower wages at that establishment, than at others at great distance, which are esteemed to be upon the best plans in the country, with all the newest improvements. [. . .]

Do you think that the regulations which are in force at New Lanark, would apply to a large populous manufacturing town, where the inhabitants are not utterly dependent upon a manufactory? — The same principles, I conceive, may be applied, under different modifications, to any situation, where there are few or many.

What employment could be found for the children of the poor, in those situations, till ten years of age? — It does not appear to me that it is necessary for children to be employed under 10 years of age, in any regular work.

If you did not employ them in any regular work, what would you do with them? — Instruct them, and give them exercise.

Would not there be a danger of their acquiring, by that time, vicious habits, for want of regular occupation? — My own experience leads me to say that I have found quite the reverse, that their habits have been good in proportion to the extent of their instruction.

That proceeds upon the supposition that they are to be instructed. — Most assuredly; if the children are not to be instructed, they had better be employed in any occupation that should keep them out of mischief. [. . .]

3

"LETTER, DATED JULY 25 AND 16, 1817, CONTAINING A FURTHER DEVELOPMENT OF THE PLAN CONTAINED IN THE REPORT TO THE COMMITTEE OF THE ASSOCIATION FOR THE RELIEF OF THE MANUFACTURING AND LABOURING POOR, WITH ANSWERS AND OBJECTIONS" (1817), IN *A SUPPLEMENTARY APPENDIX TO THE FIRST VOLUME OF THE LIFE OF ROBERT OWEN, CONTAINING A SERIES OF REPORTS, ADDRESSES, MEMORIALS, AND OTHER DOCUMENTS, REFERRED TO IN THAT VOLUME. 1803–1820* (LONDON: EFFINGHAM WILSON, 1858) APPENDIX I.2, 65–78.

Robert Owen

[Published in the London newspapers of 10 September 1817, this explanation of Owen's plans for the reorganisation of society shows how his system matured and radicalised between 1815 and 1820 following his growing interest in Poor Law reform. In March 1817, Owen had presented his proposal for the establishment of self-supporting communities for the poor, or "Agricultural and Manufacturing Villages of Unity and Mutual Co-operation" to the Select Committee of the House of Commons on the Poor Laws. When his plan was rejected by Parliament, he launched a publicity campaign to further his cause, and his *Further Development*, written in dialogue form, was sent to the London press in that context. During the post-Waterloo crisis, several hundred schemes in the Spencean vein had been put forward, such as Lieutenant General Craufurd's *Observations* or Henry Barnet Gascoigne's *Antidote to Distress*, both published in 1817(Hilton 1977, 1–66; Berg 1980, 97; Siméon 2017, 91). Owen's proposal was original insofar as he rejected purely agrarian, "back-to-the-land" approaches in favour of a balance between agricultural and industrial activities, in a bid to reconcile the best of both the old and new economic orders. The *Further Development* also acknowledged the intellectual influence of the Quaker philanthropist John Bellers' *Proposals for Raising a Colledge of Industry* [(1695)1818], an attempt to establish agricultural colonies as an antidote to the Old Poor Law (Davis 1983, 388–390; Siméon 2017, 92).[1] The response was mostly negative. In his *Paper on the Means of Reducing the Poor Rates*, the Whig political economist Robert Torrens (1780–1864) considered that Owen belonged "to the order of political alchemists" (1817, 514). Though he was personally acquainted with Owen and was involved in a committee to examine his reform proposals in June 1819, David Ricardo showed little actual commitment to the "Villages of Co-operation" (Ricardo to Trower, 8 July 1819, cited in Sraffa, 1952, 46; Berg 1980, 70). For abolitionists like the Jamaica-born, mixed-race radical Robert Wedderburn (1762–1835?), Owen had devised "pauper barracks" meant to "rear up a community of slaves" (*Black Dwarf*, 20 August 1817, 469, cited in Morris 2018, 122). Despite the hostile response, Owen's publicity campaign helped popularise his system, which became colloquially known as his "Plan" (Harrison 1969, 8, 14; Claeys 1987, xviii).]

[. . .] Communities of 500 to 1,500 persons, founded on the principle of united labour and expenditure, and having their basis in agriculture, might be arranged so as to give the following advantages to the labouring poor, and through them to all the other classes – for every real benefit to the latter must come from the former. All the labour of the individuals under this system would be naturally and advantageously directed; first to procure for themselves abundance of all that was necessary for the comfortable subsistence; next, they would obtain the means to enable them to unlearn many, almost all indeed, of the bad habits which the present defective arrangements of society have forced upon them: then, to give only the best habits and dispositions to the rising generation, and thus withdraw those circumstances from society which separate man from man, and introduce others, whose entire tendency shall be to unite them in one general interest that shall be clearly understood by each. They will afterwards be enabled to cultivate the far more valuable, the intellectual part of their nature; that part which, when properly directed, will discover how much may yet be put into practice to promote human happiness.

They will then proceed to create that surplus which will be necessary to repay the interest of the capital expended in the purchase of the establishment, including all its appendages; or, in other words, the rent of it. And lastly, to contribute their full share to the exigencies of the State, in proportion to the value of their property. By these arrangements they will add a new strength to the political power of the country, that few are yet able to estimate. [. . .]

Q. But should many of these villages be founded, will they not increase the products of agricultural and manufacturing labour, which are already too abundant, until no market can be found for them, and thus injure the present agriculture, manufacture, and commerce of the country?

A. This is a part of the subject that requires to be understood better than, at present, it appears to be by any party. Is it possible that there can be too many productions desirable and useful to society? And is it not the interest of all, that they should be produced with the least expense and labour, and with the smallest degree of misery and moral degradation to the working classes; and, of course, in the greatest abundance to the higher classes, in return for their wealth? It is surely to the interest of all, that everything should be produced with the least expense of labour, and so as to realize the largest portion of comfort to the producing classes: and there are no means of effecting these desirable ends that will bear any comparison with the combined agricultural and manufacturing villages, colleges of industry, county or district establishments for the poor and industrious, or by whatsoever name they may be called. It is true that as they increase in number they may come into competition with the existing agricultural and manufacturing systems, if society shall permit them so to do; otherwise, they can restrain them to the amount of their own immediate wants; and, constituted as they will be, they can have no motives to produce an unnecessary surplus. When society shall, however, discover its true interests, it will permit these new establishments gradually to supersede the others; inasmuch as the latter are wretchedly degrading, and directly opposed to the improvement and well-being of those employed either in agriculture or manufactures, and consequently are equally hostile to the welfare and happiness of all the higher classes. We know full well the misery and vice in which the manufacturing population is involved; we know also the ignorance and degradation to which the agricultural labourer is reduced; and it is only by such a rearrangement of this part of society that these enormous evils can ever be removed. [. . .]

Q. By thus altering the general habits and existing arrangements of the lower orders, would it not give an increased value to manual labour?

A. My intention was to combine the means of accomplishing objects which appear to me to be inevitably required by the existing state of the country; and to prevent the violent derangement of society, arising from the distress and extreme demoralization which is hourly advancing and must go on till effectual and counteracting measures shall be adopted. I saw the poor and working classes surrounded by circumstances that necessarily entailed misery on them and their posterity; that if they were allowed to continue and proceed much longer, they would further demoralize and violently subvert the whole social system. To prevent this catastrophe, it becomes absolutely indispensable that their habits be changed; and this cannot be done without altering the existing arrangements with regard to them and to the rising generation. If the plan proposed shall be found to be much, nay, infinitely, more complete, in all its parts, and in its entire combination, than any hitherto suggested, and if it can be immediately and gradually introduced without causing the least shock to society, or prematurely disturbing existing institutions, then is the proper time arrived – then are the circumstances duly prepared, for its reception; and I fell a perfect confidence in saying, that however, through mistaken private interests, it may be attempted to retard it, it will be inevitably introduced, and firmly established, even against all opposition. It is, indeed, of that nature, that opposition will but hasten its adoption, and fix the principles more generally and deeply in and through society. The circumstances that have been silently, for nearly twenty years past, preparing for this end, are so far completed, as to answer all the purposes intended; and the future welfare of mankind, in this and also in other countries, may be considered secure, beyond the power of accident. Combined labour and expenditure, for a common object, among the working classes, with proper training and instruction for their offspring, and surrounded by the circumstances devised for the whole, will create and secure the present safety of society, the present and future comfort and happiness of the individuals, and the ultimate well-being of all. I may, therefore, confidently believe, that no combination of human powers can now be formed to prevent its permanent adoption. After having made this statement, it is necessary for me to add, that the knowledge I have acquired on this subject has been forced upon me by a long and extensive experience, which, under similar circumstances, would have been acquired by the generality of mankind. None, I believe not one, of the principles, have the least claim to originality; they have been repeatedly advocated and recommended by superior minds, from the earliest periods of history. I have no claim even to priority in regard to the combinations of these principles in theory; this belongs, as far as I know, to John Bellers, who published them, and most ably recommended them to be adopted in practice in the year 1696.[2] [. . .]

Q. *Is it then your decided opinion, that land, labour, and capital, may be employed under a new combination so as to produce more valuable results to all parties than they do at present?*

A. If I have derived any distinct knowledge by my long experience and extensive practice, I am enabled to say, with a confidence that fears no refutation, that any given quantity of land, labour, and capital, may be so combined as to support at least four times the present number of human beings, and in tenfold comfort that the same is maintained at present, under the existing practices in this country; and, of course, that the intrinsic value of land, labour, and capital, may be increased in the same proportion: that, consequently, we possess the most ample means to carry now, without loss of time, the prosperity of the country to a point it has not before attained – to a height that no country has ever yet experienced. If nay parties suppose these to be mere assertions without sound foundation, or to be a visionary scheme derived from the regions of fancy, they will be mistaken; for they are the result of a patient and unwearied attention to discover accurate and practical data, and to try an endless variety of experiments, to enable me to draw correct conclusions, and thus bring the theories of learned men in their closets to the only test of truth. By thus proceeding I have been more and more satisfied of the errors of mere theories, and of the little real value they have hitherto been to mankind. I have no wish, however, that any more confidence should be placed in what I say, than to induce the public to give a fair trial of the plan. If I am in error, the loss and inconvenience, compared with the object, will be small; but if I am right, the public and the world will be gainers indeed! I ask nothing for myself; and, except goodwill and the interchange of kind and friendly offices, I will not accept anything from any party. I merely ask to be permitted to relieve the poor and working classes from their present distress, and to render an essential service to the wealthy and to all the higher classes. I am, therefore, desirous that competent persons of business should be named to investigate all the details which I have to propose; knowing, as I do from experience, that this is the only practical measure that can be adopted to enable the public to comprehend a subject so extensive and important as this will ultimately prove to be.

Q. On the supposition that the plan may be unexceptionable in all its parts, how can it be carried into execution, as far as relates to the poor who receive parochial aid?

A. First, by passing an Act of Parliament to nationalize the poor. Secondly, by borrowing, from time to time, on the national security, sufficient sums to build these villages, and to prepare the land for cultivation; the Government holding security upon these establishments until both interest and capital shall be paid; by which means the whole process would be straightforward, equitable, and just to all the parties; and the country would enable the Government to carry it into execution, without opposition from any interested party.

Notes

1 Robert Owen was introduced to John Bellers' reform scheme by Francis Place, who had remarked great similarities between the "Colledges of Industry" and the "New View of Society". Owen financed a reprint of Bellers' pamphlet in 1818 ([1695] 1818), and also included it in the appendix to his autobiography in 1858 (vol. 1.A., 157–204).
2 The actual publication date was 1695.

4

REMARKS ON THE PRACTICABILITY OF MR. ROBERT OWEN'S PLAN TO IMPROVE THE CONDITION OF THE LOWER CLASSES (LONDON: S. LEIGH, 1819), 25–28.

Philanthropos [John Minter Morgan]

[John Minter Morgan (1782–1854) was a wealthy London philanthropist and author. After hearing Owen's infamous speech at the City of London Tavern in August 1817, Minter Morgan became part of Owen's early coterie of middle- and upper-class backers. Yet, unlike many of his fellow members of the British and Foreign Philanthropic Society, he embraced Owen's radicalisation while trying to appease those who feared that his schemes had dangerously veered towards 'visionary' territory (see Part 2). A founder of the London Co-operative Society in 1825, he supported the community scheme at Orbiston and was a prominent figure at the Cooperative Congresses in the 1830s. Minter Morgan's *Remarks* were an attempt to popularise Owen's views and garner financial support for his Plan, at a time when it was attracting backlash from Radicals and Conservatives alike. To this end, and in contradiction with Owen's religious scepticism, he assured prospective patrons that the future "Villages of Co-operation" would include religious instruction for the poor, thus framing what would later be known as "socialism" as a respectable system.]

Mr. Owen, in his Report to the Committee,[1] has given so full an account of the details of the system that I forbear entering minutely into them. I will only observe, that the interest of the capital at first expended, and the rent of the land, would be paid out of the poor-rate; and as the labour of each individual with the aid of machinery, and under proper management, yields ten times more than he can consume, nine tenths of the products, or whatever the overplus may be, would so much profit, which would go towards the repayment of the capital and to the speedy abolition of the poor-rate.

I cannot be satisfied merely with suggesting that this plan is superior to any mode of relief to those who are destitute of employment, since there will be no difficulty in showing that it is eminently calculated to hasten the return of that period when the rural virtues were the best preservative of good order in the lower classes of society: for although manufactures will form a part of the establishment, there will be no necessity for any individual to work at them but for a few hours in the day; all can be instructed in the management of machinery, which requires attention rather than great skill, and from its highly improved state it will be a source of pleasant or light employment rather than of fatigue and labour. — It is not unusual to hear the fallen character of our peasantry lamented, as if the change had not been brought about by the altered circumstances in which they have been placed. In the villages want will not be known, the temptation of public-houses will be withdrawn, and all the vices arising from ignorance will give place to the morality and good conduct resulting from early religious instruction.

It has been thought that the poor, however comfortable their condition may be rendered, would be averse from any plan that placed them in continual confinement. And certainly, if such was *really* the case with regard to the villages of mutual co-operation, it might, in many instances, be an objection difficult to overcome. If you give the poor man comfortable clothing and habitation; if you give him a sufficiency of good food; if you require of him only moderate labour; if in sickness his family have the best advice and attendance; if you instruct his children in every branch of useful knowledge, and after all allow him to depart whenever he thinks proper, — does common society hold out any inducement for him to quit a situation of such substantial happiness?

As these new independent establishments are not likely to revert back to the old state of society, we will examine some of the more popular objections to the system, considered as a permanent community: but in so doing we shall be obliged to contrast the existing state of society with that which will be found in the villages; and without some preliminary explanation, we might be liable to the misconception of recommending a revolutionary scheme. Against this construction of my views I must here enter my protest: I disclaim all idea of interfering with any of our established institutions. As the opponents of the plan derive their chief arguments from whet they conclude to be an irremediable defection in human nature, it will be necessary to show to how great an extent crime may be traced to the unfavourable circumstances influencing individuals, and which it is the interest no less than the duty to remove. The remedy now proposed, so far from injuring a single individual in any respect whatever, will prove highly beneficial to all. It removes to a distance that part of society which is at present an annoyance or an incumbrance to the rest; that part which endangers the security of property, and furnishes inhabitants for our prison, and victims of punishment; and which, is suffered to go on in its present course, will lead to the entire subversion of the social system.

Note

1　The Select Committee of the House of Commons on the Poor Laws, which convened in March 1817 (Owen 1817).

5

"ON THE CAUSES OF THE DISTRESS PREVALENT IN GREAT BRITAIN", IN *REPORT OF THE COMMITTEE APPOINTED AT A MEETING OF JOURNEYMEN, CHIEFLY PRINTERS, TO TAKE INTO CONSIDERATION CERTAIN PROPOSITIONS, SUBMITTED TO THEM BY MR. GEORGE MUDIE, HAVING FOR THEIR OBJECT A SYSTEM OF SOCIAL ARRANGEMENT, CALCULATED TO EFFECT ESSENTIAL IMPROVEMENTS IN THE CONDITION OF THE WORKING CLASSES* (LONDON: THE MEDALLIC CABINET, 1821), 4–5.

George Mudie

[George Mudie (1787–1855) was a printer, newspaper editor and author from Edinburgh. He and Robert Owen met in Leeds in 1816, and Mudie soon embraced the Welshman's "science of society" and communitarian ideals. Having moved to London in 1820 as the editor of the *Sun*, he set out to form an Owenite group in the capital. This led him to address a committee of fellow radical printers in August 1820, when he suggested establishing a community based on Owen's plan to resolve the country's state of economic distress. Mudie's analysis of Britain's economic situation drew upon Owen's arguments. The chief cause of poverty remained the "depreciation in the value of manual labour" due to the irrational use of machinery. But Mudie's proposals were highly original, as he was probably the first of Owen's followers to advocate co-operation as a solution to the pauperisation of the working classes (Claeys 1987, chapter 3). The printers, one of whom was Henry Hetherington, responded favourably, thus leading to the formation of the first Owenite community experiment – the Co-operative and Economical Society (CES), which was founded in Spa Fields, London, in 1821 (Hardy 1979, 43–46; Claeys 1982; Bennett 2016, 45).]

[...] Notwithstanding [...] the just admiration in which the British Constitution is held, it must be admitted, that even in this favoured land, Statesmen and Philosophers (with but a few exceptions) appear to take it for granted that a large mass of the people must necessarily endure the evils of Poverty; in other words, that Population will ever have a tendency to outrun the means of comfortable Subsistence.

In the course of our enquiries, our attention has been particularly called to the fact, not less true than paradoxical, that the people of this country are experiencing an unprecedented degree of general Distress, at a moment when the kingdom is abounding in Wealth; and when it is admitted by the most competent authorities, that the soil is capable of producing a sufficiency of food for, at least, twice the number of its present inhabitants. The immediate cause of this state of thins may, most certainly, be traced mainly to the wonderful progress which Mechanical Inventions for abridging human labour, have made within the last 25 or 30 years:— a progress which, far from being interrupted by the lamentable effects already produced, is still advancing with accelerated force. While we chiefly attribute the difficulties of the country, however, to the substitution of Mechanical Agency for human labour, it is proper also to remark, that this injurious and seemingly paradoxical result of useful invention would not have arisen, but in an exceedingly ill constructed frame of society; and that, under a better system, the extension of scientific and mechanical power is certain to be of the highest benefit to mankind at large.

Deplorable as is the prospect which the present state of things presents to the minds of reflecting men, it is obvious that it would be wholly impracticable, even if it were desirable, to discontinue the use of machinery; since, if our steam-engines were to be destroyed, the knowledge of the scientific principles on which they are constructed is so widely diffused by means of the press, that their reconstruction would be easy and certain; and as it is highly improbable that nations envious of our wealth, and not smarting under the effects of an imaginary excess of population, would follow so rash, though self-devoted an example, its effect must necessarily be to reduce the manufacturing importance of this country far below the par of our Continental Rivals. The obvious remedy for the manifold and growing evils of our present condition, is, doubtless, to render machinery subservient to the real interests of the whole population, and to employ a portion of the manual labour which machinery has displaced, in the cultivation of the myriads of acres which are now lying waste, and to enable an increased agricultural population to exchange the produce of the soil thus rescued from sterility, for our superabundant manufactures.

There are, besides, various other arrangements of obvious and easy introduction, which would facilitate the production and distribution of new wealth in a ratio of rapidity which would almost instantly enlarge and secure the comfort and abundance of the whole people, and carry ultimately the prosperity of this and of all other countries to the highest pitch.

Mr. Mudie proceeded to shew that, to the co-operation of man with man, society owes every advance which it has made from the most barbarous state, to the present stage of civilization; while, on the other hand, almost all the evils with which civilized man has been afflicted, may be traced to his early, numerous, and continued deviations from this principle — deviations which have compelled each individual to seek the promotion of his own interests and happiness at the expense, or at least independently, of those of others, and which in every society hitherto constructed, have finally resulted in the wretchedness and ruin of all.

6

"RIGHTS OF INDUSTRY. FOUNDING OF THE NATIONAL REGENERATION SOCIETY IN FAVOUR OF THE EIGHT-HOUR DAY", *CRISIS*, 7 DECEMBER 1833, 117.

Joshua Milne

[The National Regeneration Society was founded on 25 November 1833 in support of the eight-hour working day, under the auspices of Robert Owen, trade union leader John Doherty, radical industrialist John Fielden, and the Oldham cotton factory owner Joshua Milne. Support for the eight-hour day had been on the rise since 1832, when Michael Thomas Sadler's Ten Hour Bill failed to include adult workers. The National Regeneration Society therefore must be created with the intention of it acting as a lobbying organisation with a twofold plan of action: petitioning the most prominent Short Time Committee advocates (Sadler, Richard Oastler, the Reverend G.S. Bull, of Bradford, and John Wood, MP for Preston) to adopt the eight-hour regulation, and encouraging factory operatives to stop working after eight hours. Proponents of the Ten Hour Bill deemed these demands economically unsound. Owen argued, on the contrary, that factory operatives needed more time for education and general improvement, and that the personal benefits derived from such arrangements would foster productivity, with no harm to the general economy of the country (see Chapter 2). By February 1834, the National Regeneration Society had opened about 30 branches, mostly among Lancashire cotton mill workers. It had garnered support from the radical press, including William Cobbett's *Black Dwarf* and Henry Hetherington's *Poor Man's Guardian*, but failed to convince industrialists, with the exception of Milne and Fielden. The organisation was one of the many Owenite ventures to collapse in the year 1834, along with the Labour Exchanges and the Grand National Consolidated Trades Union (GNCTU) (Macfarlane 2016, 74; Cunningham 2014, 95; Kirby and Musson 1975, 272–274, 281; Weaver 1987, 268).]

At a meeting called at the above time and place of the working people of Manchester, and their friends, after taking into their consideration –

That society in this country exhibits the strange anomaly of one part of the people working beyond their strength – another part working at worn out and other employments for very inadequate wages – and another part in a state of starvation for want of employment:

That eight hours' daily labour is enough for any human being, and under proper arrangements, sufficient to afford an ample supply of food, raiment, and shelter, or the necessaries and comforts of life, and that to the remainder of his time every person is entitled for education, recreation, and sleep:

That the productive power of this country, aided by machinery, is so great, and so rapidly increasing, as from its misdirection to threaten danger to society by a still further fall in wages, unless some measure be adopted to reduce the hours of work, and to maintain at least the present amount of wages.

It was unanimously resolved, –

1. That it is desirable that they who wish to see society improved and confusion avoided, should endeavour to assist the working classes to obtain 'for eight hours' work the present full day's wages', such eight hours to be performed between the hours of six in the morning and six in the evening; and that this new regulation should commence on the first day of March next.
2. That in order to carry the foregoing purposes into effect, a society shall, be formed, to be called 'The Society for promoting National Regeneration'.
3. That persons be immediately appointed from among the workmen to visit their fellow-workmen in each trade, manufacture, and employment, in every district of the kingdom, for the purpose of communicating with them on the subject of the above resolutions, and of inducing them to determine upon their adoption.
4. That persons be also appointed to visit the master-manufacturers in each trade, in every district, to explain and recommend to them the adoption of the new regulation referred to in the first resolution.
5. That the persons appointed as above shall hold a meeting on Tuesday evening, the 17th of December, at eight o'clock, to report what has been done, and to determine upon future proceedings.
6. That all persons engaged in gratuitous education on Sundays and during the week days, be respectfully invited to make arrangements for throwing open their schoolrooms to the working classes for two hours a day (say from one to three o'clock, or from six to eight, or any other two hours more convenient), from the 1st of March next, and that all well-disposed persons be invited to assist in promoting their education when time for which purpose has been secured to them.
7. That subscriptions be now entered into in aid of the fund to be raised by the working classes for the execution of their part of the proposed undertaking.
8. That another and distinct subscription be also entered into for defraying the expenses of the persons appointed to visit the master-manufacturers, and for other general purposes.
9. That the workmen and their friends use their utmost efforts to obtain further subscriptions, and that all well-disposed females be respectfully requested cordially to co-operate in this undertaking.

10. That a committee of workmen and their friends be now formed*, with power to add to their number, and to appoint a secretary and treasurer for the Manchester district of the society, described in the second resolution.
11. That this committee be instructed to procure as soon as possible a convenient office in Manchester, which shall be called "The Office of the Society for National Regeneration".**
12. That circulars reporting the proceedings of this meeting be immediately printed, and sent to the masters in every trade in the United Kingdom.
13. That such masters as may be disposed to adopt the proposed regulation for reducing the hours of work, and paying the same wages, are hereby respectfully invited to signify their consent by letter (post paid), addressed to the office of the society in Manchester.
14. That the catechism now read, entitled "The Catechism of the Society for Promoting National Regeneration", be adopted.
15. That Messrs. Oastler, Wood, Bull, Sadler, and others, be urgently requested to desist from soliciting Parliament for a ten hours' bill, and use their utmost exertions in aid of the measures now adopted to carry into effect, on the 1st of March next, the regulation of 'eight hours work for the present full day's wages'.
16. That the thanks of the meeting are hereby given to the aforesaid gentlemen, for their long-continued invaluable services in the cause of the oppressed of the working classes, and especially in the cause of the children and young persons employed in factories.
17. That Mr. Owen be requested to establish committees of the society for national regeneration in every place or district which he may visit, especially in the Potteries, Birmingham, Worcester, Gloucester, Leicester, Derby, and London; and that he be also requested to report to the office of the society at Manchester the names of such individuals as will assist in the present undertaking.
18. That in the first week in January next, the working men in every district throughout Great Britain and Ireland shall make application to their employers for their concurrence in the adoption of the regulation of 'eight hours' work for the present full day's wages', to commence on the 1st day of March next.
19. That this meeting earnestly appeal to their fellow-men in France, Germany, and the other countries of Europe, and on the continent of America, for their support and co-operation in this effort to improve the condition of the labourer in all parts of the world.

JOSHUA MILNE, Chairman.

* The following is a list of the committee: - John Fielden, Esq., M.P., Joshua Milne, Esq.; George Condy, Esq.; Messrs. John Travis jun., J.W. Hodgetss, George Marshall, William Clegg, Joshua Fielden, Thomas Fielden, John Doherty, George Higginbottom, James Turner, Wm. Taylor, Philip Grant, John Wyatt, George Scott, John Scott, Joseph Scott, Henry Greaves, John Brodie, Wm. Wills, and Robert Owen, Esq.

** The office of the society is N°. 48, Pall-mall, corner of King Street.

7

"MASTER V. SLAVE. ON PAID LABOUR IN COMMUNITIES", *NEW MORAL WORLD*, 2 FEBRUARY 1839, 228–229.

Benjamin Warden

[To early socialists, the wage system, based on the vagaries of an unregulated capitalistic market, constituted one of the main causes of labour exploitation (see Part 4). Following Owen's *Report to the County of Lanark* (see Part 4, Chapter 21), Labour Exchanges tried in the years 1832–1834 to implement "labour notes", an alternative paper money based upon the value of skilled work. The wage system debate resurfaced in 1839 with the founding of the communities of Queenwood and Manea Fen. In January, contributors to the *New Moral World* like Thomas Hunt, leader of the future Equality community (see Part 9, Chapter 60) argued that socialists, who mostly hailed from urban areas, should hire agricultural workers to till the land of their communities due to their own lack of farming skills.[1] This was anathema to veterans of the Labour Exchange movement like the Marylebone saddler Benjamin Warden, who likened the inequalities of the wage system to slavery. Little is known about his early years, but Warden was an early convert to the co-operative cause. In February 1832, he opened the First Western Union Exchange Bank, which was the first Owenite bazaar to use labour notes, and he was later active in the Finsbury branch of the Association of All Classes of All Nations (*Poor Man's Guardian*, 10 March 1832, cited in Bennett 2016, 45).[2] In this letter to the editor of the *New Moral World*, Warden argued that paid work, and money more generally, were the "root of all evil", and refused to condone an inegalitarian system that the Owenite communities were precisely meant to subvert (Harrison 1969, 202; Prothero 1979, 244; Langdon 2000, 67).]

Friends, — Much has been said and written on *paid labour* in the *first Communities*. I will not attempt to go over the arguments for and against the question, but at once give you my reasons for denouncing the system of *paid labour, alias* white slavery, in our first communities. One error on the formation of the human character, by mankind, has led to the most appalling and fearful results, —that one error is the cause, and the fundamental cause, of all our miseries. The error of introducing paid labour into our first communities would, no doubt, to that community, produce results as fatal to them as the other error has to society at large. Why? because money, the root of all evil, must be introduced, and the equality of right and condition destroyed; and inequality of remuneration introduced, which would engender a thousand evils in its train,—the inferiority of the producers of food would be felt and seen by the prostration of independence in them, and the loss of peace of mind, contentment, and a recklessness of character, as is seen at the present day among our agricultural classes, would be perpetuated; the beer shop, and other receptacles of vice, would find their advantage in money wages. Beware then, I say, how you commit *felo de se*,[3] by the introduction of any part of the old leaven. Do we want farm labourers, gardeners, &c.? Let us go amongst them, let us convert them to our principles, let use [sic] make them socialists, we have the power. I hope this warning will produce the inclination to arouse that part of our fellow men to a sense of their condition in society. Last year I was in the midst of farm servants; I found no difficulty to make them understand our benign principles: of all men farm servants are the most unsophisticated, the most ready to converse with strangers, and to listen to anything you may have to advance. Besides farm operations, on our superior principles, would be a recreation or pleasure. They also can be easily learned: how many farm servants did the Rappites and Shakers hire?[4] Are they not men, and do we not know the force of circumstance? If we are going to re-act the old farce of competition, then, indeed, value men's lives by gold and wages; but, even *in the transition state*, so easy is a knowledge of farm labour acquired, that with three or four weeks' training of our young able mechanics, they would acquire all the necessary skill to perform the labour required, and that as a recreation and amusement. If indeed we are to labour for the outer market, then the outer market will govern the value of our labour; but, as I hope this will not be the case, as I expect we shall first look at home, inequality in the value of labour will cease amongst us.

I say we can acquire a knowledge of farm operations in a short time, I say it advisedly, from careful enquiry amongst gardeners, farm servants, and others: they assured me that in a moth they could make any willing man to understand the general operations of gardening and farm work. But there is the trenching of the land; ah! The trenching, what is there so alarming in digging a trench? really one would suppose it required a vast amount of skill: I would venture to assert not one thousandth's part of the skill that the practice of driving the shuttle does. Mechanical operations require the practice of the hand, as well as the head; farm work requires very little practice, and often more strength than judgment is required. Besides, we have many good, strong, able men as gardeners, navigators, and farm servants, who would be able to direct the labour of others, and who long to form some of the first occupants in that dreadful attempt, *the transition*! My friends, I think the difficulties lay in our own imagination, and, when we get to practice, we shall find them so, is the firm conviction of

Yours truly,
B. Warden,
The original member of Branch 16.
Hall of Science, City Road, Finsbry [sic]
London, January 1839.

Notes

1 Thomas Hunt, "Explanation of Resolutions Respecting an Estate Fund", letter to the editor of the *New Moral World*, 26 January 1839; J.H. Billson, "Hired Labour in Communities", letter to the editor of the *New Moral World*, id.
2 Prior to the 1830s British Owenite movement, labour notes were also used at New Harmony (Harrison 1969, 169).
3 Latin for "felon on himself". An archaic term in English common law, referring to the act of suicide, which remained a felony in England and Wales until the Suicide Act 1961.
4 The Rappites and Shakers are religious movements, mostly based in the United States, with an emphasis on frugality, communal living and manual work. Robert Owen admired the Shakers' simple lifestyle and he helped reprint an account of the sect by the Quaker author William S. Warder (1818). The Rappites, or Harmonists, were founded in 1791 by the German Pietist pastor Johann Georg Rapp (1757–1847). The sect developed in the duchy of Württemberg and later established the commune of Harmonie, Indiana, in 1814. The settlement was sold to Robert Owen in 1824, and renamed "New Harmony".

Part 2

VISIONS OF THE FUTURE

The political legacy of Robert Owen rests on a paradox. Hailed as the "Father of British Socialism" since the late nineteenth century for his pioneering critique of modern capitalism, he has also been widely derided for the most "utopian" aspects of his system, i.e. his millenarianism and his reliance on intentional communities as the sole vehicle of his promised "New Moral World" (Claeys 2005; Siméon 2014). These accusations actually predate Karl Marx and Friedrich Engels's *Communist Manifesto* ([1848] 1992), and can be traced back to Owen's radicalising phase in the years 1815–1820. In 1816, William Hazlitt ([1816] 1819, 97–98) had likened Owen's *New View of Society* to Thomas More's *Utopia* ([1516] 2010); three years later, upon a visit to New Lanark, Robert Southey ([1819] 1929, 262–263) had praised Owen's benevolent management, while questioning his ability to apply its principles to the wider world. This chasm between New Lanark and Owen's communitarian schemes dominated public discussions of his Plan between 1815 and 1825, and it explains why they ultimately garnered little support from government officials and philanthropists. As an enlightened master-manufacturer Owen was worthy of praise, but not as a utopian or visionary.

Until the latter part of the twentieth century, historians of Owenism likewise struggled to reconcile the movement's practical side (especially its link to modern co-operation) and its millenarian strand. E.P. Thompson's famous quip, which claimed that Owen "simply had a vacant place in his mind where most men have political responses" (1963, 783–785) summed up general perceptions of Owenism until the movement was reassessed, following J.F.C. Harrison's seminal study of early Transatlantic socialism (1969). Part of the new historiographic trend was rooted in a readiness to accept the early socialists' insistence that their visions for the future were inherently practical because they rested on scientific foundations. The claim seemed especially relevant in Owen's case, as he had spent more than a decade of carefully planning and putting his social system to the test at New Lanark before making it open to public scrutiny. Moreover, the apparent success of the New Lanark experiment gave his proposed plans an aura of legitimacy and superiority over those of other reformers, and this provided in turn a platform for his subsequent political career as leader of Britain's first socialist movement.

There is no doubt that Owenism, and early socialism at large, had a strong millenarian strand. In Owen's eyes, "the benefits of community were to be so self-evident that the world would follow by emulation – for the community was the law of nature re-established" (Garnett 1971, 42). But far from being at odds with what is conventionally regarded as "scientific" socialism, early socialism showed a near-constant overlap between providential visions of the future and the reliance on scientific discourses and methods to realise this very vision. Owen claimed that his system was a science, not a theory, as it proposed a range of solutions that were not only empirical, but whose very practicality was bound to bring a *definitive* answer to the social question (Poynter 1969, 259; Kumar 1990, 29; Royle 1998, 12). If early socialism was therefore millenarian, this was largely secular and Enlightenment-inspired. But change was not to occur in a negative way, through the vengeful intervention of a transcendent entity; it was to unfold positively, through the revelation of the immanent laws of nature, which would provide a truthful, practical, and legitimate basis for the general reform of society (Harrison 1969; Siméon 2017, 9). Owenism's messianic overtones did not contradict his wish to implement a science of society. It was in fact a direct consequence of his rationalist outlook, rooted in an absolute confidence that his theories were economically, politically and morally true.

8

ADDRESS DELIVERED TO THE INHABITANTS OF NEW LANARK, ON JANUARY 1ST, 1816, ON THE OPENING OF THE INSTITUTION ESTABLISHED FOR THE FORMATION OF CHARACTER (LONDON: HATCHARD, 1816).

Robert Owen

[Robert Owen's speech at the City of London Tavern, which he gave in August 1817, is usually considered his "millennialist moment" (Oliver 1971, 166). It was the opportunity for him to reveal his comprehensive reform programme of general harmony. This entailed the rejection of what he identified as the three main sources of social division – unchecked capitalism, established religions and private property. Yet a previous address, given on 1 January 1816, had already set the tone of Owen's "science of society", thereby constituting the first recorded instance of Owen's shift from classical philanthropy to millennialism (Harrison 1969, 76–77). Given on a highly symbolic date, the speech marked the opening of the Institute for the Formation of Character, New Lanark's educational and cultural centre. With its nursery, primary and evening schools, assembly room, library and non-denominational chapel, it aimed to improve the conditions of the factory village inhabitants through life-long instruction and the promotion of harmonious community feeling – a programme which had been at the core of Owen's *New View of Society* (Siméon 2017, 1). But the 1816 inaugural address also revealed a set of new purposes. Relying heavily on biblical imagery, Owen professed that his comprehensive re-education scheme was now geared not only towards the emancipation of the labouring classes, but to that of mankind itself. The promise of the Institute for the Formation of Character would usher in a "New Moral World", free from the social and economic divisions of the day.]

We have met to-day for the purpose of opening this Institution; and it is my intention to explain to you the objects for which it has been founded.

These objects are most important.

The first relates to the immediate comfort and benefit of all the inhabitants of this village.

The second, to the welfare and advantage of the neighbourhood.

The third, to extensive ameliorations throughout the British dominions.

The last, to the gradual improvement of every nation in the world.

I will briefly explain how this Institution is to contribute towards producing these effects.

Long before I came to reside among you, it had been my chief study to discover the extent, causes, and remedy of the inconveniences and miseries which were perpetually recurring to every class in society.

The history of man informed me that innumerable attempts had been made, through every age, to lessen these evils; and experience convinced me that the present generation, stimulated by an accession of knowledge derived from past times, was eagerly engaged in the same pursuit. My mind at a very early period took a similar direction; and I became ardently desirous of investigating to its source a subject which involved the happiness of every human being.

It soon appeared to me, that the only path to knowledge on this subject had been neglected; that one leading in an opposite direction had alone been followed; that while causes existed to compel mankind to pursue such direction, it was idle to expect any successful result: and experience proves how vain their pursuit has been.

In this inquiry, men have hitherto been directed by their inventive faculties, and have almost entirely disregarded the only guide that can lead to true knowledge on any subject — experience. They have been governed, in the most important concerns of life, by mere illusions of the imagination, in direct opposition to existing facts.

Having satisfied myself beyond doubt with regard to this fundamental error; having traced the ignorance and misery which it has inflicted on man, by a calm and patient investigation of the causes which have continued this evil, without any intermission from one generation to another; and having also maturely reflected on the obstacles to be overcome, before a new direction can be given to the human mind; I was induced to form the resolution of devoting my life to relieve mankind from this mental disease and all its miseries.

It was evident to me that the evil was universal; that, in practice, none was in the right path —no, not one; and that, in order to remedy the evil, a different one must be pursued. That the whole man must be re-formed on fundamental principles the very reverse of those in which he had been trained; in short, that the minds of all men must be born again, and their knowledge and practice commence on a new foundation.

Satisfied of the futility of the existing modes of instruction, and of the errors of the existing modes of government, I was well convinced that none of them could ever effect the ends intended; but that, on the contrary, they were only calculated to defeat all the objects which human instructors and governors had proposed to attain.

I found, on such a patient consideration of the subject as its importance demanded, that to reiterate precept upon precept, however excellent in theory, while no decisive measures were adopted to place mankind under circumstances in which it might be possible to put those precepts in practice, was but a waste of time. I therefore determined to form arrangements preparatory to the introduction of truths, the knowledge of which should dissipate the errors and evils of all the existing political and religious systems.

Be not alarmed at the magnitude of the attempt which this declaration opens to your view. Each change, as it occurs, will establish a substantial and permanent good, unattended by any counteracting evil; nor can the mind of man, formed on the old system, longer interpose obstacles capable of retarding the progress of those truths which I am now about to unfold to you. The futile attempts which ignorance may for a short time oppose to them, will be found to accelerate their introduction. As soon as they shall be comprehended in all their bearings, every one will be compelled to acknowledge them, to see their benefits in practice to himself and to each of his fellow creatures; for, by this system, none, no not one, will be injured. It is a delightful thought, an animating reflection, a stimulus to the steady prosecution of my purpose, beyond—nay, far beyond—all that riches, and honour, and praise can bestow, to be conscious of the possibility of being instrumental in introducing a practical system into society, the complete establishment of which *shall give happiness to every human being through all succeeding generations*. And such I declare was the sole motive that gave rise to this Institution, and to all my proceedings.

To effect any permanently beneficial change in society, I found it was far more necessary to act than to speak. I tried the effect of the new principles on a limited scale in the southern part of the island. The result exceeded my most sanguine anticipations; and I became anxious for a more enlarged field of action. I saw New Lanark: it possessed many of the local circumstances proper for my purpose; and this establishment became at my disposal. This event, as many of you may recollect, occurred upwards of sixteen years ago. Sixteen years of action is not a short period: extensive changes are the result. You have been witnesses of my proceedings here, from the time I undertook the direction of the establishment to the present hour. I now ask, and I will thank you to make either a public or a private reply,—have any of you discovered even *one* of my measures that was not clearly and decisively intended to benefit the whole population? But I am satisfied that you are all now convinced of this truth. You also know some of the obstacles which were opposed to my progress; but you know not a tithe of them. Yet, after all, these obstacles have been few, compared with those which I expected and was prepared to meet; and which I trust I should have overcome.

When I examined the circumstances under which I found you, they appeared to me to be very similar to those of other manufacturing districts; except with regard to the boarding-house, which contained the young children who were procured from the public charities of the country. That part of the establishment was under an admirable arrangement, and was a strong indication of the genuine and extensive benevolence of the revered and truly good man (the late David Dale of Glasgow) who founded these works and this village. His wishes and intentions towards you all were those of a father towards his children. You knew him and his worth; and his memory must be deeply engraven upon your hearts. Little indeed could he be conscious, when he laid the first stone of this establishment, that he was commencing a work, from whence not only the amelioration of his suffering countrymen should proceed, but the means of happiness be developed to every nation in the world.

I have stated that I found the population of this place similar to that of other manufacturing districts. It was, with some exceptions, existing in poverty, crime, and misery; and strongly; prejudiced, as most people are at first, against any change that might be proposed. The usual mode of proceeding on the principles which have hitherto governed the conduct of men, would have been to punish those who committed the crimes, and to be highly displeased with every one who opposed the alterations that were intended for his benefit. The principles, however, upon which the new system is founded, lead to a very different conduct. They make it evident, that when men are in poverty,—when they commit crimes or actions injurious to themselves and others,—and when they are in a state of wretchedness,—there must be substantial causes for these lamentable effects; and that, instead of punishing or being angry with our fellow-men because they have been subjected to such a miserable existence, we ought to pity and commiserate them, and patiently to trace the causes whence the evils proceed, and endeavour to discover whether they may not be removed.

This was the course which I adopted. I sought not the punishment of any delinquent, nor felt anger at your conduct in opposition to your own good; and when apparently stern and decisive, I was not actuated by a single feeling of irritation against any individual. I dispassionately investigated the source of the evils with which I saw you afflicted. The immediate causes of them were soon obvious; nor were the remote ones, or the causes of those causes, long hid from me.

I found that those which principally produced your misery, were practices you had been permitted to acquire—of falsehood, of theft, of drunkenness, of injustice in your transactions, want of charity for the opinions of others, and mistaken notions, in which you had been instructed, as to the superiority of your religious opinions, and that these were calculated to produce more happiness than any of the opinions impressed on the minds of an infinitely more numerous part of mankind. I found, also, that these causes were but the effects of others; and that those others might all be traced to the ignorance in which our forefathers existed, and in which we ourselves have continued to this day.

But from this day a change must take place; a new era must commence; the human intellect, through the whole extent of the earth, hitherto enveloped by the grossest ignorance and superstition, must begin to be released from its state of darkness; nor shall nourishment henceforth be given to the seeds of disunion and division among men. For the time is come, when the means may be prepared to train all the nations of the world—men of every colour and climate, of the most diversified habits—in that knowledge which shall impel them not only to love but to be actively kind to each other in the whole of their conduct, without a single exception. I speak not an unmeaning jargon of words, but that which I know—that which has been derived from a cool and dispassionate examination and comparison, during a quarter of a century, of the facts which exist around us. And, however averse men may be to resign their early-taught prejudices, I pledge myself to prove, to the entire satisfaction of the world, the truth of all that I have stated and all that I mean to state. Nay, such is my confidence in the truth of the principles on which the system I am about to introduce is founded, that I hesitate not to assert their power heartily to incline all men to say, "This system is assuredly true, and therefore eminently calculated to realize those invaluable precepts of the Gospel—universal charity, goodwill, and peace among men. Hitherto we must have been trained in error; and we hail it as the harbinger of that period when our swords shall be turned into ploughshares, and our spears into pruning-hooks; when universal love and benevolence shall prevail; when there shall be but one language and one nation; and when fear of want or of any evil among men shall be known no more."

Acting, although unknown to you, uniformly and steadily upon this system, my attention was ever directed to remove, as I could prepare means for their removal, such of the immediate causes as were perpetually creating misery amongst you, and which, if permitted to remain, would to this day have continued to create misery. I therefore withdrew the most prominent incitements to falsehood, theft, drunkenness, and other pernicious habits, with which many of you were then familiar: and in their stead I introduced other causes, which were intended to produce better external habits; and better, external habits have been introduced. I say better external habits; for to these alone have my proceedings hitherto been intended to apply. What has yet been done I consider as merely preparatory.

This Institution, when all its parts shall be completed, is intended to produce permanently beneficial effects; and, instead of longer applying temporary expedients for correcting some of your most prominent external habits, to effect a complete and thorough improvement in the internal as well as external character of the whole village. For this purpose the Institution has been devised to afford the means of receiving your children at an early age, as soon almost as they can walk. By this means many of you, mothers of families, will be enabled to earn a better maintenance or support for your children; you will have less care and anxiety about them; while the children will be prevented from acquiring any bad habits, and gradually prepared to learn the best.

The middle room of the story below will be appropriated to their accommodation; and in this their chief occupation will be to play and amuse themselves in severe weather: at other times they will be permitted to occupy the enclosed area before the building; for, to give children a vigorous constitution, they ought to be kept as much as possible in the open air. As they advance in years, they will be taken into the rooms on the right and left, where they will be regularly instructed in the rudiments of common learning; which, before they shall be six years old, they may be taught in a superior manner.

These stages may be called the first and second preparatory schools: and when your children shall have passed through them, they will be admitted into this place (intended also to be used as a chapel), which, with the adjoining apartment, is to be the general schoolroom for reading, writing, arithmetic, sewing, and knitting; all which, on the plan to be pursued, will be accomplished to a considerable extent by the time the children are ten years old; before which age, none of them will be permitted to enter the works.

For the benefit of the health and spirits of the children both boys and girls will be taught to dance, and the boys will be instructed in military exercises; those of each sex who may have good voices will be taught to sing, and those among the boys who have a taste for music will be taught to play upon some instrument; for it is intended to give them as much diversified innocent amusement as the local circumstances of the establishment will admit.

The rooms to the east and west on the story below, will also be appropriated in bad weather for relaxation and exercise during some part of the day, to the children who, in the regular hours of teaching, are to be instructed in these apartments.

In this manner is the Institution to be occupied during the day in winter. In summer, it is intended that they shall derive knowledge from a personal examination of the works of nature and of art, by going out frequently with some of their masters into the neighbourhood and country around.

After the instruction of the children who are too young to attend the works shall have been finished for the day, the apartments shall be cleaned, ventilated, and in winter lighted and heated, and in all respects made comfortable, for the reception of other classes of the population. The apartments on this floor are then to be appropriated for the use of the children and youth of both sexes who have been employed at work during the day, and who may wish still further to improve themselves in reading, writing, arithmetic, sewing, or knitting; or to learn any of the useful arts: to instruct them in which, proper masters and mistresses, who are appointed, will attend for two hours every evening.

The three lower rooms, which in winter will also be well lighted and properly heated, will be thrown open for the use of the adult part of the population, who are to be provided with every accommodation requisite to enable them to read, write, account, sew, or play, converse, or walk about. But strict order and attention to the happiness of every one of the party will be enforced, until such habits shall be acquired as will render any formal restriction unnecessary; and the measures thus adopted will soon remove such necessity.

Two evenings in the week will be appropriated to dancing and music: but on these occasions every accommodation will be prepared for those who prefer to study or to follow any of the occupations pursued on the other evenings.

One of the apartments will also be occasionally appropriated for the purpose of giving useful instruction to the older classes of the inhabitants. For, believe me, my friends, you are yet very deficient with regard to the best modes of training your children, or of arranging your domestic concerns; as well as in that wisdom which is requisite to direct your conduct towards each other, so as to enable you to become greatly more happy than you have ever yet been. There will be no difficulty in teaching you what is right and proper; your own interests will afford ample stimulus for that purpose; but the real and only difficulty will be to unlearn those pernicious habits and sentiments which, an infinite variety of causes, existing through all past ages, have combined to impress upon your minds and bodies, so as to make you imagine that they are inseparable from your nature. It shall, however, ere long be proved to you, that in this respect, as well as in many others, you and all mankind are mistaken. Yet think not, from what I have said, that I mean to infringe, even in the most slight degree, on the liberty of private judgment or religious opinions. No! they have hitherto been unrestrained; and the most effectual measures have been adopted by all the parties interested in the concern, to secure to you these most invaluable privileges. And here I now publicly declare (and while I make the declaration I wish my voice could extend to the ear, and make its due impression on the mind, of every one of our fellow-creatures), "that the individual who first placed restraint on private judgment and religious opinions, was the author of hypocrisy, and the origin of innumerable evils which mankind through every past age have experienced." The right, however, of private judgment, and of real religious liberty, is nowhere yet enjoyed. It is not possessed by any nation in the world; and thence the unnecessary ignorance, as well as endless misery, of all. Nor can this right be enjoyed until the principle whence opinions originate shall be universally known and acknowledged.

The chief object of my existence will be to make this knowledge universal, and thence to bring the right of private judgment into general practice; to show the infinitely beneficial consequences that will result to mankind from its adoption. To effect this important purpose is a part, and an essential part, of that system which is about to be introduced.

I proceed to show how the Institution is to contribute to the welfare and advantage of this neighbourhood.

It will be readily admitted, that a population trained in regular habits of temperance, industry, and sobriety; of genuine charity for the opinions of all mankind, founded on the only knowledge that can implant true charity in the breast of any human being; trained also in a sincere desire to do good to the utmost of their power, and without any exception, to every one of their fellow creatures, cannot, even by their example alone, do otherwise than materially increase the welfare and advantages of the neighbourhood in which such a population may be situated. To feel the due weight of this consideration, only imagine to yourselves 2,000 or 3,000 human beings trained in habits of licentiousness, and allowed to remain in gross ignorance. How much, in such a case, would not the peace, quiet, comfort, and happiness of the neighbourhood be destroyed ! But there is not anything I have done, or purpose to do, which is not intended to benefit my fellow-creatures to the greatest extent that my operations can embrace. I wish to benefit all equally; but circumstances limit my present measures for the public good within a narrow circle. I must begin to act at some point; and a combination of singular events has fixed that point at this establishment. The first and greatest advantages will therefore centre here. But, in unison with the principle thus stated, it has ever been my intention that as this Institution, when completed, will accommodate more than the children of parents resident at the village, any persons living at Lanark, or in the neighbourhood anywhere around, who cannot well afford to educate their children, shall be at liberty, on mentioning their wishes, to send them to this place, where they will experience the same care and attention as those who belong to the establishment. Nor will there be any distinction made between the children of those parents who are deemed the worst, and of those who may be esteemed the best, members of society: rather, indeed, would I prefer to receive the offspring of the worst, if they shall be sent at an early age; because they really require more of our care and pity; and by well training these, society will be more essentially benefited, than if the like attention were paid to those whose parents are educating them in comparatively good habits. The system now preparing, and which will ultimately be brought into full practice, is to effect a complete change in all our sentiments and conduct towards those poor miserable creatures whom the errors of past times have denominated the bad, the worthless, and the wicked. A more enlarged and better knowledge of human nature will make it evident that, in strict justice, those who apply these terms to their fellow-men are not only the most ignorant, but are themselves the immediate causes of more misery in the world than those whom they call the outcasts of society. *They* are, therefore, correctly speaking, the most wicked and worthless; and were they not grossly deceived, and rendered blind from infancy, they would become conscious of the lamentably extensive evils, which, by their well-intended but most mistaken conduct, they have, during so long a period, inflicted on their fellow-men. But the veil of darkness must be removed from their eyes; their erroneous proceedings must be made so palpable that they shall thenceforth reject them with horror. Yes! they will reject with horror even those notions which hitherto they have from infancy been taught to value beyond price.

To that which follows I wish to direct the attention of all your faculties. I am about to declare to you the cause and the cure of that which is called wickedness in your fellow-men. As we proceed, instead of your feelings being roused to hate and to pursue them to punishment, you will be compelled to pity them; to commiserate their condition; nay, to love them, and to be convinced that to this day they have been treated unkindly, unjustly, and with the greatest cruelty. It is indeed high time, my friends, that our conduct—that the conduct of all mankind, in this respect, should be the very reverse of what it has been; and of this truth, new as it may and must appear to many of you, you shall, as I proceed, be satisfied to the most complete conviction.

That, then, which has been hitherto called wickedness in our fellow-men has proceeded from one of two distinct causes, or from some combination of those causes. They are what is termed bad or wicked—

First,—Because they are born with faculties and propensities which render them more liable, under the circumstances, than other men, to commit such actions as are usually denominated wicked. Or—

Second,—Because they have been placed, by birth or by other events, in particular countries; have been influenced from infancy by parents, playmates, and others; and have been surrounded by those circumstances which gradually and necessarily trained them in the habits and sentiments called wicked. Or—

Third,—They have become wicked in consequence of some particular combination of these causes.

Let us now examine them separately, and endeavour to discover whether any, and which of them, have originated with the individuals; and, of course, for which of them they ought to be treated by their fellow-men in the manner those denominated wicked have to this day been treated.

You have not, I trust, been rendered so completely insane, by the ignorance of our forefathers, as to imagine that the poor helpless infant, devoid of understanding, made itself, or any of its bodily or mental faculties or qualities: but, whatever you may have been taught, it is a fact, that every infant has received all its faculties and qualities, bodily and mental, from a power and cause, over which the infant had not the shadow of control.

Shall it, then, be unkindly treated? And, when it shall be grown up, shall it be punished with loss of liberty or life, because a power over which it had no control whatever, formed it in the womb with faculties and qualities different from those of its fellows ?—Has the infant any means of deciding who, or of what description, shall be its parents, its playmates, or those from whom it shall derive its habits and its sentiments ?—Has it the power to determine for itself whether it shall first see light within the circle of Christendom; or whether it shall be so placed as inevitably to become a disciple of Moses, of Confucius, of Mahomed; a worshipper of the great idol Juggernaut, or a savage and a cannibal?

If then, my friends, not even one of these great leading and overwhelming circumstances can be, in the smallest degree, under the control of the infant, is there a being in existence, possessing any claim even to the smallest degree of rationality, who will maintain that any individual, formed and placed under such circumstances, ought to be punished, or in any respect unkindly treated? When men shall be in some degree relieved from the mental malady with which they have been so long afflicted, and sound judgment shall take the place of wild and senseless imagination, then the united voice of mankind shall say, "No!" And they will be astonished that a contrary supposition should ever have prevailed.

If it should be asked,—Whence, then, have wickedness and misery proceeded? I reply, *Solely from the ignorance of our forefathers!* It is this ignorance, my friends, that has been, and continues to be, the only cause of all the miseries which men have experienced. This is the evil spirit which has had dominion over the world,—which has sown the seeds of hatred and disunion among all nations,—which has grossly deceived mankind, by introducing notions the most absurd and unaccountable respecting faith and belief; notions by which it has effectually placed a seal on all the rational faculties of man,—by which numberless evil passions are engendered,—by which all men, in the most senseless manner, are not only made enemies to each other, but enemies to their own happiness! While this ignorance of our forefathers continues to abuse the world, under any name whatever, it is neither more nor less than a species of madness—rank insanity—to imagine that we can ever become in practice good, wise, or happy.

Were it not, indeed, for the positive evils which proceed from these senseless notions, they are too absurd to admit of a serious refutation; nor would any refutation be necessary, if they did not from infancy destroy the reasoning faculties of men, whether Pagans, Jews, Christians, or Mahomedans; and render them utterly incompetent to draw a just conclusion from the numberless facts which perpetually present themselves to notice. Do we not learn from history, that infants through all past ages have been taught the language, habits, and sentiments of those by whom they have been surrounded? That they had no means whatever of giving to themselves the power to acquire any others? That very generation has thought and acted like preceding generations, *with such changes only as the events around it, from which experience is derived, may have forced upon it?* And, above all, are we not conscious that the experience of every individual now existing is abundantly sufficient, on reflection, to prove to himself that he has no more power or command over his faith and belief than he possesses over the winds of heaven? nay, that his constitution is so formed, that in every instance whatsoever, the faith or belief which he possesses has been given to him by causes over which he had no control?

Experience, my friends, now makes these conclusions clear as the sun at noonday. Why, then, shall we not instantly act upon them? Having discovered our error, why shall we longer afflict our fellow-men with the evils which these wild notions have generated? Have they ever been productive of one benefit to mankind? Have they not produced, through all past ages—are they not at this moment engendering, every conceivable evil to which man, in very nation of the world, is subjected? Yes; these alone prevent the introduction of charity and universal goodwill among men. These alone prevent men from discovering the true and only road which can lead to happiness. Once overcome these obstacles, and the apple of discord will be withdrawn from among us; the whole human race may then, with the greatest ease, be trained in one mind; all their efforts may then be trained to act for the good of the whole. In short, when these great errors shall be removed, all our evil passions will disappear; no ground of anger or displeasure from one human being towards another will remain; the period of the supposed Millennium will commence, and universal love prevail.

Will it not, then, tend to the welfare and advantage of this neighbourhood, to introduce into it such a practical system as shall gradually withdraw the causes of anger, hatred, discord, and every evil passion, and substitute true and genuine principles of universal charity and of never-varying kindness, of love without dissimulation, and of an ever-active desire to benefit to the full extent of our faculties all our fellow-creatures, whatever may be their sentiments and their habits,—wholly regardless whether they be Pagans, Jews, Christians, or Mahomedans? For anything short of this can proceed only from the evil spirit of ignorance, which is truly the roaring lion going about seeking whom he may devour.

We now come to the third division of the subject, which was to show that one of the objects of this Institution was to effect extensive ameliorations throughout the British dominions. This will be accomplished in two ways—

First,—By showing to the master manufacturers an example in practice, on a scale sufficiently extensive, of the mode by which the characters and situation of the working manufacturers whom they employ may be very materially improved, not only without injury to the masters, but so as to create to them also great and substantial advantages.

Second,—By inducing, through this example, the British legislature to enact such laws as will secure similar benefits to every part of our population.

The extent of the benefits which may be produced by proper legislative measures, few are yet prepared to form any adequate idea of. By legislative measures I do not mean any party proceeding whatever. Those to which I allude are,—laws to diminish and ultimately prevent the most prominent evils to which the working classes are now subjected,—laws to prevent a large part of our fellow-subjects, under the manufacturing system, from being oppressed by a much smaller part,—to prevent more than one-half of our population from being trained in gross ignorance, and their valuable labour from being most injuriously directed,—laws to prevent the same valuable part of our population from being perpetually surrounded by temptations, which they have not been trained to resist, and which compel them to commit actions most hurtful to themselves and to society. The principles on which these measures are to be founded being once fairly and honestly understood, they will, be easy of adoption; and the benefits to be derived from them in practice to every member of the community, will exceed any calculation that can be made by those not well versed in political economy.

These are some of the ameliorations which I trust this Institution will be the means of obtaining for our suffering fellow-subjects.

But, my friends, if what has been done, what is doing, and what has yet to be done here, should procure the benefits which I have imperfectly enumerated, to this village, to our neighbourhood, and to our country, only, I should be greatly disappointed; for I feel an ardent desire to benefit all my fellow-men equally. I know not any distinction whatever. Political or religious parties or sects are everywhere the fruitful sources of disunion and irritation. My aim is therefore to withdraw the germ of all party from society. As little do I admit of the divisions and distinctions created by any imaginary lines which separate nation from nation. Will any being, entitled to the epithet intelligent, say that a mountain, a river, an ocean, or any shade of colour, or difference of climate, habits, and sentiments, affords a reason sufficient to satisfy the inquiries of even a well-trained child, why one portion of mankind should be taught to despise, hate, and destroy another? Are these absurd effects of the grossest ignorance never to be brought to a termination? Are we still to preserve and encourage the continuance of those errors which must inevitably make man an enemy to man? Are these the measures calculated to bring about that promised period when the lion shall lie down with the lamb, and when uninterrupted peace shall universally prevail ?—peace, founded on a sincere goodwill, instilled from infancy into the very constitution of every man, which is the only basis on which universal happiness can ever be stablished? I look, however, with the utmost confidence to the arrival of such a period; and, if proper measures shall be adopted, its date is not far distant.

What ideas individuals may attach to the term Millennium I know not; but I know that society may be formed so as to exist without crime, without poverty, with health greatly improved, with little, if any, misery, and with intelligence and happiness increased a hundred-fold; and no obstacle whatsoever intervenes at this moment, except ignorance, to prevent such a state of society from becoming universal.

I am aware, to the fullest extent, what various impressions these declarations will make on the different religious, political, learned, commercial, and other circles which compose the population of our empire. I know the particular shade of prejudice through which they will be presented to the minds of each of these. And to none will they appear through a denser medium than to the learned, who have been taught to suppose that the book of knowledge has been exclusively opened to them; while, in fact, they have only wasted their strength in wandering through endless mazes of error. They are totally ignorant of human nature. They are full of theories, and have not the most distant conception of what may or may not be accomplished in practice. It is true their minds have been well stored with language, which they can readily use to puzzle and confound the unlettered and inexperienced. But to those who have had an opportunity of examining the utmost extent of their acquired merits, and of observing how far they have been taught, and where their knowledge terminates, the deception vanishes, and the fallacy of the foundation upon which the superstructure of all their acquirements has been raised, at once becomes most obvious. In short, with a few exceptions, their profound investigations have been about words only. For, as the principle which they have been taught, and on which all their subsequent instruction proceeds, is erroneous, so it becomes impossible that they can arrive at just conclusions. The learned have ever looked for the cause of human sentiments and actions in the individual through whom those sentiments and actions become visible,—and hitherto the learned have governed the opinions of the world. The individual has been praised, blamed, or punished according to the whims and fancies of this class of men, and, in consequence, the earth has been full charged with their ever-varying absurdities, and with the miseries which these absurdities hourly create. Had it not been a law of our nature, that any impression, however ridiculous and absurd, and however contrary to fact, may be given in infancy, so as to be tenaciously retained through life, men could not have passed through the previous ages of the world without discovering the gross errors in which they had been trained. They could not have persevered in making each other miserable, and filling the world with horrors of every description. No! they would long since have discovered the natural, easy, and simple means of giving happiness to themselves and to every human being. But that law of nature which renders it difficult to eradicate our early instruction, although it will ultimately prove highly beneficial to the human race, serves now but to give permanence to error, and to blind our judgments. For the present situation of all the inhabitants of the earth may be compared to that of one whose eyes have been closely bandaged from infancy; who has afterwards been taught to imagine that he clearly sees the form or colour of every object around him; and who has been continually flattered with this notion, so as to compel his implicit belief in the supposition, and render him impenetrable to every attempt that could be made to undeceive him. If such be the present situation of man, how shall the illusion under which he exists be withdrawn from his mind? To beings thus circumstanced, what powers of persuasion can be applied, to make them comprehend their misfortune, and manifest to them the extent of the darkness in which they exist? In what language and in what manner shall the attempt be made? Will not every such attempt irritate and increase the malady, until means shall be devised to unloose the bandage, and thus effectually remove the cause of this mental blindness? Your minds have been so completely enveloped by this dense covering, which has intercepted the approach of every ray of light, that were an angel from heaven to descend and declare your state, you would not, because so circumstanced you could not, believe him.

Causes, over which I could have no control, removed in my early days the bandage which covered my mental sight. If I have been enabled to discover this blindness with which my fellow-men are afflicted, to trace their wanderings from the path which they were most anxious to find, and at the same time to perceive that relief could not be administered to them by any premature disclosure of their unhappy state, it is not from any merit of mine; nor can I claim any personal consideration whatever for having been myself relieved from this unhappy situation. But, beholding such truly pitiable objects around me, and witnessing the misery which they hourly experienced from falling into the dangers and evils by which, in these paths, they were on every side surrounded,—could I remain an idle spectator? Could I tranquilly see my fellowmen walking like idiots in every imaginable direction, except that alone in which the happiness they were in search of could be found?

No! The causes which fashioned me in the womb,—the circumstances by which I was surrounded from my birth, and over which I had no influence whatever, formed me with far other faculties, habits, and sentiments. These gave me a mind that could not rest satisfied without trying every possible expedient to relieve my fellow-men from their wretched situation, and formed it of such a texture that obstacles of the most formidable nature served but to increase my ardour, and to fix within me a settled determination, either to overcome them, or to die in the attempt.

But the attempt has been made. In my progress the most multiplied difficulties, which to me at a distance seemed almost appalling, and which to others seemed absolutely insurmountable, have on their nearer approach diminished, until, at length, I have lived to see them disappear, like the fleeting clouds of morning, which prove but the harbingers of an animating and cheering day.

Hitherto I have not been disappointed in any of the expectations which I had formed. The events which have yet occurred far exceed my most sanguine anticipations, and my future course now appears evident and straightforward. It is no longer necessary that I should silently and alone exert myself for your benefit and the happiness of mankind. The period is arrived when I may call numbers to my aid, and the call will not be in vain. I well knew the danger which would arise from a premature and abrupt attempt to tear off the many-folded bandages of ignorance, which kept society in darkness. I have therefore been many years engaged, in a manner imperceptible to the public, in gently and gradually removing one fold after another of these fatal bands, from the mental eyes of those who have the chief influence in society. The principles on which the practical system I contemplate is to be founded, are now familiar to some of the leading men of all sects and parties in this country, and to many of the governing powers in Europe and America. They have been submitted to the examination of the most celebrated universities in Europe. They have been subjected to the minute scrutiny of the most learned and acute minds formed on the old system, and I am fully satisfied of their inability to disprove them. These principles I will shortly state.

Every society which exists at present, as well as every society; which history records, has been formed and governed on a belief in the following notions, assumed as first principles:

First,—That it is in the power of every individual to form his own character. Hence the various systems called by the name of religion, codes of law, and punishments. Hence also the angry passions entertained by individuals and nations towards each other.

Second,—That the affections are at the command of the individual. Hence insincerity and degradation of character. Hence the miseries of domestic life, and more than one-half of all the crimes of mankind.

Third,—That it is necessary that a large portion of mankind should exist in ignorance and poverty, in order to secure to the remaining part such a degree of happiness as they now enjoy.

Hence a system of counteraction in the pursuits of men, a general opposition among individuals to the interests of each other, and the necessary effects of such a system,—ignorance, poverty, and vice.

Facts prove, however—

First,—That character is universally formed for, and not by, the individual.

Second,—That any habits and sentiments may be given to mankind.

Third,—That the affections are not under the control of the individual.

Fourth,—That every individual may be trained to produce far more than he can consume, while there is a sufficiency of soil left for him to cultivate.

Fifth,—That nature has provided means by which population may be at all times maintained in the proper state to give the greatest happiness to every individual, without one check of vice or misery.

Sixth,—That any community may be arranged, on a due combination of the foregoing principles, in such a manner, as not only to withdraw vice, poverty, and, in a great degree, misery, from the world, but also to place every individual under circumstances in which he shall enjoy more permanent happiness than can be given to any individual under the principles which have hitherto regulated society.

Seventh,—That all the assumed fundamental principles on which society has hitherto been founded are erroneous, and may be demonstrated to be contrary to fact. And—

Eighth,—That the change which would follow the abandonment of those erroneous maxims which bring misery into the world, and the adoption of principles of truth, unfolding a system which shall remove and for ever exclude that misery, may be effected without the slightest injury to any human being.

Here is the groundwork,—these are the data, on which society shall ere long be re-arranged; and for this simple reason, that it will be rendered evident that it will be for the immediate and future interest of every one to lend his most active assistance gradually to reform society on this basis. I say gradually, for in that word the most important considerations are involved. Any sudden and coercive attempt which may be made to remove even misery from men will prove injurious rather than beneficial. Their minds must be gradually prepared by an essential alteration of the circumstances which surround them, for any great and important change and amelioration in their condition. They must be first convinced of their blindness: this cannot be effected, even among the least unreasonable, or those termed the best part of mankind, in their present state, without creating some degree of irritation. This irritation, must then be tranquillized before another step ought to be attempted; and a general conviction must be established of the truth of the principles on which the projected change is to be founded. Their introduction into practice will then become easy,—difficulties will vanish as we approach them,—and, afterwards, the desire to see the whole system carried immediately into effect will exceed the means of putting it into execution.

The principles on which this practical system is founded are not new; separately, or partially united, they have been often recommended by the sages of antiquity, and by modern writers. But it is not known to me that they have ever been thus combined. Yet it can be demonstrated that it is only by their being *all brought into practice together* that they are to be rendered beneficial to mankind; and sure I am that this is the earliest period in the history of man when they could be successfully introduced into practice.

I do not intend to hide from you that the change will be great. "Old things shall pass away, and all shall become new."

But this change will bear no resemblance to any of the revolutions which have hitherto occurred. These have been alone calculated to generate and call forth all the evil passions of hatred and revenge: but that system which is now contemplated will effectually eradicate every feeling of irritation and ill will which exists among mankind. The whole proceedings of those who govern and instruct the world will be reversed. Instead of spending ages in telling mankind what they ought to think and how they ought to act, the instructors and governors of the world will acquire a knowledge that will enable them, in one generation, to apply the means which shall cheerfully induce each of those whom they control and influence, not only to think, but to act in such a manner as shall be best for himself and best for every human being. And yet this extraordinary result will take place without punishment or apparent force. Under this system, before commands are issued it shall be known whether they can or cannot be obeyed. Men shall not be called upon to assent to doctrines and to dogmas which do not carry conviction to their minds. They shall not be taught that merit can exist in doing, or that demerit can arise from not doing that over which they have no control. They shall not be told, as at present, that they must love that which, by the constitution of their nature, they are compelled to dislike. They shall not be trained in wild imaginary notions, that inevitably make them despise and hate all mankind out of the little narrow circle in which they exist, and then be told that they must heartily and sincerely love all their fellow-men. No, my friends, that system which shall make its way into the heart of every man, is founded upon principles which have not the slightest resemblance to any of those I have alluded to. On the contrary, it is directly opposed to them; and the effects it will produce in practice will differ as much from the practice which history records, and from that which we see around us, as hypocrisy, hatred, envy, revenge, wars, poverty, injustice, oppression, and all their consequent misery, differ from that genuine charity and sincere kindness of which we perpetually hear, but which we have never seen, and which, under the existing systems, we never can see.

That charity and that kindness admit of no exception. They extend to every child of man, however he may have been taught, however he may have been trained. They consider not what country gave him birth, what may be his complexion, what his habits or his sentiments. Genuine charity and true kindness instruct, that whatever these may be, should they prove the very reverse of what we have been taught to think right and best, our conduct towards him, our sentiments with respect to him, should undergo no change; for, when we shall see things as they really are, we shall know that this our fellow-man has undergone the same kind of process and training from infancy which we have experienced; that he has been as effectually taught to deem his sentiments and actions right, as we have been to imagine ours right and his wrong; when perhaps the only difference is, that we were born in one country, and he in another. If this be not true, then indeed are all our prospects hopeless; then fierce contentions, poverty, and vice, must continue for ever. Fortunately, however, there is now a superabundance of facts to remove all doubt from every mind; and the principles may now be fully developed, which will easily explain the source of all the opinions which now perplex and divide the world; and their source being discovered, mankind may withdraw all those which are false and injurious, and prevent any evil from arising in consequence of the varieties of sentiments, or rather of feelings, which may afterwards remain.

In short, my friends, the New System is founded on principles which will enable mankind to *prevent*, in the rising generation, almost all, if not all of the evils and miseries which we and our forefathers have experienced. A correct knowledge of human nature will be acquired; ignorance will be removed; the angry passions will be prevented from gaining any strength; charity and kindness will universally prevail; poverty will not be known; the interest of each individual will be in strict unison with the interest of every individual in the world. There will not be any counteraction of wishes and desires among men. Temperance and simplicity of manners will be the characteristics of every part of society. The natural defects of the few will be amply compensated by the increased attention and kindness towards them of the many. None will have cause to complain; for each will possess, without injury to another, all that can tend to his comfort, his well-being, and his happiness.—Such will be the certain consequences of the introduction into practice of that system for which I have been silently preparing the way for upwards of five-and-twenty years.

Still, however, much more preparation is necessary, and must take place, before the whole can be introduced. It is not intended to put it into practice here. The establishment was too far advanced on the old system before I came amongst you, to admit of its introduction, except to a limited extent. All I now purpose doing in this place is, to introduce as many of the advantages of the new system as can be put into practice in connexion with the old: but these advantages will be neither few nor of little amount. I hope, ere long, even under the existing disadvantages, to give you and your children far more solid advantages for your labour, than any persons similarly circumstanced have yet enjoyed at any time or in any part of the world.

Nor is this all. When you and your children shall be in the full possession of all that I am preparing for you, you will acquire superior habits; your minds will gradually expand; you will be enabled to judge accurately of the cause and consequences of my proceedings, and to estimate them at their value. You will then become desirous of living in a more perfect state of society, —a society which will possess within itself the certain means of preventing the existence of any injurious passions, poverty, crime, or misery; in which every individual shall be instructed, add his powers of body and mind directed, by the wisdom derived from the best previous experience, so that neither bad habits nor erroneous sentiments shall be known;—in which age shall receive attention and respect, and in which every injurious distinction shall be avoided,—even variety of opinions shall not create disorder or any unpleasant feeling;—a society in which individuals shall acquire increased health, strength, and intelligence,—in which their labour shall be always advantageously directed,—and in which they will possess every rational enjoyment.

In due time communities shall be formed possessing such characters, and be thrown open to those among you, and to individuals of every class and denomination, whose wretched habits and whose sentiments of folly have not been too deeply impressed to be obliterated or removed, and whose minds can be sufficiently relieved from the pernicious effects of the old system, to permit them to partake of the happiness of the new. (The communities alluded to shall be more particularly described in a future publication.)

Having delivered this strange discourse, for to many of you it must appear strange indeed, I conceive only one of two conclusions can be drawn by those who have heard it. These are,— that the world to this day has been grossly wrong, and is at this moment in the depth of ignorance;—or, that I am completely in error. The chances then, you will say, are greatly against me. True: but the chances have been equally against every individual who has been enabled to make any discovery whatsoever.

To effect the purposes which I have long silently meditated, my proceedings for years have been so far removed from, or rather so much in opposition to, the common practices of mankind, that not a few have concluded I was insane. Such conjectures were favourable to my purposes, and I did not wish to contradict them. But the question of insanity between the world and myself will now be decided; either they have been rendered greatly insane,— or I am so. You have witnessed my conduct and measures here for sixteen years; and the objects I have had in progress are so far advanced that you can now comprehend many of them. You, therefore, shall be judges in this case. Insanity is inconsistency. Let us now try the parties by this rule.

From the beginning I firmly proposed to ameliorate your condition, the condition of all those engaged in similar occupations, and, ultimately, the condition of mankind, whose situation appeared to me most deplorable. Say, now, as far as you know, did I not adopt judicious measures to accomplish these purposes?

Have I not calmly, steadily, and patiently proceeded to fill up the outline of the plan which I originally formed to overcome your worst habits and greatest inconveniences, as well as your prejudices? Have not the several parts of this plan, as they were finished, fulfilled most completely the purposes for which they were projected? Are you not at this moment deriving the most substantial benefits from them? Have I in the slightest degree injured any one of you? During the progress of these measures have I not been opposed in the most determined and formidable manner by those whose interests, if they had understood them, would have made them active co-operators? Without any apparent means to resist these attempts, were they not frustrated and overcome, and even the resistance itself rendered available to hasten the execution of all my wishes? In short, have I not been enabled, with one hand, to direct with success the common mercantile concerns of this extensive establishment, and with the other hand to direct measures which now seem more like national than private ones, in order to introduce another system, the effects and success of which shall astonish the profound theologian no less than the most experienced and fortunate politician ?—a system which shall train its children of twelve years old to surpass, in true wisdom and knowledge, the boasted acquirements of modern learning, of the sages of antiquity, of the founders of all those systems —which hitherto have only confused and distracted the world, and which have been the immediate cause of almost all the miseries we now deplore?

Being witnesses of my measures, you alone are competent to judge of their consistency. Under these circumstances it would be mere hypocrisy in me to say that I do not know what must be your conclusions.

During the long period in which I have been thus silently acting for your benefit and for the benefit of each of my fellowmen,—what has been the conduct of the world?

Having maturely contemplated the past actions of men, as they have been made known to us by history, it became necessary for my purpose that I should become practically acquainted with men as they now are, and acquire from inspection a knowledge of the precise effects produced in the habits and sentiments of each class, by the peculiar circumstances with which the individuals were surrounded. The causes which had previously prepared my mind and disposition for the work,—which had removed so many formidable difficulties in the early part of my progress, now smoothed the way to the easy attainment of my wishes. By the knowledge of human nature which I had already acquired, I was enabled to dive into the secret recesses of a sufficient number of minds of the various denominations forming British society, to discover the immediate causes of the sentiments of each, and to trace the consequences of the actions that necessarily proceeded from those sentiments. The whole, as though they had been delineated on a map, were laid open to me. Shall I now at this eventful crisis make the world known to itself? Or shall this valuable knowledge descend with me to the grave, and you, our fellow-men, and our children's children, through many generations, yet suffer the miseries which the inhabitants of the earth have to this day experienced? These questions, however, need not be asked. My resolutions were taken in early life; and subsequent years have added to their strength and confirmed them. I therefore proceed regardless of individual consequences. I will hold up the mirror to man,—show him, without the intervention of any false medium, what he is, and then he will be better prepared to learn what he may be. Man is so constituted, that, by the adoption of proper measures in his infancy, and by steadily pursuing them through all the early periods of his life to manhood, he may be taught to think and to act in any manner that is not beyond the acquirement of his faculties: whatever he may have been thus taught to think and to do, he may be effectually made to believe is right and best for all mankind. He may also be taught (however few may think and act as he does), that all those who differ from him are wrong, and even ought to be punished with death if they will not think and act like him. In short, he may be rendered insane upon every subject which is not founded on, and which does not remain in never-varying consistency with, the facts that surround mankind. It is owing to this peculiarity in the constitution of man, that when he is born he may be taught any of the various dogmas which are known, and be rendered wholly unfit to associate with any of his fellow-men who have been trained in any of the other dogmas. It is owing to this principle that a poor human being duly initiated in the mysteries of Juggernaut, is thereby rendered insane on everything regarding that monster. Or, when instructed in the dogmas of Mahomedanism, he is thus rendered insane on every subject which has reference to Mahomed. I might proceed and state the same of those poor creatures who have been trained in the tenets of Brahma, or Confucius, or in any other of those systems which serve only to destroy the human intellect.

I have no doubt, my friends, you are at present convinced, as thoroughly as conviction can be formed in your minds, that none of you have been subjected to any such process;—that you have been instructed in that which is true;—that is evident. Pagans, Jews, Turks, every one of them, millions upon millions almost without end, are wrong, fundamentally wrong. Nay, you will allow, also, that they are truly as insane as I have stated them to be. But you will add,— "We are right,—we are the favoured of Heaven,—we are enlightened, and cannot be deceived." This is the feeling of every one of you at this moment. I need not be told your thoughts. Shall I now pay regard to you or to myself? Shall I be content and rest satisfied with the sufficiency which has fallen to my lot, while you remain in your ignorance and misery? Or shall I sacrifice every private consideration for the benefit of you and our fellow-men? Shall I tell you, and the whole of the civilized world, that, in many respects, none of these have been rendered more insane than yourselves,—than every one of you is at this moment; and that while these maladies remain uncured, you and your posterity cannot but exist in the midst of folly and misery?

What think you now, my friends, is the reason why you believe and act as you do? I will tell you. It is solely and merely because you were born, and have lived, in this period of the world,—in Europe,—in the island of Great Britain,—and more especially in this northern part of it. Without the shadow of a doubt, had every one of you been born in other times or other places, you might have been the very reverse of that which the present time and place have made you: and, without the possibility of the slightest degree of assent or dissent on your own parts, you might have been at this moment sacrificing yourselves under the wheels of the great idol Juggernaut, or preparing a victim for a cannibal feast. This, upon reflection, will be found to be a truth as certain as that you now hear my voice.

Will you not, then, have charity for the habits and opinions of all men, of even the very worst human beings that your imaginations can conceive? Will you not, then, be sincerely kind to them, and actively endeavour to do them good? Will you not patiently bear with, and commiserate, their defects and infirmities, and consider them as your relatives and friends?

If you will not,—if you cannot do this, and persevere to the end of your days in doing it,—you have not charity; you cannot have religion; you possess not even common justice; you are ignorant of yourselves, and are destitute of every particle of useful and valuable knowledge respecting human nature.

Until you act after this manner, it is impossible that you can ever enjoy full happiness yourselves, or make others happy.

Herein consists the essence of philosophy;—of sound morality; —of true and genuine Christianity, freed from the errors that that been attached to it;—of pure and undefiled religion.

Without the introduction of this knowledge into full and complete practice, there can be no substantial and permanent ameliorations effected in society; and I declare to you, that until all your thoughts and actions are founded on and governed by these principles, your philosophy will be vain,—your morality baseless, —your Christianity only calculated to mislead and deceive the weak and the ignorant,—and your professions of religion but as sounding brass or a tinkling cymbal.

Those, therefore, who with singleness of heart and mind are ardently desirous to benefit their fellow-men, will put forth their utmost exertions to bring this just and humane system of conduct forthwith into practice, and to extend the knowledge of its endless advantages to the uttermost parts of the earth —*for no other principles of action can ever become universal among men!*

Your time now makes it necessary that I should draw to a conclusion, and explain what ought to be the immediate result of what I have stated.

Direct your serious attention to the cause why men think and act as they do. You will then be neither surprised nor displeased on account of their sentiments or their habits. You will then clearly discover why others are displeased with you,—and pity them. As you proceed in these inquiries, you will find that mankind cannot be improved or rendered reasonable by force and contention; that it is absolutely necessary to support the old systems and institutions under which we now live, until another system and another arrangement of society shall be proved by practice to be essentially superior. You will, therefore, still regard it as your duty to pay respect and submission to what is established. For it would be no mark of wisdom to desert an old house, whatever may be its imperfections, until a new one shall be ready to receive you, however superior to the old that new one may be when finished.

Continue to obey the laws under which you live; and although many of them are founded on principles of the grossest ignorance and folly, yet obey them,—until the government of the country (which I have reason to believe is in the hands of men well disposed to adopt a system of general improvement) shall find it practicable to withdraw those laws which are productive of evil, and introduce others of an opposite tendency.

With regard to myself, I have not anything to ask of you, which I have not long experienced. I wish you merely to think that I am ardently engaged in endeavouring to benefit you and your children, and, through you and them, to render to mankind at large great and permanent advantages. I ask not for your gratitude, your love, your respect; for on you these do not depend. Neither do I seek or wish for praise or distinction of any kind; for to these, upon the clearest conviction, I am not entitled, and to me, therefore, they could be of no value. My desire is only to be considered as one of yourselves,—as a cotton spinner going about his daily and necessary avocations.

But for you I have other wishes. On this day a new era opens to our view. Let it then commence by a full and sincere dismissal from your minds of every unpleasant feeling which you may entertain towards each other, or towards any of your fellow-men. When you feel these injurious dispositions beginning to arise,—for, as you have been trained and are now circumstanced, they will arise again and again,—instantly call to your recollection how the minds of such individuals have been formed,—whence have originated all their habits and sentiments: your anger will then be appeased; you will calmly investigate the cause of your differences, and you will learn to love them and to do them good. A little perseverance in this simple and easily acquired practice will rapidly prepare the way for you, and every one around you, to be truly happy.

9

"PROSPECTUS", *ECONOMIST*, 19 JANUARY 1821, VIII–XII.

George Mudie

[The *Economist* was one of the first Owenite newspapers.[1] Founded and edited by Scottish journalist and author George Mudie (1787–1855) between January 1821 and the spring of 1823, it was the official voice of the Co-operative and Economical Society (CES), which Mudie also established. One of its main purposes was to be "explanatory of the new system of society projected by Robert Owen Esq.", in the hope of rallying potential supporters. To that end, the *Economist* also documented the organisation and day-to-day life of the CES, including a range of co-operative arrangements (such as bulk buying, a school for the community's children and a shared dining room). This was meant to show the benefits of Owen's plan for the condition of the working classes, and to offer a glimpse of the future communitarian world. In that respect, the *Economist* and the CES both adhered to one key Owenite principle: the will to implement social change through education and example, instead of resorting to violent means. Like the CES, the *Economist* was short-lived, lasting only fourteen months, but Mudie remained a lifelong proponent of socialism, though he bitterly resented Owen over his lack of support for the CES and other grassroots initiatives, as shown by their correspondence (1823–1848). He joined Abram Combe's Orbison community in 1825 (see Part 5, Chapter 28) and later edited a vast number of socialist publications and pamphlets, including the *Advocate of the Working Classes* (1826–1827), the *Gazette of the Exchange Bazaars* (1832–1833, see Part 4, Chapter 26), and the *Alarm Bell* (1839) (Claeys 1987, 67; Cole and Filson 1965, 207; Bennett 2016).]

The Collective Affairs of Men have hitherto been very grossly mismanaged. The true Principles of Society have been very little, if at all, understood. The real causes of vice, poverty and wretchedness, which have scourged the great mass of every people and have finally consigned the mightiest empires to destruction have, till very lately, been overlooked or entirely unknown. The powers acquired by mankind for the production and distribution of wealth, the diffusion of knowledge, the growth of virtue, the reduction of human labour, the enjoyment of comfort and the establishment of security have been rendered, with relation to the great majority of every people, nearly useless by the influence of counteracting principles, inherent in, and nearly coeval with, the frame of society itself.

The ECONOMIST undertakes to PROVE these assertions, by a few self-evident, intelligible, common-sense statements, as plain, as simple, and as palpable, as they are true.

He will take England as the portion of the globe on which his proofs are to be exhibited: England, with all her means, with all her power, all her glory, all her wealth, all her learning, all her beneficence,—England, (strange, and hitherto unaccountable anomaly!) with all her wretchedness, all her vice, all her poverty, all her ignorance, all her religious and political dissensions and moral degradation.

England possesses the means and the power of creating more Manufactured Goods than the world can consume; and her soil is capable of furnishing several times the number of her present population with food.

Notwithstanding this power, and this inalienable source of superabundant subsistence, millions of her own people are but imperfectly supplied with some, and are entirely destitute of most, of the necessaries and comforts of life, and of the numberless articles of convenience or of elegance which inventive skill has contrived for the accommodation or embellishment of society.

Here, then, is a source of wealth which is far from being fully opened, and a power of production which is not exerted;—and here, on the other hand, are unsatisfied wants, which the inert power, if we remove the causes that now restrain its activity, is much more than adequate to supply.

The sphere of wretchedness (to state the case again,) enlarges, the wants of the people increase; yet the productive power, which is able almost immediately to satisfy those wants, and in a short time to pour a superabundance upon the whole nation, becomes more and more inert.

The manufacturer, the merchant, the farmer, even some political economists, and all who have not yet looked to the bottom of this long perplexing subject, are in the habit of remarking, or rather complaining, that there is no demand for goods; that the market is overstocked; and that the times are bad; because, say they, more goods are produced than can be consumed.

The ECONOMIST utterly denies the truth of these allegations. He hesitates not to declare that the parties advancing them are mistaken; nor to pronounce that they have deceived themselves, and are guilty, however unintentionally, of deceiving the public, on a question of the highest importance: a question involving our very existence, as individuals and as a nation.

For what description of goods is there no demand? With what commodities is the world overstocked! Of what articles, the product of land or of industry, does there exist a greater quantity than can be consumed!

Is it of bread, or any other necessary of life, the product of the soil? —I will shew the landholder, even in this rich and flourishing land, hundreds of thousands of half-starved wretches, whose cry of distress, whose clamorous demand for bread, has at length penetrated the palaces and the breasts of their astonished and alarmed superiors.

Does the complaint come from the clothier, the hatter, the hosier, the tanner, the cutter, the potter, the joiner, the upholsterer, the founder, the builder, or even the scholar, the teacher, and the moralist?

I will take the first four through the streets of London; and I will shew them, in London alone, a multitude in abject poverty and squalid attire, the supply of whom, with comfortable apparel, would empty their full warehouses, and for a season exhaust their stores.

I will carry the cutler, the potter, the joiner, the upholsterer, the bedding maker, the founder, &c. into the miserable abodes of millions of Britons; and I will exhibit to them an almost endless succession of bare and dreary dwellings, the equipment of which with the necessaries and comforts, to say nothing of the elegancies of life, would, for a time, engross all their means and employ all their industry.

I will expose to the builder multitudes of human beings, crowded together in filthy, incommodious, and unhealthful hovels, languishing in garrets, and expiring in damp and dismal cellars, in workhouses, in hospitals, in jails. I will even shew him thousands of houseless and unsheltered wretches, inhaling their mortal malady with the distillations of the night, or perhaps breathing their last sigh on the inhospitable threshold, which is closed upon the pleading eloquence of Nature and Humanity, and repels the heart-breaking demand of silent Misery; and I will ask him, If he does not think there is ample scope for the extended consumption of our inexhaustible materials for building, and for the increased employment of him and all his labourers.

I will exhibit, even to the scholar, to the teacher, and to the moralist, millions of intelligent minds, shrouded in the darkness of ignorance. I will shew them the best principles of human nature, perverted to the worst and most unnatural purposes, by the neglect, the cruelty, and the disgraceful allurements, prepared by society for the destruction of the ignorant and the unwary. I will shew them Vice and Crime, and all the monstrous ministers of Corruption and Demoralization, let loose by society amongst the haunts of men, every day destroying thousands of their fellow creatures; and, I will ask them, Whether there is not a boundless field for the progress of intellect—for the exertion of all their zeal,—the operations of all their genius,—the diffusion of all their knowledge,—the realization of all their projects, for the happiness, the improvement, the elevation of their fellow creatures.

Did the narrow limits of a Prospectus admit it, I would prove that the same opposing extremes exist in all the affairs and circumstances of life.

That, though there is ignorance on the one hand, there is more knowledge on the other than is sufficient for its removal—knowledge, the blaze of which would speedily illumine the darkest recesses of ignorance, did society merely open channels adequate to the diffusion of the mighty and effulgent flood:

That, though Vice and Crime, (the progeny of Political Errors) are rapidly decomposing the elements of society, and preparing the volcanic mass of conflicting principles for an explosion that shall level the proud institutions and distinctions of civilization with the ground, and bury in their ruins all the graces, the charities, the intelligence, which ages of assiduous culture have brought to their present growth,—we nevertheless possess the certain means of averting the catastrophe which threatens us, and of almost instantly allaying those portentous grumblings, which too plainly indicate the approach of a terrible convulsion, that would hurl mankind back into barbarism:

That, though hundreds of thousands of English families are inadequately supplied with food, and though this country even depends upon Foreign Nations for a portion of the first necessaries of life; yet that our own soil, and our vast unemployed powers of production, are capable of immediately furnishing a superabundance of produce for the satisfaction of the first urgent and indispensable demand of nature:

That, though we have an immense population, not only ill-instructed and ill-fed, but inadequately lodged, uncomfortably clothed, and wholly unfurnished with innocent pleasures, with healthful and agreeable recreations, with all the articles and arrangements of convenience or of comfort which engage the minds, cheer the spirits, adorn the persons, and embellish the abodes of mankind,—yet we have materials,— we have the command of means,— we have hands,—above all, we have science and mechanism, capable of surrounding each individual with more of all these goods than his utmost wishes can desire.

"Well," it may be said, "these are indeed self-evident truths. It undoubtedly appears that there may be produced more than enough for all, though so many thousands have but a scanty competency, and though so many hundreds of thousands have not even that. But," it will be asked, "How is this most desirable object to be effected?— How are mankind, after so many ages of disappointment, of wretchedness, and of peril, to enter upon that happy state, which poets and philosophers have indeed anticipated, and which the sacred volume of Christianity has foretold, but the arrival of which seems to have been for ever obstructed by circumstances, over which mankind have hitherto had no control? The melancholy facts which you have stated may indeed excite a sigh for the condition of poor, perplexed, contradictory human nature; but unless you point out with more distinctness than former projectors have done, the means of overcoming the manifold evils which you have depicted, mankind will be little better for being convinced of the extent and reality of their wretchedness."

The ECONOMIST does undertake to point out, and to prove, and to carry into practice, the means by which the sum of vice and poverty, and consequently of misery, shall be rapidly diminished: and, if it be capable of diminution, what is to hinder its final extinction?

He undertakes this on no uncertain theory, but on principles, the whole of which have been demonstrated in practice; on combinations, the knowledge of which is the result of extensive observation, of profound research, and of enlarged experience; principles and combinations, the true knowledge and right use of which will enable mankind immediately to improve the character, promote the comforts, and secure the abundant subsistence, of the present generation, and to establish on a rock the happiness of the next.

The measures which are calculated to effect this great change, may be commenced almost without an effort.

All the persons who at present have employment may instantly begin to climb the ascent without soliciting a helping hand from those who stand above them.

The utterly destitute will require less aid to render them and their descendants happy and independent, than that which must, under the present system, be afforded them for the prolongation of a miserable existence, from public and private charity.

The poor will be relieved from their wretchedness, and the rich will be benefited by the process.

The ignorant will be instructed, while the learned will derive vast accessions to the sum of human knowledge and wisdom.

The vicious will be reclaimed, while the virtuous will, in a great measure, be withdrawn from temptation.

The humble will be placed in a situation of safety, and of gradual elevation, while the great will gain security.

Land and labour will become of greatly increased value, and will always command their true worth.

Of the latter (labour) there will for a long time be too little for the demand, though there is at present so great a scarcity of employment.

The present money wealth of the country will become many times more valuable, active, and useful, than it now is;—so truly and obviously so, indeed, that the effect will be the same as if foreign nations were suddenly to pay us a tribute, equal to several times the amount of our present money wealth; and as if that vast accession of wealth were equally divided among the population.

Plenty will overspread the land!—Knowledge will increase!— Virtue will flourish!—Happiness will be recognized, secured, and enjoyed.

All that the ECONOMIST has at present to request is, that no one will pronounce against these expectations, until the grounds on which they are entertained have been examined;—that he may not be condemned as a visionary, merely because he seems to promise more than can be realized;— that no one will refuse to accompany him in the investigations, merely because he may appear to unfold prospects too brilliant to be real,—hopes too flattering to be gratified,—happiness too great to be enjoyed in this world. Language of this kind has already been too long held. There are few things so great that man cannot attempt their accomplishment. There are many seeming impossibilities which he possesses powers to overcome. Science has already achieved triumphs, which remain as so many standing miracles effected by human agency. If you repeat to an uninstructed person the steps of a mathematical problem, and announce to him its result, he can neither comprehend the process, nor acknowledge its truth. The result, however, is not the less true, because to him it is unintelligible. If he has been frequently told, indeed, that all mathematical demonstrations are unerring, he may assent to the truth, merely because it is a mathematical truth. In like manner, when the principles and combinations of which we are about to treat shall be more generally understood, their truths will be universally acknowledged. In like manner, it is impossible for any of the persons who are as yet uninstructed in those principles (however intelligent or even enlightened they may be in other respects) to comprehend the nature of the combinations, or to assent to the truth of the results which the ECONOMIST announces. They must accompany him, step by step, throughout the investigation. They must be taught to comprehend each individual step separately, and the laws by which its relations with all the rest are determined, before they can comprehend the magnificent whole which arises from their union. The ECONOMIST pledges himself to prove, in his succeeding papers, the truth and accuracy of the parts, and of the whole. He only entreats that his readers will patiently attend,—that they will diligently examine,—and, above all, that they will dispassionately decide.

He has already shewn that there are almost boundless wants, and that we possess equally boundless powers of production, for the creation of all the goods by which those wants are to be satisfied. He hopes we shall at least hear no more, therefore, of there being no market for our produce,—of there being no demand for our commodities,— of the necessity of looking into every corner of the globe for customers, while we have so many millions of ill-supplied consumers at home. He trusts that mankind, at length convinced of this great truth, will set about emancipating themselves from the thraldom of ignorance, which has hitherto rendered all their energies nearly nugatory;—that they will now complain, not of the want of goods, of means, or of power, but of the errors which prevent the exercise of their power, the command of their means, and the distribution of their goods;— that, having at length discovered, that their multifarious evils arise, not from the absence of markets,—not from the limited extent of the demand,—not from the paucity of consumers,—but from the prevalence, of erroneous principles, which continually interpose between the consumers and the producers, and which tend perpetually to close the channels of circulation;—they will set themselves seriously to remove the real causes of all their calamities,—to break down the barriers which have shut out man from man, and so to open, renovate, and enlarge the channels through which alone their boundless treasures can be circulated, as to afford an easy passage to the full-swelling tide of their wealth, knowledge, and happiness.

The Economist points confidently to his future pages for the full development of those principles, simple when regarded separately, but wonder-working in their combination, which will assuredly [be] placed under the control of associated man all those elements of the moral and physical worlds, the true knowledge and command of which are indispensable to his happiness, and which will enable him, under the tutelage of the Great Author of Nature, to re-create the Earth, which he is destined to inhabit, and which he was commissioned to "subdue."

He appeals fearlessly to his ensuing Numbers, as the humble medium through which will be exhibited, by the co-operative aid of energetic minds, a bold, luminous, and correct outline of the Temple of Truth, for which men have so long sought in vain; but to which the researches of enlightened humanity have at length led the way. The progress of the first discoverer was slower than that of succeeding travellers; for he not only opened and cleared the passage,—he has rent the veil, which had hitherto concealed the glorious edifice, even from those who had approached the nearest to its precincts.—It may now be descried afar off. The mind, without stopping to examine the approaches, bounds at once, and with transport, into the habitation for which she has so long sought; and it is only in retracing her flight, that she finds the imperishable track over which she has passed, is formed of all the facts and all the experience of all mankind, that every single material is in itself a truth;—and that, in the broad and unbending course which she has so rapturously found, there are no deviations from the direct line of unerring precision, merely because the principles of error and of falsehood, with fill their devious inclinations, are wholly excluded from the work.

If, in this first paper, the ECONOMIST has succeeded in establishing the fact, in convincing his readers that there must be some mischief in the frame of society,— that there is some fatal error which thus prevents men from using and enjoying the bounties of creation;—which has turned their very blessings into curses,—has held them in ignorance while they have been cultivating knowledge,—has led them into poverty while they have been creating affluence and power,—and which daily and hourly defrauds them of the treasures diffused over the fair and fertile face of the globe,—he has already gained an important point, all indeed which he could hope to attain in the first instance; and has already effected all that he at present intended to accomplish. The knowledge of the evil is half the cure. Having clearly ascertained the disease, the public will be the better prepared to administer to the principles of health. Having distinctly marked the wide spreading roots of that destroying cancer which devours the substance of society,—which is drying up the healthful springs of life,—tainting and contaminating all the intercourses of social existence,—they will be enabled with the greater certainty to set about the extirpation of the evil.

The remedies which the ECONOMIST has to suggest are entirely emollients and restoratives; he purposes neither to amputate nor destroy: his aim is to produce a new and renovating action, which shall restore the diseased organs of society to health and vigour, and even promote their enlarged growth, their rapid improvement in size and strength, in beauty of form, and elegance of proportion.

Note

1 The first Owenite periodical was John Bone's *Age of Civilization*, published intermittently between 1816 and 1818 (Claeys 1987, 68).

10

THE REVOLT OF THE BEES (LONDON: PRINTED FOR LONGMAN, REES, ORME, BROWNE AND GREENE [1826] 1839), 22–27.

John Minter Morgan

[Drawing upon Bernard Mandeville's *Fable of the Bees* (1714) and upon Robert Owen's New Lanark experiment, John Minter Morgan's parable was serialised in the *Co-operative Magazine*, which was one of the leading socialist publications in Britain during the late 1820s and early 1930s. Using the bees as an allegory for human society, Morgan showed how the insects were now in a state of misery after having traded their natural state (communal, industrious life within the beehive) in favour of competition and private property. Embracing communitarian socialism was the only way to bring about a better future which would reconcile the advantages of modern technical innovation and the harmonious co-operation of old. *The Revolt of the Bees* proved very successful, and was key in promoting Owen's views while the latter was living in New Harmony between 1825 and 1828. Morgan helped popularise the imagery of the beehive, which later became a prominent working-class and co-operative symbol ("Minter Morgan, John", *Maitron*, 2010).]

So many difficulties had the influential bees experienced in attempting to reform the abuses of the hive, and to relieve the indigent, that they were disposed, previous to the publication of this dogma, to resign the cause in despair, if they could have reconciled it to themselves to pass by with indifference so much accumulated and increasing misery. But now they were overjoyed to find that they were sanctioned by the inexorable laws of nature, in abandoning the impoverished to their fate, and that they could resume without remorse their jollity and feasting. The drone who had made the grand discovery did not go unrewarded, for he was lodged in one of the choicest cells and fed with the royal jelly.

After the failure of the various theorists, an experimentalist[1] arrived, and announced his discovery of the source of all their moral evils. He came to promulgate a code of regulations in which no principles that had not stood the test of experiment were admitted, and which therefore could not fail to be as true and correct in practice as all theories formed upon a rigid adherence to inductive philosophy.

"I have had," said he, "under my direction a swarm of bees settled on the banks of the Clyde[2]; they came from the Pentland Hills[3] after the revolution, and had contracted the habits and peculiarities of your present policy. Having ascertained that the real causes of intemperance, vice and misery, were to be found in the altered circumstances under which they were placed, I removed many of the unfavourable circumstances, and replaced them with such as were productive of health and contentment. The hours of employment with the working bees were limited, their cells improved, and temptations withdrawn. The happiest results followed, and I had scarcely any occasion for the *Judicatores*. Thus far, however, nothing more has been effected than some improvement of your present system; but the plans which I now recommend, require an equal participation in the division of the honey, equal employment in proportion to bodily strength;—in short, they form in all respects a system of mutual assistance."

Now, although it was evident that this was the identical constitution of apiarian society from which they had departed, the principles of which were so obvious and simple, a singular phenomenon occurred. The bees of all classes,—*Judicatores, Ecclesiastes,* and *Legislatores*, were unable to comprehend it,—not even the working bees, who would have been most benefited by the change. The *Judicatores* had been so long occupied in the adjustment of individual claims, that they could not understand the identity of particular with general interests. The *Ecclesiastes* rejected the scheme, because the necessity of belief in particular doctrines was not enforced. And the apiarian economists repeated their favourite theory of Number *versus* Honey.

The experimentalist had the welfare of his species so much at heart, that he was determined to meet the objections of all parties: and accordingly to the working bees he stated, that although they might unite under his arrangements in order to secure a due proportion of honey, yet they could retain their individual cells and their privileges of privacy; that they could even regale themselves in their own cells, if they objected to feed upon the bee bread in the large cell constructed for those who wished to take their repasts with the community. He earnestly dissuaded them from committing any acts of violence, as being both unjust and calculated to retard his ameliorating measures. He clearly showed that the characters of their directors, even of those the most tyrannical, were not formed *by* themselves, but *for* them, partly in the pupa state, but chiefly by the institutions of the hive. Above all, he exhorted them to leave the affluent in the undisturbed possession of their ample stores, and to begin under his system to gather honey for themselves. But the workers had contracted habits which rendered them unwilling to submit to a change, the advantages of which they were as yet unable to appreciate.

Of the *Legislatores* he demanded how they could reasonable expect order in the hive, while their institutions were the obvious cause of dissatisfaction and turbulence, of inequality in the distribution of honey, and all the evil consequences resulting therefrom, both to the saturated and to the indigent; presenting to one class an over-excitement, and depriving the other of the means of temperate gratification. Then appealing to the *Judicatores*, he inquired how they could reconcile it to themselves gravely to sit in judgment upon their fellow citizens, while they must be conscious, that had they possessed the same nature dispositions, and been subject to the influence of the same circumstances, they would have been equally guilty. In reply to the objections of the *Ecclesiastes*, he remarked, that no bee had any control over his belief; he must assent to that opinion only, the truth of which was obvious to his understanding: it was therefore inflicting deep injustice on the community, to reject the proffered assistance of an experienced individual, merely because he could not conscientiously subscribe to peculiar doctrines; more especially when, so far from impending the exercise of any religious ceremony, his scheme offered equal facilities to all sects, and the most perfect freedom of opinion. Then turning to the apiarian economists, he observed, that their fears of an overgrown hive were groundless;—could not each bee gather more honey than was sufficient for his own subsistence, since the working bees already not only supported themselves and the rest, but also produced large quantities for exportation? Therefore every increase in their numbers was attended with a larger proportionate increase in the power of collecting honey; and until the heather on the Pentland Hills was completely exhausted of its nectar, and the whole globe had become an entire flower-garden, they might continue to lead forth their swarms without any apprehension of a famine. But his arguments were fruitless; for all the powerful bees declare the scheme to be visionary; while they admitted the benevolence and practical experience of the projector. He therefore flew away, and established a colony upon his own principles in a distant region.[4]

Notes

1 Robert Owen saw himself as a social scientist and a man of action, as opposed to classical political theorists: "Hitherto the world has been tormented by useless talking — by much speaking; all of which has proved to be of no avail. Hence-forward, acting will render precepts unnecessary: and, in future, systems for the government of mankind will be estimated and valued by their effects in practice only" (Owen [1817] 1972, 188).
2 A direct allusion to New Lanark, which was built in 1785 on the banks of the River Clyde, about two miles south-west of the royal burgh of Lanark.
3 A mountain range south-west of Edinburgh.
4 For example, New Harmony, Indiana.

11

"THE SOCIAL SYSTEM, CHAPTER V [CONTINUED], CONSTITUTIONS, LAWS AND REGULATIONS OF A COMMUNITY", *NEW HARMONY GAZETTE*, 21 FEBRUARY 1827.

Robert Owen

[This text, published in five instalments in the *New Harmony Gazette* between November 1826 and March 1827, is based on a manuscript dating back to 1821 (National Library of Wales).[1] Building upon the *Report to the County of Lanark* (1820), it provides in vivid detail a comprehensive account of community arrangements, rules and regulations in the proposed "Villages of Co-operation". In contrast to earlier versions of the "Plan", the *Social System* puts greater emphasis on social and economic equality in the form of communal living (including the rearing of children) and the abolition of private property (Claeys 1987, xviii–xix; Kolmerten 1998, 46; Langdon 2000, 10). This text also popularised the phrase "social system", which was used as a variant of Owen's "science of society", and from which the word "socialism" is derived in English (Gans 1957; Claeys 1986).]

To prepare individuals for these communities, measures should be adopted according to the localities, character and condition of the parties who are to form them, but when they shall be ready to enter upon the practice required to give success to these associations, the writer proposed as an outline, the following Rules and Regulations, and for the most important of them he subjoins the reasons for the recommendation.

CONSTITUTION, LAWS AND REGULATIONS OF A COMMUNITY

It is recommended,
I. That the community consist of persons who shall have agreed to unite their labor, skill and capital for mutual benefit, to cooperate in measures for producing and distributing, in the most advantageous manner for all, a full supply of

the necessaries and comforts of life, as well as in forming arrangements which shall enable them to enjoy in the highest degree the use of those productions, and secure to their children the best training and education.

II. That, to avoid on the one hand, the evils and inconveniences resulting from the congregation of mankind into large masses, and on the other hand to preserve that limit, below which, the full benefits of combination could not be attained, the number of persons composing a community shall not (including their families) exceed 2,000, not be less than 500.

III. That, in order to provide for an increase of population, the numbers at the commencement shall not considerably exceed the minimum, or 500. (In many situations the number associating together *at the commencement* may with great advantage be much less than 500).

IV. That the community buildings be arranged in the form of a square or parallelogram, the dwelling houses, dormitories, &c. occupying the sides, and the public buildings, comprising kitchen and dining halls, library and committee rooms, schools and lecture rooms, being placed in the center. The vacant spaces of the area may be ornamented with trees, and laid out in public walks and exercise grounds for the children. Gardens are proposed to be formed around the exterior of the square.

The plan should be arranged to admit of the most beneficial application of scientific improvements in all the departments of domestic economy, to afford increased comfort and enjoyment, at a less expense of labor and capital, to give superior accommodations of the dwelling houses, and to render the external circumstances of the establishment in a high degree agreeable and favorable to health.

V. That the village be situated as near to the center of the land to be occupied by the community as local circumstances may permit.

VI. That as exclusive employment in manufactures and all occupations carried on within doors, is incompatible with a sound state of health, and as the union of agriculture and manufactures presents many facilities to both, and as it is also of great importance that the community should produce within itself, a full supply of the first necessaries of life, the land attached to the establishment shall be of sufficient extent to render it essentially agricultural.

VII. That the manufactories, workshops, granaries, stores, washing and drying houses, be placed at the most convenient distance beyond the gardens surrounding the village; and that the farm offices be situated according to the localities of the land.

VIII. That as cordial union and cooperation never have existed and cannot exist under a system of family and individual interest, or inequality of condition; there shall be a full community of interests among all the members of the society, and as much equality as can be advantageously introduced into practice during the change from old habits to the new.

IX. That when all shall have been equally well educated, and the society shall have repaid such part of the capital, invested in the establishment, as may have been advanced by its own members, a full and complete equality shall prevail; the necessary and natural inequality of age, being the only distinction existing; and to advanced age every advantage, comfort and deference being given.

X. That the community shall at this period be under the direction of a committee composed of all the members between certain ages, of those, for example, between 35 and 45, or between 40 and 50.

XI. That in the mean time, the management of affairs be vested in a committee consisting of twelve persons, to be elected by all the members of the community.

XII. That the committee be elected annually, the members of the old being eligible for the new committee.

XIII. That the committee elect from the members of the society two treasurers and a secretary, who shall be members of the committee in virtue of their offices.

XIV. That the committee meet every Monday, and oftener when particular circumstances require their attention, such extra meetings to be called by the secretary or by any two of the members.

XV. That the oldest member present, exclusive of the treasurers and secretary, preside at these meetings, and that the minutes of proceedings at each be signed by him.

XVI. That the treasurers be empowered to receive all moneys due to the community, and pay its disbursements on orders signed by the secretary; that they balance and report their accounts every week to the committee, who shall appoint two of their number to examine and pass them under their signatures.

XVII. That the secretary be directed to keep a regular, detailed, daily statement of all the accounts and transactions of the community; and that such statement be presented weekly to the committee and submitted to the examination of two of their number who shall pass it under their signatures with such observations as may occur to them.

XVIII. That the books of accounts, and transactions of the society be open to the inspection of all its members.

XIX. That the business of the community be divided into the following departments.

1st. Agriculture and gardening.

2nd. Manufacture and trades.

3rd. Commercial transactions.

4th. Domestic economy; comprehending the arrangements for heating, ventilating, lighting, cleaning, and keeping in repair the dwelling houses and public buildings of the village —the arrangements connected with the public kitchen and dining halls, those for the furnishing of clothes, linens and furniture, and for washing and drying and the management of the dormitories.

5th. Health, or the medical superintendence of the apartments for the sick and lying in apartments, and general arrangements to prevent contagion and sickness.

6th. Police, including the arrangements for lighting and cleaning the square—for the repair of the roads and walks, and for watching to guard against fire and to protect the property of the community against external depredation.

7th. Education, or the formation of character from infancy; to this department will also belong the means of recreation, or of mental and physical exercise and improvement for all ages.

XX. That a weekly report from each of these departments be laid before the committee at their weekly meetings to be examined and passed with such observations as may be deemed necessary.

XXI. That, for the general superintendence of the departments the committee appoint sub-committees from their own number or from the other members of the society.

XXII. That in case there be not at first a sufficient number of persons in the community fully competent to the management of all the operations in the different branches of industry which it may be desirable to establish, or in any other department, the committee be empowered to engage the assistance of skillful,[sic] practical men from common society, until the increased experience of the members of the community can advantageously dispense with such services.

XXIII. That in regulating the employments of the members according to their age, abilities, previous acquirements and situation in life, the committee, at the same time, pay every regard to the inclinations of each, consistent with the general good; and that the employment be equalized as far as possible, and so ordered as to permit every individual who may be thus disposed to occupy part of his time in agriculture.

Great facilities may be afforded to agriculture by the power which the community will possess of calling out an extra number of hands, to assist in its operations, at those seasons and moments, when it is of great importance to have the command of additional aid.

XXIV. That as under the proposed arrangements, every machine, invention and expedient for the abridgement of human labor will bring an increase of benefits to all, it be a primary object with the committee to introduce to the utmost practicable extent in every department of the establishment, all those scientific improvements of modern times, which if rightly applied, are calculated to render manual labor only a healthy and agreeable exercise.

XXV. That the productive powers of the community be applied in the first place, to create a full supply of the necessaries and comforts of life for domestic consumption, and as far as localities will admit, to obtain them directly from their own land and labor.

XXVI. That the system of garden cultivation be gradually introduced as the population increases, and as it shall be found to be advantageous.

XXVII. That the surplus products of the community, which will be derived from manufactures and the useful trades and agriculture, more or less from each, according to the peculiar circumstances of the establishment, shall consist of intrinsically valuable and staple commodities; to be regulated by the demand of the neighboring markets.

XXVIII. That the persons, whom the committee appoint to conduct the commercial transactions of the community, be instructed to buy and sell for ready money only, to avoid the evils arising from a system of credit; that these transactions on the part of the community be always performed in good faith, and without the slightest attempt to deceive in any respect, buyer or seller; and when any individuals with whom they deal, shew a disposition to impose upon the community, all dealing with such individuals shall from that time cease.

XXIX. That in regard to domestic consumption, each member of the community shall be equally supplied with the necessaries and comforts of life.

XXX. That all the members of the community be equal in rights, privileges and accommodations, according to their respective ages.

XXXI. That the surplus proceeds of the united exertions of the community, which remain after discharging rent, interest, taxes, and other expenses, be regularly applied to the liquidation of the capital borrowed upon the establishment until it shall be repaid; and when this debt is cancelled, it is proposed that the future surplus proceeds be invested to form a fund for the creation of a second community, as soon as the increased population of the first may require it.

XXXII. That in the domestic department, the following arrangements and regulations be adopted:

1st. The heating, ventilating and lighting of the dwellinghouses [sic] and buildings in the square shall be effected according to the latest and post approved methods.

2nd. An ample supply of water shall be provided and distributed to each, for domestic purposes and to guard against fire.

3rd. provisions of the best quality only shall be cooked in the public kitchen; and it shall be a special object for the attention of the sub-committee of domestic economy, and of the superintendent who has the immediate direction of this department to ascertain and put in practice the best and most economical means of preparing the most nutritious and agreeable food.

Any parties being ill, or having an aversion to eat with their friends in the public dining hall, may have their meals sent to their private apartments.

4th. The furniture of the dwellinghouses [sic], dormitories and public buildings (as far as the same is provided for out of the public funds) shall be such as to afford every accommodation, which persons living in such a community can require, being devised with reference to intrinsic use and comfort and not mere fashion or capricious ornament.

5th. A similar regulation will apply to the clothing of the community. The best materials shall be provided, and that form of dress adopted, which may be best calculated to promote the comfort and health of the wearer. With regard to the children, whose habits are yet to be formed, very essential improvements may in this respect be introduced, which will not only save much useless expenses of labor and capital, but be the means of increasing in a very high degree the strength of the constitution.

6th. Modern scientific improvements, which supersede the necessity of any severe or disagreeable manual labor, shall be applied to the processes of washing and drying.

7th. The dormitories, designed for the children above two year of age, and the youth of the community until the period of marriage, shall be divided into compartments, and furnished with accommodations suited to the different ages.

XXXIII. That the employments of the female part of the community consist in preparing food and clothing—in the care of the dwellinghouses [sic], dormitories and public buildings—in the managements of the washing and drying houses—in the lighter operations of gardening, and other occupations suited to the female character. By the improved domestic arrangements proposed, one female will with great ease and comfort perform as much as twenty menial servants can do at present; and instead of being the drudge and slave which the wife of a working man with a family has hitherto been, she will be engaged only in healthy and cleanly employment, and possess sufficient leisure for mental improvements and the rational enjoyment of life.

XXXIV. That it be a general rule, that every part of the establishment be kept in the highest state of order and neatness, and that the utmost personal cleanliness be observed.

XXXV. That the following objects and regulations connected with the department of health be attended to and adopted.

1st. On the first appearance of indisposition in any of the members, immediate attention be given it, and every possible care taken of the patient till complete recovery; the prevention of serious complaints being always far more easy, than to effect a cure after the disease has fixed itself in the constitution.

2nd. The complaint of indisposition by an individual shall place him on the invalid list, on which he will remain, until the medical attendant pronounces his complete recovery.

3rd. The arrangements of the apartments for the sick shall be so formed and conducted as to afford every possible comfort to patients, and provide much more effectual means of recovery, than their private dwelling could admit of.

4th. In the lying-in apartments the best accommodations shall be prepared for the quiet and recovery of the female members of the community during their confinement.

5th. Removal to the apartments for the sick, as well as to the lying-in apartments, shall at the same time be at the option of the individual.

6th. As the health of the community may be materially improved or injured by their situation with respect to public buildings, by dress, food, employment, the temper, and general state of the mind, and by various other circumstances, the attention of the sub-committee of this department shall be continually directed to these important considerations.

Note

1 The original manuscript from 1820 has been lost, and the only surviving copy was made in 1821, probably by Owen's eldest son, Robert Dale Owen. The text differs slightly from the version published in the *New Harmony Gazette*.

12

"ONE OF 'THE PEOPLE'", "TO THE WEALTH-PRODUCING CLASSES OF ENGLAND", *MAGAZINE OF USEFUL KNOWLEDGE AND CO-OPERATIVE MISCELLANY*, N°1, JANUARY 1830, 7–10.

William Lovett

[Though William Lovett (1800–1877) is mostly known as a founding member of the London Working Men's Association in 1836 and as a leading Chartist, he was also one of the main actors in the early Owenite movement. Born in Cornwall into a working-class family, he moved to London in 1821, where he worked as a cabinet-maker. Wishing to better his education, he attended Thomas Hodgskin's (see Part 4, Chapter 22) evening classes on political economy at the London Mechanics' Institute. Lovett joined the co-operative movement around 1823. He and his wife Mary were the shopkeepers of the First London Co-operative Trading Association. He was later appointed Secretary of the British Association for the Promotion of Co-operative Knowledge, one of the movement's leading organisations in the late 1820s and early 1830s. Lovett also wrote for various publications, including the *Magazine of Useful Knowledge and Co-operative Miscellany*, a monthly periodical whose editor, William Carpenter (see Part 5, Chapter 31 and Part 6, Chapter 38), aimed to introduce Owen's system to a working-class audience (Holyoake [1875] 1908, 86–87; Cole 1944, 23; Marsh 1998, 124). Addressing his fellow-working people, Lovett attempted to demonstrate the potential of co-operation for the advancement of their class. Adapting Owen's vision of community to the more immediate concerns of poverty and unemployment, he argued in favour of the self-employment of the productive classes in co-operative stores and workshops where the means of production and distribution would be owned in common (Holyoake [1875] 1908, 303; Taylor 1983, 93; Langdon 2000, 19).]

ONE OF THE PEOPLE

To the Wealth Producing classes of England.

MY FELLOW COUNTRYMEN,

You have by your industry, and genius, combined with that of your ancestors, changed this once almost barren island, into a blooming garden, and like the industrious bees, have explored every part of the globe, for wherewith to beautify and enrich it. In the place of stagnant waters, and barren heaths, you have caused the valleys to smile with plenty, and the fair bosom of the earth to teem with abundance; you have made the deep recesses of the ocean to contribute to your support, and have wafted on its surface, the produce of your industry to every clime. You have made every elements subservient to your purposes, for executing the most minute, up to the stupendous. And in addition to this, your courage, combined with your industry, have enabled you to defend these; thus then, my friends, it is to you, to the Wealth producing classes, that England is indebted for England's greatness. You having done thus much, *What is now your condition?* Surely! you who have produced those beneficial changes and effects, enjoy every comfort, have satisfaction and peace written on your brow, while prosperity and happiness, gladden your abodes. No! no! alas, the reverse is your fate, for while you contribute to the enjoyments of others, are wanting the necessary of existence yourselves; while you erect sumptuous edifices for others, are often without a home, or habitation; while you bedeck others in silk and gold, often want a garment to shield you from the storms of the winter, or the scorching sun of summer; while your labour contributes to load with delicacies the tables of others, have not wherewith to satisfy your hunger; and while excessive labour wastes your frames of body, your minds are lacerated with anguish and despair, to think that with all your industry you must still condescend to solicit, the scanty pittance of charity.

The wealth producing classes of this country who at one time possessed a courage that was proverbial, have now that courage blasted and almost every fond endearment that bound them to their country removed, the natural power of resistance to defend their native country had been crushed; by having nothing left to defend. In fact, every thing that cherishes self-esteem, that call forth the most noble feelings of manhood, has been clouded by poverty, and chilled by despair.

And why, let us ask, have such been *their* fate? Because others have reaped the fruits of their industry, and scarcely left *them* the gleanings. Why have they not enjoyed the produce of their own labour themselves? Because at first their ignorance, their dissentions, their carelessness and indifference, and above all their bad propensities and vices; that prepared the way for others to take the advantage, and to manage *that* for them, which they managed so badly themselves. How far those persons have managed for their own benefits, many of *you now feel*, and how reluctant to give up the management most of you perceive, nay, though their future peace is likely to be effected by your wretchedness, they are indifferent of the results, and careless of the consequence.

Nay, such has been the disposition of persons whose duty and interests should have urged them to make every inquiry, relative to the justice, or even the policy of protecting labour, or capital, that hitherto they seem disposed to think in favour of the latter; never considering that by depressing the labourer, by reducing him to a state of wretchedness, and want, that they ultimately foil him on their own estates, in the shape of poor rates, &c. It is time some few have taken the alarm, lest their estates will be soon swallowed up altogether, but they seek for the cause of the evil any where, and ascribe any thing, and every thing, but the right.

Is it not in this particular the protection afforded by law to the capitalists, by persons of rank and influence, encouraging and supporting them in all their measures, however, arbitrary, to crush the labourer; that having finally ground him down to such a state of destitution, and wretchedness, so that with all his industry, he cannot provide bread for his family unless he has recourse to parochial assistance.

Let then those persons who have hitherto protected the CAPITALIST, let them, if they would keep their property secure, and secure at the same time the blessings of their countrymen, let them for the future protect the LABOURER, let them give every encouragement to his industry. Let them at the same time, renounce the great burden of taxation from the elastic springs of LABOUR and Industry, and ere long England will rise in her own estimation, be loved at home, and respected abroad. But my friends, whether persons of power, or riches, will become alive to their best interests nor not, it behoves us, it is a part of our duty to inquire what can we do to remedy the evil? By what means can we ourselves effect a beneficial change in our condition? Shall we, my friends, by uniting our powers take our cause in our own hands and manage for ourselves? THE CO-OPERATIVE SYSTEM presents us with this remedy. What is Co-operation, some may inquire, Co-operation in its fullest sense is the opposite to Competition, instead of competing and striving with each other to porcure [sic] the necessaries of life, *we make common cause, we unite with each other*, to procure the same benefits, nay, to add to our happiness; for *competition* engenders every bad feeling, that the human mind can conceive. Co-operation, my friends, is to prevent this, is to place us in a situation where conflicting interest will not present those evils; but when industry, union, and good feeling, will procure happiness for all, and to which all contribute. When we can satisfy all our wants, and administer consolation to the unfortunate, without harming ourselves, when the widow may be consoled, and the orphan provided for, when the sick man be comforted and when old age will be exempt from toil and care, and when kindness and respect, comfort and peace will increase the desire for long life; persons may smile and consider these Utopian hopes: but can we suppose that man is not capable of such enjoyments; is man always to be unhappy, always destined to persue [sic] peace and never find it, surely not, when we trace back and find what civilization has done for us, ought we to despair that much greater things may not be effected.

But how say you, is it possible for us to effect this desirable change, it may take some time to realise all the benefits that will result from Co-operation; but a beginning has already been made, successfully made, *it is a glorious step to be convinced of its importance*, and yet further steps have been made. But you have not wealth to begin with, you may say, you have that which beget all riches; you have your labours: but you want some means to render this labour effective. A plan has been adopted by many societies to obtain this, they have united to make purchases of the necessaries and conveniencies [sic] of life, at the wholesale prices; thus they save the profits of the retail dealer; thus by this means (if each take an active part, and it depends on this) they will be able to realise a sum sufficient to employ some of their members, the profits on this will enable them to employ others, and so on till all are employed, till all are taken out of the power of employers, they may then erect suitable habitations for their comforts or conveniency, and thus may the poor wretched and depressed Labourer, under such a system as Co-operation presents, become a healthy, wealthy, and happy race, united in one great family, and having corresponding links of brotherly affection throughout the universe.

ONE OF "THE PEOPLE"

13

"TO THE SOCIALISTS OF GREAT BRITAIN. LETTER FROM TYTHERLY COMMUNITY", *NEW MORAL WORLD*, 30 NOVEMBER 1839, 920–922.

George Fleming

[When the Rational Society set up its own official community at Queenwood (or Tytherly) in Hampshire in 1839, it seemed that Owen's promised "New Moral World" was now close at hand. This glowing account of the community's early days remains in line with orthodox Owenism and its insistence on large-scale communities funded through a system of shares, with the help of wealthy, upper- and middle-class backers. That it was published in the *New Moral World*, the movement's official newspaper, and penned by its editor, George Fleming, adds to the propagandist feel of the piece. The aim was undoubtedly to garner support around a project which had failed to receive unanimous approbation within the various Owenite branches from the onset, due to concerns regarding expenses and undemocratic modes of governance – a range of grievances which would later prove fatal for Owenism at large (see Part 8, Chapter 41). Yet the article also sheds light on the genuine faith in reform and general optimism for the future that were shared by Owen's followers, even in the face of various practical and financial setbacks. Along with the debacle of their co-operative and unionist ventures in 1833–1834, the inadequacy of relief policies in the context of the New Poor Law encouraged the socialists to "build a new society for themselves" (Taylor 1983, 222–223).

George Fleming (1808–1878) was one of Robert Owen's most loyal supporters. Born into a working-class family in Berwick-upon-Tweed, he later moved to Salford where he worked as a journeyman housepainter and became active in the local co-operative movement. A founding member of the Salford Community Association in 1836, he lectured at the Salford Social Institution, became a Social missionary and rose within the ranks of the Association of All Classes of All Nations. In 1838, he was appointed editor of the *New Moral World* and became an early proponent of the Queenwood community scheme. After the demise of the Owenite movement, he was a member of the Co-operative League and the League of Social Progress (Yeo 1971, 110; Langdon 2000, 109).]

Tytherly Community, Nov 21st, 1839.

Sisters and Brothers,

The deep interest which you all naturally feel in the practical measures now in progress for relieving mankind from the bondage of competition and its attendant miseries, induces me to think that I cannot better occupy the space usually allotted to leading articles, than by giving you an account of the principal events of my journey here.

No words that I am master of can adequately express my emotions, on finding myself at last seated in this farm-house, and looking out upon the rich and varied prospect which spreads around; with the high gratification of thinking that all is OURS; and that already arrangements are fast progressing, which will place a portion of you and your children amid these sylvan scenes, beyond the reach of those evils which now oppress you, and which will put within your power, by skill, intelligence, and union, to add to its natural beauties, and increase its productiveness. I shall not anticipate, however, but process with my narration. [. . .]

Mr. HOBSON[1] and I left London at two o'clock yesterday afternoon; we proceeded as far as Basingstoke by the London and Southampton Railway, and afterwards by coach to Wallop, from whence we hired a phaeton to convey us to Queenwood. The full unclouded moon shed a flood of light over the landscape, and as we passed the lodge and entered the noble avenue which leads through the estate for nearly two miles, a thrill of gladsome and buoyant ecstasy shot through our frames. We were at last on the long promised land, and happiness too great for expression held us mute; they were *our* tress through which the moon beams gleaned and quivered — *ours* were the soft green park-like glades upon which we emerged, —it was no dream.

This was the place destined to exhibit to mistaught and suffering man the means whereby mental and moral excellence can be permanently secured to all, and plenty for the supply of all healthy wants be continually supplied to its inhabitants.

It is needless to say, we were warmly received by our friends, now on the estate—Messrs. ALDAM, ALEXANDER, SPRAGUE, and BOWER.[2] Tea was speedily prepared; and, after an interchange of mutual greetings and information, they accompanied us to Broughton, where we put up for the night, in consequence of the paucity of convenience as yet collected on the Estate.

This morning we were up before the sun and on our way to Queenwood. A misty morning was succeeded by a bright warm forenoon, which brought out the feathered warblers of the woods, and cheated them into summer music, with its bland and balmy breeze. Under these auspicious influences, accompanied by Mr. ALDAM, we went forth to perambulate this pleasant land, and feast our eyes with its extensive prospects of hill, dale, woodland, and meadow. Nor are streams wanting—glittering in the sunlight; and, like the good man, marking their course and existence by benefits, they wend their sinuous way along the bottoms of the vallies, fringed by a brighter green, and studded with rural dwellings. Our first visit was the extra-parochial lands, upon which the Community buildings are to be erected. They lie to the west of the farm-house, with a gentle acclivity; the old Roman road from Sarum[3] to Winchester, passes through this portion of the Estate.

The spot selected as the site of the buildings, has a beautiful exposure to the south; a fine grove of trees being situate at no great distance, in front, and forming the foreground to a small richly wooded valley, which opens beyond. The road to them will pass through a portion of the avenue formerly spoken of, after which it will wind through an open lawn or park, till it comes on a line with the Roman road. The buildings will be well sheltered from the north, by the rising grounds behind; on the east they will be shut in by the avenue; and, on the west, the scene stretches away among a succession of woody vallies, till it rises into some hills of considerable altitude. Altogether, the selection seems a most felicitous one; although some parts of the Queenwood or parochial lands seem to me to offer still greater *pictorial* advantages. These, however, are trifling, compared with the substantial benefits to be derived from that fixed upon.

Leaving this part of the ground, we walked the boundaries of the Queenwood Farm; on the north and east, an extensive prospect opens out, the village of Broughton being in the foreground; to the south, the country grows more decidedly woodland. The ploughmen were at work here; and, in one field, some wheat sown by Mr. ALDAM is coming up most beautifully; in fact, there is nothing like it to be seen in the district; it speaks strongly for the intelligence which presides over this department of our affairs. We here again entered the avenue; and, after proceeding southward along it for some time, we made a slight turn to the left, and were suddenly brought in view of a scene which far eclipsed all we had hitherto witnessed. This was a natural alley of yew trees, the straight and polished stems of which shoot up to a considerable height, and then throw their branches across the road in such a manner as to form a close resemblance to the aisle of a Cathedral. It is scarcely possible to convey in words a correct idea of this beautiful walk; the perspective effect is most striking; and what is very singular, is, that it terminates immediately on reaching our boundary, though the wooded way is continued for nearly two miles farther. Many aged and picturesque yews are scattered over the surface of the Estate, and will afford, under their ample shade, the most favourable opportunities for erecting seats, and other conveniences, either for study or recreation.

The farm buildings are commodious, although some of them are not the best state of repair. One large barn will be converted into joiners', wheelwrights', and smiths' shops, and will serve for present purposes in these respects.

The land possesses great capabilities for improvement, and in the course of two or three seasons will be made, by spirited and liberal management, to assume the appearance of a garden, as compared with its present fertility. Water is collected in considerable quantities in reservoirs on various parts of the estate, and can always be had in sufficient quantities for all ordinary purposes; it can also be had by sinking wells on any part of the land, and of excellent quality.

It would be premature to say more on the present occasion respecting the plans which are to be adopted and carried into immediate effect: it would be an intrusion on the province of the different managers, alike unwarranted and uncalled for. They will, themselves, explain their plans and report progress in future numbers of the *New Moral World*, which will thus add new interest and attractiveness to any claims it now possesses upon public attention.

A great and important experiment is commencing upon these lands; whatever may be its ultimate fate, the principles it involves, its bearings upon the whole system of existing society and the future destiny of man, cannot fail to render the proceedings at least an object of curiosity to all who feel the slightest interest in these subjects. It will be the duty of all parries to give faithful and unvarnished accounts of their progress; and so far as I am personally concerned, it will be my endeavour to *under* rather than *over*-state anything connected with these important practical measures. A good cause needs not resort to exaggeration or deception of any kind.

Socialism has long been derided as a visionary and impracticable system. That it is every day becoming more a matter of reality, the facts of our numerous Halls of Science, and my writing from this estate, abundantly demonstrate. Its ultimate success will, of course, depend entirely on the skill, prudence, perseverance, and capital which are expended upon it. I may say that every difficulty which, at any period, has presented itself to my mind, seems as though it would be easily overcome. The difficulties have been magnified like objects in a mist, because of our distance from them; a nearer approach shews them in their true dimensions, and while here, in the seat of our operations, they appear diminutive indeed.

Let us then, my friends, go forward with undoubting confidence and the cheerfulness inspired by our present position. It is now in our power to demonstrate to the world the benefits to be derived from the general adoption of the system we advocate, and while doing so, to be effectually advancing our individual interests in whatever light these are considered. That we may all be found "walking worthy of our high vocation".[4]

Is the earnest wish and hope
Of your Friend and Brother,
GEO. A. FLEMING

Notes

1. Joshua Hobson (1810–1876), a joiner and prominent Huddersfield Owenite. He was also a Chartist, and the editor of the *Northern Star* in 1838–1844.
2. Heaton Aldam, an agriculturist from Whaley Bridge, Derbyshire, and the farm superintendent at Queenwood; John Alexander, a joiner, and William Sprague, a harness-maker and saddler, were both members of branch A.1 in London; Samuel Bower was a farmer from Yorkshire, and had joined the Bradford Owenite branch. The four men were among the first to join the Queenwood community in the autumn of 1839 (Royle 1998, 85, 244). Samuel Bower wrote a vindication of emigration, *The Peopling of Utopia*, in 1838, and later joined the short-lived utopian commune of Fruitlands, near Harvard, Massachusetts (Langdon 2000, 312).
3. Old Salisbury.

4 Liberally quoted from Ephesians 4:1–3, King James Version: "I therefore, the prisoner of the Lord, beseech you that ye walk worthy of the vocation wherewith ye are called, With all lowliness and meekness, with long suffering, forbearing one another in love; Endeavouring to keep the unity of the Spirit in the bond of peace."

Part 3

CONCEPTS OF POLITICAL CHANGE

While the idea of community was the overarching principle of the Owenite movement, it covered a variety of nuances. These included the establishment of brick-and-mortar colonies on the land, and more abstract endeavours to foster harmonious co-operation to the detriment of individualistic and selfish traits for humans and nations alike. Given the sheer range and variety of Owenite literature, concepts of political change remained an evasive and often conflicted notion, despite a broad agreement that community principles should inform political structures and modes of governance. Following Gregory Claeys's analysis (2005, vol. 1, 11) Owenite writers fell on a continuum ranging from an "overly 'anti-political' stance to 'social democratic' efforts to wed a socialist economic analysis to radical democratic practice" (see Part 6).

Robert Owen epitomized the first end of the spectrum. Failure to be elected MP for Linlithgow Burghs in 1820, and to secure support for his "Plan" in Parliament encouraged him to adopt an increasingly anti-political approach, though he never stopped courting "those who have influence in the affairs of men"(Owen 1813–1816, vol. 1, 10). This was partly an act of prudence, given the general climate of repression that pervaded William Pitt's premiership, especially after the Peterloo Massacre. But Owen's stance was also a moral jab at political institutions, which he came to identify as beacons of factionalism and individualism, two aspects of modern society that he was otherwise keen on defeating.

Political institutions were consequently treated as neutral entities, while economic equality became the core of Owen's communitarianism. As long as the producers' labour was rewarded to its full and just value, and as long as peace was maintained, "Villages of Co-operation" and the "New Moral World" would flourish under any regime (Garnett 1971, 42). Furthermore, once the economic and moral superiority of his system had been acknowledged, Owen was certain that state and government institutions would naturally wither away, superseded by a global network of harmonious communities. The "science of society was meant ultimately to replace older sciences of government as well as the practice of 'politics' in general" (Claeys 1989, 24, cited in Siméon 2017, 102–103).

In practice, various early socialist institutions like George Mudie's Co-operative and Economical Society and the *Co-operative Magazine* (1826–1830) refrained from engaging in political controversy. More generally, many Owenites chose education and preparation for community life as agents of political change, rather than party politics (Langdon 2000, 99). This included the promotion of popular education, political propaganda and the forging of communal bonds at branch level, thanks to a variety of leisure activities that included lectures, concerts, banquets and balls (see Chapters 19 and 20).

Yet the call for immediate political action remained a valid claim in the eyes of many. Some early socialists like Archibald Hamilton, William Thompson and Anna Doyle Wheeler had come to Owenism through their support for radical thinking. Added to the urgency of the post-war crisis, the repeal of the Combination and Gagging Acts in 1825 brought parliamentary reform back to the fore of public debate. For many co-operators, the promise of economic equality in the "Villages of Co-operation" was now contingent upon the extension of the franchise (Claeys 1989, 172, 187). This would create unsurmountable rifts from which the Owenite movement never recovered (see Parts 5 and 6).

14

A NEW VIEW OF SOCIETY, OR, ESSAYS ON THE FORMATION OF THE HUMAN CHARACTER: PREPARATORY TO THE DEVELOPMENT OF A PLAN FOR GRADUALLY AMELIORATING THE CONDITION OF MANKIND (LONDON: PRINTED FOR LONGMAN, HURST, REES, ORME AND BROWN, 1816), FOURTH ESSAY, 143–170.

Robert Owen

[While *A New View of Society*'s first three essays had explored Owen's deterministic theories of character formation in relation to the New Lanark experiment, the fourth instalment was a call to action. In the context of the post-Waterloo crisis, Owen wished to bring the reforms introduced at his factory village not just to the distressed working classes, but to the country as a whole. In particular, he urged for the establishment of a nationwide network of educational provisions inspired by New Lanark's Institute for the Formation of Character, which had been inaugurated on 1 January 1816 (see Part 2, Chapter 8). In his eyes, education was not merely a matter of individual improvement, but the main agent of political change through social and moral regeneration (Donnachie 2011, 15).This interest in the collective dimension of education was first publicly expressed in 1812, when Owen gave an address in Glasgow in honour of the pedagogue Joseph Lancaster (1778–1838). The latter's "monitorial" system applied the principle of the division of labour to the schooling of poor children; teachers were assisted by a corps of elite students, or "monitors", and used rote learning to foster imitation by example. These methods had been garnering support from a variety of business owners and reformers, among whom were three of Owen's future business associates, Joseph Fox, William Allen and Jeremy Bentham. The New Lanark schools were consequently reorganised along Lancastrian lines in 1813. But by 1816,

Owen had parted ways with the monitorial system, and dismissed it as a mechanical, impersonal teaching method with a limited range of subjects providing a breeding-ground for ignorance (Crook 1999; Siméon 2017, 83). The Institute for the Formation of Character was designed as a polar opposite. Minimal training and rote learning were abandoned in favour of an extremely broad curriculum (that included history, geography, science, music and dancing lessons in addition to the "3Rs") and participative pedagogy. In what probably constitutes the most ground-breaking aspect of Owen's pedagogy, all children, regardless of class and/ or gender, were to receive such comprehensive education. At a time when most reformers recommended only a minimal training for poor children, based on their supposed low social worth,[1] Owen wished to train the rising generations as whole persons and fully-functioning members of society.]

The fundamental principle on which all these Essays proceed is, that 'children collectively may be taught any sentiments and habits' or, in other words, 'trained to acquire any character'.

It is of importance that *this principle should be for ever present in the mind, and that its truth should be established beyond even the shadow of doubt.* To the superficial observer it may appear to be an abstract truth of little value; but to the reflecting and accurate reasoner, it will speedily discover itself to be a power which ultimately must destroy the ignorance and consequent prejudices that have accumulated through all preceding ages.

For, as it is a deduction from all the leading facts in the past history of the world, so it will be found, on the most extensive investigation, to be consistent with every fact which now exists. It is calculated, therefore, to become the foundation of a new system, which, because true and of unparalleled importance, must prove irresistible, will speedily supersede all those which exist, and itself become permanent.

It is necessary, however, prior to the introduction of this system in all its bearings and consequences, that the public mind should be impressed with the deepest conviction of its truth.

For this purpose, let us in imagination survey the various states and empires of the world, and attentively observe man as in these arbitrary divisions of the earth he is known to exist.

Compare the national character of each community with the laws and customs by which they are respectively governed, and, without an exception, the one will be found the archetype of the other.

Where, in former ages, the laws and customs established by Lycurgus[2] formed man into a model for martial exploits, and a perfect instrument for war, he is now trained, by other laws and customs, to be the instrument of a despotism which renders him almost, or altogether, unfit for war. And where the law and custom of Athens trained the young mind to acquire as high a degree of partial rationality as the history of preceding times records, man is now reduced, by a total change of laws and customs, to the lowest state of mental degradation. Also, where, formerly, the superior native American tribes roamed fearlessly through their trackless forests, uniformly exhibiting the hardy, penetrating, elevated, and sincere character, which was at a loss to comprehend how a rational being could desire to possess more than his nature could enjoy; now, on the very same soil, in the same climate, characters are formed under laws and customs so opposite, that all their bodily and mental faculties are individually exerted to obtain, if possible, ten thousand times more than any man can enjoy.

But why proceed to enumerate such endless results as these, of the never-failing influence of training over human nature, when it may be easily rendered self-evident even to the most illiterate, by daily examples around their own dwellings?

No one, it may be supposed, can now be so defective in knowledge as to imagine it is a different human nature, which by its own powers forms itself into a child of ignorance, of poverty, and of habits leading to crime and to punishment; or into a votary of fashion, claiming distinction from its folly and inconsistency; or, to fancy, that it is some undefined, blind, unconscious process of human nature itself, distinct from instruction, that forms the sentiments and habits of the man of commerce, of agriculture, the law, the church, the army, the navy, or of the private and illegal depredator on society, or that it is a different human nature which constitutes the societies of the Jews, of Friends, and of all the various religious denominations which have existed or which now exist. No! Human nature, save the minute differences which are ever found in all the compounds of the creation, is one and the same in all; it is without exception universally plastic, and by judicious training THE INFANTS OF ANY ONE CLASS IN THE WORLD MAY BE READILY FORMED INTO MEN OF ANY OTHER CLASS; EVEN TO BELIEVE AND DECLARE THAT CONDUCT TO BE RIGHT AND VIRTUOUS, AND TO DIE IN ITS DEFENCE, WHICH THEIR PARENTS HAD BEEN TAUGHT TO BELIEVE AND SAY WAS WRONG AND VICIOUS, AND TO OPPOSE WHICH, THOSE PARENTS WOULD ALSO HAVE WILLINGLY SACRIFICED THEIR LIVES.

Whence then the foundation of your claim, ye advocates for the superiority of the early prepossessions of your sect or party, in opposition to those taught to other men? Ignorance itself, at this day, might almost make it evident that one particle of merit is not due to you, for not possessing those notions and habits which you now the most contemn. Ought you not, and will you not, then, have charity for those who have been taught different sentiments and habits from yourselves? Let all men fairly investigate this subject for themselves; it well merits their most attentive examination. They will then discover that it is from the errors of education, misinstructing the young mind relative to the true cause of early prepossessions, that almost all the evils of life proceed.

Whence then, ye advocates for the merit and demerit of early prepossessions of opinion, do you derive your principles?

Let this system of misery be seen in all its naked deformity! It ought to be exposed; for the instruction which it inculcates at the outset of forming human character is destructive of the genuine charity which can alone train man to be truly benevolent to all other men. The ideas of exclusive right and consequent superiority which men have hitherto been taught to attach to the early sentiments and habits in which they have been instructed, are the chief cause of disunion throughout society; such notions are, indeed, in direct opposition to pure and undefiled religion; nor can they ever exist together. The extent of the misery which they generate cannot, however, be much longer concealed. They are already hastening fast to meet the fate of all errors; for the gross ignorance on which this system of misery has been raised, is exposed to the world on its proper foundation, and, so exposed, its supporters will shrink from the task of defence, and no rational mind will be found to give it support.

Having exhibited the error on which ignorance has erected the systems by which man has been governed, or compelled to become irrational and miserable; and having laid an immovable foundation for a system devoid of that error, which, when fully comprehended and adopted into practice, must train mankind 'to think of and act to others as they would wish others to think of and act to them', we proceed further to explain this *system without error*, and which may be termed a *system without mystery*.

As then children collectively may be formed into any characters, by whom ought their characters to be formed?

The kind and degree of misery or happiness experienced by the members of any community, depend on the characters which have been formed in the individuals which constitute the community.

It becomes, then, the highest interest, and consequently the first and most important duty, of every state, to form the individual characters of which the state is composed. And if any characters, from the most ignorant and miserable to the most rational and happy, can be formed, it surely merits the deepest attention of every state to adopt those means by which the formation of the latter may be secured, and that of the former prevented.

It follows that every state, to be well governed, ought to direct its chief attention to the formation of character; and thus the best governed state will be that which shall possess the best national system of education.

Under the guidance of minds competent to its direction, a national system of training and education may be formed, to become the most safe, easy, effectual, and economical instrument of government that can be devised. And it may be made to possess a power equal to the accomplishment of the most grand and beneficial purposes.

It is, however, by instruction only, that the population of the world can be made conscious of the irrational state in which they now exist; and, until that instruction is given, it is premature to introduce a national system of education.

But the time is now arrived when the British Government may with safety adopt a national system of training and education for the poor and uninstructed; and this measure alone, if the plan shall be well devised and executed, will effect the most importantly beneficial changes.

As a preliminary step, however, it is necessary to observe, that to create a well-trained, united, and happy people, this national system should be uniform over the United Kingdom; it should be also founded in the spirit of peace and of rationality, and, for the most obvious reasons, the thought of exclusion to one child in the empire should not for a moment be entertained.

Several plans have been lately proposed for the national education of the poor, but these have not been calculated to effect all that a national system of education of the poor ought to accomplish.

For the authors and supporters of these systems we feel those sentiments which the principles developed throughout these Essays must create in any minds on which they have been early and effectually impressed; and we are desirous of rendering their labours for the community as extensively beneficial as they can be made. To fulfil, however, a great and important public duty, the plans which they have devised must be considered as though they had been produced and published in the days of antiquity.

The plans alluded to are those of the Rev. Dr Bell,[3] Mr Joseph Lancaster, and Mr Whitbread.[4]

The systems of Dr Bell and Mr Lancaster, for instructing the poor in reading, writing, and arithmetic, prove the extreme ignorance which previously existed in the *manner* of training the young; for it is in the manner alone of giving instruction that these new systems are an improvement on the modes of instruction which were formerly practised.

The arrangement of the room and many of the details in Mr Lancaster's plan, are, in some respects, better calculated to give instruction in the elements enumerated, than those recommended by Dr Bell, although some of the details introduced by the latter are very superior, and highly deserving of adoption.

The essence, however, of national training and education is to impress on the young, ideas and habits which shall contribute to the future happiness of the individuals and of the state; and this can be accomplished only by instructing them to become rational beings.

It must be evident to common observers that children may be taught, by either Dr Bell's or Mr Lancaster's system, to read, write, account, and sew, and yet acquire the worst habits, and have their minds rendered irrational for life.

Reading and writing are merely instruments by which knowledge either true or false, may be imparted; and, when given to children, are of little comparative value, unless they are also taught how to make a proper use of them.

When a child receives a full and fair explanation of the objects and characters around him, and when he is also taught to reason correctly, so that he may learn to discover general truths from falsehood, he will be much better instructed, although without the knowledge of one letter or figure, than those are who have been compelled to *believe*, and whose reasoning faculties have been confounded or destroyed by what is most erroneously termed learning.

It is readily acknowledged that the manner of instructing children is of importance and deserves all the attention it has lately received; that those who discover or introduce improvements which facilitate the acquirement of knowledge are important benefactors of their fellow creatures. Yet the *manner* of giving instruction is one thing, the *instruction* itself another; and no two objects can be more distinct. The *worst* manner may be applied to give the *best* instruction, and the *best* manner to give the *worst* instruction. Were the real importance of both to be estimated by numbers, the manner of instruction may be compared to one, and the matter of instruction to millions: the first is the means only; the last, the end to be accomplished by those means.

If, therefore, in a national system of education for the poor, it be desirable to adopt the best *manner*, it is surely so much the more desirable to adopt also the best *matter*, of instruction.

Either give the poor a rational and useful training, or mock not their ignorance, their poverty, and their misery, by merely instructing them to become conscious of the extent of the degradation under which they exist. And, therefore, in pity to suffering humanity, either keep the poor, *if you now can*, in the state of the most abject ignorance, as near as possible to animal life, or at once determine to form them into rational beings, into useful and effective members of the state.

Were it possible, without national prejudice, to examine into the matter of instruction which is now given in some of our boasted new systems for the instruction of the poor, it would be found to be almost as wretched as any which can be devised. In proof of this statement, enter any one of the schools denominated national, and request the master to show the acquirements of the children. These are called out, and he asks them theological questions to which men of the most profound erudition cannot make a rational reply; the children, however, readily answer as they had been previously instructed; for memory, in this mockery of learning, is all that is required.

Thus the child whose natural faculty of comparing ideas, or whose rational powers, shall be the soonest destroyed, if, at the same time, he possess a memory to retain incongruities without connection, will become what is termed the first scholar in the class; and three-fourths of the time which ought to be devoted to the acquirement of useful instruction, will be really occupied in destroying the mental powers of the children.

To those accustomed attentively to notice the human countenance from infancy to age, in the various classes and religious denominations of the British population, it is truly an instructive although melancholy employment, to observe in the countenances of the poor children in these schools the evident expression of mental injury derived from the well-intentioned, but most mistaken, plan of their instruction.

It is an important lesson, because it affords another recent and striking example to the millions which previously existed, of the ease with which children may be taught to receive any sectarian notions, and thence acquire any habits, however contrary to their real happiness.

To those trained to become truly conscientious in any of the present sectarian errors which distract the world, this free exposure of the weakness of the peculiar tenets in which such individuals have been instructed, will, at first, excite feelings of high displeasure and horror, and these feelings will be acute and poignant in proportion to the obvious and irresistible evidence on which the disclosure of their errors is founded.

Let them, however, begin to think calmly on these subjects, to examine their own minds and the minds of all around them, and they will become conscious of the absurdities and inconsistencies in which their forefathers have trained them; they will then abhor the errors by which they have been so long abused; and, with an earnestness not to be resisted, they will exert their utmost faculties to remove the cause of so much misery to man.

Enough surely has now been said of the manner and matter of instruction in these new systems, to exhibit them in a just and true light.

The improvements in the manner of teaching children whatever may be deemed proper for them to learn improvements which, we may easily predict, will soon receive great additions and amendments have proceeded from the Rev. Dr Bell and Mr Lancaster; while the errors which their respective systems assist to engrave on the ductile mind of infancy and childhood, are derived from times when ignorance gave countenance to every kind of absurdity.

Mr Whitbread's scheme for the education of the poor was evidently the production of an ardent mind possessing considerable abilities; his mind, however, had been irregularly formed by the errors of his early education; and this was most conspicuous in the speech which introduced the plan he had devised to the House of Commons, and in the plan itself.

The first was a clear exposition of all the reasons for the education of the poor which could be expected from a human being trained from infancy under the systems in which Mr Whitbread had been instructed.

The plan itself evinced the fallacy of the principles which he had imbibed, and showed that he had not acquired a practical knowledge of the feelings and habits of the poor, or of the only effectual means by which they could be trained to be useful to themselves and to the community.

Had Mr Whitbread not been trained, as almost all the Members of both Houses of Parliament have been, in delusive theories, devoid of rational foundation, which prevent them from acquiring any extensive practical knowledge of human nature, he would not have committed a plan for the national education of the poor to the sole management and direction of the ministers, churchwardens, and overseers of parishes, whose present interests must have appeared to be opposed to the measure.

He would surely, first, have devised a plan to make it the evident interest of the ministers, churchwardens, and overseers, to co-operate in giving efficacy to the system which he wished to introduce to their superintendence; and also to render them, by previous training, competent to that superintendence for which now they are in general unprepared. For, trained as these individuals have hitherto been, they must be deficient in the practical knowledge necessary to enable them successfully to direct the instruction of others; and had an attempt been made to carry Mr Whitbread's plan into execution, it would have created a scene of confusion over the whole kingdom.

Attention to the subject will make it evident that it never was, and that it never can be, the interest of any sect claiming exclusive privileges on account of professing high and mysterious doctrines, about which the best and most conscientious men may differ in opinion, that the mass of the people should be otherwise instructed than in those doctrines which were and are in unison with its peculiar tenets; and that at this hour a national system of education for the lower orders, on sound political principles, is really dreaded, even by some of the most learned and intelligent members of the Church of England. Such feelings in the members of the national church are those only which ought to be expected; for most men so trained and circumstanced must of necessity acquire these feelings. Why, therefore, should any class of men endeavour to rouse the indignation of the public against them? Their conduct and their motives are equally correct, and therefore, equally good, with those who raise the cry against and oppose the errors of the church. And let it ever be remembered, that an establishment which possesses the power of propagating principles, may be rendered truly valuable when directed to inculcate a system of self-evident truth, unobstructed by inconsistencies and counteractions.

The dignitaries of the church, and their adherents, foresaw that a national system for the education of the poor, unless it were placed under the immediate influence and management of individuals belonging to the church, would effectually and rapidly undermine the errors, not only of their own, but of every other ecclesiastical establishment. In this foresight they evinced the superiority of their penetration over the sectaries by whom the unexclusive system is supported. The heads of the church have wisely discovered that reason and inconsistency cannot long exist together; that the one must inevitably destroy the other, and reign paramount. They have witnessed the regular, and latterly the rapid progress which reason has made; they know that its accumulating strength cannot be much longer resisted; and, as they now see the contest is hopeless, the unsuccessful attempt to destroy the Lancastrian system of education is the last effort they will ever make to counteract the dissemination of knowledge which is now widely extending itself in every direction.

The establishment of the Rev. Dr Bell's system of initiating the children of the poor in all the tenets of the Church of England, is an attempt to ward off a little longer the yet dreaded period of a change from ignorance to reason, from misery to happiness.

Let us, however, not attempt impossibilities; the task is vain and hopeless; the Church, while it adheres to the defective and injurious parts of its system, cannot be induced to act cordially in opposition to its apparent interests.

The principles here advocated will not admit the application of any deception to any class of men; they countenance no proceedings in practice, but of unlimited sincerity and candour. They give rise to no one sentiment which is not in unison with the happiness of the human race; and they impart knowledge, which renders it evident that such happiness can never be acquired until every particle of falsehood and deception shall be eradicated from the instructions which the old force upon the young.

Let us then in this spirit openly declare to the Church, that a national unexclusive plan of education for the poor will, without the shadow of doubt, destroy all the errors which are attached to the various systems; and that, when this plan shall be fully established, not one of the tenets which is in opposition to facts can long be upheld.

This unexclusive system for the education of the poor has gone forth, and, having found a resting place in the minds of its supporters, it will never more return even to the control of its projectors; but it will be speedily so improved, that by rapidly increasing strides it will firmly establish the reign of reason and happiness.

Seeing and knowing this, let us also make it equally evident to the Church, warn it of its actual state — cordially and sincerely assist its members quietly to withdraw those inconsistencies from the system, which now create its weakness and its danger; that it may retain those rational principles alone which can be successfully defended against attack, or which rather will prevent any attack from being attempted, or even meditated.

The wise and prudent, then, of all parties, instead of wishing to destroy national establishments, will use their utmost exertions to render them so consistent and reasonable in all their parts, that every well-disposed mind may be induced to give them their hearty and willing support.

For the first grand step towards effecting any substantial improvement in these realms, without injury to any part of the community, is to make it the clear and decided interest of the Church to co-operate cordially in all the projected ameliorations. Once found a national church on the true, unlimited, and genuine principles of mental charity, and all the members of the state will soon improve in every truly valuable quality. If the temperate and discerning of all parties will not now lend their aid to effect this change by peaceable means (which may with the greatest ease and with unerring certainty be done), it is evident to every calm observer, that the struggle by those who now exist in unnecessary misery, to attain that degree of happiness which they may attain in practice, cannot long be deferred. It will therefore prove true political wisdom to anticipate and guide these feelings.

To those who can reflect and will attend to the passing scenes before them, the times are indeed awfully interesting; some change of high import, scarcely yet perhaps to be scanned by the present ill-taught race of men, is evidently in progress: in consequence, well-founded, prompt, and decisive measures are now required in the British councils, to direct this change, and to relieve the nation from the errors of its present systems.

It must surely then be the desire of every rational man, of every true friend to humanity, that a cordial co-operation and unity of action should be effected between the British Executive, the Parliament, the Church, and the People, to lay a broad and firm foundation for the future happiness of themselves and the world.

Say not, my countrymen, that such an event is impracticable; for, by adopting the evident means to form a rational character in man, there is a plain and direct road opened, which, if pursued, will render its accomplishment not only possible but certain. That road, too, will be found the most safe and pleasant that human beings have ever yet travelled. It leads direct to intelligence and true knowledge, and will show the boasted acquirements of Greece, of Rome, and of all antiquity, to be the mere weakness of mental infancy. Those who travel this road will find it so straight and well defined, that no one will be in danger of wandering from the right course. Nor is it yet a narrow or exclusive path; it admits of no exclusion: every colour of body and diversity of mind are freely and alike admitted. It is open to the human race, and it is broad and spacious enough to receive the whole, were they increased a thousandfold.

We well know that a declaration like the one now made must sound chimerical in the ears of those who have hitherto wandered in the dark mazes of ignorance, error, and exclusion, and who have been taught folly and inconsistencies only from their cradle.

But if every known fact connected with the subject proves that, from the day in which man first saw light to that in which the sun now shines, the old collectively have taught the young collectively the sentiments and habits which the young have acquired; and that the present generation and every following generation must in like manner instruct their successors; then do we say, with a confidence founded on certainty itself, that even much more shall come to pass than has yet been foretold or promised. When these principles, derived from the unchangeable laws of nature, and equally revealed to all men, shall, as soon as they will, be publicly established in the world, no conceivable obstacle can remain to prevent a sincere and cordial union and co-operation for every wise and good purpose, not only among all the members of the same state, but also among the rulers of those kingdoms and empires whose enmity and rancour against each other have been carried to the utmost stretch of melancholy folly, and even occasionally to a high degree of madness.

Such, my fellow men, are some, and yet but a few, of the mighty consequences which must result from the public acknowledgement of these plain, simple, and irresistible truths. They will not prove a delusive promise of mockery, but will in reality speedily and effectively establish peace, goodwill, and an ever-active benevolence throughout the whole human race.

The public avowal of these principles, and their general introduction into practice, will constitute the invaluable secret, for which the human mind, from its birth, has been in perpetual search; its future beneficial consequences no man can yet foresee.

We will now show how these principles may be immediately and most advantageously introduced into general practice.

It has been said that 'the state which shall possess the best national system of education, will be the best governed'; and if the principle on which the reasoning of these Essays is founded be true, then is that sentiment also true. Yet (will future ages credit the fact?) to this day the British Government is without any national system of training and education even for its millions of poor and uninstructed!! The formation of the mind and habits of its subjects is permitted to go on at random, often in the hands of those who are the most incompetent in the empire; and the result is, the gross ignorance and disunion which now everywhere abound!!

Instead of continuing such unwise proceedings, a national system for the training and education of the labouring classes ought to be immediately arranged; and, if judiciously devised, it may be rendered the most valuable improvement ever yet introduced into practice.

For this purpose an act should be passed for the instruction of all the poor and labouring classes in the three kingdoms.

In this act, provision should be made:

First,—For the appointment of proper persons to direct this new department of government, which will be found ultimately to prove the most important of all its departments; consequently, those individuals who possess the highest integrity, abilities, and influence in the state, should be appointed to its direction.

Second,—For the establishment of seminaries in which those individuals who shall be destined to form the minds and bodies of the future subjects of these realms should be well initiated in the art and matter of instruction.

This is, and ought to be considered, an office of the greatest practical trust and confidence in the empire; for let this duty be well performed, and the government must proceed with ease to the people and with high gratification to those who govern.

At present there are not any individuals in the kingdom who have been trained to instruct the rising generation as it is for the interest and happiness of all that it should be instructed. The training of those who are to form the future man, becomes a consideration of the utmost magnitude; for, on due reflection, it will appear, that instruction to the young must be, of necessity, the only foundation upon which the superstructure of society can be raised. Let this instruction continue to be left, as heretofore, to chance, and often to the most inefficient members of the community, and society must still experience the endless miseries which still arise from such weak and puerile conduct. On the contrary, let the instruction to the young be well devised and well executed, and no subsequent proceedings in the state can be materially injurious. For it may truly be said to be a wonder-working power; one that merits the deepest attention of the legislature; with ease it may be used to train man into a demon of mischief to himself and to all around him, or into an agent of unlimited benevolence.

Third,—For the establishment of seminaries over the United Kingdoms; to be conveniently placed, and of sufficient extent to receive all those who require instruction.

Fourth,—For supplying the requisite expenditure for the building and support of those seminaries.

Fifth,—For the arrangement of the plan which, for the manner of instruction, upon a due comparison of the various modes now in practice, or which may be devised, shall appear to be the best.

Sixth,—For the appointment of proper masters to each of the schools. And,

Last,—The matter of instruction, both for body and mind, in these seminaries, should be substantially beneficial to the individuals and to the state. For this is, or ought to be, the sole motive for the establishment of national seminaries.

These are the outlines of the provisions necessary to prepare the most powerful instrument of good that has ever yet been placed in the hands of man.[. . .]

Notes

1 For instance, Patrick Colquhoun's *Treatise on Indigence* (1806, 146), claimed that "a limited education, suitable to the condition of the poor, is all that is necessary. Everything beyond a mere channel for converging religious and moral principles would be mischievous and utopian".
2 Lycurgus (c. 820 BC), lawmaker of Sparta and promoter of a communalistic, military-like form of education
3 Andrew Bell (1753–1832) was a Scottish Episcopalian minister and pedagogue. He designed the "Madras System of Education", a rival system of Joseph Lancaster's.
4 Samuel Whitbread (1764–1815), Whig member of Parliament and the defender of a national education system.

15

"MOTION RESPECTING MR. OWEN'S PLAN", *PARLIAMENTARY DEBATES* (LONDON: HANSARD), 16 DECEMBER 1819.

House of Commons

[The Peterloo Massacre and its aftermath of general social unrest renewed Robert Owen's determination to promote his reform plans. One of his personal friends and early supporters, the Whig MP for Southampton William de Crespigny (1765–1829), agreed to argue his case in Parliament. On 16 December 1819, he presented a motion asking for Owen's "Plan" to be examined by a Select Committee. Despite positive comments regarding the New Lanark establishment, the proposal was rejected by 141 votes to 16, as it was deemed too "utopian". This particular event marked a shift in Owen's public image, from respected philanthropist to controversial "visionary". Over the next few years, de Crespigny and many others distanced themselves from him and his ideas. The backlash thwarted Owen's numerous attempts to put his "Plan" into practice in the years 1817–1825, and fuelled his ultimate rejection of classical political practice (Jones 1890, vol. 1, 198–200; Podmore 1906, 57; Escott 2011, 152–153; Siméon 2017, 120).]

Sir W. De Crespigny, in pursuance of the notice which he had given, rose for the purpose of moving that a select committee be appointed to inquire into the plan of Mr. Owen for ameliorating the condition, of the lower classes. He trusted that the same spirit of conciliation which had marked the debate of Tuesday last would be manifested on this occasion. Labouring under severe indisposition, he brought this question forward with increased embarrassment. It had been his hope that some hon. gentleman more conversant with the subject would have introduced it to the consideration of the House, and appeared in the character of an advocate for his distressed and suffering fellow-countrymen. Under these circumstances, the House, he doubted not, would extend to him its kindness and indulgence. He could assure it, that he would endeavour to contract his observations into the narrowest compass. The question was rather one of humanity than of political reasoning; and if he should be so fortunate as to obtain the concurrence of the other side of the House, he should hail the circumstance as the harbinger of better times. The interposition of the legislature was most imperiously demanded. General poverty must produce discontent, and general discontent led often to revolt. It was necessary that the higher classes should condescend to inquire into the miseries of the poor with a view to the effectual alleviation of their distress. He saw no other means of preventing the country from being involved in bloodshed and confusion. The plan which he had to recommend would, in his opinion, prove, if adopted, beneficial for the purposes he had stated. All that was required by its friends and supporters was, that it should be submitted to experiment. Let it not be said, he implored the House, that they were prodigal in furnishing the means of destroying mankind, but were resolute not to listen to any schemes for their preservation. There were some, he knew, who, on the study of half an hour, pronounced that to be visionary which was deemed practicable and useful by a man, who had devoted to the inquiry the labour and consideration of thirty years. He called upon such persons to produce a better plan, before they condemned that which he was about to recommend. It was a most important subject for the attention of the House, to investigate the consequences arising from that mechanism which had within the last few years so extensively superseded human labour. To him it appeared, that mechanism should always be made subservient to human labour. The events of the last 30 years had made a change in the internal policy of the country absolutely necessary—and the question was, whether it should take place, step by step, by reason, or be brought about by prejudices and ignorance, or, perhaps, through the convulsion of revolution. Under the present system, the unemployed poor fed on the labour of the industrious, communicated the bad habits acquired in idleness, to the general mass of the poor, amalgamated with them, and taught them their vices. The only remedy for this evil was, the prevention of the mischief at the root. One part of Mr. Owen's plan, to which he wished particularly to direct the attention of the House, was the system of education which it embraced; for education, it could not be denied, was the foundation of all virtue and order in society. He had seen the effects of it in New Lanark, and should never forget to his dying day the impression which it made on his mind. The children were there instructed in those principles which were calculated to make them useful and excellent members of society. That which most struck his mind, and which could scarcely be credited by those who had not witnessed it, was, that the education of infants was begun in this establishment at the early age of two years. He had seen at New Lanark upwards of 100 children, on a large plot of ground, engaged in various kinds of amusements, each contributing its share to the comfort and advantage of the whole; there was among them no mark of malevolence or quarrel; they were vying in acts of kindness to one another. He saw them afterwards at school, some engaged in their letters, and others at more advanced stages of improvement. From thence they were instructed in the reading of the Bible, and taught the duties which they owed to God, to their parents, and to themselves. When the hours of amusement and those of instruction were ended, he had seen them going to their little labours with an alacrity which was really astonishing.

He trusted the House would allow him to read a few of the letters which he had received on this subject. The hon. bart. then read the following letter, which he said he had received by the post of the preceding day:—"Sir William; Having deliberately considered Mr. Owen's plan, I am of opinion, that there is not any proposition yet made for the improvement of the morals and general condition of the country, worthy of a comparison with it; and I am induced thus to intrude my sentiments on you, to propose a measure which may be likely, not only to secure its trial, but its general adoption. It may perhaps be your intention to show the benefits of such a plan, and to move for a parliamentary grant, for the purpose of trying the experiment. However favourable the general opinion may be, yet in the present feeble state of the revenue, I am fearful there may be a difficulty in obtaining the grant; and should that not be the case, yet only one establishment would, by way of trial, be produced. I, however, consider it unnecessary that the country should wait whilst another experiment be tried. In addition to the plain reason of the things, the experiment has been tried with the greatest success at New Lanark. I should therefore at once propose a bill, which should have the effect of rendering any application for a public grant unnecessary, and giving more facility to an immediate application of the plan on a general scale, as follows:— "A bill to enable parishes, at a general (not a select) meeting, to make a permanent rate on the property, and to take up money on the security of such rate, for the purpose of raising an establishment on Mr. Owen's plan. To enable two, three, or four small parishes to unite for that purpose, each parish to have an interest in, and to derive a benefit from the establishment, in proportion to its amount of rate or contribution. The rates so mortgaged to be applied quarterly in the discharge of the interest, and the reduction of the principal money so borrowed, until the same be discharged. To enable lords of manors, and the parishioners, to sell and convey waste and commonable lands for such purpose with such other clauses as the wisdom of parliament may devise. I see by a little pamphlet which lately fell in my way, and which I enclose, that 96,000l. are sufficient to found an establishment for 1,200 persons; and I lately saw in the public prints, that Mr. Owen considered an establishment for 1,000 more advantageous than for a greater or less number, and that would require 80,000l., the interest of which would be 4,000l. for the first year, and as much less every succeeding year, as the principal sum should be reduced. As there is plenty of unemployed capital in the kingdom, I think the money would easily be obtained, and it would be much more creditable to capitalists (and more beneficial to the country) to lend their money on such security, than to place it in the funds of other nations. In the neighbourhood of Mr. Ricardo, there is plenty of commonable land, and the poor are very numerous; the measure would therefore be peculiarly beneficial in that district, and, although no alarmist, yet I am of opinion that the safety of property in a great measure depends more on an immediate attention to the plan of Mr. Owen, than on any coercive measures. I remain with the greatest respect, &c.,

The letter also contained some calculations as to the time when the sum borrowed might be repaid, and the manner of repaying it, with which he did not feel it necessary to trouble the House. The next letter he would read, was from the bishop of Chester. His lordship "approved of a plan which would give to the poor an interest in the better cultivation of the land, and stated that he had tried the experiment by letting out from 70 to 80 acres to poor peasants, at about half an acre to each. The result was, that the lands so given were well cultivated, even with that time which the peasant could bestow after his usual daily labour. One of the great advantages of this plan was, the creation of a feeling of independence among the peasantry—a feeling which could not be too much cultivated, as it rendered them averse to any application to the poor laws; and in the instance alluded to, relief from the poor-rates was not sought by any of the peasants so engaged." If the House, in the present situation of the country, turned, its back upon any plan which had for its immediate object the relief of the lower classes of the people, they would excite a general spirit of disaffection and discontent. He trusted, therefore, the noble lord would not show himself averse from this inquiry; there could be no mischief in it, for if, upon examination, the plan was found to be inefficient, it might be abandoned. It might not be acceptable as a whole, but it should be recollected, that there was no flower of the forest from which the industry of the bee did not extract some honey. He might, if he did not fear to occupy too much of the time of the House, go on reading to eternity the letters which he had received from various parts of the country in favour of this plan. He, however, should only trouble the House with the reading of one more. He then read another letter in favour of the plan, which described the great advantages that might result from it, by the practice which it would encourage, of spade cultivation. A gentleman in the neighbourhood of Newcastle had proved that by this mode of cultivation, the produce of land had been raised to 7 or 8 quarters per acre. Before he submitted his motion, he begged to make one observation further. At the period when Adam Smith wrote his treatise on the Wealth of Nations, the great object was to increase the wealth of the country. This object had been since achieved by the increase of machinery, so as almost to increase the production of some articles much beyond consumption. Now, Mr. Owen's plan, to remedy this—to render the production of the necessaries of life fully adequate to the increase of population—would effect a reorganization, and a remoralizing of the lower classes, which there was no man of virtue who would not, he was persuaded, be most glad to see. He concluded by moving, "That a select committee be appointed to inquire into the nature of the plan proposed by Robert Owen, esq., and to report there on: and how far the same, or any part thereof, may be rendered available for ameliorating the condition of the labouring classes of the community, or for affording beneficial employment of the poor, by an improved application of the sums raised for their relief."

Lord Archibald Hamilton[1] seconded the motion. He was so well acquainted with the practical effect of Mr. Owen's plan, and with the great distress which existed in that part of the country near which his establishment was situated, and particularly he so well knew the anxiety which existed among the great body of those who were so distressed to have the plan inquired into, that he conceived the House ought to take the matter into consideration. At the same time that he asserted this, he did not mean to give his support to those numerous theories which had been founded upon Mr. Owen's plan. He saw, however, that a great part of it had produced an excellent effect, and he conceived that one ground why it was entitled to an examination. He did not look upon the present motion as one which went to embrace the whole of Mr. Owen's plan (which he feared, if taken up in a national or general view, would be attended with too great an expense), but to extract and separate the useful parts of it from those numerous and extensive projects with which it was combined. He would support the motion, in consequence of the good effects which he understood to have resulted from some of Mr. Owen's exertions, and from the feeling which he was aware existed among the poorer classes, that a trial of it might be made with advantage to them. One thing had resulted from the operation of this plan at New Lanark—that it had united large bodies of human beings in the strongest bonds of kindness and affection towards each, other; in such a manner indeed as he believed was never seen or known before. This was a strong reason with him in support of the inquiry, and he thought that inquiry alone was sought by the motion. He would strongly recommend the reference of the subject to a committee, to which it should be understood that every thing eligible should be submitted, and that the House should not be troubled with any details of improvement, except such as should appear in the report the committee might finally agree upon.

Mr. Brougham[2] said, that he was anxious to state the grounds upon which he was disposed to vote for the present motion, without being understood in any degree to support the general principles with which it was connected. In the first place he thought, that in the present distressed state of the country, that plan which proposed to alleviate such distress should be very wild and exceptionable, indeed, against which the House should peremptorily shut its ears. It was no doubt among the misfortunes belonging to the distress of the people, that they were too ready to attend to any visionary scheme that promised them relief; that they were disposed, as it might be said, to catch at straws, in the hope of saving themselves from sinking. This was, however, too generally the consequence of popular calamity. But parliament should be guarded, not to give the sanction of its high authority to any visionary project, because that sanction might do considerable mischief, especially in this way, that if such an impracticable plan were recommended by the House, that recommendation would weaken its power of carrying into effect any plan of less extent, but more practicability, as the people would naturally be disposed to say—"What comparison do the advantages of this plan bear to the prospects held out by the project of Mr. Owen?" This was, therefore, with him one reason why the House should look with extreme caution to any of those measures which were proposed in the present shape. At the same time he did not wish that the House should reject all inquiry on the subject before them. He was desirous not to be understood as meaning to agree to Mr. Owen's plan. He conceived the theory on which it was founded to be wholly erroneous. It was founded upon a principle which he denied—that of the increase of population being a benefit to the country. On the contrary, he had no hesitation in stating, that the excess of population was one of the great causes of the distress which at present afflicted the country. Yet this proposition, which, from the best consideration which he had been able to give to the subject, he was fully prepared to maintain was quite discarded by the theory of Mr. Owen. But it was amongst the most melancholy malpractices of the low part of the press, to depreciate this, which was the soundest principle of political economy. Nay, the worst expedients were used to calumniate the writers by whom that principle was mainly supported, although among those writers were to be found men of the most exalted morals, of the purest views, of the soundest intellect, and even of the most humane feelings. An endeavour was made to raise an outcry against those writers, principally upon the ground, forsooth, that they proposed, to interfere with the main comfort of human life, by deprecating early marriages. But was it not incumbent upon any man who had enlightened views of philanthropy, or even a sense of common justice, to dissuade people from imprudent marriages—from forming connexions which they had not the means of subsisting? Could any thing serve more to aggravate the distress or mortify the feeling of man than the collection of a family for which he was incompetent to provide? Yet against the writers who sought to guard society against this great evil, the utmost obloquy was directed. Nay, an attempt was made to excite a clamour against the men who had the wisdom to devise, and the manliness to support, that which was agreeable to the soundest principle of political economy. The present was not, however, the time in which he thought it advisable to propose the adoption, or to enter into the discussion of that to which he had devoted a great deal of his time and attention, and which he deemed the true radical remedy upon the subject of population; for if a plan to remedy this evil were now brought forward, there was reason to apprehend, from the disturbed state of the public mind, that an outcry might be raised against it which would be but too likely to interfere with the usefulness, and prove detrimental to the interest of the plan itself. The proposition of such a plan must therefore be deferred to some calm period which would be more suitable for deliberate and candid consideration. But to return to Mr. Owen's plan—although he differed from the theory upon which that plan was founded, especially upon the subject of population, and thought it would increase the evil of which it was the ostensible remedy, he still agreed with the hon. baronet who brought forward the motion, and the noble lord by whom it was seconded, that there were certain parts of that plan peculiarly entitled to the consideration of the House. He meant especially upon the subject of education. The system proposed and acted upon by Mr. Owen in training infant children, before they were susceptible of what was generally called education, was deserving of the utmost attention. This indeed was the sound part of Mr. Owen's plan, and agreeable to the wisest principles. By all means then, he would say, let the House appoint a committee to inquire into the means by which those parts of Mr. Owen's plan, against which no objections could be made, might best be put in general practice. That which was wild or visionary might be slighted; but the useful and the practicable ought not to be discarded. But with respect to education he must say, that the assistance of government or parliament was not so essential to its advancement: as the interests of that subject might be very safely trusted to the public spirit and private benevolence of the country. This, indeed, he found to be the case from his own observation, with regard to the education of children taken from their parents, who were thus enabled to pursue their own industry. But he had had some experience upon this subject, where education alone was given to children without any food or clothing, and where children were taught moral, attentive and cleanly habits at that period of life when curiosity, the great spring and element of all education, was most active and ardent—when in consequence, that which at another period of life would have been felt as a burthen, was enjoyed as a pleasure. Thus the children were educated while the parents, or at least the mother, who would have been otherwise obliged to stay at home and take care of them, was released and left at liberty to work. This system then was useful, not only to the children but to the parents, where they were disposed to industry. But the training up of infant children was in every view a point of great importance. He had given this subject a considerable degree of attention, and the experience of several years strengthened him in the opinion which he had been led to form on it. He had seen in Switzerland an establishment, the plan of Mr. Fellenberg for infant education, carried on with excellent effects.[3] That gentleman's plan was, however, better suited to an agricultural district, where the population were scattered, than to a manufacturing town, where the population was crowded together. For Mr. Fellenberg took the children to his school both night and day, thus separating them from their parents. Mr. Owen proceeded upon the same principle as to education, but then he did not separate the children from their parents, unless for the day, and therefore his plan was more applicable to manufacturing or populous districts than that of Mr. Fellenberg in Switzerland. The plan of Mr. Owen was, indeed, so much better, as it was calculated to improve the domestic habits of the people; the child being allowed, by remaining with its father and mother, to acquire those social and domestic habits which were of so much value in life, which begat those strong ties of affection, some of the best and most secure bonds of mutual assistance. With the example of what Mr. Owen had effected on the subject of the education of children, it would, he conceived, be impossible to refuse an inquiry into the practicability of extending it. If it were not vouched by such undeniable proofs, it could scarcely be believed that so much good had been done by the plan as was known to be produced at New Lanark. The example set there was, he conceived, much better than that produced in Switzerland. This system tended also, by a sort of reflex operation, to improve the habits of the parents themselves; for in the presence of children so trained, they would be ashamed of intoxication, or swearing, or any habits that might pollute the minds, or offend the feelings of those who were the objects of their attachment. This consideration, then, combined with the improved impressions of the children, was likely to produce the most salutary effect upon the morality and general conduct of parents, by checking the expression or exhibition of any impropriety, and hence he preferred the plan of Mr. Owen to that which he had witnessed in Switzerland. With a view to make an experiment of this plan, the hon. member for Bramber, the hon. member for Nottingham, had, with himself and a few other friends, made up a stock purse. He had proceeded in this experiment with the more alacrity, as he had the highest respect and esteem for Mr. Owen, whom he really believed one of the most humane, simple-minded, amiable men on earth. He was indeed a rare character; for although a projector, Mr. Owen was one of the most calm and candid men he had ever conversed with. You might discuss his theories in any terms you pleased—you might dispose of his arguments just as you thought proper; and he listened with the utmost mildness. His nature perfectly free from any gall, he had none of the feverish or irritable feeling which too generally belonged to projectors. But to revert to the committee association, of which he had the honour to be a member, he had to express their acknowledgments for the assistance which they had received from the right hon. gentleman the chancellor of the exchequer, who was always found ready to promote that which was most useful, namely, any plan of practical philanthropy. Through this association a school had been established in Westminster, according to Mr. Owen's plan; and if the experiment of that school were found practically useful, as there was every reason to expect, it was fairly to be calculated that the same experiment would be made elsewhere. The establishment in Westminster was a day-school, for which Mr. Owen had furnished the committee with an excellent superintendent, and it was going on in the most satisfactory manner, so satisfactorily indeed, that although originating in the charity of individuals, it was soon likely to be supported by the interest of those who were immediately benefitted by its existence. This was a most gratifying consideration. For although charity might begin, interest alone could continue or perpetuate institutions of this nature. If any person doubted the practical success of this plan, let him go into the school at Brewer's green, in Westminster, and he would sec both the nature of the plan and the benefits that attended it. There was indeed reason to expect that the schools established upon this system would soon and very generally enter into competition with those dame schools which had heretofore proved so very useful, and to which (while children of nine or ten years old were too often allowed to walk about almost as ignorant as beasts) infants were sent, to keep them out of harm's way, while their mothers went to work.—Of this indeed there could hardly be a doubt, as the schools to which he alluded would be conducted upon a better plan, and therefore parents would naturally rather pay quarter-pence to the one than to the other. Satisfied as he was that the success of this plan was likely to be promoted by inquiry, he was an advocate for the appointment of a committee of that House, by which that inquiry might be fully gone into, and effectually concluded. With respect to the spade husbandry which was recommended in Mr. Owen's plan, he must confess himself incapable of forming any judgment upon that part of the plan, as he was wholly unacquainted with the subject; and this was another reason with him for supporting the proposition of inquiry. But he was an advocate for inquiry, with a view to separate the wild and impracticable part of this plan from that which was sound, useful, and practicable; and he trusted that the House would not reject the latter along with the former.

The Chancellor of the Exchequer[4] said, there was nothing more usual, out of the House, than to see gentlemen of opposite political opinions uniting cordially and substantially in efforts for the benefit of the poor; and he was convinced that no spectacle could be more consoling than the display of the same spirit in parliament. It showed that that House did not act on party grounds when the welfare of the people was the subject of discussion; it showed that when they could see their way clearly, they would all agree in measures for alleviating the public distress. It would have given him great pleasure to concur in the present motion, if he had not thought that the House by going into the inquiry would give the sanction of parliament to a plan not only visionary and impracticable, but in the highest degree dangerous to the country. While he opposed the plan, however, he wished to do every justice to the character of Mr. Owen, whose humane and benevolent intentions could not be too highly praised. Though he was not particularly acquainted with the nature of the establishment at Lanark, he believed all that had been said of it. Indeed, some years ago he had visited Lanark, and though the establishment had not then attained its present state of excellence, the impression on his mind at that time was, that it was productive of great benefit, and reflected the highest credit on Mr. Owen. He had then thought the general system superior to any other that he had ever seen; and from what he had heard, he believed it to have been improved since that time. But, notwithstanding all this, he could not agree to the adoption of Mr. Owen's general system; and he should state to the House the grounds of his objections. In the year 1817, two public meetings were called at the city of London Tavern at Mr. Owen's request, at which he delivered a full explanation of the plan he had in view for the amelioration of society, and which explanation had since been given to the public. If he was incorrect in what he was about to state, he would thank a worthy alderman opposite, who was at the meeting, to correct him. At one of those meetings held on the 21st of August, 1817, Mr. Owen made a speech, from which he would now read the following extracts:—

"Why should so many countless millions of our fellow-creatures through each successive generation, have been the victims of ignorance, of superstition, of mental degradation, and of wretchedness?—My friends, a more important question has not yet been put to the sons of men. Who can answer it? Who dare answer it, but with his life in his hand; a ready and a willing victim to truth, and to the emancipation of the world, from its long bondage of disunion, error, crime, and misery? Behold that victim! On this day, in this hour, even now, shall those bonds be burst asunder, never more to unite while the world shall last. What the consequences of this daring deed shall be to myself, I am as indifferent about as whether it shall rain or be fair to-morrow. Whatever may be the consequences, I will now perform my duty to you, and to the world; and should it be the last act of my life, I shall be well content, and know that I have lived for an important purpose. Then, my friends, I tell you, that hitherto you have been prevented from even knowing what happiness really is, solely in consequence of the errors, gross errors that have been combined with the fundamental notions of every religion that has hitherto been taught to men. And, in consequence, they have made man the most inconsistent, and the most miserable being in existence. By the errors of these systems, he has been a weak and imbecile animal, or a furious bigot and fanatic; and should these qualities be carried, not only into the projected villages, but into Paradise itself, a Paradise would no longer be found.—In all the religions which have been hitherto forced on the minds of men; deep, dangerous, and lamentable principles of disunion, division, and separation, have been fast entwined with all their fundamental notions; and the certain consequences, have been, all the dire effects which religious animosities have, through all the past periods of the world, inflicted with such unrelenting stern severity, or mad and furious zeal!—If, therefore, my friends, you should carry with you into these proposed villages of intended unity and unlimited mutual co-operation, one single particle of religious, intolerance, or sectarian feelings of division and separation—maniacs only would go there to look for harmony and happiness; or elsewhere, as long as such insane errors shall be found to exist!—I am not going to ask impossibilities from you—I know what you can do, and I know also what you cannot do. Consider again on what grounds each man in existence has a full right to the enjoyment of the most unlimited liberty of conscience; I am not of your religion, nor of any religion yet taught in the world!—to me they all appear united with much—yes, with very much—error!—Am I to blame for thinking thus? those who possess any real knowledge of human nature know that I cannot think otherwise—that it is not in my power, of myself, to change the thoughts and ideas which appear to me true. Ignorance, bigotry, and superstition may again, as they have so often done before, attempt to force belief against conviction—and thus carry the correct-minded, conscientious victim to the stake; or make a human being wretchedly insincere.—Therefore, unless the world is now prepared to dismiss all its erroneous religious notions, and to feel the justice and necessity, of publicly acknowledging the most unlimited religious freedom, it will be futile to erect villages of union and mutual co-operation; for it will be vain to look on this earth for inhabitants to occupy them, who can understand how to live in the bond of peace and unity; or who can love their neighbour as themselves; whether he be Jew or Gentile, Mahommedan or Pagan, Infidel or Christian; any religion that creates one particle of feeling short of this, is false, and must prove a curse to the whole human race!—And now my friends—for such I will consider you to the last moment of my existence, although each of you were now armed for my immediate destruction—such, my friends, and no other, is the change that must take place in your hearts and minds, and all your conduct, before you can enter these abodes of peace and harmony, you must be attired in proper garments before you can partake of all the comforts and blessings with which they will abound.—Such are my thoughts and conclusions, and I know you will hereafter ponder them well in your minds, and truth will prevail! When you shall be thus prepared, if life be spared to me, I will be ready to accompany you, and to assist with all my power in every particular step that may be necessary to secure your immediate happiness and future well-being.—Now, my friends, I am content that you call me an infidel; that you esteem me the most worthless and wicked of all the human beings who have yet been born! Still, however, even this will not make what I say one jot less true, or more false. No name can make falsehood truth; how can any name whatever make truth more true? Of what use, then, can names be, except to give a false validity to gross error? The interest of those who govern has ever appeared to be, and under the present systems ever will appear to be, opposed, to the interest of those whom they govern. Law and taxation, as these are now necessarily administered, are evils of the greatest magnitude; they are a curse to every part of society; but while man remains individualised, they must continue, and both must unavoidably still increase in magnitude of evil."[5]

In reading these extracts from the speech of Mr. Owen, he did not wish to call down the spirit of persecution against him. He admired Mr. Owen's treatment of the persons under his care; and as to his religious opinions, he only regretted the aberrations of his mind. But it was evident, that he looked to the adoption of a plan subversive of the religion and government of the country; and however philanthropic his views might be, that House could not adopt the plan proposed by the hon. baronet, without countenancing those dangerous theories. But it appeared that Mr. Owen's plan was discountenanced by the unbiassed judgment of the public; for at the first meeting which he addressed at the City of London Tavern, his propositions were rejected. After Mr. Owen had spoken, several other gentlemen took part in the discussion. A worthy alderman proposed an amendment to one of the resolutions, and the purport of that amendment was, that no effectual relief could be given to the people without a fair representation in parliament. This amendment was adopted, so that it appeared, whenever a plan was proposed for ameliorating society, the grand panacea, parliamentary reform, was sure to be brought forward. He should regret, if the rejection of this motion led to the rejection of what was good in the plan; but he thought the hon. and learned gentleman who had preceded him in the debate, had cleared the way so well, as to show that this would not be a necessary consequence. It was, no doubt, true, that at a second public meeting a committee was appointed, for the purpose of considering Mr. Owen's plan, and a subscription had been opened for its advancement, to which the worthy baronet had liberally contributed. It appeared, however, that in this country of unbounded liberality—that in a city of unbounded wealth, the subscription completely failed. Only a small sum had been subscribed; and it was surely a strong prima facie case against the plan, that after it had been so long submitted to the public, it had received so little encouragement. He concluded by declaring, that as an official individual, he could not agree to a grant of the public money for the establishment of a plan that had been introduced to the public by a speech, in which all religions were pronounced false, and all systems of government bad.

Mr. John Smith[6] eulogised the character of Mr. Owen, who had long exerted himself to alleviate the distresses of his fellow creatures. It appeared that the right hon. gentleman (the chancellor of the exchequer) was not disposed to give assistance to the plan, because it was proposed by a person who differed from himself on the subjects of religion and politics. In that respect he dissented from the views of the right hon. gentleman. No man could more lament than he did, the course which Mr. Owen had pursued; and indeed, he had told him, that if he introduced those obnoxious sentiments, he would prevent people from supporting his plan. Still he could not agree with those who thought this a sufficient ground for rejecting it. It was indeed a part of Mr. Owen's system to teach men to make allowance for such differences of opinion. He had never in the course of his life known a person so thoroughly exempt from prejudice or self-interest as Mr. Owen. The right hon. gentleman would allow him to remind him of an extraordinary circumstance attending the establishment at Lanark, and which particularly demanded his notice. Such was the nature of that establishment, managed as it was by a man of Mr. Owen's unfortunate religious belief, that during the last 14 years there was not one solitary instance of a man connected with it being convicted of a crime. Could the same be said of any other establishment in this country? Surely that system which produced such effects was at least worthy of consideration. He should perhaps have been silent on this occasion, had it not been for what had fallen from the learned gentleman (Mr. Brougham) in his excellent speech. On the subject of education he would speak out, and he denied that Mr. Owen's views on this point were visionary, for he knew them to be correct from the practical results which he had himself witnessed. Mr. Owen's plan embraced the education of children from the age of three years and upwards. He had seen the plan reduced to practice at Lanark, and Mr. Owen had there, by his system of instruction, taught those little creatures to do away all the contentious passions so common at that age. No man could see one of those little boys of nine years of age, without wishing that his own children had been similarly educated; that, he would freely confess, had been his own feeling. As to many parts of the plan of Mr. Owen, he did not pretend to understand them, and he could not give an opinion on what he did not understand. If a committee were granted to inquire into the subject, although he did not think they should go into the whole question of the poor-laws, still they might consider the present state of distress in which the population of the country was involved. He would take the liberty of asking the right hon. gentleman and his colleagues, whether they were prepared to come forward with any plan for the relief of the poor? If they were not, with what face could they refuse this committee? He did therefore hope, that if the right hon. gentleman persisted in his opposition to the appointment of this committee, he would, for the satisfaction of those who were anxious on this subject, state what he intended to do.

The Chancellor of the Exchequer explained he did not object to Mr. Owen's plan, because Mr. Owen himself rejected the authority of all religions and all governments, but because Mr. Owen had stated the plan to be founded on those principles. As to the relief of the poor, it was only necessary for him to say at present, that there was a motion on that subject already before the House, and when it came to be discussed, he should take that opportunity of stating his opinions.

Mr. Ricardo[7] observed, that he was completely at war with the system of Mr. Owen, which was built upon a theory inconsistent with the principles of political economy, and in his opinion was calculated to produce infinite mischief to the community. Something had fallen from an hon. member on a former night, on the subject of the employment of machinery. It could not be denied, on the whole view of the subject, that machinery did not lessen the demand for labour; while, on the other hand, it did not consume the produce of the soil, nor employ any of our manufactures. It might also be misapplied by occasioning the production of too much cotton, or too much cloth; but the moment those articles ceased in consequence to pay the manufacturer, he would devote his time and capital to some other purpose. Mr. Owen's plan proceeded upon this—he who was such an enemy to machinery, only proposed machinery of a different kind: he would bring into operation a most active portion of machinery, namely, human arms. He would dispense with ploughs and horses in the increase of the productions of the country, although the expense as to them must be much less when compared with the support of men. He confessed he did not agree in the general principles of the plan under consideration, but he was disposed to accede to the proposition of a committee. Spade husbandry Mr. Owen recommended as more beneficial to production. He was not informed enough on the interests of agriculture to give an opinion, but that was a reason for sending the subject to a committee. For what did the country want at the present moment? A demand for labour. If the facts stated of spade husbandry were true, it was a beneficial course, as affording that demand. And though government or the legislature would not be wisely employed in engaging in any commercial experiment, it would be advantageous that it should, under present circumstances, circulate useful information and correct prejudices. They should separate such considerations from a division of the country into parallelograms, or the establishment of a community of goods, and similar visionary schemes. Before he sat down, he trusted the House would excuse his offering a few observations on what he considered the cause of the distresses of the country. He fully concurred in what had fallen from his hon. and learned friend on the subject of population. The proportion of the capital to population regulated the amount of wages, and, to augment them, it was important to increase the capital of the country. But when he heard honourable members talk of employing capital in the formation of roads and canals, they appeared to overlook the fact, that the capital thus employed must be withdrawn from some other quarter. The causes of the insufficiency of capital, and the consequent disproportion between wages and population, were to be attributed to many circumstances, for some of which government were not to blame. Supposing a country with a numerous population, large capital, and a limited soil, the profits of that capital will be smaller there, than in a country populous, with lesser portion of capital, and with a great extent of soil. This country was one of large capital, but of increasing population and of an extent of soil necessarily limited; of course profits would be lower in it than in countries which had not the same limitation: still, though the profits were smaller, the capital continued in this kingdom, not only because persons felt a solicitude to keep their property under their own eye, but because the same confidence was not reposed in the security of others: the moment, however, other kingdoms, by their laws and institutions, inspired greater confidence, the capitalist would be induced to remove his property from Great Britain to a situation where his profits would be more considerable: this arose from no fault in the government; but the effect of it was to produce a deficiency of employment and consequent distress. Then came the question, had we taken the proper steps to prevent the profits upon capital from being lower here than in other countries? On the contrary had we not done everything to augment and aggravate the evil? Had we not added to the natural artificial causes for the abduction of capital? We had passed corn laws, that made the price of that necessary of life, grain, higher than in other and neighbouring countries, and thus interfered with the article which was considered the chief regulator of wages. Where grain was dear, wages must be high, and the effect of high wages was necessarily to make the profits on capital low. A second cause arose out of the fetters upon trade, the prohibitions against the import of foreign commodities, when, in fact, better and cheaper than our own. This was done in a spirit of retaliation; but he contended, that whatever line of policy other nations pursued, the interest of this nation was different: wherever we could obtain the articles we wanted at the cheapest rate, there we ought to go for them; and wherever they were cheapest, the manufacture would be the most extensive, and the amount of it, and invitation to capital, the greatest. Another cause of the existing disposition to send capital out of the country was to be found in the national debt. Instead of paying our expenses from year to year, Great Britain had constantly pursued a system of borrowing, and taxes were accumulated not only to pay the simple interest, but sometimes even the compound interest of the debt; and the amount was now so enormous, that it became a matter of calculation, whether it was worth a capitalist's while to continue in a country where he not only obtained small profits, but where he was subjected to a great additional burthen. Every pecuniary motive impelled him rather to quit than to remain. For a great many of the various causes of the evil, some of the principal of which he had touched upon, there might not exist any immediate remedy. We had, however, a beneficial precedent in the proceedings of the last session. He alluded to the measures taken for a return to payments in specie; and he saw no inconvenience in keeping steadfastly to that system. Parliament had wisely extended the operations of that system over a number of years. They should follow the same course as to the corn laws. After the quantity of capital employed under the faith of legislative enactments in agriculture, it would be a grate[sic] injustice to proceed to an immediate repeal of those laws. But that House should look to the ultimate good, and give notice, that after a certain number of years, such an injurious system of legislation must terminate. The same observation applied to our prohibitory commercial code. From the variety of interests now in operation under that system, it would not only be necessary to look, but to look steadfastly, to a distant but certain period for its repeal. With respect to the national debt, he felt that he entertained opinions on that point which by many would be considered extravagant. He was one of those who thought that it could be paid off, and that the country was at this moment perfectly competent to pay it off. He did not mean that it should be redeemed at par; the public creditor possessed no such claim—were he paid at the market price, the public faith would be fulfilled. If every man would pay his part of the debt, it could be effected by the sacrifice of so much capital—With respect to the objection, that the effect of that sacrifice would be to bring so much land into the market, that purchasers could not be found for such a glut, the answer was, that the stockholder would be eager to employ his money, as he received it, either in the purchase of land, or in loans to the farmer or landowner, by which the latter might be enabled to become the purchaser, particularly when the government was no longer in the market as a borrower. He was persuaded that the difficulty of paying off the national debt was not so great as was generally imagined; and he was also convinced that the country had not yet nearly reached the limits of its prosperity and greatness. It was only by a comparative reference to the state of other countries that the opposite opinion could be entertained, and such opinion would gain ground as long as so many unnatural temptations, by our policy at home, were held out to withdraw capital from the country. He repeated his conviction that Mr. Owen's plan was in many parts visionary, but yet he would not oppose the appointment of a committee, if it were only for the purpose of seeing whether it was probable that the advantages which that gentleman expected from the use of spade husbandry could be realized.

Mr. N. Calvert[8] opposed the motion. He saw no benefit that could arise from the appointment of a committee. Spade husbandry, whatever good effects it might otherwise be attended with in some places, would not afford permanent relief! because it would not afford permanent employment.

Mr. Alderman Waithman[9] disapproved of the plan as a general one. It was however much more objectionable when first brought forward than at present. With all the prejudices that were entertained against it, he saw no reason why it should not be sent to a committee, if it were only for the purpose of satisfying the public, and showing the impracticability of it Mr. Owen having succeeded in one instance upon a small scale, was convinced that he would be successful upon a larger one. This he (Mr. Waithman) was convinced was a visionary expectation. He would not follow his hon. friend who had spoken last but one through the various topics upon which he touched with so much ability. His hon. friend had gone over a large extent of matter worthy of most serious inquiry. The distress of the country might be traced to various causes; but the great one was the excessive and exorbitant taxation. The consequence was, that the profits of every species of produce were greatly reduced, and vast numbers, whose income was not sufficient to support them in this country, went to reside on the continent; so that what they received from the taxes here, as the interest of their capital, was sent abroad.

Lord Althorp[10] was sorry to differ in some respects from his hon. friend the hon. member for Portarlington. He agreed with him however, in the leading principles he laid down with respect to the causes of the present distress, and the mode of applying a remedy. He was not of the same opinion with his hon. friend on the subject of the corn laws. In principle they were wrong; and he opposed them when the subject was before the House. Still, he felt that in a period of war they would be of advantage in procuring an independent supply of that most necessary article. It was also a great object to secure the employment of capital in agriculture. It might indeed be said that it was bad economy to grow corn at home when it could be had cheaper from other countries. The answer to this was, that they could not secure a supply at home in time of war unless by imposing some tax on corn of foreign growth. He agreed with what was said respecting their commercial system, and was surprised that no means had been adopted for opening a more extensive market with foreign countries, particularly France. He did not allude to a commercial treaty; that, in his mind, was not desirable; but by admitting the wines and silks of France, the produce of this country would be taken in return, and produce mutual advantage. He did not think it would be prudent to agree to the present motion. All were agreed that the plan proposed was absurd; where, then, was the necessity for appointing a committee to prove its absurdity? If they were to engage in inquiry upon such grounds there would be no end to committees. With respect to spade husbandry, if advantageous it would soon be adopted. The public were sufficiently awake to their own interest, and it was better to let individuals pursue it in their own way. An experiment, if necessary, might be made by the board of agriculture, whose funds were adequate to the purpose.

Mr. Calcraft[11] said, that the wording of the motion, supposing it were otherwise unobjectionable, would induce him to vote against it, as it in fact recognized Mr. Owen's plan. It was impossible that he could give his support to any plan, which in its results could only, he thought, tend to delusion and disappointment. He did not intend to delay the House by entering at all into questions of employment of capital, or amount of revenue, to which indeed, he felt quite incompetent. Unquestionably a great deal was expected of them by the country; of that hon. gentlemen must be aware; and while he must admit that there was much which they could not do, he was not the less disposed to assist most warmly in the development of any measure which might have a tendency effectually to relieve the suffering poor.—But he really thought that, if the hon. baronet had the interest of Mr. Owen warmly at heart, he would not make an unfavourable impression on the public mind with respect to it, by pressing his motion to the division, which must, if he persisted, shortly take place.

Sir Charles Burrell[12] opposed the motion. He was desirous to offer a few observations on the state of husbandry, in reply to some remarks which had been made upon the subject. In many cases, spade husbandry had been already tried, particularly in the hop counties, and most especially in Kent. This, therefore, was no new system. With regard to the printed papers which had been widely circulated—drawn up with the intention of displaying the large benefits likely to arise from, and the property to be rapidly accumulated by, the practice of spade husbandry, they were founded in mere delusion. It was quite impossible, he would venture to say, that any such quantity of corn could have been grown upon the same extent of land, as was said to have been raised by the superiority of spade husbandry. In particular instances, no doubt, much good might be effected by these means; but their general practice would be, in fact, the bringing back of agriculture, generally, to a state of nature. There were, besides, many parts of the country where lands could not be so tilled. It had been said that this sort of husbandry would increase the food of the whole people. He denied that assertion; but suppose it did, what good would be done? What sale could there be for it, while no encouragement was given to the home growth of the British farmer—while foreign corn was allowed to be imported at a price which must defeat the British grower?—As to the corn laws, he thought it would be well to revise them in such a manner as to make corn yield a revenue to the British grower; and by doing so, he had no doubt, the state of the country would be materially improved.

Mr. Wilberforce[13] could not give his consent to this plan. His right hon. friend opposite, had already stated, as part of his objection to Mr. Owen's plan, the nature of his religious principles. This observation did not appear to be correctly understood by his hon. friend on the bench behind him. It applied, as he apprehended, not to the principles of any particular sect of any religion, but to those avowed by Mr. Owen himself; and if Mr. Owen, as he understood, objected to all the systems of religion at present established—if his whole plan proceeded upon a system of morals founded upon no religion whatever, but rather upon considerations of moral rectitude of conduct only, he was of opinion that it behoved the House to be cautious how it gave its sanction to an institution, which did not acknowledge as one of its essential features, that doctrine, on whose truth and piety it was not for him now to enlarge. In the year 1817, he had read a paper connected with this subject, which he presumed all who heard him had also seen. Till that paper came under his observation, he had really felt disposed to vote for the plan. That paper had, however, altered his opinion. It seemed an object of Mr. Owen, to establish a number of little communities, with each a certain allotment of ground throughout the country. This, it was contended, would increase the quantity of sustenance. The conclusion implied that man would labour more diligently for the advantages to be distributed throughout a little community, than for his own individual profit. It was a position at variance with daily practice and constant experience. Societies which were to enjoy a sort of community of goods. He (Mr. Wilberforce) had not had the benefit of attending personally at the Lanark institution, but he had seen those who had; and he thought he understood the nature of it, from the very admirable speech in which it had that night been described. He was ready to admit that all those who visited it expressed themselves favourably of the system that prevailed there. It had been brought to its present stale however, not by any particular rules of Mr. Owen's (though the exclusion of public houses and other circumstances must have greatly assisted) but by the good old system of Christianity. He trusted, however, while he could not support the present motion, that the House would not break up without at least expressing its inclination to devise some measure which might alleviate, if it failed to remove, the grievances of the lower classes. With respect to what had been said by the hon. gentleman about the misapplication of the public revenue, it was with the profoundest respect that he differed from a gentleman who had so greatly distinguished himself upon questions of political economy which had exercised the pens of some of the ablest writers this kingdom ever could boast of, and who, in that science, if he had not advanced any great new principles, had yet applied existing ones in such a manner as to claim for him the warmest esteem and admiration from his contemporaries. But, for himself, he must deny that we were in "an unnatural state." The idea of the application of capital to the prosecution of public works had been very generally entertained; but as to the capital, which some persons seemed to imagine as identified with land, it was well known that from various circumstances the value of land was too fluctuating and uncertain, to be considered as a species of fixed capital. Without instancing any particular cases, he would say generally, that when he saw great wealth on the one hand, and great distress on the other, he could not but be solicitous that some mode should, if possible, be devised of bringing them together; so as to render them mutually productive and beneficial. He believed, with an honourable gentleman who had spoken in the core of the debate, that this country had not yet seen her best days. He did trust, and think, that she would go on increasing in strength, in greatness, and in happiness. We were, in fact, journeying in that road which was sure to conduct us to wealth, prosperity, and power; we were diffusing education. The reason why former states had been in all ages assimilated to the human frame, in its advance from infancy to youth, from youth to manhood, from manhood to decay, was this—the parallel proceeded upon this fact, that the religion of those states was founded on false principles. They went on from stage to stage of intellectual improvement, emerging from ignorance to knowledge, till the light of day beamed upon the fabric, and betrayed the rotten imposture upon which it was built. The pillar of our greatness, however, was raised upon that basis of all intellectual and religions improvement—the Christian religion. The pledge of our superiority was in the support of those doctrines, which, the more they were examined, were found to be the more excellent in their truths, the more beneficial in their effects. He was confident that the country would proceed in her mighty march of improving excellence, as she had hitherto proceeded; and that she would remain, to the end of time, the sanctuary of morals, the refuge of liberty, and the region of peace and happiness.

Mr. Alderman Wood[14] said, he would not detain the House more than a few minutes. The objections urged against Mr. Owen's plan were general, and yet almost every person so objecting, made some admission in its favour. It certainly ought not to be thrown out, as seemed to be the prevailing disposition, merely because it was Mr. Owen's plan. The great difficulties under which the country laboured, as had been repeatedly acknowledged, was the want of employment for labour and capital. This subject had been frequently before parliament, and, in some instances, it was deemed proper for government to interfere and lend its assistance to remedy the difficulty. Now, what said the excellent report of the commissioners who had been four years in Ireland, to examine into the state of agriculture; and to ascertain the quantity of waste lands? According to them, there were 2,500,000 acres lying waste in Ireland. And what did they assign as the cause of its so lying waste?—Why, the want of capital. There were, besides, the wastelands in England. He knew of one waste spot, which, if properly cultivated, would yield sustenance for 20,000 families, valuing them as 80,000 persons, and return 200,000l. to government besides. Although he objected to many parts of Mr. Owen's plan, he thought that the part which related to the cultivation of the waste land was highly deserving of attention, especially when it was considered how large was the annual importation by this country of foreign corn. The plan ought certainly to be referred to a committee. It had been successfully adopted in commerce; what should prevent its efficacy in agriculture? Those who objected to it, from the dread of too greatly increasing the quantity of grain, did not consider that the country paid thirteen millions annually for grain beyond what the country could produce. Many more millions were also paid out of the country for flax and other commodities, and which he insisted might be and ought to be produced from the waste land and surplus labour of the country. This was the first motion that had been made for the appointment of a committee to consider of the best means of employing the poor, and it ought not to be rejected by the House merely because they did not altogether approve of the plan recommended. All who had seen the establishment at new Lanark, admitted that the course pursued by Mr. Owen had succeeded there; and why might not its benefits be extended? He was by no means partial to the whole of that gentleman's plan, but he conceived that a portion of it might be adopted with great advantage to the country. If his Majesty's ministers would come forward and say that they were prepared with any measure which might equally benefit the poor, by employing them in redeeming the waste lands of this country, he had no doubt the hon. baronet would cheerfully withdraw his motion: but he trusted he would not do so in any other case.

Sir C. Burrell in explanation observed, that no surplus grain was grown, simply for want of encouragement.

Mr. Maxwell[15] expressed his hope that the House would not refuse to grant the committee moved for by the hon. baronet.

Mr. D. W. Harvey[16] contended, that the hon. member for Bramber had wholly misrepresented Mr. Owen's intentions, and his theological views. He had read the paper drawn up by a committee who had been appointed at Leeds to inquire into the nature of the establishment at New Lanark, and who had declared, that they never saw a purer system of morality than was there practised. While Mr. Owen did not disguise his own views of polemical subjects, he was not so extravagant as to think of introducing those views into his infant institution. To state, therefore, that it was an infidel institution, and almost an atheistical college, and that its tendency was to undermine Christianity, when the little community were as celebrated for their religious and moral deportment as for their intelligent useful, and industrious habits, was a gross misrepresentation. For himself, he was never aware that Christianity was aided by secular support, but on the contrary, he always imagined that it was wholly independent of it. The House were not called upon to discuss Mr. Owen's polemical or theological views. They had before them the fact, that a community of above 2,500 persons were, by that gentleman's system, brought into a state of great morality, of happiness, at a moment when the whole of the rest of the country was, comparatively speaking, in the greatest distress. Were they to be blind to that fact, because one honourable member thought that Mr. Owen wished to undermine Christianity, and another conceived that there was some miscalculation as to the advantage of spade cultivation? Unless his majesty's ministers would say that they had some other plan to propose, he thought the House bound to acquiesce in the honorable baronet's motion, were it only to show the people that they sympathized with them under the diversity of misery which they were suffering.

Sir W De Crespigny replied. An argument had been urged against the motion, which was scarcely to be justified.—He owned that he felt extremely sore at that argument; recollecting, as he did, that in his life he had never witnessed a purer religion than that established at Lanark. It was true that more of the inmates belonged to the Methodistical church than to the Established; it was, however, a fine sight (and had the hon. member for Bramber been present he would have thought the same) to see them on each Sunday proceeding to their different places of worship. A right honourable gentleman, who had attacked Mr. Owen's plan, had coupled with it parliamentary reform. Now, he understood that to parliamentary reform Mr. Owen was decidedly hostile. Something had also been said about a community of property. There was no such thing at Lanark. Every man had his little cottage, purchased what he required, received his profits, and either deposited them in his own name in the savings banks, or did with them what he thought fit. Undoubtedly, such a general combination as that recommended by Mr. Owen would, in his (sir W. De Crespigny's) opinion, be highly beneficial; but that was not his present object. It was evident that something must be done for the relief of the poorer classes of the community. This was the first time that a proposition for considering a particular plan for that purpose had been submitted to parliament. He now asked his majesty's ministers, whether they had themselves any plan to propose on this important subject, as if so he would consent immediately to withdraw his motion?

After a pause, sir W. De Crespigny repeated his question. No answer being given, the House divided: Ayes 16, Noes 141. Majority against the motion 125.

List of the Minority.[17]

Aubrey, Sir J.
Rancliffe, Lord
Barnett, Jas.
Ricardo, D.
Compton [sic], Samuel
Smith, J.

Gaskell, B.
Sinclair, G.
Graham, Sandford
Waithman, alderman
Harvey, W. D.
Wood, alderman
Lamb, hon. G.
Nugent, Lord.
Pringle, J.
Palmer, F.

TELLERS.

Crespigny, Sir W. De
Maxwell, John

Notes

1 Archibald James Hamilton of Dalziel (1793–1834). A Scottish aristocrat, Hamilton was the son of the laird of Dalziel and Orbiston. After serving in the Scots Grey at Waterloo, he set out to improve his estate, and was a frequent visitor of Owen's at New Lanark, after meeting him in 1816. As a Liberal MP for Lanarkshire (1802–1807), he supported political reform and opposed the church. Though Hamilton first doubted the feasibility of Owen's 'Plan', he became a lifelong convert to communitarianism. After attending the general meeting during which Owen addressed the issues which would later form the bulk of his *Report to the County of Lanark* in 1820, Hamilton joined forces with Abram Combe at Orbiston, and provided the land for the community experiment (see Part 5, Chapter 28; Hamilton Papers, Motherwell Public Library; Harrison 1969, 40–44).
2 Henry Brougham (1778–1868), Whig MP for Knaresborough, educational and parliamentary reformer and advocate of the 1833 Slavery Abolition Act. Brougham was critical of Owen's millenarianism, but admired his efforts in support of popular education. In 1819, he co-founded a primary school in Westminster based on the New Lanark system. Along with Archibald Hamilton, who was a personal friend of his, Brougham subscribed to Owen's British and Foreign Philanthropic Society, which failed to establish a Village of Co-operation at Motherwell, Lanarkshire.
3 Philip Emmanuel von Fellenberg (1771–1844) a Swiss educationalist and the founder of an experimental boarding school at Hofwyl, near Bern. Robert Owen was personally acquainted with von Fellenberg, as his four sons Robert Dale, William, David and Richard were boarders at Hofwyl (Dale Owen 1858, 137). Though Owen was not directly influenced by von Fellenberg's educational theories, he shared his wish to promote co-operation between the classes through rational training, as well as his emphasis on the regenerative character of rural life as opposed to the modern, industrial city (Silver 1965, 232–233; Siméon 2017, 72).
4 Nicholas Vansittart (1766–1851), Tory MP for Harwich; served as Chancellor of the Exchequer from 1809 to 1822.
5 From Owen (1818, 59–60).
6 John Smith (1767–1842), banker and Tory MP for Midhurst.
7 David Ricardo (1772–1823), economist and MP for Portalington.

8 Nicolson Calvert (1764–1841), Whig MP for Hertford.
9 Robert Waithman (1764–1833), master draper, political reformer, alderman of the Corporation of London and Liberal MP for the City of London.
10 John Spencer, Viscount Althorp (1782–1845), Whig MP for Northamptonshire and later Chancellor of the Exchequer (1830–1834).
11 John Calcraft (1765–1831), English military officer and Liberal MP for Wareham.
12 Sir Charles Burrell (1774–1862), Tory MP for New Shoreham.
13 William Wilberforce (1759–1833), Whig MP for Bramber, political reformer and chief proponent of the 1833 Slavery Abolition Act.
14 Sir Matthew Wood (1768–1817), Whig MP and Lord Mayor of London (1815–1817).
15 John Maxwell (1791–1865), Whig MP for Renfrewshire.
16 Daniel Whittle Harvey (1786–1863), Radical MP for Colchester, future Chartist and Commissioner of the City of London Police (1839–1863).
17 Aside from some aforementioned names, the minority voters were Sir James Aubrey (1739–1826), Tory MP for Steyning; James Barnett (c. 1760–1836), Whig MP for Rochester; Samuel Crompton (1785–1848), Whig MP for East Redford; Benjamin Gaskell (1781–1856), Whig MP for Maldon; Sandford Graham (1788–1852), MP for Ludgershall and supporter of Catholic emancipation; the Hon. George Lamb (1784–1834), barrister, writer and MP for Westminster; George Nugent-Grenville (1789–1850), Whig-radical Irish politician and MP for Aylesbury; John Pringle (1796–1831), Whig MP for Lanark Burghs; George Parkyns, 2nd Baron Rancliffe, godson of King George IV, radical Whig MP for Minehead and future supporter of Chartism, and George Sinclair (1790–1865), Whig MP for Caithness and abolitionist. "F. Palmer" probably stands for Charles Fyshe Palmer (c. 1770–1843), parliamentary reformer and Whig MP for Reading.

16

LECTURES ON AN ENTIRE NEW STATE OF SOCIETY: COMPREHENDING AN ANALYSIS OF BRITISH SOCIETY, RELATIVE TO THE PRODUCTION AND DISTRIBUTION OF WEALTH, THE FORMATION OF CHARACTER, AND GOVERNMENT, DOMESTIC AND FOREIGN (LONDON: J. BROOKS, 1830) III, 42–45.

Robert Owen

[Robert Owen originally gave these six lectures in 1830 at London's Burton Street Chapel. Delivered one year after his disastrous departure from America, these addresses publicly marked the start of his new-found interest in co-operation as a major agent of political change. This was another step in his personal radicalisation, thanks in no small part to the strand of working-class Owenism that had emerged in Britain from the early 1820s onwards. Though Owen's approach still viewed community and education as beacons of change, his new co-operative outlook reinforced his critique of private property and general economic inequalities (Harrison 1969, 258).]

[. . .] There is but one mode by which man can possess in perpetuity, all the happiness of which his nature is capable of enjoying, that is, by the union and co-operation of all, for the benefit of each. But one of the necessary consequences of the imaginary notions of man's free agency over his thoughts and feelings, and his consequent responsibility, was to individualize mankind; to create self-interest, from which emanated an ever-fertile source of disunion and misery.

Private property produced inequality of condition, exclusive privileges, and arrangements intended to benefit a few at the expense of many:—hence vanity, pride, luxury, and tyranny, on the one hand; and, on the other, poverty and degradation. Hence insincerity, deception, and hatred; traffic, robbery, murder; and a system of law, or artificial justice, covering the grossest injustice.

[. . .] Let us then, at once, set aside this origin of evil upon earth; and, in future, make the only use of the miseries it has produced, to which they can now be rationally applied. Let an impartial history be compiled of the past transactions of man, explained in accordance with the now ascertained laws of human nature, and let it be given to our children through all succeeding generations, that they may learn the horrid, mental, and physical degradation to which their predecessors were subjected, by a single error of the imagination.

Trained from infancy, free from this error, they will discover that the volume transmitted to them contains the history of human nature, through the irrational period of its existence, during which the imaginary notion of free agency respecting our thoughts and feelings, and the consequent assumed responsibility for them, produced in practice a system of punishments, rewards, emulation, separate interests, almost continual warfare and misery to all; that the abandonment of that notion was the commencement of a new era, when by the knowledge of the influence of circumstances over human nature, a system was established which exhibited in practice the union and co-operation of all, for the benefit of each; when scientific arrangements were first introduced, to secure, for every child, good habits and dispositions, the highest intellectual attainments, and a superfluity of all things necessary for his happiness

Let this change be now effected, and the whole earth will gradually acquire a new aspect, and the mind of man will be born again. He will then become a rational being; all his thoughts and feelings will be consistent throughout his life; old habits, vices, difficulties, sufferings, and miseries will disappear; and the human race emancipated from that fatal error which has hitherto counteracted every attempts to ameliorate its condition, will bound forward in a course of real improvement, never retrograding nor standing still, but always advancing at a ratio continually increasing, and by which the whole circle of human knowledge will be daily extended.

17

AN ADDRESS, DELIVERED TO THE MEMBERS OF THE NEW MECHANICS' INSTITUTION, MANCHESTER, ON FRIDAY EVENING, MARCH 25, 1831: ON THE NECESSITY OF AN EXTENSION OF MORAL AND POLITICAL INSTRUCTION AMONG THE WORKING CLASSES (MANCHESTER: W. STRANGE, 1831).

Rowland Detrosier

[The adopted son of a Manchester tailor, Rowland Detrosier (c. 1800–1834) was an active member of the Lancashire co-operative movement. As an autodidact, he was particularly keen on furthering the cause of working-class education. In keeping with Owen's views on character formation, Detrosier stated that only comprehensive moral and intellectual training would emancipate the poorer echelons of society. A Nonconformist liberal rather than a radical, he agreed with Owen that democratic reforms were useless unless they were preceded by extensive individual education and moral training. Accordingly, he took part in two local Owenite institutions which aimed at providing quality education to the people: the Manchester and Salford Association for the Dissemination of Co-operative Knowledge, which he co-founded in 1831, and the Scientific Society, an offshoot of the First Salford Co-operative Society which provided evening classes for adults and a Sunday school (Yeo 1971 90–91). Detrosier's views on popular education were outlined in his 1831 pamphlet, *On the Necessity of an Extension of Moral and Political Instruction among the Working Classes.* Two years earlier, he had broken away from the Manchester Mechanics' Institute and had founded a competing organisation, the New Mechanics' Institute, which had strong ties with the local Owenite co-operators, and which would later be integrated into the Manchester Hall of Science. This was not an isolated case, as Owenite meeting rooms in Coventry and Sheffield were founded by Mechanics' Institute renegades (Taylor 1983, 213). In addition to a presentation of the classical Owenite theory of character formation, the book provided a scathing critique of the inadequate provision of popular education at the time, a situation that the Mechanics' Institute had come to symbolise. In contrast, Owenite education was presented as a remedy against the trappings of the "Old Immoral World." The New Mechanics' Institute was no longer controlled by a board of middle- and upper-class patrons, but by "elected representatives from the working-class student body" (Yeo 1971, 91). Detrosier's diatribe also targeted the Institutes' curriculum, which focused on technical subjects and lacked intellectual and political insight. He countered that instruction should focus on essential moral questions, to be made available to men and women alike (see Part 8).]

Two years have elapsed since I had the honour and gratification of addressing the members of the New Mechanics' Institution, and their friends, on the interesting occasion of its being opened for public instruction. If, on that occasion, it was gratifying to my feelings to address you on the advantages of education, and the prospects of our infant Institution, how much more gratifying must it be to me now, to congratulate you on the realization of our hopes, and the establishing of a property in books and materials, which has so greatly increased our means of usefulness. Met together at this time, to commemorate that interesting event, I trust the subject on which I have chosen to address you, namely, the great necessity for an extension of moral and political knowledge among the working classes, will not be deemed inappropriate. To direct the attention of man to the attainment of moral excellence, cannot be considered as an act of supererogation; and, as knowledge is valuable only in proportion as it tends to increase the sum of human happiness, those institutions must be imperfect in which no provision is made for the communication of moral and political knowledge. It is, however, a lamentable fact, that this part of education not only occupies individual attention the least, but is also most imperfectly taught. Yet, it will not surely be denied, that moral cultivation is as necessary to the superiority of civilized over savage man, as the extension of knowledge in the physical sciences. Man is neither born wise nor good; his wisdom and goodness are the results of education; and the differences of character which exist in the extremes of society, in what are called civilized countries, arise not from natural incapacity on the one hand, or inherent superiority on the other, but from controlling circumstances in both. Man is the creature of education, and circumstances; and the general acknowledgment of this important truth would do more for the advancement of individual happiness, than can possibly be effected by acting on a supposition, of an opposite tendency. It is in the circumstances by which he is surrounded, and in the erroneous education of which, he is the victim, that his misery and self degradation originate. If, however, we would judge correctly of the effects of education, and the influence of circumstances, we must compare the extremes of society; and, in order to form a correct estimate of the progress of moral culture, we must separate the results of scientific education from those of moral improvement. In taking this view of the subject, it will not be difficult to discover, that the civilized nations of the present day are more indebted for their vast superiority to the increase of scientific knowledge, than to the individual extent of their moral cultivation. However humiliating it may be to our pride, it is nevertheless true, that our physical knowledge is far in advance of our moral attainments. The development of human powers in society is first physical, then mental; and this condition of our nature still remains with us, and is still strikingly manifest, though little attended to in the present state of our boasted civilization. We come into the world at a period of time when the records of the past, and the development of present discoveries, confer on us an incalculable advantage over our predecessors; yet we stop not to inquire to what it is that we owe our superiority. Dazzled with the splendid discoveries of science—proud of the almost immeasurable distance at which we have left the men of former ages, in the application of mechanics to the purposes of life—still prouder of the discovery of that Leviathan of modern times, the power of steam—and elevated beyond measure at the rapid creation of wealth which has resulted from this union of individual talent and national industry, we forget, in our delirium of joy, to ask the important question, whether morality, in the most extended signification of the word, has progressed in the ratio of scientific acquirement;—whether the great mass of our population is made better and happier:—whether governors are wiser and more honest? To no part of society are these inquiries of greater moment than to the working classes; for history bears testimony to this most important truth,—POLITICAL MELIORATION IS THE RESULTING CONSEQUENCE OF MORAL PROGRESSION. What is the reiterated apology for refusing even a limited extension of acknowledged political rights to the great body of the people? Their political ignorance and moral degradation. As the friend of the working man, I cannot but deplore that, in thousands of instances, there is but too much truth in the latter accusation, and that the former has even a more extended application. It ill becomes those, however, who are instrumental to the continuation of that ignorance and degradation, to seek in its existence an apology for the perpetration of injustice, monopoly, and oppression. It ill becomes that class of society which receives, as a body, millions a year for the dissemination of knowledge, to permit moral and political ignorance to exist to so degrading an extent. Institutions are valuable only in proportion as they tend to promote the general welfare: when they cease to do this, they sink in the public estimation, and the progress of their dissolution, though slow, is sure Is it not a fact, which reflects the greatest disgrace; on those whose especial business it is to chase moral ignorance from the land, and to leave not an abiding place for vice, that even in England, notwithstanding its boasted civilization, human nature exists in all its various grades of knowledge and ignorance, except, indeed, that of positive cannibalism! Is it not a fact, that thousands of her inhabitants are still shamefully ignorant and brutal—still, to a very considerable extent, uncivilized, degraded, and inhuman? Yes, I repeat it, repeat it with regret, thousands of both sexes exist in this country, whose claims to the character of civilized beings are of the very lowest kind. They are human machines for the creation of wealth, whose physical education in the adaptation of their power to mechanical purposes is all that is thought of.

Let us neither be deceived by names nor by appearances: neither let us flatter ourselves that this, the boasted seat of every art, is a civilized country, because a portion of its inhabitants are intelligent and virtuous. Still more would I guard you against the injustice of attributing the whole of the blame to the unhappy victims of that ignorance which is the basis of domestic misery, and the stronghold of national slavery. I repeat the important philosophical truth,—man is the creature of education and circumstances. And are there not thousands in this enlightened country, whose circumstances bequeath to them little beside rising to labour and lying down to rest? Are there not thousands in this humane country, with whom labour commences almost before infancy has passed; thousands, the whole of whose education presents to them scarcely anything more edifying than the examples of ignorance and brutality? Where is the individual bold enough to say no? They have, however, one redeeming virtue—industry! matchless industry ! — to develop which no pains are spared, no means left untried, that avarice can dictate, or poverty oblige its victims to submit to. They are consequently, in the generality of cases, considerably advanced in their knowledge of the mechanical arts; and beyond this, it is still presumed by some, the education of poverty ought not to extend. To govern, is assumed to be the peculiar province of the few; to labour and submit, the becoming duty of the many. Our labouring population are indeed no longer the serfs of the land, but they are the slaves of commerce, and the victims of bad government. Urged to exertion by the powerful stimulus of recurring wants, the imperious demands of their necessitous situation, the whole of their energies are directed to the attainment of one all-engrossing object, sustenance for the body; and this necessity has been taken advantage of, to push their powers of production to the greatest extent. Hence the experienced eye, and the practised hand, are enabled to effect more, much more, than man can effect in a state of inexperience and infantine society; and so far, indeed, our peasantry are civilized.

In the individual application of mind to the modifications of matter, a power has been created, the limits of which it would be difficult to define. By this power we are enabled to fabricate some of the physical means of happiness, to an extent and at a price, of which, even in the memory of existing individuals, society had no previous conception. But is this the great end of social institutions? Does this comprise the total of human requirements? Is man the creature of physical wants only:—or are there other subjects that ought to be included in the catalogue of essentials to human happiness? SCIENCE CREATES WEALTH; BUT IT IS MORALITY THAT PERFECTS man; and the greatness, the prosperity, the happiness of a nation, demand the inseparable union of both. Were some catastrophe of nature instantly to destroy the records of human intelligence at present existing in this country, to sweep away in an instant all those things, on the existence and possession of which the comforts of life, in the different grades, of society depend; to strip the land of all those witnesses of existing and past intelligence by which it is at present ornamented; and, sparing the population, to leave them the alternative of remaining destitute, or of constructing for themselves the requisites and comforts of life; who can doubt, for a moment, our physical power, or mechanical capacity, to extricate ourselves even from so forlorn a situation? But, let us ask the important question—are we as powerful in moral excellence as we are in mechanical skill? Were some political catastrophe to leave every man to be governed solely by the degree of knowledge which he individually might possess, what would be the scene presented to the eye of the spectator? What would be the moral consequence? What proportion of our population would be disposed to fulfil their moral engagement? What proportion would have principle enough to be a law unto themselves? Every one must feel the importance of these questions; the answer to which, were it possible to give it, would decide our claim to the character of a civilized nation, and shew the amount of our moral excellence. A nation is civilized or savage, not in proportion to the morality or intelligence of the few, but of the many; for as the author of the Wealth of Nations has well remarked:— "Though a few individuals may possess great abilities, all the nobler parts of the human character may be obliterated and extinguished in the great body of the people." I will add, that where those qualities are ever called into active existence, in the great mass of the people, the result is as fatal, the consequences as serious, and as much, to be regretted, as their entire obliteration and extension. The great end of social institutions ought to be the melioration of the moral, physical, and intellectual state of the poorest and most numerous class of society. Is this the end of the great institutions of England, where nine millions a-year are secured to one class of society, for the communication of knowledge, the cultivation, of finer feelings, and the extension of vice? Ask from that system of patronage and pluralities which at present disgraces the annals of our country—ask from that system of fiscal oppression by which placemen, pensioners, sinecurists, and lean-jobbers, are supported—ask from that system of legislative morality which, whilst it tempts poverty with a bribe, to become the slave of drink, makes use of the produce to enslave its victim.

Is it not a lamentable truth, that whilst almost every part of society is educated to provide for the physical wants of life, comparatively no portion of it is educated to promote the happiness of all? That whilst every faculty of the human edifice is pressed into the service of the belly and the back, the moral capacities of the great mass of our population are either left without cultivation or are vitiated by a system of false education? Every where we may discover apprentices to mechanical traded; but! which among them is apprenticed to morality? That which ought to be the business of all is confined to a few; and our national character is degraded, not from physical incapacity, but from a want of proper cultivation. The little that we teach is taught badly; it is deficient not only in matter and in manner, but also in the existence of approving and confirming circumstances. Ignorance is edified by a system of command: and "thou shalt," or "thou shalt not" constitutes the enlightened substitute for the explanation of necessity and moral obligation. It is the despotic morality of ages gone by, and is admirably adapted to the perpetuation of moral ignorance. Shall I be told that my assertion is not founded in truth? My reply will be a call for the code of morality that gives reason for its requirements. Where are the children of poverty taught the *necessity* of moral obligation ? "Thou shalt not steal" is a command; but why is it not stated,—To bear false witness is forbidden; but to what page of the moral code shall the attention be directed to discover what constitutes the nature of the crime? Who thinks of teaching poverty the nature of vested rights, or of explaining to the child of the operative the history of property, or the use of its institution? Where is the youth who understands the evils of lying and deceit; or who could explain the serious consequences to society of a system of general falsification?— Amidst this dearth of appropriate moral teaching, is it not preposterous to expect the consistent performance of political duty, or the existence of noble and patriotic sentiments among the people? The ancients taught patriotism as a virtue; and it is important to enquire if it has ceased to be such? If it has not, what code of the moderns contains its precepts, and where is poverty taught to revere them? if, however, our morality and patriotism are, in the great mass, the offspring of chance, our national industry is not committed to the same fostering hand. On every side may we hear the debasing sentiment, "Take care of number one;" but where are the advocates of the ennobling virtues of patriotism and the love of mankind?

It is more than probable, that whilst putting these questions, some minds are whispering to themselves—the SUNDAY SCHOOL —the infant Hercules of modern times, whose task it is to cleanse the Augean stable of ignorance, brutality, and vice. Infant, indeed; for though it has increased the extent of its operation, its practices have been almost stationary in improvement. Think not, however, that I mean to deny the amount of good of which the Sunday School has been the medium. To acknowledge it; as a lover of my species, gratefully acknowledge it. But oh! how much it short of what might be effected! They are the children of the poor who are taught there, and the day to them is of infinite value. Every moment of that day which is spent in the school, should be devoted to instruction and that instruction should be *practical and useful*. Is it so? I reply, without hesitation, that the greater portion of it is not. Let no man accuse me of an improper motive in making these remarks. I may err in judgment, certainly not in intention. My anxious desire is, that this powerful medium of moral and political regeneration may be rendered effective to national purposes; and impelled, by considerations of social duty, at the risk of misrepresentation, I put the following questions:— How much of the precious time of this fast day of poverty from labour is taken up in listening to prayers, the language and the bearings of which, however, well intentioned they may be, are beyond the comprehension of infancy? How much of that time is devoted to the reading of matter which is foreign to the purposes of every day life? The great object of such an institution ought to be the formation of character, and the development of mind; and the most powerful means will be found to be—PRIDE AND INTEREST. Engage their pride on the side of knowledge and virtue, and let the discipline of the school be calculated to inspire them with a conviction that it is their interest to attain the one, and to practise the other. Elevate the character, and teach poverty that it has something to labour for, independent of riches—the greatness of moral worth. At no period of life are proper subjects for contemplation of greater importance than during childhood and youth; and the curiosity incident to these portions of our existence, when properly directed, becomes one of the most important coadjutors in the formation of character. Seize upon this disposition of our nature, and secure it in the cause of human progression, by gratifying its anxious inquiries with useful information and philosophical facts. Let the youthful mind be stored, each succeeding week, with natural truths or moral principles, on which it may employ the activity of its thoughts; and it will, discover, by degrees, an increase of its strength, in that increase of knowledge on which the mind re poses with satisfaction. The affections will then be engaged in favour of knowledge and virtue, and the true foundation for an abhorrence, of brutality and vice will be implanted. Let our Sunday Schools become the UNIVERSITIES OF THE POOR, in which the infant mind, shall be taught to look through nature up to nature's source, by teaching it the simple elements and rudimental facts of natural philosophy. And let our first books contain them. Teach it the dignifying truth, *that the only acceptable service to that source is*—to love and serve their fellow-men. Let a reason accompany every moral precept, and an illustration every principle in philosophy. Let grammar, geography, and every useful branch, of knowledge be taught there, and let writing be made subservient to all. Discard the silly practice of setting copies without meaning, and substitute the principles and truths of natural, moral, and political philosophy, so that the learning of one branch of knowledge may become subservient to many others. And whilst labouring in this holy work of human improvement, let it not be forgotten, that no sure foundation can be laid for domestic happiness, or for the full development of virtuous character, if WOMAN *be not made a full partaker of the benefits.*

I know that some minds will be startled at these propositions, and that many will be prepared to oppose them with all that warmth which characterizes zeal without knowledge. It is, however, to reason, not to prejudice, that I appeal. Assured that the day is sanctified by the deed—not the deed by the day; and convinced that no labour can be more holy than that which tends to increase the amount of human happiness, by preparing the rising generation to become the recipients of moral and philosophical truths, and the practises of every social duty, I feel confident that reason will ultimately prevail. "The Sabbath was made for man, not man for the Sabbath;" and let it not be forgotten, that "it is lawful to do good even on the Sabbath-day." It has often been remarked, that the amount of good resulting from Sunday School tuition is by no means commensurate to the labour. The fault is in the system of teaching, and the subjects on which the time is unhappily wasted. If the full development of mind, and the correct formation of character, be not the ultimate objects of that teaching, it has comparatively small, if any, merit. Let the system be reformed, and the sooner the better; for the reformation of an error cannot commence too soon. Let the formation of a national character of which we may justly be proud, become the great object of our teaching; and let the crowning stone of our labours be the patriotic love of mankind. Then, when our youth shall be taught in the Sunday School, the philosophy of nature, of morality, and of politics,—then, indeed, will it become the full-grown Hercules of truth, that will strangle the reptiles of corruption and vice, if it be supported by a proper education at home. Without this, its best endeavours will be comparatively fruitless. Education consists not merely in the learning to read and to write. Whatever tends to give a bias to the feelings, to the formation of opinions, or to the adoption of habits, constitutes a part of education. Precept should be supported by example, and habit be rendered confirmatory of both. It has been well remarked by Mr. Mill, in his Article on Education, that "early impressions form the primary habits, and that the primary habits constitute the character of the man. The consequence is most important; for it follows, that as soon as the infant, or rather the embryo begins to feel, the character begins to be formed."[1] In this respect the working classes of this country have much to learn; and they have hitherto been deplorably deficient in good practical instructors. They have been so long taught that humility is a virtue,— so long left without the knowledge requisite to distinguish between a becoming humility and a debasing submission, that the pride of character and moral worth—the dignifying consideration, that they form the base of the great social edifice, and that they have a moral and political character to sustain, of which they ought to be most tenacious, comes not within the knowledge or consideration of thousands. If the working classes of this country would redeem their children from the political evils by which they are themselves oppressed, they must aid, by every means in their power, in the formation of a character which shall be prepared to obtain relief. Truth, honesty, kindness, and sobriety must be the never-failing examples, Truth! for the parent who forbids lying, yet practices the vice, is rendered contemptible in the estimation of his child, and his precept loses its force. Honesty! for he who enjoins it, yet contracts debts he never means to pay, or is otherwise dishonest, is rendered contemptible in the eyes of all. Kindness! for it is the anointing oil of family, love and peace; is essential to the comfort of the domestic circle; and its influence in the formation of character is most important.

The youth that has been accustomed to tyranny at home, is prepared to practise it when circumstances give the power. How can a father expect his children to pay respect to their mother, if he set the example of disrespect himself? How can a mother expect obedience and deference to a father, if she set the example of indifference herself? And how shall parents expect to remain objects of esteem to their children, if their conduct be characterized by brutality and vice? The formation of a good character requires consistency of example. The man who thinks it too much trouble to thank his wife for an act of kindness, sets an example to his children which they will not fail to imitate. Let every act of kindness be accompanied by an acknowledgment, the repetition of which will form the links of that chain on the existence of which an affectionate union is dependent. It will aid in fixing each act of kindness upon the mind; the doer will be associated with the memory of the deed, and they will be less likely to treat each other with harshness, on the tablets of whose hearts exist the abiding records of love and kindness. The littleness of wealthy pride may lead it to remark, that this is an education unsuited to poverty. It may tend, however, to the edification of that littleness, to inform it, that kindness, and moral dignity become the cottage as well as the palace. It is true, they are too often wanting at the poor man's dwelling, and "pity 'tis true;" but if instruction is to be denied him in any portion of the moral domain, blame him not for the brutality that is the consequence of ignorance. The virtues that adorn the domestic circles of wealth lose none of their intrinsic value when transplanted to the cottage hearth. It is time to chase from the latter all debasing humility, and to teach its too humble inhabitants a proper and becoming pride; that pride will lead to an abhorrence of meanness, and will be the powerful support of a virtuous emulation.

Last, though not least, in the catalogue of essentials to the increase of moral force, let the poor man be too proud to be a drunkard; or let him be discarded from the society of those who advocate good government and the cause of suffering humanity. Proclaim to the working classes, from morn to night-fall, that no POLITICAL CHANGE CAN EFFECT THE MELIORATION OF HIS CONDITION WHO IS THE SLAVE OF DRUNKENNESS; and add to it this important truth, that political melioration is the resulting consequence of moral progression. With what consistency can that man reprobate the bad government of his country, who practises not good government at home? Or how shall that father reprove his child for immorality, who is himself an habitual drunkard? The vice of drunkenness is that which more especially unveils the deficiency of moral culture in this country. We affect an abhorrence of the crimes of savage life; yet, whilst exulting in the superiority of our attainments, were we to institute a comparison between the lowest state of savage existence and that of the brutal and confirmed drunkard, our pride might receive a salutary check, in the conviction, that even cannibalism is scarcely more odious than drunkenness. The cannibal exists in a state of moral infancy, in which we discover that entire absence of governing principle,—that absolute freedom of will which has so often occupied the attention of philosophers, and in praise of which, partial knowledge has frequently had so much to say. Unchecked by considerations of humanity or moral feeling—unrestrained by a sense of right or wrong—the cannibal sits down with exultation to the war-feast of victory and joy; and whilst devouring the dead body of his slaughtered foe, constitutes the true representation of freedom of will. In contemplating such a state of savage existence, in such a moral desert, enlightened humanity is shocked at the commission of crimes for which nobody blushes, because they are permitted by all. Nor is this to be wondered at. Living in a state of society in which unrestrained will is the only governing principle—in which he is most reverenced who is most to be feared—in which cruelty is the redeeming virtue, not the odious vice—every external influence operates to produce a character ruthless in principle, and cruel in deed. Murder, torture, treachery, and deceit, are among the virtues, not the crimes, of the lowest stage of human existence. Shame, in such a state, has not yet spread its tell-tale hue over the countenance of man; and a good conscience, the offspring of moral education, is unknown. With no good principle to appeal to—no law to control—what but the most despotic authority could govern a society of individuals such as these? And what principle has the brutal and confirmed drunkard? What law is strong enough to control him? What is his superiority over the cannibal? Is he checked by considerations of humanity or moral feeling, or restrained by a sense of right, or wrong, when, daily sitting down to the feast of his cups, he swallows, at each repeated draught, not, indeed, the body of a slaughtered foe, but the happiness and well-being of his wife and children, nor blushes at the deed which consigns them to wretchedness and want? And shall such beings prate about liberty and equality? The liberty they desire is the liberty to do wrong; and to descend to an equality with such individuals, is a degradation to which no honest man will stoop. Herding with society in such unrestrained will is the only governing principle—in which he is most reverenced who is most reckless—every external influence operates to the degradation of the man, and the increase of brutality. Witness the horrid spectacle of the domestic scene The sound of his foot is the signal of fear, not of joy. The father that should protect, is coming home to abuse; and the child clings to its trembling mother in a frail, fruitless, but holy effort, to form a barrier of affection between her and brutality. Almost exhausted from the want of a sufficiency of food; half-naked, and wholly wretched, the pitiable partner of this human monster sues with fear and trembling for the miserable pittance which his brutal habit has spared for them. This picture of human degradation lacks but one more character to render its odiousness complete—the drunken mother. Then, indeed, the cup of domestic wretchedness is filled to the brim, and poverty, disease, and crime, are secure of their victims. If humanity is shocked at the supposed existence of such wretchedness, what must be the state of feelings on contemplating the reality? Drunkenness is the crying sin of this country, and its debasing consequences are manifest in thousands of instances, in the poverty and immorality of its victims. Nor are the Consequences of this odious vice confined to the domestic circle; they influence the happiness and prosperity of the nation. Wealth, not wisdom, —corruption, not virtuous consistency, has hitherto been the highway to a seat in our Legislative Assembly, the members of which have sought to indemnify themselves from the labour of all; for that which they have spent in the corrupting of a herd of misnamed freemen. The corrupted voter mortgages his own and his neighbour's labour, and drinks the produce without shame or remorse; and justice and morality are outraged through the land, whilst their paid guardians remain passive spectators. The labouring population of this country cannot begin their domestic prosperity—cannot raise themselves in the scale of political greatness, until they have raised themselves in moral excellence; and have learned the habits of prudence and sobriety. It has been correctly observed by a learned German writer, that "in all that is beyond mere animal organization, nature has placed in the hands of man the care of his own destiny: deprived of the succours of instinct, by the force of reason alone he must conquer and secure all the sum of happiness and of perfection which he ought to enjoy as his proper share. The safety of his person, the invention of his clothes, the engagements which constitute the charms of life, his knowledge, his prudence, all, *even the rectitude of his will*, must be his own work."

This important remark, which relates to the general mass of mankind, is particularly applicable to the labouring population of this country. Their destiny is in their own hands; to a very considerable extent; for the endeavours of that portion of the higher grades of society which has wisdom, virtue, an humanity sufficient to induce it to labour for the good of the working classes, can effect but little, if the latter do not them by consistency of conduct and unity of purpose. "Put thy own shoulder; to the wheel" was the reply of Jupiter to the waggoner; and seeing the necessity of a change in the moral and political culture of the operative classes, I call upon them to unite in the endeavour to effect that for themselves which others do not seem disposed to do for them. Acquire for yourselves a political importance, by the force of character; by moral consistency and mental improvement; for hitherto the labouring population of this country has been powerless, except as a mob. Think not that this remark is dictated by a feeling of reproach or contempt. Far other are the sentiments that animate my mind. "The knowledge of a disease is half its cure;" and it is most important to the working classes of this country, that they should become convinced that political reform, to effect the regeneration of national happiness, must be supported by moral improvement. It is admitted on all hands, that to secure "the greatest happiness to the greatest number," ought to be the primary object of all governments—; but it is by no means so generally admitted, that, in order to effect this desirable end, two kinds of good government are essential — DOMESTIC as well as NATIONAL. The widest political institutions cannot avert the natural consequences of individual vice; but such is the force of individual virtue, that were a nation truly civilized, a vicious government could not exist. If this be true, why not make public education apart of our scheme for obtaining political reform. Why not educate our youth to public as well as to private virtue? He who is not a good citizen is but half a social man. It is by the progress of intelligence and morality that the melioration of political institutions has been effected. The change of human laws, the modifications of their severity, together with that of the kinds of punishment, which have been effected from time to time, are so many barometrical indications of the, existing state of morality and social improvement in the great body of the people, and of the decree of enlightened humanity in the governing mind, at the different periods at which they have taken place. In proportion as man becomes enlightened and moral, in such proportion he learns to appreciate his natural rights, and to husband his moral force. The iron rod of power is no longer necessary to restrain him from the commission of crime, whose corrected, judgment leads him to abhor it. Tyranny is the natural concomitant of ignorance and barbarism, and despotism the baby-step of civilization. How important, then, it is, that moral and political knowledge should be extended to the great mass of the population; that in all our institutions for the dissemination of knowledge to the working classes, the best possible means should be adopted for the formation of character and the development of mind.

As one great means to this desirable end, it behoves the working classes to cultivate a proper and becoming pride, and to support, by consistency of conduct, the enlightened efforts of that portion of the rich who are sincerely anxious for their welfare, and have laboured to promote it. The formation of a character in the rising generation, which shall be equal to the task of assisting in the obtaining and securing of wise political institutions, demands a change in the system of our moral teaching. Let its principal bearing and tendency be to increase the moral dignity and happiness of man upon earth. Listen to the language of the celebrated Adam Smith— "Wherein consisted the happiness and perfection of a man, considered not only as an individual, but as the member of a family, of a state, and of the great society of mankind, was the object which the ancient moral philosophers proposed to investigate. In that philosophy, the duties of human life were treated of as subservient to the happiness and perfection of human life. But: when moral, as well as natural philosophy, came to be taught only as subservient to theology, the duties of human life were treated of as chiefly subservient to the happiness of a life to come. In the ancient philosophy, the perfection of virtue was represented as necessarily productive, to the person who possessed it, of the most perfect happiness in this life. In the modern philosophy, it was frequently represented as generally, or rather as almost always inconsistent with any degree of happiness in this life; and heaven was only to be earned by penance and mortification; by the austerities and abasements of a monk, not by the liberal, generous, and spirited conduct of a man."

There is a saying, that "the poor shall have their good things hereafter, whilst the rich shall be sent empty away." Enlightened humanity cries with an unceasing voice,—let the poor enjoy as much as possible of good things in this life, and let all the virtuous, the humane, and the truly patriotic, unite to obtain them the restoration of prosperity, and labour to give them the moral and political knowledge that will enable them to secure it. We live at a period when the exciting causes of political changes are peculiarly active; and when, as I have before remarked, the apology for the limited extension of acknowledged political rights, to the great body of the people, is their political ignorance and moral degradation. "Till recently," says Mr. Mill, in the article which I have before quoted, "it was denied that intelligence was a desirable quality in the great body of the people; and as intelligence is power, such is an unavoidable opinion in the breasts of those who think that the human race ought to consist of two classes— one, that of the oppressors—another, the oppressed. The concern which is now felt for the education of the working classes, shows that we have made a great step in knowledge, and in that genuine morality which ever attends it." That concern, however, has hitherto manifested itself almost exclusively in the teaching of physical, not of moral and political science. And when the friends of good government ask for a restoration of the rights and privileges of the people, the answer is, they are not prepared to receive them; they are not yet sufficiently informed on political subjects. "Give them political knowledge," say the former. "They are not prepared to receive it,—they have not sufficient knowledge to be entrusted with it," reply the latter. Heaven save the mark! They are too ignorant to be taught; so that ignorance is not only made the apology for injustice, but also for the continuation of its own existence! Can we separate man from the political events of the times in which he lives; and if not, is knowledge or ignorance most preferable?

Human life is a series of experiments for the discovery of human happiness; and whatever is admired as great in the result,—whatever is acknowledged as wise or beneficial,—every part of the mental edifice which is looked up to as politically great or morally good, in the aggregate of human institutions, is the gratifying results of education to man,—the hallowed witness of the happy and redeeming influence of the extension of knowledge. Let us, then, labour to increase the sum of that knowledge; for unlike every other species of capital, it increases by division, and leaves the distributor richer. The institutions of a country are valuable only in proportion as they tend to promote the general welfare; and as it is impossible to separate the individual prosperity of a nation from the political circumstances by which it is influenced, it is a duty of paramount importance to themselves, that they should become acquainted with the general tendency of measures which involve consequences of such serious import. Let it be remembered, that the melioration which has hitherto taken place in the government of society and the happiness of man, is the result of comparatively a very partial education. How glorious will that result be, when "knowledge shall cover the land, as the waters cover the bed of the sea!" When true patriotism and the love of mankind shall glow in every bosom, and when the practice of morality shall have convinced man that there is a heaven of peace and happiness for him even here upon earth! The practical end of all our institutions must be devoted to the melioration and perfecting of the moral, physical, and intellectual state of the poorest and most numerous class of society; and then our political millenium [sic] will be at hand. Let us not despair of its attainment; for human society is not retrograding. "The age of gold" which a blind tradition has hitherto placed in the past, is yet to come. Its dawn is approaching. The doctrine of human degeneration, and its afflicting consequence, increasing misery, is contradictory to reason, and in opposition to facts, Man is progressive, and human perfectibility is not a chimera; but that perfectibility cannot be attained until the great mass of our population is morally and politically free. All the corrupt interests are leagued against the progress of freedom and good government; and it is only by the union of the patriotic and the good, of both the middle and the working classes, that those corrupt interests can be shaken from their unhallowed situations. Their stronghold is the ignorance, the vice, the corruption of the many: remove that, and they shrink into comparative littleness.

Note

1 James Mill (1773–1836), political philosopher, educational theorist and author of the article "Education" for the 1815 edition of the *Encyclopaedia Britannica*.

18

THE FIRST TRUMPET. AN ADDRESS TO THE DISCIPLES OF ROBERT OWEN, ON THE IMPORTANCE AND NECESSITY OF SPEEDILY ACCOMPLISHING A BOND OF UNION OF MUTUAL INTEREST, FOR GRADUALLY CARRYING INTO OPERATION THE NEW SCIENCE OF SOCIETY (LONDON: J. BROOKS, 1832).

William Cameron

[A Scottish tailor, William Cameron was one of Robert Owen's earliest working-class supporters. In 1823, he had expressed interest in the Motherwell community, which he had wished to join. Later moving to London, he became a prominent figure in the local radical sphere. In 1832, he founded the Philosophical Co-operative Land Association (PCLA) on Cromer Street, London, to gather financial support for a community, and published the following *Address* to that effect. While Cameron's belief in community as the ultimate vehicle of true political change was typical of mainstream Owenism, his proposed means to achieve it were original. Unlike most Owenites in the 1830s, he eschewed co-operative stores and Labour Exchanges, which he both saw as a waste of time and resources, in favour of subscriptions and direct action on the land (Langdon 2000, 98–99). Cameron also opposed Owen's view, which the latter developed after the failed New Harmony experiment, that complete re-education should precede the founding of communities. In Cameron's opinion, theory and practice were inseparable, hence his wish for the PCLA to provide weekly meetings so that prospective members "may become acquainted with, and attached to one another, the better to prepare them for acting in concert, under the contemplated arrangements of community" (*Cosmopolite*, 30 June 1832, cited in Langdon 2000, 99).]

THE FIRST TRUMPET

FRIENDS,

You who have satisfactorily inquired into the social Science of Society;—who, from time to time, have exhibited to one another, and to society generally, clear and manifest proofs of your ardent attachment to its interest, by past exertions in the co-operative cause; and who still indefatigably continue to persevere, amidst apathy, ignorance, and prejudice, in forwarding the benevolent views of the distinguished philanthropist[1]; under the sanguine expectation of ultimately witnessing his benign principles carried into beneficial practice:—to you, therefore, this Address is candidly submitted for strict enquiry and mature consideration.

The object of this Address is, the establishment of a compact and cordial bond of union of all those persons who are in reality disciples of the new system, *in deed and in truth*: in a word, that they constitute themselves into a *distinct class, or sect*, the better to carry into effect the advancement of the social science; and the sooner to realize for each and all, through the joint efforts of united sentiment, its incalculable advantages. The Union to embrace the fellowship of all of similar minds to be found throughout the three kingdoms; that all may act in concert with each other in the one great cause of diffusing universal love, by the formation of local associations, guided by such laws as are in accordance with professed objects, calculated to produce the new state of things. Such a union as is here, slightly noticed—such a system of mutual organization would doubtlessly ensure success; public opinion would thereby be increased and accelerated, gradually tending towards a complete consolidation of the general mass. To take a retrospective view of what has been done by MR. OWEN and his friends, in their attempts to introduce a something into actual operation; the necessity of adopting such a measure becomes the more palpably apparent to every reflecting mind. You are aware of what is here meant, as some of you were actors in some of the new dramas; and have witnessed, with a piteous eye, the last scene of the piece, and—the curtain dropped; but, to *your honour*, have not ceased to shrink from the task of doing good; though disappointment, vexation, chagrin, the loss of wealth, of labour and of sleep stood in your way, another, and another rally, prepared the road for other formations—bidding fair for success at times; but dissolving at last: nevertheless, phoenix-like, you have as uniformly arisen out of the furnace of affliction, undaunted, still determined, to re-construct another more promising fabric. It cannot be hid, however, that your present condition is still as helpless, as the past was found to be forlorn: for, isolated as *you are*, while no bond of union exists—no fraternal tie of friendship—no care as to how you sink or swim in your struggles through life, in quest of a new state of being—your *efforts paralized* from following the *old system*, and *exhausting fruitlessly* in endeavouring to get up the *new system;* and what is there in the future, which the present would seem to indicate, that a change is at hand?—why nothing: and nothing can possibly be anticipated without union—a union of those who know and understand the workings of circumstances—the formation of character—the power, which *can* be rendered available through a well digested system of organization, capable of giving effect towards a speedy creation of *new* circumstances, that will usher into life the social science of society:—and *you* are the individuals with whom it now remains to lay the germ, in order that it may have birth. You have identified a part of your system with the practice of the "Primitive Christians"—'in their having all things in common', with the "Society of Friends"[2]—in their morals, cleanliness, and respectability—'the result of the formation of character;' with the "Moravians, Rappites, and Shakers"[3]—'as working communities;' and with the "St. Simonians," in France, whose objects, you say, are nearly the same as yours, viz. 'an equal system of education, and equal means of enjoyment.' '*They* are making rapid progress on the Continent'—are coming into high repute'—'nine in ten are reported to be *literary* character;' 'and a number of them possessing *extraordinary merit!*'—'are capable of supporting a *daily* Paper, and can even afford to give it away gratuitously: moreover, *can support the charges of travelling Missionaries!*' Let us again apply the glass of the mind's eye, and take a more extensive view of the past. From the year 1817 we may date the commencement of Mr. Owen's public career: since that period, a vast fund of co-operative information has diffused itself all over the country; experiments on large and small scales have been attempted; various Cooperative Societies have been formed; and considerable sums of money have been expended by bodies and individuals. What has been intrinsicly [sic] gained from all that has been said or done? Knowledge, certainly; but have any of the actors been made a whit the better in their untoward circumstances; who constitute but a small fraction compared to the population of the world, which the system is intended to embrace? '*They have been made worse.*' What did Orbiston, Harmony, and Devonshire effect?[4] From which, at least, *some* good was anticipated. Little good, however, was anticipated on the part of those who possessed the power of discrimination, touching—'the formation of character;' *they* expected that the wisdom of the founders would have led them to make a *complete* selection of character, instead of an indiscriminate admission of individuals, actuated by no common internal regulating principle, as regards the simple proposition—"That, in proportion as every one knows and endeavours how and in what manner to promote the good of the whole community, would be the amount of happiness and prosperity enjoyed by each individual." In not attending to this grand pre-requisite,* Mr. Combe[5] was evidently foiled as to what

---

* Regarding the Establishment at Orbiston, let it be understood on the part of the public, that Mr. Owen had no connexion with it. It was got up in consequence of Mr. Owen having abandoned the Motherwell Community, choosing rather to close in with the offer made by Count Rapp, of the Harmony estate; which could be purchased at the cost required to complete that establishment. Mr. A. Combe was the chief proprietor of the Orbiston establishment; and A. Hamilton, of Dalzell, the principal proprietor; whose names will ever be held dear by all the 'friends.' Had they been better assisted in the commencement, so as to have enabled them to create a producing power from within, in order to command a return of capital, the inhabitants would not have been such a drag upon those philanthropic individuals, who from time to time generously yielded supplies. From the want of a sufficiency of capital, its failure is attributed: the evils of 'indiscriminate admission.' Experience would lead to a cure.

he had previously imagined would have followed by the operation of surrounding circumstances; that is, 'he supposed' that the heterogeneous collection of individuals, comprising a variety of existing character, would in time become as one, in morals, religion and politics; one in sentiment, and one in action: had there been no other operating cause, *that*, of itself, if persevered in, was quite sufficient to have produced a failure. Harmony, also betrayed *its* symptoms of purblind philosophy. Persons from all quarters of the States flocked to the place; treble the number appeared than could be received; and the hearts of the friends at home leaped with joy at the flattering tale. Upon Mr. Owen's return to England, he met with a few staunch disciples at Red Lion Square,[6] who had not been idly employed during his absence, in giving scope to the system: it is needless to say, 'he was greeted' by all, as all were elated by the intelligence he had to communicate; still there existed the smothered doubts of the more penetrating in point of success, from Mr. Owen having overlooked the proper selection in living materials; at the same time, there were three pre-requisites required to guarantee an admission of membership, viz. a good moral character, a knowledge of some useful trade or occupation, and a knowledge of the system of mutual interests; yet, they were unknown to each other as such; consequently, the place constituted *New Harmony*, became at last *Old* Harmony indeed. Nevertheless, though this sombre state of things lay in the futurity of time, a number of the friends then expressed their anxiety to cross the Atlantic; but were fortunately prevented, on being told—"You need not, my friends, put yourselves to the trouble of going to America, the social system is applicable to all countries, and to all places: for in the course *of a few years*, I expect to see you all comfortably situated *within* communities!" "As the time has arrived !! when, &c." (The general who hazards an undisciplined army of raw recruits into the field of action, allowing that one in five have been trained to war, whilst the opposing foes is five to one advanced in skill, how in the course of *things* could he succeed?) The readers are left to apply the case. It is somewhat astonishing, however, that neither Mr. Owen nor Mr. Combe was solicitous about such a very essential step; had the friends of the system had a fair preponderance in point of number, the reverse, in all likelihood, would have taken place.

The friends of Red Lion Square, not being content to trust *too long* to hope, issued a prospectus for commencing a community within fifty miles of the metropolis.[7] You are aware of what followed the news of "the New Harmony Community" being abandoned, or what was termed "the Preparatory Community," or "Half Way Community, &c."[8]— ten small colonies came next into being, said to be composed of persons who had voluntarily agreed to associate together under more promising auspices, by and with such congenial minds, as could be brought within each of their respective circles. Some short time after, it was reported that they were flourishing and doing *well*: but since that, no news has as yet been received on this side of the water as to the state of their success; and silence warrants the conclusion, that *they neither* have been destined to see "That glorious day." Well. What next? Mr. Thomson, [sic] the principal projector of the London Community, determined that nothing should prevent his getting up an experiment, obtains land in Ireland, and generously offers it in behalf of the cause: expectations are again raised; but, alas, no success![9]

Previous to this, MR. OWEN is requested, on the part of several extensive proprietors, to take the colonization of a large tract of land in the province of Texas, in South America: he proceeds on his journey; arrives, and is kindly received by all; has an agreeable interview with the head bishop, who seems delighted with, and professes himself to be a *convert* to the new social science; and, in proof of which, promises to write to the Pope of Rome to *win him over* in its favour; but he did not succeed; as it is a law of the province, that *no* religion, except the *Catholic* religion, can be tolerated in the country; but the bishop, unwilling to part with his guest without imparting *some* rays of hope in reference to the future, declares that by *next* year a meeting of Congress would take place, and that *that* obnoxious law which stood in the way, would most probably meet with a hearty repeal. Whether an exchange of letters has taken place between the parties (the Pope included), either for or against, the "friends" have yet to learn.[10] Upon MR. OWEN's last return to this country, he found, to his surprise, that the principles of cooperation had not only taken deep root in the metropolis; but had spread over almost every county in England. The laudible [sic] and persevering exertions of J.V. of Devonshire, in rousing the attention of the working classes; the formation of "the Society for Promoting Co-operative Knowledge", with its unremitting labours; the enlightening periodical of Brighton[11]; and the contributions and donations cheerfully given by the rich and poor acting in the cause, could not fail of contributing largely to its advancement, and calling forth the attention of a discerning public. "The Revolt of the Bees," that inestimable work, pourtraying [sic] in striking language the situations of the two states of society, opened up a rich field for rational inquiry; in exposing the inequalities of wealth, through the misapplication and trickery of machinery and competition, in exposing the jugglery and crudities of political economy and over-population; in exposing the quackeries of government in affecting to ameliorate the miseries of unfortunate Ireland; and in exposing its cruel and vindictive penal code, and its wanton disregard of the morals and education of the people—a people starving in the midst of abundance. 'How great the contrast the amiable author holds up to view! Happy for society were such authors more numerous.' It therefore performed *its* share in furtherance of the great object—mutual co-operation.[12] The agreeable surprise, which MR. OWEN received, as to the progress of co-operative knowledge on the part of others, made him redouble *his* efforts.

The next series of projects, then, which fall under notice, is MR. OWEN's gracious interview with Lord Aberdeen and other Foreign Secretaries. A union of interests in trade and commerce between France, England, and America, constituted the ground work; and high expectations with the government are held up; but it turns out, that the Duke of Wellington (then in power) is said to decline granting a personal interview; at all events, he requests to have submitted to him a plan of the proposed Union—the thing at last drops, and sinks into oblivion.

Continuing, however, unshaken in the path of unwearied benevolence, a plan of arrangements for remodelling society now makes its appearance before the public; a plan which would have the tendency of keeping up the best feelings of charity and good will between poor and rich. The higher, the middle, and the lower classes, were each to inhabit distinct localities, which was to give to the whole the advantages of town and country, by all acting in concert—still he did not succeed. Fifteen addresses now find their way into the columns of the public press: these addresses are to various classes of society; calling upon them, in the strongest language possible, to *prepare* for a change.[13] Sunday morning lectures next engage the public mind; a place for that purpose is obtained, and the walls of the interior attractively delineated with the laws and objects of the new Institution, Burton Street.[14] A Synopsis is published and extensively circulated, containing the laws and regulations, creed, &c. of the Rational State of Society[15]: subsequently appears the formation of a committee, containing the names of men of rank and property; the object of which was, to introduce a system of colonization into Ireland, to supersede the necessity of poor laws being resorted to in behalf of that country. Whether there are any hopes in reserve favourable towards that laudible [sic] object, a report has yet to be made; the committee, however, seems, from its silence, to have died a natural death. *"Why should Ireland be thus deserted, as is the laws of nature had doomed her to perpetual misery?"* was an exclamation energetically and feelingly expressed on the part of the distinguished philanthropist, at a public meeting held in the City of London Tavern[16]; at a time too, when poor Ireland was suffering great and unparalleled distress: finding he could not then soften the adamant hearts of those in power to bestow a grant in exchequer bills for her relief! And finding that their successors are a whit the less obdurate! To persevere in such a wayward track, appears to be the height of folly, and a waste of time. Well, what next—an "Institution of the well disposed of the Industrious Classes,"—"for beneficially employing and usefully educating ALL the unemployed and uneducated of Great Britain."[17] To prognosticate what *may* take place, as to whether units, tens, or thousands may, or may not *reap* those advantages, time has yet to determine. Its benevolent founder and governor has called it the little mustard seed, which is to bud, blossom and bear fruit, and to cover the whole earth—be it so: yet, it will not be hazarding too much, in relation to the magnanimity of the proposed project, to introduce *them* upon the present occasion. "If your person were as gigantic as your desires, the world itself would not contain you; your right hand would touch the east, and your left hand the west, at the same time: you grasp at more than you are equal too." Gain—but prepare your minds for its reception, pause after you have finished reading the sentence; gather together your past and present experience, and collect into a focus all your scattered thoughts, because the next saying is of saving importance: 'it is wisdom to the wise,' and it here intended to be to you a guide for the future. Well, "the business of every conquest is two-fold—to win, and to preserve."

Now, have you asked yourselves how long you have been converts to the system? Where are all my former associates? Have any of us become grey in the cause, and we still feeding on hope. Have the number of converts lately increased?—(supposing they have) will they continue advocating the system? And to bring the last question to a close; a question which should bring your energies into full play, or no play (as regards its answer), viz., have these young converts any thing more promisingly substantial to look forward to than what *you* have up to the present time *received*? Suffer then this kind hint to operate a little in consideration of the precept given, for the preservation and realization of yourselves, your cause, and its objects; that society may no longer treat you and your system's projector, as vain and deluded visionaries! It is to *you*, and *you alone*, that society looks up to for something practical; notwithstanding its members treat you as visionaries, because, it is solely your business to convince them to the contrary. The advice of the father to his sons, in the "fable of the Bundle of Sticks,"[18] is point in hand; with the *exception*, by the bye, that *your* father either overlooks, wilfully neglects, or does not intend to receive you as his children; but you acknowledge one another brothers: if then *he* has no counsel to give until he has *baptized* the *whole human race*; no counsel to *you*, who *ought* to be the objects of *his first love*; do, I beseech you, pay regard to the virtue of the fable, and *take care of your younger brothers and sisters!* Recurring to the past, it is a matter of surprise that the public press has ceased, as it were, from noticing what is going on at the late public meetings of the "Institution?" Did some of the leading journals overhaul their columns regarding all which has, from time to time, been projected, descanted upon, and held up to public view, with assurances which indicated that something would be effected by *this, that*, or the other arrangement, it would only go to verify the appellation given to the system—as being *visionary* throughout: because, in comparing a succession of results, they could scarcely come to any other decision: their silence, therefore, should rather be applauded than censured; aye, and until you can show *them* that you are in a fair way of practical progress. "The time is at hand;" "the time has now arrived, my friends;" "the new era has begun, &c." are expressions which have been repeatedly reiterated from paper to paper, and from ear to ear. You are well aware of the tenor of the fifteen addresses to the various classes of society, calling upon them in the strongest language possible, to prepare for a change; the expostulations, the promises, the warnings, and the *threatenings* [sic], were, without doubt, intended for the best of purposes, to awaken society from its morbid condition, to sense of the appalling misery existing around it; and, in being thus importuned, to lend a helping hand in calling into operation a better state of things: but what did these addresses produce? Nothing; ignorance, as a matter of course, will be the plea set up, as 'the cause of inaction;' *but let the knowing ones of the different grades first shew an example.* The language of the address to the conductors of the periodical press has probably been held in remembrance; and the late invidious resolution passed at the "Institution", in reference to their silence, has had its effects by two-fold! But are you not yet sufficiently numerous and wealthy to support a press of your own?* A word more about the addresses in question, and done. The one to the mechanics, artizans, and labourers contained a promise, that MR. OWEN would no longer seek to importune those in power; 'but least a mistake occur,' he so promised or declared in some subsequent appeal, that such was his avowed intention; and, that he would *now* throw himself upon the working classes. Since that, however, he has not thrown himself much out of his way, save the opening of the "Institution," yet, the fact is, to be successful, he must endeavour to catch the tide as it flows—"to win, and to preserve". The *name* of the Institution *merely*, without *other* substantial attractions, may for a while engage an audience to pay the rent for a season or two; but MR. OWEN must still keep in mind his promise to the working classes. I have said, "It is to you, and to you alone, that society looks up to for something practical." "What have the Owenites done?" 'say some sneeringly'—others, "Such a wild system never can success"—some again, "I should like to see it tried—MR. OWEN is a most benevolent man; he means good, but I have my doubts;" and, 'as to the mass,' how many are there who trouble themselves little about it? And should some of them be in the way of hearing any thing of the system being read in the papers or other works—"Oh!" say they, "enough of that, I am sick of it; pray read something else." You, therefore, must bestir yourselves, and shew society that you are henceforth unanimously determined to give the lie to ignorance and prejudice. Scattered as you have hitherto been, like sheep without a shepherd, without the connecting link of friendship to cement the ties of brotherly union; though your past endeavours have made additions to your numbers, they have only served to prolong your hopes. The revolutions of co-operative societies; the changing of names, men, and measures; the heartburnings, the vexations and consequent disappointments, arising from fraud, ignorance, and misguided republicanism, could not fail of yielding to the faithful disciple ought but bitter fruits; from which, its will be your greatest wisdom for the future to profit by: and, in proportion to your success, the misfortunes of your other brethren will the sooner be alleviated. A number of you have long struggled to obtain, by some one project, what would ultimately lead onward to comfortable independence, by weekly contributions and profits on goods and trade, with the view of locating upon land—the summit of your greatest wish; but your struggling has been to no great purpose. The community project, which emanated from the Birmingham Co-operative Society, afforded favourable prospects in the out-set[19]; yet it does seem, that a sufficiency of principle and moral courage is much wanted to secure such an excellent experiment. £30 from 200 Societies, backed by an intelligent co-operator, might be easily raised, did anything like unanimity exist among them; such being the lamentable case, it furnished another strong proof of the desirableness of missionary exertion; but even *that*, which was resolved upon at last Congress, 'as regards an appointment, has been *lost* in its application.[20] The

---

* All hail!! to the "CRISIS."

St. Simonians *know* how to act. What the Congress will do at its third sitting in April, time will divine: as to passing resolutions, nothing is more simple. It is highly probably, that "the exchange of labour system," will constitute considerable attention in the way of inquiry, which may, in all likelihood, upset the whole of its past proceedings; and *it* also, I am afraid, will have to give way in its turn to something new. As already noticed, 'a number of you have struggled long;' how many then can each of enumerate, who went hand in hand with you for a tolerable season, who have either gone asleep or deserted the cause? Where is —, —, —, men of rank, talent, wealth, of common honesty, and industrious habits? Some of them, independent of the contemplated circumstances, as set forth in the new social science; yet, did the science but once begin to dawn, would prefer the change. And where will your present admirers be in a few years, if you still mean to continue separated from being alive to each other's interest? In short, were I not fully persuaded of the powerful and irresistable [sic] effects which could be called into action by the operation of circumstances; the doctrine of which, is in very deed the lever of the system; which accounts for all the past and present circumstances which have taken place in the world—notwithstanding the variety of opinion, in morals, religion and politics; customs, habits, riches, poverty and crime: which, when once applied, will most assuredly root out of society every thing which engenders the curse of our race; and secure unto all succeeding generations the blessings of human life! If such could not be effected; instead of summoning you together, I would advise one and all—"to your tents, O Israel," and henceforth *content* yourselves and abide in them.[21] It is under this view of the subject, which prompts MR. OWEN to speak so universally of the system; his extensive knowledge of the formation of character, as founded upon the facts deducible from human nature; and, whilst reflecting upon what is wrong in society; and what might be made right; the comprehensiveness of his mind *propels* him forwards without reserve, in declaring to the public its impressions, couched in language of studied benevolence. *You* therefore *must* begin to make use of this mighty lever by the world of *command*. I grant, that you were badly assisted by the greater number of your help-mates; why, because patience and perseverance did not accompany knowledge: and knowledge being deficient, the power to overcome difficulties is lost to the whole. By making use of the lever, 'by the word of command' it is meant, that an organization of sentiment and action be forthwith established, to include *all* the disciples of the new science to be found throughout the country, governed and directed by the most intelligent of its votaries, under the most approved laws which can be brought to bear towards the mutual harmonization of the united whole. To test the sincerity of the friends, let it be understood—that nothing short of an approach to common property, (as far as present circumstance can make it convenient) will be absolutely required to carry the introduction of the system into something bordering upon a practical operation: and without *that* measure be cordially met by *all* classes, high, low, rich and poor, their pretensions to 'enlightened benevolence' 'to labour being the source of all wealth' 'numbers beings strength, and knowledge power,' they and their pretensions in the estimation of society are *sheer humbug*—deceiving, and being deceived as regards *themselves*; and forsooth, the public at large! Should the measure proposed, find a ready concurrence even on the part of a few, voluntarily disposed so to act; the die, for producing the new chain of circumstances may then be said to be struck of an extended line; indissoluable [sic] in its essence; sure of advancing in its progress, towards a nearer and nearer approach to that science of society; from which, it would be utterly impossible for any of its recipient to recede. Men of wealth, would then think of the propriety (for interest sake) of laying their fortunes at your feet: men of science, would come forward as teachers of knowledge, in consideration of the superior facilities the new system would give to each, for the happiness of both: the working classes, the producers of all wealth, would then really find, that the system was admirably calculated to awaken their supineness, when *they* saw the new commandement "reciprocal love," being generated in the first instance—*among yourselves!* Such being the base, you could not possibly fail of affording to the most sceptical, lively sensations of its efficacy; and in a desirableness to assist in extending the connexion would naturally follow in furtherance of an approximation, to human perfectability! [sic] Whether MR. OWEN has any such union in contemplation at some distant period or other, his writings warrant very little on the subject. What he meant by an exposition of his sentiments to be found in his two lectures, "on the advantages and disadvantages of religion"[22]—is best known to himself: but surely the classification which he so minutely characterises and delineates, bespeak something approaching thereto. The lectures in question were publicly delivered on October and December 1830, and were published accordingly; and, of 'Class No. 4,'[23] 'he thus speaks.' "These men look around them in *every direction* to ascertain in what manner they *must* commence *their* task, to accomplish the great and good objects they have in view; and, when a *sufficient* number of men, shall know what *is true*, and perceiving, place that truth in plain language before the public, all error must give way before them, and no government can resist their influence. The advocates of *truth* possess a moral power which sets *all physical force at defiance*". If there *be* not a *sufficient* number of converts to commence the task, what may be the amount required, hundreds, thousands, or millions? Of this, you are still ignorant. If you have not reached the smaller number, how long are you to linger; supposing its commencement depends upon a national conversion, either from public opinion on the side of the people, or, among their governors? If either is to be the case, you may safely tell your children, that your children may tell their children, that their children may tell another generation; and, that the next generation after *that*, need not look for any further advance than their great, great, great, great grandfathers were led to anticipate: but the very next generation that will follow after that, that, and *that &c. &c.* are *sure* to be the happy offspring (who shall fully realize even to the end of prosperity) *the golden vision of happy days!!!* To be serious, however; has not MR. OWEN from first to last bored too much at governments, foreign and domestic—in pushing the universallity [sic] of his object? The first few years are admissible: but to persevere, subjecting himself to repeated rebuffs, betrays a useless waste of precious time: hence, it is full time, he was beginning to act the part of—*what*—'a decided experimentalist.' Now attend to Mr. ROSSER, while I reiterate a fraction of his cheering "Thoughts on the new era of Society"[24]—"The knowledge of the formation of character is pregnant with the most important consequences, these consequences, the forerunner of the new era are immediate; they may be said to commence the dawn of the golden age, let us, my friends, *exert our utmost to expedite its arrival*; if we cannot obtain *all* that we wish, *let us endeavour to obtain all that we can.*" Listen again to the kindly feeling thoughts of another friend to human improvement! From "Thoughts on education, union of classes, and co-operation—occasioned by the late riots at Bristol."[25] The amiable author after having pointed out the causes which led to the tumults and destruction of property, puts the question: *where* shall we search for a remedy? He adds, "In the *immediate* association of *all* classes, and to the *utmost* extent, by kindly and familiar intercourse and *communion of interests*—by the abandonment of *pride* and *distance* on the part of the *rich*, of *supineness* and *jealousy* on the part of the *poor*—by the mutual offer and participation of all those advantages, *which, being shared, enriches the receiver, and impoverishes not the donor*". As to the conduct of co-operators, he says—"They do not inflame their audiences with political harrangues [sic], full of sound and fury;—they do not encourage opposition to any human being, or any one established ordinance;—they do not merely teach the vague doctrines of harmony and good will, and brotherhood, but demonstrate and detail the excellent means of applying these holy principles in a mode conducive to general happiness."

Now, whether MR. OWEN may judge it expedient or inexpedient, to commence with the present collective force, allowing that he *has* such an object in contemplation at some period of his existence; "ere the eye becomes dim, and the breath wax cold in the body"—at all events, let a general muster be made, and the collective opinion of all ascertained, and that within the shortest possible time: *and let every man and woman, reason rationally upon the merits of its importance.* Great impressions must have been made upon the minds of many of late years: greater still could be effected, by opening up various places in the metropolis, &c. for lectures and discussions: other learned individuals might be made available, to act in concert, who could arrange matters so as to keep up an alternate change of person and place;—with regard to this; I would fain allude to a few names, the names of persons who are generally deemed well qualified to be coadjutors in the great work; but I forbear—Yet, there is *one* that cannot be passed over in dead silence, viz:—the author of "An Address on the necessity of extending moral and political knowledge among the working classes." Mr. DETROSIER[26]—'Thou hast acknowledged the doctrine of circumstances, and its efficacy: let the enlightened Philanthropist not dispair [sic] of meeting his due reward; for, although society as at present constituted, hold out little or no encouragement to moral regenerators, save in the cultivation of *Physical* science, the time must come, when it shall be otherwise—go on, exerting thy energies—form a centre; and in the mean time seriously consider the importance of the proposed union: knowledge is most successfully acquired and disseminated by united endeavours'—Ah! But that requires organization; and brings us back to the union of interests: nothing permanently effective can proceed from isolation: it would be a waste of time to say much more upon its importance, its necessity, and its incalculable utility. The subject of discourse should now be—has there been enough said and written—has there been enough of money and labour expended that will guarantee a fair trial (judging that your past labours have not been uselessly employed;—that they have not been like water spilt upon the ground which cannot be gathered up again) are we still to draw upon the resources of the humane and enlightened from day to day: while one becomes stripped—a second becomes soured—a third careless, and a fourth let to the vacillating motions of mind, of time, and of pence—the services of the first forgot, or his person shunned—of the second and third, indifference and contumely—but the fourth, 'how are you to day sir'—have you heard of our progress? Had we only so and so—we would, &c. &c. Now pay strict attention to what follows:—

Were the wealthy placed in the situation of the working classes, having nothing to support them but what they had to expect from the fruits of their industry; and, whether or not they were in possession of a knowledge of the new science, with what they do know of political economy, they would soon emancipate themselves from a continuance of misery—a second generation would not pass away ere that would not be fully accomplished: not even the fourth of the time: place any portion of them in such circumstances (say one hundred) and the same effect would result from the united few, as it would from the united many. 'This you will say' would arise from knowledge and union, 'Yes,' the first prerequisite you have, or ought to have; and that in a superior degree, is you have really satisfactorily made the social science a subject of inquiry? But the second pre-requisite—union, you want, without which you will ever remain powerless and imbecile: presumptuously proud however, that by to-morrow or next day, or the next after *that*, you yet will accomplish great mighty things. If the day star has dawned in each of your minds—shew to society it has arisen in your hearts: if the numerical rays have hitherto twinkled within remote and detached spheres—henceforth encircle and revolve upon one common orb; and, by thus giving testimony to its splendor, others will become erradiated [sic] in their turn, still adding to the effulgence of the scene; gradually tending towards the general and universal illumination of a benighted world. Having got this length in the prosecution of the Address, I have just fallen in with a slip of paper—headed "New Religion, or universal bond of unity, affection and confidence; founded upon indisputable facts, intended to remove the present agitated state of men's minds, and to relieve them by a system of prevention from moral and physical evils."[27] It contains, the *facts* on which the new religion is founded—the creed, &c. &c.—declaration of principles for practice; and convictions produced by the preceding facts, creed and principles. Your attention is requested to article 5th, under "convictions produced"—"That before this system can be successfully commenced, *governments* must be convinced of the truth of the principles on which it is founded!" How does that declaration harmonize with the declaration quoted from "The advantages and disadvantages of Religion?"—turn over the leaf and compare the two together—their consistency is much of a piece with the facts on which the *new religion* is founded, for the creed does not admit of what religionists would call '*bona fide* facts'; hence, its treats all ceremonial worship as useless service: herein MR. OWEN has greatly erred; beware therefore of calling the system by the name of "*New Religion*". Well, governments must be first convinced &c. before the system can be successfully commenced—what consolation, and what contradiction politics and religion afford—Yes, *governments* will be convinced, when priests are convinced of the "*new religion;*" may *he* live to see it; but do you keep in mind—"the Bundle of Sticks"—"the Mouse and the Lion," and "the Crow and the Jug",[28] and be guided more by principle than by precept; by measures more than men, as founders of systems may themselves be deceived. Religion having been accidentally introduced, it may not be amiss to remind you of the repeated asseverations of some of its more acute advocates, who have cheerfully gone with you a part of the way, as pioneers of the new system: but, like Lot's wife, have stopped short on the road and looked back upon old society with greater complacency than ever. What then is this: MR. OWEN's system will *never* succeed, without it be *based* upon religion: and MR. OWEN has said, "that religion is the very bane of society; and yet, he has called the system a "new religion!" Ten years ago, the Edinburgh Christian Instructor was led to designate Mr. OWEN a Nondescript."—A Monster in the moral world"—the first epithet still holds good, and *cannot* be withdrawn as regards 'religion:' the second is alone applicable to those, whose interest it is (by religion) to permit and perpetuate the moral monstrosities which exist in society, to the degradation of its base (religion) the materials of whose superstructure should be every thing that is good, lovely, and desirable; but, like your system, it has yet to be tried. Society has all along been theorizing; there has been almost nothing else but theory; the theory of the one has been long tried: for ignorance sake—for humanity sake—and for virtue sake, it is more than full time for another system to be substituted in its place. To aver that the system never will success, without being based upon religion; this will be acknowledged, when it is ascertained which, of all the known religions, is the best religion for the whole human race; and that fully proven by the common consent of its several votaries; till that *is* done, have nothing to do with religion? In addressing you as the disciples of MR. OWEN, let it be understood, that I do not wish that you should follow him any farther than his doctrines appear consistent with demonstrable fact; '*this is also his most decided desire*; but take proper heed to what may be deemed expedient, accommodating, &c. Now, my friends, to draw nigh to a close: by this time, it is presumed, you have passed some judgment on the proposed union; and that the result has been favourable; if not on the part of many, at least on the part of a few—of a few, resolutely determined to put the system in a fair way for practical operation, with that degree of zeal and enthusiasm, which true knowledge directs and love imparts to the genuine sons of the social science, in the prosecution of their great object. If, then, only a few but heartily concur together for the purpose of forming a *nucles* [sic], they may then, 'but not till then, begin to date the commencement of '*a new era*'. Suffer not one another to languish under your present devided [sic] circumstances, without affording yourselves more tangible hopes: like the rest of mankind, you have cares, trials, and disappointments to contend against; and your object is to alter that system. Why brood over them much longer—to be continually telling yourselves and society, that all suffer in a country abounding with plenty; and that union is strength, knowledge power, and labour wealth? Whilst you, who tell the people all this, and do not set an example, is passing strange! Let these professions be at once brought to the stake, that society may be the better enabled to judge of their merits, *and of your sincerity*; and, as already noticed, nothing short of an approach to a communion of property, on the part of the adherents of the new system, will be the test of their soundness in the faith. Let a preliminary meeting take place, and all the friends, who are known as such, be invited to give their attendance. All the advantages rendered available by co-operation would, under such a union, be better reduced to practice; and the benefits arising therefrom, made more certain and secure. Say, each subscribes to a fund, according to his circumstances, in proof of a willingness to bear and make light [of] one another's burdens, while sojourning through the paths of competition; and let that fund, or the greater part thereof, be appropriated towards purchasing or renting LAND. Thus, I have sounded the trumpet—I have given the first blast; he that hath ears to hear, let him hear; and in hearing, learn to understand, *what is his true interest*. Lo! the Saint Simonians have taken up theirs—a herald from Gaul has arrived on your shores[29]—an address has gone forth—the saint, the politician, and the philosopher of every rank and sect, are invited to listen to the sound; but follow them *no* further than their steps mark out to you, that such are rational? If religion is to have the precedence of philosophy, now is the time to enter the field of competition, as to who shall best effectuate the greatest possible amount of good. It is absolutely necessary that a fair trial of each should be made: do you not trifle away your time much longer. The eminent of past past ages have progressively urged upon mankind an attention to future prospects; and, of late years, those future 'prospects of society' have become more and more popular with the present generation: nothing will effect that sooner than a union of all those who are convinced of the utility of the change, and are willing to manifest charity towards each other, on account of religious difference; whatever be their religious belief, their rank, or their skill. Such, therefor, possessed of such knowledge should strenuously co-operate without further delay; and proclaim to the world, that the long-looked-for Millenium [sic] shall no longer wait for *practical* measures to secure its approach. The clergy possess a power that is omnipotent, did they but go hand in hand in the task of doing good. The philosophically enlightened possess omnipotent sway, did they but make known their numbers, and give testimony to moral courage: void of this, nothing can be anticipated! The want of which makes them the prey of malevolent laws, arising from the existence of malevolent opinions; and their supineness subjects them to persecution, imprisonment, ignominy, and reproach—hypocrisy, desertion and cowardice! It was shrewdly remarked by an old friend to physical and mental liberty, "that the manner in which MR. OWEN combatted error, no jury could possibly find him guilty of transgression." Let all interested in the diffusion of useful knowledge take the hint, and do likewise: as the St. Simonians are on the alert; let us see what we can dot in the contest for victory. However, to give both good encouragement, listen to the benevolent aspirings of *another* sincere friend to human improvement, from* a pamphlet lately published[30]; and let those of whom he speaks, those who are called the messengers of love and peace, no longer dare to sport with the sufferings of the people in the midst of existing poverty, while they possess the power of immediately giving to society a noble and generous example in their persons, in proof of the name they assume, and the respect which they claim. "If then," says our author, "if the ministers of religion would unite in this cause of holy brotherhood and charity, there would not be a single individual in Great Britain and Ireland, in five years from this time, feeling the miseries of destitution; and they might at once announce the Millenium [sic] to the gaze of a rapturous world. It is difficult to conceive how the Christian morality should ever be perfectly exmplified [sic], unless it be in communities: and the bishop or clergyman *who shall first come forward* with charity and intelligence to drawn men into communities, and denounce as wicked the individual accumulations of wealth, and the odious and demoralizing competition of trade, which are fast consigning three-fourths of society to ignominious beggary and despair, *shall do more for his country and the world*, than *all* the fires that blazed at the Reformation! Let him expect at first, opposition, obduracy, and derision; but, in a few ears, he shall hear the plaudits of all Christendom, and his name shall resound through the distant ages of futurity." Dr. Wade[31]—what say ye to this? The Rev. Messrs Groves, Hepburn, Gordon, Marriott, Dunn, and M'Connell,[32] come, form a league with thy class, and do make a beginning: prepare the way, in order that the starving multitude may receive, through your united exertions, a greater share of the good things on earth, the better to give them a relish for heaven. All that is wanted to bring about a consummation, 'that faith may give place to sight, and hope to full enjoyment,' is a combination of sentiment and action! And who more qualified to the undertaking than those who have spoken and written upon the subject? To conclude, and to leave those suggestions to your "candid inquiry and mature consideration," let me once more remind you of the *heartless* 'prospect' of waiting, upon the *conversion* of governments, or as to what may take place with *'future generations;'* which would require, on the part of the present generation, the possession of two things; that is, 'what Job had by nature,'— and 'what King Hezekiah received

---

* National advancement and Happiness considered in reference to the equalization of Property, and the formation of Communities. Effingham Wilson, Royal Exchange.

through grace;'[33] fully as much as the one, and a *trifle* more of the other. Now listen, before *I bid you* farewell*—"intellect cannot arrive at any great and illustrious attainment, however much the nature of intellect may carry us towards it, without feeling some pressages [sic] of its approach: and it is reasonable to believe, that the *earlier these pressages* [sic] *are introduced*, and the more DISTINCT they are made, the sooner and more auspicious will be *the event*." Well, look now to the scattered rods, the finger pointing, and the hand held forth—and behold the bird of Paradise hovering over you, with the cord in its bill, to bind you together in the bonds of Love and Truth! It *awaits* your assent—your *assent*—to UNION. To a *union* which will display the sterling tokens of reciprocal love—based, shielded, and directed by the dictates of *truth* and *reason*. And Love, Truth, and Reason, thus combined, will then teach your *friends* and your *foes, that such a threefold cord will* NOT *be so* EASILY *broken!*

Notes

1 Robert Owen.
2 The formal name of the Quakers. The group is traditionally attached to ideals of simplicity and charitable action. In the years 1813–1825, most of Robert Owen's business partners at New Lanark were Quakers, including the leading scientist and philanthropist William Allen (1770–1843).
3 The Moravians, Rappites and Shakers are three Protestant religious groups with a strong focus on a pared-down lifestyle, manual labour and communal living. Many of them had emigrated to America before 1825. Robert Owen bought the land at New Harmony from the Rappites' founder and leader, Johann Georg Rapp, with whom he had been corresponding since 1820 (Owen 1835, cited in Siméon 2013, 348). Overall, the communalism of these three groups had a strong influence on Owenism in America, and in the United Kingdom to a lesser extent. One of Robert Owen's earliest followers in the New World, the New York physician and health reformer Cornelius Blatchly (1773–1831) was also an admirer of the Shakers. As argued by Carol Kolmerten (1998, 42) "Like the Shaker missionaries before him, Owen converted many Americans to his communal ideas through the promise of equality in communal living, but, unlike the Shakers, Owen promised a utopia for everybody."
4 The Devonshire Community, was another short-lived Owenite experiment, like Orbiston (1825–1827) and New Harmony (1825–1828). The scheme was founded in 1826 by Jasper Vesey, a draper and a prominent member of the Devon and Exeter Co-operative Society. Vesey and thirteen colonists settled on a small farming estate, but he soon withdrew his financial support, thus leading to the community's collapse. Some of the residents formed another venture of their own, the Dowlands Devon Community, on a nearby farm. The latter probably folded by the end of 1827 (Harrison 1969, 218–219; Hardy 1979, 46–48).
5 Abram Combe (1785–1827), Owenite socialist, early co-operator and leader of the Orbiston community, Lanarkshire (see Part 5, Chapter 28, and Part 7, Chapter 43).
6 The London Co-operative Society Headquarters in Holborn.
7 See Part 5, Chapter 29.

---

* National Advancement, &c.

8 In the beginning, New Harmony was ruled according to a provisional constitution, while the community attracted an ever-growing contingent of would-be residents. In 1826 and 1827, opposition to Robert Owen's proposals for a definitive constitution arose, especially in relation to the expenses that the new regime would entail. Some also resented Owen's proprietorship of the New Harmony estate, asking for immediate community of property. By 1827, New Harmony had split into at least three dissident communities.
9 William Thompson. See Part 4, Chapter 23, and Part 5, Chapter 29. William Thompson's death in 1833 prevented the establishment of an Owenite community on his estate in County Cork. Though he granted the land to a trust of socialist friends that included his long-time collaborator Anna Doyle Wheeler, his family successfully campaigned against the project.
10 For Robert Owen's failed Texas community project, see Part 6, Chapter 37.
11 *The Co-operator*, edited from 1828 to 1830 by Dr. William King (not to be confused with William King, the London socialist and pioneer of the Labour Exchanges, see Part 5, Chapter 30). *The Co-operator* was an offshoot of Dr. King's Brighton Co-operative Benevolent Fund Association. Though he was not an Owenite, his publication achieved great prominence among British co-operators. J.F.C. Harrison credits Dr. William King with popularising the method of raising "capital for a community by means of cooperative trading" (1969, 255).
12 John Minter Morgan, *The Revolt of the Bees* (1826). See Part 2, Chapter 11.
13 Robert Owen, *The Addresses of Robert Owen, as Published in the London Journals, Preparatory to the Developement* [sic] *of a Practical Plan for the Relief of All Classes, without Injury to Any* (London: Stephen Hunt, 1830).
14 Burton Street Hall, Bloomsbury, was built in 1811 as a Particular Baptist chapel. The venue was used by socialists throughout the 1820s and 1830s. The London Co-operative Society's inaugural meeting was held there in 1824, and Robert Owen made it his principal meeting hall in the years 1830–1831, until he relocated his headquarters to nearby Gray's Inn Road (Colville 2011).
15 Robert Owen, *Outline of the Rational System of Society, Founded on Demonstrable Facts, Developing the Constitution and Laws of Human Nature; Being the Only Remedy for the Evils Experienced by the Population of the World* (London: B.D. Cousins, 1830). The book was re-printed at least fifteen times between 1830 and 1872, including an American edition (1839) and two translations in French and Welsh in 1837 and 1841 respectively (Thomas 2007, 36–40).
16 Robert Owen's speech was later reprinted as *Address to the Operative Manufacturers and Agricultural Labourers in Great Britain and Ireland* (1830).
17 The Institution of the Intelligent and Well-Disposed of the Industrious Classes, also known as the "Institution of the Intelligent and Well-Disposed of the Industrious Classes, also known as the "Institution of the Industrious Classes for Removing Ignorance and Poverty by Education and Beneficial Employment" was founded by Robert Owen in 1831 to federate his followers (Siméon 2017, 152).
18 Æsop's *Fable of the Bundle of Sticks*, also known as *The Old Man and His Sons*, advocates the idea that unity is strength.
19 For the Birmingham Co-operative Society and its community plans, see Part 4, Chapter 24.
20 The idea of appointing Missionaries did take root, however, and became a fixture of the later Owenite movement from 1835 onwards. For examples of writings by Social Missionaries, see this Part (3), Chapter 20, and Part 5, Chapter 33.
21 1 Kings 12:16.
22 Robert Owen, *The Advantages and Disadvantages of Religion, as it has been Hitherto Taught, in Forming the Character of Man, and in Governing the World; Containing*

an Address, Delivered by Robert Owen, to a Public Meeting in London, on Wednesday Oct. 20th, 1830 (Glasgow: R. Harrison, 1830).

23 The middle- and upper classes in Robert Owen's parlance. According to him, the "New Moral World" would be divided into four classes: the parish paupers (1), the working class (2), the working classes with property (3) and the "Voluntary and Independent Class" (4). The distinction was introduced as a basis for the formation of "Villages of Co-operation" in 1817, and was later used throughout the history of the Owenite movement (Owen [1817] 1858, 128).

24 Charles Rosser, *Thoughts on the New Era of Society: A Lecture Delivered at Mr. Owen's Institution, November 13th, 1831* (London: W. Strange, 1831). Rosser was a London Owenite and a frequent speaker on the socialist circuit (Claeys 1987, 153–154).

25 This pamphlet, published anonymously in 1831, advocated co-operation as an alternative to the climate of violent political tension that had led to the Bristol riots of that same year. Protests arose in the city after the House of Lords dismissed the second Reform Bill. The riots lasted three days, and were heavily repressed by the army.

26 See Part 3, Chapter 17.

27 An anonymous Owenite pamphlet from 1831, equating co-operative principles with a new creed.

28 Some of Æsop's fables.

29 Here Cameron presumably alludes to the first Saint-Simonian mission in Great Britain, carried out by Gustave d'Eichtal (1804–1886) and Charles Duveyrier (1803–1866) in January 1832 (Pilbeam 2013, 89–92).

30 The pamphlet was published in 1832 by Thomas Wayland (1800–?), a London Owenite who later emigrated to the United States.

31 Presumably John Wade (1788–1875), mostly known for his anti-clerical work, *The Black Book, or Corruption Unmasked* (London: Effingham Wilson, 1820–1823).

32 A list of Christian Owenites that includes Thomas "Tommy" Hepburn (c. 1795–1864), a Ranter preacher, Yorkshire coal miner and trade union leader; the Rev. Thomas Gordon, a contributor to the *Co-operative Herald*; the Rev. Joseph Marriott (1794–?), a Lancashire-based Baptist preacher, phrenological lecturer, contributor to the socialist press and chairman of the First Co-operative Congress in 1831; Christopher Blencoe Dunn (1798–1833), the Anglican vicar of Camberworth, Lincolnshire and a prominent co-operator; and Thomas MacConnell, a Finsbury radical and socialist lecturer.

33 That is, faith and a long life respectively (Job; 2 Kings 16: 20–20–21).

19

"LIVERPOOL - FIRST PUBLIC SOCIAL FESTIVAL AND BALL", LETTER TO THE EDITOR OF THE *LIVERPOOL CHRONICLE*, 29 NOVEMBER 1838, REPRINTED IN THE *NEW MORAL WORLD*, 1 DECEMBER 1838, 91.

John Finch

[In 1834, the collapse of both the Labour Exchanges and the Grand National Consolidated Trades' Union ushered in a second phase in the history of the Owenite movement, one geared towards a concerted effort to establish an exemplary community. To that effect, local Owenite branches played a key role, as they were deliberately designed to serve as educational hubs in the virtues of community. This report by John Finch (1784–1857), written on the occasion of the first socialist festival held at the Liverpool Hall of Science in November 1838, shows how leisure activities such as dances, public lectures, tea parties and banquets were designed as a "part-time version" of Owen's "Villages of Co-operation", especially as the Queenwood community project was getting underway (Harrison 1969, 188; Taylor 1983, 202–203). The intention was to foster bonds of harmony and mutual respect, hence Finch's insistence on sobriety. Temperance was popular amongst the early socialists, including Owen himself, as drunkenness was deemed incompatible with their ideal of brotherly love (Yeo 1971, 95). John Finch was an iron merchant and co-operator based in Liverpool. Born into humble circumstances, he was, in addition to his entrepreneurial activities, a keen Unitarian preacher and an active member of the temperance movement. He joined the co-operative movement in 1829 and became a personal friend of Owen's, whom he had probably met through the Rathbones, a prominent dynasty of Liverpool philanthropists. As one of Owen's closest lieutenants, he held key positions in the socialist movement. Appointed Secretary of the Liverpool branch of the Association of All Classes of All Nations from 1837 onwards, he was a frequent contributor to the *New Moral World*, and became one of the voices of orthodox Owenism.

A trustee of Queenwood, Finch was appointed Acting Governor of the community in 1839 (Rose 1958, 160; Langdon 2000, 88, n. 51; Harrison 1969, 103–104).]

The first public festival and ball of the Liverpool Branch of the Asosciation [sic] of all Classes of all Nations, and of the National Community Friendly Society, was held in the Clare-street school-rooms, on Monday evening last, at seven o'clock. About two hundred well-dressed males and females, principally of the working classes, sat down to an abundant supply of excellent bun-loaf, bread and butter, tea and coffee. A band of good musicians was in attendance, and the evening's amusements, consisting of dances, marches, songs, duetts [sic], recitations, &c., commenced at about eight, and were kept up with great spirit and mirth until twelve o'clock, when, as by previous appointment, and as it is intended to do on all future occasions, the meeting broke up, and all parties retired home, highly delighted with the evening's entertainment, and ardently wishing for its speedy repetition. Lemonade, gingeretta,[1] peppermint, &c., were provided for those who wished for them; but, as is the custom at all social festivities, congresses, &c, not a drop of intoxicating drink was used. Some slight inconvenience was experienced by the ladies in finding their bonnets, shawls, &c, at the close of the meeting, owing to the want of a convenient dressing-room for them, which we shall endeavour to obviate on future occasions. By these means, for the small sum of one shilling, for each male, and ninepence for each female, a rational entertainment, and a whole evening's amusement were provided, which far surpassed, in real enjoyment, any of the still, formal, gaudy pleasures of the wealthy, purchased at twenty hues the cost; affording, at the same time, to the members of our society, a foretaste of the pleasures that will be within the reach of every member of a community, male and female, every evening of their lives. "The kingdom of heaven is like unto a certain king, that made a marriage for his son. We strongly recommend tee-total societies, for their own sakes, to adopt this method of alluring the working classes from the besotting pleasures of the public house. For if these means be much longer neglected, they may depend upon it that their well-meant endeavours to reform our whole population, despite of all their preaching, praying, and hymn and doxology singing will, in the end, prove abortive; it will be impossible, by such means as they are now using, permanently to keep up the present excitement; the meetings will begin to be badly attended, the advocates will become discouraged, and many will fall back into their former habits of intemperance. So fully satisfied are we that this will be the case, that, in order to prevent it, we have determined to commence a tee-total society, from which all party politics, and all religion (except the religion of charity and good will) shall be excluded. We shall receive into our society persons of all religions, and of no religion at all, and shall confer office upon every consistent member of every sect and party; we shall allow perfect freedom of speech at every meeting, to every person, friend or foe, that attends; and shall endeavour to provide entertainments, such as I have described, for our members, as often as we can make it convenient Let us not be Liverpool; the fault does not rest with us. Many, we believe the majority, of our members, are good staunch tee-totallers; some have been efficient speakers and active members of their committees, against whom they have no shadow of complaint, except as to the way in which we worship our God; but they have reviled, persecuted, cast us out of their committees, and silenced us at their meetings. It is true they have not actually turned us out of their societies, kind souls; they still allow us to pay our money, and to sit still at their meetings and hear them abuse us "Father, forgive them, for they know not what they do." They are not aware that, by these proceedings, they have excluded five-sixths of the population of Liverpool from taking an active part in their proceedings, for they will find, by referring to the town mission reports, that not one in six of the working classes of Liverpool, regularly attend public worship of any kind, and that not one in ten has actually joined any religious society in town.

The following is an address delivered by the writer to the company assembled at the Social ball on Monday last, before dancing commenced— "Ladies and gentlemen—You are aware, or at least my social friends know, that the great principle of our system is, that 'The character of man is formed for him, and not by him.' This great truth teaches us that we ought to cherish and exercise no feelings but those of charity and kindness towards each other, and towards every individual of the human race. It teaches that 'man is the creature of circumstances.' Should there be, therefore, any among you not so well dressed as others, remember it may be owing to the poverty of their circumstances. Should there be any whose manners are not so polite, or whose speech is not so polished as your own, remember they have not been so well educated, or have not had opportunities of mixing in so good society, or gaining so much experience as yourselves. Another of our principles is, 'That all mankind are by nature equal' We are all equal when we come into the world—we are all equal when we leave the world, and no good reason can be given why we should not always remain equal. I trust, therefore, that there will be no aristocracy of feeling manifested among you this evening, but that you will treat each other with the greatest kindness, like children of one family. You have met this evening to be happy, and to make each other happy; you will not, therefore, be found quizzing each other's dresses, language, and manners, but each individual will do all in his and her power to put right those who are wrong, and to increase the general happiness; for, in fact, this, my friends, is the practice of our religion, which consists in "The unceasing practice of promoting, to the utmost extent of our power, the happiness of every man, woman, and child, without the least regard to sect, party, sex, or colour." I will not detain you longer from your amusements; I am very happy to meet so many of you upon this joyful occasion, the anniversary of the formation of our society; and it gives me particular pleasure to see so many of the fair sex among you. I hope that you will all enjoy yourselves, and that we shall have many such opportunities of meeting together."—I am, very respectfully, dear sir, yours, &c., JOHN FINCH.
Liverpool, 29th November, 1838.

Note

1 Ginger-flavoured lemonade.

20

"PROGRESS OF MORAL REFORM. MR. CAMPBELL'S MISSIONARY TOUR", *NEW MORAL WORLD*, 30 MARCH 1839, 362.

Alexander Campbell

[This document highlights the importance of political propaganda in the attempt to bring about the "New Moral World", and the key role that the Social Missionaries played to that effect within the Owenite movement (Royle 1998, 65). From 1834 onwards, the British Owenites developed a nationwide network of local branches. The Social Missionaries were 28 men and three women appointed by the Central Board, each of them assigned with the supervision of political activities and outreach within a given region. As the public faces of the movement, they gave lecture tours, spoke at the annual congresses and sent weekly reports to the *New Moral World* in an attempt to chart the progress of Owenite ideas and practices (Harrison 1969, 164, 185, 274). Alexander Campbell (1796–1870) was one of the longest-serving Social Missionaries, a charge he performed between 1834 and 1842. Originally a joiner from Glasgow, he was Owen's secretary at New Lanark for a while and later joined the Orbiston community in 1825, where he worked as the boy's schoolmaster (see Part 5, Chapter 28). Following the community's demise two years later, he was imprisoned for outstanding debts, but this did not abate his faith in socialism. Campbell was a pillar of the co-operative and trade union movements in Glasgow; he was jailed again in 1834 for editing an unstamped newspaper, the *Tradesman*. As a Social Missionary, he was responsible for the Glasgow and Paisley area. Campbell remained politically active after the end of the Owenite movement, giving lectures at the John Street Institution, London, and remaining faithful to the ideal of community through his involvement with the League of Social Reform (founded in 1849), which promoted home colonisation as a means to achieve social and economic equality (Langdon 2000 283, 297; Owen-Campbell Correspondence, 1828–1856).]

CHELTENHAM.—I arrived here on Saturday afternoon, the 16th of March, and found our friends busily engaged in preparing the new institution[1] for my course of lectures, the first of which was to be given next day. To any person but a Socialist, from the confusion of the place at six o'clock on Saturday afternoon, it would have appeared impossible that the place should be fit for the reception of an audience on the following day; but the spirit of Socialism soon became evident; carpenters, painters, glaziers, and other willing assistants, in a few hours change the place from a state of confusion to a comfortable lecture room, capable of containing 500 persons. On Sunday evening the body of the hall was well filled, and a number occupied the gallery. My lecture was on the religion of the New Moral World, compared with religion as it has hitherto been practiced, in forming the character of man. The respectable audience listened with breathless attention, and several times gave evidence of their feelings by bursts of applause, which I endeavoured to suppress. No questions were asked. On the evenings of Monday, and Tuesday, and Wednesday, I delivered a course of lectures, on "the best means of providing useful and beneficial employment for the working classes, and a rational system of education for all." On the two last evenings a young gentleman, a native of Glasgow, defended the present system of religious education, but, at the same time, he admitted that the social system contained many good points, and hoped soon to see a community commenced, in order to remove the "moral pest" which Socialists were producing in society. I have made arrangements for a public discussion at Cheltenham with the Rev. Mr. Cunningham, which is to take place on Tuesday, April 2nd, and two subsequent evenings; the question is to be —"Is Socialism radically erroneous, and injurious to the happiness of the human race?"

WORCESTER.—I arrived here on Thursday expecting to have a discussion with a Mr. Thomas Harris, who had written a letter in the *Worcestershire Guardian* against Socialism, in which he stated, that he was prepared to prove his assertions in any way before the public; but he had not consulted his "medical adviser" before he wrote his letter, for it appears from the "certificate" which he produced, that he is predisposed to inflammation, which would render it very dangerous for him to speak in public. Thus, for the present, has this "Goliath" of the old world retired from the contest.

BIRMINGHAM.—On Sunday evening, in the institution, I gave an account of my late missionary tour, to an overflowing audience, who appeared much pleased with the progress of the Social system. — A. CAMPBELL, social missionary.

Note

1 The local Hall of Science.

Part 4

POLITICAL ECONOMY

From the 1820s onwards, following the publication of Robert Owen's *Report to the County of Lanark* (1820), early socialists formulated a distinctive critique of classical political economy. Writers such as William Thompson, John Gray and John Francis Bray were some of the most prominent voices to emerge from that locus, while the issue of political economy was widely discussed in the socialist press. Others, like Thomas Hodgskin, were not directly affiliated to the Owenite movement, but their ideas were, nevertheless, instrumental in shaping an "alternative ideal of industrialisation, the division of labour, and commercial relations" (Claeys 1989, xv).

Divisions arose mainly with respect to the extent of state intervention in economic matters. Though William Thompson publicly resented Owen's dismissal of working-class democratic politics (see Part 5, Chapter 29), he fully embraced his system of decentralised, self-sufficient "Villages of Co-operation". Conversely, John Gray and George Mudie advocated economic planning as a remedy to the blind force of an unregulated market (Harrison 1969, 88; Claeys 1987, 71–75; Siméon 2017, 117).

Yet the socialist political economists had also much in common. All, following Owen's attempts at solving post-war distress, believed that the new industrial age had rendered traditional relief systems obsolete, and advocated the need for large-scale economic reforms that would benefit labourers. All shared the belief that the capitalist market and its offshoot, the factory system, were governed by selfish interests, and had thus failed to properly reward labour, in a blatant disregard for the wealth-producing working classes.

Due to their attachment to the labour theory of value, Owenite economists have often been labelled "Ricardian socialists", due to the writings on the concept by David Ricardo. Though Owen was personally acquainted with Ricardo, there is little evidence that early socialists – with the exception of Thomas Hodgskin – were directly indebted to him. It seems more likely that they took cues from Adam Smith's *Wealth of Nations* to establish labour as the sole measure of economic value, and therefore as the source of all wealth (Harrison 1969, 54; Claeys 1989, xxii–xxiii). Poverty was defined as the artificial appropriation of wealth by idle profiteers and middlemen. These unproductive classes – which, according to

Owen, but not to other socialists, did not include master-manufacturers like himself – had therefore no right to the produce of labour, which should be directed solely towards the creators of wealth under a fair, co-operative system.

The originality of socialist political economy was twofold. First, in keeping with the concept of "embeddedness" developed by Karl Polanyi (1944; 1957) it posited the constant overlapping of economic and social issues. This was at odds with classical political economy's assumptions that the laws of the market are independent and self-regulatory, thus framing the triumph of economic individualism and the depreciation of labour that followed the rise of modern industrialism as necessary evils. Second, this alternative view of economic phenomena was not seen as an end in itself, but as the stepping stone for a long-awaited "New Moral World", a new state of civilisation in which the fruits of technical progress would be enjoyed by all, for the good of all (Thompson 1984, 82; Claeys 1989, xxi–xxii).

21
REPORT TO THE COUNTY OF LANARK, OF A PLAN FOR RELIEVING PUBLIC DISTRESS (GLASGOW: WARDLAW & CUNNINGHAME [1820] 1821), 1–7.

Robert Owen

[In 1820, Robert Owen was invited to submit his plans for social and economic reform by a group of concerned Lanarkshire landowning philanthropists, in the context of the post-Waterloo crisis. The *Report* is a seminal text in the history of early socialist thought, as it provided the first refined version of Owen's economic theories. If one wished to bring about a system based on equality and co-operation rather than on competition, then a complete reorganisation of economic processes was necessary. This entailed the establishment of a new wage system based on the value of labour itself, in the joint quest for financial independence and fair profit. With this argument, Owen drew heavily upon Adam Smith's contention that labour is the source of all wealth. But his contribution to political economy was original insofar as he was determined to reward the workers themselves, not the middlemen who were appropriating the value generated by the labour of industrial, agricultural and artisanal labourers. The value of labour was thus determined not so much in monetary but in utilitarian terms, based on the producer's perceived contribution to the nation's economy. To ensure fair pay, wages would no longer be based on the unequal law of the market, but on labour time. Producers would earn their living in the form of labour notes, a paper money which could then be exchanged for various goods and commodities within the "Villages of Co-operation", thus putting an end to economic and social disparities (Siméon 2017, 97).]

The Evil for which your Reporter has been required to provide a remedy, is the general want of employment, at wages sufficient to support the family of a working man beneficially for the community. After the most earnest consideration of the subject he has been compelled to conclude that such employment cannot be procured through the medium of trade, commerce, or manufactures, or even of agriculture, until the Government and the Legislature, cordially supported by the Country, shall previously adopt measures to remove obstacles, which, without their interference, will now permanently keep the working classes in poverty and discontent and gradually deteriorate all the resources of the empire.

Your Reporter has been impressed with the truth of this conclusion by the following considerations: –

1st. – That manual labour, properly directed, is the source of all wealth, and of national prosperity.

2nd. – That, when properly directed, labour is of far more value to the community than the expense necessary to maintain the labourer in considerable comfort.

3rd. – That manual labour, properly directed, may be made to continue of this value in all parts of the world, under any supposable increase of its population, for many centuries to come.

4th. – That, under a proper direction of manual labour, Great Britain and its dependencies may be made to support an incalculable increase of population, most advantageously for all its inhabitants.

5th. – That when manual labour shall be so directed, it will be found that population cannot, for many years, be stimulated to advance as rapidly as society might be benefited by its increase.

These considerations, deduced from the first and most obvious principles of the science of political economy, convinced your Reported that some formidable artificial obstacle intervened to obstruct the natural improvement and progress of society.

It is well known that, during the last half century in particular, Great Britain, beyond any other nation, has progressively increased its powers of production, by a rapid advancement in scientific improvements and arrangements, introduced, more or less, into all the departments of productive industry throughout the empire.

The amount of this new productive power cannot, for want of proper data, be very accurately estimated; but your Reporter has ascertained from facts which none will dispute, that its increase has been enormous; that, compared with the manual labour of the whole population of Great Britain and Ireland, it is, at least, as *forty to one*, and may be easily made as 100 *to one*; and that this increase may be extended to other countries; that it is already sufficient to saturate the world with wealth, and that the power of creating wealth may be made to advance perpetually in an accelerating ratio.

It appeared to your Reporter that the natural effect of the aid thus obtained from knowledge and science should be to add to the wealth and happiness of society in proportion as the new power increased and was judiciously directed; and that, in consequence, all parties would thereby be substantially benefited. All know, however, that these beneficial effects do not exist. On the contrary, it must be acknowledged that the working classes, which form so large a proportion of the population, cannot obtain even the comforts which their labour formerly procured for them, and that no party appears to gain, but all to suffer, by their distress.

Having taken this view of the subject, your Reporter was induced to conclude that the want of beneficial employment for the working classes, and the consequent public distress, were owing to the rapid increase of the new productive power, for the advantageous application of which, society had neglected to make the proper arrangements. Could these arrangements be formed, he entertained the most confident expectation that productive employment might again be found for all who required it; and that the national distress, of which all now so loudly complain, might be gradually converted into a much higher degree of prosperity than was attainable prior to the extraordinary accession lately made to the productive powers of society.

Cheered by such a prospect, your Reporter directed his attention to the consideration of the possibility of devising arrangements by means of which the whole population might participate in the benefits derivable from the increase of scientific productive power; and he has the satisfaction to state to the meeting, that he has strong grounds to believe that such arrangements are practicable.

His opinion on this important part of the subject is founded on the following considerations:

1st. —It must be admitted that scientific or artificial aid to man increases his productive powers, his natural wants remaining the same; and in proportion as his productive powers increase he becomes less dependent on his physical strength and on the many contingencies connected with it.

2nd. —That the direct effect of every addition to scientific, or mechanical and chemical power, is to increase wealth; and it is found, accordingly, that the immediate cause of the present want of employment for the working classes is an excess of production of all kinds of wealth, by which, under the existing arrangements of commerce, all the markets of the world are overstocked.

3rd. —That, could markets be found, an incalculable addition might yet be made to the wealth of society, as is most evident from the number of persons who seek employment, and the far greater number who, from ignorance, are inefficiently employed, abut still more from the means we possess of increasing, to an unlimited extent, our scientific powers of production.

4th. —That the deficiency of employment for the working classes cannot proceed from a want of wealth or capital, or of the means of greatly adding to that which now exists, but from some defect in the mode of distributing this extraordinary addition of new capital throughout society, or, to speak commercially, from the want of a market, or means of exchange, co-extensive with the means of production.

Were effective measures devised to facilitate the distribution of wealth after it was created, your Reporter could have no difficulty in suggesting the means of beneficial occupation for all who are unemployed, and for a considerable increase to their number.

Your Reporter is aware that mankind are naturally averse to the commencement of any material alteration in long-established practices, and that, in many cases, such an innovation, however beneficial its tendency, cannot take place unless forced on society by strong necessity.

It is urgent necessity alone that will effect the changes which our present situation demands; one of which respects the mode of distributing the enormous supply of new wealth or capital which has been lately created, and which may be now indefinitely increased. To the ignorance which prevails on this and other subjects connected with the science of political economy may be attributed the present general stagnation of commerce, and the consequent distress of the country.

Your Reporter, undismayed by any opposition he may excite, is determined to perform his duty, and to use his utmost exertions to induce the Public to take into calm consideration those practical measures which to him appear the only remedy adequate to remove this distress.

One of the measures which he thus ventures to propose, *to let prosperity loose on the country* (if he may be allowed the expression,) *is a change in the standard of value.*

It is true that in the civilised parts of the world gold and silver have been long used for this purpose; but these metals have been a mere artificial standard, and they have performed the office very imperfectly and inconveniently.

Their introduction as a standard of value altered the *intrinsic* value of all things into *artificial* values; and, in consequence, they have materially retarded the general improvement of society. So much so, indeed that, in this sense, it may well be said, 'Money is the root of all evil.[1] It is fortunate for society that these metals cannot longer perform the task which ignorance assigned to them. The rapid increase of wealth, which extraordinary scientific improvements had been the means of producing in this country prior to 1797, imposed upon the Legislature in that year an overwhelming necessity to declare virtually by Act of Parliament that gold ceased to be the British standard of value.[2] Experience than proved that gold and silver could no longer practically represent the increased wealth created by British industry aided by its scientific improvements.

A temporary expedient was thought of and adopted, and Bank of England paper became the British legal standard of value;—a convincing proof that society may make any artificial substance, whether possessing intrinsic worth or not, a legal standard of value.

It soon appeared, however, that the adoption of this new artificial standard was attended with extreme danger, because it place the prosperity and well-being of the community at the mercy of a trading company, which, although highly respectable in that capacity, was itself, in a great degree, ignorant of the nature of the mighty machine which it wielded. The Legislature, with almost one voice, demanded that this monopoly of the standard of value should cease. But it was wholly unprepared with a remedy. The expedient adopted was to make preparations for an attempt to return to the former artificial standard, which, in 1797, was proved by experience to be inadequate to represent the then existing wealth of the British empire, and which was, of course, still more inadequate to the purpose when that wealth and the means of adding to it had been in the interim increased to an incalculable extent. This impolitic measure involved the Government in the most formidable difficulties, and plunged the country into poverty, discontent, and danger.

Seeing the distress which a slight progress towards the fulfilment of this measure has already occasioned, by the unparalleled depression of agriculture, commerce, and manufactures, and the consequent almost total annihilation of the value of labour, it is to be hoped that the Government and the Legislature, and the enlightened and reasonable part of society, will pause while they are yet only on the brink of the frightful abyss into which they are about to precipitate the prosperity and safety of themselves and the country.

The meeting may now justly ask of the Reporter, what remedy he has to offer, and what standard of value he proposes to substitute for gold and silver?

Before proceeding to this part of the subject he begs to claim the indulgence of the meeting for occupying so much of its time, trusting that the intricacy, difficulty, and importance of the question, added to the daily increasing poverty and distress of the working classes, (going on apparently without limitation,) and the consequent alarming and dangerous state of the country, will be accepted as some apology for him; and more especially when it is considered that he is not advocating any private interest, but simply stating a case in which the prosperity and well-being of all ranks in the community are deeply concerned.

To understand the subject on which your Reporter is now about to enter requires much profound study of the whole circle of political economy. A knowledge of some of its parts, with ignorance of the remainder, will be found to be most injurious to the practical statesman; and it is owing to this cause, perhaps, more than to any other, that the world has been so wretchedly governed; for the object of this science is to direct how the whole faculties of men may be most advantageously applied; whereas those powers have been combined, hitherto, chiefly to retard the improvements of society.

Your Reporter, then, after deeply studying these subjects, practically and theoretically, for a period exceeding thirty years, and during which his practice without a single exception has confirmed the theory which practice first suggested, now ventures to state, as one of the results of this study and experience, THAT THE NATURAL STANDARD OF VALUE IS, IN PRINCIPLE, HUMAN LABOUR OR THE COMBINED MANUAL AND MENTAL POWERS OF MEN CALLED INTO ACTION.

And that it would be highly beneficial, and has now become absolutely necessary, to reduce this principle into immediate practice.

It will be said, by those who have taken a superficial or more partial view of the question, that human labour or power is so unequal in individuals, that its average amount cannot be estimated.

Already, however, the average physical power of men, as well as of horses (equally varied in the individuals,) has been calculated for scientific purposes, and both now serve to measure inanimate powers.

On the same principle the average of human labour or power may be ascertained; and as it forms the essence of all wealth, its value in every article of produce may also be ascertained, and its exchangeable value with all other values fixed accordingly; the whole to be permanent for a given period.

Human labour would thus acquire its natural or intrinsic value, which would increase as science advanced; and this is, in fact, the only really useful object of science.

The demand for human labour would be no longer subject to caprice, nor would the support of human life be made, as at present, a perpetually varying article of commerce, and the working classes made the slaves of an artificial system of wages, more cruel in its effects than any slavery ever practised by society, either barbarous or civilised.

This change in the standard of value would immediately open the most advantageous domestic markets, until the wants of all were amply supplied; nor while this standard continued could any evil arise in future from the want of markets.

It would secure the means for the most unlimited and advantageous intercourse and exchange with other nations, without compromising national interests, and enable all governments to withdraw every existing injurious commercial restriction.

It would render unnecessary and entirely useless the present demoralising system of bargaining between individuals; and no practice perhaps tends more than this to deteriorate and degrade the human character.

It would speedily remove pauperism and ignorance from society, by furnishing time and means for the adequate instruction of the working classes, who might be rendered of far more commercial value to themselves and to society than they have yet been at any period of the world.

It would supply the means of gradually improving the condition of all ranks, to an extent not yet to be estimated.

And, as it would materially improve human nature, and raise all in the scale of well-being and happiness, none could be injured or oppressed.

Notes

1 1 Timothy 6:10.
2 The Bank Restriction Act 1797 (37 Geo. III. c. 45) suspended the obligation for the Bank of England to convert banknotes in gold. The measure was brought back between 1819 and 1821, thus causing deflation.

22

LABOUR DEFENDED AGAINST THE CLAIMS OF CAPITAL OR THE UNPRODUCTIVENESS OF CAPITAL PROVED WITH REFERENCE TO THE PRESENT COMBINATIONS AMONGST JOURNEYMEN (LONDON: KNIGHT AND LACEY, 1825), 83–92.

Thomas Hodgskin

[A naval officer during the Napoleonic Wars, and later a journalist, co-founder of the London Mechanics' Institute and socialist economist, Thomas Hodgskin (1787–1868) was a peripheral figure to the Owenite movement. Though he publicly dismissed Owen's belief in the community of property[1], his influence on early co-operators and later socialists was nevertheless strong, as his writings, often adapted from the classes on political economy that he gave at the London Mechanics' Institute (Hodgskin 1827), helped popularise the socialist theory of labour exploitation.[2] Published in 1825, *Labour Defended* was a response to James Mill's *Commerce Defended* (1808). In the context of the repeal of the Combination Acts, Hodgskin argued that it was skilled labour, not capital or commerce, that formed the most productive and dynamic element in the economy. Workers were consequently entitled to the full product of their labour, while trade unions should be allowed to "absorb profits into wages" (Cole and Filson 1965, 200–201), thus putting an end to the exploitation of labour by middlemen. The book became extremely popular in the co-operative movement, with positive reviews in the *Co-operative Magazine* (n°2, February 1825). Though his *Labor Rewarded* (1827, see Chapter 23 below) was partly a critique of Hodgskin's defence of free trade and free competition, William Thompson praised it as an "excellent pamphlet" (1827, 1) due to its support of trade unions (Prum 1994, 1–8; Stack 1998, 144).]

[…] Whatever division of labour exists, and the further it is carried the more evident does this truth become, scarcely any individual completes of himself any species of produce. Almost any product of art and skill is the result of joint and combined labour. So dependent is man on man, and so much does this dependence increase as society advances, that hardly any labour of any single individual, however much it may contribute to the whole produce of society, is of the least value but as forming a part of the great social task. In the manufacture of a piece of cloth, the spinner, the weaver, the bleacher and the dyer are all different persons. All of them except the first is dependent for his supply of materials on him, and of what use would his thread be unless the others took it from him, and each performed that part of the task which is necessary to complete the cloth? Wherever the spinner purchases the cotton or wool, the price which he can obtain for his thread, over and above what he paid for the raw material, is the reward of his labour. But it is quite plain that the sum the weaver will be disposed to give for the thread will depend on his view of its utility. Wherever the division of labour is introduced, therefore, the judgment of other men intervenes before the labourer can realise his earnings, and there is no longer any thing which we can call the natural reward of individual labour. Each labourer produces only some part of a whole, and each part having no value or utility of itself, there is nothing on which the labourer can seize, and say: "This is my product, this will I keep to myself". Between the commencement of any joint operation, such as that of making cloth, and the division of its product among the different persons whose combined exertions have produced it, the judgment of men must intervene several times, and the question is, how much of this joint product should go to each of the individuals whose united labours produce it?

I know no way of deciding this but by leaving it to be settled by the unfettered judgments of the labourers themselves. If all kinds of labour were perfectly free, if no unfounded prejudice invested some parts, and perhaps the least useful, of the social task with great honour, while other parts are very improperly branded with disgrace, there would be no difficulty on this point, and the wages of individual labour would be justly settled by what Dr Smith calls the "higgling of the market."[3] Unfortunately, labour is not, in general, free; and, unfortunately there are a number of prejudices which decree very different rewards to different species of labour from those which each of them merits.

Unfortunately, also, there is, I think, in general, a disposition to restrict the term labour to the operation of the hands. But if it should be said that the skill of the practised labourer is a mere mechanical sort of thing, nobody will deny that the labour by which he acquired that skill was a mental exertion. The exercise of that skill also, as it seems to me, requiring the constant application of judgment, depends much more on a mental than on a bodily acquirement. Probably the mere capacity of muscular exertion is as great, or greater, among a tribe of Indians as among the most productive Europeans; and the superior productive power of Europeans, and of one nation over another, arise from the different nature of their fixed capital. But I have shown that the greater efficacy of fixed capital depends on the skill of the labourer; so that we come to the conclusion that not mere labour, but mental skill, or the mode in which labour is directed, determines its productive powers. I therefore would caution my fellow labourers not to limit the term labour to the operations of the hands.

Before many of our most useful machines and instruments could be invented, a vast deal of knowledge gathered in the progress of the world by many generations was necessary. At present also a great number of persons possessed of different kinds of knowledge and skill must combine and cooperate, although they have never entered into any express contract for this purpose, before many of our most powerful machines can be completed and before they can be used. The labour of the draughtsman is as necessary to construct a ship as the labour of the man who fastens her planks together. The labour of the engineer, who "in his mind's eye" sees the effect of every contrivance, and who adapts the parts of a complicated machine to each other, is as necessary to the completion of that machine as the man who casts or fits any part of it, without being sensible of the purpose for which the whole is to serve. In like manner the labour and the knowledge of many different persons must be combined before almost any product intended for consumption can be brought to market. The knowledge and skill of the master manufacturer, or of the man who plans and arranges a productive operation, who must know the state of the markets and the qualities of different materials, and who has some tact in buying and selling, are just as necessary for the complete success of any complicated operation as the skill of the workmen whose hands actually alter the shape and fashion of these materials. Far be it, therefore, from the manual labourer, while he claims the reward due to his own productive powers, to deny its appropriate reward to any other species of labour, whether it be of the head or the hands. The labour and skill of the contriver, or of the man who arranges and adapts a whole, are as necessary as the labour and skill of him who executes only a part, and they must be paid accordingly.

I must, however, add that it is doubtful whether one species of labour is more valuable than another; certainly it is not more necessary. But because those who have been masters, planners, contrivers, etc., have in general also been capitalists, and have also had a command over the labour of those who have worked with their hands, their labour has been paid as much too high as common labour has been under paid. The wages of the master, employer or contriver has been blended with the profit of the capitalists, and he may probably be still disposed to claim the whole as only the proper reward of his exertions. On the other hand, manual labourers, oppressed by the capitalist, have never been paid high enough, and even now are more disposed to estimate their own deserts rather by what they have hitherto received than by what they produce. This sort of prejudice makes it, and will long make it, difficult even for labourers themselves to apportion with justice the social reward or wages of each individual labourer. No statesman can accomplish this, nor ought the labourers to allow any statesman to interfere in it. The labour is theirs, the produce ought to be theirs, and they alone ought to decide how much each deserves of the produce of all. While each labourer claims his own reward, let him cheerfully allow the just claims of every other labourer; but let him never assent to the strange doctrine that the food he eats and the instruments he uses, which are the work of his own hands, become endowed, by merely changing proprietors, with productive power greater than his, and that the owner of them is entitled to a more abundant reward than the labour, skill and knowledge which produce and use them.

Masters, it is evident, are labourers as well as their journeymen. In this character their interest is precisely the same as that of their men. But they are also either capitalist, or the agents of the capitalist, and in this respect their interest is decidedly opposed to the interest of their workmen. As the contrivers and enterprising undertakers of new works, they may be called employers as well as labourers, and they deserve the respect of the labourer. As capitalist, and as the agents of the capitalist, they are merely middlemen, oppressing the labourer, and deserving of anything but his respect. The labourer should know and bear this in mind. Other people should also remember it, for it is indispensable to correct reasoning to distinguish between these two characters of all masters. If by combining the journeymen were to drive masters, who are a useful class of labourers, out of the country, if they were to force abroad the skill and ingenuity which contrive, severing them from the hands which execute, they would do themselves and the remaining inhabitants considerable mischief. If, on the contrary, by combining they merely incapacitate the masters from obtaining any profit on their capital, and merely prevent them from completing the engagements they have contracted with the capitalist, they will do themselves and the country incalculable service. They may reduce or destroy altogether the profit of the idle capitalist – and from the manner in which capitalists have treated labourers, even within our own recollection, they have no claim on the gratitude of the labourer – but they will augment the wages and rewards of industry, and will give to genius and skill their due share of the national produce. They will also increase prodigiously the productive power of the country by increasing the number of skilled labourers. The most successful and widest-spread possible combination to obtain an augmentation of wages would have no other injurious effect than to reduce the incomes of those who live on profit and interest, and who have no just claim but custom to any share of the national produce.

Notes

1 Thomas Hodgskin and Robert Owen locked horns over the issue of private property during the inaugural meeting of the London Co-operative Society, held on 26 September 1825 at the London Mechanics' Institute. Hodgskin argued that communities would stifle individual creativity while positing a threat to free trade (*Weekly Free Press*, 2 October 1825, 181; Thompson 1984, 109–110; Claeys 1987, 197, n. 11; Stack 1998, 144).
2 Karl Marx extensively wrote about Thomas Hodgskin in the "Addenda" to his *Theories of Surplus-Value* ([1862–1863] 2000), the unfinished draft to the fourth volume of the *Capital*. Marx saw Hodgskin's insistence that skilled labour formed a set of "living knowledge" as a precursor to his distinction between "living" and "dead labour" (Prum 2012).
3 "There may be more labour in an hour's hard work than in two hours' easy business; or in an hour's application to a trade which it cost ten years' labour to learn, than in a month's industry at an ordinary and obvious employment. But it is not easy to find any accurate measure either of hardship or ingenuity. In exchanging, indeed, the different productions of different sorts of labour for one another, some allowance is commonly made for both. It is adjusted, however, not by any accurate measure, but by the higgling and bargaining of the market, according to that sort of rough equality which, though not exact, is sufficient for carrying on the business of common life". (Smith [1776] 1998, Book 1, chapter 5, 37).

23

LABOR REWARDED. THE CLAIMS OF LABOR AND CAPITAL CONCILIATED: OR, HOW TO SECURE TO LABOR THE WHOLE PRODUCTS OF ITS EXERTIONS. BY ONE OF THE IDLE CLASSES (LONDON: PRINTED FOR HUNT AND CLARKE, 1827), 75–88.

William Thompson

[Born into a wealthy family from Cork, William Thompson (1775–1833) met Robert Owen during the latter's tour of Ireland in 1822–1823 (see Part 9). As an improving landowner, Thompson approached socialism from a philanthropic stance, but his atheism, political radicalism and support for the French Revolution put him at odds with the rest of Owen's upper-class, earliest followers (Harrison 1969, 51; Taylor 1983, 89–91). In 1822, Thompson relocated to London following an invitation from his mentor Jeremy Bentham, who was also Owen's business partner at New Lanark. Despite his privileged upbringing, Thompson embraced the cause of working-class, co-operative Owenism and became one of the movement's most prominent intellectuals thanks to his anti-capitalist views (Langdon 2000, 15–16). Published in 1824, his *Inquiry into the Principles of the Distribution of Wealth* blended Owenite economics with Bentham's utilitarian calculus, arguing that human happiness could only be achieved through "complete equality in the distribution of wealth" (Harrison 1969, 63). As a follow-up to the *Inquiry, Labor Rewarded* (1827), explored how co-operatives could secure workers the entire produce of their labour. Against Thomas Hodgskin, Thompson argued that any system of competition and unregulated trade ultimately favoured the interests of capital against the labouring classes. Before a co-operative economy could be fully implemented in Owenite "Villages of Co-operation", Thompson recommended that co-operative workshops and, most originally, trade unions be set up as halfway houses towards a communitarian and egalitarian society (Claeys 1987, 100–102). With its insistence that labourers should "become capitalists"(p. 73) and therefore take full responsibility for the improvement of their condition, *Labor Rewarded* was immensely influential on the development of working-class Owenism in the late 1820s and early 1830s.]

Hopes too sanguine, it is to be feared, have been excited amongst the industrious of the direct efficacy of unions to increase wages. To give more energy to the principle of union or combination, we shall suppose it uniformly connected with prudence as to marriage; not that prudence which pretends to calculate the demand for children in a dozen years, but which refrains from increasing the number of children without the *actual* means of supporting them in what is called the comfort of their class.

Union Societies, or Combinations, endeavour to attain their end in different ways. Those which existed in a covert way, before the repeal of the combination laws,[1] always availed themselves in corporate towns, of the corporate laws or rules of excluding from labor or competition within their district, all those of their craft who had not served the number of years apprenticeship which the general corporation law or their particular guild regulations prescribed, though the skill of the new competitors might be ever so great. The craftsmen of a district monopolized the supply of the district; and by force, sometimes legal, sometimes not legal, prevented competition within the sphere of their power. The second expedient, common to all unions, for keeping up or advancing the wages of their labor, is by *voluntary* agreement amongst the industrious themselves of every particular trade, to forgo as against each other the selfish short-sighted advantages arising from individual Competition, and to join in mutual co-operation for the single and specific object of keeping to the highest that circumstances will afford, the remuneration of labor.

Of these two great expedients of Union or Combination, it may be remarked, that they both recognize, and direct all their efforts against, the evils of *individual competition*, of the efforts of individual workmen to undermine each other's reputation, and undersell each other's labour. The apprenticeship or excluding system, endeavours to accomplish the object of putting down the evils of individual competition, by *mere force*; and not only will not permit other laborers to *undersell*, but will not permit them to come into the market to sell at all, to offer their labor at any price. It signifies not whether that force, as in the case of corporations, be the gift of the law, or whether it be assumed by the tradesmen in spite of the law: it is equally mere force, unjustly depriving the skilled laborer of the right of exchanging his labor or its products for whatever equivalent he may be satisfied with: the grand principle of the freedom of exchanges, is violated equally in both cases. The expedient, on the contrary, by which *voluntary* unions endeavour to avert the evils of individual competition from their particular trades or departments of labor, is quite pure and unobjectionable: it seeks not to exclude any from improving themselves and exchanging their labor: it endeavours only to persuade them not to exchange it under the terms which the majority of laborers think actual circumstances will afford. Such voluntary unions cannot be prohibited without entailing upon society all the evils of Force, and Force-supported

Fraud. Let us keep steadily in view, that the main evil, which both corporation restrictions, depending on freedom, apprenticeship, and such like contrivances of ancient days, and voluntary unions or associations of the industrious of modern times, aim to guard against, is individual competition amongst the industrious themselves against each other. This species of competition they both aim equally to root out; the one by the gentle means of mutual agreement, the other by rude force, law supported or in despite of law. The competition between the capitalists and the industrious, employers and employed, or as it is variously called between masters and men, it leaves to work out its own cure, to find, by the "higgling of the market" amongst large masses, its level.[2]

Corporations were erected in times of ignorance, when lawless force and plunder overspread every country, in order to protect groups of the industrious against external attacks. The possessors of the largest quantity of governing power in every country, generally countenanced the associations of the industrious, to aid in reducing to their authority the possessors of smaller portions of power. It is quite pernicious to uphold under present circumstances, when industry is as much protected from direct open force in the country as in the towns, any sort of local privileges, which are necessarily enjoyed at the expense of society at large, in raising the price of commodities, and narrowing the market of labor for the industrious. The administration of justice, and the enjoyment of political and civil rights, should be equal and uniform through town and country. Labor and all exchanges should be every where free. The consequence of the high price of *trade-labor*, kept up by exclusions, legal exclusions rendered more operative by combinations necessarily secret amongst the men, in corporate towns, has been to keep away from such towns the seat of almost all large branches of manufacture, or of such as were liable to corporate regulations, for foreign supply, or for extensive home supply: thus demonstrating the inefficiency of force-supported regulations, though backed by political power, to keep up generally throughout a country the remuneration of any species of labor; though they certainly have tended, along with other circumstances, to keep up the remuneration to the few within the circle of the combination. When thus artificially kept up in corporate towns, it is always done at the expense of the equal right of the great mass of the industrious to acquire skill, and exchange their labor or its products, where and how they may. Corporation laws, putting down individual competition amongst the workmen, not by voluntary association but by force, must give way to those enlarged voluntary and peaceable associations amongst the industrious, which are now aiming to procure for manufacturing industry an increased portion of the products of its labor.

The word, *Combination*, having been used as a general legal term expressing many actions, some of them moral, some immoral, it may be well to dismiss it altogether, and to use always the terms, Unions or Associations of Trades, or Voluntary Unions or Associations. We shall thus avert the antipathy of those who cannot disassociate in their minds the ideas of way-laying and assaults from the term Combination.

Capital being in the hands of one set of men, labor in the hands of another; the *Industrious* seek to procure for their own use the whole products of their labor, or as near an approach as possible to this highest natural remuneration, by means of Voluntary Unions amongst all those in one place or district. They engage not to undersell each other for the same quantity and quality of work, but to abide by the decision of the majority as to the prices which circumstances may enable them to demand for their labor. These Unions of Trades being assisted by no corporation laws of apprenticeship or other similar expedients, being liable to the free competition of all not within the Union, must depend altogether on the knowledge and good habits of the members, for whatever partial success they may obtain in bettering their condition, by repressing amongst themselves the evils of Individual Competition; aided by some external funds added to their own wretched previous savings, to *keep them alive* in case of absolute disagreement with the capitalists, who are emphatically termed *their masters*.

The highest price which Free Competition will enable Unions of the industrious to obtain for their labor, is not anything like the products of their labor, but that rate of remuneration which will permit the capitalists in their line of industry to reap the same profits that other capitalists in the same line, or in other equally hazardous lines, reap from their capital. Why so? Because if any particular Union is imprudent enough to demand more of capitalists, they will transfer their capital to those other lines; or if they obtain higher wages than, as it is termed, "the trade can afford," the capitalists, proceeding in their usual rate of expenditure, (or, if the demands of wages be very unreasonable, even diminishing their expenditure,) will gradually lose their capital; at which period the remuneration of those exacting such forced wages, would of course cease altogether. This result, even the really benevolent capitalist, yielding what under the system of competition must be deemed extravagant wages, cannot avert; because, being liable to be undersold by other capitalists not only at home within the same country, but abroad in any part of the world, and the products of such cheap labor being, under free competition, admissible—and equal justice commands that they should be admitted—into even his own home market, he could not long, without ruin, continue his trade in competition with such rivals.

Hence it is evident that the benefit of these voluntary unions to the industrious classes, are almost entirely limited to times of ordinary and extraordinary prosperity of their trades. In a declining state of trade, particularly when the decline is no limited to a particular branch, voluntary unions to guard against the evils of the under-bidding of the industrious against each other, or to support those losing employment, must be inoperative. The motives arising from individual want become so strong, and the mass of misery so immense, during the decline or even stagnation of trades, that adequate relief is altogether out of the reach of unions. These are amongst the inherent, irremediable, mischiefs of the competitive system. The *finding the level*, is the sole and philosophic remedy for evils like these. The thinning of the number of the industrious by premature deaths, brought on, more or less quickly, by insufficient or bad food, exposure, dirt, and mental anguish, is the beautiful regenerating principle of the system of labor by isolated, individual exertion, or Individual Competition.

Here then we have the limit of the benefits to the industrious which the union of those of any particular trade in any particular district, can, in times of ordinary prosperity, effect. It will prevent wages from falling by individual competition amongst the workmen for any length of time, much beneath that remuneration which capitalists elsewhere give, retaining the usual rate of profits. Those of the industrious who are discharged by the avarice of individual capitalists for not underworking, being supported by the general fund of the union while out of employ, a very strong bar is thus raised by the industrious against any partial, unjustifiable reduction of wages, leading naturally to more extensive reductions, to privations, want, and misery. This is the utmost of the triumph to which such unions can look forward. They merely ward off a portion of the avoidable evil of the Competitive System. Every one of the Industrious Classes, however, who wishes to ward off from himself and his fellow-creatures this portion of evil, ought to be a member of such voluntary and peaceable associations.

But the competition of those of the same branch of trade in any one district being guarded against, the friends of Trades-Unions advance a step further, and invite those in similar trades in all the great marts, or over the whole of a country of the same language or governed by the same laws, to join in a more extended union, in order to put down a second branch of the evils of competition,—that practised by *remote* bodies of the industrious of the same occupation, in underselling each other. A great difficulty, however, here presents itself to the friends of union. Habits differ in remote districts; provisions vary in price; and skill in the mode of finishing work also varies. Under these circumstances the same pecuniary remuneration would not be the same real remuneration to laborers so differently circumstanced. The comparatively unskilled in cheap districts, would complain that the exaction by them of the same pecuniary remuneration, the lower price of provisions and inferiority of skill considered, would in point of fact be demanding a higher real remuneration, and would therefore be unjust to their employers, and deprive themselves of work altogether. If, to obviate this inconvenience, a scale of remuneration were agreed on for every district, this scale would still be liable to vary with every change of circumstances; so that it would perhaps be found necessary to leave to remote unions the fixing, according to their varying circumstances, the prices to be demanded for their own labor within their respective districts. The certainty to the members of any particular union of obtaining support from the common fund of the general union, in case of deficiency of their own district funds, when out of employment through the supposed unreasonableness of masters, would be something like an efficient check to counteract the tendency of unions in cheap and remote districts against fixing too low the rates of their remuneration. Under these circumstances, if the employers or capitalists think the demands of the industrious unreasonable, they can either suspend their business or teach their trade to new hands, the facility of doing which is much greater than the lovers of mysteries and apprenticeships in trades will allow.

Voluntary unions, local and general, of the industrious in every particular line of trade and manufacture, being thus established; new evils of competition remain to be guarded against. Are the wages of labor in any particular line brought up to the highest, through the whole country, that the usual profits of capital will permit? Those not so well paid in other trades, will become competitors for the higher wages of their neighbours. Those of the same trade in other countries where scantier remuneration is given, will also become competitors for the high wages. Those employed in labor at large, termed common or unskilled laborers, will be competitors also at home for the high wages. Here are three new sources of competition pressing exactly in proportion to the success of the local and general union of the industrious in any particular branch of trade or manufacture in attaining a fair remunerating price for their labor. The young just entering life, can be easily trained and directed to any line of industry. To endeavour to limit the number of apprentices or learners, or to aim to exclude poor foreigners, would be as vain as unjust. It would be a conspiracy, which could never but by force be rendered effectual; of the well-paid amongst the industrious, against the ill-paid,— of the few against the many of their brethren.

What new measures remain to be taken by the industrious against these new evils? Against the competition of the underpaid of surrounding trades, the ready remedy is a central union of all the general unions of all the trades of the country. The remuneration of all the different branches of artizans and mechanics in the country, might there be fixed at those rates which would leave such an *equalized* remuneration to all as would take away the temptation from those in one branch to transfer their skill in order to undersell the labor of the well remunerated in another branch; the central union fund being always ready to assist the unemployed in any particular branch, when their own local and general funds were exhausted; provided always their claims to support were by the central union deemed to be just.

What is the remedy for the local and the general union of each particular trade, and for the central union of all trades, against competition from the general fund of labor of the country, of under-paid agriculturists and common or day laborers and their children? Ought the labor of these, who are exposed to the most severe and repulsive exertions, who are liable to excesses and alternations of heat and cold, and to all causes injurious to health, who had the same faculties and the same inclination as others to learn, *if they could*, more profitable employments, to be worse remunerated than those exertions which are carried on under shelter, and are comparatively easy and agreeable? Ought they, or ought they not—in my opinion they ought not to be worse remunerated;—the fact is, that in every country they are, and under the system of Individual Competition, they ever will be, worse remunerated than mechanics and artizans*: the question therefore is, how the well paid trades can guard against the competition of the underpaid laborers around them? As information by means of Mechanics' Institutions and otherwise,

---

* In the free parts of the N. A. United States, however, the difference of remuneration between mechanics and day-laborers, is comparatively trifling, only about 50 per cent.

becomes generally diffused; as competition becomes really free, and trades' mysteries, like all other mysteries, are reduced to contempt, and legal compulsory apprenticeships abolished, the quantum of skill requisite for trades' work, will be acquired with great facility by ordinary laborers and their children. What measures of persuasion, of peace and justice, can guard the well-paid trades with their triple barrier of unions, from the competition of the great mass of the industrious? No such measures can protect them from this all-surrounding, all-pervading competition. Will they then resort to *force*, law-supported as to apprenticeships, or illegal as to intimidation—in all cases equally hateful—to put down the competition of the great majority of the Industrious, and thus erect a bloody— for force will lead to blood, and without blood no aristocracy can be supported— *aristocracy* of Industry? What would be the consequence? The unskilled laborers would every where form a league with the capitalists; and being the majority in point of physical strength, and having, moreover, justice and the legally armed bands of the country on their side, they would by the under-bidding of their labor defeat every where all the efforts of Trades-Unions, local, general, and central, to keep up the remuneration of skilled, i.e. of easy, labor, to what the average rate of profits would afford. The Central Union of All Trades, must therefore extend its operations, and enlarge its sympathies: it must comprehend All the Industrious, agricultural and day-laborers, in the sphere of its operations: thus only can the evils of competition amongst the industrious themselves of the same country, liable to the same laws, be mitigated by unions. Here, however, difficulties thicken round the friends of unions. Amongst agricultural and day-laborers, scattered abroad, isolated as they are, how shall unions be formed? how attenuated the force of public opinion amongst them! how much exposed are they to the ill-offices of their employers! how much in dread of their frowns! how little able to comprehend the utility of general arrangements! how liable to yield to the pressure of want, the food of the day often depending on the labor of the day, when labor is scarce, and low prices are offered! Let us suppose, however, that the spirit of union and general benevolence has surmounted all these difficulties, and that local and general unions of agriculturists and day-laborers are every where established, hand in hand with the local and general unions of mechanics and artizans, and that the grand Central Union of the agriculturists and day-laborers has coalesced with the Central Union of Trades, thus forming a holy league of All the Industrious of one country living under the same laws ; the two great central unions uniting, and forming a National Union. Are the Industrious Classes, then, of that country secured by this magnificent system of Unions, against all the evils of individual competition, amongst the industrious themselves, against the interests of each other? Far, very far from it. Another host of difficulties remains.

What remedy have the local and general Unions of each particular trade, what remedy have the Central Unions of all trades and of all agricultural and every-day labor, crowned by the National Union of all the Industrious of England, Scotland, and Ireland, against the evils of *individual competition on the part of the poor laborers of contiguous countries*? We suppose that the prudential check as to population-increase, is every where prevalent at home, and that the payment of every species of labor is at the highest that the general system of competition, or the existence of capital in one set of hands and of labor in another, will permit; all the other institutions of society remaining as they are, or even in any way modified, *competition remaining*. To exclude the competition of foreigners under the system of Free Competition, would, as before observed under the head of population checks, be as contradictory in principle as malevolent and inoperative in practice. If the cheap laborers from abroad did not come over to the capital and skill, the capital and skill would take wings together, and form an alliance with the cheap laborers abroad. To exclude, also, the competition of cheap foreign laborers, would be inefficient, without at the same time excluding the cheap goods they make,—grain, cottons, silks, woollens, &c. Who will advise a recurrence to the exploded smuggling and preventive-service system? not when opposed to mere unskillful taxes on importation, but to absolute prohibitions ? Or— will our Central and National Unions, under our complicated tythe and taxation and currency system at home, *persuade* the whole of the Industrious, not to use foreign articles that come in competition with the home-made? Immense must be their powers of persuasion. But, under the competitive system, there are necessarily the Idle Classes, the one tenth, the few, the men of merit, who draw the prizes and consume the products of the labor of the industrious necessarily under competition, the law-makers. Will our Unions also persuade them not to buy where they can buy cheapest? The effort will be vain. Persuasion and benevolence can never go hand in hand with such a complicated system of force and fraud. Individual short-sighted interests will overwhelm every thing. What then in the last resort is the feeble remedy of our National Union? To persuade all the industrious of contiguous countries, and not only of contiguous countries, but of all countries on the globe, whose labor might come in competition with home labor, to form local, general, central, and national Unions of all the industrious in their respective countries. What obstacles are here to be surmounted ! Laws, superstitions, prejudices of all sorts, the opposition of the chance possessors, hereditary or otherwise, of political power, the mistaken short-sighted interest of the Idle Classes, building their hopes of rivalship with prosperous manufacturing countries on the comparative cheapness of labor of the poor around them, the fabricated ignorance of the industrious themselves, national antipathies, differences of language;— these are amongst the obstacles in the way of persuasion. In what number of centuries will Unions, though aided by the diffusion of knowlege [sic], be able to surmount them? The bitterness of the opposition given at home to voluntary peaceful Unions, not only by capitalists and others of the Idle Classes, but by many of the leaders of what are called the liberal party, is an intimation not to be misunderstood of the more appalling difficulties to be encountered abroad. If foreign European competition have laughed at reason, humanity, and its own pledged faith, in the continuance of the debasing slave-trade, how very long and very pertinacious will be its opposition to a system of union that demands the most comprehensive exercise of reason and benevolence!

Shall we say then that Trades-Unions or Voluntary Associations of the Industrious Classes, bound together by notions of their utility and public opinion alone, can be of no use to the industrious? That would be asserting too much, and would be like the language of partizans. How far then are they likely to be useful?

As to the remuneration of labor, the aid given from the general fund to those thrown out of employment, will operate as a check to the partial oppression or caprices of individual employers, but particularly of capitalists employing many persons. It will keep up generally the wages of labor to the highest that the usual rate of profits will afford. It will even contribute to keep down to the lowest this general rate of profits. Whatever inconveniences and difficulties remain in the way of competitors from the same or other trades not in Unions, or of ordinary laborers, and still more of foreign competitors, in their efforts to deprive the well-paid of their labor,— these difficulties will be enhanced by the influence of the public opinion of the Unions; and the value of these inconveniences will be reaped by members of Unions in the higher remuneration of their labor. These Unions, like prudential population checks, and operating with them and with the diffusion of knowledge, will prevent a great deal of misery that would otherwise have existed.

The general and *open* establishment of Unions amongst the Industrious Classes, will tend very powerfully to call their intellectual powers into full activity on subjects hitherto neglected by them, but most directly concerning their happiness. Statistics, political economy, legislation, (the reasons and effects of laws,) general morals, will soon cease to be regarded by them as subjects beyond their ken or out of their sphere. They will find these subjects to be intimately connected with the remuneration of labor. Notwithstanding the denunciations of the men of merit amongst them, who may hope by the sublime arts of the "higgling of the market" to rise into capitalists, they will find themselves imperatively called upon, by the utter inefficiency of other expedients for securing to themselves the products of their labor, to investigate the pretensions and arrangements of co-operative political economy, to accomplish this one thing needful to their happiness; from which all other blessings will flow. Every member of a Union, will also see the necessity of becoming a member of a Mechanics or Agricultural Institution in order to become acquainted with physical knowledge, particularly the principles and processes of his own art; and all trades-crafts and mysteries, like all other crafts and mysteries, will cease to delude.

Hand in hand with the intellectual improvement of the Industrious Classes, will proceed the improvement of their moral habits. The influence of the public opinion of large numbers voluntarily associated together, when that opinion is founded on reason, and can have no other object but the interest of the associated, is irresistible. A striking instance of this occurred lately in Mr. Owen's settlement at New Harmony, Indiana. In a country where spirituous liquors may be made for a little more than a shilling a gallon, the members being American small farmers, artizans and laborers of the neighbourhood, it was resolved after four months association by the Industrious themselves; "Henceforth no spirituous liquors shall be retailed in New Harmony." The sharpening of the intellect of the members of these Unions, will necessarily lead to inquiries into the *consequences* of actions, both as they affect the individual and his associates. The knowledge of these consequences, will serve as a permanent motive to the discarding of bad habits. It is always the interest of all persons associated together, that every one amongst them should act justly and beneficently, and should not by private vices of intemperance incapacitate himself from contributing to the common good, or become burthensome on the common funds. The most wicked and profligate member, even in his own view of the case, is *interested* in the good conduct of all but himself. The reputation of all those voluntarily associated, is inevitably connected with the excesses of individual members. Kindly offices necessarily follow the kindly dispositions excited by those whose habits are moral, i.e. tend to the general good. Hence arises the great and useful influence of public opinion amongst numbers of the industrious thus voluntarily associated. Prudential habits exercised in every other department of life, will also be exercised respecting the increase of children, the facts respecting population in every line of trade through a whole country being easily ascertained by means of Unions, but utterly beyond the reach of isolated individuals. Were Unions general, the mutual influence of their public opinion would be useful to each other. In proportion to their numbers, compared with the community at large, they will beneficially influence, or be injuriously affected by, the habits of the community at large. By the very act of voluntary association, every member loses the mere selfish individuality of his character: he acknowledges that his interest is united with that of numbers: his benevolence is drawn forth towards them: instead of looking upon them, as before, from being in the same trade, as his rivals and enemies, fearing their competition,—similarity of employment, pursuits, and interest, will lead him to sympathize with their wants; not only with the wants of his own little local union, but of his brethren through every part of the country; and an extension of the same views, as Unions extend and comprehend different trades, will lead him to embrace larger circles of the industrious in his good wishes, till he shall ultimately feel an interest in the happiness of all the industrious, agriculturists and day-laborers as well as mechanics, from perceiving that the interests of all are the same. Thus will the sphere of benevolence expand by means of universally diffused peaceable Unions of the Industrious; thus will partial interests, exclusive privileges, and the exercise of force or intimidation, legal or illegal, fall into disrepute and abhorrence; and thus will drunkenness and whole days of pernicious revelry, now too often consuming occasional high wages, retreat for ever from the glance of the well-informed public opinion of the industrious themselves. Lying and thieving will be of course every day more and more falling into disrepute, as increase of comforts or diminution of miseries, caused by union and intelligence, takes away the motives to their practice.

    The Industrious Classes, thus rendered, by Unions for keeping up the remuneration of labor, and by Institutions for the diffusion of knowledge, more intelligent, moral, and comfortable, will rise in their own opinion, and will command the respect, the forbearance, if not the sympathy, of the Idle Classes, capitalists and other competitive jugglers, who must continue to live on the products of their labor; and, while the system of Competition remains the main spring of human actions, must form an unsocial league of interests opposed to theirs, the victims of short-sighted views of human nature and human happiness, and of the complicated and pernicious social arrangements upheld by such views, suffering and inflicting misery. If universal good-will, incompatible with competition, do not prevail between the Idle and the Industrious Classes, their mutual jealousies and antipathies will, be softened, and an opening will be afforded for reason to convince both parties of their real interests in Universal Union.

Though the keeping up of wages, by means of Unions and increased knowledge amongst the industrious, to the highest point compatible with the exclusive possession of capital by one set of persons and of labor by the rest, may tend to prevent as great an accumulation of capital *amongst capitalists* as would take place without union and intelligence amongst the industrious; it does not follow that capital would be less speedily accumulated throughout the country. Capital may be accumulated *out of the savings from the wages of well remunerated labor*, as well as out of the profits of stock. So wretchedly has labor in all parts of the world been hitherto remunerated, that in point of fact very little accumulation has arisen from this source: but the cause, general low wages, ignorance, and love of immediate sensual gratifications from the impossibility of looking forward to any other gratifications, being removed, the effect will cease. All articles of permanent use, furniture, dwellings, tools and machines, materials for work, food or dress, permanent improvements in land or dwellings, constitute capital, and may be accumulated or effected in a small way by each individual, giving independence and happiness to each individual; as well as in a large way by capitalists, entailing dependence and misery on the industrious, and serving as the means of extorting from them the greater part of the products of their labor. It is in this way, by promoting the acquisition of capital amongst the industrious themselves, that Unions must operate in order to make any real advance towards securing to the industrious the products of their own labor. Till the industrious become capitalists as well as laborers, each possessed of that portion of capital which is requisite to make his labor productive, they must pay, and pay dearly, the full competition price, to those who may have got into their hands the land on which they live, and which by their labor produces their food, the materials on which they work, the buildings, tools, and machines, by means of which they work, for the use respectively of all the articles. Land being kept out of the market of the Industrious by our aristocratic political institution, the ownership of it out of their reach—unlike the state of America or even France—greater efforts should here be made, by Unions of the industrious, to acquire all other species of capital within their reach. In those trades which require large buildings and machinery, the funds of the general union, of every particular manufacture, should be permanently devoted to the erection of suitable buildings, and the purchase of the best machinery to give employment to the industrious in that line, who might, from time to time, be thrown out of employment in any part of the country through disagreement with their employers ; the general union approving of their conduct, and entitling them to work at the Trades-Manufactory. These buildings should be always made, by purchase, rent free, or as nearly so as possible. Then, in case of want of employment, whether from refusing work on the part of employers, or refusing labor on the part of the employed, the industrious, instead of spending their time in irksome and corrupting idleness, instead of wasting without return the contributions of the employed in their or other lines of trade, would be able to support themselves while out of their regular employ. The funds of all Unions should be every where directed to *supplying work to the unemployed from unjust conduct of their employers, not to support them in idleness*. Near the largest seat of every extensive branch of manufacture, these buildings and workshops should be erected. The unemployed and ill-used from every part of the country, would, in their turn, find refuge in these peaceful sanctuaries of industry. Out of the products of the labor of those employed in these Trades-Manufactories, nothing should be withheld from the laborers but the head-rent, if any, and the cost of management; that cost to be, like remuneration to that paid to the laborers, to as many persons, mutually agreed on by the Trades-Unions and the Laborers themselves, as might be necessary to perform that easy and honourable duty. If, as would probably happen, the laborers working in these Trades-Manufactories, should wish themselves to become the proprietors of them, paying the Trades-Unions out of savings from their earnings or from any other resources, the cost of such buildings and machinery,—such laudable wishes for an approach to real independence, should by all means be encouraged by the Unions. The whole cost of the buildings and machinery should be divided into shares, according to the number of people they were capable of employing; and every individual paying the amount of a share should become a capitalist-laborer, and would thus enjoy an increased part of the product of his labor. The same facilities for independence should of course be opened in every department to women as to men; no person being permitted to purchase more than one share. As these Trade-Manufactories would thus come to be possessed by *joint-stock companies of the laborers themselves*, other buildings and always improved machinery should be erected with their funds by the Unions, to keep up a constant refuge for the honest and industrious losing their employments. These establishments of capitalist-laborers would be something *approaching* (and but approaching) to an efficient check on the exactions of mere capitalists. They would prove that capital can be accumulated without the aid of capitalists.

Notes

1 The Combination of Workmen Act 1824 (5 Geo. 4c. 95) repealed the Combination Acts of 1799 and 1800, which had prohibited trade unions and collective bargaining. However, due to a wave of industrial action in 1824, the new act was amended the following year, and the right to strike was outlawed.
2 A reference to Adam Smith's *Wealth of Nations* ([1776] 1998, 37).

24

"LAWS OF THE BIRMINGHAM CO-OPERATIVE SOCIETY, AND TRADING FUND ASSOCIATION", IN *AN ADDRESS DELIVERED AT THE OPENING OF THE BIRMINGHAM COOPERATIVE SOCIETY* (BIRMINGHAM: PRINTED FOR W. PLASTANS, AND PUBLISHED BY THE SOCIETY, 1828), 27–32.

William Pare

[Born in Birmingham, William Pare (1805–1873) played a major role in the development of co-operative stores and Labour Exchanges in the Midlands. After 1834, he was involved in the Birmingham branch of the Association of All Classes of All Nations, and was appointed governor of Queenwood from 1842 to 1844. He was a lifelong friend of Robert Owen's and remained at his side after the collapse of the Owenite movement. As a founding member of the First Birmingham Cooperative Society in 1828, William Pare was keen to combine the theoretical and practical sides of Owenite political economy. This inaugural address, which outlines the Society's objectives and regulations, formed the basis of a circular which was later approved by the first Co-operative Congress in May 1831 (Langdon 2000, 37). Pare thus helped define the modus operandi of the early Owenite movement. While stressing the need for individual co-operatives to pool their financial resources at national level in order to establish communities, he provided an organisational framework which was to dominate socialist initiatives until 1834, while confirming William Thompson's rising intellectual influence over that same period, to the relative detriment of Owen's top-down economic reform schemes (Garnett 1973).]

Laws of the Birmingham Co-operative Society, and Trading Fund Association

Definition

A Co-operative Society, like all other Societies, such as Benefit Clubs, Trade Societies, Savings Banks, &c., is for the purpose of avoiding some evils which men are exposed to when acting singly, and of obtaining some advantages which they must otherwise be deprived of.

Objects

The objects of this Society are, 1st. The mutual protection of the members against *Poverty*. 2nd. The attainment of a greater share of the *Comforts* of Life. And 3rd. The attainment of *Independence* by means of a common capital.

Means of obtaining these Objects

These means consist, 1st. In a weekly subscription to a COMMON CAPITAL. 2nd. In employing that capital in a different way to what is usually done, namely, not in investment, but in TRADE. 3rd. When it has accumulated sufficiently; IN MANUFACTURING for the Society: and lastly, when it has further accumulated, in the purchase, or rental of land, and living upon it in COMMUNITY OF PROPERTY.

Constitution of the Society

1. The Society shall consist, 1st. Of those persons who may, immediately on the adoption of the laws, enter their names as members: 2ndly. Of all those who not being more than *Forty* years of age, may join within one month after Public Notice is given of the existence of the Society: and lastly. Of such persons Male or Female, who may wish to join them, being of good character, industrious, sober, of general good health, not liable to any constitutional disorder, and not exceeding *Thirty-five* years of age.

Admission of Members

2. Every person wishing to join the Society, must be proposed by a member, stating his or her address, trade, or occupation, age, &c. one month previous to the ballot for his or her admission, during which time the character of such candidate shall be inquired into.
3. No person can be admitted a member who belongs to another Co-operative Society, and is he or she has formerly belonged to one, such Society shall be written to for a testimonial of his or her character, cause of leaving, &c.
4. At the proposing of a candidate, the members present shall be at liberty to make any inquiries which they may think fit, and if any member (whether present or absent, knowing such candidate is about to be proposed) shall know any cause

why he or she should not be admitted, it shall be considered their bounden duty to make known the same.

5. The majority of the members present at the final proposing of a candidate, shall decide by ballot whether such person be admitted or not.

Admission Fee, Rate of Subscription, &c.

6. Every person on becoming a member must pay his or her proportion of the Common Stock already accumulated, as stated in the last estimate, in such manner as the Committee may think fit.

7. Each member shall contribute Four-pence per week to the common fund, unless any individual may choose to contribute more than that sum, but in no case are members to reckon on any peculiar advantage as a compensation for extra contributions.

8. Sons and Daughters of members between the ages of Twelve and Eighteen may join the Society without paying a proportion of the common Stock, but will not be allowed to vote on any question until they arrive at the age of Eighteen.

Exclusion of Members

9. The members may any amount of their subscription in advance, but if any member's subscription be two months in arrear, he or she shall receive a notice thereof from the Secretary, and if the arrears be not paid within one month from the date of such notice, such member shall be suspended for six months; if at the expiration of that time, all arrears together with the interest thereon are not paid, he or she shall be no longer a member, unless two-thirds of the members assembled at the general meeting may think proper from some peculiar circumstance to extend the time.

10. If any member shall misconduct himself, or herself, or refuse to comply with the laws, or if it be proved that he, or she has used any deception for the purpose of becoming a member, it shall be lawful for nine tenths of the members assembled at a Special Meeting, called for that purpose, to exclude such person from the Society; a member so excluded shall receive back the whole amount of *Subscription* which he, or she, shall have paid into the Fund.

Transfer of Shares

11. No member on leaving the Society, (unless excluded according to law 10,) shall have any claim on the Stock or Fund, but in case of death, or removal to a distance, such member may bequeath or transfer, (not withdraw) his, or her share, subject to this condition, namely, the person to whom such share is bequeathed or transferred must be approved by a majority of the members in General Meeting assembled for that purpose: in case the claim is not made within six months from

the death or removal of a member, or if the Society should reject the candidate for such share, it shall be forfeited to the common fund.

Government

12. The Society shall elect a President, Secretary, Treasurer, and Six Committee-men, who together shall form a board of management, four shall be a quorum, provided there be but two superior officers in such quorum.

Mode and Time of Election

13. The President, Secretary, and Treasurer shall be annually elected at the first meeting of the Society in January, and those who have already served shall be eligible to be re-elected to the same offices.
14. The Committee-men shall be elected for one year, and three shall go out by rotation every half year, so that there shall always be three new Committee-men to be chosen at the first meeting of the Society in January and July in each year, the first three to go out by ballot.
15. No member of the committee going out of office shall be re-elected for the same till after the lapse of six months.
16. Printed lists of all the members' names shall be given to each member, (on application to the Secretary,) at least one week previous to the election; on which list the members shall distinctly mark the names of those persons they wish to fill the several offices, and deliver the same folded up, to the chairman of the meeting at which the election takes place.
17. Three persons not members of the Committee, shall be appointed Scrutineers, and if the suffrages for two or more candidates are equal, lots shall be prepared which shall be drawn by the chairman.

Duties of Officers

18. The President shall be expected to preside at all the meetings of the Society; in his unavoidable absence, a President shall be appointed for the evening from among the members present.
19. The Secretary shall attend all meetings of the Society, or in his unavoidable absence shall depute a member to officiate for him: he shall keep a correct record of the proceedings of the Society, and shall generally do as an executive Officer such acts as may be resolved on by the members: he shall receive all monies and shall pay the same every week to the Treasurer, who shall thereupon give him a receipt or acknowledgment, which shall be produced at the weekly meetings of the Society.
20. All payments on account of the Society of one Pound and Upwards, shall be made by drafts on the Treasurer drawn by the Secretary, by order of the Committee, or general meeting, and signed by a member of the Committee: accounts

under Twenty Shillings may be paid by the Secretary if ordered by the Committee, or general meeting.

21. The Committee shall audit the accounts of the Agent weekly, and shall take stock every three months, and report to the Society the exact state of its affairs at the first meetings in January, April, July, and October in each year, and the accounts shall be made up to the Twenty-fifth day of the preceeding [sic] month for that purpose.

Trustees

22. The property of the Institution, shall be vested in Trustees to be elected by the members from among their own body; in case of death or resignation, the vacancy shall be filled up at the next general meeting of the Society.

Private Meetings

23. Once every week a private meeting of the Society shall be held. The business shall commence at half-past Seven o'Clock, and be open to all members male and female and to no other persons without leave having first been obtained from the members then assembled.
24. Twelve members at least, beside the Secretary or his substitute, shall be present to constitute a private meeting.
25. The members shall, at their private meetings, pay their subscriptions, admit members, and transact such other business as may come before them.
26. The minutes of the last meeting shall first be read by the Secretary, he shall then report the names (if any) of the candidates for admission as members.
27. The majority on all questions (except the admission of members,) shall be ascertained by open votes, unless a ballot be demanded by any member present.

Public Meetings

28. Public meetings of the Society shall be held occasionally of which due notice shall be given by advertisement or otherwise.
29. The business of the meeting shall be announced from the chair by the President, and before the dissolution of the meeting the business proposed for the suceeding [sic] public meeting shall be announced, if practicable.
30. The public meetings shall be devoted to Lectures, Discussions, and such communications from the chair as may be deemed expedient.
31. The President shall keep order, and shall exercise rigid impartiality towards persons wishing to speak, and permit of no irregular interruption, and his decision on points of order shall be supported and obeyed.
32. Any person, male or female, member or not, may speak on any question before the meeting, not more than fifteen minutes to be allowed each speaker at one time.

33. No theological discussion shall be permitted, nor any other *irrelevant* to the subject before the Society.
34. As the dispassionate pursuit of truth is one of the principle [sic] duties of this Society, and in order that its members may avoid the appearance of party and partisanship, it is expected that they will abstain from the expression of any approbation or the contrary, during the speech of any person whatever.
35. No proposition respecting the rules, the management of the funds, or the internal arrangement of the Society shall be discussed at a public meeting.
36. After the business announced from the chair shall have been concluded, any person present may address to the chair any observations connected with the objects of the Society.

Mode of Trading

37. The trade shall be carried on with the fund arising from the Subscriptions and Loans by laying in a stock of goods at wholesale prices, such as the Society may choose to sell by retail at the usual profits, and the profits of the trade shall be at all times added to the capital of the Society.
38. In the purchase, or sale of goods no credit shall be either given or received.
39. Nothing in the way of profits of trade, or any part of the capital shall ever be divided among the members, as *Community of Property in Land and Goods is the great object of this Society.*
40. All the members shall be expected to purchase from the Store, such articles as they may want, and are kept for sale.

Agent

41. An Agent shall be elected from among the members at a salary, who shall have the custody of the stock in trade of the Society, which he shall lay in and sell out under the direction of the Committee.
42. All monies received by him shall be paid to the secretary once a week, or oftener if required.
43. The Committee shall have the power of suspending the Agent from his office at any time they may deem it expedient: in which case his conduct shall be investigated by a meeting of the Society, to be specially convened for that purpose with as little delay as possible.

Donations, Legacies, and Loans

44. Donations and Legacies may be received, as also loans of money, for which latter, interest at 5 per cent per annum will be allowed: sums lent, under Fifty Pounds, shall not be withdrawn under six months notice, to be given in writing to the Secretary; above Fifty Pounds, twelve months notice must be given in like manner.

Rights of Members

45. The members shall be at liberty to attend the meetings of the Committee, but shall not take part in the proceedings thereof, they shall also be entitled to examine the books and writings of the Society at all convenient times.

Alteration of Laws

46. No addition to, or alteration of these laws, shall be made except it be resolved on at two succeeding private meetings by a majority of the members present, and notice of such alteration or addition shall be read from the chair at least two private meetings previous to the decision.

25

"SKETCH OF A COMMERCIAL CONSTITUTION", IN *THE SOCIAL SYSTEM: A TREATISE ON THE PRINCIPLE OF EXCHANGE* (EDINBURGH: WILLIAM TAIT, 1831), 30–39.

John Gray

[Originally from Scotland, John Gray (1799–1883) first came into contact with Robert Owen in August 1823, when he realised that they shared a similar view of labour as the source of all wealth (Gray-Owen Correspondence, 1823). Two years later, he bought shares in the Orbiston community (see Part 5, Chapter 28) but never joined due to his increasing weariness towards communitarianism, a view which he expounded in his *Lecture on Human Happiness* (1825) and later in his *Social System* (1831). Though still a socialist, Gray now advocated a system of economic planification, or "National Communal Association," to guarantee a fair reward of productive labour within a co-operative, egalitarian society. Under the aegis of the Association, a National Chamber of Commerce and a National Bank would respectively regulate the production and distribution of goods on a co-operative basis, and calculate wages based on labour time. This social system was at odds with Owen's, as Gray shared George Mudie's contention that master-manufacturers were not productive labourers (*Political Economist*, January 1823, 11–25, quoted in Claeys 1989, 77; Thompson 1988, 105–108).]

As it is the object of this chapter to describe, in a connected form, the leading features of the plan about to be advocated, rather than to present, in all the stiffness of language with which such a document would require to be invested, a commercial constitution, the chapter itself might perhaps have been more properly entitled "Principles of the Social System;" but the term, "Commercial Constitution" has been preferred, as containing in itself a description of one of the ingredients conceived to be necessary to the attainment of national prosperity.

SKETCH OF A COMMERCIAL CONSTITUTION

The principles about to be specified will be accompanied here with but little either of argument or illustration; but, after the whole plan has been described, such general observations will be made upon it, as will tend to shew why, in the author's opinion, so vast and important a change in our commercial affairs is imperatively called for.

It is proposed, then, that, whenever a sufficient number of persons shall be induced to combine their capital, for the purpose of more effectually supplying themselves with the necessaries, conveniencies [sic], comforts, and luxuries of life, by making the production thereof the unfailing cause of a demand for them to an equal extent, they should proceed to act upon the following principles:—

I. That a president, and a sufficient number of representatives, be chosen in an equitable manner, to control, direct, and regulate the affairs of the association; that the persons so elected be invested with supreme power, during the time they may be in office, and that they be denominated collectively, The National Chamber of Commerce.

II. That, in their public capacity, the members of this Chamber do abstain from all political and religious discussion; that they engage to treat, with equal justice, men of every political opinion, and of every religious creed; that they do bind and oblige themselves to devote their undivided attention to the interests of commerce; to submit themselves, in all things, without complaint, to the established authorities of the country; to renounce the right even to petition parliament, and that, whenever any change in the commercial law of the country shall appear to them to be desirable, or necessary, they represent the same to their constituents, leaving it for them to petition for the necessary alteration.

III. That all persons possessed of land, or capital, be invited to join this association, and that all other persons be admitted members of it as rapidly as its progress will allow.

IV. That all members of this association, who shall be possessed of land, or capital, shall have an estimated value put upon the same, and shall consent to receive a fixed annual remuneration for the use thereof, proportionate to its value, in lieu of retaining, in their own hands, the chances of gain or loss, by its cultivation or employment.

V. That the direction and control of all cultivation, manufactures, and trade, be vested in the Chamber of Commerce.

VI. That the cultivation of land, and the management of all trades and manufactures, be intrusted to servants or managers, to be hired at fixed salaries by, and to act under the direction and control of, the Chamber of Commerce.

VII. That produce of every description, manufactured and agricultural, be lodged in national warehouses, and intrusted to the care of servants or managers, who are to be remunerated by salaries fixed by the Chamber of Commerce.

VIII. That, from these national warehouses, or depots, all shops for the disposal of goods by retail, be supplied; these shops, also, to be committed to the care of servants or managers, appointed at fixed salaries by the Chamber of Commerce.

IX. That all wages and salaries be paid in money of no intrinsic value; and that the price of commodities consist, first, of the cost of the material; secondly, of the wages of labour; and, thirdly, of such a per centage or profit, as shall be sufficient to ensure a gradual and sufficiently rapid increase of capital, as also to pay all the expenses of rent, interest of capital, salaries, depreciation of stock, unproductive labour, incidents, and all national charges, to be hereafter more particularly specified.

X. That the land, capital, and labour of the association, be devoted, in the first instance, to the stocking of the national warehouses with the various commodities which constitute the ordinary necessaries, conveniencies [sic], and comforts of life.

XI. That, whenever any commodity shall be found to be unduly accumulating in the national warehouses, thereby proving that it is unnecessary to continue its production to the same extent as formerly, a portion of the capital and labour employed in the production of the said article, be forthwith devoted to another purpose, that is, to the production of some other article of which there does not appear to be any such superfluity.

XII. That the loss or damage, whenever any shall be sustained by these changes, be charged to the national account, and form one of the items to be paid by a per centage on the sale of the produce of the labour of the association.

XIII. That, during the time that shall necessarily elapse between the relinquishing of one employment, and devoting themselves to another, the operatives be paid the full weekly sum that they shall have been accustomed to receive : this expense also to be charged to the national account.

XIV. If, from great improvements in machinery, or from any other cause, the productive powers of labour should be greatly increased, so that a small portion of the number of persons at present necessarily employed in producing the ordinary marketable supplies should prove to be sufficient to meet the demand for them, then let this simple rule be followed: As fast as we come to be supplied with the ordinary necessaries and comforts of life, let us apply our labour and capital to the production of that which is more ornamental and luxurious; and it is as impossible that production should ever overtake demand, as that mankind should ever cease to desire something which they do not possess. This rule has no restriction no condition no qualification. It may be acted on with certain advantage, so long as the earth shall continue to revolve.

XV. That the National Commercial Association be held and considered to be one body of commercial partners, upon the same principle, to the same extent, and only to the same extent, that all men are now political partners in the respective states to which they belong, being alike subject to, and protected by, the same general law; but without the smallest mixture of private property, or sacrifice of individual right.

XVI. That it be a main object of the association to pay off, as rapidly as possible, the borrowed or hired capital with which it, must commence, and that, with all convenient speed, it provide itself with sufficient land and capital of its own.
XVII. That regular accounts be kept by a national bank of the whole proceedings of the association, in a manner to be hereafter described; and that an annual balance sheet be published, exhibiting its whole receipts, expenditure, and the state of its finances.
XVIII. That a given number of members be, at all times, entitled to demand and to receive an explanation of whatever may appear to be unsatisfactory or obscure in the national balance sheet.
XIX. That a Commercial Constitution, in a detailed and explicit form, be drawn up, and that his majesty' government be humbly solicited to sanction and patronize the National Commercial Association, under the restriction, that it adhere strictly, in all its proceedings, to the principles of its constitution.
XX. That the Commercial Constitution never be altered, but with the mutual consent of the established political government, and the Chamber of Commerce.

An intelligent friend, who recently did me the favour to cast his eye over these pages whilst they were in manuscript, was immediately struck with the resemblance which appears to exist between the principles of the social system, as here defined, and the rules of an ordinary joint stock company. That a resemblance does exist, at first sight, is at once admitted, but it extends not one jot farther than that resemblance which exists between a mushroom and a toadstool, or between gold and gilded brass. The difference lies here. An ordinary joint stock company is merely an assemblage of persons and of capital, whose primary object is to carry on some branch of trade, commerce, or manufacture, for the purpose of competing with other traders, or for the sake of endeavouring to monopolize a trade altogether, as, for example, in the case of the East India Company, and private advantage is the ultimate object of the whole affair.

The specific object of the proposed commercial association, on the contrary, is to make production the infallible cause of demand, and to give the greatest possible effect to labour and capital, by whomsoever the former may be exerted, or the latter possessed, by means of a thoroughly organized plan of production, exchange, distribution, and accumulation. The ultimate object here, therefore, is, to give to the public, and to every individual composing it, in portions proportionate to his industry and wealth, the entire advantage of the compact. And although this subject is rather too extensive, and too complicated, to be seen through at a glance, and understood with that degree of attention which is given to a new novel by a professional critic, who reads for the sake of reviewing it, a very little reflection will convince any man, who is at all capable of forming an opinion upon such a subject, that national prosperity of a very exalted character, would inevitably spring from the plan of operations that is here recommended. For, the labouring classes could never suffer from the want of employment for a single hour : individual anxieties respecting business would also be done away with, for, although industry and attention would be no less necessary than they are now, unmerited misfortune, in the shape of bankruptcy, or failure, would be entirely prevented. The higher classes, too, would be provided with an excellent fund for the investment of their money; and the government, as will be duly shewn, would be saved the very disagreeable and expensive business of collecting the taxes. And, lastly, the nation would know no other limit to its wealth than the exhaustion of its industry, the exhaustion of its productive powers, or the satisfaction of its wants.

26

GAZETTE OF THE EXCHANGE BAZAARS, AND PRACTICAL GUIDE TO THE RAPID ESTABLISHMENT OF THE PUBLIC PROSPERITY, 20 OCTOBER 1832, N°5.

George Mudie

[Undeterred by the failure of the Spa Fields and Orbiston communities, George Mudie relocated to London in the early 1830s, embracing the cause of the Labour Exchanges in 1832. Despite his enthusiasm, he found himself increasingly at odds with Robert Owen's views on the subject, which were put to the test at the Gray's Inn Road National Equitable Labour Exchange (see Part 5, Chapter 30). In retaliation, Mudie founded the short-lived *Gazette of the Exchange Bazaars*, where he attacked two of Owen's policies – the decision to lower the value of labour notes to attract new customers, and the suggestion that part of the Labour Exchange's profits should be given to the government to reduce the national debt. Mudie saw this as an attack on working-class economic independence, and advocated producer-operated Labour Exchanges and a minimum wage to guarantee a fair reward of labour. He attempted to found a bazaar upon these principles, but to no avail. His rift with Owen never healed (Mudie-Owen Correspondence 1823–1848; Claeys 1989, 83–84; Bennett 2016, 119–126).]

It can no longer be denied that, whatever the Governor of the Grays [sic] Inn Road Bazaar[1] may imagine to the contrary, his past and present proceedings, and the constitution and practices of the Institution under his management, are very far from being calculated to advance the real and immediate interests of the Working Classes of the people, any more than they are calculated to serve the interests of small Dealers of any kind, or even those of small Master Tradesmen, small Manufacturers or small Capitalists.

The principles and practices in question are avowedly not favourable to the interests of small capitalists, dealers and master tradesmen; for the Governor of the Bazaar has repeatedly explained, and it has been repeated confirmed by official publications authorized by him and the Directors, that the large Capitalist and the great Manufacturer can alone operate with advantage, – that the second-rate Capitalists and Manufacturers come next in order as to the power of producing goods economically, and as to the power of disposing of them advantageously for themselves, – that the third-rate and lowest order of Capitalists and Manufacturers, and also Journeymen, produce goods the least economically, and always find it very difficult, if not impossible, to dispose of their goods with advantage to themselves, – and, finally, that Dealers in commodities being mere middlemen between producers and consumers, they ought to be altogether dispensed with, – that it is in the very nature of the proceedings of the Exchange Bazaars to extinguish all their occupations and all their present means of subsistence, – and that the system of exchanges was therefore destined to cast confusion into and to effect the overthrow of all the existing commercial arrangements of society. Therefore it was, that a Committee was sapiently formed for the purpose of contriving the means of keeping alive the fated Shopkeepers and Merchants, before measures were or even as yet have been formed for permanently securing the supply of a pound of bread for the Productive Classes. The mountain has groaned and laboured; and while the wizard so excited the commotion all expected to see the Temples of Commerce totter to their fall, the mountain has brought forth, not a ridiculously little mouse, but only a greatly ludicrous Committee. Even one whom we believe to be a very worthy man, – an embryo Member of Parliament, who is a manager of the Grays' [sic] Inn Road Bazaar, who is a member of the Shopkeepers' Committee, and who is moreover himself a respectable and flourishing shopkeeper, after placarding the public streets with imitations that the Exchange Notes would be "taken at his shop" for goods, has already turned his back upon the Notes which were but the other day proclaimed to be more valuable than gold. The Notes are not now received in payment even at his shop. Nothing will do there but gold, silver, and the "rags of Threadneedle Street". Commerce sits secure in her hundred thousand marts, not only unmoved by but insensible to the puny efforts that have been made to derange her multitudinous transactions. There has been confusion, and discord, and disappointment, and discomfiture, and malediction, nowhere but in the Grays' [sic] Inn Road Bazaar itself! Not only do the old shopkeepers continue their occupations without interruption, but new shops are entered upon daily without dread of the system of Exchanges. The Philosophers of Grays'[sic] Inn Road Bazaar have alone been obliged occasionally to shut up their shop – and they alone have thought it necessary to close their doors altogether against industrious Poverty, by refusing to transact business with all persons offering them deposits of less value than twenty shillings! The principles, therefore, are not only against the poor man, if the poor man's necessities compel him to submit to their operation; but the practices altogether exclude the very poor man from even the glimmering of hope which he might have been induced to cherish; and the practices also deprive the Institution itself of what might have been the only redeeming feature of its character, – that of being in some respects a refuge for the destitute, and a substitute for the pawnbroker!

The occasion will no longer permit the truth upon this most important subject to be blinked. Every other consideration must give place to that of protecting the true system of Exchanges from the dogmatic misinterpretations of those who have either taken it up without understanding it, or who by erroneous practices pervert it to purposes the very reverse of those for which it was devised. Every man has long known that the possessors of large capital and extensive machinery enjoy advantages over the possessors of small capital and less extensive machinery. Every one is aware that all Capitalists, – whether large or small, – all holders of machinery, – all directors of arrangements and combinations, – whether more or less extensive, – possess great advantages, – excessive, inordinate, and sometimes even unjust advantages, – over the small master mechanic, the journeyman mechanic, the small farmer, the agricultural labourer, and the poor in the aggregate. There is nothing more certain than all this, – there is nothing more certain than that all this is a great, a crying, and an increasing evil. It was to counteract this great and growing evil that the Co-operative Societies were devised and founded by the Editor of this Publication, twelve years ago, and that these Societies have been formed in every part of the Kingdom. It is for the purpose of counteracting the same evil, that the Exchange Bazaars, which originated in and are undeniably the offspring of, the Co-operative Societies, have been set on foot. While the Exchange Bazaars are yet in their infancy, and while their Managers were still seeking for such practices as shall enable them to effect the real object of the Institutions, there starts into existence the Grays' [sic] Inn Road Bazaar, and not only preposterously claiming to be the leading Institution, but plunging at once into practices, which, if it were not possible for them to be continued on a large scale, could have no other tendency than to frustrate altogether the beneficial purposes for which the legitimate Institutions had been formed. The productive classes were for a moment dazzled and deluded by the high pretensions of this ephemeral and illegitimate establishment. Israel, as heretofore, hearkened unto false teachers and bowed itself before false Gods, whose own dispensations, however, have speedily scourged the people from their folly.

These charges are grave and serious in their nature, and therefore it is incumbent upon us to show that they are well founded. The admitted evil is, that industry, and skill, and labour, are depressed and injuriously controlled by capital and machinery. The remedy, then, must be to fix a value upon labour, below which it shall not be depressed, and to render labour from the first less dependent upon capital than it is now, by as far as possible uniting the interests of the capitalist and the labourer; and to render the labourer eventually altogether independent of the capitalists, by immediately commencing and perseveringly continuing the creation of a capital for the exclusive benefit of the labourers, out of their own transactions in the Exchange Bazaars

It was therefore that we have proposed, both in this Publication and elsewhere, that 4 per cent out of the 8 ⅓ per cent. now charged upon the transactions of Depositors in Exchange Bazaars, shall be appropriated to the formation of a capital for working out the independence of the depositors. It was therefore that we proposed to allow the capitalists all the profits they can make to themselves out of the remaining 4 ⅓ per cent, after defraying from the same the charges of rent, taxes, management and services, in order that capitalists may thus be induced to assist in working out the independence of the depositors. And therefore it was that we proposed to fix the labour of mechanics, artisans, and husbandmen at a certain valuation, below which it shall not be possible for it to fall, while the immediate, direct and infallible operation of the accumulating fund shall be to raise the value of the labour to several times the amount of what it is at present. [...]

He appears to be willing to confer power upon any body of men except labouring men, and to assign advantages and profits to any parties excepting those by whose labour alone all advantages and profits are created.

Here therefore, so lately as only the other day, is a palpable invitation to Government to lay its hands upon the profits of the Exchange Bazaars, and to defray out of them the whole charges now borne by all the taxation of the country!!! The profits are not to be reduced, if the Government will but take the hint. The profits are not even to go to the foundation of charity schools and charity workshops, if the Government will only condescend to transfer them to the Exchequer, together with as much more in the shape of an exaction as shall enable them to pay all their expenditure, "extravagant as that expenditure has been!" This is really most monstrous; and as being such, it shall be further exhibited in its truly monstrous character and colours in our next number.

Note

1 Robert Owen.

27

"AN OUTLINE OF A SOCIAL MOVEMENT", IN *LABOUR'S WRONGS AND LABOUR'S REMEDY; OR, THE AGE OF MIGHT AND THE AGE OF RIGHT* (LEEDS: DAVID GREEN, 1839), 154–176.

John Francis Bray

[The British-American John Francis Bray (1809–1897) was born in the present-day American state of Washington to a family of singers and comedians. In 1822, he and his parents moved to the latter's hometown of Leeds. In the following years, upon his father's death, Bray became an apprentice to a printer and bookbinder. Over the next decade, he joined the Yorkshire co-operative and Chartist movements and wrote for the local radical press. Bray's first pamphlet, *Labour's Wrongs and Labour's Remedy*, was based on a series of lectures he had given to the Working Men's Association in Leeds, which he had helped to establish in 1837. He returned to the USA in 1842, settling as a printer in Detroit and engaging in socialist activism until his death. Based on Robert Owen's theory of value, *Labour's Wrongs* argued that only working people were entitled to the full produce of their labour. But contrary to Owen, and in keeping with his Chartist beliefs, John Francis Bray was adamant that working people had to free themselves from the shackles of the competitive system, without following middle- and upper-class leaders. To foster working-class agency, Bray recommended the founding of a trading network of co-operative joint-stock companies (Bray Papers; Thompson 1988, 109–112; Prum 1993).]

If sufficient proof has not been given of the corrupt tendencies and the unimprovable character of the present system, those who wish for more evidence have not far to look for it. Let us go where we will — see and hear what we will — read of the past and the present what we will — all places, actions, and times, have the same tale to tell. History and experience bear evidence, in characters of fire, and blood, and misery, that this social system never has been, is not now, and never can be, anything but a dark and chaotic sea of evil, in which oppression is unpunished, virtue and morality unregarded, merit unrewarded, and the tears of the widow and the orphan unpitied and unheeded. Thus, from its very nature, and the irremediable evils connected with it, there is nothing to induce us to retain the present system, even were its subversion attended by treble the difficulty which stands in the way of its accomplishment.

Changes are ever taking place, more or less important in regard to their effects upon society. Man is a progressing being; and he looks to the past, therefore, not so much to take pattern of that which was good, as to derive warning from that which was evil. In regard to any forward movement which may be made, the considerations which have been already entered into respecting what is well and what is ill in the present system, and what is requisite to the establishment and the progression of a better system, will enable us to determine what should be given up and what retained. Keeping all these things in view, we can at once briefly proceed to the consideration of a mode of subverting the present system, independent alike of change of character or the accumulation of capital among those making the attempt— two requisites almost indispensable to the success of any of the plans which have been examined.

Of the six millions of adult men in the United Kingdom, it has been calculated that about five millions assist in producing and distributing wealth; and that of this number, four millions belong to the division called the working class. It has been shewn that, by the present arrangements of society, this last great division receive scarcely £200,000,000 of the £500,000,000 of wealth annually created, which averages about £11 per head for the men, women, and children comprised in this class; and that for this miserable pittance they toil, on the average, 11 hours a day.

A consideration of the principles of production has shewn us, that three things only are necessary to the creation of any amount of wealth, namely, raw material, labour, and capital; and it has likewise taught us the best means of regulating the various powers at our disposal — by union of forces and division of labour — so as to produce the greatest quantity of wealth with the least expenditure of capital and labour. The best exemplification of the power which man may wield by union of forces and division of labour, is afforded by the working of a joint-stock company. These companies are usurping, in all directions the places and occupations hitherto confined to individual capitalists and traders; and the systematic and extended manner in which this joint-stock system of trading has been acted upon during late years, has given almost every person some knowledge of the principles and mode of action from which its strength is derived. The gigantic power of such companies is beheld in innumerable roads, railways and canals, and in the creation and distribution of almost every description of wealth. It is known that the power of these companies arises solely from the skilful application of capital and labour; and it is self-evident that the like application of capital and labour under similar circumstances, will ever produce similar results.

We have already, as it were, taken stock of the real capital and the employed and unemployed labour in the United Kingdom. We have found the capital to be worth no less than five thousand millions sterling, which, under present arrangements, gives employment only to about four millions of working men and one million of half-employed distributors — thus leaving unused and mis-used the effective strength of one million of men, in connection with uncultivated land, and unemployed machinery and tools, in every factory and workshop, sufficient to fill the hands of all men. Thousands now starve in unproductive inaction because the capitalist cannot employ them — the capitalist cannot give them work because he cannot find a market for his produce — there is no market for the produce because those who want the produce have nothing but their labour to give in exchange for it — and their labour is unemployed because the capitalist does not know how to set them to work — and thus the evils of the present system run round in a circle, one connected with and dependent upon another, and every one individually incurable.

Therefore, in respect to a social change: — it is not disputed that there is in the United Kingdom a sufficiency of the raw material of wealth to employ all the labour which can be brought to bear upon it — it is universally known that there are tens of thousands of half-starved men in unproductive inaction — it has been proved, by flushes of trade at different times, that there are implements and machines to fill the hands of all — the experience of many years has proved that there is generally food enough in the country to support comfortably all the inhabitants from one harvest to another, and that any amount can be had by exchanging our productions for the corn of foreign countries—it has been shewn that a medium of exchange, or money, can be manufactured in such abundance as to set in motion all the unemployed labour and implements in the country— and as there are all these requisites and facilities, why should they not be made a proper use of, and all the advantages obtained which can be made to result from the combined operation of so many powers ?

Without, for the present, entering into a consideration of the possibility of effecting this change, let it for a moment be supposed that the whole five millions of the adult producers in the United Kingdom are formed into a number of joint-stock companies, containing from 100 to 1,000 men each, according to locality and other circumstances — that each of these companies is comprised of men of one trade, or confines its attention to the production or distribution of particular commodities — that these companies have in use, by hire or purchase, the land and fixed capital of the country — that they are set in motion and kept moving by a circulating bank-note capital equivalent to £100 for each associated member of the community, which, taking into account the women and children connected with the five millions of producers, will comprise, altogether, about twenty millions of individuals, and a capital of two thousand millions sterling. Supposing the productive classes of the United Kingdom to be thus associated together, for the production and distribution of wealth — that they trade together with a floating capital of £2,000,000,000 — that all their affairs are conducted through the instrumentality of general and local boards of trade, comprised of the most able and business-like men that can be found— that the members of all the companies, after the manner of the present system, are paid weekly wages for their labour — what is there now accomplished in respect to production and distribution, either by joint-stock companies or individual capitalists, which could not likewise be accomplished by the productive classes thus associated? The wonders which are wrought everywhere around us, by means of joint-stock companies, shew what even a very limited union of forces is capable of accomplishing; and if individual and unallied companies can effect thus much, what may not be achieved by the united powers of thousands of such companies — all having a common interest, working for a common end, and deriving a common benefit from all that is produced?

A few very simple arrangements would enable a change like this to be effected; and such change would at once set in motion the whole of the unemployed labour in the empire — it would, without inflicting injury on any trade or any individual, allow of the introduction of an unlimited quantity of machinery — and the power of this gigantic union of labour and machinery would be maintained by a circulating medium of two thousand millions of pounds sterling. The imagination, chained down to the molehill mountains of the present system, cannot at once embrace the vast prospect and the almost omnipotent powers unfolded in a change like this!

A social movement of this character would require no fundamental alteration in disposition, or character, or habits, in the parties acting. There are no new feelings to be acquired, no old associations to be shaken off, more than would be requisite in any simple governmental change, such as men are yearly subjected to. The whole movement would require only cooperation in its simplest form, such as at the present moment exists in every trade and in every workshop, where persons of the widest extremes in respect to character, strength, and opinion, harmoniously cooperate together to effect some definite object in production. The path to action is thus already prepared, and we should only have to go forward, as it were, upon a beaten and a well-known road.

Competition could have no existence in a change like this; and the economists, considering competition as the mainspring of production, unhesitatingly predict that any social arrangements which take away this stimulus — which remove the fear of future want or the hope of future gain— will be injurious to production, and subversive of the prosperity and harmony of society. Instances are brought forward to shew that, in proportion as men are secured against the future, they relax in their endeavours, and become careless of labour, and of the production of wealth — that men are not so willing to exert themselves in procuring that which will be enjoyed by all, as if the enjoyment were confined exclusively to themselves— that when production is the business of every body it is the business of nobody, and each man endeavours to escape at the expense of his neighbours.

Although the testimony of experience goes to prove the general truth of these objections, when they are applied to the world as it is, it has been shewn that they have no force when opposed to a social system combining a change of character and new social arrangements, or to the joint-stock modification now under consideration. Competition is only a secondary cause of production; for men compete with each other for the possession of certain things, because they desire these things, and because, under the present system, *they can obtain them only by competition.* It is the natural desire for things, and not the competition, which originally incites men to action; and so long as this desire exists, production will go forward efficiently, unallied with and independent of competition. If there were plenty of work for all men, there would now be no competition for it; nor would there be any competition for the possession of particular commodities, if there were a sufficiency of every thing produced to supply the wants of all; and yet men would work together, and produce commodities in greater abundance, and enjoy themselves in a far greater degree, in such a state of things, than if one-half of them were idle, and the other half, by competition, were reduced to the necessity of labouring for what may be called a nominal existence. Competition, likewise, can be dispensed with as a stimulant to enterprise and invention; for it is notorious that the majority of inventors and intellectual labourers, instead of expecting or receiving any reward, now live and die in a state of poverty and misery exceeding even that of the most mindless being who makes use of their discoveries. If it be contended that men will not do their duty to their fellows without being spurred on by a stimulus more or less connected with their animal wants — that if the men of all trades and professions receive one uniform rate of wages, a carelessness will be engendered as to whether much or little is produced— that if all be insured a future provision, they will become indifferent to present exertion — if these and similar arguments be brought forward against the contemplated change, they will be of no more weight than if applied to individuals under the present system. Under the joint-stock movement, there will be all the incentives to action which exist at present — there will be a Public Opinion to give its award to particular actions — and the provision for the future will, as is now the case, depend upon the labour of the past. In almost all trades, the workmen now receive a stated weekly sum, although the powers of production of various individuals differ considerably; and yet such uniformity in the rate of payment does not encourage idleness. The opinion entertained of a man by his fellow-workmen is generally sufficient to excite him to honest exertions; and the advantages held out by the joint-stock system — in which every person would ultimately receive *the whole* fruits of his labour — are so superior to any now enjoyed, that they could not fail to create one universal spirit of enterprise and activity.

It can be easily determined in what manner such a system would work in regard to individuals and to society at large. We have already supposed that an indefinite number of joint-stock companies are formed — that their transactions are governed by general and local boards of trade, which would regulate production and distribution in gross —that their minor details are superintended by managers and overlookers, as at present — that the members of these companies work the same number of hours and receive one uniform rate of wages. Under the present system, the hours of labour vary from eighty to forty, and the wages from fifty to ten shillings per week; but in scarcely any instance have the wages any dependence on the hours of labour, for it generally happens that those receive the least wages who work the greatest number of hours. Under the joint-stock system, however, so great would be the amount of labour and machinery of every kind set in motion, that, in a short time, sufficient wealth would be produced for the enjoyment of all persons by an expenditure of not more than five hours' labour a day. But even at its first institution, it would require no more than from eight to ten hours' labour per day from each associate producer; and this moderate exertion would yield him an equivalent equal to two shillings an hour. Cost of production would in every instance determine value; and equal values would always exchange for equal values. If one person worked a whole week, and another worked only half a week, the first would receive double the remuneration of the last; but this extra pay of the one would not be at the expense of the other, nor would the loss incurred by the last man fall in any way upon the first. Each person would exchange the wages he individually received, for commodities of the same value as his respective wages; and in no case could the gain of one man or one trade be a loss to another man or another trade. The labour of every individual would alone determine his gains and his losses.

The arrangements respecting the production of food could be adjusted on the same principle of equality as would prevail in manufactures of various kinds. As the land, like the houses and machinery, would be held as common property, the value of all its products would be estimated on an equitable principle, such as should afford equal advantages to every member of society. Those employed in agriculture would be remunerated according to their labour, and not by amount of crop; and society at large would receive the benefit, or bear the loss, of productive or unproductive seasons.

Under this joint-stock modification of society, as under a more perfect system, ample provision could be made for the young, the aged, and the infirm, without subjecting parents or relatives to the least trouble or anxiety. With regard to employment, every company would be open to the admission or persons whose labour had been superseded by machinery; and who, by being immediately provided with a suitable occupation, would neither suffer loss themselves, nor inflict an injury upon society. There is so much of all kinds of work to be done, that there never can be too much labour set at liberty, or superseded by machinery. But if any man, or any body of men, be made to suffer from an improvement which confers a benefit upon society at large, an act of gross injustice is committed; for as every individual ought to confer as much benefit as possible upon society, so, likewise, is society equally bound to contribute to the welfare of all its members. But society can do this only by instituting such social arangements [sic] as, while they enforce the principle and practice of universal labour, take care that employment shall always be procurable. It is easy enough for the overgorged capitalist to say to the working man whose labour, under the present system, has been superseded by machinery — "Turn to some other employment " The world now offers the workman no such employment, and he is therefore compelled to combat against his steam and iron adversaries until he is worked to death, or perishes from disease and starvation.

At the present time, it would be useless to enter into minute details of what could and what should be done under a new social system such as that under consideration. We have experience to guide us in almost every thing; for the present movement is not an introduction of new principles and modes of action, but simply the application of existing principles and modes to a new object —the universal and equal benefit of society at large, instead of the aggrandisement of particular individuals and classes. There is always, if it be rightly managed, a fund of common sense in the world sufficient for all emergencies. Almost every man is aware of the order and precision with which the transactions of companies and individuals are at present carried on, however extensive or complicated they may be. By means of general and local boards of trade, and the directors attached to each individual company, the quantities of the various commodities required for consumption—the relative value of each in regard to each other— the number of hands required in various trades and descriptions of labour — and all other matters connected with production and distribution, could in a short time be as easily determined for a nation as for an individual company under the present arrangements. Statistics of every kind would acquire a degree of correctness and perfection such as they can never attain to under the existing system. The simple principles of equality are of such a nature that they can be acted upon in all transactions and all emergencies; for, like the compass of the mariner, they can guide alike in the darkness as in the sunshine—in the storm as in the calm.

The social change under consideration, great and beneficial as would be its own immediate effects, would be an easy preparatory step to the more perfect change already considered. There is nothing in the movement which can arouse the fears of the most faint-hearted. It is not to be expected that society can become perfect at once — that the vicious propensities and wrong notions which have grown with our growth and strengthened with our strength, can be eradicated or changed in a moment. But as comparative wealth and increased leisure shall take the place of hopeless poverty and inordinate toil — when better arrangements than those which now exist shall diffuse education universally — when the present narrow views and warped sympathies of classes shall be expanded and adjusted, and men made to regard all their fellows as members of one great family, having a common interest and progressing towards a common end — then will society gradually and imperceptibly glide into the state desired, and establish those institutions and usages which are so essential to the highest scale of civilization.

Every whole is but an aggregate of parts, and a nation will ever be broken up into communities or divisions of some kind. As individuals compose families, and families towns, under the existing system, so likewise would they after the joint-stock change had been effected. The present distribution of people in towns and villages, bad as it is, would not be directly interfered with; nor would there be any immediate destruction and re-erection of the buildings now in existence, unhealthy and uncomfortable as they are. We have all, more or less, imbibed feelings of attachment to our present habits, pursuits, and modes of action. We are thus morally incapacitated from acting upon a more perfect division of society into communities comprised of many families, in which there is but one feeling and one manner of living. It is not pretended that society, in these days, has knowledge enough, or morality enough, or honesty enough, for such a system. The trammelled minds of men cannot yet grasp the great and glorious destiny which is conceived for them in the womb of the future. But if perfection cannot be attained at once, there is nothing to deter men from planting the seed of future good.

Although society will ever be broken up into parts, it does not necessarily follow that those parts shall always maintain the same jarring and hostile relation to each other as they now do, and always will do, when classified as rich and poor. Man is not naturally the enemy of man; nor would he ever be so, if the interest of one were not opposed to the interest of another. This opposition of interests does not exist in joint-stock companies. If one shareholder gain or lose anything by a company, all the other members do so likewise; and this universality and equality of interest at present exists under no other circumstances. Thus, either under the joint-stock division of society, or in any other modification of the principle of community, where labour is universal and remuneration in proportion to the labour, the interest of any one man will be equally the interest of all; and this reciprocity and equality of interests would extend from one company to all.

Thus, taking society as we find it— with all its irrational habits and prejudices, its ill-arranged and incommodious habitations and modes of production, its depraved tastes and ignorant appliances of the means of enjoyment —no arrangements can bring into operation powers so extensive in their application and gigantic in their results, as those existing in connection with a joint-stock modification of the principle of community of possessions. Such a system would be simple and effectual in regard to the creation and distribution of wealth — it would, as far as possible, insure equality of exchanges, and give to every man that true independence which, under the present system, must ever be unknown to the workman — it would instantly alleviate the poverty, and crime, and vicious habits, produced by too little and too much work — it would allow of a comfortable provision for the young, the old, and the infirm, without discomfort to themselves or loss to the community. Under such social arrangements, one class would not, as at present, be dependent upon another for employment; nor could the gains of one man be an accumulation of the losses of another.

The objections which have been urged by the economists against the more perfect system of community of possessions, do not apply to this joint-stock modification of the principle. The present could not be called the trying of a mere experiment — the feeling of our way in the dark — the precursor of universal apathy, and poverty, and immorality. Throughout this change, society would act upon well-known principles — principles which the experience of every day proves to be the more efficacious and powerful in proportion as they are the more extensively acted upon, it would be simply an extension of the union of a few individuals, to effect a definite object, into the alliance of the people of a nation, to effect the same object; and as a joint-stock company is stronger than an individual, so will a nation of such companies be superior to any isolated combination.

The production and distribution of an unlimited quantity of wealth, although the first, is not the only requisite to the welfare of society. The next class of arrangements of importance are those relating to education as a whole — to the moral and physical culture of man — to the teaching him his rights and his duties — to the entire formation of his character. Under the joint-stock modification of society, this great object could be speedily and effectually attained. The time and the means which are now so ill-applied to this purpose, could be at once turned into a proper channel, and be indefinitely increased — the demoralizing circumstances which now more or less surround and influence every human being from birth to death, would shortly cease to have existence — and, by a few simple arrangements, every child might receive the best training without either trouble or anxiety on the part of its parents, or loss to the community at large.

In connection with this joint-stock system, as well as in the more perfect form of community, arrangements might be made for the support of women and children, without the former being dependent on their husbands, or the latter on their parents, for the means of subsistence. When rationally viewed, the maintenance and education of children by their parents is a glaring defect in every social system in which the practice prevails. It may be affirmed, truly enough, that all parents have a natural desire to provide for their offspring — that the same stimulus to parental exertion exists even among animals — and it may be from hence inferred, that, by establishing institutions which throw this burthen upon society at large, we act contrary to, and endeavour to subvert, the natural desires of the human breast. Such an objection as this arises from a contracted view of the subject. The inherent feelings of parents can never be annihilated, either in human beings or in brutes; but it does not follow, because mankind happen to have these feelings in common with brutes, that they should act in the same manner, and individually provide for the childhood of their little ones. We are placed in a very different position, in respect to means, to that of any class of beings around us; and we are possessed of much higher faculties than those enjoyed by any of the modifications of intelligence with which we are acquainted. We take pattern by them in nothing; and although man and brute are alike possessed of similar natural feelings in regard to their offspring, yet, while the brute is guided in the preservation of its young by instinct only, man has reason as well as instinct to direct him. Thus, while instinct ever compels human beings to provide for their children, reason only can direct them how to do this in the most effectual manner.

Experience, fraught with innumerable troubles and sorrows, shews every parent — and especially every parent in the productive class— how lamentably imperfect are the present arrangements of society for the protection and welfare of children, The greater part of the sum total of human discomfort is now comprised of parental anxiety for the preservation and happiness of offspring. In consideration of his children, how long and patiently does the workman toil — how many of the insolences of upstart authority does he silently receive — how enduringly does he bear the galling of every chain which the present accursed system fastens upon him ! Although solicitude will ever exist, yet fear and doubt, respecting the welfare of their children are no ingredients in parental happiness. By the present irrational arrangements of society, mankind are degraded to the level of brutes, — over which they suffer their boasted reason to give them no pre-eminence, in respect to the preservation of their offspring. Society, when viewed as a whole — in its composition, its constitution, and its intention —ought to know, as society, of no such limited distinctions as those of parents and children. Every child ought to be regarded and protected as the child of society; and society, in its turn, ought to be as a helping child to every aged parent. Every individual, besides his natural relationship to other individuals, has a relationship likewise to society at large; and society, by instituting arrangements for the punishment or protection of its members, tacitly acknowledges this relationship even under the present system. But under a rational organization of society, the immediate dependence of children upon their parents would be, as it ought to be, entirely done away with; and society, taking upon itself the physical, moral, and intellectual culture of all its foster-children, would leave to their parents, as individuals, no offices to perform but the caressings [sic] of parental love.

There can be neither wrong nor loss inflicted upon society by thus maintaining its children. The considerations which have been already entered into respecting the nature and origin of wealth, and the experience which man has of his powers of production, go to shew, that, while there is a sufficiency of raw material there never can be too much labour. Every child contains in embryo more or less of labour, mental and corporeal; and consequently, under arrangements which enforce universal labour, and at the same time keep in view the accumulation of sufficient capital to set this labour in motion as it arrives, every child, instead of being a loss, will be a profit to society. It is society, and not the individual parents, which receives the benefits arising from the male and female children born into the world; and upon society, therefore, have they a just claim for an outfit. There would exist under the social system of community, none of the incentives to celibacy which now influence so many thousands. The facility for marriage would be co-extensive with the desire for it. All parents would contribute to the support of all children, in an indirect manner, through proper social regulations; and thus children would not be, as at present, unjustly visited and punished by the sins of their parents.

Bad as are the social arrangements which leave children immediately dependent upon their parents for education and subsistence, a still worse feature in the present system, and one productive of the greater part of the demoralization and vice which surround us, is that custom of society which leaves woman dependent upon individual man for subsistence. Woman should be altogether as independent of man, in respect to her occupation and her maintenance, as man is independent of her or of his fellow-man. Woman is not naturally, and never can be legally, the slave or the property of man; but, in regard to every right appertaining to human existence, she stands with man on a footing of the most perfect equality. Under the present system, woman is dependent upon and is regarded as inferior to man — she is by turns his slave and his plaything — she has no equal social rights, and no political existence. Spoiled by a pernicious and deficient education, half-despised for the apparent want of those mental powers which are not permitted to be called forth and exercised, and degraded by her dependent position, — woman is now fixed in a labyrinth of tyranny and injustice from which she cannot be rescued by any means which do not afford her entire independence of the control of her self-styled superior, in the same degree as he is independent of her mien released from such dominion — when relieved from the fear of future want, and made a co-equal with man — when fostered and protected by social institutions calculated to make her physically, morally, and mentally, what she should be — then will she stand in her true position—then will the unknown and now unappreciable treasures of her heart and mind be poured out, and she will be to man "a help-mate meet for him."[1]

This joint-stock modification of society would in a short time prepare the way for the introduction of social arrangements calculated to effect all these objects, and every other which philanthropy can desire and intellect discover for the happiness of society. There is ample scope afforded, for philosophical inquiry, and invention, and experiment, by the establishment of national institutions provided with every requisite that unfettered ingenuity and labour can bring into existence. Old age and impotency could be provided for in a manner such as worn-out Labour well deserves for the honest exertions of its better days — and this, too, as a matter of right, and apart from all the feelings now existing in connexion with charity and alms-houses. All losses to individuals and companies, by fire, shipwreck, and other disasters, could be made, as in justice they ought, to fall upon society at large. There would be one great gainer and one great loser — the nation — for society would form, as it were, one vast insurance company, in which the profits only would be known, and the losses be unfelt and unseen.

Upon the establishment of such a system, every social, political, and ecclesiastical grievance under which men now suffer, and with which they have ineffectually combated for centuries, would be almost instantly annihilated. Intolerance would give place to liberality; and a just, natural, and rational equality of rights and possessions would succeed the present system of exaltations and abasements — of tyranny and slavery — wherein the hand of every man is raised against his fellow, and a wide-spread conventional hypocrisy of love exists in the place of that sympathy and kindness which nature prompts us to entertain towards each other. Under this joint-stock system, the same as under that now existing, every individual would be at liberty to accumulate as much as he pleased, and to enjoy such accumulations when and where he might think proper. The savings of every man would be his own, and would in no way affect the savings of his fellow ; for equal exchanges, and individual independence of individual, render wealth an almost powerless instrument of mischief. By the imposition of a direct tax on individuals or on articles of consumption, together with the rents of buildings, &c., ample funds could be secured to meet all the expenses connected with the proper government of society, the education of all its children, the maintenance of the infirm, the prosecution of scientific research, the progressive demolition and re-erection of the habitations now in existence, the formation of roads, and the establishment of every institution required to meet the wants and the exigencies of society.

Thus, with a social change like this, although the face of society would retain for a time, its present appearance, its whole inner constitution would be daily undergoing a purification, a reviviscency, which would shortly extend to its outward aspect. The abominable wickedness and vice of every kind — the unmitigated moral putrescency— which now exists in the very heart's core of society, and stinks in the nostrils of Truth and Justice, would speedily give place to a purity and vitality such as society has never yet enjoyed; and the swelling torrent of human happiness, flowing from the rock of right, would bound from heart to heart, until all had drunk of its waters and felt their soul, cheering influence.

To those, then, who deem that a social change is necessary, and to those who decry all such changes as the hallucinations of misguided visionaries or the artful impositions of designing miscreants, the outline of a social movement is before them for consideration. Founded as it is upon established principles of production, and acting throughout upon a well-known and well-tried plan of operations, there can be little doubt that it would tend to the speedy progression of the human race towards that ultimate degree of happiness and perfectibility by which all finite things are bounded. Such a change would give increased wealth and increased leisure to society at large, and thereby remove the poverty and ignorance which now exist — it would be destructive of the present class and caste division of society, as well as of the social and governmental tyranny engendered by this division — and, by allowing of the introduction of circumstantial regulations favourable to the object in view, would enable all persons to acquire a degree of physical, moral, and intellectual excellence to which, under the present system, they can never attain.

A change like this, as well as the more perfect change already considered, presupposes that all the real capital of the country— the land, buildings, machinery, vessels, and every other description of reproducible wealth, except the personal property of individuals — is possessed and controlled by society at large; that the occupations and authority of the present capitalists and employers, in their individualized capacity, are superseded; that society is, as it were, one great joint-stock company, composed of an Indefinite number of smaller companies, all labouring, producing, and exchanging with each other on terms of the most perfect equality. The idea of such a thing is easily conceived; and to act upon the conception will be as easy a matter as to conceive it.

Hitherto, we have regarded this social movement only as an established change, without taking into consideration the means whereby such a change is to be accomplished, and the real capital of the country obtained possession of by the productive classes. It has been shewn that, under the present system, wealth is acquired by individuals in two ways — by labour, and by trading — the first being dependent on its own exertions, and the latter being derived, by unequal exchanges, from the exertions of others. Gold and silver coin and bank-notes are the exponents of wealth; and when a man has obtained possession of these —no matter by what means—he can find multitudes of persons willing to give him lands, houses, or anything else, in exchange for his coin and banknotes. It has been shewn that coin and notes are valuable only by conventional usage; and that such value depends upon the existence of the real capital, of which they are no more than the representatives.

This was exemplified by the fact, that the wealth or the poverty of a nation depends, not on the amount of the gold and silver possessed by the people, but upon the buildings, ships, machinery, and commodities in the country; and that, were we now without these things, and shut out from communion with other countries, we should be no better off than so many starving beggars, even if every individual were possessed of a million of sovereigns; because these would be no produce to be purchased from each other for the maintenance of life. But, under present arrangements, a man will give up his real capital— his buildings, and machinery, and food— for its worthless representatives, gold and bank-notes; and he does so only because he is well assured, by his experience of the conventional usages of society, that he can at any time receive for his gold and notes *an amount of real wealth equivalent to their apparent value*. He knows that this money will procure him lodgings, food, and clothing, or any other requisite of life, for twenty or forty years to come, as the amount may be. It matters not whether any of these things be in existence at the time a man receives his money guarantee for them: he knows that there is real capital, somewhere, to the amount of his bond, and that men will toil for and give to him, in exchange for this gold or paper bond, real wealth of every kind to the full amount. It is from these considerations that men buy and sell with money, and give up the real thing for its representative; and upon the same principle, and by the same means, may the working classes purchase from the capitalists all those vast accumulations which the present system of unequal exchanges has enabled them to obtain possession of.

The real capital of the country has been estimated to be worth five thousand millions of pounds sterling; and it has been shewn that the value of the wealth annually produced in the United Kingdom does not fall short of £500,000,000, of which the working classes receive and enjoy less than £200,000,000. If the working classes had only themselves to maintain, at the present rate, and were they to produce annually no greater an amount even than this £500,000,000, they would, in the course of seventeen years, create wealth sufficient to purchase all the present fixed capital of the empire. But it has been shewn that their position, and the enormous burthens which they have to sustain, will ever prevent them from being accumulators to any considerable amount under the present system; and that the subversion of this system, by such means, is an event to be looked for only in the course of centuries, during which the greatest part of the working class must suffer, with unmitigated severity, all the evils entailed upon them by the existing state of things. As it is necessary, however, to the success of any social change, that the real capital of the country should be possessed by the productive classes — as they must acquire such capital by purchase — as they have no means, under present circumstances, of accumulating sufficient wealth to purchase this capital during many generations—it is apparent that the productive classes must still remain the prey and the slaves of their fellows, unless some plan be adopted different to any hitherto made use of by them.

The discovery and adoption of such a plan will be anything but difficult. To accomplish the end desired, let it for a moment be supposed that the desire for a social change is almost universal among the productive classes — that each trade establishes within itself the germs of a future company—that a provisional government of delegates from each is appointed and convened— that paper money, and a coinage of pottery, bearing the two denominations of amount of labour and amount sterling, is created for the purpose of superseding the present medium, and carrying on the future transactions of society— and that a bargain takes place between the producers thus united and the capitalists, and the fixed capital is transferred from the one to the other.

In none of these suppositions—not even in the last—is there anything impossible. It is not indispensable to the success of the movement, that the whole of the capitalists and producers should at once concur in the settlement of the question. The change might be accomplished just so far as there might be capitalists and producers willing to agree in the matter. Assuming, however, that all parties are willing to sell and to buy on the terms proposed— that the capitalists receive their vouchers and give up their property— that the vast amount of unemployed labour and machinery which now exists is set in motion— that new inventions and new appliances are brought to bear in the business of production— that the combined labour and energies of the productive classes are brought into one focus and directed to a common end— the whole of the two thousand millions of debt might be wiped off within twenty years, and the capitalists would be enabled to enjoy this vast sum as they pleased, in the most perfect security, and uninterfered with by the busy world around them.

What are the real difficulties which stand in the way of a transaction such as this? On the one side there is nothing needed but union and industry— on the other, confidence is the sole requisite. The purchase of the real capital of the country, in the manner under consideration, would be as much a legal and proper purchase as any transaction which now takes place between a seller and a buyer. The magnitude of the contract does not alter its character. If the working classes had gold in their possession where, with to pay in advance for the things wanted, thousands of capitalists would be willing to make the bargain: and no difficulty would stand in the way of selling the same property to known capitalists, even if they were not possessed of gold, but were simply to give, as security, a promise to pay at some future specified time. If a working man pay gold to a capitalist, or one capitalist pay gold to another, he merely gives a representative of the things which labour has produced — if he give a bond to pay at a future time, he merely promises to pay what labour will produce. The past, the present, and the future transactions of Capital all depend on Labour for their fulfilment. Such being the case, why should not Labour itself make a purchase? Why should not the bond of Labour, to pay at a future time what itself only can produce, be as valuable as the bond of Capital, to pay what this very same Labour is to produce ? If gold be paid at once to the capitalist for his machinery and buildings, this gold is no more than a voucher that the capitalist shall receive other wealth to the full value of the things obtained from him: if a bond be given, it is equally a voucher that the contract shall be made good. The gold and notes would now be taken by the capitalist for his commodities, simply because the gold and notes form the common circulating medium: and as, in the contemplated change, the notes issued by the productive classes would likewise form the circulating medium, they would in every respect be equally as valuable as the gold. If security be wanted by the capitalist, that the contract shall be abided by, is the security offered by a people of less worth than that offered by an individual? There are innumerable instances of individual breach of faith — the page of history teems with records of governmental treachery — but there cannot be found one solitary instance of the infringement of a contract by a people.

The considerations entered into respecting the wrongs necessarily endured by the working classes under the present system, have shewn us that these wrongs owe their origin to unequal exchanges, and the consequent division of society into employers and employed, or rich and poor; and the first object of every social change is the ultimate subversion of the relations and the inequality existing between these classes. Such being the end in view, it is scarcely to be expected that the capitalists, with their present habits and prejudices, will generally consent even to sell their property for this object. As a class, they will, at the moment, abhor any transaction which tends, however remotely, to take from them their supremacy, to destroy class and caste associations and feelings, and to equalize the present distinctions in society. But the inquiry relating to the nature, origin, and transmission of wealth has proved that the capitalists, abstractedly considered, have no rightful title to the land which they now hold, nor to the vast accumulations of capital which they have obtained possession of. The title by which the capitalists hold these things is no more than a conventional privilege — a privilege conferred and sanctioned by the common usage of society, without particular limitation as to time. It is likewise a common usage of society, when the property of individuals interferes with the welfare of the body politic — in regard to roads, railways, canals, and other effects — to have such property equitably valued, and, paying its owners the price fixed upon, take the property, independent of their consent. The maintenance of a title to property in perpetuity, without regard to any circumstances which may arise, and independent of any extraneous control, is a thing which even now is never dreamed of. Thus, although the conventional privilege by which the capitalists hold possession of their wealth is, in the eye of justice, as sacred as that by which the producers hold the scanty reward of their labour, it is, nevertheless, in the power of society at large to alter at any time its existing arrangements, independent of the consent of a particular individual or a particular class. But the purchase of the wealth now possessed by the capitalists, in the manner considered, has in it nothing which can tend to interrupt the peace or destroy the happiness of one individual being.

With regard to the union of a number of producers adequate to effect a change in the present system, it is the easiest, as it is the first, step in the movement. Even at the present moment there are no less than two millions of producers united together in societies of various kinds. Almost every working man is or has been a member of a trades' union or trade society; and the number of this class in benefit societies does not from late returns, fall short of 1,500,000. Those at present united in societies will have dependent upon them eight or nine millions of women and children—the whole mass thus forming no less than one-third of the population. Here is at once material amply sufficient to accomplish any change, whether social or governmental—material more or less bonded together, and organised, and containing intelligence as well as numbers — material suffering a common wrong from the present state of things, and even now united together for the purpose of destroying or neutralising this wrong. But when the unimprovable nature of the present system is perceived by them—when they become aware of the fixity of their doom, and the utter futility of all mere governmental changes—there can be little doubt that the whole working class will unite as one man to demand a social change ; and when they thus demand it, there is no power on earth that can say it shall not take place. This oppressed class alone, if even partially united in one body, and devoting their now divided energies to one purpose, could instantly effect the deliverance of their order and their country— could overturn, by one movement, the whole social fabric, and institute arrangements calculated to produce as much of good and as little of evil as the most sanguine philanthropist can desire.

Such, then, is one mode of accomplishing a social change —such are the means possessed by society for effecting the end desired — such are the results which will follow its consummation. The object is just, the means are simple, the issue will be satisfactory. The change may for the moment startle some by its novelty, or frighten others who view it through the distorting medium of prejudice; but when the subject has been attentively examined—when the good has been balanced against the evil, the cost against the enjoyment — all these feelings of dislike and distrust will insensibly disappear, and the whole movement will take the hue and excite only the emotions of an every-day occurrence. In the principles and modes of action considered, neither truth nor justice is outraged — the physical, moral, and intellectual powers of every individual cannot be made worse, but must be made better, by the change — there is no avenue left open through which Despotism, with its galling fetters and its long train of military and judicial massacres, can be let in among the people, but every source of governmental evil will be dried up and destroyed for ever. There is nothing in the movement which can lead to social anarchy, or to those innumerable ills which ever follow in the train of simple governmental revolutions. What, then, has society or individuals to fear? The productive classes have only to move on with confidence, for Truth is with them—Justice is with them — all the elements of success are with them!

Note

1 A reference to the creation of Eve in Genesis 2:18: "It is not good that the man should be alone; I will make him an help meet for him".

Part 5

WAYS OF ORGANISING

The diversity and vitality of the Owenite movement was mirrored in the various ways it was organised. Early rejections of Owen's "Plan" and his subsequent departure to New Harmony in 1825 gave his British supporters ample latitude to adapt and reinterpret the "science of society". A myriad of institutions emerged, ranging from intentional communities, producer and retail co-operatives to trade unions, meetings halls and local branches.

They all aspired to establish a communitarian society, but the definition of that very ideal existed on a broad spectrum (Taylor 1983, 92–93; Langdon 2000, 74). For the millenarian wing, community life, as embodied by the Queenwood project for instance, was viewed as a quasi-religious New Jerusalem. Whereas the more practical wing thought that banding together would offer a more immediate response to their pressing needs – finding a way out of pauperisation and unemployment, and gaining access to affordable, quality food and other necessities. The stakes were high in the context of the post-war crisis, and the sense of urgency heightened with the passing of the New Poor Law in 1834 (Gurney 2017, 50). Not that the two approaches were incompatible. In the late 1820s and early 1830s, co-operative stores, Labour Exchanges and trade unions all appeared to offer an effective way to raise funds for the establishment of future communities on the land, while paving the way for a fairer economic system within those same communities.

The means of achieving community, however, were a more contentious issue, and revealed profound divisions between patrician and plebeian Owenism (see Part 6). The failure of early attempts to adapt his "Plan" at Spa Fields and Orbiston had convinced Owen that the general public, socialists included, were not ready for his notion of community. He therefore insisted that the initiative and leadership of social reform should come from above, thanks to benevolent, middle- and upper-class philanthropists like himself. Consequently, most of his organisational efforts were focused on education and preparation for future community life. This sat uneasily with most working-class Owenites and their allies, who believed that grassroots initiatives and self-help would usher in the "New Moral World" (Taylor 1983, 92). Taking cues from George Mudie's early community experiment at Spa Fields, they accordingly favoured smaller sized ventures which could be set up quickly, on a small budget and outside middle-class interference. Inspiration also came from William Thompson, whose intellectual influence grew during Owen's absence in the USA, and whose handbook for community formation, *Practical Directions* (1830), advocated a system of radical and democratic communitarianism.

Approaches to community building did shift in the second phase of the Owenite movement. Following the collapse of the Grand National Consolidated Trades' Union, Labour Exchanges and the early co-operatives, the locus of Owenite activism transferred to schools and meeting halls, such as the Social Institutions and the Halls of Science, especially after Owen tightened his hold over the Rational Society in 1843 (see Chapter 34). But for most local members, community on the Queenwood model remained unattainable, mainly for financial reasons. Six months after the founding of the Rational Society, more than 3,000 Owenites had subscribed to the General Fund, which financed activism in the local branches through a variety of lectures, balls and other social gatherings. However, only 783 individuals had given money to the Community Fund in support of Queenwood. Just like in the early, co-operative phase of Owenism, efforts remained concentrated at branch level. For socialists, "Owenism was and remained primarily an educational and ethical movement to make life more bearable in the old immoral world to which most of them were necessarily confined" (Royle 1998, 95).

28

"ARTICLES OF AGREEMENT OF THE ESTABLISHMENT AT ORBISTON", *REGISTER FOR THE FIRST SOCIETY OF ADHERENTS TO DIVINE REVELATION, AT ORBISTON*, N°1, 10 NOVEMBER 1825.

[The Orbiston community (1825–1827) was one of the first attempts to put Robert Owen's large-scale community plans into practice. Co-founded by two of his earliest followers, Alexander Hamilton of Dalzell (see Part 3, Chapter 15) and Abram Combe (1785–1827), Orbiston was meant to pick up where the failed Motherwell scheme had left off the same year. Combe, whose younger brother George was the pioneer of phrenology in Britain, was an Edinburgh tanner who converted to Owen's views after a visit to New Lanark in 1820. One year later, with financial support from Hamilton, he founded the Edinburgh Practical Society, a discussion group for local Owenites, co-operative shop and general training ground for future community living. The project came to fruition in 1825, when community buildings were established at Orbiston, Lanarkshire, on land belonging to Hamilton's family estate. Members included George Mudie (see Chapters 5 and 9) and two former New Lanark schoolteachers, Joseph Applegarth and Catherine Vale Whitwell (see Part 8, Chapter 48; Harrison 1969, 134–139; Siméon 2017, 151). As shown by the articles of agreement, ambitious community arrangements – including a vast range of amenities like schools, workshops, a dining-hall and communal dwellings – were meant to dazzle by example and facilitate conversion to Owen's principles. However, Orbiston failed to attract sufficient financial backing from wealthy investors, as Owen's visionary schemes and anti-religious stance were facing an increasing backlash (see Part 3, Chapter 15). This, in addition to Combe's untimely death in 1827, meant that the grandiose plans of its articles of agreement were never realised (Hardy 1979, 36–37).]

INTRODUCTION

[…] The following are the principles upon which the proprietors consider it necessary that the tenants should act: —

1st, That the Establishment at Orbiston be conducted upon the principles of union and mutual co-operation, for the purpose of removing vice and poverty; that its arrangements exclude all force and violence, all division and opposition of interest; and that its members be respected in proportion as their efforts tend to promote the general welfare of the community.

2d, That the private rooms be let to individuals at a yearly rent, and that, if the demand for apartments shall exceed the accommodation, in no case shall more than *one* private apartment be let to *one* individual, and more than *two* individuals shall not have the use of *one* apartment,—children under three years of age, with their parents, excepted.

3d, That no cooking of provisions, or cashing of clothes, or any mechanical operations, be carried on in the private apartments of the Establishment; and that no individual children be introduced to the public rooms of the Establishment which are intended for the use of adults.

4th, That the principal public rooms in the Establishment be *equally open to all* who are cleanly in their person and dress, and equally shut against all who are offensively filthy or slovenly, in any respect, in their manners, person, or dress.

5th, That as the smoke of tobacco is exceedingly disagreeable to those who consider the of it "a bad habit, and calculated to injure the health and intellect of those who practice it", if possible, the feelings of such individuals shall not be hurt by the open or public indulgence of such habits.

6th, That all the individuals in the society who belong or wish to join one trade or profession, will form a committee of management for conducting their own business, under a superintendent of their own appointment. They will have the advantages of the workshops, machinery, and utensils, and of the inclination on the part of the proprietors to assist them with capital. Each, from the first, will be entitled to the value of his own labour, and the profits will be divided *either* equally, *or* in proportion to the labour of each, as they themselves shall voluntarily determine. But, at the outset, each class will act entirely upon their own account, until experience shall show the propriety and safety of a more general union.

7th, That the children of all the Members of the Community shall be trained and educated together, upon a footing of equality, as the children of one family, upon the principles of undeviating kindness, without any artificial reward or punishment, and without any other distinction than that which unavoidably attend superior habits and attainments.

8th, That all inclinations and habits which are at variance with justice, temperance, industry, and personal and domestic cleanliness, are opposed to the New Views, and not likely to find either encouragement or protection in the Orbiston Establishment.

9th, That the invariable characteristic of false principles, and bad practices, is "*a rooted antipathy to defend them before those who think and act more rationally*"; and that no individual can be a suitable Member of this Community who is inclined to adopt any notions, or to practise any habits, which he is not inclined to persevere in defending before the world.

10th, That those who adhere to Divine Revelation in the New Community have a just title, and full liberty, to state, and to teach to their own children, the facts and truths which God reveals to the senses and to the understanding—though it is probable that those whose faith has been founded on mere human testimony will feel unable to act towards them according to the principles of genuine charity.

11th, That the formation of the judgment and inclinations of individuals is not in any way under their own control, and that from these alone do the voluntary actions of every human being proceed; and almost all violence, may be justly ascribed to the prevalence of notions which are opposed to these truths.

12th, That at the expiration of every year as the individual Members acquire more experience in the practical measures of a Community, the Rules and Regulations shall undergo such revision as the majority of Members may decide upon.

13th, That the Community, acting upon the principle of utility (or that which tends most to promote the happiness of the greatest number), has the sole management of its own affairs, and has equal and complete control over all its individual Members, and that all ignorantly selfish attempts to promote our own interest, at the expense of others, must tend to our own material injury.

14th, That the Community claims the privilege of publishing to the world the particulars of all the actions which the individual members may persevere in practicing openly before the Community, and that they consider this circumstance as the most effectual restraint upon vice, and a great incentive to virtue.

15th, That the suitableness of the members in the New Society will depend upon the consistency which their conduct shall manifest with their principles.

29

"PROCEEDINGS OF THE LONDON CO-OPERATIVE SOCIETY. AN ADDRESS DELIVERED BEFORE THE SOCIETY, ON NEW YEAR'S-DAY", *CO-OPERATIVE MAGAZINE AND MONTHLY HERALD*, N°2, FEBRUARY 1826, 54–59.

[Founded in 1824 with Owen's support, the London Co-operative Society (LCS) was another attempt to raise funds to establish communities on a larger scale. Prominent members included William Thompson and William Lovett. Following the instructions outlined in the *Report to the County of Lanark* (1820), the LCS proposed to raise a capital of £20,000 to develop a "Village of Co-operation" some 50 miles from London. To that end, it sought help from rich backers, offering them a return of 5% on investment. But the project suffered from Owen's departure for the United States in 1825 (where he remained until 1828). By January 1826, the fund had only gathered £400. This was mainly due to a lack of support for co-operative ideals outside radical and socialist circles, as Owenism proposed to give producers a power hitherto reserved to the economic elite, thus blurring and threatening social hierarchies (Holyoake [1875]1908, 442). The failure of the LCS encouraged Owenites to embrace co-operative trading and production as a means to raise money for community-building. Many, including Thompson and Lovett, thus joined the London Co-operative Trading Association and the British Association for the Promotion of Co-operative Knowledge, which were founded as splinter groups from the LCS in that context (Langdon 2000, 75).]

When a traveler has long journeyed through a country which he has never before explored, and in a path but imperfectly marked out, in which he has continually met with unlooked for obstructions, it is a pleasing compensation for the toil he has undergone, to rest for a time on the summit of an eminence, whence he can see before him, at no great distance, the spot to which his steps have been directed, and whence he can look back with complacency on the obstacles he has surmounted, and on the difficulties which once appeared invincible, but which he has overcome.

We are now placed in a similar situation. The termination of the old, and the commencement of a new year, is a period which seems to invite us to pause awhile in our course, to consider the circumstances by which we are now surrounded, to contemplate the bright and cheering prospect before us, and to take a retrospective glance at the various incidents of the past, which have accelerated or retarded our progress.

More than eight years have now elapsed since Mr. Owen stood forward as the public advocate of a new combination of circumstances, by which he proposed to remove from society its greatest evils—poverty and ignorance. At that period Mr. Owen himself, and many of his friends, probably expected to see the benefits of the plan more immediately realized than has been answered by the event. Yet, if we take into the account the numerous impediments it was first necessary to remove, we shall not be surprised that the march of the New System has not been more rapid, and we shall find reason to congratulate ourselves upon what has been effected.

Mr. Owen had not been long before the public, when he was joined by many persons in the upper walks of life, who professed themselves willing to give his plans every support. A little time, however, proved that these individuals were not sufficiently grounded in the principles to render efficient aid, or to second Mr. Owen's views to that extent which was necessary to give the system a fair trial. Mr. Owen failed, therefore, in obtaining able coadjutors from the higher or richer classes; but it was by no means an idle, or an [sic] useless measure, (as some have supposed,) when he directed his first appeal to them. Had he acted otherwise—had he addressed himself exclusively to the laboring classes—it is highly probable that prejudice and misrepresentation would have raised an unfounded alarm among the members of the Aristocracy; and that those who at that time had power in their hands, would have made use of it to arrest his further proceedings. Now, however, we may rest in perfect confidence, that, however indisposed the Legislature may be to come forward and support the system, no active opposition need be apprehended from that quarter.

When we consider the total change that will be effected by the new arrangements, in the habits and circumstances to which individuals have been accustomed from childhood, it is but reasonable that it should not be an easy task to satisfy them that this change would be altogether beneficial and desirable, and then to convince them if its practicability.

Many of us can remember the time, when, if not altogether hostile to the system, we ourselves looked upon it with distrust; when we could see a thousand objections, which have now all disappeared. But those objections were not removed from our minds in an instant, and not without much thought, investigation, and canvassing of the subject in all its different bearings; and, in like manner, it was not to be expected that society generally should at once see the beauty and propriety of a scheme so novel, so much at variance with established usages and institutions, so contrary to the existing order of things, as was the new system of social arrangements when first proposed by Mr. Owen.

The London Co-operative Society was formed to facilitate the removal of these difficulties, by lectures, public discussions, by publications of various kinds, and by every means that could be adopted, to place the subject in a clear point of view. This Society has hardly been in existence more than fifteen months. About fourteen months back, the few individuals who then composed it, hired rooms in Burton-street[1], Burton-crescent, and advertised questions for discussion relative to the merits of the two systems—of Individual Competition, and Mutual Co-operation. It was found that this situation was not sufficiently central to command a numerous assemblage, and the public discussions were there discontinued, and immediately resumed at the Crown and Rolls Rooms, in Chancery-lane.

On the 9th of January, 1825, Mr. Hamilton, of Dalzill [sic][2], being in town, gave a public breakfast at the York Hotel, in Bridge-street, Blackfriars. At this meeting Mr. Coombe [sic][3] exhibited the plans for the buildings which have since been erected at Orbiston. From this period it has been the practice of the Society to hold weekly social breakfasts, at which more than fifty persons have very commonly been present, and which have been at once of great utility, and a source of much pleasure and gratification.

In the same month a lecture was delivered at the Crown and Anchor, on the System, which met at the time with some opposition, and afterwards gave rise to an animated discussion, prolonged for several months, at the Crown and Rolls Rooms, and which, on many evenings, drew overflowing audiences. On these occasions much ability was displayed by the Political Economists who came forward to expose what they considered the weak points of Mr. Owen's plan. The chief argument urged against the System, was the Malthusian doctrine, of "the tendency of population to press against the means of subsistence." It is not assuming too much, when we assert that they went away convinced, that whether this position be true or not, it proves nothing against the proposed arrangements; for, should the period ever arrive when a really superabundant population need be apprehended, the numbers of mankind would be much more easily kept within their proper limits in the new state of society than in the old, since there would be less ignorance and improvidence, and more intelligence and forecast, and consequently greater ability to guard against the dreaded evil.

In the month of April the Society hired a first-floor in Picket street, Temple-bar, for the private meetings of the members, which it continued to occupy for seven months; when, finding its members rapidly increasing, it became necessary to seek more commodious apartments; and, in November, the Society removed to the house, No. 36, Red Lion Square, which will probably be a permanent station.

Among the most interesting and important features of the past year, must be mentioned the Public Meeting held at the Theatre of the London Mechanics' Institution, on the 26th of September. It was highly gratifying to witness the theatre crowded to excess: the applause with which Mr. Owen was greeted on his entrance; the marked attention paid to all the observations he delivered; and the almost unanimity with which the resolutions he proposed were adopted. Those among us who remembered the time when, at a public meeting called by Mr. Owen, all his propositions were treated as idle fantasies, and negatived, with hardly one hand held up in their favour, hailed these facts as delightful evidences of the progress of the new system, as silently and secretly made in the minds of men, and as a happy omen of the approaching period when it shall be universally embraced.

The Society has also done much in the course of the past year in printing and publishing various pamphlets relative to the system; and as it has every reason to anticipate a great addition of members, and consequently an increase of funds, it will be enabled in a short time greatly to extend its usefulness.

With the new year commences the *Co-operative Magazine and Monthly Herald*, of the new System of Social Arrangements. The conductors of the work cannot be too frequently reminded of the motto affixed to the *New Harmony Gazette*:—"*If we cannot reconcile all opinions, let us endeavour to unite all hearts.*" Our object must not be to wage open war with all opinions that may be at variance with our own, and that are not necessarily connected with the practical tenets we advocate. Already much mischief has been done by the injudicious conduct of some of our best friends. The new system has unfortunately been too much identified with speculations on other subjects, which the public mind is not yet prepared to discuss, which will not be listened to with candour and forbearance, which have therefore been extremely ill timed, and have served only to strengthen the prejudices already imbibed, and to render them more inveterate. Let us avoid this rock: let us rather endeavour unremittingly to inculcate the precept of universal charity. The time will never arrive when mankind on all subjects will think alike; but the time will come, and we will endeavour to hasten it, when persecution and intolerance, and all illiberality shall cease, and when men shall agree to differ.

Our labours will now be continued under circumstances highly encouraging. That which was theory alone is now reduced to practice. The assertion of the impracticability of the system must soon be set at rest for ever. We can now point to the western hemisphere, and show it in operation: in a few months also an experiment, on a somewhat smaller scale, will commence at Orbiston. By presenting the public with the details of the progress of these establishments, we shall do more than by volumes of dissertations on the subject.

The plan which the Society put forth for establishing a community within fifty miles of London, has yet met with but partial success. Shares have been taken out to the amount of 4,000*l*. About the middle of this year, Mr. Owen is expected back to assist our operations; and there is little doubt but a trial of the principles will then speedily be set on foot in this country. We must, however, be careful not to take any premature steps: when we build let it be on a sure foundation. If the time should not be yet, do not let us despair: although circumstances do not now bend to our wishes, they are in a proper train:—we are certain of ultimate success, but it is not for us to know the times and the seasons.

We are now delayed only by the backwardness of our friends. There are thousands in this country who are favourably disposed towards our views, and who collectively possess sufficient capital to carry them into effect; but they are discouraged by difficulties which they might easily overcome. They will not come forward to oppose popular ignorance and prejudice; they are intimidated by the derision and ridicule, abuse and opposition the new system has sometimes experienced, and which the true philanthropist has invariably met with, in the commencement of his labours, in every age, and in every country of the world. We, at least, will stand to our post, and not desert our colours. The time is not far distant when we shall remember with pride that we did not shrink from bearing our part of "the burthen and the heat of the day." Even if life should fail us before our wishes should be realized, the object we have before us would still be worthy of pursuit, for there is no pursuit more noble; and there is nothing that affords a satisfaction more sweet than the reflection, that in our day and generation we have served the cause of truth—we have studied the welfare of the human race—we have devoted our strength, have spent our best energies in the endeavour to bring into operation the only effectual means of meliorating the condition of our fellow-creatures, and of removing that misery and wretchedness, the sight of which now makes the heart bleed.

The magnitude of the change we propose to effect, is an idle argument to offer in support of the assertion, that our expectations are visionary. Changes as great have been effected in the history of the world, but had the individuals through whose instrumentality they have been wrought, listened to the suggestions of the faint-hearted and the indolent, what great and good object ever would have been effected?

The time was when our present solar system was unknown, when it was the popular, the universal belief, that the earth was stationary, and that the sun moved round it once in twenty-four hours. When Galileo denied the truth of this doctrine, it was at the peril of his life. Ignorance, prejudice, and fanaticism, raised a clamour against him. It is easy to imagine the representations which were made to him by his friends. No doubt they advised him to consult his personal safety, and to remain silent; no doubt they insisted that it was wholly impracticable to stem the torrent of public prejudice, and to enlighten the minds of the people on this subject; no doubt they told him that it was a visionary expectation, that mankind would ever embrace his mathematical calculations, opposed, as they appeared to be, to the evidence of the senses; that men ever would believe that the sun was the fixed centre of a system, when they could see it traversing the heavens, rising in the east and setting in the west, and performing, each day, one half its journey before their eyes. For the honour of human nature, there have been individuals who have not been dismayed by these considerations, but have laughed them to scorn. Galileo persevered: he drew upon himself unmerited obloquy and persecution: twice he suffered imprisonment: his hooks were publicly burnt at Rome; and, when nearly seventy years of age, he was dragged before the fathers of the Holy Inquisition, to answer for promulgating a doctrine which was denounced as dangerous to the then existing "civil and religions institutions," and as proceeding from the instigations of the devil. *Not quite two centuries ago* was this old man compelled to abjure his philosophy; and, kneeling to read a solemn recantation of what was termed his "pernicious error." We are told, that as he rose from the earth, with feelings of ill suppressed indignation, brushing the dust away from his knees, he said,— "It moves, however." Yes, it moves, in spite of the blind guardians of what is called "the venerable fabric of antiquity," who sit "clothed in purple and fine linen, and who fare sumptuously every day."[4] Yes, and as it moves on in that undeviating, uninterrupted order, which is at once sublime and beautiful, each revolution in its orbit marks a change in the character of the human race, and a progressive advance from ignorance, barbarism, and wretchedness, towards knowledge, true civilization, and happiness. Innumerable as have been the moral evils which have arisen out of the errors of the past, they have yet been highly salutary: they have furnished us with data, from which we may now draw correct conclusions; they have given us a light by which, henceforward, we may direct our feet; they have taught us by experience, to discern good from evil; and come at length it will, when knowledge shall cover the earth as the waters cover the channels of the great deep, and when the whole family of man shall learn to refuse the evil, and to cleave to that which is good.

We shall not live to witness this general, this desirable consummation; but we shall, ere long, see the opposition we now experience rapidly die away. Once brought into full operation, and the practical advantages of our principles must silence all objections; and we may quickly expect to see the new system adopted in many parts of Europe and of the western world. Our present conflict will then terminate with the song of triumph, and we shall rejoice, not over our enemies, if any we have, but with them; not that we have trampled them under our feet, but that we have made them our friends.

Notes

1 In Bloomsbury, London.
2 Alexander Hamilton of Dalzell.
3 Abram Combe (see Part 7, Chapter 43).
4 Luke 16:19.

30

"RULES AND REGULATIONS OF THE EQUITABLE LABOUR EXCHANGE, GRAY'S INN ROAD, LONDON, FOR THE PURPOSE OF RELIEVING THE PRODUCTIVE CLASSES FROM POVERTY, BY THEIR OWN INDUSTRY, AND FOR THE MUTUAL EXCHANGE OF LABOUR FOR EQUAL VALUE OF LABOUR", *CRISIS*, N°27, 8 SEPTEMBER 1832, 105–106.

[The National Equitable Labour Exchange was inaugurated by Robert Owen on 17 September 1832 at 277 Gray's Inn Road, London, following a series of earlier grassroots initiatives in London, Glasgow and Birmingham (Harrison 1969, 202; Prothero 1979, 244; Langdon 2000, 67; Hayes 2001). Labour Exchanges aimed to combine co-operative trading with Owen's theories of political economy, and especially his wish to reward labour as the source of all wealth (see Part 4, Chapter 21). Within the new shops, also known as "bazaars", co-operative producers could bypass middlemen and trade their goods directly for labour notes based upon the estimated labour-time used to perform skilled work, thus enjoying the full produce of their craftsmanship (Lovett [1867] 1967, 35; Taylor 1983, 93). The *Crisis*, which was the main Owenite newspaper at the time, became the official voice of the Labour Exchange movement. But the bazaars faced a variety of setbacks, and folded after less than two years. As most Owenites were artisans, supply was dominated by craft goods, to the detriment of food produce and other staples. Complaints also rose over the paltry rate of pay that was six pence an hour. By the end of 1833, Owen had become engrossed in trade unionism, and had lost interest in the Labour Exchanges (Cole and Filson 1965, 262–263; Claeys 1991, xviii–xix; Siméon 2017, 145).]

I.—Considering that great distress has arisen among the Industrious Classes for want of means to circulate the wealth they can so easily produce, and that their

RULES AND REGULATIONS

distress is daily increasing, individuals desirous of removing this grievous evil, have determined to attempt its accomplishment: and for this purpose have formed themselves, into an Association for relieving the productive classes from poverty by their own industry, and mutual exchange of labour for equal value of labour under the denomination of the EQUITABLE LABOUR EXCHANGE, as now established in the Institution of the Industrious Classes, Gray's Inn Road, with a capital unlimited.

II.—This capital shall be employed, first, in the carrying on and extending the operation of the Exchanges, and afterwards in providing arrangements to give employment to the industrious classes and education to their children.

III.—The capital shall be raised by deposits of £20 each, which shall never be recalled by the depositors.

IV.—The depositors of £20, or upwards, shall be proprietors, and may sell and transfer their shares in the profits of the Exchange.

Members

V.—The members of this Association shall receive annually Labour Notes to the value of forty hours, as interest in consideration of every twenty pounds, or eight hundred hours' labour, which they may deposit.

VI.—Any depositor of goods for exchange in the Exchange, who shall become possessed of Labour Notes to the value of eight hundred hours, or more, shall be entitled, with such notes, with the Governor and Directors, and conforming to the Rules and Regulations of the Association, to become a member thereof, and shall be entitled to all the privileges of a member.

VII.—All surplus profit beyond the amount necessary to pay the necessary expences [sic], and five per cent. interest to the proprietors, shall be applied to extending the exchanges, by providing employment for the industrious classes and educating their children.

VIII.—Each member of the Association shall receive, at the time he makes his deposit, a Certificate, signed by the Governor, a Trustee, and a Director, in the following form:—

Equitable Labour Exchange.
Gray's Inn Road, London.
Established, 1832.

No.
    Date.
This is to certify that—of—has this day become a member of this Association, which entitles him to receive annually from the stores of the Exchange, goods to the value of forty hours laborr [sic]. Entered,

Governor.
Trustee.
Director.
Secretary.

IX.—The governor and directors shall issue annually Labour Notes to the value expressed on each certificate to any person presenting the same, unless notice shall have been given to them in writing by the member to whom any certificate may belong, that such certificate has been lost.

TRUSTEES.

X.—The property of the Association shall be vested in three trustees, who shall be named and appointed by the Members in general meeting assembled.
XI.—When any vacancy occurs in the number of Trustees, by death, resignation, or otherwise, it shall be filled up at the first General Meeting of the thereafter.

TREASURERS.

XII.—The Governor and Directors for the time being shall be joint Treasurers to the Association, and shall appoint a banker whenever it may appear to them necessary so to do.
XIII.—All drafts upon the banker shall be made by the Governor, and signed by at least one Director, and countersigned by the Secretary.

MANAGEMENT.

XIV.—The Management of the affairs of the Exchange shall be vested in a Governor, five Directors, and a Council of seven Proprietors, all of whom shall be elected by Ballot.
XV.—The Governor shall be elected once in three years by the Proprietors voting by ballot.
XVI.—The Directors shall be elected by ballot at the formation of the Association, and the two lowest of them on the ballot shall retire from office at the end of the first year. The two next lowest at the end of the second year, and the remaining Director and Governor at the end of the third year.
XVIII.—The vacancies in the direction either by death, resignation, or otherwise shall be filled up by the Proprietors voting by ballot, and those Directors or Governors who have retired from office shall be eligible to be re-elected.

THE COUNCIL

XIX.—A Council consisting of seven Members of the Association shall be nominated and elected annually by ballot, without salary, whose duties shall be to inspect and investigate all the books, accounts, and every other matter whatsoever, connected with the Association, and to report thereon, to the Proprietors monthly, and to the Public quarterly.

XX.—Any four Members of the Council may call a special general meeting of the members, and may present, at such meeting, any report which may appear to them to affect the interests of the members.

GOVERNOR AND DIRECTORS.

XXI.—The Governor and Directors shall have the entire management and control [sic] of the affairs of the Exchange: shall appoint all officers and servants necessary to assist them in the management, and may dismiss such officers or servants when it shall appear to them expedient so to do.

XXII.—The Governor shall preside at all meetings of the Directors, or meeting of Directors and Council, when he is present, shall be entitled to vote; and, upon all occasions of equal voting, he shall have, in addition, a casting vote.

XXIII.—The Directors shall contract with the Proprietors of the Institution, in Gray's Inn Road, for premises for carrying on the business of the Exchange, at a rental not exceeding 23 per cent. on the exchanges effected, or upon the best terms that can be obtained.

XXIV.—The Governor and Directors shall not make any contract or engagement that will extend beyond the time they continue to be Directors, or that would bind or fix their successors to any payment, engagement, or performance, unless such contract, covenant, or engagement shall have been approved at a general meeting of the Proprietors.

XXV.—The Governor or Directors shall not deposit any goods for exchange while they continue in office.

XXVI.—The Governor and Directors shall appoint such persons as they shall deem competent to value the goods deposited in the Exchange.

XXVII.—When the Directors have decided upon the value of the goods submitted to them, they shall issue Labour Notes to the amount in hours, which notes shall be signed by the Governor and a Director, and countersigned by the Secretary.

XXVIII.—The Directors shall make up a return monthly of the Exchanges made in the Exchange; of the salaries paid to officers and servants, and other incidental expences [sic], all which returns shall be laid before the Council.

XXIX.—The Directors shall also keep minutes of their proceedings which shall always be open to the inspection of the members of the Council.

XXX. —The Directors shall also report at the annual general meeting the state of the affairs of the Association.

XXXI.—The Directors may, at any time, call the Council together to assist them in their deliberations.

NOMINATION OF OFFICERS.

XXXII.—Any member may nominate another member for the office of Governor or Member of the Council; and any person, whether a member or not, as a Director.

XXXIII.—All nominations must be made at least twenty-one days before the election, and delivered to the Secretary in writing.

XXXIV.—A list of the Members nominated, and the office for which each of them has been nominated shall be delivered to the Council, and also hung up in the exchange at least fourteen days before the day of election.

XXXV.—No name shall be inserted in the list to be hung up, unless the person named shall have given his consent to take the office for which he is nominated.

XXXVI.—Balloting lists shall be prepared for the use of the members, and shall be delivered by the Secretary to such members as shall apply for them at the day of election.

MODE AND TIME OF BALLOTING.

XXXVII.—At the annual general meeting on the last Wednesday in August, every member who votes shall deliver to the Chairman his balloting list folded up, who shall, in his presence, put it into the balloting box. The Secretary shall then mark off the name of the Proprietor who delivered it.

XXXVIII.—When the Ballot is about to be commenced three persons shall be appointed Scrutineers by the members assembled.

XXXIX. —As soon as the balloting is closed the Scrutineers shall cast up the number of votes, and report the same, in writing, to the Chairman, who shall announce the result to the members assembled.

XL.—If the votes for two or more candidates should be equal, lots shall be prepared by the Scrutineers, and drawn by the Chairman.

XLI.—Candidates in this manner elected shall have the management of the affairs of the Exchange for the year ensuing, or such other term as by the foregoing Rules they may be elected for.

XLII.—The Secretary shall make a List of the Officers elected, which List shall be hung up in the Exchange.

GENERAL MEETINGS.

XLIII.—The annual general meeting of the members shall take place on the last Wednesday in Aug. The business of which meeting shall be to consider the Report of the Governor and Directors of the proceedings of the Exchanges for the year immediately ended, and to elect by Ballot the Directors and Council of the Association.

XLIV.—Special general meetings may be called at any time by the Directors, or by four of the Members of the Council.

XLV.—No special general meeting shall be called till seven clear days notice shall have been given to the members.

XLVI.—No business shall be brought forward or discussed at any special general meeting, unless included in the notice for calling such meeting.

RULES AND REGULATIONS

XLVII.—All general meetings may adjourn from time to time, and any new matter may be adopted at an adjourned meeting provided that seven days' notice of the introduction of such new matter be given to the members.

XLVIII.—No member shall be entitled to vote at any annual or general meeting till he shall have been a member for six months.

XLIX.—No member shall be entitled to vote at any Annual or special general meeting of the members of this association, who has become a member by purchasing a certificate of any member, until six months after he shall have given notice to the Directors, in writing, that he has so become a member.

L.—No member shall be entitled to more than one vote at any meeting in respect of any number of shares he may possess.

LI.—All alteration in the Laws of the Association shall be made by a Committee appointed at a general meeting to consider such alterations, which Committee shall report to a subsequent general meeting; and, if their Report be adopted, the laws shall be altered accordingly.

31

"INCIPIENT COMMUNITY" IN *PROCEEDINGS OF THE THIRD COOPERATIVE CONGRESS, HELD IN LONDON* (LONDON: W. STRANGE, 1832), 85–95.

[The third Co-operative Congress was held in April 1832 at the Owenite movement's headquarters on Gray's Inn Road, London. Since the previous annual meeting held in Birmingham, discord over the nature and the means to achieve community had reached a breaking point between Owen and his working-class followers. In 1831, a committee appointed to fund a community based on William Pare's proposals (see Part 4, Chapter 24) had failed to gather sufficient funding. This encouraged William Thompson, who sided with the Congress delegates and had become their de facto spokesman, to air his grievances publicly. Blaming Owen for his refusal to take immediate action and his contempt for grassroots initiatives, he urged for the appointment of a new committee intent on establishing smaller-scale, more practical and more affordable communities. Owen refused to give way, countering that the world was at present too ignorant to comprehend and implement his plans – an argument that would be reiterated throughout the history of his movement (Langdon 2000, 16, 50–51). The proceedings of all Co-operative Congresses were edited by William Carpenter (1797–1874), a radical journalist and essayist. The son of a London tradesman, he was self-taught and an apprentice to a Finsbury bookseller from an early age, before finding employment as a newspaper editor. By 1829, he had joined the British Association for Promoting Cooperative Knowledge. Along with fellow BAPCK member Henry Hetherington, Carpenter was a defender of the free press, and was jailed in May 1831 for his *Political Letters*, which he had published that same year as a critique of the stamp duty (Harrison 1969, 166). In the late 1830s and 1840s, he supported suffrage reform and the Chartist movement (see Part 6, Chapter 38).]

Mr. Pare[1] then read the resolutions (5, 7, 8) of the last congress (held at Birmingham), for the appointment of a committee to take the necessary steps towards the immediate formation of a community upon the social system; and also the report of the Committee, as follows :—

REPORT OF THE COMMITTEE APPOINTED BY THE SIXTH RESOLUTION OF THE LAST MEETING OF CONGRESS,

To take the necessary steps towards the immediate formation of a Community upon the Social System, in accordance with the Seventh and Eighth Resolutions of the Meeting of Congress, held in Manchester, in May, 1831.

Your Committee report that they held several meetings, immediately after the breaking up of Congress, at Robert Owen's Institution, Burton Street, Burton Crescent, London. F.D. Massey Dawson, Esq. was appointed Honorary Secretary, and Mr. Benjamin Warden[2] Sub-Secretary, *pro tempore*. Messrs. Samuel Austin[3], Francis French, and John Dempsey, were appointed Trustees, and Messrs. Prescott, Grote and Co. of Threadneedle Street, London, Bankers. In October, the following Circular was adopted and printed, and, after some unavoidable delay, 250 copies were forwarded to as many societies in the country, and to each member of the committee not residing in London.

CIRCULAR TO THE CO-OPERATIVE SOCIETIES OF THE UNITED KINGDOM OF GREAT BRITAIN AND IRELAND, AND TO SUCH INDIVIDUALS AS MAY WISH TO FURTHER THEIR VIEWS

At the Second Co-operative Congress held at Birmingham, October 4th and 5th, 1831, and continued by adjournment to the 6th, it was resolved,

I. That a council be now appointed to carry out the resolution of the First Congress held at Manchester, viz. 'That a Co-operative Community be formed.'

II. That this Congress considers it highly desirable that a Community, on the principles of 'Mutual Co-operation, United Possessions, and Equality of Exertions, and of the Means of Enjoyment,' should be established in England, as speedily as possible, in order to show the practicability of the co-operative system; and, further, it is the opinion of this Congress, that such Community may be formed by the means recently suggested by the 'First Birmingham Co-operative Society,' contained in the following resolution of that society, and published in 'Carpenter's Political Letter.' April 30, 1831.[4]

That this society, fully sensible of the great advantages that would result from the speedy formation of an Incipient Co-operative Community, upon the plan laid down by Mr. William Thompson[5], will make immediate application to one hundred and ninety-nine other Co-operative Societies, in order to obtain their concurrence to a project of electing a member of each society, and supplying him, in such a manner as they shall deem best, with the sum

of 30*l*., in order that an Incipient Community of 6000*l*. may immediately be formed in some part of England.
III. That Subscriptions of 3*l*. deposit, on shares of 30*l*. each, for the purpose of forming a Community on the basis and plans contained in the foregoing resolution, be received from the Trading Fund Associations, or from individuals wishing to join the Community; and that, as soon as 900*l*. shall be engaged, the Secretary shall call a meeting, where he may deem it most convenient to the majority of the Subscribers, to proceed in the formation of such Community.

Co-operative Societies, or individuals desirous for the formation of a Community, are requested to forward their deposits, as soon as possible, to the account of the Trustees, Messrs. Samuel Austin, Francis French, and John Dempsey, at Messrs. Prescott, Grote, and Co., Bankers, Threadneedle Street, London, or to either of the members of the Council residing in their neighbourhood, that it may be forwarded, without loss of time, to the Bankers in London. No part of these deposits will be used by the Council, or any other persons but the future Community itself, for any purpose whatever. All deposits shall be returned, if demanded, should the land not be purchased within one year after the 300 shares shall have been taken up. As soon as the shares are all disposed of, a meeting of the shareholders shall be called in London, or any place more convenient to a majority of the shareholders, when they shall (assisted by the Council) take all subsequent arrangements into their own hands.

N. B. Societies and individuals, after making a deposit, must send an intimation of the same to the Sub-Secretary, Mr. Benjamin Warden, at Robert Owen's Institution, Burton Street, Burton Crescent, London, post paid, with name and address, for registry by the Secretary,

(Here followed the name and address of the Secretary.).

Your Committee regret to state, that they have received replies from only two societies, namely, the "First Birmingham," who have sent to the bankers 6*l*., as deposit for two shares, and from the Kendal Society, who have expressed their desire to subscribe for a share or shares, but who have not remitted any deposit. Your Committee conceive that one reason why so little has been done towards the formation of the proposed Community is, that many of the societies have embarked their capital in purchasing raw materials and machinery, for the purpose of employing their members in manufactures, whilst others have been appropriating their share of capital, in the way of subscriptions, to assist in the formation of the "North-West of England Co-operative Company,"[6] which they have considered the best calculated, for the present, to advance their interests.

Your Committee trusts that the steps these societies have severally taken will enable them, at no distant period, to join the projected Community.

The SECRETARY[7] also read such letters and documents as had been received by the committee, containing offers and suggestions relative to the community.

Mr. WARDEN requested to withdraw as secretary, *pro. tem.* to the committee.—Agreed to.

Mr. THOMPSON[8] explained the reasons why the committee had done so little in this business. Six persons, living in different parts of the kingdom, were upon the committee, the majority of them being resident in London; and it was of course expected that the latter would meet and act more efficiently than the others. Himself, however, with another or two of those resident at a distance, had come to London for the purpose of beginning practical operations; and as far as preliminary measures were concerned, they had done their duty. A circular had been drawn up, and sent round to the societies. Mr. Owen, however, who was upon that committee, proposed that they should form themselves into a committee for universal correspondence, alleging that to be the large object for which they were really appointed, and not for the mere petty or little purpose of forming a committee. For his (Mr. Owen's) part, he would not consent to have his name associated with any committee who was for making a beginning with a smaller sum than 240,000*l*. That had rather startled the committee, and Mr. Owen deliberately withdrew his name from the committee, saying, he would give them all the assistance he could, as an individual, but he would have no responsible connection with a thing not started upon a proper basis. This circumstance had paralysed the exertions of the committee; but he (Mr. T.) was always not only ready, but anxious to co-operate with the rest, whenever he saw that any thing was likely to be done. He trusted that the congress would now appoint another committee, consisting of practical men, who would be ready and determined to go forward in realising their object.

Messrs. STYLES[9], AUSTIN, and WARDEN, severally explained the circumstances in which the committee had been placed, for the purpose of showing, that although they had effected nothing, it had not arisen from negligence or apathy on their parts.—The report was then adopted.

Mr. BISHOP[10] read a resolution passed by the first society at Birmingham, explanatory of their views of the importance of forming an incipient community, and enforced upon the congress the propriety and necessity of maturing and acting upon some plan for this purpose.

Mr. PARE was sure that there was a sufficient number of societies in the kingdom to realize an incipient community, if the measures necessary for the purpose were now taken. For his part, he had been disappointed that so few shares had been subscribed for, the fact being, that persons were desirous to know something about the details of the project. A full prospectus, comprising all the necessary information should be drawn up and circulated, and then there would be no want of subscribers. On the previous evening, the result of a desultory conversation among a few of the delegates had been a subscription of twelve pounds.

Mr. LOVETT[11] concurred with Mr. Pare, and felt assured that if ever the world was to realise the happy state of society promised by Mr. Owen, it must be through the medium of such incipient communities as they were now contemplating. Living, as they now did, in the midst of difficulties and distresses, weighed down by anxiety for the subsistence of themselves and their children, they were not only prevented from acquiring the requisite knowledge for a perfect state of community, but the requisite dispositions also. He urged upon the congress to prepare and adopt some plan of proceeding before they left this subject.

The Rev. Mr. MARRIOTT[12] was also desirous to see an incipient community formed, and if it were necessary he would give up his profession, and with his family enter such a society.

Mr. NASH[13], of Sheffield, doubted whether the co-operators were yet sufficiently informed to realise a community, and also whether they could compete with capitalists in the market.

Mr. OWEN next addressed the congress. He said he had heard much about the necessity of forming a community, but he had heard nothing proposed that was likely to be successful. It would be necessary first to understand the principles on which the community was to be formed. If it were intended that the members should subsist upon the produce of their own labour, independent of all transactions with the external world, the arrangements must be very different to what they would be, did they intend to come into competition with it. The former plan was the one to which he thought the congress should look; and if so, they had a most important object before them. They would find, in this case, that no small community could succeed; and he was of opinion, indeed, that a small community would not do, even if it were intended to compete with the external world. In fact, he was fully satisfied that a large community might be formed with more ease, and in a shorter time, than a small one; besides which, the one would give satisfaction to the members and the public, while the other would disappoint all, and throw back most materially the progress of the cause. It was in consequence of repudiating his opinions, that the Orbiston Society failed.[14] That society was not the tenth part of a community; it was not formed upon community principles, but in direct opposition to them, and that from the beginning to the end. It had been said that the community at New Lanark and the community at New Harmony had failed; but nothing could be more ridiculous, for there had been nothing like a community in either place. He had found the people to be in a state not to act in community; they were not competent to govern themselves. The moment they began to act, he found they could not do so much in a year, as he and those who acted with him could do in a day: their whole time was spent in talking. After all, however, he was glad to see the anxiety on this subject; he was glad to see so many persons at length convinced that there were no means of mending the old state of society. Had there been the same anxiety manifested in 1817, when he (Mr. O.) came forward, the world would by this time have been a perfect paradise. If they were now ready for this, however, he had no doubt that their object might be realised. A friend had offered 420 acres of good land, within seventeen miles of London, at 1*l*. 2*s*. 6*d*. an acre, tithe-free; and it was of great importance that land for a community should be tithe-free. This land—which adjoined 1100 acres belonging to a gentleman who would, he had no doubt, do what he could to serve them—might be had upon lease for twenty-one years, with liberty to extend the term to any period they chose, or to purchase it for ever. Its situation, too, was admirably adapted or their purpose; for their first community should be within a circle of thirty miles from London—not nearer than twelve miles, nor farther than thirty. Then, also, he had no doubt, if they were sufficiently advanced for this, that they might find men of capital and builders, who would assist them with what they might want, upon such security as they would have it in their power to offer. To succeed as a community, however, their arrangements must combine a due proportion of capital and labour to produce the various kinds of wealth the inhabitants would require, both for their own use, and for the purpose of exchanging for such articles as they could not themselves produce. It must also comprise a proper combination for distributing their productions beneficially for each individual, and also for training and forming the character of each individual in the most beneficial and economical manner. It must also comprise arrangements which would give them the most simple, cheap, and efficient government. All this was capable of being effected in a rightly constituted community. Every person present, probably, had his own views of a community; but he believed them all to differ most materially from his views; and he further believed that none of their plans, when attempted, would succeed. It was on that account that he withdrew his name from the committee that had been appointed at the last congress, for he would not give the sanction of his name to what he believed would be a failure. But let no man suppose that he was indifferent upon this subject; he could not be indifferent. No man could feel more deeply interested in it than he did: and no man would sacrifice more, than he would to see a community realised. All he wanted was, that those who were now so desirous to effect this object should see the difficulties as well as the advantages of the undertaking. Mr. Owen concluded his remarks by observing, that he was satisfied that our own government, as well as all the governments of Europe, was fully satisfied of the truth and value of his principles, and was extremely desirous to adopt them. At present they could not do so, for the people were not prepared for the change. They only waited for the public opinion to be formed and matured to effect those happy changes which co-operation was adapted to realise.

Mr. LOVETT rose, and said that himself, Mr. Pare, and Mr. Styles had taken an opportunity to retire for a few moments to draw up a resolution upon this subject, which he would now submit for adoption. It was to the following effect:—

"Resolved, that this Congress, deeply impressed with the growing evils of the present competitive system, and anxious that arrangements should be made to place the industrious classes beyond its devastating and irritating influence, are determined to renew and redouble their exertions to establish, as speedily as possible, a community upon the principles of mutual co-operation, united possessions, and equality of exertions, and of the means of enjoyments."

In supporting the resolution, Mr. Lovett replied to some of Mr. Owen's arguments against the kind of incipient community they now proposed, and forcibly urged upon the congress the necessity of doing something for themselves and the working class, generally, without waiting for the government to take them by the hand.

Mr. PARE seconded the resolution, and expressed his opinion that Mr. Owen had not only too highly estimated the contingent results of his own proceedings in opening the purses of the affluent, but that he had also too meanly estimated the capabilities and powers of the labouring classes.

Mr.FINCH, Mr. MANDLEY, the Rev. Mr. DUNN and Mr. STYLES, severally supported the resolution; as did Mr. SIMPSON also. This delegate, in the course of his remarks, defended the inhabitants of Orbiston community, and attributed its failure to the mismanagement of the monied proprietors, who had an interest in direct opposition to that of the working members.[15]

Mr. WIGG corroborated the statement of Mr. Simpson relative to the Orbiston community, and supported the motion before the chair, as did also Messrs. Beatson and Caldwell.[16]

Mr. FLATHER[17] contended that the co-operators were not yet fit for community; there was neither enough knowledge nor enough good feeling amongst them for such a state.

Mr. WARDEN combatted the statements of his colleague, Mr. Flather; but even if he admitted them to be true, he could not see that they furnished any argument against a community. Was it likely, he asked, that they could become much wiser or better while they remained in the present wretched state of society? He denied that they could, and therefore he was for an attempt to form an incipient and experimental community.

Mr. OWEN then addressed the congress. What wisdom (he would ask) would there be in taking a savage from the wilds of America, who could not tell the difference that existed between the numbers 5 and 10; and placing him in Cambridge University to teach the professors mathematics? None!— Practicable methods must be tried. For forty years had he been labouring to try the effects of a community. He purchased Lanark of its proprietors, for the purpose of establishing his system, but he knew that he would not make any great progress, except he returned a profit for the capital embarked in the establishment. He carried on his arrangements there for 14 or 15 years, and during the last five years he was enabled to pay six per cent, interest for the capital. When he first took the establishment, the population was idle, dissolute, inefficient, and immoral in the highest degree. The first effect of his system, was to produce a complete change in their character, and he left them a most moral and industrious body. The next object obtained, was that the children were educated at 3$s.$ per year, and got as good instruction as they would for 300$l.$ in London. The next good object attained was that the children were not overworked, they were not put to labour until they arrived at the age of ten years, and then the labour was proportioned to their strength.[18] During twenty-nine years, there was not a single instance where it was necessary to apply to a magistrate. He himself was a magistrate[19], but never acted in his capacity,—the punishments were pecuniary fines, and went towards the establishment of a sick fund. He was told at first, that his plan was visionary; but the reason was, because it was not understood. Extensive combination was in no way new to him. He had never ceased to labour to discover the shortest time it would take to form a successful community, and he looked forward to the great good that would result from meeting congress? The meeting had mentioned that £6,000 ought to be advanced towards Mr. Thompson's plan. Now, he (Mr. Owen) had the greatest possible esteem for Mr. Thompson, but he begged leave to assure him that he knew little of this matter. 6,000*l.*, 20,000*l.*, or even 60,000*l.*, would be of little avail; but if they were united as one man, and fully determined to prosecute their plan, many a man on the stock exchange would be willing to advance capital. There were many money-holders favourable to co-operation, when they found it just in a practical point of view—men of good genuine principles; and some had said, that if an intelligible and satisfactory statement were put before them, they would advance capital to almost any amount, at four per cent. Mr. Owen then proceeded to make some observations on the excellent security a community could offer—a security of land—of buildings about to be erected, of a superior kind—and of the daily industry of the people, who by their exertions would enhance the value of the property. He was glad to see the meeting so impatient to proceed, and he advised them strongly to lose no time in making proposals to monied men to advance capital at four per cent, on the security he mentioned.

The meeting then adjourned until seven o'clock.

Mr. WATKINS having been called to the Chair, the Congress resumed its sitting at the hour just mentioned.

Mr. CARSON[20] rose and said, that many persons in Lancashire had serious intentions of forming a community. The Worsley co-operatives were also eager to form one, having found that they might get a vast quantity of uncultivated land at 1*l.* per acre. Near Liverpool, he also thought they could find means to get 1,000 acres, and the only thing wanting to make it valuable, was labour. One man ought to be sent from every co-operative society. They would support and erect a cottage for him; but pay no wages. If such a plan were adopted, in a few years it would be made a valuable estate. After reading the works of Messrs. Owen and Thompson, the people were anxious to commence a community.

Mr. HIRST[21] said, no subject delighted him more than the present, and nothing should be wanting on his part towards attaining such a desirable object. It appeared to him, that all things were working for their good. He earnestly beseeched them, however, not to allow themselves to be carried away by wrong calculations; they should not attempt a community without a certainty of success.

The Rev. Mr. DUNN felt great pleasure in perfectly coinciding with Mr. Owen's sentiments.

Mr. PETRIE said he stood on principle; he was a true disciple of Mr. Owen's, and had a wife who would follow him into community. Though a humble mechanic, he had applied himself diligently to the study of co-operation.

Mr. THOMPSON said, they imagined two kinds of communities; one of which would be a state of bliss, the other a kind of superior workhouse or workshops for the poor. The fabric should be erected at once, which imagination conceives to be the most perfect, if they had the means. If, however, he could get a sufficient capital, and 2,000 individuals together, he would not despair but that in a short period he would show to the world, an institution that might even please Mr. Owen; he thought the security Mr. Owen offered would not be satisfactory enough to the money holders.

Mr. OWEN said, one of the capitalists told him within a short period, that he had not sufficiently understood his system; but that now, finding it excellent, he was willing to aid it

Mr. THOMPSON said, if we cannot get up a first-rate community at once, let us begin on a small scale; if we wish to ameliorate the condition of the poor, we should be content with a community such as he described. He then alluded to the Dutch communities[22], which were on such a bad sandy soil, but, in a few years, became a most excellent and bountiful one, by unceased labour and tillage. Their object was, to put a stop to beggary; and if we could not accomplish what they did, we must be stupid indeed. As to the consideration whether or not we should proceed to operations without the assistance of great wealth, he would say that it could well be dispensed with, as Mr. Vandeleur's establishment in Clare[23] clearly demonstrated; and where they were employing many Irish labourers who had only 5*l*. per year to support themselves and families, and to purchase clothes, &c. &c. There was one wise part of Mr. Vandeleur's system. It was extremely difficult to get ignorant people to work, when they considered that they had not some individual motive for it; committees, therefore, regulated every evening the work for the ensuing day, for every man, woman, child, and beast; there were, therefore, no idlers among them, and each worked with cheerfulness. They soon found out the secret, that if one or two stopped working, the whole produce would soon be lessened; and the force of *public opinion*, caused each person to exert himself the more.

Mr OWEN said, to ensure success, a complete unity must pervade the whole—committees and majorities would never answer; there would be too much confusion. He had found by thirty years' experience, that people could not act for themselves in a community. There must be some conducting head. He went to America to try the experiment, and would have no objection to try any experiment.

Mr. LOVETT did not like that one man should have the absolute government of many useful and practical men. It savoured, he thought, of despotism. Committees of arrangement were of great use; though a little time might be lost, valuable information might be gained. The meeting had wandered from the question, which was, whether they should commence an incipient community.—Mr. Owen was against going into a community without very large funds. Now, why wait for others to do that which they could do for themselves? He thought working men ought to come forward, and commence operations at once.

Mr OWEN said, no one was more opposed to despotism than he was; but such a combination as they had in view, could only be effected by the direction of one mind. He would put an end to despotism, and would give to every child, when it was born, his full share in the government of the world. He would wish perfect equality. He acknowledged no man as above him, and no man was beneath him.

Mr. THOMPSON asked Mr. Owen if he had taken care to give to the world, after his own death, the valuable knowledge he possesed. [sic]

Mr. OWEN replied, that it had always been present to his mind, and that he had taken all the steps that occurred to him to render his own life of as little importance as possible. He had written his opinions, and had constructed models; but it was impossible he could convey in books or models the whole of the experience he had, or the spirit of the interesting conversations he had held with Monroe, Jefferson, and other great minds, who had ceased to exist in this world[24]. He believed, however, that the aristocracy were better acquainted with the system than his friends were aware of, and that they were only waiting for the people to be prepared for it, in order to join them. He intended, as soon as funds admitted of it, to have a large model erected which practical men could work from. Mr. Owen concluded the discussion by saying, that now was the time for every man to exhibit his moral courage, and that if they were determined, and would follow up the plan of co-operation, this pandemonium of existing society would soon be changed to a state of happiness—to a terrestrial paradise. Let them adhere to the *truth* and they had nothing to fear; the victory was won. (Cheering.) He did not care if all men deserted him; he would be of the same opinion still, for he knew they would all come back to him.

Mr. LOVETT's resolution was then put and carried, as were also the following :—

"That every delegate and visitor to the Congress here present, and so disposed, do now sign his name to a paper prepared for that purpose, whether on his act, or for the society he represents as a subscriber to the proposed community, and pay at least one pound deposit."

"That Messrs. Thompson, Pare, and Wigg, be appointed to draw up a prospectus for a community."

The meeting then adjourned till seven o'clock on the following morning.

Friday morning, 7 o'clock.

The discussion on the Incipient Community was resumed.

Mr. LOVETT said, he hoped that when the plan was matured, and carried into effect, the members of the community would be chosen from among co-operative and working persons, and that no one would be allowed to buy five or six shares, and put in who he liked.

Mr. THOMPSON moved, that as soon as 100 names were subscribed, individuals be appointed to take at least 400 acres of land, on lease for ever, or with liberty of purchase ; and that they be responsible, as trustees, for this purpose.

Messrs. Thompson, Hamilton, Hoskins, and Bromley, were then appointed as fit persons to determine on the choice and purchase of lands.

Mr. PARE said, he hoped it would be remembered, that when individuals subscribed, the subscription included only themselves, and not their wives, should they be married.

Mr. STYLES then moved that a committee be formed, consisting of the following persons, in London, whose duty it shall be to make the necessary arrangements to convene a meeting of subscribers so soon as 100 names shall be on the list, and to render any assistance and facility in correspondence, &c. to the gentlemen appointed to purchase the land.

—Names, Messrs. Lovett, Simpson, Wigg, Tucker[25], Warden and Styles.

Notes

1. William Pare (see Part 4, Chapter 24).
2. See Part 1, Chapter 7.
3. Samuel Austin was Secretary of Robert Owen's National Equitable Labour Exchange, Gray's Inn Road, London.
4. William Pare's First Birmingham Co-operative Society had suggested that British cooperative associations should join forces in building a community on the land (see Part 4, Chapter 24). Their resolutions were published under the title "Co-operation.—Extracts from Correspondence with the Committee of the British Association for the Promotion of Co-operative Knowledge", in William Carpenter's *Political Letters and Pamphlets*, 30 April 1831 (Langdon 2000, 37).
5. See Thompson (1830) for his advocacy of small-scale, cheap and efficient community building.
6. The North-West of England Co-operative Company was an early wholesale co-operative association, with no communitarian goals (Purvis 1987, 91, n. 48).
7. The Rev. Thomas MacConnell (see Part 3, Chapter 18).
8. William Thompson (see Parts 4 and 8).
9. Joseph Styles, a Westminster carpenter and veteran socialist. A friend of William Lovett's, he was a member of the British Association for the Promotion of Co-operative Knowledge (BAPCK), and a union leader in the Friendly Society of the Operative Carpenters and Joiners in 1833. After the demise of the Owenite movement, Styles was one of the architects of the post-Rochdale co-operative revival, and co-founded the Cooperative League in 1833.
10. Peter Bishop, delegate for Birmingham.
11. William Lovett (see Part 2, Chapter 12).
12. The Rev., Joseph Marriott, delegate for Rochdale (see Part 3, Chapter 18).
13. The Rev. Nash, a Sheffield co-operator and proponent of the Labour Exchanges.
14. See Chapter 28 above.
15. John Finch (see Part 3, Chapter 19 and Part 9, Chapter 59); George Mandley, a leading Manchester co-operator; George Simpson, a fellow Manchester co-operator. Simpson was among the working-class committee that took over Queenwood in August 1844. A clerk by trade, he was appointed community secretary (Royle 1998, 249).
16. Robert Wigg, a Finsbury shoemaker and former member of the BAPCK. He later supported the Chartist cause; Jasper Beatson, a lawyer and the author of a vindication of socialism, *An Examination of Mr. Owen's Plans for Relieving Public Distress* (1823).
17. James Flather, a London co-operator and Mechanics' Institute lecturer.
18. See Part 1, Chapters 1–2.
19. Robert Owen was appointed Justice of the Peace for Lanarkshire around 1813, when he published his *New View of Society* (1813–1816).
20. William Carson, delegate for Wigan, Christian co-operator and lecturer.
21. Thomas Hirst (?–1833), delegate for Huddersfield, local co-operative leader and lecturer.

22 The *Maatschappij van weldedigheit* (Benevolent Society) was founded in 1818 by the Dutch reformer Johannes van den Bosch. The Society managed a network of agricultural settlements in the country, and employed beggars, foundlings and orphans. Robert Owen was an admirer of the scheme (*The Examiner*, 25 April 1819, cited in Owen 1858, 213; Gijwijt-Hofstra 2017, 267).
23 Ralahine community in County Clare, Ireland (see Part 9, Chapter 57).
24 While the New Harmony experiment was under way, Robert Owen also travelled extensively throughout the United States to propagate his views. In early March 1825, he addressed members of the Congress in Washington. John Quincy Adams and James Monroe were in attendance. That same month, thanks to letters of introduction from Monroe, Owen visited Thomas Jefferson at Monticello (Bestor 1950, 112–113).
25 James Tucker, a coal merchant and pioneer of the Labour Exchange movement in London.

32

RULES AND REGULATIONS OF THE GRAND NATIONAL CONSOLIDATED TRADES' UNION OF GREAT BRITAIN AND IRELAND: INSTITUTED FOR THE PURPOSE OF MORE EFFECTUALLY ENABLING THE WORKING CLASSES TO SECURE, PROTECT, AND ESTABLISH THE RIGHTS OF INDUSTRY (LONDON: HARJETTE AND SAVILLE, 1834).

[Trade unions were legalised in 1825 following the repeal of the Combination Acts, and while industrial action remained prohibited, many unionists lent a favourable ear to Owen's claim that labour was the source of all wealth, and that producers were subsequently entitled to fair wages and humane working hours. The co-operative ideal of a general union and workers' parliament took even greater hold after the passing of the Great Reform Act 1832, which had chosen to exclude working-class men from the franchise. Many thus felt that ordinary labourers had no choice but to rely upon their own exertions to advance their cause via direct political action (Chase 2017, chapter 5; Siméon 2018, 23). In February 1833, spurred by Owen's increasing support for trade unions as a means to implement economic co-operation, a group of Owenite tailors from London set up the Grand National Consolidated Trades Union (GNCTU). According to its *Rules and Regulations*, the new union was not merely intended as an instrument of working-class relief, but as a means to bring about "a different state of things" (art. XLVI), in which co-operation between workers and employers would not only end capitalist exploitation, but pave the way for the regeneration of mankind. Owen joined the GNCTU in April 1834 and became its chairman, but his gradualism found itself increasingly at odds with the rank-and-file's openness to industrial action. The rift became insurmountable in May 1834, when the London tailors embarked on a strike of their own, campaigning for fair wages and universal male suffrage with the support of the *Crisis* editor, James Elishama Smith (1801–1857). The GNCTU also suffered from external pressure. As the authorities saw unions as a hotbed of sedition, two undercover agents from the Home Office were tasked to infiltrate the movement and report on its activities. The Tolpuddle Martyrs, who were affiliated to the GNCTU, were unlawfully transported to Australia, and syndicalist activities in the spring and summer of 1834 were heavily repressed. Owen officially dissolved the union in the winter of that same year (*Crisis* 12 July 1834; Parssinen and Prothero 1977, 80).]

GENERAL PLAN AND GOVERNMENT

I. Each Trade in this Consolidated Union shall have its Grand Lodge in that town or city most eligible for it, such Grand Lodge to be governed internally by a Grand Master, Deputy Grand Master, and Grand Secretary, and a Committee of Management.

II. Each Grand Lodge shall have its District Lodges, in any number, to be designated or named after the town or city in which the District Lodge is founded.

III. Each Grand Lodge shall be considered the head of its own particular trade, and to have certain exclusive powers accordingly; but in all other respects the Grand Lodges are to answer the same ends as the District Lodges.

IV. Each District Lodge shall embrace within itself all operatives of the same trade, living in smaller towns or villages adjacent to it, and shall be governed internally by a president, vice-president, secretary, and a committee of management.

V. Each District Lodge shall have (if necessary) its Branch Lodge or Lodges, numbered in rotation; such Branch Lodges to be under the control of the District Lodge from which they sprung.

VI. An unlimited number of the above-described Lodges shall form and constitute the Grand National Consolidated Trades Union of Great Britain and Ireland.

VII. Each District shall have its Central Committee, composed of a Deputy, or Deputies, from every District Lodge of the different trades in the district; such Central Committee shall meet once in every week to superintend and watch over the interests of the Consolidated Union in that District, transmitting a report of the sale, monthly, to the Executive Council in London, together with any suggestions of improvements they may think proper.

VIII. The general government of the G.N.C.T.U. shall be vested in a Grand Council of Delegates from each of the Central Committees of all the Districts in the Consolidated Union, to be holden every six months, at such places as shall be decided upon at the preceding Council; the next meeting of the Grand Council of the Consolidated Union to be held on the first day of September, 1834, and to continue its sitting so long as may be requisite.

IX. During the recess of the Grand Council of Delegates, the government of the Consolidated Union shall be vested in an Executive Council of five; which executive will in future be chosen at the Grand Delegate Council aforesaid.

X. All dispensations or grants for the formation of new Lodges shall come from the Grand Lodge of each particular trade, or from the Executive Council. Applications to come through the Central Committee of the District or by memorial, signed by at least 20 operatives of the place where such new Lodge is proposed to be founded.

XI. The Executive Council shall act as trustees for all funds provided by the Consolidated Union, and for the adjustment of strikes, the purchasing or renting of land, establishing provision stores, workshops, etc.; or for any other purpose connected with the general benefit of the whole of the Union.

XII. All sums for the above purposes to be transmitted from the Lodges to the Executive Council through some safe and accredited medium.

XIII. District and Grand Lodges shall have the control of their own funds, subject to the levies imposed on them by the Executive Council.

XIV. The ordinary weekly subscription of members to be three-pence each member

XV. No strike or turn-out for an *advance* of wages shall be made by the members of any Lodge in the Consolidated Union without the consent of the Executive Council; but in all cases of a *reduction* of wages the Central Committee of the District shall have the power of deciding whenever a strike shall or shall not take place, and should such Central Committee be necessitated to order a levy in support of such strike brought on by such reduction of wages, such order shall be made in all the Lodges; in the first instance, in the District in which such reduction hath taken place, and on advice being forwarded to the Executive they shall consider the case, and order accordingly.

XVI. No higher sum than ten shillings per week each shall be paid to members during a strike or turn out.

XVII. All Lodges shall be divided into local sections of twenty men each, or as near that number as may be.

MISCELLANEOUS AND AUXILIARY LODGES

XVIII. In all cases where the number of Operatives in a particular Trade, in any District, is too limited to allow of such Trade forming a Lodge of itself, the Members of such Trade shall be permitted to become Unionists by joining the Lodge of any other Trade in the District. Should there be several Trades in a District thus limited with respect to the number of their Operatives, they shall be allowed to form together a District Miscellaneous Lodge, with permission, in order to extend the sphere of the brotherhood, to hold out the hand of fellowship to all really useful Labourers employed productively.

XIX. And, in order that all acknowledged Friends of the Productive Classes may attach themselves to the Conciliated Union, an Auxiliary Lodge may be established in every City or Town in the Kingdom. The members of which Lodge shall confirm to all the Rules and Regulations herein contained, and be bound in the same manner, and subject to all the Laws of the Grand National Consolidated Trades' Union; and shall not, in any manner, or at any time or place, speak or write any thing in opposition to these Laws or the interest of the Union aforesaid. The Auxiliary Lodge shall be liable to be dissolved according to Article xxii.

XX. Lodges of Industrious Females shall be instituted in Every District where it may be practicable; such Lodges to be considered, in every respect, as part of, and belonging to, the Grand National Consolidated Trades' Union.

EMPLOYMENT OF TURN-OUTS.

XXI. In all cases of strikes or turn-outs, where it is practicable to employ members in the making of production of such commodities or article as are in demand among their brother Unionists, or any other operatives willing to purchase the same, each Lodge shall provide a workroom or shop in which such commodities and articles may be manufactured on account of that Lodge, which shall make proper arrangements for the supply of the necessary materials; over which arrangements the Central Committee of the District shall have the control, subject to the scrutiny of the Grand Lodge Committee of the trade on strike.

XXII. The Grand Lodge of each Trade to have the power of dissolving any District Lodge, in that Trade, for any violation of these Laws, any outrage upon the Public Peace, or for gross neglect of Duty. All Branch, Miscellaneous, or Auxiliary Lodges to be subject to the same control.

XXIII. The internal management and general concerns of each Grand or District Lodge are vested in a Committee of Management, composed of at least Seven and not more than Twenty-five, Members, each to be chosen by Ballot, and elected by having not less than three-fourths of the Votes of the members present, at the time of his election, in his favour. The whole of this Committee to go out of office Quarterly, eligible however to re-election. The Grand Master, or President, and the Secretary, or Grand Secretary of a Grand or a District Lodge, to be considered Members of its Committee of Management by virtue of their Offices.

XXIV. Each Grand Lodge, in this Consolidated Union, to be considered the centre of information regarding the general affairs of its particular Trade; each District Lodge to communicate with its Grand Lodge at the end of each month, and to give an account to it of the number of payable Members in the District Lodge,—the gross number of hours' labour performed by them in that District,—the state of its funds,—and any local or general intelligence that may be considered of interest to the Grand Lodge.

XXV. The Committee of Management in each Lodge shall sit at least on one evening in every week for the dispatch of business,—and oftener if necessary.

XXVI. Each Grand or District Lodge to hold its meetings on one evening in every month; at which meeting a Report of the Proceedings of the Committee, during the past month, shall be laid before the Members; together with an Abstract of the state of the Funds, an Account of the prospects of the Society, and any proposition or By-Laws which the Committee may have to suggest for adoption, and any other information or correspondence of interest to the Members. All nominations of fresh Officers to be made at Lodge meetings, and all complaints of Members to be considered and discussed therein.

XXVII. The Grand Master, or Deputy Grand Master, President, or Vice-President, or both, shall preside at all meetings of Grand or District Lodges, to keep order, state and put questions according to the sense and intention of the Members, give effect to the resolutions, and cause them to be put in force; and they shall be addressed by Members, during Lodge hours, by their proper titles.

XXVIII. No subject which does not immediately concern the interests of the Trade shall be discussed at any meetings of Committees or Lodges; and no proposition shall be adopted in either without the consent of at least three-fourths of the Members present at its proposal,—the question to be decided by ballot if any Member demand it. Not less than five Members of Committee of Management to constitute a Quorum, provided the rest have all been duly summoned; no Grand or District Lodges to be considered open unless at least Thirty Members be present. XXIX. Each Grand or District Lodge shall have the power to appoint Sub-Committees to inquire into or manage any affair touching their interests, of which Committees the head officers of the Lodge are always to be considered Members.

OF SECRETARIES

XXX. The Duties of a Secretary to a Grand or District Lodge, are—

To attend Lodge and Committee Meetings, and take minutes of the proceedings, entering the same in a book to be kept for that purpose.

To conduct all the correspondence of the Society.

To take down the names and addresses of parties desirous of being initiated into the order; and upon receiving the initiation fee from each, and entering the amount into a book, he will give each party a card, by which they may be admitted into the place appointed for the ceremony.

To receive the subscriptions of members, entering the same into a small account book, numbering the Subscribers from No. , and following up the sequence in regular order, giving to each Subscriber a card, on which his contribution or payment shall be noted.

To enter all additional weekly payments, and all levies, into separate small books; all subscriptions and payments to be afterwards copied into a ledger, ruled expressly for the purpose.

The Secretary to be paid an adequate weekly salary, and to be allowed an Assistant if the amount of business require it.

The Secretary of each Grand or District Lodge shall balance his books once every fortnight, and the Managing Committee shall audit them, going over each item of receipt and expenditure with strict attention, checking the same with scrupulous care; and if found correct, three of the Committee shall verify the same, by affixing their signatures to the page on which the Balance is struck.

INITIATION.

XXXI. Any of the Officers or Members of a Lodge may be appointed by the Committee of Management to perform the Initiation Service; and to have charge of the Robes, &c., for that purpose; for which the Committee may allow him a reasonable remuneration.

Any party applying to be initiated must bring forward two witnesses as to character and the identity of his trade or occupation.

OF BRANCH LODGES.

XXXII. Branch Lodge Meetings shall be held on one evening in every week, in the respective localities; at which Lodges any motion, proposed by law, &c., may be discussed and considered by the Members previous to its being finally submitted to the Grand or District Lodge Committee.

XXXIII. The Members of each Branch may elect a President to preside at the Branch Lodge, and a Secretary to collect Subscriptions or levies for their Grand or District Lodge, who shall also attend meeting of the Committee of Management for instructions and information, and to submit suggestions, complaints, &c., from his Branch Lodge. No salaries or fees to be allowed to officers of Branch Lodges, unless by the unanimous consent of their Members.

WARDENS, ETC.

XXXIV. In addition to the Officers before mentioned in these regulations, there shall be, in each Grand and District Lodge, a Warden, an Inside Tyler, an Outside Tyler, and a Conductor; whose principal duties are to attend Initiations, and see that no improper persons be admitted into the meetings. These officers to be elected in the same manner, and at the same periods, as other officers.

MISCELLANEOUS ARTICLES

XXXV. Any Member shall be liable to expulsion from the Lodges for any improper conduct therein; and shall be excluded from the benefits of the Society if his subscriptions be more than six months in arrear, unless the Committee of Management shall see cause to decide otherwise.

XXXVI. The "Grand National Consolidated Trades' Union Gazette"[1] to be considered the official organ of the Executive Council, and the general medium of intelligence on the affairs of the Union.

XXXVII. Each Lodge shall, as soon as possible, make arrangements for furnishing the means of mental improvement to their Members, and for the cultivation of good habits among them, by instituting Libraries or Reading-rooms, or any other arrangements, affording them every facility for meeting together for friendly conversation, mutual instruction, and rational amusement or recreation.

XXXVIII. In all cases, where it be practicable, each Lodge shall establish within its locality one or more Depôts for provisions and articles in general domestic use, in order that its Members may be supplied with the best of such commodities at little above wholesale prices.

XXXIX. Each District and Grand Lodge shall endeavour to institute a Fund for the support of sick and aged Members, and for defraying the funeral expenses of deceased Members, on a similar principle to that of benefit societies; such fund to be kept up by small monthly contributions from those Unionists who are willing to subscribe towards it.

BY-LAWS.

XL. Each Grand or District Lodge to have the power of making its own By-Laws, for purposes not comprised in these Regulations; but such By-Law, or Laws, must not be in opposition to, or in counteraction of, any of the Articles herein specified.

XLI. No Member can enter Lodge-meetings without giving the proper signs, and producing his card to prove his membership, and that he is not in arrears of subscriptions for more than one month, unless lenity has been granted by order of Committee.

XLII. That a separate Treasurer be appointed for every Twenty Pounds of the Funds collected; and that such Treasurers shall not suffer any money to be withdrawn from their hands without a written order, signed by at least Three of the Managing Committee, and presented by the Secretary, or one of the other officers of the Society.

XLIII. All sums under Thirty Pounds shall be left in the hands of the Secretary, for current expenses; but no outlay shall be made by him without an express order from the Managing Committee, signed by at least Three of its Members.

XLIV. That every Member of this Union do use his best endeavours, by fair and open argument, and the force of good example, and not by intimidation or violence, to induce his fellows to join the brotherhood, in order that no workmen may remain out of Union to under-sell them in the market of labour; as, while that is done, employers will be enabled to resist the demands of Unionists, whereas, if no operatives remain out of Union, employers will be compelled to keep up the price of labour.

XLV. That each Member of the Consolidated Union pay a Registration Fee of three-pence, to defray the general expenses; which fee is to be transmitted to the Executive once in every month.

XLVI. That although the design of the Union is, in the first instance, to raise the wages of the workmen, or prevent any further reduction therein, and to diminish the hours of labour, the great and ultimate object of it must be to establish the paramount rights of Industry and Humanity, by instituting such measures as shall effectually prevent the ignorant, idle, and useless part of society from that undue control over the fruits of our toil, which, through the agency of a vicious money system, they at present possess; and that, consequently, the Unionists should lose no opportunity of mutually encouraging and assisting each other in bringing about A DIFFERENT ORDER OF THINGS, in which the really useful and intelligent part of society only shall have the direction of its affairs, and in which well-directed industry and virtue shall meet their just distinction and reward, and vicious idleness, its merited contempt and destitution.

XLVII. All the Rules and Regulations herein contained, to be subject to the revision, alteration, or abrogation of the Grand Delegate Council.

THE END.

Note

1 Probably the *Crisis*, which was the official Owenite periodical in the years 1832–1834.

33

"PROGRESS OF SOCIAL REFORM", *NEW MORAL WORLD*, 6 AUGUST 1843, 46–47.

[In the early 1830s, the Owenites had sought to establish their own meeting halls, as church and city officials were often unwilling to provide space to a group with a reputation for immorality and infidelity (see Part 7). Originally known as the "Social Institutions", these buildings were later renamed as "Halls of Science" following the establishment of the Association of All Classes of All Nations (AACAN), as the Owenite movement was now focused on preparing its members for community life – hence the need for institutions where the "science of society" could be taught to a large audience (Harrison 1969, 275). As part of these propagandist activities, full reports on the Halls of Science such as this one appeared weekly in the *New Moral World*. They reveal a rich social life at branch level and an array of universal aims. As a base for both militant, educational and leisure activities, Halls of Science were meant to foster community bonds while promoting a radical culture firmly set against the individualism and selfishness of capitalistic society (Yeo 1971, 87–94).]

LEEDS, July 22.–It is now a long time since our friends had a report from this quarter; and the opponents of our principles have represented us as dead. We are glad to say that we are at last in a position to show them that we are neither dead nor asleep. It is about a year and a half since we lost the Music Saloon, during which time we have been looking out for other premises. Last week we were so fortunate as to secure a building for a short period; which, though it is not exactly what we would like to have, yet we hope it will be the means of our obtaining better. The premises consist of a room capable of holding 600 persons, a room that will accommodate 200, a library-room, and two small anti-rooms [sic]. We are busily engaged in cleaning, and intend to open the institution to the public on Sunday, July 31. Fortunately Mr. Speirs [sic][1] has taken up his residence in Leeds, and we intend to engage him to be our lecturer. With his valuable assistance we hope to make a good impression upon the public mind. He will commence, on the first Sunday in August, a course of lectures on "Home Colonization." These we expect, from the feeling which is being created in this district in favour of spade-husbandry, will be well attended. Besides the letters of J. G. Marshall, Esq., on the subject of spade-husbandry[2], there has appeared in the *Leeds Conservative Journal* a long letter from Mr. Atkinson (a solicitor in this town), in favour of colonizing the crown lands and other public property. And in the charge of the chairman (R. Paley, Esq.) of the quarter sessions lately held at Ripon, we find the following passage:– "Another source of crime may be attributed to arise from the want of employment and, I think it incumbent on every gentleman in the neighbourhood to find as much employment as he possibly can for the labouring class, and thereby, to the utmost of his power, to endeavour to remove the evil. I would suggest that small portions of land be allotted them to cultivate, without regard to parties mixing it up either with religion or politics. Two or three years ago I adopted this plan on a small scale, and let some waste land to the workmen at Bishopton Mill. One man, who had half a rood of land, and for which he paid me £5 yearly, grew thereon last year as many potatoes and other vegetables, as supplied himself, wife, and two children the whole year, besides disposing of 50s. worth to the public; and his wife informed me, that by having this land to cultivate, he had been kept sober, and she and the children provided for, instead of his leisure time and money being spent in the public-house. Now I think if this plan was carried out practically, the bad would be made better, and the good virtuous." Trade in this town is in a very depressed state. Hundreds of working-men may be seen in the streets, with hunger and misery in their appearance. A great number of our friends are out of employment, and several have emigrated, thinking to mend their condition in a foreign country. Some of our friends who had withdrawn themselves have again come forward; the differences which have existed are likely to be removed, and there is good reason to expect that the Leeds Branch will take up the position it formerly held in the society.

John Melson.[3]

SHEFFIELD, July 29–There was a general meeting of the members of this branch last Sunday morning, at which a unanimous vote of confidence in the present officers of the society was passed, and a resolution pledging the members to use their best energies to place the affairs of the society in a prosperous condition. One of our magistrates has written to a gentleman residing very near Harmony, requesting some information relative to that establishment. The answer was read to me last Tuesday, and was to the effect, that the society had been there rather more than two years, that they had lived together in a very orderly manner, that they had effected great good in the neighbourhood, by having employed the poor upon the land, and the new buildings, which had been completed in an expensive and substantial manner, but that there had been such a frequent change of the members, that it was impossible to form a solid judgment of the working of the system at present. Let this have its due weight in our future proceedings. On Wednesday there was a public meeting here of at least 15,000 persons to memorialize the Queen on the subject of the Corn-Laws. A Chartist Memorial was moved as an amendment, and I moved a second amendment in a speech of more than half an hour's length, in which I gave them something to think about. The Chartist Amendment was carried. I have been told since by my friends, the free traders, that a very serious responsibility rests upon me for acting as I did; that I had the meeting, entirely in my hands, and could have turned it any way I liked. They (the free traders) certainly looked most wofully.[sic] I showed the pernicious effects of their doctrines, and the impossibility of any scheme, short of Home Colonization, effecting any substantial relief. From what I have heard since, it has caused the principles to progress in the estimation of the public.

Isaac Ironside.[4]

Notes

1 William Spiers (or Spier), formerly a Social Missionary for the Liverpool area.
2 James Garth Marshall (1802–1873), a liberal politician and Fellow of the the Royal Agricultural Society of England, had written to the *Leeds Mercury* in May 1841 to advocate the practice of spade husbandry as a means of employment for the poor. The measure was commended in the *New Moral World* (25 June 1842).
3 John Melson, printer from Leeds and Social Missionary. In December 1844, he joined the Queenwood community with his wife Elizabeth and their six children (Royle 1998, 249).
4 Isaac Ironside (1808–1870). Originally a founder, he joined New Harmony around 1826. Having returned to England after the community's collapse, he joined his father's accountancy firm and became one of the leaders of the Sheffield Owenite movement, helping build the local Hall of Science. He also supported Chartism (Langdon 2000, 119).

34

UNIVERSAL COMMUNITY OF RATIONAL RELIGIONISTS, *THE CONSTITUTION AND LAWS OF THE RATIONAL SOCIETY: AS AGREED TO AT THE ANNUAL CONGRESS, HELD AT HARMONY HALL, HANTS., MAY 10, 1843* (LONDON: PRINTED AND PUBLISHED FOR THE SOCIETY BY W. JOHNSTON, 1843).

[In 1839, the Universal Community Society of Rational Religionists was established during the annual Socialist Congress as a merger between the Association of All Classes of All Nations (AACAN) and the National Community Friendly Society. As the latter had been the official body responsible for the Queenwood project, the new organisation (known as the 'Rational Society' for short) reaffirmed what Owen saw as his movement's sole purpose: the founding of "Villages of Co-operation" (Royle 1998, 95; Taylor 1983, 241). At first, the Rational Society retained much of the AACAN's institutional structure, which coupled a London-based, top-down executive (the Central Board), as well as a relative degree of autonomy and democratic practice in the branches, which were usually managed by "elected committees of working-class shareholders" (Yeo 1971, 92). But things changed when Owen attempted to take control of the fledgling Queenwood community amidst a storm of infighting and financial difficulties. At the 1843 annual Congress, which was held at Harmony Hall (Queenwood's main building and showpiece) to drive the point home, a new constitution was adopted for the Rational Society. In addition to confirming Owen as the community's governor, the document approved a new, paternalistic governance system which sought to extend the Central Board's powers to the detriment of the local branches. The 1843 constitution widened the existing gap between the Owenite executive and the grassroots, and the conflict would later play a prominent part in the movement's collapse (Claeys 1989, 241; see Part 6 below).]

[Enrolled under the statutes 10 Geo. IV. c. 56. and 4 and 5 Will. IV. c. 40.][1]

NAME.

1. This Society shall be called the Rational Society.*

OBJECTS.

2. The objects of the Society are as follow:—

Universal Charity.—To establish over the world, in principle and practice, charity for the convictions, —feelings, and conduct of every human being, without distinction of sex, class, sect, party, country, or colour.

Education and Employment—To well educate and advantageously employ ALL, so as to insure their health, permanent prosperity, intelligence, union, and happiness.

Rational Economy.—To produce and distribute, in the best manner, the best qualities of all kinds of wealth abundantly for ALL.

Government.—To govern most beneficially for all,—without force or fraud, and, ultimately, without artificial rewards or punishments, by the removal of the causes which produce evil, and the institution of those which produce good.

Peaceful change.—Thus to effect peaceably, and by reason alone, an entire change in the character and condition of mankind.

MEANS

3. These objects are to be attained by the following means:

Public Opinion.—By creating a new public opinion in favour of this entire change in the character and condition of mankind, through the medium of public meetings, lectures, discussions, missionaries, cheap publications, and mutual exchanges of productions, upon equitable principles, without individual competition.

Schools.—By instituting infant, and other schools, in which, by means of the new circumstances in which the individuals will be placed, a new and very superior character will be formed for them, by being daily taught truth, unconnected with error, and by exhibiting a conduct in strict accordance with the principles of this Society.

Funds.—By raising from time to time, by subscriptions among the members, or by voluntary contributions or donations, or bequests or loans from members or others, various stocks or funds, for the mutual assistance, maintenance, and education of the members, their wives and children, or nominees, in infancy, advanced

---

* By enrolment of 3d August, 1843.

age, sickness, or other natural state or contingency; also funds for defraying the incidental expenses of the Society.

Communities.—By applying such stocks or funds for the purchase or rental of land, whereon to establish COMMUNITIES of UNITED INTERESTS, or for the purchase or rental of dwellings or other buildings, wherein the members shall by united labour support each other, under every vicissitude.

PRINCIPLES.

4. The following are the fundamental principles of this Society:

Formation of Character.—That man is a being formed to have a compound character; first, as he is organized at birth, before he has received any direct impressions from external objects; and second, as he is subsequently made to become, by the influence of external objects upon his organization, especially by the action of experienced man or society on infant or inexperienced man.

Feelings.—That all man's *feelings* are formed *for* him, by external objects acting upon his organization, and its reaction.

Convictions.—That all his convictions are formed for him by the action of external objects upon his organization, and its reaction.

Will.—That his will, or decision to act, is formed for him by the convictions or feelings separately, or by the convictions and feelings unitedly, which have been formed for him by the action of external circumstances upon his organization.

Actions.—That man is so organized as to act in accordance with his convictions or his feelings, whichever may be the strongest at the moment of action, or to act in obedience to these convictions and feelings when united, and which nature and society combined have caused him to receive.

LAWS.

5. *Their Scope*—The laws and regulations required for the progress and government of the Society, during the transition from the irrational to the rational state of society, have been conceived in the spirit of charity, kindness, good will, and equal justice to all; and it is intended that they shall be applied to practice, on all occasions, in the same spirit.

DIVISIONS OF THE SOCIETY.

6. The Society shall consist of a Centre, with Branches and Classes.

7. *Central Society.*—The Centre shall be composed of members and candidates, resident in all parts of the United Kingdom, or abroad, enrolled in books kept at the office of the Central Board; and each paying £1 annually to the General Fund, which amount, in peculiar cases, may be reduced to ten shillings, at the discretion of the Central Board. Persons may also be constituted life members by one payment of £10.

8. *Branches.*—The Branches and Classes shall be composed of members and candidates, enrolled in the books of the Branch or Class to which they are attached, each paying one shilling quarterly to the General Fund, with such additional amount as may be required to defray the local expenses of the Branch or Class.

MEMBERSHIP.

9. *Candidates.*—Persons shall be admitted as candidates, on payment of the subscriptions, and making a declaration that they have studied the principles and laws of the Society, and approve of them, and desire to aid in carrying them into practice.

10. *Members.*—Candidates shall be admitted as members only with the approval of the Central or Local President and Board of Directors.

11. *Arrears.*—All members or candidates whose payments to the general or local funds are allowed to be in arrears for two quarters, shall thereby cease to belong to the Society; but may be reinstated, if sufficient cause is shown to the Central or Local President and Directors.

12. *Right of Voting.*—Members alone shall have the privilege of speaking and voting relative to the general funds and other business of the Society; and the election of officers shall be settled by them solely. Members paying to the Community Fund shall alone have the decision of matters affecting that Fund. No member shall be entitled to more than one vote.

GOVERNMENT OF THE SOCIETY.

13. *Executive.*—The government of the Society shall be administered by a President and Central Board of Directors, who may, in all cases during the intervals of the sittings of Congress, act for the Society in such manner as may appear to them conducive to its interests.

14. *President.*—The President of the Society shall be elected by the Congress, and shall retain his office so long as he shall conduct the affairs to the satisfaction of the Society; but, in case of dissatisfaction, the Congress may make a new appointment at any of its annual meetings, or a Special Congress may be summoned for the purpose, at any intermediate time, if desired by a majority of the members of Congress, with the exception of any members of the Central Board who may be members of Congress.

15. *Change of President.*—In the event of the death or resignation of the President, the Central Board shall, within seven days, summon a Special Congress, to be held within fourteen days from the date thereof, to elect his successor.

16. *Central Board.*—The Central Board shall consist of the President, Vice President, General Secretary, Governors of Communities, and not less than three, nor more than seven, other members, nominated by the President and confirmed by the Congress; and the Board shall meet periodically, and record the minutes of their proceedings.

17. *Removal of Directors.*—The President of the Society may change those members of the Central Board nominated by himself to Congress, and replace them by others.

18. *Treasurer and Auditors.*—The Treasurer and General Auditors shall be elected in the same manner as the President, and shall in like manner retain their offices, or be subject to removal by Congress; and in case of such removal, a new election shall be made as before. The Treasurer shall be an xi member of the Central Board.

19. *Additional Treasurer, &c.*—An additional Treasurer and two additional Auditors shall be appointed, in the same manner as the principal Treasurer and Auditors, who, in the event of decease, resignation, or refusal to act of any such principal officers, shall succeed to the respective offices of Treasurer or Auditor, until new elections shall be deemed requisite, or can be conveniently made.

20. *Trustees.*—Three persons shall be appointed, by the Congress, as Trustees of the Society, and they may be changed at any time the Congress shall think fit. The Trustees shall be *ex officio* members of the Central Board.

21. *Central Board Meetings.*—The Central Board shall meet weekly, or oftener if necessary, at such time as they shall appoint, at the general office of the Society, on the estate of Harmony[2], in the county of Hants, at London, in the county of Middlesex, or at such other place, in the counties of Hants and Middlesex as the enrolment of these laws may authorize.

GOVERNMENT OF BRANCHES AND CLASSES.

22. *Branches, &c.*—Each Branch or Class shall be under the immediate direction of a Local President and Board of Directors.

23. *Local President.*—The Local President shall be elected by the members of the Branch or Class, and shall retain his office so long as he shall conduct its affairs to the satisfaction of the members; but, in case of dissatisfaction, the Branch or Class may make a new appointment, at any of its stated meetings, (provided a month's notice has been given of such intention), or at a special meeting called for that purpose.

24. *Local Boards.*—The Local Boards shall consist of the President, Vice-President, Secretary, and not more than seven other members, nominated by the President, and confirmed by the Branch or Class. Such Board shall meet periodically, and records of the proceedings of such meetings shall be kept, and be, at all reasonable times, accessible to the members.

25. *Change of Local Boards.*—The Local Presidents may change the members of the Board, and replace them by others, who shall also be submitted to the approval of the Branch.

26. *Change of Local President.*—If any local President shall act in opposition to the principles and laws of the Society, the Central Board may require the election of a new President, in the place of such officer; and in the event of the decease

or resignation of a local President, a general meeting of the members shall be held within fourteen days, to elect a successor to the office.

27. *Change of Secretary.*—If the Secretary of any Branch or Class be found incompetent to the discharge of his duties, the Central Board may require the Local President to appoint another Secretary in the place of such officer.

28. *Powers, &c.*—The Local Presidents and Boards of Directors shall carry into effect the rules as to membership; the collection and transmission of funds; the management of institutions, and other local affairs; so far as pertaining to them; and generally co-operate to carry out the objects of the Society.

29. *Local Collectors, &c.*—The Local Collector and Auditors shall be chosen by the members of the Branch or Class, in the same manner as the President; and the Collector shall be *ex officio* a member of the Local Board.

30. *Sanction of the Executive.*—No Branch, Class, or member of the Society shall, at any time, act in the name of the Society, except under the written sanction of the General Executive.

31. *Elective Board.*—Should any Branch or Class prefer a Board for the administration of its affairs, elected by the members, such Branch or Class may adopt such form of appointment.

CONGRESS.

32. *Sessions.*—A Congress shall be held annually, or oftener if required. The annual session shall commence within three days before or after the tenth of May, at the discretion of the Central Board.

33. *Branch Delegates.*—A Branch, having not less than thirty paying members on its books, may elect one member of Congress. A Branch having one hundred and fifty paying members and upwards, may elect two members. Each member of Congress to be elected annually, and to hold his office until his successor be appointed.

34. *Community Delegates.*—The members of every Community established by this Society may send Delegates to Congress, in proportion to the numbers resident in each establishment, according to the law respecting Branches, and at the expense of each Community.

35. *Qualifications of Delegates.*—No person shall be eligible as a Delegate, who has not been a member of the Society at least twelve months; unless the Branch for which he is elected has not been so long in operation. Nor shall any person be eligible unless he is the holder of a certificate in the Community Fund of the Society.

36. *Ex-officio Members.*—Members of the Central Board, Governors of Communities, and the Trustees of the Society, may sit and speak in Congress, though not elected to represent any Branch; but in such case they shall not vote.

37. *Powers.*—The Congress shall have power to make and revise the laws of the Society; to appoint the seat of government; to elect the Trustees and such other

officers as it may deem requisite; and generally to transact all such business as may come before it.

38. *Place of Meeting.*—The annual or special sessions of Congress shall be held at the Society's estate of Harmony, near Stockbridge, Hants; in London, in the County of Middlesex, or at such other place in Hants and Middlesex as the enrolment of the laws may authorise, and as may be determined on by the annual Congress, or by the President of the Society.

COMMUNITY FUND SUBSCRIPTIONS.

39. *Subscribers.*—Members of the Society, only, shall be subscribers to the Community Fund, and their current payments to that fund shall be liable for arrears to the General Fund, so long as they continue members of the Society; but certificates granted for subscriptions to the Community Fund shall be free from such liability.

40. *Payments.*—Subscriptions to the Community Fund of £1, or of any number of pounds, shall be paid direct to the Central Board. Smaller subscriptions shall be made in the Branches or Classes by such means as the Central Board shall direct; but the General Society shall not be responsible for such subscriptions until the amounts and the reports thereof have been sent to the Central Board, and certificates granted for the same.

41. *Interest.*—Until Congress shall otherwise determine, interest at a rate, not exceeding five per cent. per annum, shall be allowed on subscriptions to the Community Fund.

42. *Certificates.*—The certificates to be granted by the Central Board for Community Fund subscriptions, shall be transferable, and in such form as the Central Board may from time to time direct, in the Hand-Book of the Society.

PREFERENCE CAPITAL.

Whereas it is expedient, in pursuance of a resolution of the Congress of 1843, and under the powers of law No. 13, of the Rational Society, to obtain an additional capital of £25,000, in five thousand Preference Shares, of £5 each. The Directors shall have power to raise the same on the undermentioned CONDITIONS.

43. *Shareholders.*—Subscribers to the Community Fund to have precedence in the appropriation of the Preference Shares.

44. *Deposit and Calls.*—A deposit of ten shillings per share shall be paid on appropriation, and the Directors shall have the power to make calls of ten shillings per share at intervals of not less than two months, until the whole amount be paid. Notice of such calls shall be inserted in the weekly Gazette of the Rational Society, and such notice shall be deemed sufficient.

45. *Interest on Shares.*—Each share shall bear interest at the rate of five per cent per annum, payable half-yearly; such interest to commence from the period

fixed by the Directors for the payment of the third call; and shall be paid before any division of the profits accruing from the property of the Society, or any other interest except that on ordinary loans.

46. *Interest on unpaid Calls, &c.*—Interest at the rate of five per cent. per annum shall be charged upon all unpaid calls; and at the expiration of six months from the time of any call being made, the share or shares of the defaulters shall be forfeited, together with the monies paid thereon, and all privileges belonging thereto.

47. *Privileges of Shareholders.*—Every holder of Preference Shares shall be eligible to become a candidate for membership in Community, if nominated according to the laws of the Society.

48. *Right of Nomination to the Schools.*—Shareholders shall have the power of nominating children, as Pupils in the Schools, on the terms following, viz.:—

Holders of three Preference Shares may nominate one child, *to be received upon the lowest terms fixed by the Directors, and which shall not exceed the cost to the Establishment of maintenance, clothing, and education.* The admissions to take place from time to time, as vacancies occur in the Establishment, the calls on the shares being then fully paid up. The children to be admitted in the order in which the shares have been subscribed for, unless in case of disease or other unfitness.

Holders of less than three shares may nominate children for reception in the Schools, at such advanced terms as the Directors may think fit: such advanced terms to be reduced annually, at the discretion of the Directors, so long as the children so nominated remain at the School, until it reaches the aforesaid actual cost.

Holders of Community scrip may nominate in the above proportion; but the nominees of holders of Preference Shares shall have priority of admission into the Schools.

49. *Membership of Pupils.*—If the Directors shall be of opinion that any of the pupils, upon attaining the age of sixteen, may be rendered permanently useful to the Establishment, the school charge to such pupils shall be reduced, at a graduated scale per annum, until it be entirely dispensed with, and upon the payment, in shares or money, of a sum to be fixed by the Directors, they shall become free members of the Establishment.

50. *Liability of Shareholders.*—To prevent any personal liabilities attaching to the shareholders, for more than the amount of their respective shares, the Directors shall not have power to contract any debts on behalf of the Society, unless they shall be in possession of funds equal to the payment of such debts, and any deviation from this rule shall be upon their own personal responsibility.

51. *Transfers.*—Any shareholder, or his legal representative, may transfer his shares; but no transfer shall be valid until the same has been confirmed by the Directors, and registered in the books of the Society

52. *Fee for Transfers.*—The person to whom any transfer is made shall pay one shilling for the confirmation and registration thereof.

53. *Paying off Preference Shares.*—The Directors shall have power to pay off, from time to time, (at par, with such interest as may remain due) such proportion of the Preference Shares as they may think fit, giving the holders of such shares the option of retaining them, subject to the regulations affecting the original subscribers to the Community Fund.

LOANS.

54. *Power to Borrow.*—The Central Board may from time to time borrow, by way of mortgage, or otherwise, any sums of money required for the purposes of the Society.

55. *Certificate of Loan.*—For every sum of money borrowed by this Society, on the security of the Community Fund, a certificate shall be granted to the lender, in such form as the Central Board may direct in the Hand-book of the Society, which shall pledge the Community property of the Society for repayment of the sum borrowed.

56. *Interest.*—Upon all loans of money, interest shall be paid half yearly, as follows:—

   1st. On loans from individuals,

   (a) For periods of not less than five years a rate of interest not exceeding five per cent. per annum.

   (b) For periods of not less than one year, with three months notice of withdrawal, a rate not exceeding four per cent. per annum.

   2nd. On Loans from Societies.—For periods of not less than three months, with fourteen days notice of withdrawal, a rate not exceeding four per cent. per annum.

57. *Priority of Claim.*—Should a dissolution of the Society, or of any of its establishments, be determined on, all monies and the fixed amount of other valuables contributed to such establishment, shall be first repaid; and the remaining balance, if any, shall be divided equally among the members, resident and non-resident.

58. *Transfer of Loans.*—Any member, or his legal representative duly qualified as such, may transfer the certificates of loans held by him; and such transfers shall be made by the holder, stating on the back of the document the name of the member to whom it is transferred, and signing the same with his own hand.

59. *Special Mortgages.*—The Central Board may from time to time borrow, at such lawful interest as they may think fit, any sum of money, upon the security of mortgage of any estate or property belonging to, or which shall have been contracted to be purchased by, or for, or on behalf of the Society, and may cause the mortgage to be made either for a term of years, or in fee, and either with or without a power of sale over the estate or property, and generally in such form as the lender shall reasonably require.

PROFITS.

60. *Division*—When a clear surplus profit shall have been made by any Community, after paying the interest of capital, supplying the necessary and reasonable wants of the members residing in it, and defraying the expenses of repairs, and other incidentals, such profit shall be appropriated in the following manner:—

> One fourth to the parties who have advanced the capital;
> One fourth to the General Fund of the Society; and
> The remaining half to the liquidation of debts.

ACCOUNTS AND STATISTICAL RETURNS.

61. *General Control.*—The accounts and reports of the Society's affairs, kept at the office of the Central Board; and also the local accounts to be kept, and reports made, by the local Presidents and Boards, for the right conduct of the local affairs of Branches and classes of the Society, shall be subject to the rules and directions of the Central Board, established from time to time in the Hand-Book, and given to the respective officers of the Society. A general statement of the funds and effects of the Society shall be prepared, at least, once in every year, in terms of the statute.

GOVERNMENT OF COMMUNITIES.

62. *Officers.*—The government of each Community shall be administered by a Governor, who shall appoint a Deputy Governor, Secretary, heads of departments, and such other officers as may be requisite.
63. *Governor.*—Each Governor shall be appointed by the Congress at its annual meetings, or by the Central Board in case of a vacancy by death, resignation, or otherwise; but such appointment shall be subject to the confirmation of the Congress at its next meeting. The Governor shall enjoy all the rights of a member equally as if he had been selected in the same manner as other members.
64. *Council.*—The Governor of each Community shall form a Council, composed of the Deputy Governor, Secretary, and heads of departments: such Council to hold periodical meetings, the proceedings of which shall be recorded, and be at all reasonable times accessible to the members of the Community.
65. *Deputy Governor.*—In the event of the decease of any Governor, he shall be succeeded in his office by his Deputy Governor, until a new appointment is made.

RESIDENTS IN COMMUNITY.

66. *Selection.*—The persons admitted to reside in any Community shall be selected by the Governor, from lists of members of the Society kept by the Central Board;

but each Governor shall have discretionary power, under peculiar circumstances, to admit other persons who may appear to him to be desirable.

67. *Probation.*—Every person admitted to reside in any Community, who desires to become a member of the Community, shall undergo at least twelve months probation as a candidate, and shall be admitted a member only by the consent of the Governor.

68. *Agreement.*—Every person, upon entering a Community as a probationer, shall sign an agreement to abide by any and all rules and regulations established by the Society and the Governor of such Community, or to withdraw from the Community when required so to do.

69. *Removals.*—The Governor may at any time remove any resident, candidate, or member, from the Community under his direction; but the individuals so removed may appeal to the Central Board, whose decision shall be final.

70. *Withdrawal, &c. of Members.*—If any member leave any establishment of the Society, of his own desire, or be dismissed by the Governor for con-conformity [sic] to the regulations of the establishment; or, if any member die [sic], the said withdrawn or dismissed member, or the heirs or nearest of kin or nominees of a deceased member, by virtue of the will or deed of gift which such member may have made, shall receive interest on the amount of his share; and the said members, or the heirs or nearest of kin or nominees of a deceased member, may transfer such funds to any other member, or other person, subject to the laws of the Society.

SETTLEMENT OF DISPUTES.

71. *Arbitration.*—All disputes between the Society and any member or person claiming on account of any member, shall be submitted to arbitration, pursuant to the statute 10 Geo. IV. c. 56, § 27., and at the first meeting of the Central Board, after the rules are enrolled, five arbitrators shall be named and elected, none of them being directly or indirectly beneficially interested in the funds of the Society; and in each case of dispute, the names of the arbitrators shall be written on pieces of paper and placed in a box or glass, and the three whose names are first drawn out by the complaining party, or by some one appointed by him or her, shall be the arbitrators to decide the matter in difference.

DISSOLUTION OF THE SOCIETY.

72. *Consents.*—This Society shall not be dissolved or determined, so long as the intents or purposes thereof, or any of them, remain to be carried into effect, without the votes and consents, and guarantee for the division of the funds required by the statute.

BYE-LAWS.

73. *Hand-Book.*—The Central Board may, pursuant to 10 Geo. IV. c. 56, § 9., enact such bye-laws, and issue such instructions from time to time as they deem

requisite for carrying into effect the general laws of the Society, or for the right conduct of the business of the Society in any of the Branches; and such bye-laws and instructions, when duly certified, shall be published for the use of the members in a Hand-Book, and also in the *Gazette* of the Society.[3]

PUBLICATION OF THE LAWS.

74. *Printed Copies.*—The laws and Hand-Book of the Society shall be printed and published at the general expense of the Society, and each member furnished with a copy, for which he shall pay a sum to be fixed by the Central Board.

INTERPRETATIONS.

75. *Meanings of Words.*—In giving effect to the foregoing laws, and bye-laws, the following meanings shall be assigned to expressions, unless either the subject or the context otherwise requires.

The singular number shall include the plural number as well as the singular.
The masculine gender shall include females as well as males.

[Certificate annexed to the rules generally.]
I hereby certify that the foregoing rules are in conformity to law, and with the provisions of the Act 10 Geo. IV. c. 56., as amended by 4 and 5 Will. IV. c. 40.

JOHN TIDD PRATT,

The Barrister appointed to certify the rules of Savings' Banks. London, August 3, 1843.
Copy sent to Clerk of Peace for Hants.
J. TIDD PRATT.

[Certificate annexed to the "Preference capital" rules.] I hereby certify that the foregoing alterations are in conformity to law, and with the provisions of the Act 10 Geo. IV. c. 56, as amended by 4 and 5 Will. IV. c. 40.

JOHN TIDD PRATT,

The Barrister appointed to certify the rules of Savings' Banks. - London, Sept. 21, 1843.
Copy sent to Clerk of Peace for Middlesex.
J. TIDD PRATT.

Robert Owen, President.
DAVID VINES, Vice President.[4]
FREDERICK BATE, Treasurer.[5]
JAMES ATKINSON, Gen. Sec.[6]
G. A. FLEMING, Editor of the *Gazette*, and General Missionary.[7]
LLOYD JONES, General Missionary.[8]

THOMAS WILLEY, Accountant.[9]
JAMES CROSS.
J. CAMPBELL SMITH.[10]
Robert ALGER.[11]
John FINCH, of Liverpool, Trustee.[12]
WILLIAM CLEGG, of Manchester, Trustee.[13]
CHARLES FREDERICK GREEN, of Indiana, United States, Trustee.[14]

Central Board Office,
44, Bloomsbury Square,
London, September, 1843.

Notes

1 The Society was registered under the Friendly Societies Acts 1832 and 1834.
2 Queenwood Community, also known as "Harmony" after Harmony Hall, its main building and showpiece.
3 The *New Moral World*.
4 David Vines, Secretary of the Reading branch of the Rational Society since 1839.
5 Frederick Bate, originally a printer's draughtsman from Dublin. He was secretary of the Burton Street Hall (the hub of London Owenism in the late 1830s) and the treasurer of the Home Colonisation Society since 1840. The organisation raised funds for the Queenwood community. Bate later joined James Pierrepont Greaves's Concordium community experiment.
6 James Atkinson, a silk mercer from Leeds and Queenwood's secretary from January 1842 to August 1844.
7 George Alexander Fleming (see Part 2, Chapter 13). He joined the Queenwood community in January 1845, and edited the *New Moral World* there until the venture collapsed later that same year.
8 Lloyd Jones (1811–1886), a Manchester fustian cutter and early co-operator. A personal friends of E.T. Craig (see Part 9, Chapter 57), he was appointed Social Missionary around 1835. After the demise of the Owenite movement, Jones was involved in the co-operative revival and became one of Robert Owen's earliest biographers (Jones 1890; Harrison 1969, 220; Langdon 2000, 102).
9 Thomas Willey (1795–1861), a Cheltenham printer and Chartist. Willey was an ardent defender of the Chartist Land Plan, and also supported Owenite communitarian ventures.
10 James Campbell Smith, a member of the Rational Society's London Branch A1, founded in 1835 on Great Queen Street, Lincoln's Inn Fields. By April 1840, it was moved to a larger meeting hall on John Street. The branch had 160 members, and was the second largest after Manchester (Garnett 1972, 164, n. 108).
11 Robert Alger was the first editor of the *New Moral World* from 1834 to 1837. That year, he was appointed secretary of the Rational Society's London District Board, an umbrella organisation for Owenites in the capital and the surrounding counties (Claeys 2008, 243–244).
12 See Part 3, Chapter 19 and Part 9, Chapter 58. John Finch was Queenwood's first acting governor.
13 A Manchester Owenite, William Clegg had been involved in the Queenwood project since 1837, when he joined Robert Owen's National Community Friendly Society alongside John Finch and George Alexander Fleming.

14 Born in the United States, Charles Frederick Green was a butcher by trade and one of London's leading Owenites. He was a member of the London District Board since 1839, and the President of the capital's Branch A1. He joined Queenwood with his wife Martha in March 1840 and was appointed community governor until August of that same year. Thomas Hunt (see Part 9, Chapter 59) replaced him as President of Branch A1 (Royle 1998, 249).

Part 6

DEMOCRACY AND THE STATE

Democracy and the role of the State in a co-operative society were some of the most contentious issues in the history of the Owenite movement. Divisions over the very definition of community and the means to achieve it were wed to competing approaches to working-class agency. These ranged from Robert Owen's top-down, apolitical stance (see Part 3) to William Thompson's insistence that the socialist promise of economic self-sufficiency was conducive to another ideal, that of political self-determination (see Part 4).

Owen's dismissal of working-class politics stemmed from his deterministic outlook. Considering that the poor were the victims of circumstances – such as economic downturns, inadequate relief provisions and entrenched class prejudice – to a greater extent than the wealthy, he deemed them incapable of ensuring their own salvation. Moreover, the poor were not educated enough to be able to make informed political decisions. Consequently, during the Reform Act debate in 1830–1832, Owen opposed the extension of the electoral franchise to working men, arguing that they were as yet too ignorant to be granted political agency. In the interim, guidance and education had to come from above (Carpenter 1832; Lovett [1876] 1967, 40–41; Holyoake 1908, 120). Owen was also keen to point out that his followers' political aspirations were an illusion, for only his "science of society" would foster true political equality. In his eyes, democracy was no better than aristocracy, as both systems fed the interests of one class against the other. On the contrary, his "Villages of Co-operation" would be governed by committees of elders. Under this gerontocratic regime, once they reached the age of sixty, community members would exercise power in turn, thus establishing a natural aristocracy based on the knowledge and experience acquired over one's lifetime (see Part 2, Chapter 10). Class divisions would thus be erased, once communities had superseded all state institutions.

In reality, Owen's gerontocratic system was never put into action; though the majority of his followers did support the idea of self-governing communities, his focus remained firmly set on re-educating an increasingly working-class membership. Such was the paradox of a system whose precise aim was through co-operation, to transcend all social and economic divisions. This top-down governing style, along with renewed calls for parliamentary reform in the late 1820s and early 1830s, caused long-standing rifts among early socialists. In the run-up to the Great Reform Act 1832, most Owenites campaigned for universal male suffrage, and many later embraced Chartism. Though they never formally broke away from co-operative socialism, two of the Chartist founders, William Lovett and Henry Hetherington, embraced the cause, in part as a critique of Owen's autocratic leadership. By 1838, according to the *New Moral World*, half of the London Owenites supported the Charter, while most of the provincial branches favoured democratic governance based on elected committees (Yeo 1971, 91; Taylor 1983, 300, n. 15). For all those who had grown weary of Owen's benevolent despotism, political reform was the groundwork upon which to found economic equality and personal improvement, not the other way around.

Aligning with working-class movements was less of a priority for American Owenites, who often came to socialism via religious nonconformity and usually hailed from more privileged backgrounds than their British counterparts. Their bids for democracy were rather focused on the abolitionist cause, as they deemed slavery incompatible with the ideal of freedom as enshrined in the Constitution of the United States (Bestor 1950, 216; Kolmerten 1998, 145). During his New Lanark days and afterwards, Owen never directly addressed the fact that his factory's fortunes, and those of the British textile sector as a whole, actually relied on slave labour.[1] According to his own "doctrine of circumstances", he considered slavery to be an irrational and therefore undesirable practice as he did not believe, contrary to many in favour of slavery, that people had a particular character, or an inferior status, merely due to their skin colour or race. By the early 1820s, most of Owen's American admirers, like reformer and New Harmony resident George Flower or Cornelius Blatchly, a New York physician, were also staunch abolitionists. Once settled in America, all of Owen's children also embraced the cause (Owen 1906, 63–64). All saw his community schemes as an alternative to the plantation system, especially as settlements for former slaves were being promoted at the time in Haiti and Liberia by the American Colonization Society (Kolmerten 1998, 31).

As per usual, Owenite abolitionists favoured a gradualist approach in order to avoid class conflict and limit the financial burden on planters. In contrast to the ideal of immediate emancipation, which was promoted in the 1820s by the *Freedom's Journal*, the first African-American periodical, the Owenites were keen to "devise a set of relationships, economic and social, that might safely supersede the peculiar institution" (Bestor 1950, 216). These principles would be put to the test in 1827 by Frances Wright at Nashoba community in Tennessee (see Chapter 36).

Nevertheless, the Owenites held ambiguous views on race. Owen, Frances Wright and others denied that Black people were inherently and naturally inferior to Whites, but they did think that decades of slavery had degraded them. Under the present state of things, slaves and recently emancipated Black Americans were therefore deemed incapable of becoming fully-functioning citizens and productive members of society, unless they were properly educated (Bederman 2005,

443). This line of reasoning explains why Owen prohibited "persons of color" from becoming members of the New Harmony Community (1825, reprinted in Lockwood 1905, 84–90). Such a paternalistic stance had also much in common with Owen's dismissal of working-class democratic demands in the United Kingdom. It informed his distrust of both the American and British abolitionist movements (see Chapter 37), as well as practical experiments at Nashoba. On both sides of the Atlantic, the possibility of political agency for those at the very bottom of social hierarchies was left unanswered.

Note

1 Owen's views on slavery have generally remained underexplored, with the exception of Morris, 2018.

35

AN ADDRESS TO THE WORKING CLASSES (1819), REPRINTED IN *A SUPPLEMENTARY APPENDIX TO THE FIRST VOLUME OF THE LIFE OF ROBERT OWEN...* (LONDON: EFFINGHAM WILSON, 1858), 225–231.

Robert Owen

[Originally published in the *Star* newspaper on 15 April 1819, this document provides a link between Owen's theory of character formation and his mistrust of democratic, grassroots-led political practice. Arguing that the time was ripe for the definitive improvement of working-class conditions, he attempted to present his "science of society" as an alternative to any antagonistic means of achieving change, especially political agitation. For Owen, the working-classes first needed to allow themselves to be re-educated in the truth of his doctrine of circumstances. Once they understood that all human beings were equally the product of their environment, and that class-based divisions were therefore mere social constructs, the poor would be able to better themselves without encroaching on the lives and riches of the wealthy.]

The truly intelligent in Europe and America, by their silence when publicly called upon, now admit the truth of those principles which I have advocated as preliminary to the introduction of a New System for the government of mankind. Hitherto, no individual, either in this country or abroad, who possesses any knowledge of the theory and practice of governing men or of forming their character, has attempted to prove error in any one of the principles developed in the "New View of Society." On close examination they are all found to be nature's laws, and therefore unassailable.

Yet all men have from infancy been forced to think and act as if other notions were true; and, as they have never seen any part of mankind placed under circumstances in which they could act on those principles which, they are now obliged to admit, are true in theory, they very naturally from past experience conclude that, although the principles of the "New System" are capable of the most evident demonstration, they cannot be applied to practice. All this however means no more than that they who come to this conclusion are incompetent to reduce erected principles into beneficial practice: and the persons who thus hastily decide, without having sufficient data on which to form any accurate judgment, would have made the same random assertions respecting any of the great improvements in science, prior to their introduction. Such individuals forget that it is a modern invention to enable one man, with the aid of a little steam, to perform the labour of 1,000 men.

What would these unbelievers in human improvement say, if the truths of the Copernican System were now for the first time to be introduced to their notice?

But we will leave them to brood over their melancholy fancied wisdom until facts shall overcome their disbelief; for the time is at hand when they will behold with astonishment the simplicity and beautiful order of those movements, the combination of which they now deem to be impossible.

Yet before this change, so much to be desired by you and every other class, from the highest to the lowest, can be permitted to take place, one formidable obstacle must be removed. From infancy you, like others, have been made to despise and to hate those who differ from you in manners, language, and sentiments. You have been filled with all uncharitableness, and in consequence cherish feelings of anger towards your fellow-men who have been placed in opposition to your interests. Those feelings of anger must be withdrawn before any being who has your real interest at heart can place power in your hands. You must be made to know yourselves, by which means alone you can discover what other men are. You will then distinctly perceive that no rational ground for anger exists, even against those who by the errors of the present system have been made your greatest oppressors and your most bitter enemies. An endless multiplicity of circumstances, over which you had not the smallest control, placed you where you are, and as you are. In the same manner, others of your fellow-men have been formed by circumstances, equally uncontrollable by them, to become your enemies and grievous oppressors. In strict justice they are no more to be blamed for these results than you are; nor you than they; and, splendid as their exterior may be, this state of matters often causes them to suffer even more poignantly than you. They have therefore an interest, strong as yours, in the change which is about to commence for the equal benefit of all, provided *you* do not create a more formidable counteracting interest on *their* parts; of which the result must be, to prolong the existing misery of both classes, and to retard the public good.

The existing order of things has placed some of your fellow-men in situations of power and emolument, and in the possession of privileges on which they have been taught to set a value. While you shew by your conduct any desire violently to dispossess them of this power, these emoluments, and privileges,—is it not evident that they must continue to regard you with jealous and hostile feelings, that the contention between the rich and the poor will never have an end, and that, whatever relative changes may take place among you, there will ever be the same oppression of the weak by the party who has attained to power? Before your condition can be ameliorated this irrational and useless contest must cease, and measures must be adopted in which both parties may have a substantial interest. Then will anger and opposition subside, and those arrangements which now appear impracticable to the inexperienced, be carried most easily into practice. And these changes are at hand; for a crisis has arrived, new in the history of mankind.

The experience of ages has now developed truths which demonstrate, "That all men have been forced by the circumstances which have surrounded them from birth to become mere irrational and localized animals, and who in consequence have been compelled to think and act on data directly opposed to facts, and of course to pursue measures destructive alike of their own happiness and of the happiness of human nature." I am well aware of the feelings which the development of this truth will at first excite in those who are now deemed rich, learned, and powerful, and in all those who have been taught to imagine that they possess some knowledge. The truth however is not thus declared to inflict unnecessary pain on a single human being. On the contrary, it is held up to the light of the world, solely to shew mankind the first step of knowledge which can lead them to rationality, and out of the ignorance and misery in which they have hitherto existed. The pain which the development of this all-important truth must create will be transient and pass away without real injury to any one; while the substantial benefits which it will produce will be perpetually experienced by the whole of human nature through all succeeding generations. It is from a thorough knowledge of this truth, and of the infinite beneficial consequences which will result to mankind from its being universally known, that I now bring it before your minds, not as an abstract theory to amuse speculative men, but to shew you the source of all the errors which afflict society, and which must be removed before your condition can be ameliorated.

There is no knowledge except this which can make human nature truly benevolent and kind to the whole of the species, and, with the certainty of a mathematical demonstration, render all men charitable, in the most enlarged and best sense of the term. It will force on the human mind the conviction that to blame and to be angry with our fellow-men for the evils which exist, is the very essence of folly and irrationality, and that notions which can give rise to such feelings never could enter into the composition of any human being that had been once made rational.

Are you then prepared to look upon all your fellow-creatures, in power and out of power, rich and poor, learned and unlearned, good and bad, as beings formed solely by the circumstances of their birth, and who have been made as they are, whatever they may be, from causes which exclude the possibility of the smallest control on their parts in the formation of those faculties and qualities they may happen to possess? If you cannot see and comprehend this truth, then is the time not yet to come for your deliverance from the depths of mental darkness and physical misery. But I trust the light is not now too strong for you to receive without injury; for I have been gradually preparing you for years for its reception, and if the experience which I have been permitted to acquire of human nature does not very much deceive me, it is not now a premature disclosure.

DEMOCRACY AND THE STATE

If you then can bear to be told that human beings possessing the most attractive form and the highest intellectual attainments which the world has yet seen, can justly claim no other appellation than that of localised animals, peculiar to some of the innumerable districts into which irrationality has divided the world; and if your minds can now comprehend the principles which place this truth among those which are capable of the easiest demonstration; then is the time of your deliverance from mental slavery come, and the period is approaching when you may acquire some title to be considered rational creatures.

If you are in this advanced mental state, so much to be desired for your happiness, then you will at once cease to blame others for the evils which you suffer; anger, revenge, and hatred, almost to the very recollection of them, will be withdrawn from your feelings; you will not longer [sic] dissipate all your energies in attempting to find the cause of your miseries among any of your fellow men, and thus destroy your minds and happiness by creating unceasing, useless irritation.

No! In all respects your conduct will become the very reverse of this. You will regard all your fellow-men, without distinction, as beings who are soon to become your friends and active co- operators in the attainment of the substantial happiness to which human nature is evidently destined. You will say to those who are now in possession of riches, honours, power, and privileges, which they have been taught to value,— "Retain these in perfect security as long as you can hold them in estimation. Our whole conduct and proceedings shall be a pledge to you that we will never attempt to dispossess you of any part of them; nay, while you can derive pleasure from additional wealth, we will add to that which you now possess. The cause of contest between us will henceforth cease. We have discovered its irrationality and utter uselessness. We will not, except to acquire experience from it, recur to the past, in which all have been compelled to act an irrational part; but we will earnestly apply ourselves to the future; and having discovered the light of true knowledge, we will henceforward walk by it."

All this you may with confidence say to the higher classes, whose supposed privileges you will soon cease to envy. For, without entering into contest with them, without infringing on any of the imaginary privileges which prior circumstances have placed in their hands, a new view of your interests shall be speedily opened to you, by which, without interfering with the rights of any class, without exciting any feeling of opposition to your proceedings, you shall be enabled to relieve yourselves and your descendants from poverty, from ignorance, and from the innumerable causes of misery to which you have hitherto been victims. When you shall thus be enabled to understand your real interests you will have no desire for any of the fancied advantages now possessed by the higher classes.

Had those who are of this order in the civilized world been permitted to discover what human nature really is, they would have distinctly known long ago that, by being raised, as it is termed, to the privileged ranks, they are placed under circumstances which render their successors, except by some extraordinary chance, increasingly useless to themselves and to society.

They are taught from infancy to set an inordinate value on themselves because they possess what are miscalled privileges, the only real effect of which is to surround them by circumstances which must inevitably make them more helpless and dependant than other men.

They are trained from the cradle (and therefore call for our pity, not blame,) to take pride to themselves for pursuing measures which deprive the great mass of mankind of the most essential benefits that belong to human nature, in order that they, a most insignificant part in point of numbers, may be distinguished by advantages over their fellows.

The feelings which this absurd conduct generates throughout society, keep the whole population of the world in a lower degree of enjoyment and rationality than most of the animal creation. They are the very essence of ignorant selfishness. You will now soon pass this error.

You will discover that there is no comparison between the result of such conduct and the pleasure to be derived from the most active exertions to give to all your fellow-creatures the same privileges and benefits which you yourselves possess, and, by this means, so far increase the aggregate of human enjoyment, that the least gifted member of society will experience a larger share of continued and permanent happiness than has hitherto fallen to the lot of the most fortunate. The motives which lead to the former conduct are altogether irrational, and will not bear the glance of an enlightened mind; while those which will compel you to adopt the latter are in unison with every sound principle and just feeling, and defy the most rigid scrutiny to detect in them any error.

Let me however guard you against a mistake which exists to a great extent among the unprivileged orders. The privileged classes of the present day, throughout Europe, are not, as this mistake supposes, influenced so much by a desire to keep *you* down, as by an anxiety to retain the means of securing to *themselves* a comfortable and respectable enjoyment of life. Let them distinctly perceive that the ameliorations which you are about to experience are not intended or calculated to inflict any real injury on them or their posterity, but, on the contrary, that the same measures which will improve *you*, must, as they assuredly will, essentially benefit *them*, and raise them in the scale of happiness and intellectual enjoyment,—and you will speedily have their co-operation to carry the contemplated arrangements into effect. It must be satisfactory to you to learn that I have had the most evident proofs from many individuals, high in these classes, that they have now a real desire to improve your condition; but, from the unfortunate situation in which they have been placed by birth, they cannot, of themselves, devise measures by which you can be benefited and their own circumstances improved. Such changes must proceed from practical men.

What has been said is sufficient for your minds to digest at one time. When you are prepared to receive more, it shall be given to you.

Heed not what men with fanciful theories and without practical knowledge may say to you. Many of them, I have no doubt, mean well. But be assured that whatever tends to irritation and violence proceeds from the most gross ignorance of human nature, and evinces an utter inexperience in those practical measures by which alone society can be relieved from the evils which it has so long suffered.

My fixed intention has long been to develop truths which it is of the utmost importance to the well-being of mankind to make publicly known at this period; and I have been gradually preparing the public mind to receive them. Where great darkness has ever existed, a sudden admission of strong light would destroy the infant powers of vision. Unless the most salutary truths, when they are opposed to centuries of prejudice, are introduced with due care to those whose minds have wandered in a labyrinth of error from their birth, the tender germ of rationality would likewise perish, and ignorance and misery must continue to prevail over knowledge and happiness.

As you become acquainted with these truths, one after the other, your long injured minds will acquire strength, and your rational powers gradually expand, until the knowledge of human nature, which now appears so incomprehensible to you, will discover itself to be as simple as any of the other facts which surround you, and with which you are now the most familiar.

What I have now stated is intended to prepare the public mind for the following conclusions:—

1st. That the rich and the poor, the governors and the governed, have really but one interest.
2nd. That the notions and arrangements which at present prevail throught [sic] society are necessarily destructive of the happiness of all ranks.
3rd. That a correct knowledge of human nature will destroy all animosity and anger among men, and will prepare the way for new arrangements, which will be introduced without violence and without injury to any party, and which will effectually remove the cause from which all the errors and evils of society now proceed.
4th. That the higher classes in general no longer wish to degrade you, but in any change that may be proposed for *your* benefit, they demand only that advantages should be secured to *them*, at least equal to those which they now possess: and this feeling is quite natural; it would be yours if you were in their situation.
5th. That you now possess all the means which are necessary to relieve yourselves and your descendants to the latest period from the sufferings which you have hitherto experienced,—except the knowledge how to direct those means.
6th. That this knowledge is withheld from you only until the violence of your irritation against your fellow-men shall cease; that is, until you thoroughly understand and are influenced in all your conduct by the principle, "That it is the circumstances of birth, with subsequent surrounding circumstances, all formed for the individual, (and over which society has now a complete control,) that have hitherto made the past generations of mankind into the irrational creatures exhibited in history, and fashioned them, up to the present hour, into those localised beings of country, sect, class, and party, who now compose the population of the earth."

7th and, last. That the past ages of the world present the history of human irrationality only, and that we are but now advancing towards the dawn of reason, and to the period when the mind of man shall be born again.

ROBERT OWEN.

New Lanark, March 29, 1819.

36

FANNY WRIGHT UNMASKED BY HER OWN PEN. EXPLANATORY NOTES, RESPECTING THE NATURE AND OBJECTS OF THE INSTITUTION OF NASHOBA, AND OF THE PRINCIPLES UPON WHICH IT IS FOUNDED, ADDRESSED TO THE FRIENDS OF HUMAN IMPROVEMENT, IN ALL COUNTRIES AND OF ALL NATIONS (NEW YORK: PRINTED FOR THE PURCHASERS [1827] 1830).

Frances Wright

[Nashoba was an experimental settlement in Tennessee, founded in November 1825 by Frances Wright (1795–1852), in order to enable the gradual emancipation of American slaves. Born in Scotland into an upper-class, liberal family, Wright was a freethinker, a feminist and an abolitionist who saw Robert Owen's communitarian schemes as a potential solution to the slave-based plantation system (Harrison 1969, 116). After she acquired Nashoba, Frances Wright purchased fifteen slaves. Over the course of a five-year tenure, they would be able to earn enough to buy their freedom, while receiving an education to prepare them for their future life as free citizens. Wright hoped they would eventually emigrate to either Liberia or Haiti, two countries founded for and by emancipated slaves (Bederman 2005, 446). She also anticipated that the plan, once imitated throughout the United States, would eventually remove slavery from the nation's territory, without any bloodshed and at no great cost to the planters (Kolmerten 1998, 111–142; Stowitzky 2004, 31). However, Nashoba was soon plagued by difficulties and scandals. The slaves remained subordinate and were submitted to a paternalistic regime, as they were governed by a committee of white trustees.[1] To the dismay of many, even among abolitionist circles, Nashoba's doctor, James Richardson, entered into a relationship with Joséphine Larieu, a free woman of colour from New Orleans who had been hired as a schoolmistress, along with her mother Charlotte (Stowitzky 2004, 58).[2] Frances Wright's *Explanatory Notes*, penned in 1827 and published the following year in an anti-slavery paper, the *Genius of Universal Emancipation*, were written to find financial backers, recruit new trustees and defend her and her friends' own distrust of the institution of marriage (Bederman 2005, 449). She argued in favour of co-operative production, or "united labour" as the only viable economic alternative to slavery, and also advocated mixed-race unions as the answer to America's system of racial and political inequality. But these proposals were never put into practice at Nashoba, so strong was the backlash against Wright's vindication of racial amalgamation. The community disbanded by January 1828, and two years later, Wright took the now emancipated slaves to Haiti.]

This institution was founded in the autumn of 1825, in the western district of the state of Tennessee, North America, by Frances Wright. The object of the founder was to attempt the practice of certain principles, which in theory had been frequently advocated. She had observed that the step between theory and practice is usually great; that while many could reason, few were prepared to proceed to action and that yet mankind must reasonably hesitate to receive as truths, theories, however ingenious, if unsupported by experiment. In the individual who should first attempt an experiment opposed to all existing opinions and practice, she believed two requisites to be indispensable; mental courage, and, as some writers have defined it, a passion for the improvement of the human race. She felt within herself these necessary qualifications; and, strongly convinced of the truth of the principles which, after mature consideration, her heart and head had embraced, she determined to apply all her energies, and to devote her slender fortune, to the building up of an institution which should have those principles for its base, and whose destinies, she fondly hoped, might tend to convince mankind of their moral beauty and practical utility. Actuated, from her earliest youth, by a passionate interest in the welfare of man, she had peculiarly addressed herself to the study of his past and present condition. All her observations tended to corroborate the opinion which her own feelings might possibly, in the first instance, have predisposed her to adopt— *that men are virtuous in proportion as they are happy, and happy in proportion as they are free.* She saw this truth exemplified in the history of modern, as of ancient times. Every where, knowledge, mental refinement and the gentler, as the more ennobling. feelings of humanity, have kept pace, influx or reflux, with the growth or depression of the spirit of freedom.

But while human liberty has engaged the attention of the enlightened, and enlisted the feelings of the generous of all civilized nations, may we not inquire if this liberty has been rightly understood? Has it not been with limitations and exceptions, tending to foster jealousies, or to inspire injurious ambition? Has it, in short, been pure and entire in principle, universal in the objects it embraces, and equal for all men and classes of men? Liberty without equality, what is it but a chimera? and equality, what is it also but a chimera, unless it extend to all the enjoyments, exertions and advantages, intellectual and physical, of which our nature is capable?

One nation, and as yet, one nation only, has declared all men "born free and equal," and conquered the political freedom and equality of it; citizens—with the lamentable exception of its citizens of color. But is there not a liberty yet more precious than what is termed *national*, and an equality more precious than what is termed *political*? Before we are citizens, are we not human beings, and ere we can exercise equal rights, must we not possess equal advantages, equal means of improvement and of enjoyment?

Political liberty may be said to exist in the United States at America, and (without adverting to the yet unsettled, though we may fondly trust secured republics of America's southern continent) *only there*. Moral liberty exists *no where*.

By political liberty we may understand the liberty of speech and of action without incurring the violence of authority or the penalties of law. By moral liberty may we not understand the *free exercise of the liberty of speech and of action*, without incurring the intolerance of popular prejudice and ignorant public opinion? To secure the latter where the former liberty exists, what is necessary "but to will it." Far truer is the assertion as here applied to moral liberty than as heretofore applied to political liberty To free ourselves of thrones, aristocracies, and hierarchies, of fleets and armies, and all the arrayed panoply of organized despotism, it is not sufficient to will it. We must fight for it and fight for it too with all the odds of wealth, and power, and position against us. But when the field is won, to use it is surely ours; and if the possession of the right of free action inspire not the courage to exercise the right, liberty has done but little for us. It is much to have the fetters broken from our limbs, but yet better is it to have them broken from the mind. It is much to have *declared* men free and equal, but it shall be more when they are rendered so; when means shall be sought and found, and employed to develop all the intellectual and physical powers of all human beings without regard to sex or condition, class, race, nation or color; and when men shall learn to view each other as members of one great family, with equal claims to enjoyment and equal capacities for labor and instruction, admitting always the sole differences arising out of the varieties exhibited in individual organization.

It were superfluous to elucidate, by argument, the baleful effects arising out of the division of labor as now existing, and which condemns the large half of mankind to an existence purely physical, and the remaining portion to pernicious idleness, and occasionally to exertions painfully, because solely intellectual. He who lives in the single exercise of his mental faculties, however usefully or curiously directed, is equally an imperfect animal with the man who knows only the exercise of his muscles.

Let us consider the actual condition of our species. Where shall we find even a single individual, male or female, whose mental and physical powers have been fairly cultivated and developed? How then is it with the great family of human kind? We have addressed our ingenuity to improve the nature and beautify the forms of all the tribe of animals domesticated by our care, but man has still neglected man; ourselves, our own species, our own nature are deemed unworthy, even unbecoming objects of experiment. Why should we refuse to the human animal care at least equal to that bestowed on the horse or the dog? His forms are surely not less susceptible of beauty; and his faculties, more numerous and exalted, may challenge, at the least, equal developement [sic].

The spirit of curiosity and inquiry, which distinguished the human animal, and which not all the artificial habits and whimsical prejudices of miscalled civilization, have sufficed to quench, seems as yet, for the most part, to have been idly directed. Arts and sciences are multiplied wants imagined, and luxuries supplied; but the first of all sciences is yet left in the germ: the first great science of human beings, the science of human life, remains untouched, unknown, unstudied; and he who should speak of it, might perhaps excite only astonishment. All the wants and comforts of man are now abstracted, as it were, from himself. We hear of the wealth of nations, of the powers of production of the demand and supply of markets, and we forgot that these words mean no more, if they mean any thing than the happiness, labor and necessities, of men. Is it not the unnatural division of mankind into classes—operative, consuming, professional. Enlightened, ignorant, &c., which inspires this false mode of reasoning, and leads the legislator and economist to see in the most useful of their fellow creatures only so much machinery for the creation of certain articles of commerce, and to pronounce a nation rich, not in proportion to the number of individuals who enjoy, but to the mass of ideal wealth thrown into commercial circulation. Surely it is time to inquire if our very sciences are not frequently as unmeaning as our teachers are mistaken and our books erroneous. Surely it is time to examine into the meaning of words and the nature of things and to arrive at simple facts, not received upon the dictum of learned authorities, but upon attentive and personal observation of what is passing around us. And surely it is more especially time to inquire why occupations the most useful and absolutely necessary to our existence and well being, should be held in disrepute, and those the least useful, nay, frequently the most decidedly mischievous, should be held in honor. The husbandman who supports us by the fruits of his labor, the artisan to whom we owe all the comforts and conveniences of life, are banished from what is termed intellectual society, nay, worse, but too often condemned to the most severe physical privations and the grossest mental ignorance while the soldier, who lives by our crimes, the lawyer by our quarrels and our rapacity, and the priest by our credulity or our hypocrisy, are honored with public consideration. and applause.

Were human life studied as a science, and, as it truly is, the first and most important of all sciences, to which every other should be viewed only as the handmaiden, it would soon appear that we are only happy in a due and well proportioned exercise of all our powers, physical, intellectual, and moral; that bodily labor becomes a pleasure when varied with mental occupation, and cheered by free and happy affection, and that no occupation can, in itself, be degrading, which has the comfort and well being of man for its object.

It will appear evident upon attentive consideration that equality of intellectual and physical advantages is the only sure foundation of liberty, and that such equality may best, and perhaps only, be obtained by a union of interests and cooperation in labor. The existing principle of selfish interest and competition has been carried to its extreme point; and, in its progress, has isolated the heart of man, blunted the edge of his finest sensibilities, and annihilated all his most generous impulse, and sympathies. Need we hesitate to denounce the principle as vicious, which places the interests of each individual in continual opposition to those of his fellows; which makes of one man's loss another's gain, and inspires a spirit of accumulation, that crushes every noble sentiment, fosters every degrading one, makes of this globe a scene of strife, and the whole human race, idolators of gold? And must we be told that this is in the nature of things? It certainly is the nature of our antisocial institutions, and need we seek any stronger argument to urge against them?

Man has been adjudged a social animal. And so he truly is; equally, we might even hazard the assertion, *more* capable of being moved to generous feeling and generous action through his affections and his interests rightly understood, than he is now moved to violence, rapine and fraud by hard necessity, and his interests falsely interpreted. Let us not libel human nature! It is what circumstance has made. But, as profiting by experience, we shall change the education of youth, remould our institutions, correct our very ideas of true and false, of right and wrong, of vice and virtue, we may see human nature assume a new form and present an appearance rich in peace and enjoyment—yet more rich in future hope.

How great soever the differences stamped on each individual by original organization, it will readily be conceded, that by fostering the good, and repressing the evil tendencies, by developing every useful faculty and amiable feeling, and cultivating the peculiar talent or talents of every child as discovered in the course of education, all human beings, (with the single and rare exceptions presented by the malconformation of the physical organs,) might be rendered useful and happy. And admitting only a similar capability of improvement in our own species that we see in other races of animals, we may with justice set no limits to our expectations respecting it, so soon as it shall become, through successive generation, the object of judicious care, and enlightened and fearless experiment.

But if we should hazard the assertion, that of children we may make what we please, we must accord that it is otherwise with man. The simplest principles become difficult of practice, when habits, formed in error, have been fixed by time, and the simplest truths hard to receive, when prejudice has warped the mind.

The founder of Nashoba looks not for the conversion of the existing generation; she looks not even for its sympathy. All that she ventures to anticipate is, the cooperation of a certain number of individuals acknowledging the same views with herself; a similar interest in the improvement of man, and a similar intrepidity, to venture all things for his welfare. To these individuals, now scattered throughout the world, and unknown probably to each other, she ventures to address herself. From their union, their cooperation, their exertions, she ventures to expect a successful experiment in favor of human liberty and human happiness. Let them unite their efforts (their numbers will not be too many) and in a country where human speech and human actions are free, let them plant their standard in the earth—declare fearlessly their principles, however opposed to the received opinions of mankind, and establish their practice accordingly, with consistence and perseverance,

This has been attempted at Nashoba: not in a spirit of hostility to the practice of the world, but with a strong moral conviction of the superior truth and beauty of that consecrated by the legal act of the founder. By a reference to that act it will be seen that the principles on which the institution is based are those of human liberty and equality without exceptions or limitations—*and its more especial object, the protection and regeneration of the race of color, universally oppressed and despised in a country self-denominated free.* This more immediate object was selected and specified by the founder, first, because her feelings had been peculiarly enlisted in behalf of the negro; and secondly because the aristocracy of color is the peculiar vice of the country which she had chosen as the seat of her experiment.

The limits of the present address will not admit of a detailed defence of the principles, and explanation of the practice of cooperative labor. And, however great their advantages, the founder of Nashoba views them as entirely subordinate to the one great principle of human liberty which she believes them calculated to further and secure.

She sees in the cooperative system, as it has been termed, *the means, not the end*, but, after mature consideration of its theory, and some observation of its practice, believing it the best means yet discovered for securing the one great end—that of human liberty and equality; she has for that reason and that reason only, made it the base of the experiment at Nashoba.

The institution of Nashoba being thus founded on the broad basis of human liberty and equality, every provision made by the legal act of the founder as well as the subsequent regulations of the trustees, are shaped in accordance with it. It will be seen by a reference to that public record, of which it is recommended to attach a copy to this address, that the personal independence of each individual member of the society is effectually secured, and that, without disputing the established laws of the country, the Institution recognizes only within its bosom the force of its own principles.

It is declared, in the deed of the founder, that no individual can be received as a member, but after a noviciate of six months, and then only by a unanimous vote of the resident proprietors. It is also provided that the admission of a husband shall not involve that of a wife, nor the admission of a wife that of a husband, nor the admission of either or both of the parents that of children *above the age of fourteen*. Each individual must pass through a separate trial, and be received or rejected on the strength of his or her merits or demerits. And, as in the reception of members the individual character is the only one recognized, so by the principle of the society that character can never be forfeited. The marriage law existing without the pale of the institution, is of no force within that pale. No woman can forfeit her individual rights or independent existence, and no man assert over her any rights or power whatsoever beyond what he may exercise over her free and voluntary affections. Nor, on the other hand, may any woman assert claims to the society or peculiar protection of any individual of the other sex, beyond what mutual inclination dictates and sanctions; while, to every individual member of either sex, is secured the protection and friendly aid of all.

The tyranny usurped by the matrimonial law, over the most sacred of the human affections, can perhaps only be equalled by that of the unjust public opinion, which so frequently stamps with infamy, or condemns to martyrdom, the best grounded and most generous attachments which ever did honor to the human heart, simply because unlegalized by human ceremonies equally idle and offensive in the form and mischievous in their tendency.

This tyranny, as now exercised over the strongest, and at the same time, if refined by mental cultivation, the noblest of the human passions had probably its source in religious prejudice or priestly rapacity; while it has found its plausible and more philosophical apology in the apparent dependence of children on the union of the parents. To this plea it might perhaps be replied, that the end, how important soever, is not secured by the means: that the forcible union of unsuitable and unsuited parents can little promote the happiness of the offspring; and that supposing the protection of children to be the real source and object of our code of morals and of our matrimonial laws, what shall we say of the effects of these humane provisions on the fate and fortunes of one large family of helpless innocents, born into the world in spite of all prohibitions and persecutions, and whom a cruel law and yet more cruel opinion disown and stigmatize. But how wide a field does this topic embrace! how much cruelty—how much oppression of the weak and helpless does it not involve!

The children denominated illegitimate or *natural*, (as if in contradistinction of others who should be out of Nature because under law) may be multiplied to any number by an unprincipled father, easily exonerated by law and custom from the duties of paternity, while these duties and their accompanying shame are left to a mother but too often rendered desperate by misfortune! and should we follow out our review of the law of civilized countries, we shall find the offspring termed legitimate, with whom honor and power and possession are associated, adjudged, in case of matrimonial dissentions, to the father, who, by means of this legal claim, has not unfrequently bowed to servitude the spirit of a fond mother, and held her as a galley slave to the oar.

But it is not here that this subject can be discussed in all its bearings. The writer of this article will, however, challenge all the advocates of existing institutions, and existing opinions, to test them by the secret feelings of their own bosoms, and then to pronounce on their justice. She will challenge them to consider the wide field of human society as now existing, to examine its practice and to weigh its theory, and to pronounce on the consistency of the one and the virtue of the other. She will challenge them to determine how many of the moral evils, and numerous family of physical diseases, which now torture the human species, have their source in the false opinions and vicious institutions, which have perverted the best source of human happiness—the intercourse of the sexes, into the deepest source of human misery. Let us look into our streets, our hospitals, our asylums; let us look into the secret thought of the anxious parent, trembling for the minds and bodies of sons starting into life, or mourning over the dying health of daughters condemned to the unnatural repression of feelings and desires inherent to their very organization, and necessary alike to their moral and physical well being.

Or let us look to the victims—not of pleasure—not of love—nor yet of their own depravity, but of those ignorant laws, ignorant prejudices, and of that ignorant code of morals which condemn one portion of the female sex to vicious excess, another to as vicious restraint, and all to defenceless helplessness, and slavery: and generally the whole of the male sex to debasing licentiousness, if not to loathsome brutality.

And must we be told that "private vices are public benefits," that the units of individual misery make the sum of the general good? or that the immolation of some, and suffering of all, are requisite to secure public order, and to moderate human population to the supplies yielded for its support. As if living creatures could ever for any space of time positively exceed the means of subsistence; or as if their tendency to increase beyond a healthy sufficiency of these means, could ever be repressed save by the increase and spread of real knowledge, which should teach human beings to consider the creation of other human beings as the most important of all actions; and the securing to the beings of their creation a sound and healthy organization and equally a sound and healthy education with all the means of a happy existence, as the most important of all duties. In the moral, intellectual, and physical cultivation of both sexes, should we seek, as we can only find, the source and security of human happiness and human virtue. Prejudice and fear are weak barriers against passions which, inherent in our nature, and demanding only judicious training to form the ornament and supply the best joys of our existence, are maddened into violence by pernicious example and pernicious restraint, varied with as pernicious indulgence. Let us correct our views of right and wrong, correct our moral lessons, and so correct the practice of rising generations ! Let us not teach that virtue consists in crucifying the affections and appetites but in their judicious government! Let us not attach ideas of purity to monastic chastity, impossible to man or woman without consequences fraught with evil, nor ideas of vice to connections formed under the auspices of kind feeling! Let us inquire not if a mother be a wife, or a father a husband, but if parents can supply, to the creature they have brought into being, all things requisite to make existence a blessing. Let the force of public opinion be brought against the thoughtless ignorance or cruel selfishness which, either with or without the sanction of a legal or religious permit, so frequently multiplies off spring beyond the resources of the parents. Let us check the force of passions, as well as their precocity, not by the idle terror of imaginary crime in the desire itself, but by the just and benevolent apprehension of bringing into existence unhappy or imperfect beings! Let us teach the young mind to reason, and the young heart to feel; and, instead of shrouding our own bodies, wants, desires, sense, affections, and faculties in mystery, let us court inquiry, and show, that acquaintance with our own nature can alone guide us to judicious practice, and *that in the consequence of human actions exists only true test of their virtue or their vice.*

We need only to observe the effects of the present system to be convinced of its error. When is the repressive force of public opinion perceived? Whom does it affect? The poor, the ignorant, the unhappy pauper, the diseased profligate, the licentious hypocrite? Is it they who feel the force either of just or unjust censure; or who hesitate to call into existence sentient beings, born to ignorance, want, or disease? No! is it not rather upon that class whose feelings and intellects have been most cultivated, and who consequently are best fitted to give life to a healthy and intellectual race, upon whom the weight of coercive prejudice falls?

Let us advert to the far more important half of the human species (whether we consider their share in the first formation and rearing the infant, or their moral influence on society). Let us consider the effects of existing institutions and opinions as exemplified among women. In what class do we find the largest number of childless females and devoted victims to unnatural restraints? Certainly among the cultivated, talented, and independent women, who (in England more especially,) shrink equally from the servitude of matrimony, and from the opprobrium stamped on unlegalized connexions.

But again, the writer of this address must observe, that she can here only touch upon subject, which she feels herself prepared to examine in detail; but which she must defer until a suitable medium be supplied in the periodical publication, which it will be the object of the society to issue, as soon as it can be done consistently with its interests.

It is considered that the peculiar object of the founder, "The benefit of the negro race," may best be consulted by the admission and incorporation of suitable individuals of that, and the mixed race, on the same principles of equality which guide the admission of all members; and farther, that such individuals may best be found among the *free citizens of color*, who form no inconsiderable, and frequently a very respectable body in the American population, more especially to that of the southern cities.

As it was the object of the founder to attempt the peaceful influence of example, and silently to correct the practice and reach the laws through the feelings and the reason of the American people, she carefully forebore outraging any of the legal provisions in the slave state in which she ventured to attempt her experiment, or those of any of the slave states with which she is acquainted, and trusted confidently to the national good sense, and to the liberality fostered by the national institutions, for the safety of any experiment however exposed to the national prejudices, which should be undertaken in a spirit of kindliness to all men, and conducted within the limits of private, or, as in the present case, of associate property.

It is not supposed that (with some rare exceptions) human beings raised under the benumbing influence of brutal slavery can be elevated to the level of a society based upon the principles of moral liberty and voluntary cooperation. The experiment, therefore, as respects *slave* population, is intended to limit, at Nashoba, to the first purchase of the founder, excepting in cases where planters, becoming members, may wish to place their negroes under the protection of the institution. And looking to effect the more especial object of the institution through the present free race of color, and more especially by the education of colored children, the founder judged that she should best conciliate the laws of the southern states, and the popular feelings of the whole Union as well as the interests of the emancipated negro, by providing for the colonization of all the slaves emancipated by the society, in a free country, without the limits of the United States. Personal observation had taught her the danger of launching a freed slave into the midst of an inimical population. And if unfit, as he must of necessity be, for incorporation into society as a free proprietor, it appeared consistent with justice and humanity to enjoin his being sent to a country of safety for his color, when ejected from the protection of the institution.

While occupied, as they fondly hope, in paving the way for the moral regeneration of American citizens, of color, the trustees of Nashoba believe that *slavery* may safely be left to work its own ruin. The falling price of cotton must soon reduce to zero the profits of the upland planter, and fortunately the growth of sugar is restricted by climate to a small portion of the American slave territory. But when the bankrupt fortunes of the southern planters shall have put an end to the *internal slave trade* of the United States, and Maryland, Virginia and Kentucky, the *Guinea* of the states farther south, shall have lost their last staple *commodity of profit*, the principles avowed in this paper may attract the national attention, and the olive of peace and brotherhood be embraced by the white man and the black; and their children, approached in feeling and education, gradually blend into one their blood and their hue.

The writer of this address is fully aware that the topic most offensive to the American public is that now under consideration. But so, to that public is it more peculiarly addressed; not, it will be believed, with *a view to offend*, but with the single view of exposing the principles of Nashoba to the American people, and calling their attention to the cool investigation of a subject unhappily seldom approached but with the anger of sectional, or the pride of national feeling.

The strength of the prejudice of color, as existing in the U. [sic] States and in the European colonies, can in general be little conceived, and less understood in the old continent; yet, however whimsical it may thee appear, is it, in fact, more ridiculous than the European prejudice of birth? The superior excellence which the one supposes in a peculiar descent, or merely in a peculiar name, the other imagines in a peculiar complexion or set of features; and perhaps it is only by considering man in many countries, and observing all his varying and contradictory prejudices, that we can discover the equal absurdity of all.

Those to whom the American institutions and American character are familiar, and who have considered the question of negro slavery in all its hearings, will probably be disposed to pronounce, with the writer of this address, that the emancipation of the colored population cannot be *progressive through the laws*. It must, and can only be p*rogressive through the feelings*; and, through that medium, be finally complete and entire, involving at once political equality and the amalgamation of the races.

And has Nature (as slave apologists would tell us) drawn a Rubicon between the human varieties of physiognomy and complexion, or need we enter into details to prove that no *natural antipathy* blinds the white Louisianian to the charms of the graceful Quadroon—however the force of prejudice or the fear of public censure makes of her his mistress, and of the whiter skinned, but often not more accomplished or more attractive female his wife? Or must we point to the intercourse in its most degraded forms, where the child is the marketable slave of its father? Idle indeed is the assertion that the mixture of races is not in Nature. If not in Nature, it could not exist; and, being in Nature, since it does happen, the only question is whether it shall take place in good taste and good feeling, and be made at once the means of sealing the tranquillity and of perfecting the liberty of the country, and of peopling it with a race more suited to its southern climate than the pure European,—or whether it shall proceed, as it now does, viciously and degradingly, mingling hatred and fear with the ties of blood—denied, indeed, but stamped by Nature herself upon the skin. The education of the race of color would undoubtedly make the amalgamation more rapid as well as more creditable ; and so far from considering the physical amalgamation of the two colors, when accompanied by a moral approximation, as an evil, it must surely be viewed as a good equally desirable for both. In this belief, the more especial object of the founder of Nashoba is to raise the man of color to the level of the white. Where fitted by habits of industry and suitable dispositions to receive him as a brother and equal, and, after due trial, as proprietor trustee of the property; to educate his children with white children, and thus approaching their minds, tastes and occupations, to leave the affections of future generations to the dictates of free choice.

It may be necessary to advert to one provision of the deed of trust, which establishes a difference between trustees and associates, and fixes a period (fifty years from the date of the gift of the property) when the distinction shall cease, and every proprietor possess the full character of trustee.

The founder being greatly anxious that the principles of moral and intellectual liberty, enumerated in her deed, should be preserved pure in practice as in principle, and that its more especial object—the protection and regeneration of the race of color, should never be lost sight of, so long as the oppression of the race shall find a sanction in the laws, or in the feelings of the more numerous population, she was desirous of confining *the moral trust* of the institution within very special limits. And yet at the same time believing that many individuals might constitute useful and happy members of the institution, whose intellectual faculties or moral courage might not be of that strength as to render them safe guardians of the principles, in practice, at least, so novel, or of the peculiar interests of a proscribed race, she judged it a less evil to admit of a distinction in the powers, not the rights of future proprietor, than to restrict too scrupulously their number, or to endanger the great moral objects of the institution itself.

The duration of such a distinction was limited to fifty years, in the belief that before that period the great majority of adult members must be supplied from the schools of the institution, and consequently absolved from those prejudices with which we of the present generation are all of necessity more or less imbued.

The limits prescribed to the present address are already exceeded. But however imperfectly elicited many of the principles here touched upon, it is believed the present observations will sufficiently explain the nature of the institution, and bearing of the different provisions made in the deed of the founder. It remains only to explain a few regulations adopted by the trustees, and to present a few observations applicable to those who may image, in the institution, a mode of life and moral practice suitable to their feelings and opinions.

First. It must be premised that Nashoba offers only a life of exertion, and, at the present time, one of privation: rough cabins, simple fare, and active occupation. Yet although based upon the principle of co-operative labor, no less than upon that of united interest, the imperfect education and pernicious habits which have unfitted many of the present generation for regular active exertion, who may *morally* be the most fitted to advance the interests of the institution, and to receive happiness therein, it is provided that an equivalent may be rendered in money by such members as cannot furnish by their labor suitable assistance to the society. This highest sum demanded of an individual is *two hundred dollars per annum* The pecuniary demand within this sum, will of course be proportioned to his, or her, fitness for useful occupations.

Secondly. Such as may possess the gifts of fortune and the moral feeling to devote their property, or any part of it, to forward the object of the institution, will do so voluntarily, and must then place property so given at the disposal of the society, by a writing under their hand duly arrested, and of which a record will be kept. But it will never be expected of any individual to bring with him more than the practical knowledge of a useful employment, agricultural or mechanical, with industry to pursue it steadily; or as above stated a sufficient equivalent in property to warrant exemption from the name.

Thirdly. The moral requisites which can alone ensure admission to any individual, must, it ill feared, circumscribe the admission of adults within narrow limits. An amiable and willing disposition, kindly affections, simple tastes a high tone of moral feeling with a liberal tone of thinking must be evinced by those who aspire to the character of trustees of Nashoba.

Fourthly. It will sufficiently appear from the substance of this address and from the observations appended to the deed itself, that religion occupies no place in the institution, and the rule of *moral practice* there proposed has simply and singly in view human happiness: considering as virtuous whatever practice tends to promote that happiness, as vicious whatever tends to counteract it. It is indeed usual to attach as many meanings to the word religion, as there are varieties in human opinion. So that it may sometimes mean the faith of the Jews, at others that of Christ, at others the peculiar doctrines of Rome or Geneva, or sometimes the worship of the mystical first cause of simple theism, and not unfrequently the moral principle acknowledged under various names by all teachers of what school soever. But as it is the special object of the writer of this address to explain as far as possible, and without risk of misapprehension, the principles of the society to which she appertains, she would expressly specify that she uses the term *religion* as distinct from *moral practice,* and as signifying *belief in, and worship rendered to, a Being or Beings not cognizable by the senses of man.* And though it will of course never be demanded of any individual to adopt the shades of opinion held by the existing proprietors, yet it is equally due to them, and to the world, to remove all mystery from their principle, as from their practice, and to declare explicitly those opinions which they hold conscientiously. Candor is here the more necessary, as it is important that no one should seek the sanctuary of the institution, without thoroughly understanding the opinions and practice of its members. Let it therefore be understood that, without making their opinions a law, they will ever claim for themselves that which they accord to others, perfect liberty of speech as of thought; and holding the exercise of this liberty one of the first pleasures of life as also, in their public character, one of its first duties, they will *never forego its exercise.* Those, therefore, acknowledging religious feelings will do well to examine the extent of their liberality before entering the precincts of a society whose opinions might wound those feelings.

Fifthly. The existing resident trustees of the institution have also decided that no religious doctrines shall be taught in the school, whenever it may be organized; but the reason of the children be left to its free developement [sic], and encouraged to examine all opinions, and to receive or reject them, according to the bearings of facts, and the strength of their moral testimony.

Sixthly. In conformity with the provisions of the deed, which binds the trustees to the opening of a school for children of color, and with a view to consult the best interest of the race peculiarly recommended to their care, as well as the best interests of humanity in general, they propose, as soon as measures shall be taken, and means supplied for the reception, to receive children, either as pensioners for the sum of *one hundred dollars per annum,* all expenses included, or without payment, upon condition that the parents or guardians shall transfer to the institution all rights over the children so received—such children to be in all things treated and cared for the same as the children born in the institution

Seventhly. Any persons of property, sympathizing with the objects of the institution, and desirous of contributing to forward the same, could not better apply their succor than to the building up of its schools either by devoting a sum of money for raising the necessary buildings at the present much wanted, or, by supplying them with books, maps, globes, a philosophical apparatus &c. Donations of book, to aid the formation of the library of the institution, will be at all times highly valuable

Eighthly. It is conceived that with some exceptions, the institution of Nashoha will be found most suited to young persons, of both sexes, of independent minds and liberal education: men under the age of thirty, who have yet their attachments to form, and whose feelings are unblunted by long commerce with the world, and by the debasing spirit of trade; and young women of mental energy, amiable manners and dispositions, and small independent property, or in place of the latter and which were yet better, possessing the knowledge of some useful occupation in the house, the dairy, or the school, adequate to cater their expenses, and to promote the well being of society. It is particularly recommended to every young man, before he visits the institution with a view of being received therein, that he apply himself to some useful trade, by making a short, but active apprenticeship to a good artisan or mechanic, blacksmith, carpenter, sawyer, brickmaker, bricklayer, shoemaker, tanner, weaver, &c., or to a farmer, gardener, &c. The grafting, pruning, and proper treatment of fruit trees, and skilful raising of vegetables, planting and dressing a vineyard, and, above all, the manual labor of a farm, the care and management of cattle, &c., will furnish employment of the first utility. It is, also, equally recommended to young women to acquire previous knowledge of some useful employment. Plaiting and making straw hats, spinning, weaving, simple cookery, baking, or any of the various occupations necessary to human life and social comfort. By this is meant not a *general* or *imperfect* knowledge of any employment, but a thorough and practical one. Let no one seek Nashoba, with a view of reaching the *science* of a business, or superintending the work of others. All must bring hands as well as heads, and, above all, kind and willing *hearts*, ever disposed to make light of inconveniences, and to find the best enjoyment in promoting the happiness of others. Moreover, let none imagine that they can enter an institution based on the novel principle of cooperation, without experiencing inconveniences and difficulties both moral and physical. *They will experience many*, and nothing but a strong moral purpose — a real heart interest in the success of the undertaking, a deep conviction of the truth of the principles, which it aspires practically to illustrate, can strengthen them to weather such difficulties. Possessed of the moral requisites, they will succeed and ensure the success of the institution. But, until a sufficient number possessed of these qualifications shall be collected at Nashoba, the experiment must remain as it is — in embryo only.

Ninthly. It would be well for every individual to bring with him the tools necessary in his particular trade; and Europeans, reaching New Orleans, may also bring with them a mattrass [sic], blankets, linen, and any other convenience, which their habits may render agreeable, and with which a young and remote settlement is but scantily provided. Among these, should always be included a good knife, fork, spoon, and drinking cup. Strangers will always render a service to the institution, by bringing with them them any valuable seeds of superior quality, for the garden or farm, cuttings of valuable trees, or grafts of fruit.

Nashoba is situated fourteen miles from the little town of Memphis, which stands on the eastern bank of the Mississippi river, 300 miles above the city of New Orleans. Those reaching it from Europe by the route of New Orleans, should be careful to avoid arriving in that city during the midsummer and early autumnal months. By leaving any of the European ports during the months of

October, November or December they may expect to make the pleasantest southern passage, and will arrive in New Orleans during a delightful season. From New Orleans, steamboats, which migrate the Mississippi at all seasons, will land passengers and luggage at Memphis, where they will find themselves within a short ride, or even walk, of Nashoba. Those preferring the northern route by New York or Philadelphia, can make the voyage during any of the summer or autumnal months, from April till November, and may then traverse the most interesting part of the United States, and take a steamboat for Memphis, on the upper waters of the Ohio. For this route, the spring and early summer months are the most convenient, the rivers being then full and navigation open. It may be well to observe, that this route is the most interesting, but the most expensive.

It is proposed to establish regular communications between the society and suitable correspondents in the leading countries of Europe, Great Britain, France, Germany, Holland, and Switzerland.

At present it will suffice to name the Cooperative Society, Red Lion Square, London, and count de Lasteyrie[3], Paris.

At sea, 4th December, 1827.[4]

Notes

1 The trust was founded in 1826, at a time when Frances Wright became seriously ill with malaria. The arrangement was meant to secure the future of Nashoba in the event of her death. It included a group of resident trustees with governing powers (Frances Wright, her sister Camilla Wright, James Richardson, George Flower and Robert Dale Owen, who lived in Nashoba for some time) and a group of non-resident members that included General Lafayette, Robert Owen and William Maclure, who provided financial and political backing.

2 Other scandals included accusations of sexual harassment among Nashoba's Black residents, and the use of corporal punishment.

3 Charles Philibert de Lasteyrie (1759–1849) was a French agronomist, a personal friend of Frances Wright's and a fellow supporter of Robert Owen. In 1819, de Lasteyrie translated two of Owen's publications into French – the *Address to the Sovereigns of the Holy-Alliance United in Congress at Aix-la-Chapelle* (1818) and the *Address to the European Governments* (1818).

4 Frances Wright wrote her *Explanatory Notes* while sailing back from Europe to Nashoba. She had spent the previous months in Britain and France to recover from a severe bout of malaria, while trying to find potential backers for her community venture.

37

"MR. OWEN'S MEMORIAL TO THE REPUBLIC OF MEXICO, AND A NARRATIVE OF THE PROCEEDINGS THEREON", IN *ROBERT OWEN'S OPENING SPEECH, AND HIS REPLY TO THE REV. ALEX. CAMPBELL...* (CINCINNATI: PUBLISHED FOR R. OWEN, 1829), 184–190.

Robert Owen

[After the collapse of New Harmony in June 1828, Robert Owen returned to England, only to sail back to the American Continent in November of the same year, intent on establishing a new co-operative community in Mexico.[1] It is little known that on his way to Veracruz, he made two short stops in Haiti and Jamaica. Though the Mexican government ultimately rejected Owen's Texan project, his *Memorial to the Republic of Mexico*, which outlined his community plans, was published in 1828. The book was reissued the following year with a supplementary account of Owen's West Indian journey (Bestor 1950, 216). At the time, discontent was mounting among British abolitionists, who acknowledged that the abolition of the triangular trade in all British colonies in 1807 had failed to significantly improve the condition of the enslaved people. The Anti-Slavery Society was founded in that context in 1823 by William Wilberforce, Thomas Clarkson and others. Over the years, many of its members, including mixed-race radical Robert Wedderburn, Quaker activist Elizabeth Heyrick, Church of Scotland evangelical Andrew Thompson and William Allen (Owen's former business partner at New Lanark) came to support immediate emancipation. Owen opposed the latter, and used what he saw in the Caribbean to justify his rejection to such proposals. In the wake of the Haitian Revolution (1791–1802), a slave revolt which had led to the country's independence and the emancipation of its Black population, but at the cost of protracted political turmoil, Owen believed the Haitian government to be too new and inexperienced to guarantee peace and prosperity post-emancipation. To avoid repeating such violence in the British West Indies, Owen advised that Jamaican slaves be kept in their state of blissful ignorance until the island's white population and the British government could come up with a peaceful solution to their plight. Owen was not opposed to emancipation in itself, and he did not believe in any notion of natural racial superiority. But his arguments mirrored those put forward by the very slave owners who had entertained him in Jamaica. Thus, Owen bought into the myth of the "grateful slave", according to which, due to the supposed protection offered by their masters, the condition of Black slaves was much superior to that of the "white slaves" toiling away in British factories. This myth would come to dominate and justify racist and imperialistic discourses in the second half of the nineteenth century (Boulukos 2008; Morris 2018, 127).]

[...] I left London on the 17th, and Falmouth, in the new packet ship Spey, on the 22d of November [1828]. [...] on the last day of the year, at evening, we saw land, which the next day was discovered to be Antigua. The same day we saw St. Kitts, St. Nevis, Rondo Rock, Montserat [sic] and Guadaloupe [sic] in the distance. After passing within our view Santa Cruz and Porto Rico, we came in sight of St. Domingo; and on the 6th, landed the mail for that island, at the small port of Jacquemel [Jacmel].[2] I went on shore in the boat with captain James, expecting to see a few huts and wretched inhabitants. I was most agreeably disappointed. I found a large town, with many good and commodious houses, and a respectable looking mansion for the president when he visits that district. Although not Sabbath, it was a religious holiday; and as I fortunately met, upon my landing, a gentleman who had been a few years before at New-Lanark; he enabled me, in a short time, to take a hasty general view of the town and its inhabitants. This was my first landing in any of the West Indian settlements, and every thing was new to me, and more new in consequence of its being the first free colored population I had seen. As a population living, as I understood it did, by its own industry, it was better drest [sic], cleaner, more orderly, and mild and polite in its demeanor the one to the other, than any working or trading population I had ever seen in any civilized country. There was less corroding anxiety, and more urbanity in the expression of countenance, than I had witnessed in any population in Europe or America. I was introduced to see one of the dances, which I was informed, was made up of those who were not considered of the higher orders of the place; but the neatness and elegance of their dress, their general outward appearance, and their conduct to each other, and to us as strangers, would have done credit to any town population I had ever seen collected together for a similar purpose. I returned to the Spey with different impression of the town and people of Jacquemel, from those which I had taken with me on shore. I left a copy, for the president, of the before mentioned memorial, to be sent that night by a messenger who was to cross over to Port-au-Prince. I sent it under the expectation that it might be of some use to a new government, which had much experience to acquire.

On the 8th, the Spey arrived in Port Royal, Jamaica. [...] I now proceeded with captain James to Kingston, to deliver some letters of introduction; [...]. We returned from Kingston in time to dine on board the Barham[3], where, among the officers of the fleet and other gentlemen, we met the venerable general Grant[4], the newly appointed governor of Trinidad, who had just arrived from his late government of the Bahama islands.

The next day, I went early to see some of the interior of the island; and after breakfasting with one of the merchants in Kingston, who had been a visiter [sic] at New-Lanark, I was introduced by the admiral to the bishop, Dr. Lipscomb.[5] I had been introduced the day before to sir John Keane, the lieutenant-governor and commander-in-chief, with whom I had promised to dine, if the detention of the Spey permitted; but it did not.[6] We, however, partook of an excellent breakfast, *a la fourchette*, with the collector of the customs, Mr. M'Dougal Grant, at whose residence, upon our return from the bishop, we found Mrs. Fleeming[7]— also Captain Deere and other officers. The governor of Trinidad had been of the party to visit the head of the church, and returned with our party to Mr. M'Dougal Grant's. We then proceeded to the vice-admiral's *penn*, as a country residence is called in Jamaica; and after being joined there by Sir John Keane, who came in a dashing style, driving an open carriage four in hand, in the practice of which he seemed an adept, we returned on board the Barham, and again met more of the officers of the fleet, with other gentlemen, at dinner. [...]

In sailing out of the harbor at sunrise of the 9th, we had a delightful view of the scenery around, even to the top of the highest hills and mountains; in the numerous hollows of which there were a few floating, and some stationary white clouds, just sufficient to give variety without hiding a single beauty. The air at that hour was delicious. It came from the land, and after a heavy shower of rain, which fell the preceding evening, was filled with a fragrance so exhilarating as to put all on board in good spirits.

[...]

I was much pleased with my short visit to Jamaica, independent of the circumstances which I have narrated. It afforded me an opportunity of seeing the slave population of one of our West India islands, and comparing their general condition and state of feelings with those of the working classes in Great Britain and Ireland. I found one day's personal inspection gave me more valuable knowledge upon the subject, than all the partizan writings I had ever read. If the slave population in and around Kingston be a fair specimen of slavery in the West Indian islands, then I have no hesitation in saying, that their condition, in a great many respects, is much to be preferred to that of a large majority of the working classes in England, Wales, Scotland and Ireland.

Wherever I go, I find philanthropy and religion mere names to confound the understanding, and deceive the very best intentioned individuals. If Thomas Clarkson, Mr. Wilberforce, William Allen, Fowel [sic] Buxton[8], and other British philanthropists, could make an unprejudiced comparison between the present state of the manufacturing and other laboring classes in the islands of Great Britain and Ireland, and the slave population of the West India colonies, they would discover that they had a task equal to all their united powers of body, mind and means, to advance the former to the same enjoyments that are now in the actual possession of the latter.

The slaves whom I saw in the island of Jamaica, are better dressed, more independent in their look, person and manners, and are greatly more free from corroding care and anxiety, than are a large portion of the working classes in England, Scotland and Ireland. What the condition of these slaves was in former times, I know not. But I request, with all the earnestness such a subject demands, that our good religious people of England will not attempt to disturb these slaves in the happiness and independence which they feel in their present condition. For while they are under humane masters,—and almost all slave proprietors are now humane, for they know it to be their interest to be so,—the West Indian slave, as he is called, is greatly more comfortable and happy than the British or Irish operative manufacturer or day laborer. These slaves are secure in a sufficiency for the enjoyment of all the animal wants; and they are, fortunately for themselves, in the present stage of society, too ignorant to desire more. If their present condition shall not be interfered with by the abolitionists on one hand, and the religionists on the other, these slaves cannot fail to be generally the happiest members of society for many years to come—until knowledge can no longer be kept from them, or until it would be desirable not to keep it from them; and then an entire change must be made in their condition. Because a little reflection is sufficient to make it evident, that slavery and knowledge can never long exist in the same individuals. It is this very circumstance, that, at this period, renders a great moral and political change over the civilized world unavoidable. The degradation of the producing classes, by the hourly diminishing value of manual labor, through the extension of scientific power, and their daily advance in real knowledge, has elicited a state of things, frightful to contemplate, if that knowledge did not bring a remedy with it to restrain violence. Let not, therefore, the existing slave population be urged forward beyond the present happy ignorant state in which they are, until some wise arrangements, between the existing white producers and non-producers, shall be adjusted for their future benefit.

I conversed with a slave in Kingston, who, I was informed, was one among many, who could any day purchase his freedom with the money he had earned by his own industry, and retained by his good conduct. The slaves have all now a certain time to themselves, which is employed as they deem most beneficial. I inquired why he did not purchase his freedom from his master, as he had plenty of money for that purpose. His reply was—"I don't know, massa, who will take care of me when I am sick?—don't know how long I shall be well. My massa very good massa: he provides me with all I want, and I cannot have more." I really thought so; for he was well dressed, looked extremely well, seemed to have no care, and had his horses and carriage in as good a condition as himself. His business was to take care of these, and drive the carriage. He was not, nor did I see any of the slaves, half so hard worked as the manufacturing classes are daily in England and Scotland. If the slaves should be emancipated, without first receiving knowledge and acquiring good habits, they will be rendered wretched, and society will be injured, probably through many generations.

But the slave question is one, which must force another great political question to some practical result under all the civilized governments,—that is, What is to be done with the working classes, seeing they cannot be employed as formerly, and that they have acquired knowledge to discern right from wrong? This question must be met, and first met by the British government, because it is in advance of all other governments upon the old error or civilization of society, and will the soonest experience all its evils.

Notes

1 In August 1828, Robert Owen was approached by two supporters of the Mexican Revolution, Benjamin R. Milam (1788–1835) and the Scottish general Arthur Goodall Wavell (1785–1860), who had recently been granted permission by the newly independent state of Mexico to establish a colony in the provinces of Coahuila and Texas. Owen was offered an allotment in Texas and drew up new community plans in the autumn of 1828, despite the opposition of the Mexican representative in London, Vicente Rocafuerte (Milam to Owen, 30 August 1828; Rocafuerte to Owen, 17 October 1828, Robert Owen Collection, Manchester).
2 A town in southern Haiti, founded by the Spanish in 1504.
3 The Barham was the ship of Charles Elphinstone Fleeming (1774–1840), the viceadmiral of Jamaica and commander-in-chief of the West Indies from 1828 to 1829.
4 Ludovick (or Lewis) Grant (1776–1852), Scottish Army general and colonial administrator in the Caribbean from 1801 to 1833, and a staunch opponent to emancipation.
5 Christopher Lipscomb (? –1843), first Anglican Bishop of Jamaica from 1825 to 1842.
6 John Keane, 1st Baron Keane (1781–1844). Born in Belmont, Ireland, Keane was commander-in-chief in the West Indies and governor of Jamaica during Owen's visit.
7 Née Doña Catalina Alejandro de Jimenez, a Spanish lady and Fleeming's wife since 1816.
8 Thomas Clarkson (1760–1846), co-founder of the Society for the Abolition of the Slave Trade in 1787; William Wilberforce (1759–1833); William Allen (1770–1843), Quaker philanthropist, abolitionist and Robert Owen's former business partner at New Lanark; Sir Thomas Fowell Buxton (1786–1845), Member of Parliament, abolitionist and social reformer.

38

AN ADDRESS TO THE WORKING CLASSES ON THE REFORM BILL (LONDON: W. STRANGE, 1831), 13–16.

William Carpenter

[From the early 1830s onwards, the London co-operator and journalist William Carpenter (see Part 5, Chapter 31) embraced the cause of political reform, which he promoted in various publications including *Political Letters* (1830–1831) and *Carpenter's Monthly Political Magazine* (1831–1832). The *Address to the Working Classes,* written while Carpenter was in jail due to his refusal to pay the stamp duty on newspapers, shows that he occupied a middle-ground between Robert Owen and the radical critics of the Reform Bill like James Bronterre O'Brien and William Cobbett (who was a personal friend of Carpenter's). Unlike Owen, Carpenter was firmly in favour of an extended franchise for working men, a belief that would later see him join the Chartist movement. He also wished to avoid class conflict, and maintained the necessity of an alliance between working men and the newly enfranchised middle-classes (Hollis 1973, 74; Claeys 1989, 213–214).]

If I have succeeded in convincing you, that although this plan of reform is not such a one as we should frame ourselves, nor such an [sic] one as would be framed by a statesman who took a just or statesmanlike view of the subject, it is nevertheless a great improvement upon the present system; that although it leaves many evils unredressed—many rights in abeyance—many imperfections unamended, it nevertheless suppresses many abuses—gives a great accession to popular influence in the House of Commons—and, above all, recognizes the *principle*, that the institutions of society should be modified or altered in accordance with *public opinion*; —if I have succeeded in convincing you of this, and, as a necessary consequence, that the present measure lays a basis sufficiently extensive, both in depth and in width, to carry a superstructure in which all rights shall be comprehended, and all perfection embodied—if I have succeeded in this, I am entitled to urge upon you, by every consideration which should have weight in the minds of reasonable men, your duty to give it your support. Self-interest, if no higher motive be adverted to, is in itself a sufficient motive for so doing; but when you look beyond yourselves, and witness the scenes of distress and wretchedness throughout the country—the general depression of trade and commerce—and the blighting influence of the present system upon all the great productive interests of the country; then all the better and more generous feelings of humanity unite, and in their combined force, urge you to such a course.

An association with you for a period of at least twenty years makes me bold to say, that it would have been not only superfluous but insulting thus to remind you of your duty at the present awful crisis, had you not been misled by a few mistaken men. Some of these are my personal friends—they are honest in the expression of their opinions, and it is therefore my duty as it is my inclination to speak of them with respect. But at so critical and awful a moment as the present—when a mere spark would put the kingdom into a blaze from one end to the other, and in its devastating course destroy indiscriminately good and bad, old and young, children and men of mature age; at such a moment, I cannot consent to remain silent, while others are scattering about them firebrands, arrows, and death. Listen to both sides then; reflect calmly, and having done so, form your deliberate judgement.

1. *You are told that you ought not to support the Reform Bill, because it will do* YOU *no good.*

Those who urge this argument assume that the franchise the bill proposes to confer will *exclude* YOU altogether. Now, is this the fact? Answer me this question fairly. Does the franchise which the bill creates exclude the whole of the working classes? I am afraid to write upon this matter—my pen would, unconsciously to myself, give utterance to expressions offensive to those who urge this upon you as a reason why you should not only abstain from supporting the Bill, but why you should give it your strenuous opposition. I will only say this, that if you will do as I have done—make enquiry as to the towns and boroughs, you will find the majority of the 10*l*.—or as they have been contemptuously called by the opponents of the bill—the 3s. 10d. tenants, will form the majority of the new constituency in such places.

But supposing it were true that the bill did exclude you altogether; should this induce you to oppose it? It might be a reason why you should remain neuter—why you should take no part in the affair—but surely not a reason why you should *oppose* it. The man who would oppose another in obtaining *his* rights, *because he was refused his own*, is unworthy the name of an Englishman.

2. But then, it has been said, *the enfranchisement of the* MIDDLE CLASSES, *for whom the bill is intended, will greatly injure your interests, and indefinitely postpone the time of* YOUR *enfranchisement.*

This has been pretty fully answered, in considering our second and third topics; but we may add a few words here. Those who thus address you, insist that the middle classes, or "middle-men," as they sometimes invidiously designate them, have an interest s*eparate* and adverse from yours; and it is greatly to be regretted, that the language they employ, whenever speaking of this class, is such as is calculated to alienate from each other the two classes of society—if two classes they *will* have them to be—who, united, must command all they want. I cannot enlarge upon this topic in this address; but I most confidently state, that the middle classes of 1831—whatever may have been those of 1800, when the commerce of the country was in a very different situation to what it is now; that the middle classes of 1831 are not only *not* a class of persons having interests different from your own; but that they *are not a different class from your own*. They are the *same* class; they are, generally speaking, working or labouring men—and working, too, in such a sphere as to be almost wholly overwhelmed by anxieties and difficulties, of precisely the same description, and arising from the same causes, as your own. It is quite true, that there are a few large manufacturers, and commercial men, and monopolists, who have in some sense an interest separate from your's [sic] (though this is only *apparently* the case); but then, these are not the men who are to be enfranchised by the Bill; they are enfranchised pretty well already, and those persons do not deal honestly by you, who declaim about the evil of giving to such men as these *additional power*, in connexion with the principle and details of the Bill.*

But we will give the objectors all the advantage they can desire, by assuming (1) that you are altogether excluded by the Bill (which, however, is monstrously incorrect); and (2) that the tradesmen, or "middle classes," as they call them, have a separate, if not an adverse, interest from you (but which is not true in fact). Assuming these things, then, the question is, how their enfranchisement can hurt you? I should much like to see some person who really holds the opinion that the passing of this measure *would* be injurious to the working classes, by postponing for a long period the carrying of such a measure as would include all rights, and be efficient for all purposes; I should much like to see such a person sit down, take up his pen, and fairly reason the subject. Of *declamation*—bold and unqualified *assertion*, we have had more than enough. But this is not the thing to be desired in any case where there is a reasonable diversity of opinion, and where men's understandings require to be informed and convinced. Let the question at issue be first *proved*, by cool reasoning and logical argument, and then we will not deny to the triumphant disputant that he should declaim, if he will, till doomsday. For proofs, however, we have looked in vain, and therefore

---

* The writer of the Poor Man's Guardian has from the beginning opposed the Bill by this fallacy. In the number for this day, (Friday, Oct, 14th.) he asks with much apparent rent simplicity, "Where can we find a middle man (he uses this phrase and "middle class," as convertible terms) without his half-a-dozen working men? and how many are there of this middle class who have not hundreds in employ?" If he had asked this question of his honest publisher, Hetherington, who knows a great deal more about the middle classes, than his (the writer's) station in life permits him to do, he would never have suffered it to escape his pen. If the term "middle class" is to include only such persons as have half-dozens, scores, and hundreds of men in their pay and employ, what term is to include all those who have none? The fact is, as we have already said, such persons as the Guardian contemplates have the elective franchise without the Bill.

we must put up with such *materiel* as we can get. Speaking of the Bill, the *Poor Man's Guardian* says:

> "It is a measure not only directly professing to have—but *actually possessing—the means of staying the progress of Reform*—and exactly at a point, too, where it does not the remotest good to the working classes; that is, unless it is to be admitted that the "*middle men,*" the little masters, will feel more disposed than the higher *aristocracy* to better the condition of their inferiors at their own expense—to elevate them by proportionally levelling themselves."

Would that the writer had proceeded to shew us how the measure, not only professes to have (which we admit) but actually possesses (which we deny) the means of *staying the progress of reform*; of "*completely blocking up the narrow passage,*" as he elsewhere has it, "*which leads to the redemption of the working classes.*" Why does he not shew us the means by which this is to be effected? Why does he not *prove* to us that the bill possesses these means? This is what we want; this is what we have a right to demand. But to prove this he must establish these positions. (1) That the bill neither admits you through "the narrow passage", nor recognizes and puts into operation principles that will widen the passage. (2) That the middle classes, or rather the majority of the *new constituency*, will be *more* hostile to your interests and more independent on your co-operation than the honourable and titled boroughmongers are. And (3) that the only mode of destroying that hostility, and drawing them closer to yourselves, is by your joining with their aristocratic enemies in refusing them their rights.

When these positions shall have been established, I shall be ready to acknowledge my present error, and to make all the recompence [sic] in my power for any injury I may have done, in giving it currency throughout the country. Till then, I have my own opinion.

But to advert to the point whence this digression carried us. Assuming that the 10*l.* electors is a class altogether different from yourselves, and that they have a separate interest, how is the keeping them out of the franchise to assist you in obtaining yours; or the granting it to them, to postpone the period of your enfranchisement? Do they now make *common cause* with YOU? No! Then how will you, as a class shut out of "the temple of the constitution," be rendered weaker than you now are, by the mere circumstance of their having obtained an entry? The objection necessarily implies that they are irreconcileably [sic], because constitutionally or interestedly, *opposed* to you; and yet it most strangely urges that you will be rendered weaker in your demand for reform, because they—who will not, cannot, join you in the demand—obtain a change of position! Can any man explain away this inconsistency—this outrage upon common sense and reason? But perhaps it is meant, that by a protracted denial of justice they will at last unite themselves with you! Indeed! Mind, the objection supposes that they *desire* to keep you down; that their hostility towards your constitutional right is at least as strong as that of the boroughmongers; that they believe you can only be elevated by their corresponding depression: and yet, notwithstanding all this, you are asked to believe, that if you only oppose them in their present pursuit, if you only join their other opponents in dashing the cup from their lips, in destroying their trade, in embarrassing their finances, and thus goading them on to desperation and madness, they—kind souls!—will turn round, and, in reward for your magnanimity, will throw themselves into your arms, and embrace you as brothers! Away with such nonsense! there is not a man who can cherish the idea for a moment. You must all know, if you but reflect for an instant, that no measure of reform is more than a *means*— an *instrument* for effecting the ends of good government. If the present Reform Bill furnish, either designedly or accidentally, this means or instrument, well. If it do not, fear you not that the middle classes will (even upon the assumption that they are what the objection implies, but which I deny)—you having done them justice when struggling for their rights—aid you in realizing your own; under the impression, that a necessary preliminary to all good government, and all social prosperity and happiness, is this—that all the units making up the great aggregate of the population should assume their right place, and that all the interests—making up the great aggregate interest, should be harmoniously blended and united.

In whatever light we view the attempt to set the working classes against the bill, it appears extremely foolish and mischievous. They could get nothing by it; but they must lose much. I have shewn, what must, indeed, be obvious to almost every man, that the Bill lays the foundation for securing the rights of all. It is, like a wedge, the edge of which it is proposed to put into the fissure, and leave there. You well know the power of such an instrument, and in this case no earthly means can prevent its continual propulsion into the heart of corruption. It must be urged forward till it lays it open, and exposes it to the pulverising influence of the moral atmosphere. Why, then, should *you* be called upon to prevent such a consummation, and that *only* because it is not to be brought about in some other manner? If the *end* be attained, why should you quarrel with the means? But such opposition would not only be *foolish*; it would be mischievous, also. Can you look at the state of the country, and not believe that an abandonment of this bill would produce a violent convulsion? At all events, you know that there are at least 500,000 people pledged to refuse payment of taxes, should this be the case. Such refusal must produce a revolution—in the popular sense of the word; that is, a violent breaking up of society—a civil war. It *must* do this—there is no alternative. And I beseech you to reflect upon what the consequence would be, if the calamity of such an event were to be augmented by the working classes and the middle classes being arrayed against each other? What would be the destruction of property? What the awful waste of human life? And for what purpose, and to what end? That your common enemies—the fosterers of corruption, the oligarchy who have hitherto ruled, and robbed, and pauperised you both, should diminish the number of those who now render them uneasy—entrench themselves in their fastnesses—and perpetuate their iron-handed dominion.

Friends and Fellow Countrymen— I have now filled up my limits, and must lay down my pen. Though oppressed by severe illness, I have felt it to be my duty to do what I can to prevent the calamities that must ensue upon the working and "middle classes" being placed in hostility to each other. If not the same class, identically, your interests are alike. You are equally interested in getting cheap government, and a due reward for skill and labour; but if the *enemies of reform*— the men who *hate* you both, because they love themselves exclusively—can but succeed in separating you, in arraying you against each other, in prevailing upon you to pull in opposite directions—they gain their point, and both of you become sacrificed to your own folly. I beseech you to reflect upon this—to weigh well its consequences—to estimate carefully its results—and then to act as becomes you. I have done my duty as best I could, and I have no fear of you.

King's Bench, Friday, Oct. 14th.

WILLIAM CARPENTER.

39

POOR MAN'S GUARDIAN, 14 JANUARY 1832, 245–246.

Henry Hetherington

[Henry Hetherington (1792–1849) was a radical printer and leading Chartist. The son of a London tailor, he was apprenticed to Luke Hansard, the British Parliament's official printer. After becoming acquainted with Robert Owen's writings in the early 1820s, Hetherington joined the Co-operative Printers Association and was also a member of George Mudie's Co-operative and Economical Society (see Part 1, Chapter 5). From 1822 onwards, he edited a number of radical publications, most notably the *Poor Man's Guardian* (1831–1835), in which he voiced his support for parliamentary reform. In 1836, after the Great Reform Act had failed to extend the franchise to labouring men, he formed the London's Working Men Association with William Lovett, James Watson and John Cleave, and co-wrote the *People's Charter*. Hetherington remained a lifelong supporter of "moral force" Chartism and co-operation. He died in London during the cholera epidemic of 1849. In this article, published at the height of the Reform Act debate, Henry Hetherington expressed his frustration at Owen's dismissal of working-political activism. This text epitomises the ambivalence that many socialists felt towards Owen. Though highly critical of the Welshman's incessant quest for middle- and upper-class financial support, Hetherington never lost faith in some of the main tenets of Owenism, most notably, the conviction that workers were entitled to the full produce of their labour, and the promotion of popular education as the main agent of social change (Royle 1974, 66, 88, 261; Hollis 1970; Tsuzuki 1971, 13).]

[…] Mr. Owen's principles are "practicable and beneficial," if the working people have fair play—not else. Independent Co-operation cannot be successfully established in this country—*even as an experiment*—till the working classes obtain their political rights, or an alteration takes place in the existing laws. I could, were it judicious to do so, state several important facts in corroboration of this assertion. Mr. Owen is generally esteemed, and without doubt is, a kind-hearted man—benevolently disposed to do his utmost to better the condition of mankind; but he exhibits a strange perversity of mind in expecting to realize his political millenium [sic] before working men are placed on an equal footing with the other classes of community with regard to political rights; and I consider him, on this point, in almost as hopeless a condition, as the individual who believed he was made of glass; it was useless to knock his head against the wall to convince him to the contrary—the notion was immoveable. So it is with Mr. Owen—he entertains an absurd idea, that with the aid of a plundering aristocracy he shall be able to establish Co-operative principles, notwithstanding the unjust and iniquitous laws which at present exist in this country. In his case, experience is unavailing; for after more than twenty years' exertion he is not a jot nearer the attainment of his object. His mental vision must have some peculiar defect, or he would perceive that he was "dipping buckets into empty wells, and growing old in drawing nothing up."

Conversing recently with a gentleman on Co-operative principles, he contended, "that the plausibility of Mr. Owen's views was entirely attributable to the present unequal state of things in this country; and that if we had equal political rights it would produce such important changes in the laws and condition of the country, as altogether to supersede the necessity for Mr. Owen's plan." whether a legislative remedy could, or could not, be found for the evils of competition, I am not prepared to assert; but if Co-operation would (as all co-operators believe) really benefit the condition of the wealth-producers—the destitute millions—then every sensible working man must be convinced, judging from the cruelties daily inflicted upon them, that it will be the last thing established—indeed, that it will NEVER be established unless the working classes succeed in obtaining political power. Our present unfeeling government is evidently disposed to perpetuate the misery of the poor, for not only is their right to be represented in parliament denied, on the plea of ignorance, but all those who endeavour to remove that ignorance are unjustly imprisoned. The rulers of this country, by partial and cruel "*laws*," have contrived to strip the working classes of every domestic comfort—they are inadequately paid when employed —thousands and thousands are destitute of food, of clothing, and of shelter, they receive from men in authority nothing but taunts, indignities, and oppression——and if, haply, the poignancy of their sufferings is beyond human endurance, and a momentary ebullition of feeling leads to the destruction of some of those hoards of "*property*," for want of a portion of which they are famishing, the "*paternal government*" of a "*Patriot King*," acutely sympathizing with the destitute wealth-producers, invariably administers to the unhappy victims of their complicate and abominable tyranny—special commissions, the bayonet, and the halter! What have the "*genuine*" Owenites in London done against these enormities, but paralyze the nobler efforts of others, by deprecating politics? Have they raised their voice against imprisoning poor men for vending cheap knowledge? Have they, in any way, assisted to establish a free press; or contributed a trifle, at any of their social dancing parties, to mitigate the sufferings of the poor victims of Whig tyranny? "Nero fiddled while Rome was burning!" and the benevolent Owenites are "*dancing jigs* at two shilling *hops*,"[1] while thousands and tens of thousands of their poorer fellow-countrymen are pining in want and destitution, are their minds so stultified as to believe that Co-operative principles can be established till their country is re-generated Mr. Owen depicts an Elysium, but never tells his votaries that insurmountable barriers obstruct its attainment;—I, therefore, tell them that the greatest, and first to be removed, is the want of political power in the millions; and till that is removed, Co-operation upon Mr. Owen's comprehensive plan, can never be successfully established. This novel association[2] will dwindle into a School of Industry, supported like other charitable institutions, by voluntary contributions; already I perceive that twenty-one bankers have consented to receive subscriptions. If any money is collected at these bankers it may stand a year or two. Thanks to Mr. Bromley[3], the association will surmount the first year tolerably well, having no rent to pay; but afterwards, unless some of the monied Co-operators prop it by double subscriptions, it will totter and fall. And this is the *practical experiment* that is to demonstrate the utility and efficacy of Mr. Owen's principles to save the nation! Insignificant and futile scheme! During its rickety existence, it will decoy and amuse for a few months, a few unsteady men like *"my friend"* Warden[4], who is "all by turns, and nothing long;" but it will be discountenanced by all honest intelligent workmen, because they must see that it will not, to any extent, remove either "ignorance" or "poverty." What would so rapidly and so effectually remove *ignorance* as a free press? Is the establishment of a free press one of the objects of the association ?—No, indeed; nor is there a disposition to take any one step to forward its accomplishment. Then, again, were ignorance removed from the millions would the mere possession of knowledge enable them to avoid poverty? I may be plundered of my purse by a gang of thieves—I may know how they took it—*where* they have placed it—*the best way of recovering it*; but, without the means, will this knowledge restore the purse —Certainly not. In England, a gang of thieves legislate for the community, and it is not sufficient merely that we know that to be the case, we must possess the means of protecting ourselves from their depredations. The first step, therefore, is to establish a FREE PRESS, that *ignorance* may be removed; the next is, to obtain POLITICAL POWER, that we may be enabled to adopt efficient measures *for the removal of property*, and for consolidating the prosperity and happiness of all classes of society. Let us not be diverted, then, by any party from these steps —those who are not for us, in this particular, are against us. Why are the middle classes so extremely anxious that the Reform Bill should pass, but that they may obtain the light of suffrage; which right will enable them to protect themselves against the depredations of the thieves? Have not the millions— the wealth-producers—an equal right to, and do they not stand in greater need of political protection than the middle class, being plundered to a far greater extent and consequently reduced to a much worse condition? Let the working classes, then, unanimously discountenance all illusive schemes, whether on the subject of Co-operation, or any other subject; and let them rest assumed that that man or party who would discourage the utterance of political sentiments in behalf of the un-represented at public meetings is not honest. Even-handed justice for poor honest men need never again be expected till they obtain Universal Suffrage, Vote by Ballot, and above all, the abolition of Property Qualifications.[5]

Courtesy of HathiTrust

Notes

1 A direct jab at the practice, common in Owenite meeting halls, of having banquets and balls to foster community bonds (see Part 3, Chapter 19).
2 A reference to Robert Owen's Institution of the Industrious Classes for Removing Ignorance and Poverty by Education and Beneficial Employment. Also known as the Society to Remove the Causes of Poverty and Ignorance, it was founded on 12 December 1831 to propagate Owen's views amongst his new roster of working-class supporters. Philanthropic in tone and purpose, the Institution was chaired by a committee of middle- and upper-class directors. As such, it did not "reflect any new-found confidence in the working classes as an independent force for social change" (Harrison 1969, 259). The Institution was located at 277 Gray's Inn Road. Due to its lack of success, it was replaced the following year by the National Equitable Labour Exchange on the same premises.
3 William Bromley, a disciple of Robert Owen and the proprietor of 277 Gray's Inn Road.
4 Benjamin Warden (see Part 1, Chapter 7).
5 These would later form the core of the People's Charter, which Hetherington co-wrote with William Lovett in 1836.

40

MODEL REPUBLIC: A MONTHLY JOURNAL OF POLITICS, LITERATURE, AND THEOLOGY, N°1, 1 JANUARY 1843, 1–4.

James Napier Bailey

[Very little is known of James Napier Bailey's early life. According to George Jacob Holyoake's *History of Co-operation* ([1875]1908, 377), he was originally a Lancashire schoolmaster, and one of Robert Owen's earliest supporters. Thanks to his erudition and public speaking skills, Bailey became one of the Owenite movement's Social Missionaries, and was later appointed to the Central Board of the Rational Society in 1838. As a strong proponent of democratic government, James Napier Bailey was highly critical of Owen's paternal leadership. Fearing that political rifts may tear the British socialists apart, he endeavoured to reconcile Owenism and Chartism. His publication, the *Model Republic*, was founded in January 1843 to advocate his views, which he called "Republican" or "Chartist Socialism" (Claeys 1989, 234). In this article, which can be considered his manifesto, Bailey explained that true democracy could only be implemented via universal male suffrage and a fully elected government and parliament. By being representative of all classes, the new regime would foster shared interests, thus applying the Owenite ideal of community to all areas of political life. Though indicative of the fluidity of radical allegiances in the 1840s, Bailey's dream of uniting Owenism and Chartism never came to fruition. Not only did his overtly political stance clash with the Central Board's emphasis on community building and socialist propaganda, the Chartists also showed little interest in a formal rapprochement with Owen's followers, as by 1843, their efforts were now almost entirely focused on the Land Plan.]

The men of the present age are characterized by an ardent thirst for information upon all subjects connected with the destiny of humanity. The palmy days of ignorance and superstition have rolled away into the waste of past time, and now furnish themes on which the historian may exercise his genius and horrify his reader with startling pictures of ancient brutality. The clerical despotism of the Vatican, which once trampled on the prostrate energies of Europe and made the mightiest potentates tremble at its frown, has ceased to govern the fears and sympathies of the people. Its spiritual thunders are now comparatively impotent, its lightnings play harmlessly round the chair of St Peter, its power has vanished, and its glory has been changed into darkness. The press, like a mighty giant, has burst the fetters which for ages held the human mind in bondage; and man, like a prisoner set free from captivity, now moves over the earth with a firm and elastic step, and scans with an eye of intelligence and enquiry the wonders, and beauties, and harmonies of nature.

[...]

In the political world affairs wear a somewhat similar aspect. A mighty revolution has occurred in the empire of politics as well as in that of religion. The democratic principle, which began to show itself in Europe during the dark ages, has ever since that time been gradually working itself into bolder and more perfect developement [sic], and now beats like an angry sea upon almost every vestige of the ancient aristocratic institutions. Wherever this principle has triumphed, *there also*, liberty of speech and freedom of opinion have been tacitly acknowledged as the inalienable birthrights of humanity; and, on the contrary, wherever despotism has reared its monstrous throne *there* liberty of speech has been crushed, and the press has been rendered a tame and submissive auxiliary to the designs of government. Austria, Russia, and Turkey are the principal kingdoms where despotism is in the ascendant; and France, Switzerland, England, and America form the stage on which democracy now plays its part, and on which it is destined to gain a final victory.

But many of the present generation would not be satisfied with the mere rejection of those religious opinions which have hitherto been regarded as divine, not with the triumphs of democracy, even though accompanied with freedom of opinion, were it not that they regard these events as the heralds of a change in the physical and moral condition of the people. The possession of political power they consider to be a means for accomplishing an end, and while laboring to obtain the instrument, they desire not to forget the object which alone renders it valuable. The privileges of uttering their sentiments on political topics, and of exercising the suffrage at a popular election they look upon as of little intrinsic importance, but the results to which these may give birth, they regard as of the greatest moment to the welfare of the world. They behold in almost all countries, in England especially, a bloated and pampered aristocracy, a middle class of capitalists and manufacturers, and a class of helots to possess the shadow of liberty without substance. They desire, therefore, to see the people in the possession of political power, in order that they may be able to compel the legislature to adopt measures adapted to relieve the distresses of the nation, instead of enacting laws only calculated to augment the grandeur and affluence of a few aristocratic houses.

Persons holding these views constitute a class of reforms distinct from those Chartists who would employ physical violence in accomplishing their purposes, as well as from those Socialists who would be satisfied with any form of government that would supply them with the necessaries of life and the amusements of community. The possession of political power they regard as the inalienable birthright of the people, nor would they be content with any form of government that would deny the exercise of this right, to its subjects. Paternal forms of government, whether they relate to small societies or nations, they look upon as identical with paternal forms of humbug or paternal forms of despotism. Their motto is not "war to the knife, and blood to the horse-bridle;"[1] nor it is "community under any form of government, whether despotism or democracy;" neither do they clamour "a fair day's wages for a fair day's work," which has been considered by some to be the highest object of legislatorial policy: but they sigh for a change in the political and social institutions of the world,—a change which shall afford to all equal rights and privileges, abolish mercantile competition and rivalry, and place society upon an equitable basis; in short, the objects they have in view, and for the accomplishment of which they shall not cease to labour, are, the acquirement of political power for the people, and the formation of Home Colonies on the plan originally laid down by the philosopher of Lanark.[2]

Impressed with the importance of these views, and desirous of seeing them formally advocated, the members of "The Society for the Encouragement of Socialist and Democratic Literature" have commenced this publication. The funds already in possession of the above society offer a sufficient guarantee for the regular appearance of the work, and the talent which will eventually be employed in its support, will, we have no doubt ensure its acceptance with the public. Time, however, which sweeps away all things in his mighty dragnet, will enable our readers to judge of the accuracy of these statements.

It is the intention of the society, under whose auspices this journal has been commenced, to devote the principal part of its pages to the bold and fearless advocacy of Republican Socialism. This will form its leading feature and object. In pursuance of this design, sketches of ancient and modern republican forms of government and articles exhibiting the effects of democracy on mind, morals, and national happiness shall occasionally appear in conjunction with other papers shewing the evil effects resulting from despotic and aristocratic institutions. To these will be added papers upon various literary topics, essays upon science, theology, and popular antiquities; and, in fine, no expense nor trouble will be spared to render the work a novel and popular miscellany fit for the perusal of all ranks and classes.

It is unnecessary to say more respecting our principles and objects and the line of policy we shall adopt in future numbers of this journal. We, therefore, humbly hope that the paper we now commit to the care of the public may serve the cause of truth and hasten the dawn of that happy morn—

> *"When every transfer of earth's natural gifts*
> *Shall be a commerce of good words and works;*
> *When poverty and wealth, the thirst of fame,*
> *The fear of infamy, disease and woe,*

War with its million horrors, and fierce hate,
Shall live but in the memory of time,
Who like a penitent libertine shall start,
Look back and shudder at his former years[3]

Notes

1 Two Biblical allusions from Psalm 38:17 ("Deep conviction continues to irritate the conscience; it will not endure a patched up peace; but cries war to the knife till the enmity is slain".) and Revelation 14:20 ("So the angel swung his sickle at the earth and gathered the vine of the earth and threw it into the great winepress of God's fury. And the winepress was trampled outside the city, and blood came out of the winepress up to the horses' bridles, for a thousand six hundred stadia".).
2 "the philosopher of Lanark": Robert Owen.
3 An excerpt from Percy Bysshe Shelley's *Queen Mab* (1813), in which the eponymous fairy prophesises a future utopia on earth. James Napier Bailey's quote is inaccurate, as the sixth verse should read "War with its million horrors, and fierce hell".

41

"MEETING OF CONGRESS, FRIDAY, MAY 10, 1844", *NEW MORAL WORLD*, 8 JUNE 1844, 402–404.

[After Robert Owen tightened his hold upon the Rational Society in 1842 (Part 5, Chapter 34), the gap widened between the Central Board and local branches across the country. Financial strains on the movement as a whole became a major bone of contention. Mounting expenses at Queenwood forced the residents to fire their hired help and to take on farming activities they knew little or nothing about. Meanwhile, the Halls of Science struggled to pay rent, the Social Missionaries were let go and socialist membership floundered. By 1843, half of the Rational Society's fifty branches had closed down (Garnett 1972, 195). In 1844, the level of desperation and frustration had reached an all-time high. The "inevitable revolt" occurred during the annual Congress held in May of that same year, when the socialist delegates forced Owen to step down both as President of the Rational Society and Governor of Queenwood. On 25 May, they first appointed David Vines (see Part 5, Chapter 34), a member of the Central Board and one of Owen's closest associates, but he refused the position. The "Social Father" was eventually replaced on 28 May by John Buxton, a Manchester calico-printer (Taylor 1983, 259). While Buxton promised to turn the flagship community into a democratic haven, he was unable to turn a profit, and the experiment eventually ceased in 1845, effectively ending Owenism as an organised movement.]

[…] Mr. Vines having entered the room, then said, that he was sorry to hear that Mr. Owen had not been placed at the head of the Society, and he feared that unless he was so, there would be a falling off in the funds and resources of the Society. He thought if it got abroad that Mr. Owen was not at the head of affairs, the world would have improper ideas respecting Mr. Owen's character; and he thought that the interests of the Society required that Mr. Owen should be at its head. Unless that was the case, he did not feel inclined to take office. Mr. Vines then read a document containing his views in reference to the matter, and the views therein contained, he said, were those held by Mr. Owen; so that if they wished him to be President, they might much rather: Mr. Owen. He would again repeat that out of the respect he had for Mr. Owen, he could not consent to hold any office in the Society unless Mr. Owen was President.

Mr. Nockles[1] then asked if Mr. Vines declined accepting of the Presidency.

Mr. VINES said he could not accept of the Presidency so long as Mr. Owen was alive.

Mr. BUXTON said they were now in a strange position. Mr. Owen's resignation had been given in and accepted, because the Congress could not consent to the terms he had proposed; and now Mr. Vines, who was nominated as President, refused to take any office, unless under Mr. Owen; and refused, upon any consideration, to take the office of President while Mr. Owen was alive. In reference to what Mr. Vines had said about the funds falling off, he (Mr. Buxton) thought it unnecessary to prove the converse, and he was quite prepared to accept even the resignation of Mr. Vines. It was too bad to try to force Mr. Owen upon them in such a way. He had come to Congress to transact business to the best of his abilities; and, having done so, he was prepared to sustain the character and dignity of Congress. He for one, had supported the character and dignity of Mr. Owen, by placing him as President of the Society; and Mr. Owen having resigned, he had, in a similar manner, supported Mr. Vines; but both of these had declined, except on terms which could not be accepted. He would, therefore, move that the resignation of Mr. Vines be accepted.

After a few remarks from Messrs. CAMPBELL[2] and HARTHILL[3],

Mr. JONES[4] said he never felt more painfully in all his life than at that moment. He thought both parties, viz., the Congress and Mr. Owen had been too rash. He had told the Congress so, during its sittings, at different times; and he said the same thing now of the individuals who had been appointed to office. They had appointed a President, who accepted office, and nominated his Board, declaring himself satisfied at the time. That Board of officers they sanctioned, and after all this that President came and resigned office. They accepted the resignation, and Mr. Vines was appointed the President. He had come and refused to take office unless under Mr. Owen; so what were they then to do? Although he did not agree with resolutions which had been passed by Congress, yet he was prepared to abide by its decisions. If they rescinded one resolution that had been passed, then they gave their character a mortal stab; if, on the contrary, they determined on carrying them into execution, regardless of consequences, they might be productive of much injury; and no one would accept of office on such terms. Under present circumstances, he would advise the reception of Mr. Vines' resignation, and prepare for the worst.

On the motion of Mr. Buxton, seconded by Mr. Ardill[5], the resignation of Mr. Vines was accepted.

Mr. JONES then said they were now unfettered, and he hoped they would make an honest attempt to bring matters into a satisfactory condition.

At this stage of the proceedings, considerable excitement prevailed; and it was thought advisable to adjourn for a time. It was then agreed to adjourn till nine o'clock.

After the house resumed, Mr. BATE[6] moved that the house should adjourn till the next morning; as, on a matter of so much importance, it was necessary that they should have time to think over it, calmly, and dispassionately. Several

Delegates, having stated their necessity to leave on the following day, the house proceeded.

Mr. BUXTON then moved, that Mr. John Finch be appointed President of the Rational Society. The motion was not seconded.

Mr. Ardill, of Leeds, seconded by Mr. Hawkes[7], London, then moved, that Mr. John Buxton be appointed President of the Rational Society.

No amendment being proposed, the Chairman put the motion to the house, when the following was the result.

For the motion	Against
Messrs. Ellis[8]	Messrs. Jones
Hawkes	Campbell
Simpson[9]	Pikethley[10]
Nockles	Bate
Smith[11]	Douthwaite[12]
Ardill	
Harthill	
Marshall[13]	
Meadowcroft[14]	

On the motion being passed,

Mr. BUXTON rose, and said his position was an extraordinary one, and he was sure they would believe him when he said that he had no desire to be put in nomination with such men as Mr. Owen, Mr. Vines or Mr. Finch. When he attended that Congress, his sole object had been to do justice to his constituents and to the Society, and he had not the remotes idea of holding any office, much less the presidency of the Society. At the first nomination of president, he silently acquiesced, so as not to displace Mr. Owen; and he had hoped that Mr. Owen would have continued to fill that office, along with his Board, which had also been sanctioned by Congress. But, when Mr. Owen had attended the Congress, and there distinctly stated that he did not intend to act unless upon conditions, involving the necessity of rescinding certain resolutions which had been deliberately passed by Congress, he, for one, had disagreed with such a course, and agreed rather that Mr. Owen's resignation should be accepted. Mr. Vines was then nominated by them, and had been brought from London for the purpose of nominating his Board. When that gentleman arrived, he had consulted with Mr. Owen, and with no one else; but, no doubt, he had consulted Mr. Owen considering he had the greatest mind in the Society. He would not say that Mr. Vines had acted under Mr. Owen's instructions, but nevertheless, after having considered the matter, that gentleman had declined the presidency while Mr. Owen was alive. That might be a sufficient reason for Mr. Vines, but it was not sufficiently so for Congress to rescind the resolutions which it had passed. When the adjournment was agreed to, he was requested to leave the room, along with some others, when the question was put to him whether he would be the president of the Society. He told them that he did not think himself so well qualified for the situation as the gentlemen who had been proposed; but when he urged that objection, he was told that there was no alternative, and it was from being so pressed, that he consented to allow himself to be put in office. Now, however, that the duty of president devolved upon him, he was prepared to do his duty. True it was, he was not an opulent man, and that might act against him in the eyes of many—(cries of no, no)—but he could assure them that Congress, having taken that course, would find him willingly obey their call, and do the utmost in his power to forward the great cause in which they were united. He should request of Congress to allow him to retire for some time previous to nominating his Board.

The evening being then far advanced, it was agreed to adjourn till to-morrow.

WEDNESDAY, MAY 29th.

[...] Mr. Vines having declined to act as Governor of Harmony at the same time that he declined being President, Mr. JOSEPH SMITH said he would only be following the precedent of last Congress (when Mr. Owen was appointed President of the Society and Governor of Harmony) by moving that the President, Mr. Buxton, be Governor of Harmony. The motion having been seconded by Mr. Nockles, was put to the meeting, and the result was as follows:—

For the motion	Against
Messrs. Ellis	Messrs. Jones
Hawkes	Campbell
Simpson	Pikethley
Nockles	Bate
Smith	Douthwaite
Ardill	
Harthill	
Marshall	
Meadowcroft	

Notes

1 James Nockles, Glasgow delegate.
2 Alexander Campbell, Stockport delegate and Social Missionary (see Part 3, Chapter 20).
3 Adam Harthill, Edinbugh delegate.
4 Lloyd Jones, member of the Central Board and Bolton delegate (see Part 5, Chapter 34).
5 John Ardill, Leeds delegate. Ardill was a printer and bookkeeper for Feargus O'Connor's *Northern Star*, the leading Chartist periodical.
6 Frederick Bate, Blackburn delegate and member of the Central Board of the Rational Society (see Part 5, Chapter 34).

7 John Hawkes, delegate for London's Branch A1.
8 John Ellis, delegate for London's Branch A1, teacher and Social Missionary (see Part 7, Chapter 47).
9 George Simpson, Manchester delegate (see Part 5, Chapter 31).
10 Lawrence Pitkethley (?–1858), delegate for Huddersfield and a leading Yorkshire radical. Pitkethley was involved in both the Owenite and Chartist movements, and was instrumental in establishing the Huddersfield Hall of Science.
11 Joseph Smith, Social Missionary and Oldham delegate.
12 John W. Douthwaite, socialist lecturer and Bradford delegate.
13 Thomas Marshall, London (Whitechapel) delegate.
14 Josiah Meadowcroft, delegate for Queenwood community.

Part 7

THE NEW RELIGION AND THE OLD

Due to its distinctive blend of scientific and millenarian aspirations (see Part 2), early socialism eschews clear-cut political and philosophical classification (Oliver 1971, 166–187). This rings especially true when considering the Owenites' attitudes to religion. Indeed, even though Robert Owen's deterministic "science of society" was grounded in Enlightenment-era scepticism, its aspirations and language were shot through with religious and prophetic overtones. Subsequently, in the later stage of the movement, Owenite umbrella organisations like the Association of All Classes of All Nations (AACAN) and the Universal Society of Rational Religionists (Part 5, Chapter 34) often took on a variety of sectarian terminologies and practices. Socialist meetings mirrored church services, with the singing of Social Hymns and lectures by Owenite Missionaries. Taking on the role of a tutelar figure, Robert Owen became known as the "Social Father". He and other socialist speakers conducted weddings, performed baptisms (or "naming" ceremonies) and gave funeral orations (*New Moral World*, 10 June 1837 and 26 October 1844; Bray 1879, 63). More generally, the Owenites "displayed the values associated with religious groups", such as voluntary membership, a series of shared beliefs that often stood in contradiction with those of mainstream society, and eschatological expectations that equated the advent of socialism with a New Jerusalem (Harrison 1969, 175; Taylor 1983, 151).

Though the exact origin of Owen's religious scepticism remains obscure, his system was indeed based upon an unflagging belief in human perfectibility, one that left no room for any notion of original sin. In August 1817, during a series of lectures given at the City of London Tavern, he identified established religion as a locus of superstition and sectarian division, thus branding it as one of the main impediments to universal progress and happiness. By contrast, his own "science of society" claimed to have solved the enigma of social harmony through the discovery of the laws of nature, especially the "doctrine of circumstances" (see Parts 1 and 2).

However, conflating Owenism with a religious sect is somewhat problematic. In many cases, this line of argument is fraught with misleading assumptions that betray a tendency to "pick out certain elements of interest to a later quite different theorisation of socialism, while relegating the rest to the individual 'eccentricity' or 'naiveté' of founding fathers" (Jones 1981, 141). According to Marx and Engels's *Communist Manifesto* ([1848] 1992, 89–93), the working-class, socialist credentials of early Owenism had altogether vanished by 1835. By then, Owen's utopian leanings had turned the movement that bore his name into a "mere reactionary sect", a step down that sowed the seed of its ultimate demise. Aside from its teleological leanings, this interpretation, which has somehow endured in the writings of historians such as G.D.H. Cole and Raymond Postgate (1939, 270–271), and Henri Desroche (1959), overlooks the variety and complexity of the Owenites' religious outlook (Yeo 1971, 105–106; Taylor 1983, 129). As Robert Owen himself combined deist rationalism with millenarian calls for a "New Moral World", his movement logically became a magnet and breeding ground for unorthodox opinions. These encompassed various and often conflicting forms of infidelity, ranging from freethought and unconventional religious beliefs (such as deism, agnosticism and Nonconformity) through to anti-clericalism and atheism.

Consequently, as argued by Gareth Stedman Jones (1981), Eileen Yeo (1971, 95–103) and Barbara Taylor (1983, 152–153) among others, Owenism is best seen as an anti-religion rather than a sect. Many opponents to socialism certainly perceived it as an infidel group. Throughout the 1830s and 1840s anti-socialist tracts and lectures proliferated, mostly in reaction against the Owenite critique of marriage and the nuclear family (see Part 8). In February 1840, the Bishop of Exeter asked the House of Lords to ban Owenism as a blasphemous group and to close down its Halls of Science, a call for action which was soon followed by support petitions throughout the country (Hansard, LI (1840), col. 530, 1187; Harrison 1969, 182; Taylor 1983, 192). More generally, Owen and his followers were regularly accused of infidelity and libertinage, and this intensive backlash prompted them to assert the validity and propriety of their religious unorthodoxy.

By proclaiming themselves to be "Rational Religionists", Owen's followers did not simply refute Christian dogmas. They also established their "science of society" as a complete substitute for them. Since his earliest writings, Owen had offered an alternative route to human salvation based on the positive forces of education and co-operation, in deliberate contrast with the negative, punitive character of Christian theology (Jones 1981, 139; Siméon 2017, 18, 21). For Christian Owenites such as John Minter Morgan, Benjamin Scott Jones (see Chapter 42 below) or the *Crisis* editor James Elishama Smith, this meant that the New Jerusalem could only be established in a socialist world based on economic co-operation, the union of "all classes of all nations" and a community of goods (Smith 1833, cited in Harrison 1969, 157–158). For all Owenites, socialism would therefore act, in the words of William Thompson, not only as a political movement, but as "one grand moral as well as economical experiment" (1824, 427) pointing the way towards a better future – not to be attained in the afterlife, but here and now, through the exertions of enlightened enthusiasts (Taylor 1983, 153).

42

ECONOMIST, N°51, 2 MARCH 1821, 399–408.

"Philadelphus" [Benjamin Scott Jones]

[As Owenism attracted a substantial minority of Christians, religious issues were extensively debated throughout the history of the movement. The assumption that Robert Owen's theories amounted to a form of practical millenarianism clashed with many a socialist's anti-clerical stance. As a result, there were countless attempts to reconcile Owenism with Christian teachings, based on the argument that the "science of society", with its pursuit of equality, its dismissal of ill-acquired wealth and its insistence on community ideals, was actually a return to original Christianity, as pursued by Jesus and the Apostles. One of the earliest examples of such debates is to be found in George Mudie's *Economist*. Contrary to other, less orthodox contributors to the publication, such as "N.O.", whose article is discussed here, the anonymous 'Philadelphus' (the Latin for "brotherly love") argued that faith would provide a moral foundation for Owen's co-operative ideals, which he saw as a modern incarnation of the Christian principle of "universal brotherly love" (Claeys 1981, 15). He consequently defended a policy of religious toleration within the future Owenite communities.

In a 1981 paper, Gregory Claeys identified 'Philadelphus' as Benjamin Scott Jones, a middle-class philanthropist and personal friend of Owen's. Though little is known of Jones's early life, he joined the Board of Commissioners for the East India Company in 1784, and remained employed there for the next fifty years (Tuck 1998, 268–271). A former radical and supporter of parliamentary reform in the 1790s, he later rejected partisan politics, hence his interest in Owen's peaceful reform schemes (Jones, *Economist*, vol. 2, n°33, 8 September 1821, 109, quoted in Claeys 1989, 172). By 1821, he had joined the British and Foreign Philanthropic Society, and was one of Owen's earliest followers alongside George Mudie. Though he never took part in the latter's Co-operative and Economical Society, or in any other Owenite community scheme, Jones was a frequent writer for the early socialist press, including the *Economist* (1821–1822), the *Political Economist and Universal Philanthropist* (1823) and the *Co-operative Magazine* (1826–1830). A staunch Unitarian, Jones ultimately rejected the theory of character formation that was at the heart of Owen's "science of society", but he remained a lifelong supporter of the co-operative system, writing for the *New Moral World* and joining Owen on his trip to Paris in 1837 (Jones-Owen Correspondence, Robert Owen Collection 1835–1837).]

TO THE ECONOMIST,

"You, Magnus Troil, from hard-hearted audacity of spirit,
are unworthy to look on this mystic work; and the
glance of your eyes mingles with and weakens the
spell: for the powers cannot brook distrust."

NORNA OF THE FITFUL HEAD[1]

Sir,

It appears to me, that the warfare in which we have engaged, is becoming rather too desultory, and that it will be expedient, preparatively to a new campaign, to concentrate our forces, and to settle the plan of our operations.

I had it in contemplation to recommend this course to you, at the moment when your last Number (49) reached my hands. If I am not greatly mistaken, the gentleman who decidedly responds N.O. to "Friend O. N." will put our courage and strength to a severe trial. He professes indeed to be "a plain unlettered man;" and yet, although he modestly disclaims "all, knowledge of the mysteries of science, and the depths of philosophy," he challenges you to discuss the *nature of man*, as connected with this subject. This, you will perceive, involves the whole question at issue; for, if the projected social arrangements which you are so earnestly, endeavouring to carry into effect do not accord with the nature of man, there is an end to the scheme; and The Economist may be at once consigned to the pigeon-holes of the Abbe Sieyes.[2] But, Sir, so far from depreciating the conflict to which we are thus invited, I rejoice to find that you have at length met with an antagonist who will assuredly put your sinews to war proof; "more glory will then be won, or less be lost."[3]

I really cannot perceive that the small capitalists who may be tempted to embark their whole property in this speculation, will incur greater hazards than are attendant upon many enterprises of a very ordinary nature. Let us compare their case with that of the Emigrants to the Cape of Good Hope or Van Dieman's Land[4]. If the government do not actually invite, they certainly encourage emigration to these colonies. The cases of the Emigrants, and of the parties who may join the Motherwell establishment, agree in this particular, that both seek a state of society different from that which at present exists in this country. The Emigrant has to encounter the perils of a long voyage, and the inconveniences of tropical climate; he must expend a considerable sum of money in order to reach his destination, and is often quite uncertain where he is to fix his abode; whether it is to be near to or remote from other human habitations, and whether, if he has neighbours, they are to be savage or civilized. If, after all this trouble, expense, risk, and uncertainty, he should fail, he becomes a pauper in a strange land, far re-moved from friends and relatives: the circumstance of his having a family with him, would tend rather to aggravate than to alleviate his distress.

The first occupants of the Motherwell Establishment[5], will probably for the most part consist of persons at present living near to the spot; their new quarters will be far more comfortable than those of the working classes and petty retail dealers; they will have a voice in the choice of their associates; their occupations will be as nearly as possible such as they have been used to; they will be at little or no expense for transport; and in case of failure they will still be in their native land; and may hope to find other employment, or, at the worst, to obtain relief from those charitable institutions which abound among us.

But, Sir, let us pass to the objections which our eloquent antagonist has levelled at the very basis of our theory.

In complimenting us upon the pure *originality* of the New Scheme of Society, N. O. evidently intends us to understand that he deems it *ultra utopian*. Plato, and More, and Godwin, and Spence, founded their theories, visionary as they were, on the well-known habits and propensities of human nature. While the Philosopher of New Lanark, "presumes to legislate for man as if he was an automaton devoid of passion, or bereft of reason". It was reserved for Mr. Owen [says N. O.] to make the grand discovery that man is an animal having no will, no inclination of his own, no motives, no desires, no caprices, but what are implanted or imposed by others; an animal which when the most painful wants of his nature are appeased, will become perfectly tame, contented, and docile, willing to be directed wherever duty required by the still small voice of reason and philosophy.

We are charmed, Sir, by the music of the sentence which would pronounce our doom. But is it in truth our theory that is thus condemned ; is it not rather something which has been substituted for it? I hope it will appear either that we have been misrepresented to N. O., or that he has misunderstood our object. "From the sublime to the ridiculous there is but a step".[6] Place the wig of a Judge on the head of the Appollo [sic] Belvidere, and our admiration is turned into laughter. I can assure N. O. that I laughed heartily at the merry thought of uniting every person of my acquaintance [sic] in mutual co-operation, with all their whims, habits, caprices, antipathies, likings, dislikings, family feuds, competition of talent, personal charms and accomplishments—their oddities, absurdities, and infirmities. But then, in order to enjoy the joke, I was obliged to fancy that these people had been dragged or driven into one of Mr. Owen's parallelograms, and set a digging, or spinning, dancing or singing at the word of command. How ruefully would a lawyer eye the spade which was to supersede Chancery suits, title-deeds, and marriage settlements. What pouting and glouting [sic] would there be with the belles, what grumbling and execration, with the beaus, when summoned to their daily tasks. —How suspiciously and distastefully would all parties survey their strange associates—how sulkily would they assemble to their public meals—how doggedly would they address themselves to the very recreations, which were prescribed for them.

Subtract, however, the single idea of compulsion from this fantastic assemblage, and our merriment instantly subsides. The every-day characters, quite as dissimilar as can be well conceived, mutually and actively co-operating together for a great variety of purposes, when some ruling passion is touched—some ideal good is proposed.

In answer to the *charge* of originality, let good Mr. Owen speak for himself. "None," says he, "I believe not one, of the principles of the proposed system, have the least claim to originality; they have been repeatedly advocated and recommended by superior minds, from the earliest period of history. I have no claim even to priority, in regard to the combination of these principles in theory; —this belongs, as far as I know, to John Bellers[7], who published them, and most ably recommended them to be adopted in practice in the year 1696. Whatever merit can be due to an individual for the original discovery of a plan, that, in its consequences, is calculated to effect more substantial and permanent benefit to mankind, than any ever yet perhaps contemplated by the human mind,—it all belongs exclusively to John Bellers."[8]

It is perhaps true, that Mr. Owen has done little more than to engross upon the plan of Bellers those scientific contrivances which the lapse of time has brought to light or matured. It must, however, be admitted, that Mr. Owen has connected with the adoption of his plan, many gladsome anticipations which his ingenious predecessor failed to express. It must also be granted, that Mr. Owen has built his hopes of the future happiness of the human race, upon that very basis which N. O. deems it presumptuous to assume. Mr. Owen does not indeed say in so many words, that man is an automaton: but the affirmation that, in all cases, the character is formed for, and not by the individual, amounts very nearly to the same thing. N. O. however, need not be reminded that even this proposition, startling as it is, has not the merit or demerit of novelty. It is, in other words, neither more nor less than the doctrine of necessity. N. O. is aware, that the controversy, concerning liberty and necessity, has been renewed from age to age; that it was discussed by the ancient philosophers, and not forgotten by the ancient fathers; that it was carried on by the schoolmen with all the subtlety and variety of distinctions for which they were so eminently conspicuous: that, at the time of the Reformation, Erasmus and Luther engaged in it; that it was resumed by a multitude of writers in almost every country of Europe: that during the seventeenth century the matter seemed to have been examined to the bottom by Hobbes and Bramhall; but was nevertheless re-examined again and again during the past century, by Collins and Hartley, by Priestley and Price, and Palmer and Bryant, and Dawson and Horsley[9]; and that, notwithstanding all the acuteness which these and other metaphysicians have displayed, this puzzling question has been again revived by Dr. Coplestone[10], and is at this very moment upon the tapis, as will appear on a reference to the last numbers both of the Edinburgh and Quarterly Reviews. [Edin. No. lxi. p. 252, et seq. Quarterly, No. li. p. 83, l02.

Mr. Owen, wisely abandoning the high a priori road, has conducted his enquiries respecting the nature of man according to the method prescribed by Bacon for the attainment of *every description* of knowledge[11]. He professes to have risen by continued steps from particulars to inferior maxims, and so on to the most general. "*Ab actu ad posse valet consecutio.*"[12] For an undertaking of this nature, it must be acknowledged that Mr. Owen has enjoyed great, advantages, from the extent of the population (originally, the reverse of orderly and virtuous) which has for a great number of years been subject to his superintendance and controul.[sic] During the period that he has had the management of the New Lanark establishment, he has mixed moreover very much in society, both in this country and upon the Continent, and the fame of his proceedings has attracted to his own place a great number of visitors of various countries, ranks, and creeds.

I would ask, them, whether some deference be not due, I do not say to the opinions, but to the unimpeached testimony of such a man? It appears to me that Mr. Owen does not stand so much distinguished from other philosophers in affirming that "Man is the creature of circumstances," (for this is a very trite remark) as in declaring it as the result of his own experience, that a constant unvaried course of kind treatment is far more effectual for the formation of good and for the reformation of evil habits, than the common expedient of coercion.

Even this idea, however, has not the merit of originality. It can be traced to Count Rumford, by whom its truth was verified by one of the most interesting experiments that ever was tried upon criminals and vagabonds. I glory in the fact that this man was a Briton, and I rejoice to know that the course which he marked out has been successfully pursued by our countrywoman Mrs. Fry[13], as well as by Mr. Owen and other benevolent persons in the United Kingdom.

Before I proceed to notice that part of N. O.'s letter which questions the possibility of holding together " the heterogeneous assemblage of all ranks and classes," which that gentleman supposes to have been somehow impounded in one of Mr. Owen's parallelograms, I am anxious to explain distinctly to what extent and upon what grounds I stand committed as an advocate of Mr. Owen's Plan.

There is the greater need of such an explanation, because, I suspect that N. O. is impressed with an idea which is very prevalent, that we must either reject the Plan in toto, or take it encumbered with all the speculative notions of its Projector,—that we must either use it in the mode which he has prescribed, or leave it untouched.

Now, I conceive that it is both expedient and easy to separate the idea of the Plan itself, from that of the purposes to which it may be applied. If indeed Mr. Owen had said, "I have a plan which will effectually remove all the sources of poverty and wretchedness, but you shall not profit by it, unless you engage to regulate your faith and practice by my authority," it would become us to pause before we accepted of his proffered boon. But the case is far otherwise. He has actually put us in full possession of his secret, together with his best thoughts upon a variety of curious and interesting subjects; and we are at full liberty to take the Plan with or without the opinions, and to use or abuse it at our will and pleasure. We are under no greater necessity to adopt his religious or political or commercial opinions, than are the persons who purchase his cotton twist.

In speaking of Mr. Owen's Plan, therefore, I restrict my meaning to those admirable arrangements which he has devised for facilitating the attainment of every object which can conduce to the health, comfort, and happiness of a small community, associated upon the principle of united labour and expenditure and equal rights. In the regulation of their affairs, it will be the duty of the association to avail themselves of the best opinions in every department of knowledge and science, and those of Mr. Owen must abide the test of rigid examination and impartial comparison.

But, Sir, we are checked in our very first step, by a serious question. N. O. calls upon us to produce the bond which is to hold together this Village Community. "In every considerable association from the time of Lycurgus and the primitive Christians, down even to the renowned Shakers and their celebrated establishments at Hoffwyl [sic] and New Lanark[14], there has always been some force of authority, some tie of consanguinity, some unison of feeling, some conformity of opinion, some strong necessity either for attack or defence, in fine, some strange comfort, some ruling passion, some ideal good, which served to distinguish and detach them from the mass of mankind, and which during their little day of triumphant singularity operated as a bond of union to hold them together." This beautiful sentence comprehends, I think, every description of social tie, and if in the enumeration of so many motives for union, we cannot point to any one of them as correctly designating the bond on which we rely, it must surely be no better than a rope of sand, and we have then no reason to hope that our Societies will attain even the ephemeral age of the shortest-lived fraternities.

I have however the pleasure to believe that the bond of our proposed communities is composed of the best of those ties which N. O. has concisely described. And herein, consists the pure originality of our scheme. Its power of attraction is derived from the well known fact, that any object, be it good or evil, is attained with incomparably, more, ease and certainty, when it is pursued by well combined exertions, than when a number of individuals proceed separately and without concert in the same quest. Assuming this unquestionable truth, the Plan in question, as already observed, is framed with a view to facilitate the skilful accomplishment of all the ends of civilized society.

But let us hear Mr. Owen himself. His objects, as stated in the 32d, number of your work, are as, follows:

    1st. To erect, heat, and ventilate lodging apartments for the working classes, better and cheaper than can be effected by any of the Plans now in practice.
    2d. To feed them better and cheaper.
    3d. To clothe them better and cheaper,
    4th. To train and educate them better and cheaper.
    5th. To secure to them better health than they now enjoy.
    6th. To apply their labour to agriculture, manufactures, and all the purposes of society, with science better directed than heretofore.
    7th. and lastly. To make them in all respects better members of society.

Now it surely will not for a moment be disputed, that in the above statement we have something more than ideal good; and yet in the ties of union enumerated by N. O. we find the joint pursuit of ideal good. But it appears from calculations, the accuracy of which has not been questioned, that all the real solid advantages summarily stated in the paper of Mr. Owen, are to be procured for a man, his wife, and two children, at an expense several pounds per annum within the average amount of the wages at present allowed to various kinds of labour.

The community of good and evil to which the creation and distribution of wealth, and the exercise of every description of talent, thus invite every individual of the association, affords the greatest strength which the social compact possibly can or ever did produce.

To the motives above stated might be superadded a unity of religious opinion; but it is to be hoped that in an age when the odium theologicum has lost much of its virulence, and all sects of Christians have cordially co-operated in diffusing over the world the Sacred Volume which contains the doctrines and precepts of their common faith, a community of the proposed extent might, though of different persuasions, be induced to act very cordially together.

In speaking of the attractive qualities of the Plan, I ought not to omit that it provides the means of privacy, and that it combines the advantages of a country life with many of those which are enjoyed in town.

But N. O. appears to doubt whether any force of authority could be maintained among the parties thus associated.

He does not, I am sure, deem it essential to the strength of authority, that it should either be imposed by a power extraneous to the society itself, or that it should be exercised with rigour. I really cannot conceive why there should be more difficulty in framing a government for the proposed societies than has been experienced in the case of a great variety of corporate bodies, to say nothing of the Shakers and Harmonists[15]. Where no emolument is to attach to office, and where the duty of superintending, or rather of taking the lead, will naturally fall to the most expert in each department of business, we need not apprehend on the one hand that there will arise any great violence of contention for authority, nor, on the other hand, that there will be an indisposition to undertake a charge which may be assigned on the ground of qualification. The question of government is however open, and whether it shall be founded upon the principle of seniority or of ascertained skill, and for what period of time any particular office shall be held, must be determined with due care. One thing must ever be borne in mind,—that the business only relates to bye-laws, and that the Association will, like the Moravians and Quakers, be subject to the general laws of the country.

PHILADELPHUS.

Notes

1 Adapted from Walter's Scott *The Pirate* (1822, 443). The actual quote reads: "You, Magnus Troil, from hard-hearted audacity of spirit, and you, Brenda, from wanton and

THE NEW RELIGION AND THE OLD

idle disbelief in that which is beyond your bounded comprehension, are unworthy to look on this mystic work; and the glance of your eyes mingles with, and weakens the spell; for the powers cannot brook distrust".

2 A nod to Edmund Burke's critique of the French political writer and clergyman Emmanuel Joseph Sieyès (1748–1836): "Abbé Sieyes has whole nests of pigeon-holes full of constitutions ready made, ticketed, sorted, and numbered" ("Letter to a Noble Lord", in *Further Reflections on the Revolution in France* 1796, 316).

3 Adapted from Milton's *Paradise Lost*: "Thus spoke the Cherub ... more Glory will be won then, or less lost" (1767, 167).

4 Or "Van Diemen's Land", the original name given by Europeans to the island of Tasmania before 1856.

5 A failed community project engineered by Robert Owen and Alexander Hamilton of Dalzell in 1821 on the latter's family estate at Motherwell, Lanarkshire.

6 "Du sublime au ridicule il n'y a qu'un pas". A quote attributed to Napoleon upon his return from the campaign of Russia in 1812.

7 John Bellers (1654–1725), educational theorist, Quaker theologian and author of *Proposals for Raising a Colledge of Industry of All Useful Trades and Husbandry* (1695).

8 From Robert Owen's *Further Development of the Plan contained in the Report to the Committee of the Association for the Relief of the Manufacturing and Labouring Poor* (1817, 76). See Part 1, Chapter 3.

9 John Bramhall (1594–1633), Anglican bishop and philosopher; Anthony Collins (1676–1729), deist philosopher; David Hartley (1705–1757), English philosopher; Joseph Priestley (1733–1804), theologian and the founder of Unitarianism in England; Richard Price (1723–1791), Nonconformist Welsh theologian and radical supporter of republicanism; Elihu Palmer (1764–1806), former Presbyterian preacher and advocate of deism in the United States; Jacob Bryant (1715–1804), English scholar and mythographer; Benjamin Dawson (1729–1814), Anglican minister and philosopher; Samuel Horsley (1733–1806), Anglican Bishop of Rochester and a rival of Joseph Priestley.

10 Edward Copleston (1776–1849), Anglican churchman, Provost of Oriel College, Oxford, and author of *An Enquiry concerning Necessity and Predestination* (1821).

11 Empiricism.

12 "The conclusion or induction from the actual to the possible is valid", a logical maxim meaning that one can draw conclusions in the present from envisioning future possibilities.

13 Elizabeth Fry (1780–1845), English prison reformer and philanthropist.

14 "N.O." wrongly identifies Philip Emmanuel von Fellenberg's experimental school at Hofwyl, Switzerland, and Robert Owen's spinning mill at New Lanark, Scotland, as Shaker communities.

15 "Harmonists": Johann Georg Rapp's Pietist community at Harmony, Indiana.

43

THE RELIGIOUS CREED OF THE NEW SYSTEM (EDINBURGH: PRINTED BY D. SCHAW, 1824), 3–6.

Abram Combe

[Abram Combe (1785–1827) was an Edinburgh tanner and early proponent of Robert Owen's theories. His conversion to the "new view of society" can be traced back to 1820, when he visited New Lanark with his younger brother George (1788–1858), the leader of the phrenological movement in Britain. One year later, Combe opened the Edinburgh Practical Society, which served as a school, co-operative shop and discussion group for local Owenites, including Archibald Hamilton of Dalzell (see Part 2, Chapter 15). In addition to this practical experiment, Combe sought out to publicise Owen's "new view", and especially to defend his unorthodox religious opinions. His *Religious Creed of the New System* (1823) followed an earlier pamphlet, *Address to the Conductors of the Periodical Press upon the Causes of Religious and Political Disputes* (1823). Both publications defended Owen with the help of classical deist arguments, which were known, in Combe's parlance, as "Divine Revelation". According to Combe, Owen was no infidel, but a secular prophet, whose theories were inspired by the laws of nature, which were themselves the laws of God (Harrison 1969, 104–105). In 1825, Combe established the community, the "First Society of Adherents to Divine Revelation" at Orbiston to put these principles to the test (Harrison 1969, 129; Garnett 1972, 68–73).]

PREFACE.

THE following pages have been written under the impression, That, as Rational Beings, it is our first duty, and our best interest, to respect and obey the laws which govern our nature; and whatever is advanced in favour of "Nature, Reason, and Experience," has proceeded, solely, from the idea, *That these are means which have been provided by the Supreme Ruler of the Universe*, for our instruction and direction. The past history of the world, and our present experience, have, too plainly exhibited the melancholy consequences of neglecting or despising such means, when supported by such authority. It is more than a year since Mr OWEN of New Lanark, (when publicly called upon for an expression of his sentiments on the subject of Religion,) declared to the world, "That after having, for forty years, studied the religious systems of the world, with the most sincere desire to discover one that was devoid of error, that he was persuaded that all, without a single exception, contain too much error to be of any utility in the present advanced state of the human mind"; and he also stated, that a religion which shall possess whatever is valuable in each, and exclude whatever is erroneous in all, in due time shall be promulgated."[1]

As Mr Owen has been prevented, by what he must have considered, more pressing avocations, from giving to the public his ideas on religion, I have ventured, in the mean time, to submit the following pages, for their perusal. To *say* that a production, which Mr Owen has neither seen nor heard of, *contains his sentiments on the subject of religion*, might justly be considered presumptive; but I can aver with sincerity, that the following pages contain a candid statement of the religious impressions, which an attentive perusal of his writings has made upon my mind.

The idea of a religion "without error" appears—to those who have been all their lives accustomed to think, and to act, in opposition to Nature and Reason,—extremely ridiculous. Though I am not so weak as to affirm, that the following sheets contain an exposition of such a religion, yet it appears to me, that all error proceeds from opposing Nature and Reason, and that nothing, but ignorance and the acquired prejudices of mankind, prevents them from immediately renouncing every thing that is erroneous.

It is nearly twelve years since Mr Owen laid before the public the principles upon which a discovery is founded, which is Calculated to produce the happiest effects to the whole human race, without injuring, in the slightest degree, the interest of a solitary individual. A discovery, the utility and practicability of which, may be incontrovertibly decided, by a short experiment, whenever mankind shall be induced to make it. The acquired prejudices, *of the most enlightened people in the world*, in favour of doctrines which are opposed to Nature and Reason, have been sufficiently powerful, in this instance, to induce them to prefer ignorance to knowledge; and consequently, at the end of twelve years, they know as little of this discovery, and its effects, as they did when it was first laid before them. It is the peculiar duty of the Pulpit and the Periodical Press, to "break the spell" which has produced effects so injurious. "They can best do it, and by them it ought to be done." The first step will lead them to place implicit confidence in the invincible nature of Truth; and this confidence will make them as anxious, to *examine* the evidence which exists against the truth of such doctrines, as they now feel, to *suppress* this evidence.

THE CREED OF THE NEW SYSTEM, OR A STATEMENT OF THE IMPRESSIONS WHICH

The Study of Undisputed Religion is calculated to produce on the Minds of its Followers.

1. That Man, though born ignorant, and unable to communicate knowledge to himself, is a Progressive Being, with a mind capable of acquiring new ideas;

and consequently, that his Creed of to-day, may be altered, or improved, by the progress of knowledge, tomorrow.
2. That God is the Supreme Agent—the Identical Mover,—by whose power "we live, and move, and have "our being;" and whose influence" directs the atom, "and controuls [sic] the aggregate of matter."
3. That True Faith consists in believing that God is, and ever has been, and ever will be, every where, the same.
4. That the laws of Nature are the laws of God, and that the existing works of Nature are, as it were, the "words of Deity," speaking in a language which every human being may be made to understand; and that these constitute the most valuable standard for regulating human opinions, as they have remained equally undisputed in all nations and in all ages.
5. That all human knowledge consists in a correct acquaintance with these laws, and with these works; and that the past experience of the world has invariably shown, that the happiness of Man is augmented by the observance of these laws, and by the knowledge of these works; and that the amount of his misery corresponds with the extent of his deviations from these laws, and his ignorance of these works.
6. That, as the laws of Nature are the laws of an Eternal Power, and consequently eternal and immutable, they constitute the most valuable test for distinguishing Truth from Error. Because every thing that is in unison with these laws may be true, while every thing that is opposed to them must be false.
7. That, as the actions of Man can in no shape affect the condition of Deity, it must follow, that the sole use or end of religion, is, to promote the happiness and welfare of the human species; and that this can be best attained, by a correct acquaintance with the works of God, and by obedience to the laws which govern our nature.
8. That these laws enjoin us, most peremptorily, to do Good, and to avoid Evil; while they declare as explicitly, that *"Whatever in its ultimate consequences, increases the happiness of the community, is Good; and whatever, on the other hand, tends to diminish that happiness, is Evil."*
9. That Religion consists in love to God, and love to Man, which can be evinced better by deeds than by words; while, to seek knowledge, to follow truth, to do good, and to avoid evil, under the guidance of those eternal laws which govern our nature, seems to constitute the whole duty of man, in the condition in which he is now placed.
10. That, as it is universally acknowledged that the laws of Nature are the laws of God, and that the works of Nature are, as it were, the words of Deity, and the first and only undisputed revelation from God to Man, it should follow, that those of our fellow-creatures, who have no power to believe any doctrines which are opposed to this divine revelation, or who cannot consider it their duty

to follow any practices which are opposed to these divine laws, ought not to be despised and reviled, or in any way persecuted, because they refuse to say otherwise.

Note

1 Adapted from Robert Owen, "A New Religion", *Niles Register*, 24 May 1823, reprinted from the *Limerick Chronicle*, 27 January 1823.

44
"ADDRESS DELIVERED AT THE ANNUAL CONGRESS OF THE ASSOCIATION OF ALL CLASSES OF ALL NATIONS, HELD IN MANCHESTER, FROM THE 10TH TO THE 30TH OF MAY, 1837", IN *SIX LECTURES DELIVERED IN MANCHESTER PREVIOUSLY TO THE DISCUSSION BETWEEN MR. ROBERT OWEN AND THE REV. J.H. ROEBUCK* (MANCHESTER: A. HEYWOOD, 1837), 102–112.

Robert Owen

[Robert Owen's distrust of organised religion was one of the most infamous tenets of early socialism in Britain. By the mid-1830s, following Owen's vocal rejection of the marriage institution, tensions with the various churches in the country had reached an all-time high, (Royle 1976, 47; see Part 8). In the spring of 1837, wishing to salvage his reputation while still propagating his views, Owen agreed to a series of public debates with the Reverend J.H. Roebuck, a Nonconformist minister from Manchester (Podmore 1906, 222). The following address was delivered shortly before those debates at the Socialist Congress of 1837, which was also held in the Lancashire capital that same year. While speaking to his supporters, Owen outlined the stakes of such public discussions with clerical opponents to socialism. The upcoming debate would help him reaffirm the power of circumstances as opposed to the Christian doctrine of free will, thereby confirming all established churches as forces of division and superstition. Lastly, Owen stressed the need for socialism to supersede these very same churches as a new religion in the original sense of the word (*religio*), a "bond of brotherliness and joy" (Yeo 1971, 96–97).]

At the previous annual meetings of Congress, principles of vital importance to the well-being and happiness of the human race have been promulgated, with the view of gradually preparing the population of the world for an entire change in the internal and external condition of man: a change which shall regenerate him in his feelings, thoughts and conduct, and form him to become a being of a superior order, physically, mentally and morally; a change that shall transform him from the ignorant, irrational, selfish being which the influences of superstition, and of a system of commerce founded on the principle of individual gain, or money profit, have compelled him to become, to an enlightened, rational, social being, whose individual happiness will arise from the absence of misery in others, and from a life always actively engaged in promoting the prosperity and happiness of all around him.

These principles, although most strenuously opposed by the ignorance and superstition of the old world, have, by their simplicity, and accordance with nature, made their way among the more intelligent and best disposed of the population in various nations, until considerable numbers at home and abroad, have become most anxious that the change from the irrational to the rational state of human existence should be at this period commenced in good earnest.

We now desire to extend this knowledge, in order that those accustomed to generalize their ideas, and who have had experience in extensive practical combinations to effect some important result, may adopt the principles and act upon them with the least delay; and thus relieve society from the religious, political, commercial, moral and social errors, and consequent evils, with which it is now, in every nation of the world, overwhelmed. For, under all these aspects of society, men have been made to think and to act most erroneously and injuriously.

At this moment, those deemed the most learned, wise, and experienced in all nations, are, in every department of human affairs, actively pursuing measures, the most opposed to their own happiness, and to the general good order and well-being of society. It is however the high interest of all that the cause of these errors and evils should be as speedily as possible withdrawn, without throwing society into greater disorder than now prevails.

In religion, morals, politics, commerce, and social relations and practices, every conceivable anomaly and absurdity is gravely taught and practised. From these anomalies and absurdities, wisdom and happiness are continually promised by the teachers, and expected by the taught, but, of course, can never be realised. In religion, men for ages have been contending about mysteries, respecting which, they are now ignorant as they were from the beginning; mysteries, too, which can be of no benefit to any one. But, what is most to be regretted, is that these mysteries derange the intellectual and moral faculties of all men, diverting their minds from truth to falsehood, and their conduct from right to wrong. These mysteries, varied as they are in theory and practice, in different districts, are called by all, "religion." A name, under which, are daily perpetuated the most melancholy and horrid evils throughout all the nations of the earth. But so insane are all made by the religious education forced upon them, that, in every nation of the world, men are rendered incompetent to perceive the most glaring inconsistencies in their own creed and conduct, although they can easily discover the insanities of the creed and conduct of all others. Thus are they regularly trained from infancy to believe any dogma, however incongruous, to be what they call divine and supernatural truths, and to act so absurdly as to worship reptiles, stocks or stones, or even nothing that they can see or comprehend, and to deem it a duty to compel others to believe and act, as they have been taught to think and act, and if they cannot compel them so to think and act, to consider it a still higher duty to punish them for their unbelief. These insane religions have often proceeded so far as to cause their votaries to burn and to consign to everlasting perdition, after death, those who had been forced by their education to believe in a different insane creed.

Now, one grain of common sense, or of real knowledge derived from facts, would at once put an end to this irrational state of the human mind, and the consequent insane conduct of all who have hitherto remained in this melancholy mental condition. A slight knowledge of facts respecting human nature, would make it evident to all that belief and feeling are instincts of their nature; instincts, which create the will of every individual; and, that as no man made his own organization, or external nature, or society, and as he must of necessity be, at every moment of his existence, a compound of these; he must be, what he is, and could not be other than what he is, any more than an elephant, or a lion, or a lamb could be other than what they are.

But this is but a small part of the irrationality, which the population of the world exhibits.

The intellects of men have been deranged through so many ages by these religious mysteries that they now gravely propound, as divine truths—

First, that there is a Being who made and who governs the universe, and all within it; and that without him (for they represent him as a male existence,) nothing was made. That this Being is infinite in knowledge, in power and in goodness; that he *knows* all things, *does* all things, and *can* do any thing that he wishes or desires.

Second, that he made all things, *first, perfect*, in heaven, on the earth and throughout the universe; that he had the power, if he chose, to keep all things, eternally in this perfect state; and that he alone made angels in heaven and men on earth.

Third, that yet through some other Power or Influence, an angel, although first made perfect by infinite wisdom and goodness, became, or by some unaccountable process made himself a devil, and then seduced other angels, that had also been made perfect, to follow his example; and that this party, with the devil at their head, seduced man to become the irrational being that he has been, and now is, over every part of the world, and to act continually in opposition to his own happiness, and to the will of his own creator.

Fourth, that there is eternal enmity between these two opposing parties; the first God, and his angels of goodness, always desiring to make men wise and happy; while the second power, that is, the Devil and his angels, are equally intent upon keeping men ignorant, wicked and miserable.

[As men are at this day ignorant, wicked and miserable, the unavoidable conclusion is, that the Devil and his angels are more powerful than the first Deity, or God, assisted by his angels.]

Fifth, That this eternal, infinitely wise and good being, who made human nature perfect and happy, yet so made it that the devil and his angels could so corrupt it, in the first man and woman as to render it for ever afterwards corrupt and sinful.

Sixth, That human corruption and sinfulness can be overcome and removed only by the most unaccountable proceeding of a Being said to be the Son of this first Being, and at the same time to be the first Being or God himself; that this Being, Son and Father in one, took upon himself the human form, suffering human misery and an ignominious death; and even then, that a part only of the human race are to be saved from everlasting perdition [sic] by this supernatural and most mysterious agency of this all-wise and all-good Being who desires the happiness of the universe.

From this wild combination of absurdities, millions upon millions of the most incongruous schemes, fancies and whims, have been continually forced upon the young un-resisting mind, until the human race, at this day presents the most melancholy aspect of religious frenzy and insanity, all men, afflicted with this mental disease, being made to think, speak and act, in direct opposition to their own well-being and happiness, and to the well-being and happiness of the human race.

Such is the crazy foundation upon which the human character has hitherto been formed. Such are the insanities by which, all human affairs have been involved in utter confusion; by which, men's understandings have been so perplexed that they cannot perceive the most plain and valuable truths, and they are compelled to reject what is the most beneficial for them and their children, and to cling, like maniacs, to that which is most pernicious to both.

Thus they make morals to consist in thinking, feeling and acting contrary to that nature, which they have been compelled to receive; in falsifying their sensations which are unavoidable instincts, and in saying that they believe and feel, that which they cannot understand, or be made; to comprehend. Morality is made to consist in opposing nature; in attempts to hide the truth, and in compelling all to be unnatural in their feelings, thoughts and conduct, and, therefore, unhappy in the midst of means to secure for all, great physical, intellectual and moral excellence, and a high degree of permanent enjoyment.

These religious and moral errors have engendered a political system equally false and irrational. If it be enquired what is the utility of, or end to be attained, by what men now call the science of politics, the answer is, to make and ensure the happiness of society.

Now, that which men have been trained to call the science of politics, is, in the first place, no science at all; because it is based upon error; and secondly, it produces in practice incalculable misery to the human race. It is founded on the supposition that individual man forms himself to be what he is, and that he has merit or demerit for being what he is.

Laws are, therefore, made, and governments formed, to reward ,and punish man for those matters of which it is now evident men have been most ignorant; under every code of law and form of government, over the world, all are actively engaged in devising and executing schemes to oppose their nature, and to render each other most unnatural and miserable. The policy thus produced, to govern the nations of the earth, has engendered a classification of society, which, of necessity, must while it shall be allowed to remain, disunite mankind, and make them secret or open enemies of each other; disunite them, as regards manners, habits, feelings, language and imagined interests; make and keep some far too wealthy and powerful; while the multitude, abandoned to rude ignorance, must continually sink into poverty, and experience perpetual injustice and oppression. By this error in the Polity of the world, all are detained in a condition, far below that in which any human being needs to be, if the united power of society, for the production of wealth and the formation of the human character, were understood and acted upon.

But the existing classification of mankind, most injurious as it is to all classes, is necessary to maintain the existing religions, moralities and politics of the world. In consequence of this classification, there has gradually arisen a commerce, having for its object a money profit, for individual gain. A commerce of this nature, must, of necessity, engender the most unfavorable character that man could be made to receive; and, as commerce has extended among the most civilized or wealthy nations, all the inferior feelings and passions, of which, human nature is capable of being made the victim, have been most assiduously cultivated and brought into full action. Wealth and civilization have come to be considered synonymous; and thus, by degrees, the most commercial nations have become the most selfish, cunning and deceptions; the most oppressive towards the poor, and the most regardless of each others [sic] well-being and happiness. Commerce, having for its object money-profit for the individual, has converted the best and finest feelings of human nature into a sordid love of gold. It has blinded the understandings of mankind and diverted all their faculties from the pursuit of rational happiness, to the acquisition of individual possessions, most injurious to the owner, and the very protection of which, alone entails misery upon him, and deforms his character.

These religious, moral, political and commercial errors have also produced individual family or domestic arrangements; a system of life, which, although called social, is perhaps the most unsocial and vicious, that the intellects of man could devise. If it were desired to make men and women ignorantly and viciously selfish; to make them acquire all the inferior feelings which vicious selfishness produces; to cultivate in them the worst passions; and to oppose individual to individual throughout the world, a better scheme for accomplishing these objects and rendering the whole race miserable, could not have been invented, than the existing system of single family arrangements. Like the religions, moralities, politics and commerce of the world, these arrangements have been formed at periods, when men knew not themselves; when human nature was altogether a mystery to them, and when they were incompetent to perceive that a perfect science of society, founded on a knowledge of the laws of human nature, could be introduced into practice. The experience of the past has been necessary to develope [sic] these laws to an extent sufficient to force this discovery at the present period, and this discovery will now gradually bring to a termination the reign of the religions, moralities, politics, commerce and anti-social arrangements which have so long deranged the intellectual faculties of the human race; a derangement, which has produced disunion and vice, instead of union and real virtue; which inflicts misery on all, instead of insuring the happiness which, man, by his physical, intellectual and moral organization, is so well constituted to enjoy, as soon as he shall be trained in accordance with the laws of his nature, and shall be freely permitted by man to act in accordance with these laws.

It is difficult to determine which of the erroneous systems now prevailing in society, is the most injurious. For, the religions of the world are, alone, sufficient to divide man from man, to destroy his health, and derange his faculties. The moralities of the world are, alone, sufficient to divide man from man, to destroy his health, and to derange his faculties. The politics of the world are, alone, sufficient to divide man from man, to destroy his health, and derange his faculties. The commerce of the world is, alone, sufficient to divide man from man, to destroy his health, and to derange his faculties. And the domestic, or, what is called, the social family arrangements, are, alone, sufficient to divide man from man, to destroy his health, and to derange his faculties.

But when these errors are all compounded into one incongruous system for training and governing man, from birth to death, they form together an heterogeneous mass of opposing and contradictory elements, which it is impossible by any change so to amalgamate, as that they shall constitute a combination, which will not divide man from man, destroy the health, and derange the faculties of all, who shall be subjected to its influence.

It is useless, therefore, and a waste of the most valuable time and faculties of the populations of all countries, to attempt to improve the physical and mental condition of the human race, so long as any of the existing divisions, or the existing classification of society, shall remain. These divisions render it impracticable for men to speak the truth, to acquire the habit of sincerity, to be charitable to each other, as regards their conviction and feeling, or to be truly kind and affectionate to one another. Neither will it be practicable, while this irrational arrangement continues, for the adult population ever to train the infant population to acquire those lovely physical forms and expressions, and those intellectual and moral excellencies, which, by the laws of our nature, can enable us to love one another, or rather, which will compel us to love all those around us, better than we love ourselves.

It is this entire change in the principles, classification and practices of society for which we now contend. The endless divisions, and inhuman feelings, which the religions, the moralities, the commerce, and the anti-social family arrangements produce, must be altogether abandoned, before there can be the least chance of man being made an intelligent, rational and happy being. It is therefore futile in the extreme to enter into religious, moral, political, commercial or social disputes, until the fundamental principles on which these are based, shall be ascertained and acknowledged. Until this be done, it is as irrational to discuss any of these subjects, as it would be to investigate any combination of numbers until we know on what data the calculations have been made. For, if we find that any series of arithmetical calculations has been worked out upon erroneous data, it follows of course that each result must be false. And, as we now know, beyond the possibility of mistake, that all the religions, moralities, politics, commercial and domestic arrangements of the world, have been founded upon the most crude and vulgar errors, it is a folly, and a downright waste of intellect, to discuss the details of any one of these systems. All have had their origin in vulgar ignorance respecting man and society; and those trained in this ignorance, and who retain the errors they have been taught, cannot reason; they can express only the incongruous, inconsistent and absurd feelings, and belief, which their equally misinstructed and misguided teachers forced them to receive; the teachers themselves having been, from their birth, subjected to the same insane treatment.

So insane has the mind of society been made, that at the moment when these words are impressed upon the paper, the clever men, so called by the world, over Europe and America, are suffering, as if they were upon the rack, because they cannot obtain what they call money; while the fact is, they would all be far more wise, rich and happy, were there none of such money in existence. These men have not discovered the means by which, with one grain of common sense or right judgment, the world might be made to superabound in all kinds of the most valuable wealth without risk, trouble or anxiety to any one, but, on the contrary, with the greatest pleasure and delight to all. If they possessed any real knowledge, this wealth might with ease be made always to create its own representatives; and thus, there never could be any want of the most valuable money.

But so utterly deficient are the leading minds of the world, at this advanced period, in a knowledge of facts, that the population of all countries are made miserable for the want of a shadow; while, if they did not thus insanely pursue the shadow, they might most effectually secure the substance, which would render the shadow of no value whatever.

The conduct, at this moment, of these leaders of the public mind, is not one whit superior to that of the child who cried for the moon; and yet, these men are considered wise in their generation.

All this foolery must now give way to a knowledge of plain and simple facts, which, when fairly stated, can be easily comprehended [sic] by all, and the absurdities of religions, moralities, politics, commerce and domestic arrangements, must be at once sacrificed at the shrine of common sense, or sound judgment, which, when allowed to: direct the affairs of mankind, will now easily ensure wisdom, goodness and happiness to all.

45

"POLICY VERSUS PRINCIPLE. TO THE SOCIALISTS OF ENGLAND. LETTER V", *ORACLE OF REASON; OR, PHILOSOPHY VINDICATED*, N° 11, 5 MARCH 1842, 89–91.

Charles Southwell

[Charles Southwell (1814–1860) was an anti-clerical bookseller, writer and journalist from London. He became active in the Lambeth branch of the Association of All Classes of All Nations (AACAN) around 1840, and was appointed Social Missionary for the London area. However, his radical atheism was soon at odds with the Central Board, which favoured a more conciliatory approach towards Robert Owen's clerical opponents (Taylor 1983, 145). Following the Bishop of Exeter's incendiary attacks against the AACAN in February 1840, the Central Board encouraged its Social Missionaries and lecturers to swear the oath taken by Nonconformist ministers, hoping that it would prevent them from further attacks, while securing the movement's respectability in the eyes of the law. Southwell denounced this compromise as hypocritical, arguing that socialism should not mimic religion, but help destroy it altogether (Royle 1976, 42). In 1841, Southwell co-founded the *Oracle of Reason*, Britain's first atheist publication, to further these views. However, the *Oracle* failed to attract support from mainstream Owenism, given that its anti-religious stance also had strong anti-Semitic undertones (as illustrated by the article "The Jew Book" from its fourth issue). While Owen did oppose organised churches, he otherwise championed religious toleration for the sake of universal co-operation, and was a strong proponent of Jewish emancipation, as shown by his correspondence with the financier and philanthropist Sir Isaac Lyon Goldsmid (Goldsmid Letters 1830).[1] After being tried for blasphemy in 1841, Charles Southwell stepped down as editor of the *Oracle of Reason*, and was succeeded by George Jacob Holyoake, who favoured a more moderate tone. He emigrated to Australia in 1855 and later to New Zealand, where he became a strong proponent of colonialism and white supremacy. He remains to this day a highly controversial and polarising figure in the history of early socialism (Stenhouse 2005).]

"Honesty IS the best Policy."

FRIENDS,

In the *Times* of Monday, the 7th instant, there are some remarks worthy of attention; the writer, in alluding to a pamphlet lately printed at Paris, by General Cass, which treats of the question now pending between this country and America, respecting "the right of search," observes, "Of course a political writer is quite at liberty, in plain but measured terms, to impute to his opponents such motives as he considers their actions clearly evidence. Whether he does so in a spirit of truth, it is for others to judge, not for him to proclaim; and they will not be prejudiced in his favour, by seeing that before, and whilst making his accusation, he does not manfully take up such invidium[2] as attaches to his position, but tries to shelter himself by a disclaimer from the responsibility of a suggestion by which he yet plainly intends to preoccupy the mind of the reader."[3]

I was forcibly struck with the above spirited passage, which in my present somewhat delicate position came completely home to my feelings. Though I cannot allow myself to be called an "opponent" of your party, I know that in taking my present course it is scarce possible I should escape such a charge. But I am far less anxious to ward off such a charge than to do you justice. Either in attacking or defending parties it is difficult to keep strictly to the line of moderation. Could I convey to you all, and exactly what I think, I am persuaded that no sane man among you would take offence, but to conceive is one thing, to execute another.

Lacedemonian Chilo thus profest,
Nothing too much, a mean in all is best,[4]

which was admirable advice of the Grecian sage, but advice few indeed know how to act upon. No one can deny that "the mean in all is best," but who can safely determine what is the mean, the neither too much nor For myself, whenever I attempt to put on paper said, that such was the majesty of his genius, that the English language sunk under him. I invariably find that I sink under the language. In writing to you upon matter so calculated, however carefully dealt with, to perplex and irritate, my condition reminds me of a little Scotch friend of mine, secretary to a debating society, of which I was a member, who would sometimes attempt to make a speech, but after sundry miscarriages he at length candidly said, that getting up in the midst of so many friends literally frightened the ideas out of his head, but he added very naively, "could I only say what I think, when I am sometimes crossing the road, I could make a speech with the best of you." The weakness which I do not feel when combatting the common enemy, I attribute to the excessive anxiety I feel not to be mistaken, but to convey to your minds the simple naked truth and no more; and I candidly confess, that could I entirely succeed in this particular, I should be careless about the good or bad opinions of any individuals or parties. No one can think more lightly or even contemptuously of vulgar applause, but few are more ambitious or would make larger sacrifices to obtain the approbation of wise men. I value fame as a means to an end, not to the end itself, knowing, to use the words of a modern writer, that "It is not so much action that stamps the character, as character that stamps the action."

I am by no means desirous, while making "accusations" against the policy of your party, to shrink from the *invidium* which may attach to such conduct, at the same time it is but fair that I should provide against mistakes, and "*speak* by the card, lest equivocation should undo me." I know the folly of attempting, or rather expecting, to please all men; those who are over solicitous to do so much, will probably succeed in doing very little, and like the poor old man with his ass, receive no other reward than scorn and derision. Having therefore determined to take the strictly honest course, I *am* prepared "manfully to take up such *invidium* as attaches to my position," nor will I attempt to "shelter myself by any disclaimers from the responsibility of any suggestion by which I plainly intend to preoccupy your minds." As all inuendos [sic], parables, or dark sayings of any kind, savour of servitude, and would never be used by the really free, such modes of expression will here be avoided, so that no man shall have the power to say, I wished indirectly to convey that which I dared not openly proclaim. And here I may allude to a sentence in a former letter, with a view to guard against misapprehension. I there state, that in "all that relates to thought I call no man master;" but standing as it does, it is calculated to convey a false idea, an idea it was never intended to convey. It is true, that in all that relates to thought "I call no man master," but it should have been added, that I accept thousands as friends and instructors. I am opposed to mastership and discipleship, but no less opposed to arrogance and presumption.

I have long been an ardent admirer of Mr. Owen, and to the best of my ability have defended him from the coarse, assassin-like attacks of priests and their emissaries, but my admiration never degenerated into idolatry, and I hope that I shall never so far dishonor myself as to prostrate reason before any human idol. Not a few of your party are mere Owenites, who puff Mr. Owen up as an oracle of wisdom as well as of reason, and have instituted a species of man-worship. It has long been my opinion that the worship either of god's or men is a pollution of our humanity. Mr. Owen exercises great influence in your party; and as regards the attainment of certain inferior objects, perhaps a salutary one, but if you would march towards the largest measure of freedom, he is a stumbling block in your way. I do not hesitate to affirm that Mr. Owen's connexion with your party is fatal to its progress in just ideas and the noblest practices. It is usual to flatter Mr. Owen, but I have other objects than that of pleasing individuals. There are few men who can resist the poison of flattery, and Mr. Owen is certainly not of the number. Flattery almost always, acts injuriously upon public men, but specially so upon such susceptible natures as Mr. Owen's, who, with rare benevolence and most astonishing perseverance in the cause of suffering man, is seemingly without his own knowledge, lustful of power, and strongly, I may add fatally, inclines

> To give his little senate laws
> And sit attentive to his own applause[5]

This opinion is not set forth in *spite*, but in *duty*; for, as regards Mr. Owen, personally, I have no quarrel. I think that no man of the present generation is at all comparable to him, in the essentials of a truly great and good man; but he is not infallible, nay, of late, he has manifested weakness, and displayed inconsistencies of a most glaring and pernicious character; and I must insist, that Mr. Owen puts forth claims to being a "practical man," and the only rational one; which is neither warranted by his conduct or abilities. Mr. Owen has been called by enthusiastic admirers, "the greatest luminary that ever rose above the political horizon," which if we admit, I see no reason why men should fall down and worship him. But I do not admit anything of the kind, and am clearly of opinion that Mr. Owen, though well qualified to point the way to a new and superior state of society, has no notion how to build up a science of morals. He sees a few truths, and only a few, and mistaking them for all truth, he sets to work with a perseverance which does him honor. As a friend once said to me, "A duck's leg is not a duck; and he who would expect it to lay eggs would be disappointed;" just so with Mr. Owen, he has got a duck's leg which he mistakes for a duck, and is always on the look out for eggs. If Mr. Owen were content to moderate his pretensions, they would not be so often challenged; but the most friendly cannot stifle disgust at offensive displays of excessive egotism. Besides, as my object is to infuse fresh blood into your party, and make you acquainted with the true state of your affairs, it is essential that you should be undeceived with regard to Mr. Owen. I wish to show you that he is but a man like yourselves, and not a demi-god, as some would seem to think him. Mr. Owen says that he is the only sane man in the country, all others are grossly irrational; now I only go one step further, and say that we are *all* mad together. We may safely lay it down as a rule without exception, that all are mad a *little*.

When at Congress, I was positively ashamed to hear some of the delegates pour forth their flattery. These big babies were everlastingly talking about "our dear father" doing this, and "our dear father" saying that; in fact, their conduct was preposterous, and better suited to the eunuchs of an eastern harem, than the members of a rational congress. I have heard of a monarch, who, being unfortunate enough to have a crooked neck, not a single courtier could be found with his neck straight. Another suddenly determined upon taking snuff, when all his courtiers at once became snuff-takers, and nothing was heard but sneezing about the palace; and I verily believe that Mr. Owen, had he put his neck awry, or begun to sneeze, would have found his courtiers at the Congress equally complaisant.

Mr. Owen was by no means averse to the *"popish trick"* of calling him *dear father*[6], but listened to that and the most fulsome adulations with great complacency and unmixed delight. His whole manner strongly reminded me of a certain French quack who used to parade the streets of Paris, preceded by a little boy, with pills and other cures *"for all diseases."* The boy ran before his master, crying, "My master cures all diseases, and sometimes death itself, for the small charge of six sous;" the master contenting himself by every now and then pointing to the boy and saying with great gravity, *"The lad speaks true."*

I confess that my admiration of Mr. Owen, which at one period was almost unbounded, has much cooled of late. Close contact with him has cured me of my enthusiasm, and given new value to the remark of Dr. Johnson, that men talk like angels and act like men.[7] His conduct upon one particular subject has given me great offence: I allude to his attempt to teach his "disciples" what he is pleased to term a "Rational Religion."

I shall take the liberty to consider Mr. Owen's personal merits or demerits, in other papers, my object now being merely to shake your faith in Mr. Owen's infallibility, and to protest against the idea of Rational Religion, as most absurd in itself, and if not exposed will speedily prove most disastrous in its consequences. It matters little whether Mr. Owen's opinions and conduct, with regard to this, or indeed any other question, result from what is called policy or sheer ignorance; for whether error proceed from folly or left-handed wisdom, it is always destructive to the morals and happiness of society. The overthrow of superstition has been for ages the aim of wise men, and as to the cant, or it is nought else, about all religions being destroyed, except the true and rational one, it unfortunately happens for Rational Religionists that philosophers consider all religions equally rational. They deal with them most liberally, placing all exactly upon the same footing. As to what form it may assume, it may be truly said,

> For forms of religion let fools contest,[8]

there being a settled conviction in men of sense, that whether it assume the Presbyterian, Protestant, Catholic, Jewish, or Pagan forms, or whatever may be its object, crescent or cross, one or a thousand gods, it is always a dead weight upon human intellect. Mr. Owen has lately discovered that religion is a most excellent thing, if it be of the right quality. He abhors superstition, but Rational Religion, the religion of charity, as he sometimes calls it, cannot be dispensed with. As the parsons say of prayer, it is as needful for the body as for the soul. Mr. Owen never seems to have thought deeply upon the subject, if we are permitted to judge of his latest writings. He talks about Rational Religion as though entirely ignorant that a religion, like a revelation, if proved by reason, would be destroyed by the proof. "To prove revelation by reason," said Soame Jenyns, "is to destroy it;"[9] undoubtedly, and it is not less certain that a religion proved to be true, would lose its religious character and take rank among the sciences. Belief is the essence of religion; knowledge is the essence of philosophy. Mr. Owen should have avoided the rock on which so many great reformers have split. He should not have made religion part and parcel of his system, but boldly drawing the line between conjecture and knowledge, said to the people, I will show you the way to peace, wealth, and happiness in this world; but as to the next, JE NE LE CONNAIS PAS[10], so I leave all to find that for themselves.

Your well wisher,
C.S.

Notes

1 Sir Isaac Lyon Goldsmid (1778–1859) was a personal friend of Robert Owen's and the main financial backer for the Queenwood community. He and Owen supported Jewish emancipation and popular education, and were instrumental in the founding of University College London. Goldsmid was the first Jew to be created a baronet in 1841.
2 Latin for "envy".
3 Lewis Cass (1782–1866), US Army General and US Minister to France since 1836. In 1842, the Quintuple Treaty was negotiated between Great Britain, France, Prussia, Russia and Austria for the abolition of the slave trade. The five countries discussed the possibility for their respective Navy officers to search their ships for slaves. Cass opposed the measure and attacked it in a pamphlet, *An Examination of the Questions now in Discussion between the American and British Government Concerning the Right of Search* (1842).
4 A nod to Ovid's "Metamorphosis of Lyrian and Sylvia", trans. Edward Sherburne (1639, 144): "But Lyndian Cleobulus does protest/Mean in All is best. Southwell refers to Chilon of Sparta (6th century BC), who reportedly helped overthrow the tyrannical regime in the nearby city of Sicyon, and was subsequently hailed as one of the Seven Sages of Greece alongside Thales of Miletus, Solon of Athens and others.
5 Alexander Pope, *Epistle to Dr. Arbuthnot* (1735). The poem is a direct attack on Pope's literary and political opponents.
6 During the Rational Society phase of his movement, Robert Owen was commonly referred to as the "Social Father".
7 "Be not too hasty [...] to trust, or to admire, the teachers of morality; they discourse like angels, but they live like men". Samuel Johnson, *Rasselas* ([1795] 2009 edn.), 45.
8 Alexander Pope, *Essay on Man* (1733–1734), Epistle III.
9 From Soame Jenyns, *Disquisition VI. On Rational Christianity* (1790), 249: "To prove the reasonableness of a revelation, is in fact to destroy it"
10 French for "I do not know it".

46

RELIGION SUPERSEDED, OR THE MORAL CODE OF NATURE SUFFICIENT FOR THE GUIDANCE OF MAN (LONDON: WATSON, 1844).

Emma Martin

[Born into a lower-middle class family from Bristol, Emma Martin (1811–1851) became acquainted with socialist ideas in February 1839, when she attended a lecture by the Owenite Social Missionary Alexander Campbell (see Part 3, Chapter 20). Later that year, she renounced her Baptist faith, left her husband and took her three daughters to London (Holyoake 1851). There, along with Margaret Chappellsmith (1806–1883) and Frances Morrison (1807–1898), she became one of the few female lecturers on the Owenite circuit, quickly earning a reputation as a gifted orator and polemicist. As a result, her lectures, including *Religion Superseded*, were often published in pamphlet form. Martin focused on a dual critique of gender inequalities and organised religion, which she both saw as two sides of the same patriarchal coin. In her eyes, clergymen, capitalists and politicians formed one corrupt, oppressive oligarchy with no utility whatsoever, hence the need to replace existing religious systems with Robert Owen's new "science of society", in the name of natural rights, morality and reason (Taylor 1983, 138–139; Latham 1994; Schwartz 2013, chapter 1).]

Christianity affirms that it alone possessed a true standard of morality, and would have us think that, without its assistance, the world would be a wild scene of disorder and wrong.

Pretensions so arrogant may without difficulty be proved groundless, but it would

> "Resemble Ocean into tempest tost
> To waft a sparrow, or to drown a fly."[1]

If we should enter into an elaborate refutation of such claims. It will be enough for our purpose to point to the existing christian [sic] churches, among which, if its moral principles are so good, we may expect to see living embodiments of them; but look around your own locality,—has Christianity silenced the voice of ambition in the bosom of the preacher in the neighbouring church or chapel? Will he refuse to forsake his flock even though a larger fold should be offered to him? Has he all kindness to pity, yet firmness to reprove? Is he meek and lowly of heart, seeking the honour of his master and the prosperity of his kingdom only?

Your near neighbour, the church-warden, or deacon, is he all you could desire? Has he never "laid house to house and land to land until there was no more room"?[2] has he been faithful in the discharge of his Christian duties?—And the humbler members of the flock, is there among them that Christian charity, that justice, that benevolence which is so beautiful when it is a reality, seen in the conduct, and not living only on the lip?—Are the newspaper reports filled with the delinquences [sic] of unbelievers, or are they not exclusively the record of the faults of professing Christians? His is this?

Believe me, there is no royal road to moral perfection. Religion presents no magic ground which makes those who enter it free at once from the perils and frailties of life.

Morality is a science, and as such must be studied. It is fortunately as independent of the flimsy protection of religion as the mountains of the fragment at its base. And not only is morality unassisted by religion, but it receives from it no light, no explanation, no enforcement. It stands or falls in its own strength. Conscience, so far from being its guide, is but its reflex. In the mirror of conscience, morality sees only the stature she has reached in any individual mind, differing in each; yet her resources for a universal empire are ample, as will be readily seen. The principles of morality, based on nature like other sciences, when read with candour will be found simple, universal and sufficient.

The object of Human existence, in this world, is the production of pleasurable emotions.
To this end are all the organs and functions of the human structure admirably suited. And in the same proportion as a supply of outward agents or circumstances, suitable for the creation of happiness, are withheld, is human life abridged.

The test of the morality of an act is its utility: of the utility, its tendency to the creation of pleasurable emotions.[*][3]
1.—No action is moral which produces pain to the individual, or others, unless it can be shewn, that such action will certainly, or almost certainly, produce ultimate pleasure greater than the present pain.

A patriot is justified in suffering for the establishment of the liberty or happiness of his country and posterity, and a mother in enduring privation and anxiety for the restoration from sickness, or for the cultivation of the mind of her child;

---

[*] The able dissertation of Dr. Southwood Smith, on the Philosophy of Health, (vol. 1), demonstrates this important truth in the simplest yet most scientific manner; and his work should be read by every person anxious to have *clear* notions of Man and his interests.

and both, in the use of such disciple, as, though painful, may be necessary for the establishment of the final good.

2.—No action is moral which produces present pleasure with the probability of hereafter causing a greater amount of pain.

All excessive indulgence of the animal appetite is thus shewn to be immoral, since they enervate the body, if not produce active disease.

3.—No action is moral which produces pleasures of a lower kind to the exclusion to those derivable from higher sources.

Those who content themselves with the pleasures of the mere animal nature, as eating, drinking, &c., when knowledge generosity, benevolence and justice are left untasted and unsought, necessarily suffer disappointment in their expectations of happiness; for though the pleasures of sense, when subservient to those of the moral and intellectual life are justifiable they become the avenues to misery and death when sought for their own sake alone.

To make our conduct such as may bear the foregoing tests, the following classes of duties must be understood and practised:—

Personal Duties	Social Duties
1. Preservation	1. Forbearance
2. Cultivation	2. Instruction
3. Enjoyment	3. Benevolence

Every "thinker" will be able to deduce from the general principles I have laid down, enough to guide him in every important and unimportant affair of life; but unfortunately the majority of mankind are not "thinkers." Especially on this subject they have been trained to suffer others to think for them; and though their "actions" are often very far from "the" standard, their "thoughts" of what is right generally go pretty near it. For the information of this class, I shall state at large the special duties which we deduce from the general principles already laid down.

There is also a class of persons who do not think, but who, unlike "charity which thinketh no evil",[4] delight, in making that which is not "their" school, however excellent in itself, appear unworthy the reception of mankind. It is well therefore, that I should be sufficiently explicit to leave them no room to bring unfounded charges.

THE FIRST PRINCIPLE OF MORALITY IS PRESERVATION

You have often heard that "self preservation is the first law of nature, " and the maxim would be perfect if the first word were omitted. Morality is in every respect two-fold. I cannot possible owe a duty to myself which has not its counter part for others. And the legitimate discharge of BOTH can alone constitute virtue.

"The first duty of life is to Preserve it," and the special duties involved in this will be found to be as follows:—

PRUDENCE.—The duty of self-preservation requires that men should, with prudential care, prevent the contraction of physical deformity, weakness and disease; and purchase by temperance, by exercise, and attention to the laws of health, a robust constitution and a cool temperament.

Great indeed should be the real advantage proposed, before any person should pursue an occupation which will demand the sacrifice of Health,—that sweetener of life.

If to pursue an avocation by which the constitution is impaired, be contrary to self-preservation, what can be said of the enervation or destruction of the body by the indulgence of the appetites and passions?

TEMPERANCE.—The stomach when loaded with food in improper quality or quantity, becomes oppressed and languidly exercises its function of digestion, and eventually becomes altogether unfitted for that task. Now, as life mainly depends upon the proper assimilation of foreign substances with the vital tissues, which is the function of the digestive powers, whatever tends to the weakening, or destruction of these, must shorten the period of human existence. Immoderate exercise of the mind, and the excitement of the passions have the same effects, and therefore are by the same rule condemned.

Indulgence in intoxicating drinks embraces a wider field of evil, since by their action on the brain they are liable to excite to every species of immorality. Their deadly effects upon the human frame are seen in the excitement, and then helplessness which they induce in the first instance—often concluding the tragic scene with delirium tremens, apoplexy, or madness.

How strange it is that men can believe a creative intelligence produced and is watching them through life, and yet can destroy the glorious structure they think he has bestowed! Load it with imbecility and impurity, and then impudently kneel and ask him to forgive them for the devastation they have made! Too frequently rising from the supplication, to make more food for future hypocritical confession and repentance.

CHASTITY is necessary to the observance of this law, but what is CHASTITY? Chastity consist in the calm observance of the laws of nature in the cultivation of family affections and the discharge of marital obligations. It is equally distant from the erratic flights of passion, as from conventual abstinence; the latter is denounced by nature in the maladies, the melancholy, and the sense of loneliness with which she visits it; and the former by the jealousies, the diseases, the lassitude and degradation of mind by which it is followed.

Celibacy is no virtue by natures [sic] law, for nature when she formed a diversity of sex, when she implanted the instinct of love, when she endowed us with parental sympathies, could use no stronger command to marriage.

If the interests of religion require the monitions of nature to be stifled, such religion is the enemy of nature, and it's God exists, cannot have proceeded from him, since, if he exists at all, it is as the creator of that , which we call nature, and he surely could not have given a "second" to counteract, and give the lie, to his "first" work.

The priests and devotees of the Catholic religion, have individually too often found to their cost, that their thoughts were not more undividedly Gods, because they had shut themselves from human associations, and duties. The hall smothered fires of passion have burnt more consuming in the cloister, amid all the austerities of devotion than it could have happened in the world under more "natural," and therefore " holier" circumstances.

Chastity is consistent with individual attachment; whether sanctioned by the church or otherwise. True love limits its action to a pair, and suffers no others to step in to share its sympathies during its duration; but a ceremony cannot render it more pure, or more lasting, as too many instances every day prove. Chastity is of the mind, and exists independently of law, or circumstance. Lucretia was not less chaste after the sin of Tarquin, because the mind had not been debauched by being made a consenting party; nor does the lynx-eyed Duenna succeed in preserving the chastity of her charge, whose only success has been in keeping her from outward acts. Thus it will be seen that the saying attributed to Christ, "Whosoever looketh with lust, hath committed adultery in his heart," agrees with our definition of chastity. It cannot, however, be denied, that the evils in the two cases are different and that those of the act surpass in bed results those of the thought, but it must also be remembered, that the mind once polluted, the preservation of the body from pollution also, will be very difficult, consequently, true chastity not only requires that actual offences be not committed, but urges us to guard ourselves from evil by the disciplining of the mind: and this is especially the duty of those who have the charge of youth.

The "chaste" person will not consider that a legal marriage can render pure his intercourse with one who has never been married to him by the only true tie, that of the affections; or who has forfeited that love by a variety of wrongs; nor will consider himself less so by divorce from such an one, and the consequent formation of a true marriage. Nature teaches that such union, following such separation, though iniquitous laws may brand them as infamous, are nevertheless no " adultery," which crime is only committed when the mock—that is legal marriage is allowed to exist unprotested against, and undissolved, and other engagements are made contemporaneously with it.

The counterpart of the duty of self-preservation is, FORBEARANCE to inflict or return an injury.

As tender as I should be of my own interests, nature asks me to be also of the interests of others. If to possess the highest sum of the most pleasurable emotions should be the aim of humanity, as the natural laws teach, it will be evidently my duty to guard myself, as far as possible, from being the cause of the infliction of any suffering on others. The student of realities thus discovers that society is badly constituted, that it abounds with errors, since the selfish principle prevails above the social, whereas we only then fulfil our destiny when these go hand in hand. Were nature's voice allowed to speak distinctly, war would rage no more, and man would cease to look on man as his rival or enemy, but hail him as a brother and a friend.

Tried by this rule, we find the heroes, who have trod the world's stage so majestically in past and present times, GREAT only in crime. Their toys have been human hearts, and like fretful children, they have broken and cast them away regardless. The simplest peasant who ever pitied and assisted a stray lamb, er [sic] gave a cup of milk to a weary traveller, deserves more of our esteem,—has been more valuable to society, than the proudest hero. That man is not worthless, and cannot be unhappy, who has enjoyed and distributed the blessings of earth; while he whose fevered ambition has been medicined by the sufferings of his fellows, can be neither useful nor happy.

Reader! Do you ever find pleasure in humiliating or outshining your poorer neighbour, or in annoying your richer one? Do you ever chastise your child in order to vent your anger upon him, instead of using that correction alone which you may reasonably suppose necessary? Do you ever speak to your companions even the truth with the design of hurting their feelings? Do you ever recklessly follow your own desires Without calculating what injury may follow to any or many other persons? Do you ever advise, or by the absence of reproof give countenance to intemperance in others? If you do any of these things NATURE denounces you as immoral, and entreats you to FORBEAR.

Other persons sin.—That is no excuse for you. Life is precious, misery abridges it. Life is precious, but happiness is more so, then prevent out yourself or others from the attainment of the highest amount of it of which you are susceptible.

The first principle of morality, Self-preservation, applies only to the continuation of life, and so guards against the means by which it may be impaired, but our duties as developed by the laws of nature do not end there.

THE SECOND PRINCIPLE OF MORALITY IS CULTIVATION.

We must not be content with use, but must endeavour to embody as much of life as possible in our existence. Undoubtedly there are many persons who do, on this earth, little more than vegetate. There are persons in whom only some of their qualities are developed, whose higher mental powers remain dormant, and whose sympathetic feelings have scarcely learnt glow. We must not be of such. Nature's laws unfold to us an increase of power in proportion to cultivation. The athletic frame of the peasant has not been matured without unfettered exercise, and robust occupation. Your drawing-rooms shall never rear an arm whose sinew shall match with his! The ease and grace of classic forms shall never be found in boarding school misses, whose bodies, crammed into stays, sink into deformity, who dare not move lest they disturb a ringlet, or disarrange some article of dress.

Cultivate, exercise, the powers of the body if you would purchase its best estate: And will you do less by the mind? No, for all the motives to a proper physical education are more imperative for the cultivation of the mind; the law of advance there is much more progressive and illimitable. The mind stops not its enlargement with the maturity of the body, but continues to develop itself as circumstances may encourage it. Shall we then hesitate to supply it with its legitimate food? But what is its proper food? TRUTH, from the qualities of a mite to the motives of a hero. Shall we allow others to cater for our mind's appetite? Shall we take THEIR word for what is truth? No, we must sift it for ourselves. We must not be alarmed when men raise an outcry against new opinions. We must not be steeled against the reception of new truths. Let us not starve the mind amid a world of wonders, through fear or laziness, to look into the things which are freighted with wisdom for us.

Neither must we allow the moral qualities to wither for want of use. This cold world is a barren soil for the flowers of love to blossom in. Yet we must not suffer them to die, or society is left a howling wilderness. Others may live on the miseries or ignorance of their fellows, and they may have the bitter satisfaction of success in the obtainment of gold at the expence of happiness, we envy them not. Let venal and ignorant governments hunt poverty as a crime, and then, when it has driven its victim to some desperate act, entertain the populace with a human hatchery, our philosophy teaches, and bids us hope for better things.

The counterpart of our duty to cultivate and properly develope [sic] *our own physical intellectual and moral qualities, is that of* INSTRUCTION, *or Communication of our knowledge to the world,*

Those who are misers of mental wealth sin more deeply than those who hoard their gold alone. He who roads Nature rightly will know, that in every country, the means of information should be free for all. Universal education and an unfettered press would speedily give a moral tone to any people, such as can be now but little anticipated. I hold it a sacred duty to impart to others that knowledge which I think will benefit them, and if in so doing I oppose existing institutions I cannot help it. My duty to my race must be more imperative than my allegiance to a self selected government or to priest and profligate-made laws. Should I win the derision of the thoughtless, the accusation of the malignant, the oppression of the tyrant or the curse of the priest, I am yet undaunted, posterity will right me, or should it not, I am happy in the knowledge, that I have but aimed at the dissemination of TRUTH.

THE THIRD PRINCIPLE OF MORALITY IS ENJOYMENT,

"What!" exclaims the ascetic Christian, "think you that our only purpose on earth is to enjoy life? Do you not know that 'this world is a vale of tears'? Is not 'man born to trouble as the sparks fly upward'[5]? Does not the holy Scriptures teach us that 'this is not our rest'[6]? No! I see at once your sophistry, and am not to be deceived by it! This is a state of probation, and here, as stated by the apostle, 'whom the Lord loveth he chasteneth, and scourgeth every son whom he receiveth'.[7] Your whole philosophy must be false since this principle, which refers to the grand object of life, is disproved both by scripture and experience."

Christian, listen to my answer! Scripture contradicts me, does it? Well, so let it be! I do not profess to derive my principles from that source, and its divine authority must be proved before its opposition could be fatal to my views.

And experience CONTRADICTS me also. I know it does! I know that misery IS in the world; but I know also that it need not be.

I have studied the human constitution, and I find in it no organ whose object is the production of pain. But on the contrary, the healthy action of any or all form the medium of our happiness.

The colours and fragrance of flowers—the harmony of sounds—the plumage and song of birds—in short, the myriad beauties and wonders of nature and art, perceived by my intellectual faculties, are sources of pleasure.

I find too, that length of life is generally proportioned to the number, extent and uninterruptedness of the pleasurable emotions, which the being has possessed, so that Nature speaks as plainly as possible, LIVE TO ENJOY:—ENJOY AND LIVE.

The law of Nature however, teaches me that I am not hastily and recklessly to pluck the blossom without guarding myself from the thorns. I shall not call that enjoyment by which I may purchase future pain either of body or mind. Revenge may for a moment be sweet, but its remembrance will be bitter. Men may run eagerly in the pursuit of the gratification of the organs of sense, and by the pertinacity of the pursuit miss the object of their search. The sweetest harmony palls upon the wearied ear, and the eye may wander over the richest scenes, until it becomes fatigued or disgusted with what at first charmed it.

We must use our reason in the choice of enjoyments, if we would have them preserve that character. We must use our reason in the time and alternation of our enjoyments, since the human being is of so complicated a construction, both of body and mind, that any attempt to derive our chief pleasures from one class of our physical or mental qualities, and defraud the rest of the exercise they need, leaves us bankrupt of happiness, after all our efforts.

The counterpart of our right and duty to seek enjoyment for ourselves, 1': to endeavour to promote the Diffusion of Happiness.

Shall we be content to have the means of happiness individually, and make no effort for their general diffusion? Do we know that rest, and plenty, and knowledge, are the elements of felicity, and that the masses have neither of these, and yet do nothing to alter the present state of things? Do we know that happiness must have health for its foundation, and be certain, as we are, that it is continually sacrificed at the shrine of wealth and ignorance, and yet suffer these to exist and exert their despotism almost unchecked?

Those whose uncontrollable passions are their masters, may do this, since in the misery surrounding them, they will find a theatre for their own excesses. The Christian may do so, for he consoles himself that heaven will by and by make amends for earthly sufferings; but the philosopher, the philanthropist, must look on the evils of life, not listlessly to lament, but energetically to remedy them.

ALL THESE DUTIES MUST BE PRACTISED.

No character can be deemed good which does not contain ALL the virtues named. Indeed they are so inseparable, that no one of them can exist in even tolerable perfection unless the others are existent also, as a little reflection will show.

An individual may have the best wishes for the diffusion of happiness to those around him, but if he has neglected to acquaint himself with their qualities, circumstances and requirements, how will he know what to do for their benefit?

He may be very anxious to watch and aid the helpless and unfortunate, but if he has not prudently conserved his own health, he will be incapacitated for the task.

He may long to see the smile of cheerfulness around him, but if his mind has not been disciplined into gathering from the flowers of earth their sweets, instead of ever poring over its weeds for poisons, his own soured temper will but produce its reflex in others. Nor can he steadily pursue his own conservation, or avoid the vices which wreck the body, if he has not looked to the higher qualities of his nature for enjoyment.

MOTIVES FOR MORALITY DRAWN FROM NATURE

It is true that the grand stimulus to morality, presented by the priest, is withdrawn from the student of Nature. Heaven and Hell no longer stand out in bold relief in the scenes formed in his imagination. Can it then be affirmed that he possesses no sufficient motive to choose a life of virtue?

One thing seems clear from the very necessity which produced this simple essay, that the hopes and fears of religion have not presented a sufficient motive, else would society have been pure, and my pen been excused this effort.

Morality commends its practice to mankind by its

BEAUTY.——Think, if you please, what are those sentiments which you have almost instinctively applauded when they have been uttered in the poet's words, or beamed from the orator's thought? What are the actions you have delighted to remember, or relate,—which live for you in the historian's page, or in the fancy-created tale? Are they those wherein tyranny congratulates itself on its success? — where virtue and honesty are drooping and oppressed: Is it where libertinism has triumphed, and scorn assails the victim ?

You know it is not. Every heart instinctively honors that which is noble, generous and enduring; and does homage to virtue by its admiration, and when possible, by its simulation also. Let some pathetic narrative of devoted friendship, or faithful love, or parental devotion, be uttered in any country, from the torrid to the frigid zone,—it shall affect all hearts, for

"One touch of Nature makes the whole world kin."[8]

Then try some majestic strain of gaunt ambition sacrificing myriads to a name.—Custom may have familiarized the mind to such horrors, and therefore prevent their condemning them; but the cold glory of the laurel wreath excites no sympathy, while the myrtle and the palm share the smiles and prayers of all.

Rightly constituted persons love virtue for its own sake, and recognise a sublimity in justice, a beauty in generosity, independent even of its results. But the motive to moral purity and excellence presented by its intrinsic beauty, is after all a less powerful one than that afforded by its

UTILITY.—It is the final consequences of an act which decides the reason to avoid or perform it. It is the probable consequence on our future prospects which commends or condemns it. Men are interested in the practice of virtue, because that is the only sure path to happiness. He who refuses the enticements of inordinate pleasure shall purchase that self-respect, calmness and health, which will far counterbalance the allurements he shunned. Temperance would have enough charms for man did he know all the probable and necessary consequences of discretion, and he would be able to endure the present anxieties and self-denial requisite for the dispensation of justice to all men, in all his dealings with them, were he convinced of this immutable truth,—That by our patient perseverance in the course morality enjoins, we shall both set an example which will find a host of imitators, and also obtain the pleasing conviction of having done our duty.

It is true we shall not then madly affirm, as the religionist, "we are unprofitable servants"[9]; for the PROFITABLENESS of such actions in the production of happiness, would have been strong recommendation of our course.

But there is another consideration, yet, for those especially upon whom only weak impressions can be made even by strong arguments. If moral purity has its charms so has vice its terrors; and morality commends itself by its

NECESSITY—Nature does not tell us, that "the wicked shall flourish like the green Bay-tree,"[10] but it proves that vice is a canker-worm, whose pitiless fang shall strike at the heart of the human blossom. Each vice produces its own peculiar consequence. "We gather no grapes of thorns," nor does the student of Nature expect to see an evil act visited by results of a different character to itself.

The prudent overmuch, the miser, the grasper of worldly wealth, does not share the bankrupt fate of the prodigal; but he has other misfortunes purchased by his anti-social disposition, not less fatal to his happiness.

How often has precocious vice implanted in a yet immature constitution the seeds of a rapid decay! How many a tomb is tilled with the mouldering fabrics which intemperance alone has destroyed! The Philosopher reading the melancholy history of disease, and turning over the dusty muster-rolls of Death, will recognize at once the NECESSITY for moral purity.

MEANS FOR THE ESTABLISHMENT OF A PURE MORALITY.

The reader is perhaps ready to exclaim,—If virtue is so beautiful, so useful, and even so necessary, how is it that the masses of mankind have been so blind to its requirements?

I answer,—The masses have been led away from the fields of nature to be cooped up in the enclosure of religion. They have been kept from the only study which could be really useful to them; and the majority have been placed in the most unfavourable circumstances for the developement [sic] of virtue. The means to restore them to a fair chance of happiness appear to be the following—

1. EDUCATION.—Education is the full developement [sic] of the PHYSICAL LIFE,—so that health, and ordinary perfection may be possessed:—of the MIND,—so that the judgement may be correct from the existence of just perceptions:—of the MORALS, so that the passions may be regulated by unrelaxed discipline. This education must be given to every member of the state,—must exclude religion,—and must be accompanied by the removal of all influences likely to render it nugatory, whether such influences arise from the whims or from the poverty of parents, or bad example. Its teachers must be philosopers [sic], who understand the nature of the being they must medicine.

2. OCCUPATION.—The field of idleness never yet produced a crop of virtue. Habits of industry must be established among a class where they are now unknown, or our efforts for human weal will sink abortive. While one part of a nation have no occupation but to devise schemes for the gratification of their passions, and have wealth enough to corrupt a portion of the remainder, vice will prevail, spite the dictates of reason, or the thunderings of religion.

No occupation is dishonorable which is useful, but that man is indeed infamous, who, in a world in which so many blessings reward labour, (when labour has its rights), uses his energies only for the consumption and corruption of that which the efforts of others have purchased.

On the other hand, nature as strongly interdicts unmitigated toil, and in stinting the mental energies, wasting the frame, corrupting the morals, exhibits the wreck of her own work as the result of man's rapacity.

3. RECREATION.—Little do law-makers imagine, how necessary to the morality and happiness of a nation are measures, which will ensure to all a sufficient amount of leisure, to break down the monotony of toil by a taste of varied enjoyments. Did they understand human nature better, Museums would, on ALL days, be open for the entrance of the people. Parks, Baths Concerts, aye, and even Balls! would be considered more useful than Prisons and would often prevent the necessity of Infirmaries and Lunatic Asylums.

4. PLENTY.—The people must be fed, clothed, and housed or they cannot be moral. Why should some persons inhabit palaces and fare luxuriously, and others perish for want? When did nature label her husks "for the peasant," and her grain "for the prince"? When, and where did she give the aristocrat a charter to gather her gifts, and shut out the rest of her children? Never! And never shall man be moral, until justice has no longer to weep over the prodigality of a few, and the penury of the remainder.

5. FREEDOM.—I would not be even a sleek, well-fed, idle, educated slave. To be virtuous a people must be free. Freedom consists in being subject to no man's or party's caprice,—in protection in the gratification of our desires, whenever this may not interfere with an equal privilege in others.

To be free, we must be governed by those whom we select for their superior wisdom, and integrity, to make such laws as it is our interest to obey. Such laws will have equal reference to the interests of all, and will therefore be respected and obeyed.

TREATMENT OF THE REFRACTORY

Criminal Jurisprudence is a subject our space will only allow us to glance at, and more is now scarcely necessary.

Nature exhibits evils following crime, not as a punishment for it, but as beacons which warn us of its precincts. It is the tendency of a particular line of action to produce a bad result which makes us designate and shun it as a sin. Nature inflicts no punishments, that which looks like them are only NECESSARY CONSEQUENCES.

He who reads Nature's book finds admonitions and reproofs, but no vindictive sentence. Nor are there any facts corroborative of what is called providence. I challenge the religious world for proof of their affirmations on this head, which they have so often repeated, but for which they have so few facts.

Let us then learn, that to institute reformatory discipline is all that society can have a right to do; and if it will but distribute justice to all, and educate and fraternize the people, even reformatory restraints will be unnecessary. If governments had sown the seeds of virtue alone, it would not have needed so large a body of police to pull up the weeds, or such an expensive machinery of injustice to consume them.

Notes

1 From Edward Young's poem *Night Thoughts* (1742): "Resembles ocean into tempest wrought, to waft a feather or to drown a fly".
2 Adapted from Isaiah 5:8: "Woe unto them that join house to house, that lay field to field, till there be no place, that they may be placed alone in the midst of the earth!" All of Emma Martin's Biblical references are taken from the King James Version.
3 Thomas Southwood Smith (1788–1861), English physician, public health reformer and utilitarian.

4 Adapted from 1 Corinthians 13:4–5: "Charity suffereth long, *and* is kind; charity envieth not; charity vaunteth not itself, is not puffed up, Doth not behave itself unseemly, seeketh not her own, is not easily provoked, thinketh no evil"
5 Psalm 84:6 and Job 5:7.
6 Micah 2:10.
7 Hebrews 12:6.
8 William Shakespeare, *Troilus and Cressida*, Act 3, scene 3.
9 Luke 17:10.
10 Adapted from Psalm 37:55, "I have seen the wicked in great power, and spreading himself like a green bay tree".

47

"ACCOUNT OF AN OWENITE NUPTIAL CEREMONY", *NEW MORAL WORLD*, 29 MARCH 1845, 319.

"T.B."

[In 1840, an amendment to the Marriage Act 1753 allowed any building to be certified as a venue for nuptial ceremonies. Though the change was voted to accommodate Nonconformist demands, this allowed the Owenite Halls of Science to provide weddings for their members (Taylor 1983, 191–192). As shown by this anonymous report published in the *New Moral World,* marriages soon became part of everyday life in the branches, along with a roster of activities (such as lectures, banquets and weekly meetings) meant to prepare the socialists for their future lives in the communities (Yeo 1971, 96–97). Nuptial ceremonies were particularly important as part of the Owenite propagandist strategy. Intended as a show of respectability, they signalled the movement's ability to act as an alternative to organised religion, while quashing potential accusations of impropriety and infidelity.]

Branch A1 [London], Sunday, March 16th – At an early hour this morning, our institution presented a scene of unusual bustle and confusion, in consequence of the *nuptial ceremony* between two of our members, arranged for to-day – which by the way has been noticed in some of the public journals,* with, as usual, that degree of false colouring and injustice incompatible with an honest purpose. By ten o'clock a large number of persons had assembled in the Hall, curious to witness an act of which a great portion of the public believe we take no cognizance. At about eleven, the happy couple, accompanied by their immediate friends, entered the Hall welcomed by the organ's music, and after taking their respective seats, our President[1] opened the proceedings by reading a portion of the Act of Parliament legalizing such marriages, and afterwards read from tract No. 8, our advocacy of marriage according to the late new Marriage Act. The necessary declarations in accordance with this Act were then made by our friend, under the direction of the Registrar, while, during their signatures, our choir favoured us with an appropriate chorus. Mr. Ellis[2] then rose, and delivered an excellent address upon this important

---

* The *Post*, subsequently copied into the *Sun*.

subject, wherein he strenuously enforced the golden truth, "That man's *feelings* are independent of his will", upon the right understanding and application of which, would depend much of the future happiness of our newly wedded pair; in conclusion, he heartily congratulated them upon their happy union, and the example they had now shown of our appreciation of the marriage law, apart from the trammels the priesthood of this and other countries have continually encircled this natural law of our nature. Another chorus followed, and we never saw our excellent choir more spirited in their performance. A number of our friends then retired to the "Ladies Room", where an excellent breakfast was provided, and the remainder to the "Coffee Room" to the more weighty consideration of Harmony affairs. In the afternoon at three o'clock, the ladies meet [sic] to celebrate the anniversary of their first formation into a class.[3] Between forty and fifty sat down to tea, and in the unavoidable absence of our excellent friend M. Ellis, who had promised to preside, Mr. R. Clarke kindly proffered his services. Mr. C. in his address said, it gave him great pleasure to find so much unanimity and good feeling exist, as he observed on the present occasion; and in directing their attention to that portion of their circular, relating to the formation of *Communities of United Interests*, noticed the great difficulties experienced by the want of co-operation on the part of the female sex, and hoped the time was now come when such obstructions would cease to be, that we may all go hand in hand in the formation of that state of society most desirable for the promotion of each others [sic] happiness. The thanks of the Class having been returned to those friends who had favoured them with their attendance, it was announced that a similar meeting would take place *every month*, and our young friends concluded that entertainment with several songs and duets. In the evening Mr. Peter Jones lectured on the "Study of Moral Philosophy, and its relation to Human Happiness".[4] The miscellaneous concert got up by our excellent choir, was most fully attended on Monday night. The entertainment was in fact, everything their most sanguine expectations could have anticipated. T.B.

Notes

1 Robert Clark, a London co-operator. He succeeded Thomas Hunt, who emigrated to Wisconsin in 1843 (see Part 9, Chapter 61), as branch President.
2 John Ellis.
3 Owenite women often organised associations for themselves within the branches. The "Ladies' Class" of Branch A1 was founded in March 1844, with around 60 members. The Class was self-governing, with an elected chairwoman, Caroline Holyoake Hornblower (George Jacob Holyoake's sister). In June 1844, she was also appointed on the branch executive council (*New Moral World* 13 July 1844; Kay 2012, 30).
4 Peter Jones/Kahkewāquonāby (1802–1856), Ojibwe chief, Methodist minister and author from Canada. Jones travelled to Britain three times, including a speaking and fundraising tour in 1845.

Part 8

GENDER, SEXUALITY AND FAMILY RELATIONS

It has long been assumed that the feminist debate in Britain virtually died out in the period between Mary Wollstonecraft's death in 1797 and the emergence of the suffrage movement from the early 1870s onwards (Caine 1997, 53). Yet in spite of dominant, conservative discourses and gender norms, the discussion of women's rights found a platform in the Owenite movement (Taylor 1983, 41–42).

Owen himself never put female emancipation at the core of his "science of society", but his communitarian and co-operative ideals did include a critique of traditional marriage, as well as a redefinition of domestic labour and family relations (see Part 2, Chapter 10). In an 1826 pamphlet, *Oration Containing a Declaration of Mental Independence*, he equated Church-approved unions with mere financial arrangements sanctioned by religious prejudice, in which women were turned into their husband's property. By contrast, in the society of the future, mutual affection would be the sole driving force of matrimony. Ultimately, Owenite communities would mark the end of the nuclear family, which Owen considered a breeding-ground of individualism and selfishness. Instead, children born of free unions were to be reared and educated collectively, thus allowing women to fulfil "useful and productive" occupations, no longer limited to the drudgery of domestic life (Owen 1827; McFadden 1989, 137).

Proponents of women's rights were also drawn to Owenism due to its overarching theory of character formation. If individuals were indeed moulded by their environment, then the traditional notions of "femininity" and "masculinity" were not natural, but social constructs. Consequently, "women's apparent inferiority was a product of 'vicious circumstances' rather than innate deficiencies" (Taylor 1983, 25). More generally, since socialism posited itself as a system of universal emancipation, its premise could logically be applied to the advancement of women's rights, in such fields as education, employment and suffrage (McFadden 1989, 89).

As a result, women made a vital, yet underexplored, contribution to the Owenite movement. In the 1820s and 1830s, they joined co-operatives and trade unions. Some, like Mary Lovett, ran co-operative shops. The London seamstresses and dressmakers enrolled in the Society of Industrious Females produced goods for the Labour Exchanges. In the 1840s, weekly reports from the *New Moral World* showed that lectures and social functions in the Halls of Science were attended by men and women in equal numbers (Taylor 1983, 70, 95, 274 n.1). The movement also counted within its ranks a small, yet very active group of feminists like Anna Doyle Wheeler (see Chapters 49–50 below), Frances Wright (see Part 6, Chapter 36) and Emma Martin (see Part 7, Chapter 46), whose voices were almost entirely erased from early histories of Owenism, most notably J.F.C. Harrison's otherwise seminal study (1969; Caine 1997, 55–56). The feminist critique that emerged from that locus was highly original, as it ascribed gender inequalities not only to age-old patriarchal traditions, but also to the forces of unchecked capitalism in the new industrial age. In that sense, Owen's co-operative ideals seemed to show the way towards "a free and equal partnership between the sexes" (Harris 1983, 8).

However, the Owenite movement never reached a consensus regarding the issues of gender, sexuality and family relations. First, as shown in Chapter 52 (see below), women were usually weary of "free love" as professed by their male counterparts. Many female socialists, who otherwise rejected traditional marriage, still called for alternative, legal unions to ensure their economic protection and social reputation. Second, the wish to "extend universally that love which is now pent up within the narrow circle of a family" (Bray 1839, 123) was met with even greater caution. Though Owen's supporters were happy to engage in social displays of brotherly love while attending weekly lectures, meetings and the occasional socialist festival, they were less likely to accept their leader's "Platonic scheme of education" and child-rearing (Claeys 1989, 115). At Orbiston, New Harmony and Nashoba, attempts to put such principles to the test were vehemently opposed by parents and offspring alike. Thirdly, feminist ideals were never truly applied either in the communities – where women still bore the burden of domestic chores – or in the Owenite movement more generally. As Barbara Taylor has argued, the prevalence of traditional gender roles was due to a combination of "male prejudice and female diffidence" (1983, 205). Only a small portion of relatively privileged women, like Anna Doyle Wheeler, Frances Wright, Emma Martin or Eleanor Chapellsmith could afford to make a living out of their propagandist activities. Furthermore, though women voted in most Owenite branches in the 1840s, the number of female officials remained very low. Women were underrepresented among Social Missionaries and at annual congresses, while only the Finsbury branch had a female secretary, Mary Jenneson (Taylor 1983, 204). More generally, male Owenites were often reluctant to support feminist claims, contending that the pursuit of specifically female interests contradicted co-operative ideals and the will to unite "all classes of all nations". The argument was put forward time and time again, to discourage women's involvement in co-operatives, trade unions and communities, and later in the Chartist movement.

In the end, Owenism failed to fully integrate women to its cause. Consequently, after the Queenwood community collapsed in 1845, male socialists found an outlet in the budding labour movement and in the second co-operative wave. Women, however, almost entirely disappeared from the British political stage over the next three decades, until the suffrage movement (LeGates 2001, 169).

48

"CONCLUSION, IN WHICH SOME THOUGHTS ON FEMALE EDUCATION ARE OFFERED", IN *AN ASTRONOMICAL CATECHISM, OR, DIALOGUES BETWEEN A MOTHER AND HER DAUGHTER* (LONDON: PRINTED FOR AND SOLD BY THE AUTHOR, 1818), 345–359.

Catherine Vale Whitwell

[Robert Owen and his followers all shared the belief that education was, to quote George Mudie, the "steam engine of the new moral world" (*Economist* 1821 (I), 96, cited in Harrison 1967, 98). Throughout the history of the Owenite movement and beyond, New Lanark's Institute for the Formation of Character (IFC) has accordingly been revered as the cradle of Owen's innovative pedagogy. One of its most ground-breaking aspects was undoubtedly the provision of a broad, non-gendered curriculum (with the exception of sewing classes for girls), at a time when females, especially within the working-classes, were seldom offered sufficient educational opportunities (Taylor 1983, 211; Siméon 2017, 74). Unsurprisingly, most teachers at New Lanark were also early supporters of Owen's. One of them, Catherine Vale Whitwell (1789–1873) blended socialism with a lifelong commitment to the promotion of female education. Born in London in a wealthy Nonconformist family, she was the cousin of architect Thomas Stedman Whitwell, who taught her to sketch and paint from a young age.[1] At some point in the 1810s, Whitwell opened a seminary for middle- and upper-class girls in Russell Square, London. She and Owen met in 1812 or 1813, while he was residing in the capital and working on his *New View of Society*, and they bonded over their shared belief in the potential of female education. Owen's two eldest daughters, Anne and Jane, were sent to Whitwell's school around 1820 (Anne and Jane Owen Letters 1820-1821; Allen 1990, 149–152). By then, the headmistress had fully embraced Owen's views on education and character formation, and she became a member of the New Lanark teaching staff in the autumn of 1821. She painted a number of celebrated teaching aids, including botanical charts and historical timelines. After Owen relocated to New Harmony, Whitwell joined the Orbiston community, and later resumed her activities at her London seminary (Dale Owen 1824, 33; Donnachie 2004; Donnachie 2019, 3). Written during her gradual conversion to Owen's views, her "Thoughts on Female Education" constitute the conclusion to the *Astronomical Catechism* (1818), a scientific textbook in dialogue form that she both wrote and illustrated. The book is part of a wave of popular educational texts geared specifically towards girls, at a time when the suitability and scope of female education was being highly debated. Whitwell's originality stems from the fact that she considered science (traditionally viewed as a masculine pursuit) to be as important as the arts in the education of girls and young women. Like Owen, she also believed that education should be provided on a national basis, through a government-sanctioned association of schools. (Wardlaugh 2012, 255-256; Donnachie 2019, 8–9). With this ambitious programme, Whitwell asserted the intellectual equality of genders, attempting in the process to free women from the domestic world to which they were too often confined, even within socialist circles.[2]]

Any idea I have to offer must necessarily be connected with the object of my constant attention. Female education then is the topic: a subject of such commanding importance, that it requires the head of a politician and legislator to do it justice. Education was a theme to which Milton and Locke thought it their honour to yield attention:[3] it may then, with propriety, be inquired, who is it that ventures to advance, and offer her views on such a subject? The individual is humble, indeed, but the whole of her career has furnished one act of dedication to this important topic. For seven years of her life, metaphysical works were her meat, and her drink; days and nights were devoted to the gratification of this insatiable appetite. It was impossible, thus to fail of acquiring some little insight into the established laws of the human constitution. This period has been most unexpectedly succeeded by seven years of practical investigation of these laws; and the combination of these circumstances has placed, in a most overwhelming point of view, the necessity of presenting to the youthful mind science in its simplest, its noblest, its most general, and commanding point of view: and the rapid progress in improvement, the habitual good will during the hours of business, and the amiable deportment of pupils, whose studies are directed by an attention to this rule, during the periods of relaxation, create a considerable degree of anxiety to give it a much wider circulation.

It has been an inquiry of some interest, how this may be effected; and, the most probable means appear to be, the union of forty or fifty ladies, who are heads of seminaries, and members of the Established Church, into an association, by which means there might be a constant and friendly exchange of sentiments on the subject of education. By this consolidation of work, talent, and piety, independent seminaries which have shone as so many glittering stars in the firmament, would appear with the importance and splendour of the sun; but to give this association all that weight and influence which it is desirable it should possess, to give to its laws all that wisdom which they ought to display, and all that knowledge of human nature which they must evince, it is important that it should be under the patronage and direction of one or more of the dignitaries of the church, who should be identified as the fathers of the rising generation.

Such is, very briefly, the idea I have to present. To enter more into the detail is unnecessary at this time; and as the catechetical part of this work is offered with a considerable degree of timidity, and has been withheld, till, with propriety, it could be kept back no longer, I shall have credit for descending from general topics, to a particular point, with increased emotion. The arguments I have to offer in its favour, I trust, will furnish an apology for my zeal and anxiety in the cause.

I cannot but be aware, that there are a multitude of individuals, who look upon any deviation from the beaten track, as the rash effort of a warm imagination, that may please and dazzle for a time, but can produce no real or lasting benefit. This idea might be applicable on the present occasion, were my views connected with any violent depreciation of those plans, still in use in female seminaries, or if any indecorous precipitation in the work of amendment were urged; but my object is simply to *facilitate* that mental improvement which is working its way, and to furnish a permanent foundation, upon which its towering eminence may stand secure, one effect of which would be, that, instead of individuals being borne unconsciously by the tide of popular opinion, they would recognise the fact, that the education of their daughters is reduced to a system, and that it is the subject of certain, fixed, well-known, and general laws.

Who is not anxious that such an education should become national, as would concentrate in one individual, extremes the most opposite? and this will doubtless be the result of the progress of reason, and a judicious diffusion of knowledge. Is it not desirable that the mind should possess a considerable portion of information, and yet the individual remain modest and retiring? that, with much decision of character, a polite attention to the opinions of others should be united? that, with a scrupulous regard to the value of time, there should be sweetness and complacency in the society of our connexions; so that, solitude should be bliss, and society the source of delight? that, with a mind fitted for contemplation, the attention should be alive to the ten thousand little comforts of life? that, with a keen penetration into personal defects, a mantle of tenderness should be cast around the failures of others? that, with a low estimate of personal attainments, should be united a readiness to allow whatever is excellent in others? that, profound piety should exist, without superstition; a liberal state of mind, without laxity; and a spirit of investigation, without scepticism? That such a combination is not often to be found, is the idea I have imbibed: but all this is essential to the perfection of the female character; and to the due maintenance of that exalted station which she holds in the community, by which, unseen, she gives energy to her sons, and by her virtues, or her vices, insures a nation's prosperity, or, with accelerated aggravations, hastens its downfall. Since such are the effects of female influence, and a combination of all the excellencies just enumerated is rare, yet, as the assemblage is occasionally found, it appears to be desirable, that those who would facilitate our national improvement, should trace out the general principles of our nature, which have been acted upon, when such a result has exhibited itself.

What was the object aimed at by several enlightened citizens, when the arithmetical skill of an American youth displayed itself? It was to obtain the basis upon which his deductions were founded, that the application of the principle might be rendered subservient to the more rapid progress of ordinary capacities. In connexion with this subject, how important is a remark made by Lord Bacon: "Rules," says he, "do, in some sort, equal men's wits, and leave no great advantage or pre-eminence to the perfect and excellent motions of the spirit. To draw a straight line, or to describe a circle, by aim of hand only, there must be a great difference between an unsteady and an unpractised hand, and a steady and practised; but, to do it by rule or compass, it is much alike."[4]

The rapid spread of intellectual improvement during the last twenty years, is surely encouraging to any one willing to enter upon the task of its increased advancement; and it is the first argument I offer, in soliciting attention to the idea of an association of female seminaries.

To what art or science can we direct our attention, in which the progress is not truly interesting? Shall the subjects be geography, and navigation? The glowing language of a celebrated writer, relative to the former science, cannot be improved: he says, "The reign of George III will stand conspicuous, and proudly pre-eminent in future history, for the spirit with which discoveries were prosecuted, and the objects of science promoted; and a dawn of hope appears, that ere its close, the interesting problem of a north-west passage from the Atlantic to the Pacific will be solved, and this great discovery, to which the Frobishers[5], the Hudsons[6], the Davises[7], Baffins[8], and Bylots[9], so successfully opened the way, will be accomplished."[10] And, doubtless, the increased knowledge of the science of navigation will not be without its advantages in facilitating the solution of this problem. Such are the laws to which navigation is reduced, that a seaman, though ignorant of mathematics, may apply with correctness and dexterity the rules for finding the longitude." The progress which has been made in astronomy, anatomy, and botany, is proverbial; and has this arisen from the retrograde motion of some sister science? no; but from the aid they have received from the increased proficiency of the optician. Indeed, upon the sciences of astronomy, and mathematics, the eloquent and philosophical statement of the argument by M. Condorcet[11], cannot fail to carry conviction to the mind. His words, as translated by Dugald Stewart, are, "To such of my readers as may be slow in admitting the possibility of the progressive improvement of the human race, allow me to state, as an example, the history of that science in which the advances of discovery are the most certain, and in which they may be measured with the greatest precision. Those elementary truths of geometry, and of astronomy, which, in India, and Egypt, formed an occult science, upon which an ambitious priesthood founded its influence, were become, in the times of Archimedes and Hipparchus, the subjects of common education in the public schools of Greece. In the last century, a few years of study were sufficient for comprehending all that Archimedes and Hipparchus knew; and, at present, two years employed under an able teacher, carry the student beyond those conclusions which limited the inquiries of Leibnitz and of Newton. Let any person reflect on these facts: let him follow the immense chain which connects the inquiries of Euler[12], with those of a priest of Memphis: let him observe, at each epoch, how genius outstrips the present age, and how it is overtaken by mediocrity in the next; he will perceive that nature has furnished us with the means of abridging, and facilitating our intellectual labours, and that there is no reason for apprehending that such simplification can ever have an end. He will perceive, that at the moment when a multitude of particular solutions, and of insulated facts, begin to distract the attention, and to overcharge the memory, the former gradually lose themselves in one general method, and the latter unite in one general law; and that these generalizations continually succeeding one to another, like the successive multiplications of number by itself, have no other limit, than that infinity which the human faculties are unable to comprehend."[13]

In proportion as the mind becomes familiarized with these ideas, will it be stimulated to action, not simply by the consideration of how much is done; but by the conviction of how much there still remains to do; so much that it seems to require uncommon vigour to qualify for the combat, an unusual character of mind, that dares calculate upon the bliss of victory. The immense achievements yet to be made, is my second argument.

We are still only emanating from the darkness of the sixth, and seventh centuries. We are but on the march from the tyranny of ancient prejudice, to the perfection of human reason; we are only emerging from that oppressive bondage, upon which the old system of policy was founded, and on the skilful exercise of which, its influence has been so long perpetuated. We are but half way upon our journey between the time, when every thought, on every subject, was made to yield before the terrors of the Inquisition; and that auspicious period when the perfection of human society shall render the execution of sanguinary laws unnecessary, and the whole science of legislation shall be reduced to a few, grand, and simple, precepts. But surely the greater part of our difficulties are surmounted, and the certainty of our progress, is more obvious, than could have been the advances made by our predecessors. The following argument drawn from Stewart's[14] Philosophy of the human Mind, must be truly encouraging to those whose energies fail, because the combat is severe. He observes, "Of the progress which may yet be made in the different branches of moral and political philosophy, we may form some idea, from what has already happened in physics, since the time that Lord Bacon united, in one useful direction, the labours of those who cultivate that science. At the period when he wrote, physics was certainly in a more hopeless state, than that of moral and political philosophy in the present age. A perpetual succession of chimerical theories had, till then, amused the world, and the prevailing opinion was, that the case would continue to be the same for ever. Why then should we despair of the competency of the human faculties, to establish solid and permanent systems, upon other subjects which are of still more serious importance? Physics, it is true, is free from many difficulties which obstruct our progress in moral and political inquiries; but, perhaps, this advantage may be more than counterbalanced, by the tendency they have to engage a more universal, and a more earnest attention, in consequence of their coming home more immediately to our 'business and our bosoms'. When these sciences too, begin to be prosecuted on a regular and systematical plan, their improvement will go on with an accelerated velocity; not only as the number of speculative minds will be every day increased by the diffusion of knowledge, but as an acquaintance with the just rules of inquiry, will more and more place important discoveries, within the reach of ordinary understandings."[15]

If, after what has been said, it still remains the subject of inquiry, why I am anxious to press home, the importance of female education, and to trouble the public with my views on the subject, I can only say, it was not the *solitary* exertions of a Nimrod,[16] a Hercules,[17] or a Semiramis,[18] that raised those stupendous monuments of human skill, which have excited the admiration of succeeding ages. No: it appears to be the sole prerogative of the Infinite Mind to act alone. When finite minds would effect any great object, it must be by the concentration of their powers by the union of their influence; it must be the act of the multitude, not of an individual.

It is, perhaps, almost unnecessary, as an argument in favour of the cause I plead, to point out some circumstances respecting the state of society in the United Kingdom. It is a well-known fact, that a large part of the community are not members of the national established Church: that, on the one hand, the Catholics, daily augment in number, and that the Dissenters, split into forty or fifty subordinate divisions, form a large mass of the population. In addition to this, we cannot but expect an influx of gaiety, and some revival of infidelity, from the closer and more general intercourse that exists between us, and our continental neighbours; whose vices are the more likely to be adopted by us, since they are covered with an exterior garb, which must captivate every individual of taste, and feeling.

During the season of confinement to our country, which a long war imposed,[19] there was time for many of the important truths of religion to be rivetted in the minds of our people; but how few can grasp the whole of a subject! and each department of the community pursues the division of truth, which falls in with some darling prejudice, or some favourite object. Hence, many of the precepts of the sacred writings have been imbibed by our populace, without any knowledge of the relation in which they stand to other parts of the Holy Scriptures. Hence, this doctrine of the equality of mankind, supposed to rest upon this infallible basis, has been proclaimed, without considering, that social order, and universal subordination, are founded on the laws of nature, and unavoidably impose themselves upon each individual who becomes a member of society; without considering the fact, that to enjoy liberty aright, the foundation on which it rests must be generally understood, and that the light of philosophy must first be universally extended. To the statement of one fact, without its indispensable associate being kept in view, I apprehend we may trace much of that insubordination obvious in various departments of the community. Hence, a practical exhibition of the import of these precepts, "Be courteous," "Honour all men," appears as though it might be beneficial to our associates. But while we would duly appreciate, and diligently cultivate that which is admirable in the French character, there is great danger of imbibing some of the odious maxims of their policy.

What then is to be done? Shall we place around our island a barrier more formidable than the ocean, to check the unparalleled activity of our people in their visits to the continent? Shall we do what we can to prevent their seeing an habitual exhibition of the finest feelings of our nature? Shall we seclude them from the world, and then boast of their decision of character?

This will not do; we must supply an antidote, as extensive as the malady, and exactly suited to its nature. We must give to the rising generation, solid and permanent principles; yea, principles more permanent, and more solid, than those by which the world has hitherto been governed. Need I say, then, that this is my third argument in soliciting, at this juncture, the dignitaries of our church to come forward, and fix the wavering opinions of the community, by giving the impress of their own exalted minds, to the rising generation? Their patriotic spirit, their natural and acquired endowments, and their paternal connexion with the community, render it particularly desirable that they should enter seriously upon the important business of directing the established laws of our constitution to purposes worthy of their divine origin; and that, after having devoted themselves to this important engagement, they should place the result in the hands of all those heads of seminaries who shall willingly be guided by such regulations. By this, not only, would a degree of stability be given to the opinions of the community, but the improvement of female education in the British empire would be, in a ratio infinitely greater than any thing that has been witnessed at present. Lord Bacon well observes, "expert individuals can execute, but the general counsels, and plots, and the marshalling of affairs, come but from those that are learned."[20]

Notes

1 Thomas Stedman Whitwell was also associated with the Owenite movement. In 1817, Robert Owen circulated a plan of his ideal "Village of Co-operation" in the British press, probably drawn by Whitwell. The architect was later commissioned to draw the blueprints of the Harmony Hall building at Queenwood (Owen 1839).

2 Among many instances of such willingness to enforce separate spheres for men and women, the *New Moral World* claimed that "young women should be taught the duties of housewifery (28 March 1840, cited in Taylor 1983, 213). Though Owen was committed to providing females with an education on par with that usually given to middle- and upper-class men (with a curriculum that encompassed not only the "3Rs" but the teaching of science, the humanities, dancing and music), he partly supported that

stance. At New Lanark, he had planned to introduce home economics classes for adult women. His later community schemes professed that women should not be confined to the drudgery of domestic life, but be allowed ample time to educate and entertain themselves. But these proposals also made it clear that household chores would be carried out by women alone, albeit with the help of modern machinery to alleviate their workload. (see Owen 1827, Part 2, Chapter 10).

3 John Milton, *Of Education* (1644); John Locke, *Some Thoughts Concerning Education* (1693).
4 Francis Bacon, *Cogitata et Visa de Interpretatione Naturae* ([1607] 1884) vol. 1, p. 94.
5 Martin Frobisher (c.1535–1594), English seaman.
6 Henry Hudson (c. 1565–1611), English navigator and explorer of Canada.
7 John Davis (c.1550–1605), English explorer.
8 William Baffin (c. 1584–1622), English navigator.
9 Robert Bylot (?–?), English explorer. He was first mate on Henry Hudson's ship during the latter's 1610–1611 expedition into northern Canada. Bylot later took part in William Baffin's search for the Northwest Passage in 1816.
10 Lieutenant Chappell, "Narrative of a Voyage to Hudson's Bay, in His Majesty's Ship Rosamond, containing some Account of the North-eastern Coast of America, and of the Tribes inhabiting that remote Region", *The Quarterly Review* 1817, vol. 18, 213.
11 Nicolas de Condorcet (1743–1794), French philosopher.
12 Leonhard Euler (1707–1783), Swiss mathematician, physicist and astronomer.
13 Condorcet, *Cinq mémoires sur l'instruction publique* (1791).
14 Dugald Stewart (1753–1828), Scottish philosopher.
15 Dugald Stewart, *Elements of the Philosophy of the Human Mind* (1792) vol. 1, 266–267.
16 Nimrod, the legendary king of Shinar (Mesopotamia), who ordered the building of the Tower of Babel according to the Book of Genesis.
17 An allusion to the twelve Labours of Hercules.
18 Semiramis, legendary queen of Assyria. She is credited as the restorer of the walls of Babylon.
19 Napoleon's Continental Blockade against the United Kingdom during the Napoleonic Wars (1806–1812).
20 Francis Bacon, *Of Studies* (1625).

49

APPEAL TO ONE HALF OF THE HUMAN RACE, WOMEN, AGAINST THE PRETENSIONS OF THE OTHER HALF, MEN: TO RETAIN IN POLITICAL, AND THENCE IN CIVIL AND DOMESTIC SLAVERY; IN REPLY TO A PARAGRAPH OF MR. MILL'S CELEBRATED "ARTICLE ON GOVERNMENT" (LONDON: LONGMAN, HURST, REES, ORME, BROWN AND GREEN, 1825), 198–206

William Thompson and Anna Doyle Wheeler

[One of the most celebrated feminist texts of the nineteenth century, the *Appeal* helped popularise the issue of women's rights within the Owenite movement, especially as it was probably the first publication in British history to explicitly advocate female suffrage. William Thompson was credited as sole author of the *Appeal,* but in the preface, "Letter to Mrs Wheeler", he nevertheless acknowledged it as his "joint property" with fellow Irish socialist Anna Doyle Wheeler (1785–1848). Due to her poor health, she had only penned the text's last section, but she and Thompson had developed the book's arguments together (Durant 1834, 62–63; Dooley 1995; Taylor 1983, 67–68).[1] Born, like Thompson, into the Irish Protestant Ascendency, Anna Wheeler turned to feminism, political radicalism and atheism following the breakdown of her disastrous marriage with an alcoholic aristocrat. In 1807, she left her husband and took her two surviving children to Guernsey and then to Caen, France, when she became acquainted with local Saint-Simonian circles. By 1823, she had relocated to London, where she had become a follower and personal friend of Robert Owen, most likely through their mutual acquaintance Jeremy Bentham. The latter also introduced her to

Thompson, and the two compatriots bonded over their shared anguish for Ireland's economic crisis, faith in Owen's communitarian schemes, and interest in promoting women's rights (Lane 1997, 15; Nyland and Heenan 2003, 241–260). The *Appeal* originated as a rebuke to James Mill's *Essay on Government* ([1819] 1992). Mill posited that women were in no need of the vote, as their interests were meant to be taken care of by their fathers and husbands (Moriarty 2012, 112; Cory 2004, 106). Wheeler and Thompson argued, on the contrary, that women were in dire need of political and civil rights, so unequal was their condition, under the triple yoke of the so-called "civilized" norms of religion, marriage and private property. Sexual and economic exploitation were thus intertwined, as both were the produce of an overarching system of institutionalised oppression and competition, whether between master and workers, man and woman, or husband and wife. The time was therefore ripe for the complete re-education of humankind along socialist lines. Only in intentional communities modelled on Owen's "Villages of Co-operation" could full emancipation be secured. While guaranteeing general economic security to workers of all genders, the communities would also provide a favourable environment for the exertion of full political and civil rights, including female suffrage (Dooley 1996, 313).]

You will always, under the system of individual competition and individual accumulation of wealth, be liable to the casualty of misery on the death of the active producer of the family, and occasional injustices from domestic abuse of superior strength and influence, against which no laws can entirely guard. Under the system of production by individual competition, it is impossible to expect that public opinion should be raised so high as to supply the defects of law, which can only repress— at the expense of the minor evils of punishment—the more flagrant and proveable [sic] acts of injustice, but can not take cognizance of those minute occurrences which so often form the ground-work of the happiness or misery of life. Superiority in the production or accumulation of individual wealth will ever be whispering into man's ear preposterous notions of his relative importance over woman, which notions must be ever prompting him to unsocial airs towards women, and particularly towards that women who co-operates with him in the rearing of family: for, individual wealth being under this system the thing needful, all other qualities not tending to acquire it, though contributing ever so largely to increase the common stock of mutual happiness, are disregarded; and compensation for the exercise of such qualities or talents, for the endurance of pains and privations, would scarcely be dreamed of. If man, pursuing individual wealth, condescend to be equally instrumental with you in the production of children, the whole of the pleasure he takes care to enjoy and make the most of, as his by right of superior strength; but as to the pains and privations which his enjoyments may have entailed upon another, where is the bond that his labor should afford compensation for them?

Not so under the system of, Association, or of Labor by Mutual Co-operation.

This scheme of social arrangements is the only one which will complete and for ever insure the perfect equality and entire reciprocity of happiness between women and men. Those evils, which neither an equality of civil and criminal laws, nor of political laws, nor an equal system of morals upheld by an enlightened public opinion, can entirely obviate, this scheme of human exertion will remove or abundantly compensate. Even for the partial dispensations of nature it affords a remedy. Large numbers of men and women co-operating together for mutual happiness, all their possessions and means of enjoyment being the equal property of all—individual property and competition for ever excluded—women are not asked to *labor* as much in point of strength of muscle as men, but to contribute what they can, with as much cheerful benevolence, to the common happiness. All talents, all faculties, whether from nature or education, whether of mind or muscle, are here equally appreciated if they are spontaneously afforded and improved, and if they are necessary to keep up the common mass of happiness. All talents, all faculties, whether from nature or education, whether of mind or muscle, are here equally appreciated if they are spontaneously afforded and improved, and if they are necessary to keep up the common mass of happiness. Here no dread of being deserted by a husband with a helpless and pining family, could compel a woman to submit to the barbarities of an exclusive master. The whole Association educate and provide for the children of all: the children are independent of the exertions or the bounty of any individual parent: the whole wealth and beneficence of the community support woman against the enormous wrong of such casualties: they affect her not. She is bound by no motives to submit to injustice: it would not, therefore, be practised upon her. Here the evil of losing, by any accident, a beloved companion, is not aggravated to woman by the unanticipated pressure of overwhelming want. All her comforts, her respectability, depending on her personal qualities, remain unchanged: she co-operates as before to the common happiness, and her intelligent and sympathizing associates mitigate and gradually replace the bitterness of a last separation from the friend of her affections. Here, the daughter of the deserted mother could not, from want or vanity, sell the use of her person. She is as fully supplied with all comforts as any other member of the community, co-operating with them in whatever way her talents may permit to the common good. The vile trade of prostitution, consigning to untimely graves the youth and beauty of every civilized land, and gloated on by men pursuing individual wealth and upholding the sexual and partial system of morals, could not here exist. Man has, here, no individual wealth more than woman, with which to buy her person for the animal use of a few years. Man, like woman, if he wish to be beloved, must learn the art of pleasing, of benevolence, of deserving love. Here, the happiness of a young woman is not blasted for life by the scorn and persecutions of unrelenting hypocrisy, for that very indiscretion which weaves the gay chaplet of exulting gallantry round the forehead of unrestrained man. Morality is, here, just and equal in her awards. Why so? Because, man having no more wealth than woman, and no more influence over the general property, and his superior strength being brought down to its just level of utility, he can procure no sexual gratification but from the voluntary affection of woman: in proscribing her indiscretions, therefore, he must proscribe his own: and as far as the greatest degree of common happiness might require that such indiscretions should be equally repressed in the two sexes, so far on individual men for their daily support, if the children of all the pairs of the community are educated and maintained out of the common stock of wealth and talents, if every possible aid of medical skill and kindness is afforded impartially to all, to compensate for the bitterness of those hours when the organization of woman imposes on her superfluous sufferings; what motives, under such circumstances, could lead women to submit to unmerited reproach more than men, for those very acts in which men must from the very nature of things be equal participators? *No means of persecution being left to men*, all reproach not founded on reason and justice, all attempt at exclusive reproach, would be thrown back with laughter and contempt on the fools who harboured them. Woman's love must under such circumstances be earned, be merited, not, as now, *bought or commanded*: it would not be prostituted on heartless miscreants who could first steal the gem and then murder with their scorn its innocent confiding owner. Such men, in such an Association, might love themselves! a species of love, in which they would find no rivals to molest them!

All sexual morality, and its attendant horrors of human misery, thus banished from these happy abodes of equal justice by the inevitable operation of circumstances, withdrawing the old, and affording new, motives to human exertion and judgement, the education of women being as comprehensive and useful as that of men, the inequality of chances of enjoyment to women, under the system of individual competition from average inequality of powers, being obviated, and all the compensation that human skill and kindness can afford being provided against the inevitable evils of nature or accident; what remains but that you should every where advocate, first, that partial equality which is all that equal laws, political and civil, equal morals, and an equal system of education can give you under the scheme of isolated individual, or family, exertion, now prevalent, and that you should also advocate, with an energy not inferior, the new social system of the Association of large numbers, all cheerfully contributing their exertions, muscular or mental, to the common good, and all equal in duties, rights, and enjoyments; the happiness of both men and women raised a hundredfold beyond what it now is? The scheme of Association or Mutual Co-operation, where all useful talents and efforts for the common good will be equally appreciated and rewarded, is the true haven for the happiness of both sexes, particularly of women. All motives are here taken away from men to practise injustice; all motives are taken away from women to submit to injustice. The practice of it will not, therefore, be attempted. As long as the exclusive individual possession of wealth remains the moving-spring of human society, so long will your peculiar pains and privations be disregarded and unrequited, and man will avail himself of his natural advantages of strength and uninterrupted exertion to exact an indirect domination over woman in the secrecy of domestic life, though laws and public opinion were opposed to such usurpation. It is not in human nature, possessed of power and the means of exercising it, and acting in every thing by individual competition, to abstain on all occasions from the abuse of that power. By Mutual Co-operation of large numbers, the power and the means of exercising it, and the desire of exercising it, are equally withdrawn. Women are here no more dependent on men, or on any individual man, than men are on women. Let the laws of general society be what they may, let them remain ever so brutal, even as they now are, respecting what they are pleased to term the marriage contract, no woman in these Associations of large numbers for mutual happiness, will be under any necessity, will find any possible motive, that could induce her to become the self-devoted slave to the caprices, or, capricious or not, to the *will* of any other human being. Cheerfully co-operating by personal exertion of mind, skill, or muscle, to the common good, possessing influence proportioned to her powers of reason and useful talent, sharing equally all benefits, watched over in sickness and health by equal care, what premium under such circumstances has man to offer to woman that she should be his slave in any thing? No more than woman has to offer to man that he should be the slave other appetites and capricious jealousies. Who wishes, man or woman, in these Communities to be esteemed or loved, must deserve to be esteemed or loved, and must look forward to the loss of love or esteem with the loss, or the neglect to practise, those good qualities which called esteem or love into existence. No persecution could here be practised to constrain the semblance, the mockery, of esteem or love when the reality had ceased to exist. To enjoy equal happiness with men, to associate with them on terms of perfect equality, you must be equally useful to the common good by an equal improvement and equally useful application of all your faculties of mind and body, in exchange for the state of domestic drudgery, ignorance, and insignificance to which you are now reduced, with various shades, in civilized as well as savage life. Then shall you and men salute each other with a real and mutual modesty, founded on mutual benevolence, on a just estimate of your several characters, and a knowledge of the mutual dependence of each on the other to elicit the highest degree of happiness; not, as now, with an air of superiority and condescending bounty on the one side, and on the other with downcast eyes, the willing and ignorant slaves of men's pampered and brutalizing appetites.*

Under such arrangements, women may have equal improvement and use of all their faculties with men: under these circumstances, they may derive as much of

---

* While Mr. Owen was in Scotland, at New Lanark, practically experimenting on the principles of the new Social System of Mutual Co-operation, a French writer, M. Charles Fourier (with whose eccentricities of speculation we are not here concerned) was studying the same subject at Lyons. As the result of the observations and meditations of 30 years, he has published in Paris two large volumes, which he calls a "*Treatise of Industrial Association.*" In the great leading features of the Co-operation of large numbers for the production of wealth and social happiness, and the improved, and industrious, and *equal* education of *all* the children, Fourier agrees with Mr. Owen. But *inequality of distribution* is a leading feature of Fourier's system of Co-operation; while *equality* of distribution of wealth, as of all the means of happiness, seems to be the ultimate object of Owen's. Under the systems of both, under all systems of just Co-operation, not only will equal protection of Institutions be granted to women with men, but equal means of happiness from all sources will be insured to them.

happiness from every source—of the sense, of intelligence, and sympathy—as men, according to the peculiarities of organization of each: under these circumstances, all may be perfectly equal in rights, duties, and enjoyments, according to their capabilities of acting, suffering, and enjoying. If men from an average superiority of strength, be able to add more to general happiness in the way of increasing the products of labor, where would happiness, where would men be found, were it not for the peculiar pains, privations and cares which women suffer in nourishing and rearing the infancy of the whole race? Against the almost doubtful advantage, in the present state of improved chemical and mechanical science and art, of mere superiority of animal strength on the part of men, in increasing their utility or contributions to the common happiness, may not the unquestionable usefulness of the employment of that part of the time of women which is consumed in preserving the race be opposed? Which is more indispensable for human happiness, that a few more broadcloths or cotton should be every year produced, or that the race itself should be every year increased and kindly and skilfully nurtured? Wherever the principle of Association prevailed, justice would prevail, and these mutual compensations – as nurturing infants against strength – would be fully admitted; no person cheerfully exerting his or her means, whatever they might be, for the common benefit, would be punished for the scantiness of those means, still less for the pains or privations attending their development. In this, as in all the other arrangements of Mutual Co-operation, the punishments of nature, whether arising from decrease of enjoyments or from positive pain, would not only perhaps be found sufficient for all useful purposes, but would rather demand compensation than factitious increase.

Note

1 Recent reprints have acknowledged Anna Doyle Wheeler's co-authorship (see the volume edited by M. Foot and M. Mulvey Roberts, 1994).

50

"RIGHTS OF WOMEN. A LECTURE DELIVERED BY MRS. WHEELER, LAST YEAR, IN A CHAPEL NEAR FINSBURY SQUARE", *BRITISH CO-OPERATOR*, 1830, 12–15.

Anna Doyle Wheeler

[Following the publication of the *Appeal to One Half of the Human Race* in 1825, Anna Doyle Wheeler became a public authority within the Owenite movement. She embarked on a flurry of public activity, contributing to the socialist press and giving various lectures on women's rights. One of these speeches, given in 1829, at the Unitarian chapel in Finsbury Square, London, was reprinted the following year in the *British Co-operator*, then one of the leading socialist publications in Britain. The lecture expanded upon the *Appeal*'s last section, "Letter to the Women of England", which Wheeler had authored. It was a call to direct action, at a time when Wheeler and many defenders of women's rights were growing frustrated with Robert Owen's reluctance to fully endorse the subject. Though he publicly declared his "profound sympathy" for women, he feared that the exploitation that they were submitted to had rendered them too weak to assume responsibility for their own salvation (*Crisis*, 24 August 1833). Wheeler took an opposing stance, urging women of all nationalities to acknowledge their own oppression and join forces to defend their cause, thereby voicing what may be the first instance in history of a call for an international women's movement (Anderson 2000, 81; McFadden 2015, 139). This internationalist position was also the result of Wheeler's own take on Owen's determinism. If human beings were no longer to be the passive victims of their environment, then women, as the main targets of exploitation, had a moral duty to become the driving force and agents of their own improvement. Wheeler's call to action led her to forge strong links with like-minded French socialists, such as Flora Tristan (see Part 9, Chapter 58), Désirée Véret and the editors of the Paris-based feminist publication *La Tribune des femmes* (1832–1834), which had emerged from the Saint-Simonian movement (Gans 1964, 105–118; Mallet 1980, 203–212; Moses 1982, 240–267).]

In conceding to the solicitations of the managers of this Institution, to deliver a Lecture on the: "Social Condition of Women," I have had to struggle against a two-fold obstacle, that of depressed health, and a mind robbed of much of its energy and elasticity by a deep domestic sorrow.[1] And while I feel the difficulty of employing a moderate language, in speaking of the degraded position of my sex, I am on the other hand but too well aware, that the remarks I am about to make, will draw upon me the hate of most men, together with that of the greater portion of the *very sex*, whose *rights* (at the present stage of my existence) I attempt to advocate, with a disinterestedness which finds no rallying point in Self.

But what appears to me the the most cheerless part of my task — I would almost say the "forlorn hope of my enterprise," is that I am doubtful, whether any material good can be effected by this and similar lectures, seeing as I do, the rottenness of our institutions, and those especially which smell of *rank* injustice, in the disabilities set up against half the human race: WOMAN!

Nevertheless I shall attempt this task, stimulated by hope, which some friends entertain, that by so doing I contribute to the support of a truly liberal institution (as I understand this to be) besides, offering an example, which might produce the most beneficial results, if followed up, on similar principles, and acted upon by a competent number of Women.

Should I however fail to awaken attention, in that portion of my audience, most immediately interested in my remarks, (if indeed what concerns all can be said to relate particularly to some,) I shall at least have discharged a debt to society, which its own increasing liberality enables me to pay, by permitting this public appeal!

For myself I confess, that "to die and make no sign" expressive of my horror, indignation and bitter contempt, for that state of society called civilized, which in fact is nothing more than barbarism masked, playing off its brute absurdities under wisdom's guise, (through which however the cloven foot never fails to appear, and more particularly so in the destiny it has assigned to women,) would, I feel, complete the measure of my regret for having lived only to serve and suffer, in my capacity of slave and woman; but the opportunity afforded me now, to leave *one* parting admonition to Society, will greatly mitigate those regrets which I feel, in common with every good mind, when denied the power of being more actively useful.

After this introduction to a question, that may indeed be called a PIVOT, on which all our social interests turn — it would manifest little respect for the intelligence of my hearers, were I to offer any apology for the remarks I am about to make — Men and Women, must be prepared, to find me laying aside that cheat *courtesy*, speaking to facts, and holding the mirror up — Not indeed to nature, (for man's cruel social code has stultified, if not stifled nature in him,) but to some mockery of himself, some distorted image of a goodly nature, warped in all its fair proportions by the evil genius vanity, who condemns him to be his own tormentor, in being the enemy and oppressor of Woman!

Before I proceed further, it may be necessary to say, that I have no antipathy to men but only to institutions; no leaning to the interests of one sex above the other; my object is to deprecate that narrow, stupid policy which divides their interests, and in so doing, makes a pandemonium of our earth, by forcing its inhabitants to be in constant opposition to each other!

Whatever then may be the force of the terms I employ, to decry the monstrous, degraded condition of my sex, I beg to be understood, as speaking, more in *sorrow* than in anger; more with *regret,* for the loss of happiness to both sexes, than to either in particular. It is not in the nature of Woman (when she has strength of character sufficient to preserve original feelings, and reject those which are forced upon her adoption) to wish to mete out undue proportions of good, for one sex above the other—her destiny is to be the mother of both, and nature, whose laws are general and not partial, makes no distinction in a mother's love!

When I advocate the Rights of Women then, I do it under the most perfect conviction, that I am also pleading the cause of men by showing the mighty influence Women hold over the happiness or misery of men themselves, according as they are instructed or ignorant, as they are fettered or free, as they *act on principles, not teamed by rote,* but acquired through the full development of their *own faculties,* not put into movement like machines, or led like beasts of burden, at the capricious will of a master, or in stupid routine, by that *many headed* despot custom! So true it is that, "though men make the law, it is women who mould the manners and morals of society; and according as they are enlightened or ignorant, do they spin the web of human destiny.

It may be difficult for those, who have not studied the complexity of social movement, to conceive how beings, apparently deprived of *all power,* can possess *so much,* particularly as all the ingenuity of short sighted cunning legislators, has been exhausted, not only to make, but keep them passive instruments of man's will; well knowing, that the most effectual means of perpetuating the ignorance, and consequent slavery of men themselves, was to close the door effectually to all progressive improvement in woman, by assigning to her the lowest position in the scale of being, that which connects itself solely with man's mere animal wants!

But how does nature avenge her wrongs, and those of eternal justice, in refusing to cultivate women's intellectual faculties. Men are caught in their own snares; and the ignorance, that they would exclusively confine to women, soon becomes general, and works itself into a very solid chain of fallacies and errors, which ultimately leads opinion; and opinion, whatever be the direction given to it, is always sure to be triumphant!

Woman it is, who by a stupid servile submission to man's arbitrary will, gives stability to all his selfish propensities, and which encountering no *judgment* in their passage to her mind, leaves it the recipient of every foul and monstrous error; thus, like the fabled Pandora, she spreads the contents of the fatal box through all society!

Oh! how contagious is error! *Prejudice* becomes *fixed principle,* omnipotent always, in proportion as its tendency is mischievous. Thus man, by his narrow views of mere personal interest, his jealous monopoly of rights and privileges, his absurd system of *sexual morality*, (as if indeed *this* can be a virtue and *that* a vice, which is not distinctly vice or virtue in every body); his setting up *individual*, as opposed to *general* interests has plunged him in perpetual warfare with his species! Hence the results we read of, and witness: vice, crime, and dissocial anarchy abound, misery, privation and suffering, in every degree that our nature is susceptible of; happiness is lost to all, because security is unknown to any. This alas! must ever be the case, whilst our social system is based on principles of discord, while unity of action is sacrificed, in all our arrangements, and the most striking lessons that experience can offer, are neither attended to nor understood!

But I must not lose time in vain declamations against the vicious tendency of our institutions which have been termed by hireling advocates, "*the perfection of human reason.*" What a satire this, on human reason! As well indeed might we discover perfection in the first rude attempts at sculpture, as in that mass of inconsistency and folly which our laws presents, and which is as much the *caricature* of reason, as the other is of the human face and form.

If reason means any thing, it means a *generalizing* faculty of the human mind, which finds, 'tis true, its source in *instinct*, but its limits only in *experience*. When left uncultivated we lose all the advantages which should distinguish the human from the brute animal, and thus, by *screwing* up human reason to the sticking point *perfection*, all clue has been lost to social happiness.

In the abstract we are willing to admit, that nothing can be good which produces permanently evil effects: the social history of man abundantly shows that nothing is more *perfectly imperfect* and irrational, than laws and institutions which do not recognise the general interest of all mankind.

But let us examine the grounds of disabilities set up by men, to disfranchise half the human race, Women; the effects of this treatment on us and on themselves; and whether indeed there is any essential difference between the sexes, which can authorise the superiority men claim over women? What are the causes of, and who are accountable, for the seeming difference which makes the sum of their plea?

It will, I think appear, that man's own tyranny has created the distinction which he ungenerously sets up as a just cause for its exercise.

FIRST: *Deficiency of muscular strength*, has been deemed a sufficient reason for reducing them to vassalage, not to mention the grosser barbarities, which we know to be the daily practice of men towards beings whose happiness is so inseparably linked with their own, and which the law, *the written law*, that stupendous monument of man's disgrace, not only sanctions but dictates to every known extent, save but the murderous blow, which ends the sufferings of the victim; and for this show of mercy, man's own life is forfeited. All experience proves how little reason men have to triumph, in the base possession of an authority which unnatural violence and usurpation first put into their hands, and which has not, as is presumed, found its excuse in the physical or moral organization of Women. As to to the first charge of bodily weakness, strange enough Monsieur de Chateaubriand, in his Book of martyrs (an appropriate place to find a chapter on

Women,) brings a host of evidence, from travellers and naturalists, to prove that this deficiency of strength in Woman, is nothing but a *civilized disease*, imposed no doubt, on women, to shorten the duration of life, and to provide men with a rapid succession of youthful slaves; in short a civil or civilized way of getting rid of a superfluous number; less shocking though not less cruel, than that resorted to, by other nations which cannot boast the high degree of civilization of our own.[2] So that this supposed organic weakness, which condemns women to be slaves, is by no means borne out by fact. Savage tribes acknowledge it not, and men every where choosing their occupation compel women to drudgery, while they themselves engage in the most pleasurable and profitable pursuits of life.

(*To be continued*)[3]

Notes

1 Anna Doyle Wheeler was left inconsolable after one of her daughters, Henrietta, had died in 1826.
2 François-René de Chateaubriand (1768–1848), French Romantic writer and author of *Les Martyrs ou le triomphe de la religion chrétienne* (1808).
3 It seems that the *British Co-operator* ceased publication shortly afterwards, and that the rest of Anna Doyle Wheeler's lecture was never published.

51

MORAL PHYSIOLOGY; OR, A BRIEF AND PLAIN TREATISE ON THE POPULATION QUESTION (NEW YORK: WRIGHT AND OWEN, 1830), 13–18.

Robert Dale Owen

[Robert Dale Owen (1801-1877) was Anne Caroline and Robert Owen's eldest child. An early supporter of his father's theories, he followed him to New Harmony in 1825. After the community collapsed, he became an American citizen and made a career as a politician in the United States. Though he slowly drifted away from co-operative socialism, he remained a lifelong opponent of slavery, and a defender of women's rights, under the influence of his close friend and associate Frances Wright (see Part 6,Chapter 36). In 1842, he was elected as a Democratic representative for the state of Indiana in the American Congress (Elliott 1964, 331–352). Owen's *Moral Philosophy* is one of the many pamphlets that he published throughout his life. In line with William Thompson's *Practical Directions* (1830, 246–47), he argued for the need to distinguish between sexual intercourse and procreation, mainly to manage the economic pressures of demographic growth, and recommended the use of birth control to that effect. But beyond this somewhat Malthusian line of thought, Robert Dale Owen also insisted that women had an inalienable right to exert control over their bodies without fear of social stigma (Himes 1930; Taylor 1983, 65–66).]

Among the human instincts which contribute to man's preservation and well-being, the instinct of reproduction holds a distinguished rank. It peoples the earth; it perpetuates the species. Controlled by reason and chastened by good feeling, it gives to social intercourse much of its charm and zest. Directed by selfishness, or governed by force, it is prolific of misery and degradation. Whether wisely or unwisely directed, its influence is that of a master principle, that colours, brightly or darkly, much of the destiny of man.

It is sometimes spoken of as a low and selfish propensity; and the Shakers call it a "carnal and sensual passion."* I see nothing in the instinct itself that merits

---

* See "A brief exposition of the principles of the United Society called Shakers," published by Calvin Green and Seth Y. Wells, 1830

such epithets. Like other instincts, it may assume a selfish, mercenary, or brutal character. But, in itself, it appears to me the most social and least selfish of all our instincts. It fits us to give, even while receiving, pleasure; and, among cultivated beings, the former power is ever more highly valued than the latter. Not one of our instincts, perhaps, affords larger scope for the exercise of disinterestedness, or fitter play for the best moral feelings of our race. Not one gives birth to relations more gentle, more humanizing and endearing; not one lies more immediately at the root of the kindliest charities and most generous impulses that honour and bless human nature. Its very power, indeed, gives fatal force to its aberrations; even as the waters of the calmest river, when dammed up or forced from their bed, flood and ruin the country: but the gentle flow and fertilizing influence of the stream are the fit emblems of the instinct, when suffered, undisturbed by force or passion, to follow its own quiet channel.

That such an instinct should be thought and spoken of as a low, selfish propensity, and, as such, that the discussion of its nature and consequences should be almost interdicted in what is called decent society, is to me a proof of the profligacy of the age, and the impurity of the pseudo-civilized mind. I imagine that if all men and women were gluttons and drunkards, they would, in like manner, be ashamed to speak of diet or of temperance.

Were I an optimist, and, as such, had I accustomed myself to judge and to admire the arrangements of nature, I should be inclined to put forward, as one of the most admirable, the arrangement according to which the temperate fulfilling of the dictates of this, as well as of almost all other instincts, confers pleasure. The desire of offspring would probably induce us to perpetuate the species, though no gratification were connected with the act. In the language of the optimist, then, "pleasure is gratuitously superadded." But, instead of pausing to admire arrangements and intentions, the great whole of which human reason seems little fitted to appreciate or comprehend, I content myself with remarking, that this very circumstance (in itself surely a fortunate one, inasmuch as it adds another to the sources of human happiness) has often been the cause of misery; and, from a blessing, has been perverted into a curse. Enjoyment has led to excess, and sometimes to tyranny and barbarous injustice.

Were the reproductive instinct disconnected from pleasure of any kind, it would neither afford enjoyment nor admit of abuse. As it is, the instinct is susceptible of either; just as wisdom or ignorance governs human laws, habits, and customs. It behooves [sic] us, therefore, to be especially careful in its regulation; else what is a great good may become for us a great evil.

This instinct, then, may be regarded in a two-fold light; *first*, as giving the power of reproduction: *secondly*, as affording pleasure.

And here, before I proceed, let me recall to the reader's mind, that it is the province of rational beings to bear UTILITY strictly in view. Reason recognizes as little the romantic and unearthly reveries of Stoicism, as she does the doctrines of health-destroying and mind-debasing debauchery. She reprobates equally a contemning and an abusing of pleasure. She bids us avoid asceticism on the one hand, and excess on the other. In all our enquiries, then, let reason guide us, and let UTILITY be our polar star. I have often had long arguments with my friends, the Shakers,* touching the two-fold light in which the reproductive instinct may be regarded. They commonly stand out stoutly against the propriety of considering it except simply as a means of perpetuating the species; and, apart from that, they deny that it may be regarded as a legitimate source of enjoyment. In this I totally dissent from them. It is a much more noble, because less purely selfish, instinct, than hunger or thirst. It is an instinct that entwines itself around the warmest feelings and best affections of the heart; and, though it differ from hunger and thirst in this, that it may remain ungratified without causing death, I have yet to learn, that because it is *possible*, it is therefore also *desirable*, to mortify and repress it. I admit, to the Shakers, that in the world, profligate and hypocritical as we see it, this instinct is the source of infinite misery; perhaps even, on the whole, of a *balance* of unhappiness: and I always freely admit to them, that if I had to choose between the life of the profligate man of the world and that of the ascetic Shaker, I should not hesitate a moment to prefer the latter. But, for admitting that the most social and kindly of human instincts is sensual and degrading in itself, I cannot. I think its influence moral, humanizing, polishing, beneficent; and that the social education of no man or woman is fully completed without it. Its mortification (though far less injurious than its excess) is yet very mischievous. If it do not give birth to peevishness, or melancholy, or incipient disease, or unnatural practices, at least it almost always freezes and stiffens the character, by checking the flow of its kindliest emotions; and not unfrequently gives to it a solitary, anti-social, selfish stamp.

I deny the position of the Shaker, then, that the instinct is justifiable (if, indeed, it be at all) only as necessary to the reproduction of the species. It is justifiable, in my view, just in as far as it makes man a happier and a better being. It is justifiable, both as a source of temperate enjoyment, and as a means by which the sexes can mutually polish and improve each other.

If a Shaker has read my little book thus far, and cannot reconcile his mind to this idea, he may as well shut it at once. I found all my arguments on the position, that the pleasure derived from this instinct, independent of and totally distinct from, its ultimate object, the reproduction of our race, is good, proper, worth securing and enjoying. I maintain, that its temperate enjoyment is a blessing, both in itself and in its influence on human character.

Upon this distinction of the instinct into its two-fold character, hinges the chief point in the present discussion. It sometimes happens, nay, it happens every day and hour, that mankind obey its impulses, not from any calculation of consequences, but simply from animal impulse. Thus many children that are brought into the world owe their existence, not to deliberate conviction in their parents that

---

* I call them my friends, because, however little I am disposed to accede to all their principles, I have met, from among their body, a greater proportion of individuals who have taken with them my friendship and sympathy, than perhaps from among any other sect or class of men.

their birth was really desirable, but simply to an unreasoning instinct, which men, in the mass, have not learnt either to resist or control.

It is a serious question—and surely an exceedingly proper and important one—whether man can obtain, and whether he is benefitted by obtaining, control over this instinct. IS IT DESIRABLE, THAT IT SHOULD NEVER BE GRATIFIED WITHOUT AN INCREASE TO POPULATION? OR, IS IT DESIRABLE, THAT, IN GRATIFYING IT, MAN SHALL BE ABLE TO SAY WHETHER OFFSPRING SHALL BE THE RESULT OR NOT?

To answer the questions satisfactorily, it would be necessary to substantiate, that such control may be obtained without the slightest injury to the physical health, or violence to the moral feelings; and also, that it should be obtained without any real sacrifice of enjoyment; or, if that cannot be, with as little as possible.

Thus have I plainly stated the subject. It resolves itself, as my readers may observe, into two distinct heads: first, the desirability of such control; and, secondly, its possibility.

In discussing its desirability, I enter a wide field, a field often traversed by political economists, by moralists, and by philosophers, though generally, it will be confessed, to little purpose. This may be, in a great measure, attributed rather to their fear than their ignorance. The world would not permit them to say what they knew. I intend that my readers shall know all that I know on the subject; for I have long since ceased to ask the world's leave to say what I think, and what I believe to be useful to the public. [...]

52

"TO ROBERT OWEN, ESQ.", *CRISIS*, 22 JUNE 1833, 189–190.

"Concordia"

[The anonymous "Concordia" was one of the many women who regularly contributed to the Owenite press, thus bringing feminist issues to a wider audience within the movement (Moriarty 2012, 119; Gleadle 1995, 118). In this letter to the editor of the *Crisis,* which was the leading socialist publication in the 1830s, the author voiced her reservations with Robert Owen's views on marriage reform, which he had first publicly expressed in an 1826 pamphlet, *Oration Containing a Declaration of Mental Independence* (Durieux 2005, 96). While advocating free unions outside the church, Concordia argued, Owen was being too idealistic, as he ignored how difficult it was for a woman to thrive on her own. Without specific directions to guarantee the economic independence of all, and unless men were rapidly trained to see their female companions as their equals, women would remain very much subordinates, even after the advent of the "New Moral World". As Barbara Taylor has argued, Concordia was not alone in voicing such concerns. When she accidentally became pregnant, Frances Wright decided, despite her opposition to the institution of marriage, to marry Gustave Phiquepal d'Arusmont, whom she did not love, in order to protect her unborn child from the shame and stigma of illegitimacy. In that context, Concordia believed that "increased sexual freedom for men would only be compatible with increased social power for women […] when all other sources of sexual inequality had been eliminated. Until then, greater liberty could only become greater libertinism" (Taylor 1983, 180–190).]

DEAR SIR—In the Crisis of May 11th, there is a paragraph which involves considerations so important to society, and to women, that nothing but the hope that either an explanation would have been given, so as materially to modify its meaning, or that some more eloquent pen might have pointed out its error, could have kept me so long silent. I allude to the arrangements for what you term the marriage of those parties who profess the opinions you advocate, and in which I conceive you to be premature, as it has always appeared to me a wise assertion which I have understood you to make, that in all plans relating to the especial domestic economy of the social system, the revolution must be complete, or not at all. Other regulations, of a more isolated nature, may gradually come into operation, as society advances towards truth; but one that so peculiarly involves relative claims or domestic associations, imperatively demands, not only that its propriety should be acknowledged by the public mind, but that its adoption should be the natural result of irresistible circumstances; otherwise the individuals who attempt to brave the public scorn, or to force it to reverse its decrees, only engage in a struggle which will finally end in the destruction of their happiness, and the injury of their cause. I am, of course, limiting my view to what I conceive would be the inevitable effects of such a trial as I understand you to propose, *while society is constituted as at present*; and to such a view I wish you to confine your answer. It is irrelevant to my argument to reason about what may be, or what must be; the inquiry is, how far present circumstances justify the experiment; and I venture to assert, that not only are neither men nor women yet prepared for such a change, but that, for the most part, they do not even understand your meaning. The moral feelings of the former are very far from being in the state which would alone entitle them to the privileges of your millennium; they would only cause your good to be evil-spoken of; and the latter are, generally, too much the slaves of imagination and an unhealthy sensibility—too little accustomed to let judgment lead, to enable us reasonably to expect that they could suddenly submit to its dictates. Bear with me while I say a few plain truths of both parties—not because I have a pleasure in pointing out their moral and intellectual degradation; far, very far from it; but because I would have them examine themselves more honestly; because I feel certain that a clearer and less partial view of their own habits, a more correct knowledge of their own emotions, and a better understanding of the springs by which they are compelled to act, than they at present possess, will alone teach them, that the happiness they seek can never be found in the indulgence of those base and false feelings by which they are now too often governed. I will even assume that those by whom you are surrounded, and who profess so much love for truth, feel frequently in accordance with her kind and wise laws; but it were folly to suppose that even they are divested of all the falsehood which contaminates the old system—folly to close our eyes to the reply which their actions but too plainly give. When feeling shall be pure and lasting, not the fleeting vapour of an excited fancy—when affection shall be the spontaneous result of contemplating what is noble and true —when love shall be produced by congeniality, and maintained by consistency; then, and then only, can the assertion be ventured, that with habits regulated by wisdom, with feelings guided by reason, and with a correct knowledge of themselves, men may be safely trusted with that liberty, which, unless they shall be so regulated, so guided, and so informed, would introduce nothing but misery.

On the other hand, I would observe, that neither are the women who profess to think with you prepared for accepting gracefully, or with advantage to themselves, the change you propose–to them, indeed, it would be no boon; and woe to them should it be received and acted upon as such–woe to them, if in *this* respect they should fancy themselves to have already advanced so far in the career of improvement, or to have acquired such an extensive influence in society generally, as to enable them successfully to oppose its existing customs. It would speedily convince them of their error, and pursue them with its vengeance. These are regulations—it matters not for the purposes of my argument whether right or wrong—which women may not yet set at defiance with impunity. They ever have been, and, while society continues as it is, they ever will be the victims upon whose helpless heads it pour out the vials of its wrath—

"For every woe can pity claim,
Except an erring sister's shame."[1]

Oh! for a voice which should vibrate through each female heart, while I beseech them to consider well what they do— to ponder carefully on the tremendous risk they would encounter. Let them not from enthusiasm, from romance, from a partial survey and application of that which is right only when viewed as a who only good when capable of being applied universally,—let them not overstep those limits which are at present wisely marked out:—but let us hope that happily these prejudices cannot at once be given to the winds. I say *happily*, for remove them now, and from how many a deceived and broken heart should we hear the touching language of the Indian mother, "Let not my child be a girl, for very sad is the life of a woman."[2] It is indeed sad as compared with the state of freedom and happiness for which nature has so eminently fitted her; it is, indeed, sad, owing to the ignorance which so particularly marks all the regulations at concern her. She has been carefully surrounded with prejudices and weaknesses, and has been, and is, more especially the victim of a narrow and selfish system; but unprepared as both parties now are for the change, it will not be sufficient that she is bid to cast away the shackles of society, or to burst the fetters which man has forged. Time and knowledge will alone enable him to unrivet them for her. But it may be contended, "surely these parties have a right to form what association they please." Undoubtedly they would if the consequences could be confined to themselves. It is, however, questionable whether they have a right so far to influence the interests of others as to deprive their children of that protection of which children so situated are deprived. The inconveniences consequent upon their birth are neither few nor trifling. You may tell me that there are hundreds even now, who are so placed; but you will find few who do not feel it to be a positive disadvantage, even though they may have all the care and attention bestowed upon them that paternal affection can devise. There appears a lot to me an inconsistency in attempting to compel ties to live together, unless both desire separation, for nothing is gained over the old system, but there is rather a loss.

In all that I have said, I beg to be understood as not defending the present arrangement, nor as wishing it to continue. I need not be told that it is very, very bad, but if you argue that society must, therefore, be forced to adopt a change, I reply that you will not force it to do so for the *better*, by the insulated experiment you appear to propose. It ought—it must—first experience a great revolution; till that is effected, let not the change be attempted at the expense of woman's tears, of woman's sorrow; do not expose to the fury of the conflict those whose very helplessness should rather raise up for them a shield in every manly heart.

CONCORDIA.

June 1, 1833

Notes

1 Lord Byron, *The Giaour* (1813).
2 Epigraph of Felicia Hemans's poem *Indian Woman's Death-Song* (1828). The quote is itself adapted from James Fenimore Cooper's 1827 novel *The Prairie* (vol. 1, 1852 edition.), 152.

53

LECTURES ON THE MARRIAGES OF THE PRIESTHOOD OF THE OLD IMMORAL WORLD, DELIVERED IN THE YEAR 1835, BEFORE THE PASSING OF THE NEW MARRIAGE ACT (LEEDS: J. HOBSON [1835] 1840), 3–14.

Robert Owen

[Delivered in 1835 and later compiled in pamphlet form, these lectures became the most notorious of Robert Owen's writings on the question of marriage, and were reprinted at least four times over the next few years (Taylor 1983, 173–174). The text expanded upon earlier publications on the same topic, such as the *Oration Containing a Declaration of Mental Independence* (1826). Since the mid-1820s, Owen had become increasingly critical of marriage, most likely due to the unravelling of his own relationship with his wife Anne Caroline. Using arguments seemingly borrowed from Godwin's *Enquiry Concerning Political Justice* (1793), he claimed that except in rare instances of genuine affection, the prevalence of arranged unions reduced women to the legal property of their husbands, thus locking them into a state of near-serfdom (Kolmerten 1998, 18). While not going as far as calling for the abolition of marriage itself, he recommended that both parties be equal in wealth, condition and education, and bound by true feelings of love (Durieux 2005, 96). Owen's critique became much more radical over the following decade, in part due to a growing demand for marriage reform. Since the mid-eighteenth century, only the unions blessed by the Church of England were granted legal status, to the dismay of Nonconformists and freethinkers (Taylor 1983, 54). However, in supporting non-denominational marriages and the right to divorce, Owen was also attacking the ideal of the nuclear family, in direct opposition to Christian teachings, Anglican or otherwise. As a priesthood-sanctioned institution, the family unit not only perpetuated religious superstition and the lie of unnatural, arranged unions. With the transmission of private property at its heart, it also fostered selfish interests to the detriment of community feelings, thereby constituting a vehicle of social inequality and an obstacle to true progress. By contrast, natural unions based on shared feelings of love and affection would flourish within the communities of the "New Moral World", thus uniting all human beings into one family (Taylor 1983, 55).]

LECTURE FIRST.

Mr. Owen commenced his Lecture, by stating that in that morning's Discussion a lady had brought forward three questions, which were put by the celebrated Chateubriand [sic] in a work he had written, but which was not to be published until after his death.[1] The questions showed the anxiety in the minds of the Statesmen of the world about the present state of society, which they were satisfied could not much longer be bolstered up.

The first question asked is: "What shall be the *new* state of society ?" What! does one of the leading ministers of France, and a high Tory — does he ask such a question as this; and a question, too, that shows that he and his friends have made up their minds that a change must take place? Without entering further into the subject now, I will merely say, that the new state of society will be entirely different from the present state, and will be based on principles totally distinct. I hope our friends, in investigating our plans, will make no attempt to unite the two states of society. I have said again and again, that they never can amalgamate in any proportion, and it will, therefore, be useless to draw inferences on the new system from any thing we see around us.

The second question is, "How shall women arrive at legal emancipation?" Up to the present day, society has proceeded upon the principle of classes, bodies or corporations, and of distinct families. The third is: "What *appearance* will society present when these regulations shall *no longer exist* and women become INDIVIDUAL, as is the TENDENCY that they should become?"

I rejoice that these questions have been put, and that too by so eminent and intelligent an individual; they go to confirm my own impressions on the subject.

In my previous lectures I have stated, that the chief of the Satanic institutions over the world, though somewhat varied in name and form, are the priesthood; the lawyers and magistrates; the military; the unnatural and artificial union of the sexes; individual and national competition and contest; and the single-family, or universally disuniting arrangements of society; and the metal, or any other medium liable to change in value, for the circulation of wealth. And I then hastily glanced at some of the leading evils necessarily arising from the priesthood, the laws and magistracy, and the military. I now proceed to notice, in the same hasty manner, some of the remainder of these Satanic institutions, or institutions of moral evil; and first of the unnatural or artificial union of the sexes. It seems that many of the readers of the *New Moral World*, many of my usual audience, as well as a large portion of the public, are much opposed to any thing being said openly, to a mixed assembly, on the subject of marriage, because, say they, we are none of us prepared to enter upon the consideration of this delicate subject. The disciples of our system say: "We readily acknowledge the truth of the three fundamental errors of moral evil, and the three fundamental principles of moral good. We fully understand the facts whence they are derived, and consider the developement [sic] of them, in this plain intelligible form, the greatest boon that man has yet acquired from his intellectual faculties. To know the cause of evil and of good among the human race is the most valuable knowledge that can be given to man; it is to know the *cause of misery and of happiness*: in fact, it is to learn how to make the earth a pandemonium or a paradise." All this the disciples of the system readily admit; but they add: "What has all this to do with the present marriages of the world, seeing that the prejudices of the human race are so deeply rooted in favour of their continuance?"

When I hear these sentiments repeated time after time, by many who have long professed themselves disciples of our system, and some who are esteemed the most intelligent among them, I am obliged to say, as I have often done, greatly to the annoyance of those who deemed themselves sufficiently advanced in a knowledge of the new system to be the experienced instructors of others: "You really know nothing yet about the system which you are teaching to others." And upon this occasion, as we are now about to lay a solid foundation in the minds of those who are to take an active part in our future proceedings, it is incumbent on me to declare to you, that no parties can be considered to understand correctly or practically any part of the system which I contemplate, unless they know how to apply the third fundamental principle of moral good, and to trace the third fundamental error of moral evil to practice, and also to carry them out through all their ramifications into the domestic and public arrangements of society, and to trace the endless train of moral evil, and consequent misery, which the present marriage system in all countries necessarily engenders.

Surely none of you can imagine that I decided upon relinquishing a situation, which was perhaps the most enviable that man could hold under the existing vicious system of the world, bringing me in, at the same time, many thousands a-year, merely that I might instruct my suffering fellow men in a few theoretical truths, which of themselves could never be applied to useful practice, much less to emancipate the human race from ignorance, sin and misery? Or that I gave up a situation in which I could effect much practical good, to teach *some truths*, and *refrain from teaching others*; to flatter the prejudices of any man, woman, or child; when the latter truths were essential to effect the great good intended, and which could never be attained until all ancient prejudices were removed? Or do any of you imagine that I meet you here to pander to your prejudices upon important subjects, in which your permanent happiness is involved? No, my friends; I have made the sacrifice of extensive wealth; of an extraordinary personal consideration among the great and good ones of the earth, as they are now called; that, being freed from all such shackles, I might attain the highest elevation and the most enviable condition to which a human being can aspire; that is, to be at full liberty to speak to the world a new language of truth, unmixed with error, upon subjects of the most vital interest to all of human kind, and to send forth these truths, without fear of man, to the great ones of the earth; to emperors and kings, and to the learned and wise, as they are called, until they shall attend to them, become conscious of their truth and high value, and shall willingly adopt them.

Think you that I am to be withheld from this course because a few or many of my readers or hearers are alarmed at new, and to them astounding truths? truths essential to be known and publicly acted upon for the eternal well-being and happiness of the human race.

Those who have imbibed these impressions little indeed know the early determinations of my mind, and the thoughts which have long been within me. I tell you now, I am not teaching in the midst of the metropolis of the British Empire to please my hearers, flatter their prejudices, and live upon their ignorance. I am purposely come among you to oppose all your oldest, strongest, and most inveterate prejudices; to stir them up from their *lowest foundations*, and to withdraw them, root and branch, out of your constitutions, or to sacrifice all that man holds dear in the attempt.

You are prepared, you say, to give up some of your old errors and prejudices; but you wish I would not touch upon others, and especially upon the present married state.

What would you think of the wisdom of those who were afflicted with some dreadful disorder, hitherto deemed incurable, saying to a physician, who had happily discovered a certain and effectual cure for it: "We are indeed diseased from head to foot; we feel the malady most excruciating from morning to night and from night to morning, but, pray, dear good doctor, do not touch this sad and incurable disorder, it is too bad to be interfered with ; but you may, if you please, cure our toothache, or one of our little fingers that occasionally gives us some pain!"

Such is your state and condition ; and knowing what different beings you will be when you shall be restored to sound health, I shall disregard your sickly or feverish complainings, and proceed to effect your cure.

And I now tell you, and, through you, the population of all the nations of the earth, that the present marriages of the world, under the system of moral evil in which they have been devised and are now contracted, are the sole cause of all the prostitution, of all its incalculable grievous evils, and of more than one half of all the vilest and most degrading crimes known to society. And that, until you put away from among you and your children for ever, *this accursed thing*, you will never be in a condition to become chaste or virtuous in your thoughts and feelings, or to know what real happiness is. For now almost all who are in the married state are daily and hourly practising the deepest deception, and living in the grossest prostitution of body and mind; and misery is multiplied by it beyond any of your feeble powers, in your present irrational state, to estimate; for it extends directly and indirectly through all the ramifications of life. Yes! your fathers, mothers, brothers, sisters, husbands, wives, and children, are one and all suffering most grievously from this opposition to nature ; from this ignorance of your own organization ; from this unnatural crime ; which destroys the finest feelings and best powers of the species, by changing sincerity, kindness, affection, sympathy and pure love, into deception, envy, jealousy, hatred and revenge. It is a Satanic device of the Priesthood to place and keep mankind within their slavish superstitions, and to render them subservient to all their purposes; and until you can acquire fortitude and moral courage to look this subject fairly in the face and meet it fully on the ground of common sense and right reason, and can show it to be, as it is, in direct opposition to the laws of your organization, it is eminently calculated to make you, in the greatest extreme, ignorantly selfish, wretchedly vicious, and most unhappy. And while this evil is suffered to remain you cannot reasonably expect to advance one single step in practice in the right road to real virtue and happiness. There is, therefore, no hope whatever, for you until you acquire sufficient strength of mind to overcome this evil, and openly denounce it both in principle and practice. It is now ascertained that you have not been organized to feel or not to feel at your pleasure. You, therefore, commit a crime against the everlasting laws of your nature when you say that you will "love and cherish" what your organization may compel you to dislike and to loathe, even in a few hours. Away then with this eminently false delicacy and sickly appetite for truths which are the most essential to the progressive improvement and permanent happiness of our species!

The species, man, as approaching towards a rational nature, is yet in its cradle; and if we do not soon remove it from this infant condition it will be rocked too long, and the reasoning powers of man will be not only of no benefit to him, but a grievous evil, and place him, relatively to the enjoyment of happiness, greatly below the majority of terrestrial animals.

Not speak of the present marriage state and its endless crimes: why what absurdity yet remains in the public mind! Not to speak and expose the greatest of the practical sources of vice and misery! As well may we at once close our eyes and put a seal upon our lips, that we may not see or speak of the greatest deceptions, the most abandoned wickedness, and the cause of the most extended calamities known to the human race. The time is now past for those who have a desire to ameliorate the condition of the human race upon everlasting principles of truth, to pander to the prejudices of any portion of mankind; much less to this prejudice in favour of artificial marriage and unnatural union of the sexes: of a prejudice which is one of the deepest seated in human society, and the most fatal to the happiness of men and women from their birth to their death.

Under this baneful crime against nature, man must continually degenerate in his physical, mental, and moral powers, as he has done during many past ages, in proportion as this crime has been extended, and made, through the influence of increasing wealth and superstition, more and more unnatural and artificial. The inhabitants of the British Empire, said to be the most advanced of modern nations, although, through the progress of science, the most powerful in all the means requisite to insure the highest physical intellectual and moral qualities to every member of its extensive and widely-spread population, are greatly inferior, individually, in all these respects, to the individuals of former times, who possessed greater physical powers, more intellectual strength and vigour, and more exalted notions of public virtue, and of truth and sincerity, then are to be found in modern times. When we look at the ancient inhabitants of Greece and Rome, and compare the present race of men to them, we find the comparison greatly to the disadvantage of ourselves. It is true we have scientific powers which they had not; but on these we are accustomed to place too much reliance. We, the said-to-be-envied of the world, have gradually degenerated, through all ranks and degrees, into mere pedlars and panderers for money gains, or some tomfoolery of name or personal distinction, which makes the individual appear only the more conspicuously irrational to those who understand the nature and real character of man. And instead of natural connexions being formed between those whose sympathies or qualities of mind and body are in harmony with each other, wealth, family, titles, or privileges of some kind, have been the artificial uniting motive, in opposition to natural desires or pure and chaste feelings.

It is full time that this increasing degeneration of the species, bodily and mental, should cease, and that the natural association of the sexes should be resumed, but improved by all the experience of the past.

Previous to the great change which we have ultimately in view, relative to the new position in which the sexes will be placed, many highly necessary arrangements and provisions must be made, to render these changes practicable and beneficial. For in the present irrational condition of the human race relative to the association of the sexes and to the single-family arrangements, to mix the two most opposing principles and practices together, would be to make the present confusion of ideas and feelings and conduct ten times more perplexed and irrational.

Many of our friends have, perhaps naturally, with their very limited views of the great changes which must be made in passing from a state of moral evil to moral good, supposed that the principles and practices of the one state were intended or could be made to assimilate or amalgamate with the other. Yet, had they any clear conception of these two systems, they would, at once, discover that the greatest of all impossibilities will be to unite the practice of the one with any part of the practice of the other. We have now the pure unadulterated system of moral evil, both in principle and in practice, producing a perfect terrestrial pandemonium. Were any of our friends to attempt, individually, to introduce any of our principles and practices of moral good into this pandemonium of single-family feuds and mal-arrangements, they would increase, ten-fold, the evils which now reign triumphant throughout almost all the families of mankind. But this now most interesting of all questions, at this crisis of our proceedings, must not longer be left in doubt or mystery, or in a state liable to be misunderstood by the friends and of moral good.

Therefore, *let it now be known to all*, that when the mind of man shall be regenerated, and he shall enter upon the state of moral good, in an association of sufficient numbers to support and protect itself, and its rising generation, against the ignorance and consequent prejudices of moral evil; that CELIBACY, beyond the period plainly indicated for its termination by nature, (although esteemed a high virtue under the reign of moral evil,) will be known to be a great crime, necessarily leading to disease of body and mind, and to unnatural thoughts, feelings, and conduct, and to every kind of falsification of our real impressions sympathies and sensations, all of which are of nature's most wise creation, in perfect accordance with the superior organization which it has given to man over the inferior animals.

Also, in the present state of moral evil, it is esteemed a high and superior virtue to be chaste, according to the unnatural notions and imaginations of a most degraded order of men, called the Priesthood, who, in various parts of the world, have taken upon themselves to direct the opinions and feelings of the human race, as though they were themselves divinities, and could by their fiat of absurdities and almost ceasless [sic] irrational ravings, reverse the laws of earthly things, and change the everlasting decrees of that universal and hitherto incomprehensible power which "directs the atom and controls the aggregate of nature." This order of men, to whose oppressions of mind and body no rational being will longer submit, have chosen to make chastity to consist in having sexual intercourse in accordance only with *their* most fantastic whims and unnatural notions; and whom they thus discordantly join, *"let"* say they *"no man put asunder!"* This human decree of the Priesthood is the origin of all prostitution, and of all its endless crimes, evils, and sufferings; of all impure and unchaste thoughts and desires, and of all the known and unknown, and almost unimagined multiplied crimes and miseries of the present married life; and has been the most unnatural grievous misconception of all the crudities which the various insanities of the Priesthood have engendered. They have ever been totally ignorant of the laws of man's organization, and they have been governed in all their proceedings by the imbecility of infancy or the ravings of a disordered intellect or distempered imagination.

Had they not been thus ignorant, they never would have supposed that pure and undefiled chastity consisted in men and women abiding by *their* bidding. Chastity is a feeling and sympathy mysteriously implanted in human nature, and exists only between the sexes when in their intercourse they feel a sincere and genuine affection for each other: and this delightful union of heart and mind the Priesthood never gave by their unhallowed and grossly absurd ceremonies, which they have invented for their gain, and called marriages; nor do they yet know how to create these pure affections, or to retain them when created.

Real genuine chastity is a sentiment and a feeling far too elevated and refined for their ignorant and gross conceptions, or thay [sic] could never have artificially tied bodies in their bonds of wedlock, and then said: "Be you united, mind and body, for life ; or be miserable in this world and everlastingly damned in the next." What a sacrilege of the best and finest sympathies of our nature! What ignorance of the organization of man and woman ! What horrid sacrifice of the happiness of the human life!

In the New Moral World no such destruction of common sense; of our most refined and best feelings; of our just and natural rights and privileges of our openhearted sincerity; and of our highest enjoyment and purest happiness, will ever be required or permitted. No; for the unerring laws of our nature, that guide which, when referred to, never deceives us, will alone direct the mode by which the association of the sexes shall be maintained, as well as every other arrangement for the well ordering and conducting the whole business of human life; but, assuredly, the present marriages of the Priesthood of the world, the source of so much crime and misery, will form no part of it.

Celibacy is a virtue of the Priesthood of the world, but it is a vice against Nature ; and, I ask, shall Nature or the Priesthood prevail?

When you and the public shall have had time to digest this highly important and deeply interesting subject, I will return to it, and expose, in detail, more of its innumerable crimes and miseries.

In the meantime let no one misunderstand me. The present system of society over the world is founded on notions of unmixed falsehood, leading, of necessity, to every absurdity and evil in practice; a perfect unmixed system in principle and practice of moral evil, most admirably calculated to give a false direction to all the higher qualities and best feelings of our nature, and to render the whole mass of the population of the world a compound of ignorant selfishness, of folly and absurdity, of counteraction and division, of vice and crime, and of sickening disappointment to all superior minds, and of grievous misery to all: and that the New Moral system is the reverse of it in all these particulars, and so opposite in principle and practice that it will be for ever utterly impossible to bend or blend the one to conform to the other. The world must have the whole of the one or of the other.

Now, my friends, I have just placed before you the last obstacle in our way, and the most difficult to be overcome. In 1818, I proclaimed that ignorance and error, crime and folly, had their source in the different religions of the world. I was at that time, perhaps, the most popular man in the world. No daily newspaper then refused to publish, however long, the addresses delivered by me in London.[2] I well knew I was opposing all the stronger prejudices of the world; and that when I stated what I did on the subject of religion, I was casting away from me all the popularity which I then possessed; but which I considered then, and I consider it now, not worth one straw, except when expressed in favour of truth.

I was then preparing the public mind for the principles I advocated; and it has taken me ever since, a period of seventeen years, to prepare it sufficiently for the introduction of the subject of the present evening's lecture. We are now fairly and fully before the world, and we must keep our position. I now denounce the priestly marriages of the old world, as I then denounced religions.

Do not mistake me, my friends. Were you to attempt to unite any parts of the two systems, you would be sure to fail. When you go into the world, tell your friends and neighbours, of all I have said; but tell them also that we shall reserve the practice of these principles till we are so situated, in the New Moral World, as to have a society of our own; when, and not till then, we shall be prepared to put on the marriage garment.

Can you go away, knowing all this, and not try to change the existing state of things ? We are now forming an association to effect this change soon, and which, I hope, will spread over the world.[3] I care not what some individuals may think of our little nucleus here; I hope we shall soon show them that we are the grain of mustard-seed, which shall flourish and spread until it covers the whole world.

Notes

1 François-René de Chateaubriand, *Mémoires d'outre-tombe* (1849–1850).
2 It was actually in 1817 that Owen publicly criticized established religions. See *Letter published in the London Newspapers of July 30th, 1817* (1817); *Letter published in the London Newspapers of August 9th, 1817* (1817), and *Address delivered at the City of London Tavern, on Thursday, August 14th* (1817). Reprinted in Claeys 1993, 156–194.
3 The Association of All Classes of All Nations, founded on 1 May 1835.

54

"ON THE NECESSARY CO-OPERATION OF BOTH SEXES FOR HUMAN ADVANCEMENT", *NEW MORAL WORLD*, 26 AUGUST 1843, 65.

"M.A.S."

[Published in 1843, this letter to the editor of the *New Moral World* is representative of the ambiguous response to the "woman question" within the Owenite movement. Though the anonymous male author did not deny the reality of women's oppression, he cast doubt on the possibility, and relevance even, of female agency, arguing that their emancipation would follow naturally from the general improvement of mankind under a co-operative regime. Throughout the late 1820s and 1830s, many all-female institutions emerged among British socialist circles. In 1833, the Practical Moral Union of the Women of Great Britain and Ireland tried to unite women of all classes in the fight for female suffrage. In the eyes of many, including Owen, such separatist institutions were merely a distraction from the true aims of co-operation, which commanded a union of interests, for all classes of all nations (Taylor 1983, 82).]

It is evident to all reflecting minds, that the great truths now in process of promulgation, are destined to create such a change in public opinion, as must not only revolutionize all existing institutions, but will ultimately force their reconstruction on entirely new bases.

Seeing that the many political changes and revolutions that have successively taken place in all times and nations, have hitherto failed to attain their true object, viz., social prosperity and happiness, I would here suggest one main cause of such failures, and beg the consideration of an untried remedy for the prevention (in as far as it can be efficiently applied) of like disappointments for the future.

Let not the reader anticipate any Utopian speculations, or fear that his imagination is about to be racked with any new chimera or fanciful project. No! It is simply with a view to induce WOMEN to prepare themselves for co-operation with their brethren in the cause of truth, and to obtain their assistance in a gradual re-organization of social affairs, that I have been requested to offer to the readers of the *New Moral World* (women more especially) a series of short essays on this important subject.

The part hitherto taken by women in all onward moves has, when not indeed oposive, been but partial and indirect; the advance effected has been correspondently slow and unstable; and if, at the approaching crisis, they fail to take their stand, unitedly and consistently maintaining their rights, and co-operating with men for the establishment of social and political justice, their own emancipation, and that of their race, will be very materially, if not incalculably, retarded;—then once more will the patriot's hopes be disappointed—once more will philanthropy have to mourn the protraction of human misery—and once more will nature smile derisively, if again she hear her sons declare their independence, whilst her daughters are in chains.

It has been confidently asserted, and with reason, that "the position of woman determines that of the race;" but for her retrograde influence, men would be far more advanced than they now are: there is a natural tendency in inferior minds to draw down others, for sympathy, to their standard; and, independent of social intercourse, the ties of relationship must ever effectually prevent the *isolated* advancement of either sex. Vain was America's boasted declaration —as vain her free institutions and youthful energies!—her very spirit is crushed, and her reason held in thralldom, by the sectarian serpent that subtilely [sic] luxuriates in the uncultivated, stagnant recesses of the female brain.

It would seem that men, in general, are blind to the recoil and baneful effects of their own injustice: they see not that slavery is incompatible with happiness, both as regards the enslaver and the enslaved; and that in woman's degradation their own is inevitably involved.

All that can be reasonably urged respecting the injustice and the impolicy of maintaining the present class divisions of society, as wealth producers and wealth consumers, may apply with equal force, and as drawing, if possible, worse consequences in its train, to the relative position of the sexes in society. Wealth has oppressed poverty, and brought on destitution; physical strength has taken advantage of relative weakness, and induced mental imbecility. The rich consider and treat the poor as a distinct race, formed but for their use, and supported only by their wealth: and even so do men regard women as inferior beings, born for their amusement, and incapable alike of reason or self-support. The principle is in both cases unjust, and its origin alike barbarous; but as oppressors have never yet been found wise or good enough to unyoke their victims, so neither will men, of themselves, be found possessed of sufficient enlightenment and justice to emancipate woman from her present thraldom.

In both instances the movement must proceed from beneath, and the bonds be burst asunder by the force of an upward, irresistible mental heave.

"For a nation to be free," says La Fayette, "it is sufficient that she wills it;"—and woman, once willing her freedom, is no longer a slave.[1]

But it is not by indignant invective, or useless re- pining, that an enlightened mind would seek to gain its end. Women would do well to effect their mental emancipation, before they proceed to the dissolution of their legalized bonds. At present, they should rather learn to maintain their rights, than seek to obtain them; lest any concession from men being implied, the power of male re-usurpation be still retained.

Laws cannot suddenly make equal those whom they have gradually made unequal; education is the great equalizer, and time is requisite for the fulfilment of its end. It is not now in man's power to effect woman's deliverance. Intellectual justice can alone make her free.

Let women acquaint themselves with truth—the press is open to them—the will alone is wanting to learn—and when satisfied as to the means of effecting their object, let them advance, with fixed, firm, united purpose, nothing daunted or doubting, from individual considerations, to the attainment of their goal —equality of rights and reciprocity of duties.

Seeing that to excite pity is degrading, as it implies infirmity of purpose, and inefficiency for its attainment, let none complain of injustice which themselves permit; but rather seek to prevent its continuance, by taking an individual interest in public affairs. Let them endeavour to think, read, and interest themselves, in the events of the present juncture. A new life, a new aim, a new impulse would thus be excited, for which no temporary personal advantage, however great, could compensate, or consequent misfortune destroy.

Let them learn of philosophy the inevitableness of the past—of innate philanthropy their duties for the future. The former will teach them to forgive, if not to forget, the wrongs they have sustained. The latter will bid them throw off their mental lethargy, and prepare for an active and benignant influence over the events of futurity.

M.A.S.

Notes

1 "... pour qu'une nation aime la liberté, il suffit qu'elle la connaisse; et que, pour qu'elle soit libre, il suffit qu'elle le veuille", Marquis de La Fayette, "Projet de Déclaration des Droits de l'Homme présenté par La Fayette à l'Assemblée Nationale (Séance du 11 juillet 1789)", in Philippe Buchez and Pierre-Célestin Roux-Lavergne, *Histoire parlementaire de la Révolution française* (1834) vol. 2, 93–95. The quote was popularised in England by Thomas Paine's *Rights of Man* (1791), 17: "For a nation to love liberty, it is sufficient that she knows it; and to be free, it is sufficient that she wills it".

Part 9

WAR, PEACE AND INTERNATIONALISM

Even before the emergence of the First International (the International Workingmen's Association), in the early 1860s, ideals of global, working-class solidary were pioneered in the Owenite movement (Weisser 1975, 53–57; Claeys 1988, 245). Despite Robert Owen himself aiming to unite "all classes of all nations" rather than only the proletariat, he had championed a global outlook from the onset. Since his New Lanark experiment was meant to be imitated universally, it was crucial for his message to be brought to the widest audience possible (see Chapter 55) More generally, in the aftermath of the Napoleonic Wars, he was keen to present his co-operative, communitarian schemes as an alternative to the divisive forces of European competition, be they economic, political or military (Gurney 1988, 543–544). Based on the belief that a fair economic system would inevitably limit the risk of social chaos, Owen's early writings provided "a theory of how society could be organised for the peaceful purpose of production and the satisfaction of needs rather than the destructive aims of war" (Claeys 1988, 236).

Drawing inspiration from the Enlightenment-era idea of cosmopolitanism as the vehicle for universal prosperity and peace (Hume [1772] 1994; Smith [1776] 2008, 196–197), Owen was certain that once the economic and moral superiority of his system would be acknowledged, former enemy states would be superseded by a global federation of harmonious communities (Schlereth 1977; Claeys 1989, 24). Therefore, the wish to "facilitate universal intercourse, so as to gradually destroy the idea of foreign, not only in word but in feeling" became a firm fixture within Owenism, and the movement consequently had a strong international dimension (*Proceedings of the Third Cooperative Congress* 1832, cited in Claeys 1988, 247).

In America, Owen's supporters remained politically active even after the first generation of socialist communities collapsed in the late 1820s (see Chapter 6). Some fifteen years later, the Association of All Classes of All Nations (AACAN) opened two branches in New York and Philadelphia. Many British Owenites also favoured emigration to the New World as a response to their leader's personal hold over the AACAN and the Rational Society. These ventures were part of the wider, mostly Fourierite communitarian revival of the 1840s, and included Thomas Hunt's community of Equality, Wisconsin (Chapter 59) as well as various attempts to establish socialist settlements in locations as remote as Venezuela and New South Wales (*New Moral World*, 1 February 1840; Claeys 1986; Chase 2011).

Owenism also spread into Continental Europe, and especially France, where Owen's writings had been translated as early as 1816 for the *Bibliothèque britannique* – later known as the *Bibliothèque universelle* – a celebrated collection of British sources edited by the Swiss brothers Marc-Auguste and Charles Pictet. Due to the efforts of international go-betweens, such as Anna Doyle Wheeler and Hugh Doherty (Chapter 58), bridges were built between British and French socialists. Many French radicals saw themselves as Owenites, including Joseph Rey, Jules Gay and to a lesser extent Étienne Cabet (Claeys 1988, 251; Pilbeam 2013, 23; Siméon 2020). There was also good communication with German and Italian socialists, as London acted as a magnet for exiled Continental radicals like Wilhelm Weitling in the context of the European revolutions. More specifically, the Owenites were instrumental in the founding of early internationalist groups such as the Democratic Friends of All Nations and the Fraternal Democrats (Chapter 61). Both organisations were joined by the likes of Henry Hetherington, George Jacob Holyoake and John Weston, who later attended the First International's inaugural meeting at Saint Martin's Hall, London, in September 1864.

Though they eschewed any attempt to unite all classes in favour of working-class co-operation alone, the Democratic Friends and the Fraternal Democrats were "considerably indebted to Owenite formulations of class identity. The recognition of class antagonism and the promotion of working-class consciousness did not in these groups inevitably lead all to calls for violent revolution by the mere proletariat, only to greater national and international working-class unity" (Claeys 1988, 252–253).

55
"MEMORIAL OF ROBERT OWEN, OF NEW LANARK, IN SCOTLAND, TO THE ALLIED POWERS ASSEMBLED IN CONGRESS, AT AIX-LA-CHAPELLE, ON BEHALF OF THE WORKING CLASSES, 1818", REPRINTED IN *MANIFESTO OF ROBERT OWEN...* (LONDON: EFFINGHAM WILSON, 1840), 31–41.

Robert Owen

[The aftermath of the Napoleonic Wars and the wish to secure political and economic peace in that context greatly informed the maturation of Owen's thought in the years 1815–1820. This was accompanied by various attempts to reach the widest audience possible. The doors of New Lanark were thrown open to the public; at the same time, Owen took part in innumerable lectures and meetings throughout Britain. These were followed by several foreign tours, where he hoped to garner further support. In 1818, Owen journeyed to the Continent in the company of his business partner John Walker and Swiss scientist and author Marc-Auguste Pictet, who had published the first French translation of *A New View of Society* in 1816 (Rilliet and Cassaigneau, 1995). After visiting the experimental schools of Emmanuel von Fellenberg and Johann Heinrich Pestalozzi in Switzerland, Owen made his way to the Congress of Aix-la-Chapelle, a follow-up to the Congress of Vienna (1814–1815) meant to further the balance of power in Europe. Upon his arrival, Owen handed out a *Memorial* outlining his system to various diplomatic representatives of Britain, Austria, Prussia, Russia and France. The goal was to create perpetual peace through the introduction of his co-operative economic system. But Owen's efforts were to no avail, due to widespread opposition to the anti-aristocratic and anti-capitalistic stance of his communitarian schemes (Volwiler 1922; Hasselman 1971, 289; Siméon 2017, 110).]

THAT your Memorialist has addressed a Memorial to the Governments of Europe and America, on subjects deeply interesting to the working classes and to all ranks in these countries.

That he has presented the said Memorial to many of the European governments; and will take the earliest opportunity to lay it before the remaining governments of Europe, and before the states of America.

That the said Memorial was a preliminary one, being intended to call the attention of the civilized world—

First:—To the new and extraordinary effects produced by the introduction of improved scientific power into the manufactures of Europe and America; and which has already materially affected the value of labour in these countries, and the health, comfort, and happiness of the working classes employed in manufactures. And,

Second:—To the overwhelming influence which experience has now given to the adult part of society over the rising generation, to educate them, by the arrangement of new circumstances around them from infancy, to become the best characters for their own happiness and the permanent good of the community to which they may belong.

That your Memorialist stated his willingness to develop the details of his experience on these important subjects, to all or to any of the governments whom he addressed.

That, as the unaided deliberations of governments are necessarily slow, and the people are daily injured by the effects of the new scientific power, and the want of a well-digested system of training and instruction, from infancy, applicable to every child of the poor, he deems it his duty, with a view to facilitate and accelerate the execution of an object which the allied powers must have so much at heart, and in which their immediate interest is so deeply involved, to submit to Congress, as he now does, preliminary explanations of the three general results contained in the Appendix to the Memorial, and which he divides into three parts.

PART FIRST.

The first general result was as follows :—

That the period is arrived, when the means are become obvious, by which, without force or fraud of any kind, riches may be mated in such abundance, and so advantageously all, that the wants and desires of every human being may be more than satisfied.

In consequence, the dominion of wealth, and the evils arising from the desire to acquire and accumulate riches, are on the point of terminating.

GENERAL PRELIMINARY EXPLANATIONS OF THIS RESULT.

The general proof of the truth of this statement shall be drawn from the changes which have occurred within the last quarter of a century, or since the introduction of Messrs. Watt and Arkwright's improved mechanism, first into the manufactures of Britain, and subsequently into those of other countries.[1]

At the commencement of the period mentioned, a much larger proportion of the population of Great Britain was occupied in agriculture than in manufactures; and it is probable that the inhabitants of the British isles then experienced a greater degree of substantial prosperity than they had attained before, or than they have enjoyed since.

The reasons are obvious:

— The new manufacturing system, had then attained that point which gave the highest value to manual labour, compared with the price of the necessaries and comforts of life, which it was calculated to afford; and it had not yet introduced the demoralizing effects which soon afterwards began to emanate from it.

At this period, then, the manual and scientific productive powers of Great Britain were sufficient to create a degree of prosperity which placed all her population in a state of comfort, at least equal, if not superior, to that of the inhabitants of any other part of the world. The value of her national funds was higher in 1792 than at any other period, and pauperism was but little known.

The productive powers which created this high degree of prosperity, consisted of temperate manual labour, and mechanical and other scientific power, which had been gradually and very slowly accumulating through the previous periods of her history.

The manual labour was chiefly performed by men, unaided by the premature exertions of children; and its whole amount in 1792, may be estimated at about that of one fourth of the population, which was then about fifteen millions.

The scientific power at the same period was probably about three times the amount of its labour; in which case

The manual labour would be	3,750,000
And the scientific	11,250,000
And the aggregate productive power	15,000,000
The population was also	15,000,000

Thus the aggregate productive power and the population 1792 appear to have been equal, or as one to one.

The introduction, however, of the improved steam-engine and spinning-machinery, with the endless variety of mechanical and other scientific inventions to which they gave rise, and which have been applied to almost all the useful purposes and ornamental arts of life, have created a change in the productive powers of Great Britain, of the most extraordinary amount.

Manual labour has been increased, by calling into action the unceasing long daily labour of women and children in manufactures, and, in consequence, its whole amount may be now estimated at about that of one third of the population, which, in 1817, was calculated to be eighteen millions—or in twenty-five years to have increased three millions; and this estimate will give six millions for the present manual power.

But since the introduction of Arkwright and Watts's improved mechanism there has been a real addition made in Great Britain to the power of creating wealth, equal to that of much more than two hundred millions of stout, active, well-trained labourers; or to more than ten times the present population of the British isles [sic], or than thirty times the manual labour which they now supply for the production of wealth.

The following changes have then occurred from 1792 to 1817.

The population increased from fifteen millions to	18,000,000
The manual labour form one fourth of fifteen millions to one third of eighteen millions, or to	6,000,000
The new-created productive power, from 1792 to 1817 will be under-stated at two hundred millions, say	200,000,000
While the old scientific power, if but three times the manual power in 1792, will be as stated.	11,250,000
Which together makes the aggregate productive power, in 1817	217,250,000

Or, in proportion to the population, in 1817, *as twelve and a fraction to one*.

It follows that Great Britain has thus acquired a new aid from science in twenty-five years, which enables her to increase her riches, annually, twelve times in quantity beyond what she possessed the power of creating prior to that period: and which excess she may either dissipate in unprofitable foreign commerce, waste by war, or apply directly to improve and ameliorate her own population.

This enormous accession to the productive powers of Great Britain is, however, trifling compared with that which she may now acquire. She has still capital and industry unemployed or misapplied, sufficient to create, annually, an addition to her present productive powers far exceeding the amount of her actual manual labour.

Already, with a population under twenty millions, and a manual power not exceeding six millions, with the aid of the new power undirected, except by a blind private interest, she supplies her own demand, and overstocks with her manufactures all the markets in the world into which her commerce is admitted. The merchants of Britain are now using every exertion to open new markets, even in the most distant regions; and they could soon, by the help of science, supply the wants of another world equally populous with the earth.

Instead, however, of thus contending with other nations to supply wants which they could, under better arrangements, more advantageously furnish for themselves, Great Britain might, most advantageously for herself and them, extend the knowledge which she has herself acquired of creating wealth or new productive power, to the rest of Europe, to Asia, Africa, and America. It is a principle which will be admitted by all political economists, that

> *It is the interest of society to obtain the largest amount of productions, useful and valuable to man, at the least expense of manual labour, and with the most comfort to the producers.*

And when this principle shall be judiciously applied to practice with the aid which scientific power now offers to the world, wealth may be created, in all parts of the earth where it can be required, more than sufficient for every useful purpose.

It is then strictly true, "That the period has arrived when the means are become obvious, by which without violence or fraud of any kind, riches may be created in such abundance and advantageously for all, that the wants and desires of every human being may be oversatisfied.

Thus have two men, Watt and Arkwright, by introducing improved scientific power of a peculiar description, given to the world the means of creating wealth far more rapidly than it can be used. It is presumed, no intelligent practical man, who has devoted sufficient time to the investigation of this interesting subject, will now contend against the conclusion which has been just stated.

The grand question, then, to be solved is not how a sufficiency of wealth for all may be produced, but how the excess of riches which by arrangement only can be easily created, may be generally distributed throughout society advantageously for all ranks without prematurely disturbing the existing institutions in any country.

Your Memorialist will present the second and third parts in a few days.

PART SECOND.

Statement:

> *"That the period has arrived, when the principles of the science are become obvious, by which, without force or punishment of any kind, the rising generation may be, with ease and advantage to all, surrounded by new circumstances, which shall form them into any character that society may predetermine; and any defect shall afterwards appear in those characters, except what nature has made uncontroulable* [sic] *by human means, the cause will not be in the individuals, but will be solely owing to the inexperience of the parties who attempt to put those invaluable principles into practice."*

In consequence, the continuance of ignorance, of fraud, and violence, is also on the point of termination.

GENERAL PRELIMINARY EXPLANATIONS OF THE FOREGOING RESULT.

It is a fact obvious to our senses, that children are born with certain faculties and qualities, or with the germs or seeds of them: and that these combined constitute what is called human nature.

In conformity with what appears to be an universal law in the creation, these faculties and qualities differ in each individual in strength and combination, and to so great an extent as to render it highly improbable that any two infants have been, or ever will be, born alike.

It is also a fact, obvious to our reason, that whatever these powers may be in each child, he could not create the smallest part of them; they are formed *for* him by Providence, by Nature, by that Power, (whatever name men may give it,) which creates him; and whether those faculties and qualities are inferior or superior, it is contrary to reason to say that the infant can be entitled to merit or deserve any blame for them.

He has received his natural constitution as the lamb and the tiger have received theirs; and there is precisely as much reason in finding fault with the one as with the others.

The child is also born in some country, of parents belonging to some class, and who possess characters peculiar to themselves.

Over these circumstances, also, the child can have no influence whatever; each of them have been predetermined for him before he possessed power of any kind.

These circumstances, however unheeded they may be by ordinary minds, have hitherto fixed,

> First:—Whether the child shall be a Jew, a disciple of Confucius, a Mahomedan, a Christian, a worshiper of Juggernaut, or a savage—even a cannibal.
> Second:—To what country he shall belong, and, in consequence, what national prejudices shall be forced upon him.
> Third:—What sectarian notions, if any, shall be impressed on his mind.
> Fourth :—What language he shall be taught, for it influences character more than is usually supposed.
> Fifth:—In what class he shall be trained.
> Sixth:—What peculiar habits and notions he shall imbibe from his parents and those immediately around him in childhood.

So completely, indeed, has he been hitherto enveloped within these various mediums, that it is unlikely a single individual has yet been able to resist their influence, except to a comparatively slight degree, even aided by the infinite variety of natural faculties and qualities which have been given to children in every part of the world.

Now, however, with the experience acquired, society may form new circumstances around children, in every part of the world, which shall enable each of them to pass this sixfold barrier of error and prejudice.

It is true, the power of society over the individual is not without limit. It cannot recreate and altogether change the natural faculties and qualities which are given to children at birth; nor can it make those faculties and qualities in children superior which nature has originally made inferior. But the power over human natures which it has already gained by experience may be so applied as to effect every purpose that can be rationally desired.

Such indeed is the overwhelming influence which experience has now given to society, over the rising generation, that it may surround children from their birth with new circumstances which shall form each of them, bodily and mentally, in such a manner that his habits, dispositions and general character, shall be greatly superior to the habits, dispositions, and general characters, which the circumstances of birth have yet formed for man in any part of the world.

He may also, by the same means, be so trained, placed, and employed, in proper unity with others, and aided by mechanical, chemical, and other scientific power, that he shall create a surplus of new wealth, or property, far beyond what he will or can desire for his own use.

Under these circumstances, until the whole earth shall be well cultivated, and the seas refuse to furnish additional food, each child born in the working class will become a great gain to society.

And these beneficial changes may now be created with much less expense and trouble than are required to continue the present defective and most injurious arrangements.

It is to be particularly remarked that these statements are not derived from, or supported upon, mere theory. The Memorialist has acted upon these principles for many years; and all the practical results have exceeded his most sanguine expectations. *He has proved, by the most decisive experience, the cast, the incalculable, superiority of legislating for the arranging of circumstances, over the past and present puerile system of allowing the circumstances to remain unchanged, and legislating for the individuals, which is truly laying hold of the lever by the wrong end.*

Some uninformed, inexperienced, and prejudiced persons have lightly and hastily concluded that your Memorialist is a visionary, and therefore he occupies himself with public affairs. Whenever the subject shall be thoroughly investigated to its foundation it will be found the fact is not so. He has long witnessed the happy effects of the principles which he recommends, even very imperfectly executed in practice; and, in consequence, he cannot but feel anxious to see them generally introduced and acted upon in all countries in which there are any poor, ignorant, and unprovided with proper employment.

At new [sic] Lanark, in Scotland, the Memorialist, while opposed by all the prejudices of birth existing in that part of the world, patiently, and for many years, silently occupied himself by withdrawing some of the old circumstances which he found injurious to the well-being of his little colony, and with arranging new circumstances, within which five or six hundred children and young persons are now daily educated, without punishment or individual reward of any kind; and their habits, dispositions, and general character are allowed by strangers who visit them, to be superior to the general habits, dispositions, and character of the same class, to be found elsewhere.

And about *one thousand six hundred* persons of this colony are daily employed, who, with the aid of scientific power, complete as much work, (and in a better manner,) as could have been executed in Scotland, of the same kind, forty years ago by *one hundred and sixty thousand* persons; or one now, with this new aid, performs the work of one hundred.

Extraordinary as this change may appear to many who are unacquainted with such kind of facts, society may now create new arrangements, to train, educate, and employ the ignorant and unprovided of the working classes, under circumstances far more advantageous for them and for the public, than it was in the power of the Memorialist to accomplish.

He commenced his task without education, without friends who could render him assistance, and without fortune; and he has been opposed in his whole progress by the mistaken notions of the world.

If then an individual of ordinary capacity, thus circumstanced, could create the arrangements which have been stated, solely because he was influenced by principles which are true and in strict unison with nature, how much more could have been effected in the same time for the improvement of society, by an individual so influenced, if he had possessed superior natural talents, a good education, friends in power, and a fortune sufficient to enable him to put his knowledge into practice under all the proper circumstances, and taking agriculture instead of manufactures for the foundation of his new arrangements

Yet how much more could have been attained in the same period for the permanent improvement of all classes, if, instead of an ordinary unaided individual, the whole of society had been influenced by these rational principles, and had acted upon them! With this explanation it is surely then not too much to say,

> "That the period has arrived when the principles of the science are become obvious, by which, without injury to any, the rising generation of the working classes, may be so trained, educated and employed, that they shall become, whatever character society may deem the best, and create also more riches than can be useful or desired both for private and public purposes."

Aix-la-Chapelle, 21st October, 1818.

PART THIRD.

Preliminary Explanations of the Third General Result, stated in the Appendix to a Memorial addressed to the Governments of Europe and America, by the Memorialist.

Statement:

"That it is the interest, and that it will soon APPEAR to be the interest, of each individual, in every rank, in all countries, that judicious measures should be adopted, with the least delay, to secure these beneficial results. It is, however, greatly to be desired that they should be carried into reflect by general consent, gradually and temperately, in order that no party or individual may be injured by the changes which must necessarily arise."

In consequence, any attempt to stop or retard the introduction of these measures will be unavailing. Already the principles and consequent practice are placed effectually beyond the power of human assault. It will be found that silence cannot now retard their progress, and that opposition will give increased celerity to their movements.

GENERAL PRELIMINARY EXPLANATIONS OF THE FOREGOING RESULT.

Your Memorialist submits, that in the explanations of the *first* general result, it has been shown that the means have been discovered and brought into action, by which a great accumulation of wealth has been made, and that by the extension of new scientific power, riches may be increased beyond any assignable limit.

That in the *second* general result, it has been shown that the principles of the science are become obvious, by which, without violence or punishment of any kind, the rising generation may be, with ease and advantage to all, surrounded by (new) circumstances, which shall train them into any character that society may predetermine.

Under the existing arrangements of society, the mass of the people, in all countries, derive their subsistence through a nominal value of their labour, which rises and falls on the common commercial principle of supply and demand.

This arrangement served the purpose in a tolerable degree while wealth was produced chiefly by manual labour; because the producer was also a consumer, and by this means the supply of, and demand for, labour were adjusted.

But it has been shown that, latterly, a power of production, unlimited in extent, and which scarcely consumes at all, has been introduced; that it has already created a most unfavourable disproportion between the demand for, and supply of, manual labour; and in its daily, undirected progress, this disproportion will go on increasing.

As long, however, as manual labour shall continue thus depressed, the mass of the people who derive their subsistence solely from that source, must be subjected to poverty and misery; while a few—not nearly one in a thousand of the population of the world—will be in possession of accumulated wealth which, under those circumstances, must destroy their happiness. They would be perpetually involved in the opposition, evil passions, and struggles, which would arise in such a lamentable state of society. It is not indeed possible, with the knowledge now in the world, and which is daily advancing, that such a state of society could long exist. The overwhelming strength and interest on one side, will render all contest vain, and the folly of contest will be soon distinctly perceived.

No one, therefore, can for a moment doubt that it *is* the interest of each individual, in every rank, in all countries, that judicious measures should be adopted with the least delay, to insure these beneficial results in practice. Nor can it be doubted that, with the hourly increase of knowledge in many parts of Europe and America, the period can be distant when it will appear to be the interest of all that these ameliorations should be speedily executed.

Thus, has your Memorialist given preliminary explanations of the Three General Results, stated in the Appendix to the Memorial on these subjects, addressed to the governments of Europe and America.

He submits these preliminary explanations to satisfy Congress that he has had much experience on these subjects, and that he understands them thoroughly to their foundation. And upon that knowledge he now re-states, *that all countries possess the means, and many the most ample, to give riches, good habits and dispositions, and useful learning and intelligence, to all their inhabitants*:—

That the practical measures to effect these important purposes are unknown; otherwise, as the benefits to each would be beyond estimate, they would Without loss of time carry them into execution:—

That your Memorialist is desirous of developing these measures in the most minute detail to Congress and to the governments of Europe and America, that they may take the lead in directing, under the established order of things in each country, those changes which can alone relieve the world from the practical evils of the present system, which is experienced to be now so productive of error and misery, that every one exclaims, Something must be done, though no one has yet attempted to state what should be done:—

That your Memorialist is most desirous of cordially uniting the governments and people in those measures, which he is ready to prove ought now to be put in practice, for the substantial and permanent interests of both :—

That he has hitherto, except in part, withheld this knowledge from the people, because he has been afraid they would act upon it in their present neglected and unprepared state, with too much precipitancy to benefit themselves and others. He still withholds it from them, until he shall discover that they will use it calmly and temperately for their advantage, without having the desire to apply it to the injury of any class, sect, party, or individual. This period, however, for many reasons, he considers to be rapidly drawing near, and he will patiently await its arrival.

In the common acceptation of the term, your Memorialist has no private object whatever in pursuing the measures with which he has so long occupied himself for the public benefit, and in which he has expended large sums in experiments, and in various other ways.

He asks nothing—he wants nothing—and he fears nothing, individually, either from the governments or the people.

Before he moved one step in this course, "he put his life in his hand;" and all personal objects he considered "as a feather in the balance," compared with the *immensity of good* which he knew, under such circumstances, might be accomplished for his fellow-creatures. And to attain this amelioration for them, is the sole object which now influences his conduct.

To understand this motive in all its bearings and extent, the mind must be enabled to overcome and pass through the six-fold barrier of error and prejudice, with which the circumstances of birth have hitherto encompassed every one. In fact, "the mind must be born again," by a new training from infancy on the principles that the character of man ever has been, and ever must be, formed *for* him.

Then will this motive be distinctly comprehended by all; and it will influence every action of their lives.

Under these circumstances, which your Memorialist is aware are not of an ordinary nature, he proposes that the Allied Powers assembled in Congress, should appoint a commission to examine, personally, the effects produced at New Lanark, by a very partial and defective application to practice of the principles which he recommends. Also to investigate minutely the whole of the new arrangements which, under modifications, he has to propose for adoption in all countries, and to report their opinion thereon to Congress, when it next assembles—the frequent meetings of which may be substantially useful to Europe and the world. Yes! the finest opportunity that has ever occurred in history now presents itself to Congress, to establish a permanent system of peace, conservation, and charity, in its most enlarged and true sense; and effectually to supersede the system of war, destruction, and of almost every evil, arising from uncharitable notions among men, produced *solely* by the circumstances of birth.

Aix-la-Chapelle, 22nd October, 1818.

Note

1 James Watt's steam engine and Richard Arkwright's water frame were two of the most important innovations behind the development of the textile industry in eighteenth- and nineteenth-century Britain.

56

CONSTITUTION OF THE BLUE SPRING COMMUNITY FOR THE PROMOTION OF SCIENCE AND INDUSTRY (1826).

[Formed in Monroe County, Indiana, the Blue Spring Community (1825–1826) was one of many short-lived attempts to bring Robert Owen's vision to life in the New World between 1824 and 1828.[1] The community's constitution was signed between April and May 1826 by a group of nineteen men and eight women, thus indicating a continuous influx of new members over that short period. Though Blue Spring took direct inspiration from New Harmony, its sociological profile was very different, as it was not founded by a group of well-to-do reformers and intellectuals, but by an extended family of modest settlers who had recently moved to Indiana from the East Coast. Very little is known about the residents, including why and how they came to embrace Owen's system in the first place. The Constitution is certainly indebted to mainstream Owenite principles, such as the superiority of co-operation and community life over pervading individualism in the modern age. However, the document also casts light on how the "new views" were accepted and adapted as potential solutions to the trials of life on the American frontier. Yet these very conditions proved to cause Blue Spring's undoing. Faced with chronic shortage of capital, as well as with a lack of farming skills and local amenities, the community disbanded sometime in 1826 (Harrison 1969, 224; Bakken 2011).]

(Transcript in the original spelling)

We the undersigned believing that the numberless ills which are inflicted on mankind by poverty and ignorance in the individual system of society may be effectually remedied and avoided in future by adopting the social system of society recommended to the world by Robert Owen do mutually agree hereby to enter into our association of union and cooperation of skills and labour for producing distributing and enjoying the blessings of life in the most advantageous manner and for giving to our posterity a superior education both physically and mentally – and we do adopt and agree to be governed by the following constitution

Article 1st This community shall be located near the Blue Spring in town[ship] eight north range two west in the county of Monroe and State of Indiana which shall be known by the name of the Blue Spring Community.

Article 2d We the members of the community shall cooperate by their skill and labor in measures for procuring distributing and enjoying in the most advantageous manner a full supply of the necessaries and comforts of life, for securing to their children the best physical and mental education and for gradually raising a fund for repaying the capital advanced by members and others.

Article 3d Members who furnish cash or real estate for the use of the community shall receive a certiffficate for the same, and those who furnish property of any other description shall have the same appraised by the committee and receive a certificate for the amount in other property or release of the same upon withdrawal according to [a]greement of the parties.

Article 4th Any member wishing to withdraw from the community shall have liberty to do so at any time by giving a weeks notice to the committee, and if he or she be a certificate holder may receive a scrip for the amount baring interest at six per cent per annum.

Article 5th No creditor wishing to withdraw shall have that right to claim any payment from the community under the term of five years except by special contract and whenever the funds of the community are sufficient to liquidate the debts of itself the money shall be tendered to each creditor.

Article 6th The committies of our arrangement shall be elected annually by a majority of the members in the community. They shall consist of odd numbers never less than three but may be increased to odd numbers according to the a[d]vice of the community; and the method of election in this community shall be by ballot.

Article 7th All male members eighteen years and older shall be considered legal actors in all matters pertaining to the community. Females over eighteen who are heads of families shall also be considered legal actors and all females over eighteen may have a voice in the receiving and rejecting members and all domestic matters of their own concern.

Article 8th The Treasurer shall receive all monies due or belonging to the community, disburse the same on order signed by the chairman and attested by the secretary, record all receipts and disbursements in a book kept for that purpose — and report to the committee weekly.

Article 9th The secretary shall keep a regular detailed statement of the important transactions of the community and present the same weekly to the committee two of whom shall examine and keep the same [and?] in their signatures with such observations as they may deem necessary.

Article 10th The books of the community shall at all times to the inspection of any of the members.

Article 11th As it is of the first importance that the community produce within itself a competency for the [use/care?] and convenience of all its members there shall be attached thereto a sufficient quantity of land for agricultural purposes and also for establishing manufactures and the other mechanics arts.

Article 12th Whenever the capital advanced by the members and others shall have been repaid all property both real and personal shall be held and used in common purposes.

Article 13th It shall be the duty of the committee to form rules and regulations for the government of the community and for the transactions of the daily business and submit the same for the reception or rejection of the members monthly or oftener if deemed necessary for the community.

Article 14th The business of the community shall be divided into the following departments. vis:

1st The erection of buildings and general improvements

2nd Agriculture and gardening

3d Manufactures and trades

4th Commercial transactions

5th Domestic economy comprehending the arrangements for heating and ventillating cleaning and lighting the dwelling houses and public buildings the arrangements connected with the publick kitchen and dining halls those for the suply of clothing linnen and furniture for washing and drying and for the management of the dormitories

6th Health or the superintendance of the sick including the arrangements to prevent sickness and contagion

7th Police including the arrangements of cleaning and lighting the square, repairing roads and walks guarding against fire and the protection of the property from external depredations

8th Education or the formation of character from infancy. To this department, will belong the devising of the best means of recreation

Art. 15th The aged widows and orphans shall be the peculiar care of the community and every relief that kindness can afford shall be administered.

Art 16th That, in regulating the employments of the members acording to their ages and abilities previous acquirements and situations in life. The committee shall pay due regard to the inclinations of each, consistent with the general good and that each one may if disposed occupy part of his time in agriculture.

CONSTITUTION OF THE BLUE SPRING COMMUNITY

Art. 17th That the committee introduces all modern and scientific improvements for the abridgement of labour to the greatest possible extent.

Art 18th All the memberes of the committe shall be equal in rights and privileges acording to their ages.

Art 19th As the right education of the rising generation is under divine Providence the basis on which the future prosperity and happiness of the community must be founded, the committee shall employ in this important concern those individuals whose talents attainments and dispositions render them best qualified for such a charge. The children of the community shall be educated together as one family in the school and exercise grounds provided for them, where they may at all times be under the inspection of their parents: and that each child may acquire good habits, and facility in reading and writing —— a knowledge of arithmetic, the elements of the most useful sciences, including geography and natural history, a practical knowledge of agriculture and domestic economy with a knowledge of some one useful trade or manufacture so that his employment be varyed for the improvement of his physical and mental powers; and lastly a knowledge of himself and of human nature to form him into a rational being and render him charitable benevolent and kind to all his fellow creatures.

Art 20th All the children in the community shall be entitled to membership by inheritance and when the members shall become too numerous for our community, a second shall be formed. The number of individuals in the community shall not exceed two thousand.

Art 21st as liberty of conscience religio[u]s and mental liberty will be proffessed by every member of this community, arrangements shall be made to accomodate all d[en]om[in]ations with convenient places of worship; and it shall be the duty of each individual to exibit in his whole conduct the utmost forbearance, kindness and charity towards all who may differ from him.

Art 22nd Every member who wishes to support the gospel or give anything to the poor, shall be allowed so much as may be deemed necesary to be appropriated, as he may think proper.

Art 23d The committe shall form arrangement, by which all the members shall enjoy equal opportunities of visiting their friends elsewhere, and traveling for improvements, and other objects.

Art 24th Members may receive their friends to visit them provided they be answerable, that, such visitors during their stay do not transgress the rules of the society.

Art 25 The use of spiritous liquors shall be excluded, except when prescr[i]bed as a medicine.

Art 26 The society shall not be answerable for the debts of any member further than the amount of property advanced by him.

Art 27th Every member shall furnish his own provisions and clothing, house hold furniture and kitchen furniture for the first year, for which the community shall allow him a reasonable compensation. And if he have a family, for his wife and each child sixteen years old and over, he shall receive a propo[r]tionable compensation as is provided for in receiving other property. And at the expiration of the year all of the above described articles remaining in his possession shall be valued and received into the stock of the community, except such articles as the family wish to retain as their own.

Art 28th In case of a withdrawel of any of the members from the community, such gratuity shall be allowed as a majority of the [word missing] shall agree upon.

Art 29th The committee may receive men on probation; but no person shall be received into full membership; but by the unanimous consent of all the legal voters present at a general meeting.

Art 30th Persons whose peculiar circumstances may render it inexpedient for them to be received as members, may enjoy like comforts and intelectual advantages with the members and their children enjoy like advantages as the children of the community.

Art 31st If the conduct of any individual be immoral or injurious to the community, it s[h]all be the duty of every member to use every argument that kindness can dictate to reclaim such individual; and in no case shall any members be allo[w]ed to use reproachful epithets: should this course prove ineff[ec]tual such offender shall be excluded from the community. three fourths of the members present at a general meeting concuring therein.

Art 32nd All dealings and transactions with general society shall be done by the committee or their authorised agents; provided they make no contracts over a hundred dollars without the consent of a majority of the members.

Art 33d The employment of the female part of the community shall consist in preparing food and clothing, in the care of dwelling houses and dormitories, in the management of washing and drying helping in the education (in part) of the children, and such other employments as are suited to the female capacity.

Art 34th With regard to domestic consumption every individual shall be fully supplied with the necessaries of life.

Art 35th Any member of the community who is apointed guardian and having a child or children a proportionable part (according to the number of the family) of the money and property such number may have put into the community.

Art 36th Any of the members may propose amendments or alterations in writing to the committee at the general meeting which shall lie over until the next meeting and may then be adopted by unanimous consent provided vested rights be not contravened.

In witness whereof we have hereunto set our hands this tenth day of

April AD 1826
In presence of us
Isaac Pauley
John T. Berry

Jonathan Nichols	John A. Givens
Robert Hamilton	William Berry
John M. Berry	Hannah Berry
Elizabeth Berry	Richard B. McCorkle
Amos Cox	William B. May

April 15 1826

Orion S. Crocker	Dudley C. Smith
Philip Rogers	Elizabeth Bailey
Elizabeth Cox	Elisa Nichols
Sarah Cox	Ibby McCorkle

May 11

Parker Byford	Perseus Harris
Chesley D. Bailey	James Bailey
Acquilla Rogers Sr.	William Armstrong
James Matlock	
William B. Ferguson	
Thomas Fullerton	

Committee of Management	William B. May
	Jonathan Nichols
	John A. Givens
Treasurer	Robert Hamilton

Courtesy of the Monroe County History Center
and Monroe County Government

Note

1 Aside from New Harmony (1825–1828) the other early Owenite communities in America were Yellow Springs, Ohio; an unnamed joint-stock company in Illinois; Fountain Community, Indiana and Kendal, Ohio (Bestor 1950, chapter 8; Bakken 2011, 237).

57

"RALAHINE (IRELAND); OR HUMAN IMPROVEMENT AND HUMAN HAPPINESS", LETTERS I–IV, *NEW MORAL WORLD*, 31 MARCH–21 APRIL 1838.

John Finch

[Robert Owen spent most of the years 1822 and 1823 touring Ireland, repeatedly urging local authorities to adopt his New Lanark-inspired "Plan" for the "Villages of Co-operation" in a bid to solve the country's socio-economic crisis (Owen 1857, 183; Siméon 2017, 110). Though his "new views" failed to make significant inroads, Owen nevertheless attracted support from a handful of Irish improving landowners, including William Thompson and John Scott Vandeleur, a Limerick aristocrat. In 1830, after his steward was murdered during a peasant revolt, Vandeleur decided to implement Owen's communitarian system on his estate of Ralahine, County Clare. Upon the recommendation of the prominent Liverpool co-operator John Finch (see Part 3, Chapter 19), Vandeleur enlisted the help of the young Manchester socialist Edward Thomas Craig (1804–1894), who was hired as estate manager, steward and schoolmaster. Finch visited Ralahine in the spring of 1833 to report on the community's progress, and his positive account was published as a series of fifteen letters in the *Liverpool Chronicle*, and then reprinted in the *New Moral World* five years later. Like Owen, Finch believed that co-operative and communitarian leadership should be entrusted to men of power like John Scott Vandeleur. Consequently, his letters praised Ralahine's regime of paternal benevolence as an alternative to the Poor Law system and to the spread of political radicalism in Ireland, in the context of Daniel O'Connell's campaigns for Catholic emancipation. Despite its top-down character, Ralahine was also a democratic community in some respects, as its day-to-day affairs were overseen by a committee elected by universal suffrage. Vandeleur's tenants were also granted freedom of religion. Nevertheless, as alluded by Finch in his first letter, the young aristocrat suffered from a gambling addiction, which ultimately bankrupted Ralahine. The community was sold in 1833 to Vandeleur's creditors. Former residents received no compensation. E.T. Craig later joined the Manea Fen community, founded in Cambridgeshire by William Hodson in 1838 (Harrison 1969, 218–220; Garnett 1972, 108; Geoghegan 1991).]

Letter I.

Dedication.—To the Queen's most excellent Majesty—to the Ladies of Great Britain and Ireland–to her Majesty's Ministers—to the Poor-law Commissioners, Parish Authorities, Irish Landlords, Manufacturers and Capitalists, Clubs and Trades' Unions, Patriots, Philanthropists, Political Economists, Professors of Religion, Britons of every class, party, and creed, with great respect I address you : the subject on which I am about to write is important to you all.

PREFACE

LADIES AND GENTLEMEN,

—At a time like the present, when good men of every party are much divided in opinion as to the principles and practical operation of the English Poor-law Amendment Bill[1], and whilst the poor in many parts of the kingdom regard it with horror and detestation,—when a poor-law similar to it is about being introduced into Ireland, when trades' unions are setting working men against masters, and masters against working men, when reform, conservative, and sectarian associations are dividing the people into numberless little knots and factions, hated by and hating each other, and thus threatening to destroy ultimately every thing like Christian charity among us, I think it a most favourable time for fulfilling a promise long made to my friends of laying before you, as I intend to do in the following letters, *the best means of preventing ignorance, poverty, drunkenness, and crime— superseding the necessity for the introduction of poor-laws into Ireland—relieving England from this oppressive burthen altogether— and improving the condition of all classes without any material extra outlay of capital, the least interference with private property, or with any of our public institutions either in church or state.*

It is not my intention to advance any speculative theory of my own, or the exclusive opinions and practices of any sect or party, but to give you a plain unvarnished account of a most important practical experiment made by an Irish landowner, of a highly respectable family, upon his own estate, with the successful working of which I made myself thoroughly acquainted by a minute personal examination of the plan in all its details, by conversation with all the parties engaged in it, and by inspection of all their books and documents on the spot, during a three days' visit to the institution undertaken for this purpose in the spring of 1833.

If prevention be better than cure, —If permanent remedies be better than temporary expedients,—if a thriving agricultural tenantry be better than half-naked, half-starved cottagers, if well-employed, well-fed, well-clothed, well-educated, and contented workmen are better than a wretched, unemployed, mutinous population, —if happiness be preferable to misery, —if virtue, peace, and good manners, are more to be desired than vice, violence, and crime, —and if a single successful practical experiment founded upon good principles, be far before a great number of plausible theories, the following account of Mr. John Scott Vandeleur's proceedings on his Ralahine estate in the county of Clare, in the years 1831-2 and 3, are more deserving of the serious consideration of every Christian than any that have hitherto been laid before the public, and my only regret is, that I have not talent sufficient to do full justice to the subject. M. Vandeleur, the resident proprietor of Ralahine, was of a highly respectable family, nearly related to Judge Vandeleur; he was pleasing in his manners, hospitable to his friends, well informed on most subjects, a man of experience, observation, and knowledge of the world, liberal in his principles and opinions, benevolent and kind to the poor, diligent and active, and the most scientific and skilful farmer in the whole neighbourhood. He had but one vice that I know of, and that was the great, truly aristocratic, and fashionable vice of gambling, which, like drunkenness, is the prolific source of innumerable crimes, was the cause of nearly all his errors, and eventually proved the ruin of himself, his family, and his system; for this fault he has already sufficiently suffered; lot us not forget that his character, like that of all other human beings, was formed for him, by the training he received, and the circumstances in which he was placed; over his weakness let Christian charity spread her veil. A system so just and benevolent as that of Mr. Vandeleur could have no other origin than a naturally just and benevolent mind, and among those individuals who are still disposed to condemn him, "let him who is without fault cast the first stone". May he soon be recalled and restored to his family, and learning wisdom from experience, again become an ornament to society, and a blessing to his country. —I am, very respectfully,

JOHN FINCH.

RALAHINE.
LETTER II.

Mr. Vandeleur had two estates, one of which, containing about 700 acres, was let in small farms in the way usual in Ireland, the other called Ralahine, (situated 1 and a half mile to the right hand of the road from Limerick to Ennis, 12 miles from Limerick, 3 miles from Newmarket on Fergus, and about 6 miles from Ennis, and containing about 618 English acres,) he cultivated it himself, by employing the labourers in the neighbourhood, under the direction of a steward; but the difficulty of obtaining good, experienced, steady labourers, or of getting labourers at all when most wanted in harvest (as many of them went over to England at that time); the trouble he had to manage his workmen, from their drunken and disorderly habits, and the state of insecurity and alarm in which men of property were at that time placed, owing to the extreme poverty and consequent discontent and turbulence of the people, were a constant source of annoyance both to himself and his family whilst the pity and commiseration he felt for the grievous sufferings of his poor families around him, made him extremely anxious to do something to relieve them, and if possible permanently to remove the causes of their misery. Under these feelings it was with great pleasure he attended the lectures delivered by Mr. Robert when, in Dublin, he had frequent interviews with him, and carefully read and studied his writings; the consequence was, he became a thorough convert to Mr. Owen's great principle, that the character of man is formed for him and not by him, by his original constitution or organization at birth, and the influence of the external circumstances by which he is surrounded from birth through life, and by the action and reaction of each of these upon the other, and hence that the great secret for reforming mankind consists in removing all those circumstances from the whole population, that have a tendency to make them poor, ignorant, and vicious, and surrounding them with all those circumstances that have a tendency to make them wise, virtuous, and happy, and that the arrangement of those favourable circumstances was the proper business of government, and of all good men possessed of wealth, power and influence in society, and he became fully convinced, that by acting upon this principle in the management of the agricultural labourers, and suiting it to each locality, that it was perfectly practicable to cultivate land, either in England or Ireland, in such a manner as to secure better rents to landowners, more interest for capital, and ten times more and greater advantages and enjoyment to labourers than can possibly be obtained by any mode at present adopted, and he determined, as soon as he could make the necessary preparation, to bring these principles into practice, by forming all the workmen he employed upon his estate at Ralahine into one, large family or community, living together upon the estate, working upon one common capital, for the equal benefit of all, their wants supplied from the common store, the whole under his own direction and superintendence, governed by a code of laws securing equal rights and equal means of enjoyment to all. He had built a spinning factory and weaving shop by the side of a stream, was fitting up cottages, and making other preparations, when a circumstance occurred which induced him to commence operation much sooner than he intended.

It was the custom in that part of the country then, and perhaps is so still, for the occupiers of land to let it in small lots to the labouring poor for the first year, when it was manured, for potatoes, to prepare it for a crop of grain the year following, and it was let for a very high rent in that state—at £8, £10, or £11 per acre; and it frequently happened in a bad season that the crop would not cover the rent, in which case the poor man abandoned the land, and lost all his seed and labour. This mode is called letting by conacre. But the occupiers of land were at that time beginning to discontinue the practice, and to cultivate it themselves; the consequence was, that great numbers of the poor were left without either food or labour, and this was the principal cause of the formation of the secret societies, called Terry Alts[2], which carried terror and devastation, for a considerable period through Clare and some adjoining counties. They sallied out in the night in large numbers, with spades and forks, went into the grounds of those who had offended them, and in one night would turn up whole fields, and leave them in such a state that it was not possible to cultivate them that year: they searched houses for fire arms, and committed many acts of violence and cruelty to individuals, and among the rest, Mr. Vandeleur's steward, who had made himself obnoxious by a haughty and tyrannical manner among the workpeople, was shot dead upon the estate during his employer's absence from home. Some of Mr. Vandeleur's workmen were Terry Alts, and believed to be privy to this transaction, if not actual accomplices in it, and these were the only people he dared to employ in his new experiments. They were miserably poor, grossly ignorant; they were drunken, idle, vicious, and, perhaps, some of them even murderers. In addition to this, his relatives and friends considered his scheme utopian; his wife was opposed to it, and his neighbours laughed at it; but none of these discouraged him, he was now fully determined to commence immediately; and accordingly towards the end of 1830 he came over to England to find a suitable person or persons to assist him organizing his society, and engaged Mr. Craig, of Manchester, a sensible, clever, active young man, well acquainted with the principles of the social system, as ardently desirous of seeing them reduced to practice as himself, and who cheerfully made great sacrifices, both of friends and pecuniary interests, for the purpose of being employed in this glorious cause. He left all and went to Ralahine to act as Mr. V.'s new steward and secretary, and as schoolmaster to the community. They immediately set about framing laws and regulations suited to the circumstances and characters of the parties to be employed, and the localities of the place, and finished the preparations for receiving the people on the land. Having now brought you to the beginning of my story, I shall conclude this letter with an observation of great importance to my social friends in the formation of the first communities, which is this, that Mr. Vandeleur and Mr. Craig were the only persons that knew anything of Mr. Owen's principles at the commencement of the Ralahine society, and the sequel will prove that, if all the members of a community will only consent to be governed in all their proceedings by a few well-informed, experienced officers, till they have gained sufficient practical knowledge themselves, it is not absolutely necessary at the beginning that every member should be thoroughly acquainted with all the principles and duties of our system.—I am, very respectfully,

JOHN FINCH

LETTER III.

Ralahine agricultural and manufacturing association was founded on the principle, that "that the character of man is formed for him." Its objects (as the preamble to its laws informs us) were,—1. The acquisition of a common capital. 2. The mutual assurance of its members against the evils of poverty, sickness, infirmity and old age. 3. The attainment of a greater share of the comforts of life than the working classes now possess. 4. The mental and moral improvement of its adult members; and 5. The education of their children. The great principle of the society was Mr. Robert Owen's. The arrangement of the circumstances for the production and distribution of wealth, —for instruction, and for government, and their adaptation to the situation and wants of the people in that neighbourhood, were the work of Mr. Vandeleur and Mr. Craig. These were the purposes for which this society was formed, as it respected the labourers. Mr. Vandeleur, the other party, was about to try an important experiment, altogether new in this, or in any other country, in opposition to the opinions of his family and friends. He had to encounter the deep-rooted prejudices of an ignorant and vicious population, and to entrust a large portion of his property and income in the hands of a number of labouring men and women not worth one shilling; and also to make still further advances to the in for food and clothing, till the first harvest was got in, and the crops sold. Under such circumstances, common prudence, and justice to his family, rendered it necessary that he should retain complete possession of the stock, crops, and premises: should make no larger advances to the labourers for subsistence than he would have paid to them for wages, if they had been working for him as they did before; and that he should have power to expel bad members from the society, and a veto in the choice of new members. By these means he secured himself from the possibility of loss, because he paid no more for labour than he did before, and he could get no more for his land, stock, and capital, than all that the land produced; indeed he had much better security, in the labour of the people, than he had before, because, having a motive for industry, the members of this society did twice as much work in a day as any men he ever before employed; at the same time, as the goods in their store were of the best quality, and charged to them at wholesale prices, they had most articles 50 per cent lower than they could procure them elsewhere; and as, by living together, they could live much cheaper than in single families, it was equal to doubling their wages. And I would beg leave to hint to my social friends, for their consideration at the approaching Congress, in May next, that it will be necessary for the members of the first community to give security, somewhat similar to the above, to the trustees, association, and friends who advance capital, and become responsible for rent, interest, &c.; and must continue to do so till they are out of debt, when they will be free, and will govern themselves.

Formation of the Society.—All things being now ready, Mr. Vandeleur called a meeting of those persons from among whom he wished to form the Society. The number that attended was about 40, consisting of the very poorest persons in the neighbourhood, many of them his former workpeople, without cottage, no other employment than his, not a shilling of capital, and among them six orphan youths and children. His reason for choosing such was, that, should the experiment fail, none of them might hereafter have cause for reproaching him with having made their condition worse than it was before. Being assembled, he explained to them his intentions and views, read his code of laws, and proposed that they should form themselves into a society upon these principles, to which they unanimously agreed. He then produced a ballot-box which he had prepared, explained the nature and use of the ballot, and, after cautioning them of the evils of choosing bad members, he set them to ballot each other into the society; two that were present were rejected, and the utility of choosing their members by ballot was seen soon afterwards, for the two rejected persons were transported for theft: the labourers knew them to be thieves at the time, and therefore refused them.

Agreement for Rent, &c.—To this society he let the estate of Ralahine, containing, as we have said, 618 English acres, about 267 acres of which was pasture, 285 acres was tilled, 633 acres was bog, and 2 1/2 acres was orchard; the soil was generally good, some 99 stoney.[sic] This land, together with six cottages, and an old castle, which were converted into dwellings for the married people; all the farm buildings, barns, cow-houses, stables, sheds, &c., part of which he had converted into a public dining-room, and committee and school-room, with dormitories above them, for the children and unmarried males and females. There were also a saw-mill and threshing-mill, turned by a water-wheel, and the shell of a factory, and of a weaving-shop, but no machinery in them. These premises he let to them for £700 per year, tithe and tax free. For the tools, implements of husbandry, live stock, and advances made to then for food and clothing till the harvest was got in, they were to pay (which was reckoning about £6. per cent interest) £200 more, making in all £300 per year. They were to live together upon the estate, in the buildings provided in common, and they were to work upon this common capital for their joint interest. After paying the above rent and charges, the remainder of the produce was to be the property of the adult members 17 years old and upwards, share and share alike, male or female, single or married. The tools, implements, and machinery were to be kept in as good repair as received, and when worn out replaced, and the cattle and other live stock were to be kept up both in number and value. The rent was to be paid in the produce of the estate always; the first year it was to be a money rent,—£900 worth of produce at the prices at the time in Limerick market; in future years it was to be a corn rent, consisting of as many bushels of grain, and hundred weights of beef, pork, butter, &c., as was paid the first year; and whatever improvements the society might make on the estate, no advance in rent was ever to take place; and as soon as they had acquired sufficient capital to purchase the stock, a long lease of the property was promised at the same rent. So much for the formation of the society and terms of their agreement with the landlord. Our next shall give the laws of the society, and the practical working of the system.

I am, very respectfully,

JOHN FINCH.

LETTER IV.

The annual rent of Rahaline [sic] estate, 618 acres was	£700
Interest for live stock, valued at £1500, at 6 per cent	90
Interest for buildings, valued at £1000, ditto	60
Interest for tools, implements, machinery and advances	50
	£900

The first year, 1831, the rent and interest were paid in money. In 1832, and following years, it was agreed that it should be paid in produce, the quantity and value as follows; and, if they did not grow so much of one kind, it was to be made up with another:—the society thus taking on themselves the risk of good and bad seasons, and Mr. Vandeleur the risk of high and low prices in the market:—

Annual Payment

6400 stones of wheat, at 1s. 6d. per stone	£480	0	0
3840 stones barley, at 10d. per stone	160	0	0
480 stones oats, at 10d. per stone	20	0	0
70 cwts. beef, at 40s. per cwt	140	0	0
30 cwts. pork, at 40s. per cwt	60	0	0
10 cwts. butter, at 80s. per cwt	40	0	0
	£900	9	0

The total value of the produce of Ralahine Estate, in 1832, was near c1,700; the advances made to the Society for food, clothing, seed, &c., that year, was about £550; the extra advances made for timber, slating, glazing, &c., for furniture, and for building their cottages, the first three years, took all their surplus produce; but they were increasing their comforts, and trusted they were laying the foundation of future wealth and happiness. We now give the laws and practices of Ralahine Association, and shall arrange them under the five following heads:—1st. Those relating to their agreement with Mr. Vandeleur. 2nd. The creation of wealth. 3rd Distribution. 4th. Formation of character. 5th. Government.

1st.—Laws Relating to the Agreement.

1st. For the attainment of the objects of this Society, the persons who have signed these rules agree to associate together, and to rent the lands, buildings, manufactories, machinery, &c., of Ralahine, from Mr. John Scott Vandeleur, according to agreement; and the each of them, jointly and severally, bind themselves to obey the following rules, and to use every means in their power to cause them to be observed:

2nd. that all the stock, implements of husbandry, and other property, belonging to, and are the property of Mr. Vandeleur, until the Society accumulates sufficient to pay for them. They then become the joint property of the Society.

3rd. That Mr. Vandeleur have power, during the first twelve months after the Society is formed, to direct that any member misbehaving him or herself be discharged.

4th. That any member wishing to withdraw from the Society, have full liberty to do so, by giving one week's notice thereof to the committee.

5th. If it be found that there are not a sufficient number of persons in the Society, to carry on the different branches of agricultural and manufacturing industry in a proper manner, one member shall be at liberty to propose, and another member to second, the nomination of a new member; and, that a new member having been approved by Mr. Vandeleur also, may then come upon trial for one week, during which time he or she shall receive diet and lodging only; at the expiration of the week he or she shall be balloted for, the majority of members to decide whether such person will be a fit member.

6th. That Mr. Vandeleur be President of the Society, and of the committee, the committee to nominate a substitute during that gentleman's unavoidable absence.

7th. That Mr. Vandeleur choose the secretary, treasurer, and storekeeper, and that the two former always sit on committee by virtue of their office.—[Note. the whole property entrusted to the Society was under their care and in their keeping, and part of their salaries were charged to the Society and part to Mr. Vandeleur, thus making them the servants of both parties; and, as members of the Society, they were entitled to an equal share of its profits.]

8th. Strangers wishing to visit or inspect any of the departments of this society, must request permission to do so from the president or secretary, who shall appoint a member to accompany the party through the establishment.

Practical Effects of These Laws

The advantages Mr. Vandeleur proposed to himself were—1st. To obtain a higher rent for his land. 2nd. Better interest for his capital. 3rd. To secure the punctual payment of these. 4th. Security for the advances he made upon the labour of the people, 5th. the safety of the property put into their hands. 6th. To do all this in accordance with the laws, and greatly to the advantage of every member of this Society:—

1st. The rent and interest charged were much more than the profits he had ever been able to realise when he cultivated the land himself; indeed he thought the rent too high, and intended to have reduced it.— 2nd. As he resided on the estate, close to the dwellings of the people, the whole of the property in the store, as well as the crops and stock, were still in his possession, under the care of the secretary, treasurer, and storekeeper, who were his servants, chosen by himself, and removable at his pleasure; and not a single bushel of grain, or carcase of stock, could be removed without his knowledge and consent. He had the means in his hands, therefore, at all times to pay himself, and hence he had better security for the payment of his rent, interest, and advances, than any other landlord. The only difficulty was, to avoid making larger advances to the labourers, previous to harvest, than was likely to be their share of the crops (and to this subject we must pay particular attention, because this is a subject that must be strictly attended to when our first community is formed, or it will be sure to fail.) The principle followed out was this, that the members of the Society were to work as many hours, to do as much labour, and to draw no more from the fund, than he would have paid them for wages as common labourers and workmen; and they were to continue to do so till they had a capital of their own. To effect these objects, a regular account was kept by the secretary of the time and labour of every individual each day, and at the end of the week, the same sum was paid to each, upon his or her labour, that Mr. Vandeleur, had formerly paid them for wages. The prospect of a share of the crops at harvest, afforded the strongest motive for industry, and these people did twice as much work every day as any hired labourers in the neighbourhood, thus giving them double security in their labour upon all that he advanced. The money advanced was in labour notes, payable only at their own store. This was effected with two good effects:—1st. It enabled him to support them without actual advances in cash; 2nd., as no intoxicating drinks were kept in their store, and as their money would not pass at the dram-shops, drunkenness was effectually prevented, and they all became Tee-totallers. The Society was allowed to build additional cottages, as their numbers increased, on the following terms:— There was timber growing on the land, which they were allowed to cut down on condition of their planting three young trees for every one that was removed; there was plenty of good stone for building; that stone was lime stone, and they had plenty of turf to burn it with for mortar; all these they were allowed to use for this and other purposes.

Mr. Vandeleur agreed to pay part of the expenses for slating and glazing, and their own carpenters and labourers performed all the other labour. The cottages were to be Mr. Vandeleur's, as being built with his materials (thus increasing the value of his property.) and the people were to live in them rent free for their labour in building them. Six very nice slated cottages, built on these terms, were finishing when I was there. By these common-sense means, he fully realized all—and more than all—the advantages he proposed to himself in the formation of the Society. He had a higher rent, and more interest for his money, and better security for the punctual payment of these, and of the advances he paid to them for subsistence, than any other landlord possesses; by the erection of these buildings, and the improved modes of cultivation adopted, the value of the estate was continually increasing. He was entirely relieved from the fear of Terry Alts and Assassins; he had plenty of cheerful, contented good workmen, not one drunken, idle, or disorderly person among them; and not one application was ever made, or was necessary, either to magistrate or lawyer.—The interest of Mr. Vandeleur, and of his tenants, was made to be in all cases the same; for it was equally the interest of the Society; as it was Mr. Vandeleur's, to keep up, and take care of the live stock; to cultivate land in the best manner; and to introduce the most improved modes of cultivation, so that their share of the produce was greater; and it was their interest to keep their fences, cottages, farm buildings, tools, and implements, in good order and in good repair, and to introduce the very best machinery, because these improvements served to lessen their labour, and to increase their profits and enjoyments, the natural effects of all such improvements, and these will be their only effects in a rational state of Society.

In superintending the Society he had constant rational employment, and the most exalted pleasures. He presided at the meetings of the Society as king and father of his people. His dwelling was encompassed with a guard, more faithful than surrounds the palaces of princes. and no midnight plunderer, cruel or mischievous cowardly hare-killer or sportsman, dared to break his fences, trample his crops, or trespass on his premises. And all this was accomplished in three years, with a population as poor, miserable, and depraved as any to be found [in] Ireland. I proceed, in my next, to shew the advantages derived by the people themselves. I am, respectfully,

JOHN FINCH.

Notes

1 John Finch visited Ralahine at the height of the controversial Poor Law Amendment debate. The Old Poor Law and its system of outdoor relief was scrapped under the Poor Law Amendment Act 1834 (commonly known as the New Poor Law), which normalised workhouses as the main providers of poor relief. The Act was widely criticised by the Owenites.
2 The Terry Alts movement (1828–1831) was a wave of agrarian unrest in rural Ireland, spurred by a combination of bad harvests, contested elections and support for Catholic emancipation.

58

"PROCEEDINGS OF CONGRESS, SATURDAY, MAY 16, 1840", *NEW MORAL WORLD*, 13 JUNE 1840, 1314–1316.

[Following the translation of *A New View of Society* in French (Owen 1816), Owen's ideas started gathering support among Parisian radical circles. In 1823, Charles Fourier offered his assistance in establishing "Villages of Co-operation" but Owen refused, fearing competition from his French fellow socialist (Beecher 1990, 364–370; Mercklé 2001, 168–174). In spite of this rebuttal, many bridges were built from the mid-1820s onwards between Owenites, Fourierites and Saint-Simonians across the Channel. Membership between the three groups often overlapped in the name of international socialist solidarity, regardless of the personal enmity between Owen and Fourier. In 1826, the Owenite lawyer Joseph Rey founded a Parisian branch of the London Co-operative Society, which endured until the July Revolution of 1830 (Gans 1962, 36). Co-operative ideals and the defence of popular education attracted the likes of former Babouvist and *Revue encyclopédique* editor Marc-Antoine Jullien (1775–1858), radical author Jules Gay (1809–1883) and his future wife, the feminist Jeanne-Désirée Véret (1810–1891). In 1837, Gay and Anna Doyle Wheeler, who had resided in Paris between 1823 and 1826, arranged for Owen to travel to the French capital, where he met his foreign disciples. The Irish socialist Hugh Doherty was also a major go-between. A friend of Anna Doyle Wheeler's, he settled in Paris during the early July Monarchy (1830-1848). As a disciple of both Robert Owen and Charles Fourier, he became the informal leader of a local group of socialist sympathisers. It was in this capacity that he was invited to attend the 1840 Socialist Congress, held in Leeds that year. On this occasion, Doherty presented a letter undersigned by various Parisian radicals (including Jules Gay and Flora Tristan) expressing their wish to further cross-Channel socialist co-operation. Doherty was officially confirmed as the Owenite representative in Paris, with the apparent intent of opening a branch of the Association of All Classes of All Nations (AACAN) in the French capital. In spite of support from the Central Board, the French Owenites remained but a small group, as the largely top-down, apolitical stance at the heart of British socialism clashed with French traditions of radical republicanism. Many ventures therefore collapsed, including the founding of the aforementioned AACAN branch, as well as various attempts to establish Owenite schools and publications (Desroche 1971; Baroteaux 2019). Hugh Doherty soon relocated to the United Kingdom, where he edited the *London Phalanx* (1841–1843), Britain's first and only Fourierite periodical (Grandjonc 1989, 471–474).]

[...]
Monday, May 18. — MORNING SITTING

DEPUTATION FROM PARIS

The PRESIDENT[1] then rose and said, — I have the honour to introduce to the Congress my excellent friend Mr. Hugh Doherty, of Paris, who left the French capital on Wednesday last to attend this Congress, and arrived in Leeds on Saturday evening. (*cheers*.) I understand he is charged with an Address from the French Socialists to the Congress, and in presenting that Address he will be kind enough to favour us with an account of the state of Social Reform on the continent. (*cheers*.)

HUGH DOHERTY, Esq., then rose and said he had been deputed to present to that Congress an Address from a number of ladies and gentlemen in the French capital who were sincerely attached to the cause of universal Socialism, and who were desirous of cultivating, by all available means, a closer connection between themselves and those whom they represented, and the English Socialists. The Address was as follows:— [...]

[TRANSLATION.]
To the Socialists of Great Britain, assembled in Congress.

GENTLEMEN,

"Feeling the deepest interest in the practical direction which you have given to Socialism, we have long desired to shew you how much in heart and mind, we appreciate the successful efforts you are making for the triumph of those principles which are common to you and to us; and, as Mr. Doherty, who is not less zealously interested in the good cause than we are, informs us that he intends to go to England, we, the undersigned, take advantage of that circumstance to express our sympathies for your persons, and our best wishes for the success of your labours in the cause of humanity. We regret that there is not sufficient time for us to inform our numerous friends and co-operators of the present favourable opportunity, for we know that they would gladly add their names to the list of those who have here expressed their sympathy for you, and the cause which you advocate.

"It is our most ardent desire, also, that a regular communication should be established between the Socialists of Great Britain and France; and we beg

Mr. Doherty to consult with you concerning the best means of realising that union."

Paris, the 11th of May. 1840.

F. Villegardelle[2]
Ad. Radiguel[3]
Jules Gay
C. Couturier
Muirson[4]
A.Girand
Dogliani
Dufai
Christopher Frederic Guil.
Charles de Ribeyrolle[5]
J. Moussons
L. Reymoneng
Vayron[6]
Louise Vayron[7]
Briges[8]
C. de Lasteyrie[9]
Henry Price[10]
J. Borthwick Gilchrist, L.L.D.[11]
R.H. Black, L.L.D.[12]
Clara Black[13]
Genilles[14]
Flora Tristan[15]
E.J. Kirwan[16]
Lasservolle
J. Jeane
Ricourt[17]

Mr. Doherty in continuation said, that the address would have received a larger number of signatures, had time permitted; but the fact was, not knowing the exact time of the assembling of Congress, he was afraid he might not arrive here until the session had terminated, and only a few hours had been devoted to obtain the signatures. He believed that most of those whose names he had read were known to their excellent President; but as he apprehended they were strangers to nearly all whom he then addressed, he would, for their information, state the class of society to which they belonged. They were all, more or less, people of property and influence, some holding official situations. There were among them a Colonial Agent, a Captain in the English Service, several Editors of Journals or Reviews, Professors in Medicine and Law, Architects, &c. &c.; and one of the ladies, "Madame

Tristan," was a well-known authoress who lately paid a visit to this country and had since published a work, entitled *"Promenades dans Londres,"* in which there was a chapter devoted to an account of Mr. Owen and the English Socialists. This lady had entrusted him with a copy of the work to present to that Congress. and which he now begged to hand to the President." (*cheers.*) He had much pleasure in informing them that the cause of Socialism was making great progress on the continent. There were in France a considerable number who were closely identified with the principles and objects which the English Socialists held, and had in view; and a very large number who were extremely favourable to them. There were very few indeed who were unfavourable; people, at most, were indifferent. On no occasion, so far as he knew, had the principles and objects been deprecated or misrepresented by any public writers or speakers. All the public Journals gave a fair account of the views, and of the personnel of the chief directing parties in the movement. In this respect there was a manifest difference with regard to public opinion in the two countries. There was, in France, no persecution whatever, or any disposition to it; on the contrary, when the Bishop of Exeter made his furious attack in the House of Lords, and called for the strong arm of the law to put down the Socialists, he and his party were, most severely censured by all the Journals, for their intolerance. (*hear, hear.*) He should observe that many of the Fourierites in France, who did not understand Mr. Owen's plans, fancied there was a manifest difference between them; but he (Mr. Doherty) after many years of close and searching investigation into the principles and practices of both Owen and Fourier was unable to discover any essential difference. Undoubtedly there were some differences in working out the detail, but in all the grand features, he found they were identical. Both sought, by a science, to produce social harmony, and thereby to secure to man a pleasurable and a happy state of existence; and whatever differences there might be in the mode of operation, he was convinced they would only be observable during, what might be termed, the "transitional" state. (*hear, hear.*) He was most anxious to have all who entertained their great leading principles enrolled under one grand banner of universal Socialism. (*cheers.*) This he thought would be effected, although there might be some little difficulty at first. As some proof of what was doing in France, he might mention that a Scotch merchant[18], now residing, he believed, in Antwerp, had recently given no less a sum than £12,000. for the purpose of diffusing the principles, or, what in France was called, "propogande"[sic]; and he had promised to back up this with a further sum of £20,000. for practical operations so soon as these were ready to be commenced. (*cheers.*) The first-mentioned sum had been absolutely paid, but he regretted to say it had been given to the chief of a coterie, who, though well-intentioned, could not be said to represent the Socialists of France, and who, he feared, would spend the money in a way not calculated to do any very great good.[19] He (Mr. D.) was satisfied, however, that if the English Socialists, with their brethren in France and elsewhere who held the same enlarged views, would pursue their course steadily and prudently, they would very speedily procure the assistance of the more wealthy and influential portion of society. The subject of

Socialism, on account of its benevolent, practically religious, and all-absorbing character, was commanding the attention of the leading minds of the world; and the eyes of the most enlightened men in Europe were now anxiously turned to the movements of the English Socialists, who were looked to the more on account of the practical direction which they had given to the new views of society. One of the most popular and esteemed authors in France was on the eve of completing a history of Socialism, in the compilation of which he had been engaged for some time, and had taken the greatest pains in collecting the materials. It was intended to insure for this work a wide circulation, and from the well-known talent and impartiality of the author, he (Mr. Doherty) had no doubt it would be productive of great good. (*hear, hear*.) The celebrated "Manifesto" of Mr. Owen had been translated into French, and would be widely circulated by means of the press.[20] It was also in contemplation to republish regularly the articles of progress, and other articles of an original and important character which appeared in the weekly paper of the society he was now addressing, "*The New Moral World;*" and one of the principal objects of the deputation was to arrange for a regular supply of this and other Social publications, in order that the large and increasing body of friends on the continent, and particularly in France, might be kept constantly aware of what was doing in England, particularly in a practical point of view. Mr. Doherty concluded by thanking the Delegates for the kind attention they had accorded him, and expressing a hope that much good might result from their present important labours.

The PRESIDENT said that in confirmation of what Mr. Doherty had stated, as to the attention which was now being paid to the proposed Rational System of Society, he would state that he had recently received a letter from Professor Fallati,[21] of the University of Tubingen, who evidently took a deep interest in the subject. He visited England last year and collected a great number of works, from which he was compiling a history of the rise and progress of the principles and practices they recommended, which he was about to publish in the German language. From the accounts which he, (the President) was constantly receiving, he learned that almost all the talented and influential men on the Continent, were now investigating these, to them, new truths, and he had little doubt but that great good would speedily result to the cause. (*hear, hear*.)

Mr. Hobson[22] then moved,—

"That the Congress receive with great pleasure the Address presented by Hugh Doherty, Esq., from the French Socialists, expressive of their sympathy in our efforts and objects; that the Address be entered on the minutes, with a free translation; and that Messrs. Fleming[23], Mackintosh[24], and Buchanan[25], be appointed a Committee to prepare an answer to the same."

Mr. CAMPBELL[26] seconded the motion, and Mr. FLEMING supported the same, observing that all present must have heard with deep interest the very satisfactory account which had been given by Mr. Doherty, of the progress of their holy cause on the continent of Europe (*hear, hear.*). The Congress would of course assure Mr. Doherty, and through him, their friends in the French capital, that no pains should be spared by the society of which they were the representatives, to draw closer that bond of union which already existed between them and their brethren in France. (*cheers.*)

Mr. GREEN[27] trusted that Mr. Doherty would not suppose that they gave him a cool reception. They were about to receive the Address of which he was the bearer, in that calm and business-like manner which was customary to Englishmen, but he might be assured that they hailed his presence with delight, and had already resolved in their minds to carry out the wishes of their friends in France by a more regular and constant intercourse with them.

Mr. CONNARD[28] expressed himself greatly pleased with the very interesting account which they had just heard from Mr. Doherty: he felt certain that it would gratify their friends throughout the country.

Mr. GRANT was delighted at the contemplation of the growing energies of Socialism in England, Scotland, France, Germany, and America. Every true lover of his species must hail the prospect which was before them. England and France had for a long series of years been rendered two antagonistic powers by the cruel policy of the few, who so grossly misgoverned the ignorant many, and led them forth in organized bands to destroy each other. (*hear, hear.*) What a different scene did they now behold! The growing intelligence and virtue of the working classes were forcing the influential classes into measures of peace; and now, instead of England and France destroying each other, circumstances were operating to force them into the arms of universal brotherhood. (*cheers.*)

The PRESIDENT, in putting the motion, said, he believed that the difference between themselves and Fourier was this: Fourier based his system upon thirteen imaginary passions of human nature, which he sought so to arrange as that each should be placed in opposition to its antagonistic passion, for the purpose of counteracting each others' evils. The principles upon which English Socialism was based, were distinctly set forth, in the "Declaration" he had read to them in the opening of that day's business; and he ventured to affirm that they would be found to be consonant with all truth as yet revealed to man, and therefore immutable. (*hear, hear.*) In common with all present, he had been much pleased with the account given by their friend, Mr. Doherty; and he strongly recommended that the French Socialists should appoint him their agent in England, that he might thereby facilitate the arrangements for a closer union between the two bodies, which was so desirable. (*hear, hear.*)

The motion was then put and carried unanimously.

Upon the motion of Mr. CAMPBELL, seconded by Mr. CONNARD, it was then resolved unanimously—

> "That Mr. Doherty, as the Deputy from the Socialists in France, be permitted to sit and speak in Congress, upon the same conditions as the Deputies from Yarmouth, Norwich, and Edinburgh."

Mr. Doherty briefly acknowledged the honour the Congress had conferred upon him, and said he should listen with deep interest to their proceedings.

Notes

1. Robert Owen.
2. François Villegardelle (1810–1850), Fourierite economist.
3. Adolphe Radiguel or Radiguet, former secretary of the Paris branch of the London Cooperative Society.
4. Presumably Just Muiron (1787–1881), a disciple and close friend of Charles Fourier.
5. Charles de Ribeyrolles (1812–1861), radical journalist.
6. Presumably François Benjamin Vauron, a radical printer and lithographer.
7. Presumably Marie-Louise Vauron, née Thibaux, his wife and fellow-printer.
8. Brige or Briges (first name unknown), a member of the Parisian Owenite circle alongside Jules Gay and Désirée Véret. He stated his deterministic beliefs in *De l'existence, de la destinée humaine découlant de la combinaison universelle (négation du libre arbitre)*, Paris, H. Fournier et Cie, 1839.
9. Charles-Philibert de Lasteyrie (1759–1849), a personal friend of Owen's and his first French translator.
10. Henry Price, a British captain and co-editor of a short-lived Owenite paper in Paris around 1839.
11. John Gilchrist (1759–1849), a Paris-based Scottish linguist, patron of University College London alongside Robert Owen and others, and a supporter of republicanism.
12. R.H. Black, an Edinburgh-born doctor and a member of the aforementioned editorial board around 1839.
13. Clara Black, his wife.
14. Guillaume Géniller or Génillier, a professor of mathematics and a member of Jules and Désirée Gay's Owenite circle.
15. Flora Tristan (1803–1844), writer, socialist and feminist. Flora Tristan met Robert Owen in 1837 during the latter's second journey to Paris. Her *Promenades dans Londres* (1840), which offered a positive account of Owenism, were well received by British socialists. She later embraced trade unionism and internationalism.
16. Édouard André Kirwan, merchant and socialist printer of Irish ancestry. A friend of Flora Tristan's, he testified in her favour during her divorce trial. Kirwan also edited *L'Europe*, a radical publication with internationalist leanings.
17. Presumably Achille Ricourt (1797? –1875) painter, lithographer and founder of the periodical *L'Artiste* in 1831.
18. Arthur Young, a rich British expatriate and the sponsor of the failed Fourierist community experiment at Cîteaux, Burgundy, in 1841–1842. Young also gave financial support to Fourier's disciples, or "École sociétaire" (Beecher 2001, 120–121).
19. Victor Considerant (1808–1893), Charles Fourier's main disciple and the leader of the École sociétaire in the 1830s and 1840s (Beecher 2001).
20. *Manifeste de Robert Owen. Inventeur et fondateur d'un système de société et de religion rationnelles* (1841).
21. Johannes Fallati (1809–1855), German statistician and economist.
22. Joshua Hobson.
23. George Alexander Fleming.
24. Thomas Simmons Mackintosh, an Owenite lecturer and the author of the deist pamphlet *An Inquiry into the Nature of Responsibility* (1840).
25. Robert Buchanan (1813–1866), Scottish Owenite and Social Missionary for the Manchester area.

26 Alexander Campbell.
27 David Green, a socialist publisher from Leeds and the founder of the Leeds Redemption Society in 1845.
28 George Connard, a painter from Oldham and the Social Missionary for the Wigan district.

59

REPORT TO A MEETING OF INTENDING EMIGRANTS: COMPREHENDING A PRACTICAL PLAN FOR FOUNDING CO-OPERATIVE COLONIES OF UNITED INTERESTS IN THE NORTH-WESTERN TERRITORIES OF THE UNITED STATES (LONDON: W. OSTELL, 1843), 2–10.

Thomas Hunt

[In 1840, the Owenite Benjamin Timms, formerly of the Manea Fen Community in Cambridgeshire, opened a branch of the AACAN in New York, along with a group of fellow British immigrants. This paved the way for an Owenite revival in America. Over the next three years, Robert Owen's disciples founded four new communities in the United States – Promisewell, Goose Pond (both located in Pennsylvania), Skaneateles, New York, and Equality, Wisconsin (Harrison 1969, 221–222). The latter was established by the prominent London Owenite Thomas Hunt in accordance with the enduring belief in a "new moral world". But it was also a response to ongoing tension within the British socialist movement. In September 1839, Hunt had rejected Owen's view that working men were unable to establish viable communities without the help of the middle- and upper classes. He also dismissed the "Social Father's" critique of Manea Fen, which was a renegade community in the eyes of orthodox Owenites (*Working Bee*, 28 September 1839). These arguments were repeated in the following *Report* of 1843, which urged "real", working-class socialists to establish a community of Equality abroad. Only in the New World, away from Owen's stifling governance and Europe's perceived backwardness, could material abundance and freedom be achieved through complete social and political equality (Chase 2011, 200). Twenty-one Owenites answered Hunt's call for action. These included John Green, former editor of the *Working Bee*, Manea Fen's official publication. Thomas Hunt resigned from his position as President of the London Branch A1, and the group left England for Wisconsin in June 1843, but the following winter was extremely harsh and they did not manage to produce sufficient crops to ensure self-sufficiency. The community folded in early 1847 (Langdon 2000, 323–330).]

Much surprise will doubtless be felt by those who have witnessed my zeal and anxiety in the cause of Socialism, when they shall hear that I have become an advocate of emigration, and that my conviction now is, that the United States of America is the best field for the future operations of those who are desirous of a speedy realization of the PRACTICE of our system. It will be explained that I should state the reasons which have brought me to this conclusion, and also to explain why I am dissatisfied with the practical proceedings of our society[1]. This it is my intention to do.

After a patient review of the past and present state and future prospects of Harmony[2], which I felt myself called upon to take in consequence of the evident apathy and want of confidence pervading the working portion of the members of the society, in the promotion of whose objects I feel especially interested, I have been reluctantly brought to the conclusion that that establishment has not answered their expectations, inasmuch as, after an existence of more than three years, and after an expenditure of upwards of £30,000, not more than seventy persons have been enabled to obtain a residence there. It has been contended by many parties that this sum has been judiciously and economically expended. I wish I would see this in the light that others do; and, above all, I wish I could discern in the establishment even the embryo of that wished-for future growth—a community of men and women, usefully employed and wisely directed, and whose every-day existence should give evidence of that fact, that they were approaching nearer and nearer that important and eventful period, viz. the self-supporting stage of their progress, instead of hearing its occupants making an incessant call for external support. This would have been made manifest from the beginning, if the end had been seen, and the means properly proportioned to it. As the means were limited, the object should have been proportionately small. The error of aiming at too much has been fallen into, and, in consequence, it may fairly be anticipated that little or nothing, in an industrial point of view, will be effected.

Impressed with this conviction, and having a strong desire to see a successful experiment upon the land, in order that the path to permanent relief may be opened to the members of our society, it cannot be surprising that a question like the following should have presented itself to my mind for solution:—"How is it, that after such an expenditure of time and money, our society has not succeeded in making 100 persons independent of external aid; while the Rappites, in America, with little more than £3,000 to begin with, made themselves independent of the outward world after the first harvest, and at the end of eight years they numbered 800 persons, whose property was estimated at upwards of £45,000?" I could hardly conceive that it would be contended that these persons were either more skilful, more industrious, or more economical than an equal number of persons professing the Social principles, and was consequently led to inquire whether this discrepancy might not arise from national causes, and whether America was more favourably circumstanced than this country for such an undertaking. I therefore resolved to inquire into the nature of these circumstances, and to ascertain their probable effects upon a colony of 100 persons established in that country, with a view to contrast its results with what has been effected by us in this country, taking for granted that what has been done is the best that could have been done under all the circumstances. This limited number I know to be unfavourable to the American side of the argument, the cost of maintenance being so exceedingly low, when compared with the value of labour; but I nevertheless adopted it as the most desirable, because the most controllable number; and, further, because it corresponded more closely with the greatest number of residents at any period admitted into the Harmony establishment. I was aware, too, that one year would not give a satisfactory solution of [sic] the question, and I therefore made a series of estimates of production and consumption upon a farm of 200 acres, extending through a period of three successive years, in order to ascertain, first, the sufficiency of the original outlay; secondly, the amount of production and consumption in each year; and, thirdly, whether any and what amount of surplus remained.

It will be seen by the detailed statements to be hereafter given, that at the end of three years the whole of the original outlay will be returned, after supporting the residents, improving the land, erecting a number of buildings, and greatly increasing the implements and stock of the farm. Thus, in three years, would 100 persons become possessed of a highly-improved freehold property, capable of supporting double or treble their number.

I was surprised and delighted at this result—not because it was favourable to America as a field for working out the co-operative principle, and therefore greatly to the disadvantage of our own country in this particular, but because I felt it to be a happy circumstance that any country, and more especially one possessing liberal institutions, should present to the industrious man of small capital the means of securing a permanent existence immediately, and the certainty of being enabled ultimately to surround himself with everything essential to complete his happiness, requiring only the exercise of his skill and labour upon the raw material which exists there in great abundance, which he will find himself at full liberty to use to the extent of his power; for there nearly the entire value of a commodity is labour.

Satisfied as to the accuracy of the estimates from which the result I speak of was obtained, I at once revolved upon making them the basis of a plan for an experiment on our principles in America. A rough draught of the plan having been prepared, it was quietly submitted successively to various individuals of congenial minds, and their co-operation in carrying it into practice invited and secured.

[...] As many objections to emigration are afloat in the public mind at the present moment, I propose, in this place, to answer some of them, and shall then bring under your notice the details of the plan you have met to consider.

Some of these objectors have their own peculiar remedies for existing evils. The remedy of one class is the employment of the surplus population at home on the waste and other lands; but I am not aware that any parties (except those entertaining our principles) propose to adopt the only true mode of making man permanently secure and truly happy—that is, by establishing SELF-SUPPORTING COLONIES OF UNITED INTERESTS; while the remedy of other parties rests upon an increased demand for the manufacture of the country, to be brought amongst other means, by a repeal of the corn-laws. Among these parties, we find the objections of a number of individuals formerly friendly to the principle of emigration; who, having tested the value of emigration by actual experience, and finding the competitive system as prolific of evil at New York and its vicinity, as well as at all the frontier cities and towns in the United States, as they had experienced it in England, have returned to their own country, spirit-broken and bereft of hope, exclaiming bitterly against the "promised land"[3].

[...]

It is thought by many persons attached to our system, that as there are but two principles upon which society can be founded—the competitive and the co-operative—and that as the abandonment of the former would necessitate the adoption of the latter, so would it also, in their estimation, imply the adoption of the fundamental principles of the Rational System of Society. This is a complete delusion; for, should a change from the competitive to the the co-operative principles take place—should the landed interest, who have hitherto resisted all employment to the surplus labour thrown off from our now paralized manufacturing system, by which an abundance of agricultural produce would be raised in this country, rather than be forced into a repeal of the corn-laws, and with it an extensive depreciation in the value of their land and its productions—should a change of this description be preferred by them (and they would prove themselves worse tactitions [sic] than they have hitherto had the credit of being, should they throw away the opportunity offered them), they would have the power, in organizing this new system, of stamping upon it whatever character they might desire to give it.

The physical condition of the people might in some degree be improved by the change; but as this change would not have been produced by the people themselves, but by the tyrants in heart and the depraved in morals—as it would have been imposed upon these tyrants by an uncontrolable [sic] necessity, and adopted, like every other measure, as a choice of evils, rather than from principle—as the thirst for individual gain would not have been extinguished, nor the love of dominion eradicated from the minds of these old tyrants of the world, there is not a glimmer of hope that an enlightened and humanizing philosophy would shed its equal and genial rays over colonies of their formation, or that any but a stultifying education would be given to the people. On the contrary, a despotism more complete—a tyranny more enduring than any hitherto existing in the world would be established in these colonies, because the power of resistance on the part of their inmates would be utterly destroyed by the fact of their being wholly dependent upon the landed aristocracy, and subjected to the every-day influences of a clerical domination.

[...]

Contrast the complication, insecurity, and expense of English tenures with the simplicity, security, and if it be preferred, total absence of cost in the mode of conveying land in the United States, as I find stated in a letter by "An American Citizen" inserted in the *Preston Chronicle*:—"In the purchasing of land, the deed that transfers the right of property from the general government to the individual purchasing is very simple: it is contained on a piece of parchment less than half a sheet of letter-paper, with the date, the locality of the land, the purchaser's name, and then subscribed by the President of the United States, and the agent of the general land-office. This is given free of all expense, and may be transferred by the purchaser to any other person, without the aid of a lawyer, or that of stamped paper"[4].

It has long been a practice in the United States for those who were too poor to purchase, to take possession of unsurveyed land, and consequently all the labour they might have given to its was entirely at the mercy of the government. But a law was enacted to protect these little properties, by giving their occupiers a priority of right to purchase, at the Congress price of a dollar and a quarter per acre, whenever the land they occupied should come into the market, and whatever might have been the extent of their improvements, provided these improvements included the reception of a dwelling-house of certain small dimensions.

In short the obstacles in the way of obtaining land in this country, by small capitalists, are so great as almost to amount to an absolute prohibition of its use; and even if attainable, it is so beset with legal entanglements, burdened with such a high rental, and taxed in so many different forms, as to make any experiment on the land, however well supported, lingering in its progress, doubtful as a measure of relief to those who may support it, and uncertain as to its protracted results.

To meet the never-ending exactions to which land in this country is subjected, two-thirds of the produce of the labourer's toil is drawn from him. If he take a farm at a rental, he and his fellow-slaves can only call the produce of every third acre their own, although none of these acres possessed any value without their labour. They alone have given value to them, and they alone ought to reap the fruit. This they can never do under the system which has produced the injustice. They are, and ever must be, the bond slaves, socially and politically, of the monied interest, so long as they continue under its influence. Of what value to the working man is the knowledge of a happier state of human existence, when he is met with insurmountable obstacles at every turn in his endeavours to improve his condition by the application of superior principles to practice?

It is intended to be shown that the proposed plan is not only exempt from all the objections I have stated, but that in two years from the commencement of operations, at a comparatively trifling outlay, every individual interested in the undertaking, by a safe and simple process, may be so placed as to commence a career of uninterrupted prosperity and real independence. And when it is considered that in addition to this comfort and independence the individuals thus located upon American soil will have the means in their own society for educating their children in knowledge and virtue, no further persuasion will be necessary to convince the thinking portion of the public of the utility of the Plan detailed in the following Report.

Notes

1 "our society": the Universal Society of Rational Religionists.
2 Harmony Hall, i.e. the Queenwood community.
3 An allusion to Robert Owen's failed community experiment at New Harmony, Indiana (1825–1828).
4 *Preston Chronicle*, 26 March 1842.

60

"PROGRESS OF SOCIAL REFORM ON THE CONTINENT. N° II. GERMANY AND SWITZERLAND", *NEW MORAL WORLD*, 18 NOVEMBER 1843, 161–162.

Friedrich Engels

[In November 1842, the young Friedrich Engels moved from Berlin to Manchester, where he was sent to oversee his father's spinning mill. Already acquainted with German radical thought, he became a frequent attendee at the local Hall of Science. There, he met his future life partner, Mary Burns, a young Irish cotton spinner and activist who introduced him further into the city's socialist circles (Whitfield 1988, 19; Bensimon 2018, 9–11). During this first stay in England, until August 1844, Engels not only wrote about the Owenite movement for radical German periodicals, such as the *Rheinische Zeitung*, edited by Karl Marx. He also contributed to Feargus O'Connor's *Northern Star*, the leading Chartist publication at the time, and to the *New Moral World*. His series of letters, "Progress of Social Reform on the Continent", were published in the two British newspapers during the same period between October and November 1843. Thanks to Engels's account of socialist movements in France and in his native Germany, the Owenites became acquainted with radical figures such as Wilhelm Weitling (1808–1871), who would later flee to London as a political exile (see Chapter 61 below). Engels's Manchester years were pivotal to the development of his political thinking. Much of what he learnt and saw there provided the material for his *Condition of the Working-Classes in England* (1845). The book would also see him turn his back on Owenism – certainly a socialist movement led by a former industrialist was a contradiction in terms, and could only produce "great injustice toward the proletariat in its methods" (Engels [1845] 1892, 236, cited in Tsuzuki 1971, 18). The same critique pervaded the *Communist Manifesto ([1848] 1992)*, though it somewhat mellowed in Engels's later writings. Despite the "Social Father's" "utopian" idealism and bourgeois leanings, Engels believed that "every social movement, every real advance in England on behalf of the workers [linked] itself to the name of Robert Owen" ([1880] 1970, 95).]

Germany had her Social Reformers as early as the Reformation. Soon after Luther had begun to proclaim church reform and to agitate the people against spiritual authority, the peasantry of Southern and Middle Germany rose in a general insurrection against their temporal lords. Luther always stated his object to be, to return to original Christianity in doctrine and practice; the peasantry took exactly the same standing, and demanded, therefore, not only the ecclesiastical, but also the social practice of primitive Christianity. They conceived a state of villainy and servitude, such as they lived under, to be inconsistent with the doctrines of the Bible; they were oppressed by a set of haughty barons and earls, robbed and treated like their cattle every day, they had no law to protect them, and if they had, they found nobody to enforce it. Such a state contrasted very much with the communities of early Christians and the doctrines of Christ, as laid down in the Bible. Therefore they arose and began a war against their lords, which could only be a war of extermination. Thomas Münzer[1], a preacher, whom they placed at their head, issued a proclamation, full, of course, of the religious and superstitious nonsense of the age, but containing also among others, principles like these: That according to the Bible, no Christian is entitled to hold any property whatever exclusively for himself; that community of property is the only proper state for a society of Christians; that it is not allowed to any good Christian to have any authority or command over other Christians, nor to hold any office of government or hereditary power, but on the contrary, that, as all men are equal before God, so they ought to be on earth also. These doctrines were nothing but conclusions drawn from the Bible and from Luther's own writings; but the Reformer was not prepared to go as far as the people did; notwithstanding the courage he displayed against the spiritual authorities, he had not freed himself from the political and social prejudices of his age; he believed as firmly in the right divine of princes and landlords to trample upon the people, as he did in the Bible. Besides this, he wanted the protection of the aristocracy and the Protestant princes, and thus he wrote a tract against the rioters disclaiming not only every connection with them, but also exhorting the aristocracy to put them down with the utmost severity, as rebels against the laws of God. "Kill them like dogs!" he exclaimed. The whole tract is written with such an animosity, nay, fury and fanaticism against the people, that it will ever form a blot upon Luther's character; it shows that, if he began his career as a man of the people, he was now entirely in the service of their oppressors. The insurrection, after a most bloody civil war, was suppressed, and the peasants reduced to their former servitude.

If we except some solitary instances, of which no notice was taken by the public, there has been no party of Social Reformers in Germany, since the peasants' war, up to a very recent date. The public mind during the last fifty years was too much occupied with questions of either a merely political or merely metaphysical nature — questions, which had to be answered, before the social question could be discussed with the necessary calmness and knowledge. Men, who would have been decidedly opposed to a system of community, if such had been proposed to them, were nevertheless paving the way for its introduction.

It was among the working class of Germany that Social Reform has been of late made again a topic of discussion. Germany having comparatively little manufacturing industry, the mass of the working classes is made up by handicraftsmen, who previous to their establishing themselves as little masters, travel for some years over Germany, Switzerland, and very often over France also. A great number of German workmen is thus continually going to and from Paris, and must of course there become acquainted with the political and social movements of the French working classes. One of these men, William Weitling, a native of Magdeburg in Prussia, and a simple journeyman-tailor, resolved to establish communities in his own country.

This man, who is to be considered as the founder of German Communism, after a few years' stay in Paris, went to Switzerland, and, whilst he was working in some tailor's shop in Geneva, preached his new gospel to his fellow-workmen. He formed Communist Associations in all the towns and cities on the Swiss side of the lake of Geneva, most of the Germans who worked there becoming favourable to his views. Having thus prepared the public mind, he issued a periodical, the Young Generation,' for a more extensive agitation of the country. This paper, although written for working men only, and by a working man, has from its beginning been superior to most of the French Communist publications, even to Father Cabet's[2] *Populaire*. It shows that its editor must have worked very hard to obtain that knowledge of history and politics which a public writer cannot do without, and which a neglected education had left him deprived of. It shows, at the same time, that Weitling was always struggling to unite his various ideas and thoughts on society into a complete system of Communism. The *Young Generation* was first published in 1841; in the following year, Weitling published a work: *Guarantees of Harmony and Liberty*, in which he gave a review of the old social system and the outlines of a new one. I shall, perhaps, some time give a few extracts from this book.

Having thus established the nucleus of a Communist party in Geneva and its neighbourhood, he went to Zurich, where, as in other towns of Northern Switzerland, some of his friends had already commenced to operate upon the minds of the working men. He now began to organise his party in these towns. Under the name of Singing Clubs, associations were formed for the discussion of Social reorganisation. At the same time Weitling advertised his intention to publish a book, — *The Gospel of the Poor Sinners*. But here the police interfered with his proceedings.

In June last, Weitling was taken into custody, his papers and his book were seized, before it left the press. The Executive of the Republic appointed a committee to investigate the matter, and to report to the Grand Council, the representatives of the people. This report has been printed a few months since. It appears from it, that a great many Communist associations existed in every part of Switzerland, consisting mostly of German working men; that Weitling was considered as the leader of the party, and received from time to time reports of progress; that he was in correspondence with similar associations of Germans in Paris and London, and that all these societies, being composed of men who very often changed their residence, were so many seminaries of these "dangerous and Utopian doctrines", sending out their elder members to Germany, Hungary, and Italy, and imbuing with their spirit every workman who came within their reach. The report was drawn up by Dr. Bluntschl[3], a man of aristocratic and fanatically Christian opinions, and the whole of it therefore is written more like a party denunciation, than like a calm, official report. Communism is denounced as a doctrine dangerous in the extreme, subversive of all existing order, and destroying all the sacred bonds of society. The pious doctor, besides, is at a loss for words sufficiently strong to express his feelings as to the frivolous blasphemy with which these infamous and ignorant people try to justify their wicked and revolutionary doctrines, by passages from the Holy Scriptures. Weitling and his party are, in this respect, just like the Icarians[4] in France, and contend that Christianity is Communism.

The result of Weitling's trial did very little to satisfy the anticipations of the Zurich government. Although Weitling and his friends were sometimes very incautious in their expressions, yet the charge of high treason and conspiracy against him could not be maintained; the criminal court sentenced him to six months' imprisonment, and eternal banishment from Switzerland; the members of the Zurich associations were expelled the Canton; the report was communicated to the governments of the other Cantons and to the foreign embassies, but the Communists in other parts of Switzerland were very little interfered with. The prosecution came too late, and was too little assisted by the other Cantons; it did nothing at all for the destruction of Communism, and was even favourable to it, by the great interest it produced in all countries of the German tongue. Communism was almost unknown in Germany, but became by this an object of general attention.

Besides this party there exists another in Germany, which advocates Communism. The former, being thoroughly a popular party, will no doubt very soon unite all the working classes of Germany; that party which I now refer to is a philosophical one, unconnected in its origin with either French or English Communists, and arising from that philosophy which, since the last fifty years, Germany has been so proud of.

The political revolution of France was accompanied by a philosophical revolution in Germany. Kant began it by overthrowing the old system of Leibnitzian metaphysics, which at the end of last century was introduced in all Universities of the Continent. Fichte and Schelling commenced rebuilding, and Hegel completed the new system. There has never been, ever since man began to think, a system of philosophy as comprehensive as that of Hegel. Logic, metaphysics, natural philosophy, the philosophy of mind, the philosophy of law, of religion, of history, all are united in one system, reduced to one fundamental principle. The system appeared quite unassailable from without, and so it was; it has been overthrown from within only, by those who were Hegelians themselves. I cannot, of course, give here a complete development either of the system or of its history, and therefore must restrain myself to the following remarks. The progress of German philosophy from Kant to Hegel was so consistent, so logical, so necessary, if I may say so, that no other systems besides those I have named could subsist. There are two or three of them, but they found no attention; they were so neglected, that nobody would even do them the honour to overthrow them. Hegel, notwithstanding his enormous learning and his deep thought, was so much occupied with abstract questions, that he neglected to free himself from the prejudices of his age — an age of restoration for old systems of government and religion. But his disciples had very different views on these subjects. Hegel died in 1831, and as early as 1835 appeared Strauss'[5] *Life of Jesus,* the first work showing some progress beyond the limits of orthodox Hegelianism. Others followed; and in 1837 the Christians rose against what they called the New Hegelians, denouncing them as Atheists, and calling for the interference of the state. The state, however, did not interfere, and the controversy went on. At that time, the New, or Young Hegelians, were so little conscious of the consequences of their own reasoning, that they all denied the charge of Atheism, and called themselves Christians and Protestants, although they denied the existence of a God who was not man, and declared the history of the gospels to be a pure mythology. It was not until last year, in a pamphlet, by the writer of these lines, that the charge of Atheism was allowed to be just. But the development went on. The Young Hegelians of 1842 were declared Atheists and Republicans; the periodical of the party, the German Annals, was more radical and open than ever before; a political paper was established, and very soon the whole of the German liberal press was entirely in our hands. We had friends in almost every considerable town of Germany; we provided all the liberal papers with the necessary matter, and by this means made them our organs; we inundated the country with pamphlets, and soon governed public opinion upon every question. A temporary relaxation of the censorship of the press added a great deal to the energy of this movement, quite novel to a considerable part of the German public. Papers, published under the authorisation of a government censor, contained things which, even in France, would have been punished as high treason, and other things which could not have been pronounced in England, without a trial for blasphemy being the consequence of it. The movement was so sudden, so rapid, so energetically pursued, that the government as well as the public were dragged along with it for some time. But this violent character of the agitation proved that it was not founded upon a strong party among the public, and that its power was produced by the surprise, and consternation only of its opponents. The governments, recovering their senses, put a stop to it by a most despotic oppression of the liberty of speech. Pamphlets, newspapers, periodicals, scientific works were suppressed by dozens, and the agitated state of the country soon subsided. It is a matter of course that such a tyrannical interference will not check the progress of public opinion, nor quench the principles defended by the agitators; the entire persecution has been of no use whatever to the ruling powers; because, if they had not put down the movement, it would have been checked by the apathy of the public at large, a public as little prepared for radical changes as that of every other country; and, if even this had not been the case, the republican agitation would have been abandoned by the agitators themselves, who now, by developing farther and farther the consequences of their philosophy, became Communists. The princes and rulers of Germany, at the very moment when they believed to have put down for ever republicanism, saw the rise of Communism from the ashes of political agitation; and this new doctrine appears to them even more dangerous and formidable than that in whose apparent destruction they rejoiced.

As early as autumn, 1842, some of the party contended for the insufficiency of political change, and declared their opinion to be, that a Social revolution based upon common property, was the only state of mankind agreeing with their abstract principles. But even the leaders of the party, such as Dr. Bruno Bauer[6], Dr. Feuerbach[7], and Dr. Ruge[8], were not then prepared for this decided step. The political paper of the party, the *Rhenish Gazette*, published some papers advocating Communism, but without the wished-for effect. Communism, however, was such a necessary consequence of New Hegelian philosophy, that no opposition could keep it down, and, in the course of this present year, the originators of it had the satisfaction of seeing one republican after the other join their ranks. Besides Dr. Hess[9], one of the editors of the now suppressed *Rhenish Gazette,* and who was, in fact, the first Communist of the party, there are now a great many others; as Dr. Ruge, editor of the German Annals, the scientific periodical of the Young Hegelians, which has been suppressed by resolution of the German Diet; Dr. Marx[10], another of the editors of the *Rhenish Gazette;* George Herwegh[11], the poet whose letter to the King of Prussia was translated, last winter, by most of the English papers, and others: and we hope that the remainder of the republican party will, by-and-by, come over too.

Thus, philosophical Communism may be considered for ever established in Germany, notwithstanding the efforts of the governments to keep it down. They have annihilated the press in their dominions, but to no effect; the progress parties profit by the free press of Switzerland and France, and their publications are as extensively circulated in Germany, as if they were printed in that country itself. All persecutions and prohibitions have proved ineffectual, and will ever do so; the Germans are a philosophical nation, and will not, cannot abandon Communism, as soon as it is founded upon sound philosophical principles: chiefly if it is derived as an unavoidable conclusion from their own philosophy. And this is the part we have to perform now. Our party has to prove that either all the philosophical efforts of the German nation, from Kant to Hegel, have been useless — worse than useless; or, that they must end in Communism; that the Germans must either reject their great philosophers, whose names they hold up as the glory of their nation, or that they must adopt Communism. And this *will* be proved; this dilemma the Germans will be forced into, and there can scarcely be any doubt as to which side of the question the people will adopt.

There is a greater chance in Germany for the establishment of a Communist party among the educated classes of society, than anywhere else. The Germans are a very disinterested nation; if in Germany principle comes into collision with interest, principle will almost always silence the claims of interest. The same love of abstract principle, the same disregard of reality and self-interest, which have brought the Germans to a state of political nonentity, these very same qualities guarantee the success of philosophical Communism in that country. It will appear very singular to Englishmen, that a party which aims at the destruction of private property is chiefly made up by those who have property; and yet this is the case in Germany. We can recruit our ranks from those classes only which have enjoyed a pretty good education; that is, from the universities and from the commercial class; and in either we have not hitherto met with any considerable difficulty.

As to the particular doctrines of our party, we agree much more with the English Socialists than with any other party. Their system, like ours, is founded upon philosophical principle; they struggle, as we do, against religious prejudices whilst the French reject philosophy and perpetuate religion by dragging it over with themselves into the projected new state of society. The French Communists could assist us in the first stages only of our development, and we soon found that we knew more than our teachers; but we shall have to learn a great deal yet from the English Socialists. Although our fundamental principles give us a broader base, inasmuch as we received them from a system of philosophy embracing every part of human knowledge; yet in everything bearing upon practice, upon the *facts* of the present state of society, we find that the English Socialists are a long way before us, and have left very little to be done. I may say, besides, that I have met with English Socialists with whom I agree upon almost every question.

I cannot now give an exposition of this Communist system without adding too much to the length of this paper; but I intend to do so some time soon, if the Editor of the *New Moral World* will allow me the space for it. I therefore conclude by stating that, notwithstanding the persecutions of the German governments (I understand that, in Berlin, Mr. Edgar Bauer[12] is being prosecuted for a Communist publication; and in Stuttgart another gentleman has been committed for the novel crime of "Communist correspondence"!), notwithstanding this, I say, every necessary step is taken to bring about a successful agitation for Social Reform, to establish a new periodical, and to secure the circulation of all publications advocating Communism.

Notes

1 Thomas Müntzer (c. 1489–1525) German radical preacher and theologian, and the leader of the 1525 German Peasants' War.
2 Étienne Cabet (1788–1856), French philosopher, admirer of Robert Owen and founder of the Icarian movement. He was known to his disciples as "Père Cabet" (Father Cabet).
3 Johann Caspar Bluntschli (1808–1881), Swiss jurist and Conservative politician.
4 The Icarians were the followers of French utopian socialist Étienne Cabet (1788–1856). His *Travels in Icaria* (1840) advocated workers' co-operatives, and were partly inspired by Robert Owen's theories. In the late 1840s and early 1850s, the Icarians founded intentional communities in Texas and Illinois.
5 David Friedrich Strauss (1808–1874), German Protestant theologian.
6 Bruno Bauer (1809–1882), German philosopher and historian.
7 Ludwig Andreas von Feuerbach (1804–1872), German philosopher and later author of *The Essence of Christianity* (1848), which had a profound influence on Karl Marx and Friedrich Engels.
8 Arnold Ruge (1802–1889), German philosopher.
9 Moses Hess (1812–1875), French-German philosopher, correspondent of the *Rheinische Zeitung* in Paris, and a founder of socialist Zionism. Hess is credited with introducing Engels to communism in the early 1840s.
10 Karl Marx.
11 Georg Theodor Herwegh (1817–1875), German poet.
12 Edgar Bauer (1820–1886), German philosopher.

61

"MEETING OF ENGLISH AND FOREIGN COMMUNISTS", *NEW MORAL WORLD*, 28 SEPTEMBER 1844, 109–111.

[In September 1844, the *New Moral World* published the proceedings of a meeting held in honour of the German radical Wilhelm Weitling (1808–1871), who had recently found refuge in London. The event was attended by local Owenites such as George Jacob Holyoake and the editor of the *New Moral World*, George Alexander Fleming, and also welcomed delegates from various London-based foreign socialist organisations like the French Democratic Society (Société démocratique française) and Germany's League of the Just. Through their joint support for Weitling, and following various rapprochement attempts over the previous years,[1] all parties involved expressed their desire to foster co-operation between British and foreign socialists or "communists", as the two terms became interchangeable for a while. The time was ripe, they argued, for establishing a more formal and permanent institutional framework in the name of international solidarity (Holyoake, *Movement*, 1843, n°41, 352, cited in Lattek 1988, 262). Rather than insisting on the defence of working-class interests alone, the addresses given during the meeting asserted instead the importance of universal socialist brotherhood, regardless of class divisions. A new organisation, the Democratic Friends of All Nations, was founded shortly after, on 19 October 1844 based on these Owenite principles, but nothing indicates that it was ever active. Indeed, it was seemingly superseded the following year by the Fraternal Democrats, which embraced a more Chartist stance, with a clear defence of class-based cosmopolitanism. Nevertheless, the Owenite ideal of co-operation acted for a time as the ferment for future strands of internationalism. Not only did Owen's followers pioneer contacts with socialist Continental expatriates in London. They also popularised the idea that only useful and thus productive workers deserved the name of "socialist" (see Part 4). This definition, of course, differs from Marx's understanding of the proletariat as a distinct class. Yet the power to create wealth was used by the First International as a criterion to establish "the unity of the working-classes everywhere" (Claeys 1988, 248; Claeys 1985).]

On Sunday last, a very numerous assembly of British and Foreign Socialists took place at the Institution, John-street,[2] for the purpose of welcoming Wilhelm

Weitling, the leader of the German Communists, who has recently arrived in this country, after enduring imprisonment and persecution in Switzerland and Prussia, in consequence of his labours in the Communist cause. The meeting was also intended to introduce the members of the Rational Society to the Foreign Communists resident in London. There are two societies which hold regular meetings, the one composed of natives of France, the other of Germany, and many of their members were present, with numerous continental friends besides. The number of applicants for tickets to the tea-party was so great that, notwithstanding the ample accommodation provided on the spacious floor of the Hall, the company had to be divided into two sets, and consequently it was half-past seven o'clock before the friendly repast was finished. At that time, Mr. R., Clarke[3], President of the Branch, took the chair, and the proceedings were commenced by the choir giving, in excellent spirit and style, the "*Marseillaise Hymn*," which was received with great enthusiasm, and unanimously encored.

THE CHAIRMAN then rose, and, in allusion to the chorus of the song just finished, said, he believed that all present were prepared to "march on, all hearts resolved," armed with the sword of truth, and the shield of righteousness. The Socialists needed no other armour. Their weapons were those of peaceful and rational agitation, and their victories were to be won by moral power alone. But a few weeks had elapsed since they met in that Hall for the purpose of giving a farewell festival to the great and good Robert Owen, whose departure from our shores, even for a limited period, had been viewed with regret by those attached, to his person and his principles. They were that evening again called together for the purpose of honouring communist principles in the person of their advocates, by welcoming to our island their friend and brother, Weitling, whose persecution, and whose sufferings in a foreign land, for the principles they mutually professed, would prove the best passport to their mutual acquaintance and esteem, he would not delay them longer, but introduce to them Mr. Weitling.

Mr. WEITLING then rose, amidst hearty and continued plaudits, and after stating that his limited acquaintance with the English language would not permit him to express himself as he could wish, extemporaneously, proceeded to read the following

ADDRESS:—

FRIENDS! "All's well that ends well!" I am again free, free in action and in word; I am among you according to your invitation, and I feel that I am welcome.

I, a stranger, here find hospitable and sympathizing friends, who generally wait only on the great, the learned, and the rich. But you warmly greet a stranger who is none of these, showing thus to the world, that the liberty of speech among you is not as "sounding brass or a tinkling cymbal," but a reality, which leads you to the recognition of Communist principles, and the practice of their consequences.

A sympathy springing from the principles that mutually animate us, has induced you to welcome me. This welcome will be a message of gladness to our friends on the continent, and a brand of shame for our bigoted persecutors; if, indeed, the smallest feeling of shame yet slumbers in their breasts.

What have we asked of them? What ought we to expect? Freedom of speech, free discussion, a public refutation of our principles, with arguments to prove that the present state of things is based on truth, while our ideas and propositions for its amelioration are utterly erroneous. Instead of this, what have they done They have, in a cowardly manner, avoided this great question, and introduced plans for hindering the liberty of speech and writing, by means of threats, imprisonment, fine, and banishment.

They have partly executed their plans, but what have they gained? They tried to blow out the spark of liberty, but they have only kindled it into a blaze.

Some time ago, the doctrine of Communism was, in literature, but a small uncultivated plant in a barren wilderness. But what see we now! The papers which heretofore found no interest in admitting the subject in their columns, or dared not discuss it, have advanced, by degrees, till they teem with criticism and reports of Communists and Communism.

Our philosophical and political literature, which can no longer avoid the contact, we now find becoming more and more imbued with it. Our philosophers of the new school are consequently Communists, yes, even a party of our adversaries begin to call themselves Socialists, to hide from the public, in a more pleasing garb, the onesideness [sic] of their ideas on political reform.

Is not this joyful progress? And have we not to thank our enemies, the monkeys, for throwing heavy nuts, to injure weary travellers, who, smiling and refreshed, pursue their journey with renewed vigour.

Even the people, from, whom the literary language of our philosophers and politicians is hidden, who seldom understand the terms they use—the people, who have no money for books and no leisure for reading—have thought deeply on that immeasurable world of ideas which lies in that, to them, strange-sounding word, "Communism!"

"To have all things in common would be right!" is whispered from mouth to mouth, from Berlin to Vienna, from Cologne to Königsberg, from Prague to Langenbilau.

"We will not burn their houses," said the infuriated weavers, "for the proprietors would be indemnified by the insurance company, but we will pull them down. Let them also feel what it is to be poor!"

The blind rage of persecution, the arrogant scoff, the unnatural hardening of all tender feelings, have brought on this state of things. The oppressed, the pursued, the victims, find everywhere a helper or avenger, and how can it be otherwise, when even animals sympathise with the oppressed among themselves.

Observe a little dog, bitten by a large one, how often the other little ones come enraged to attack the oppressor. And if animals have such feelings to whose dictates they must bend, how can men resist their influence?

These deep and irresistible feelings are natural, and their demands constitute our rights. Our rights, therefore, are not matter of science but of feeling. They are not to be calculated mathematically, nor by a money-standard—nor are they to be measured by fine and imprisonment. Feeling alone is the accurate barometer of our rights; if different degrees are occasionally shown, it is because some are pressed to the earth—others elevated to the clouds.

What now, in the language of lawyers, is called our right is a sophism, a deceitful play upon words, mere jugglery for making black white, or the contrary. It is a fishing book which provides food for men of useless and even pernicious professions, and which the satiated glutton passes by with impunity, whilst the half-starved and diseased bleed to death upon it.

You know, they have many rights; had they also a right to banish me? No, according to the mathematical tariff of Prussian rights, they had none! I said to them, "I have yet a right!" but they answered, "We have the might!" Such might is that of brutal force, by which an ox has more right than a man.

You see, that if in such circumstances we depend upon our rights, it will be necessary at last to connect the feeling of our right with the recollection of our power.

Our physical power is hired and turned against us by the gold of our adversaries; if it were to be used for our own benefit, no one would offer one farthing for it. But we have still our intellect, which is the creator of all that is and can be done by us.

How shall we so develope [sic] this intellectual power as to conquer and triumph? Not by Captain Warner's invention of destructive engines[4]; not by the crafty finance operations of Rothschild and Company; not by the cunning manoeuvres of diplomatists; not by the dogmatism of a useless and slavish erudition. No! it must be by freedom of expression that fears no contradiction, but, on the contrary, expects it by freedom of expression. Proved and measured by opposition, the power alone of free expression in explaining the interests of individuals as the necessary, the useful, the beautiful, and agreeable, finds in each man's breast a natural defender.

Here it is said, we have freedom of expression. If so, hail, welcome England, asylum of the liberty of speech of Europe! O, why art thou but that why art thou also the residence of Mammon, our material god?

Thy innumerable ships crossing all waters, accumulating and exchanging the products of the labour from the sweat of many millions of workmen, of different countries. Why, like a cruel step-mother, dost thou suffer thy most diligent children to sit by their hearths empty-handed, whilst, capricious to others, thou fillest their pockets with us, less toys and sweet meats?

Thou art great in thy dominion over the seas; thou hast devised, and partly accomplished, the emancipation of the black slaves. Why, England, dost thou nothing for the emancipation of the white? Canst thou be indifferent whilst thy magazines and warehouses are overstocked with the wealth of the globe, whilst thou seest the producer ragged and hungry, strolling through thy streets? See, the winter approaches; the destitute crowd in unhealthy holes, or are exposed without shelter to bitter frosts, or chilling damps, whilst the idle consumers fly to the south, their warm nests left empty.

The swallows also fly to the south, leaving empty their nests, which the sparrows take possession of for their own comfort. Why should houseless, naked creatures, in sight of splendour and luxury, slowly be frozen to death? Have not the people built and furnished all these nests? Had they not a greater right to them than the sparrows who have not built those of the swallows?

Proud England, who hast diffused among the most distant nations, the light of knowledge, improvement, and Christianity; who givest to whole nations thy language, see the ignorance and wretchedness of thine own children! See the females in the period of childhood, death depicted in her countenance, see her on the slippery brink of corruption! See her earning her bread by the most degrading debauchery. Look England behold and help thine own children:

How long, England, wilt thou beg for what thou hast a right to demand?

So long as the energies of the many are employed for the exclusive interests and enjoyments of the few; and laws are made and punishments enforced to preserve such a state of things—*so long as those who labour are poore* [sic] *than those who govern.*

A beautiful and excellent thing is freedom of expression, a powerful voice in the mouth of the oppressed, an indescribable sound of rejoicing from the lips of the mighty. But it is nothing, and falls inoperative if the ideas it evolves are of an impracticable nature.

Therefore, we see all ideas occupied with that which is essential to all, which can be proved, compared, and explained, fear no discussion, they are the lifeblood of freedom of expression. These have created that sympathy which animated the Phalanges of all European Communists.

Our power lies, therefore, in the power of our principles,—it is developed by their propagation and the best propagandism is the best means of attaining our ends. When, if finally we approach then, we shall look for a man with the principles of Owen, and with the resolution and generosity of Oscar the young King of Sweden, who offered at once voluntarily to his people, what millions have here, vainly demanded for many years.[5]

Thus I end, having freely expressed myself, and hoping though a stranger, you will not banish me for it, as the republican government in Zurich, and the liberal government in Prussia have done.

Mr. Weitling was listened to throughout with the deepest attention and interest, and on resuming his seat, was greeted with hearty and long continued cheering.

The Chairman then called upon

Mr. FLEMING[6], Editor of the *"New Moral World,"* who said, the meeting of that night was the realization of one of his earliest dreams of Socialism. Before he was made acquainted with its catholic principles, he, like others, had his mind filled with the ordinary local and narrow notions of localized beings, national greatness, national glory, national patriotism, and national prejudices, were necessary consequences of the sectional training generally imparted, and the results were to be seen in the foolish talk about "natural enemies", which was even now, so rife, and in those deplorable wars which were so frequently waged between different nations. From the moment, however, that he understood the principles of the Rational System of Society, as propounded by Robert Owen, such ideas died a natural death. A new light was thrown upon the page of history — new hopes were created for the future. He saw in mankind everywhere only brethren, and knew that the best interests of humanity could be best promoted by promoting fraternity between men of all climes and countries. What if a chain of mountains, a river, or an ocean, separated their respective birth-places ! Were they not constituted with the same elementary faculties? had they not the same desires for happiness? — was not the globe ample enough in its stores to satisfy them all? And should the mere accident of birth—the chance of being brought into existence on one or the other side of a strip of water—be a cause for antipathies or alienation among beings thus formed to promote each others [sic]welfare? For these and other reasons to which he would allude, he rejoiced in witnessing the numerous and enthusiastic meeting he then addressed, and he thanked the chairman for having selected him to stand up in the name of the Socialists of Great Britain, and on their behalf to tender a hearty and cordial welcome to Welhelm [sic] Weitling the courageous and talented leader of German Communism —(*Great cheering*). They hailed him as a brother in the best sense of that word. They were united by kindred principles in the noblest of causes, and in thus publicly testifying their respect for him, they were but pledging themselves anew to the advocacy of those great principles of Social reform of which they were the disciples—principles which led to exertions as cosmopolitan in their scope—to plans as universal in their object, as they were catholic and immutable in their foundation and essence. The meeting, however, in addition to its primary object of testifying its esteem and respect to one of the martyrs in the cause of Communism abroad, had a secondary one, that of holding out the hand of friendship to communists everywhere. Too long had they been strangers to each other, ignorant of their mutual proceedings, working sectionally — therefore ineffectively. He hoped that this meeting was the commencement of a new era, and that in future that peaceful and moral revolution which was now espoused by the leading minds in all civilized nations, would proceed more rapidly in consequence of the greater intimacy and intercourse which would flow from it. If they wished to know what the results of such an intercourse would be, they had only to think of the hostile feelings, which had lately, for a considerable period found vent in the journals of the war factions of France and England. These journals had pandered to the grossest prejudices, had raked up old quarrels and kindled old animosities. The stupid as well as immoral cry of "natural enemies," had been raised by them again, and he (Mr. F.) was sorry to find that the adherents of these journals—the keenest for war, were found among the democracy, the masses of these respective countries. In the United States the same appetite for war exhibited itself among what was called the democratic party. Deeply did he regret this. It had been said, that were "nations wise, war was a game that kings would not be allowed to play at,"[7]—what then must be thought of nations who had to be restrained from hostilities by kings? The only certain way to counteract this belligerent propensity of the masses, was to disseminate every where the peace-making and humanizing principles of Socialism. These could alone destroy anger, revenge, national or individual jealousy, and enable mankind to fraternize as members of one family. In this light the meeting of that night assumed an important aspect, and he fervently hoped it would be one of the instruments for spreading among the people of all European countries, a knowledge of those saving principles by which their highest and dearest wishes could be most effectually advanced, and of the plans which promised to make peace universal and permanent . . . Mr. Fleming then briefly alluded to the career of Mr. Weitling. He said that the first introduction of that Reformer to the notice of the British reader was through the medium of the "*New Moral World*" at the latter end of last year, in a series of well written papers on "Continental Socialism," by a young German gentleman resident in this country, and which were afterwards quoted by the *Northern Star*.[8] These papers created a deep interest in the movement, the nature and scope of which they outlined, and especially in that of its disinterested and determined originator and leader Mr. Weitling, whose imprisonment for six months, by the authorities of Zurich, for the dissemination of Communist opinions they first made known. Since Mr. Weitling's release from prison, he had been subjected to much persecution from the government of his native country, Prussia, and had at last been compelled to take refuge, at least for the present, in this "island of free speech and thought." In the very striking address which Mr. W. had just delivered, it appeared that the co-existence of the distress and injustice there alluded to, had struck him as being anomalous and inconsistent with the possession and exercise of the right of freedom of expression. It was natural that such an impression should be produced on the mind of one just arrived from countries where no such invaluable privilege was possessed. When however Mr. Weitling became a little more conversant with the peculiar structure of society in England, he would see what was almost impossible to explain to him in words— the nature of the material upon which the social and political reformer had to operate, and find in that the most satisfactory explanation of his difficulty. John Bull was very fond of grumbling (laughter), and he dearly prized his liberty of speech, because it enabled him to indulge freely his propensity; but very little reform satisfied him at any time, and in the meantime the liberty of speech served as a capital safety-valve for the social machine, and the government would be foolish indeed which meddled with it restrictively. As a proof that this view of the matter was correct, the speaker showed by various illustrations that the periods of popular commotion and agitation in England were always coincident with stagnation of trade and severe physical destitution among the masses; that immediately on the revival of trade, and the consequent partial diminution of the sufferings of the industrious classes, these agitations invariably declined. What was the present condition of that formerly flourishing body, the Anti-Corn Law League[9]— what of the still more numerous one, the Chartists, at the present moment? The truth was, that no agitation whatever could bear up against even a partial prosperity in England; the people were very easily satisfied, and the most certain way to pacify John Bull was through his stomach. Mr. Fleming applied this to the Social movement, and pointedly put it to the numerous meeting around him, the majority of whom were constant attendants at that Hall, what they had practically done for the advancement of the experiment at Harmony. Reverting to the subject of freedom of expression, Mr. F. said, that though it had not yet destroyed those anomalies, nor put down the unjust arrangements which produced the sufferings alluded to by Mr. Weitling, it was still an invaluable privilege in itself, and he had no doubt would, in due time work out the moral and physical, as it was now effecting the mental emancipation of the people. Mr. F. then alluded to the progress of Socialism in this country as a proof of its growing influence over the public mind, and an evidence of the utility of free inquiry and free discussion; their meeting that night, the audiences who were at that moment listening to lectures in similar Halls[10] in all the great towns of this country; these and many other enjoyments could not be thought of without gratification; and he was happy to see around him several of those veterans whose imprisonments and exertions had won for Britain such an invaluable right, and made it at the present moment the freest country in the world. He said this, with the imprisonment of Mr. Holyoake[11], of Mr. Southwell[12], of Mr. Paterson[13], of Miss Roalfe[14], &c. full in his recollection; nor did he forget the recent incarceration of another friend near him, Mr. Hetherington[15], for the publication and expression of opinion. These exceptions did not invalidate the main fact; they were rather confirmatory of it. In truth, some of the parties to whom he had referred provoked prosecution. They had gone into the den of bigotry, stirred it up in the most audacious manner, dared it to open combat, and insisted upon having a struggle with it. But for such conduct he thought there was little likelihood that it would have voluntarily ventured on persecution. He was not condemning the course these parties had pursued, but merely accounting for the exceptions which might be urged against his statements. Mr. Fleming concluded a long address, which our limited space will not permit us to report more fully, and which was received throughout with great cheering, by again reiterating a welcome to Mr. Weitling and the foreigners present.

Mr. HOLYOAKE, who was warmly received by the meeting, said, Some time ago, when he saw an account in the *New Moral World*—a relation of Mr. Weitling's sufferings—he little thought that they should so soon sit at the same table, and utter in his ears their sympathy for his sufferings, and their appreciation of his efforts on behalf of German humanity. He said German humanity, because a man's worth was best estimated by what he did at home. The glorious name of Lycurgus was held in esteem, because he made Sparta a model to all nations. Mr. Weitling's worth is to be estimated by his efforts on behalf of Germany. Mr. Weitling had compared the persecutor's power to that of the ox; yet, brutal as it was, it was that power which too often made good men eat their words, mystify their doctrines, and double their dealings. He (Mr. H.) was proud to stand among those who welcomed Mr. Weitling; because, though chained and treated with contumely, yet was Mr. Weitling there expressing his opinions as formerly. There was hope of improvement when our public men were not only wise but honest—not only benevolent but brave. They had heard England praised for its liberty—it was regarded as devotion to the cause of freedom regardless of personal the foreigner's home—but if England was so excellent with consequences should be inculcated. Whatever, that if the suffering was to be ten times, greater its misrule and miseries, how sunken must be continental nations! Did it not happen that we are inclined to endure what we have, because other nations are worse off? From this they learned the duty of fraternizing with their foreign brethren—for the existence of foreign slavery perpetuated English subjugation. Mr. Weitling had referred to that talismanic word, Communism—Let us hope that that manifold idea will yet rise gradually and glowingly, until its fire warms and brightens all. In that hour they could be generous to the oppressor, and even the oppressed could forget him. It was not because Communism was put forth with good intentions, or struck down by bad ones, that they stood by it—it was because its principles were consonant with right reason, in accordance with progress, and resulting from undying conviction. (Applause.)

Mr. SCHAPPER[16], a German, said, in the name of his country-men be thanked the meeting for the cordial and honourable reception they had given to his brother Welling. It would be an ample recompense for all he had endured individually; but, above all, he rejoiced at seeing that splendid, spirited meeting, inasmuch as it would convey to those who held similar doctrines abroad, the assurance that they had friends and co-labourers in England who sympathized with them. Let those who talked of "natural enemies" come there and see men of all European nations, met together as brothers, for an answer to such anti-social doctrines. Outside, those natives of other countries, who were present, might be called foreigners, but there he was certain there were no foreigners; they were all brothers. (Great cheering) The German Communists agreed with the English Socialists, in thinking that Communities could be obtained by peaceable means and free discussion alone. They wanted only free speech and writing abroad, and they would be certain of success. Sometime ago they had the notion that it was possible to thrust ideas into the brains of their rulers by force, but they had now discovered that reason and force were incompatible, and that no amount of bullets, cannon, or otherwise, could make an argument or destroy one. (Cheers.) The German Communists also agreed with their English brethren in thinking that good circumstances were the only means by which a superior character could be given to human beings; and these circumstances could not be attained except by a total reconstruction of society; therefore they would join them in their efforts to put down the real devil of the world—private property—and in instituting arrangements that would, at all times, exercise and develope [sic] the best faculties of humanity. Their cause was that of reason, truth, justice, and fraternity, and by the diffusion of these alone could it be attained. Perseverance, in a peaceable and charitable agitation, would enable us to bequeath a glorious legacy to their children, and cover, not England, but Europe, with Harmony Halls. (Great cheering.)

Mr. CHILLMAN[17] thought that some account of the progress and state of Socialism in France might be acceptable to the assembly. Ten years ago, there were not more than a dozen professed Socialists, and they were under the guidance of Buonarotti.

None were more hostile to them than the republican party. Now there is scarcely a town or village in France in which Communism has not its votaries. The great question is not now between republicanism and monarchy, but between those who advocate individual property and community of property. They have past the fear that aristocracy would form a coalition to put down communism. Some speakers have congratulated themselves upon the fact of the superior latitude allowed here by the laws. He would wish to see greater stringency and rigour adopted. The necessary stimulus would not then be wanting to incite men to energetic action. This laxity reminded the speaker of the case of a horse, on whose neck the rider threw the reins loosely and carelessly—why?—because he was so well tamed as to induce no fear of his being restive or troublesome. Why are not the movement party stronger here? Because divided and distracted by contentions—Social parties here—Chartist parties there; these divisions keep up a most injurious want of confidence, and prevent the accession of numbers from among the indifferent lookers on. Thus do our enemies keep the upper hand; be would only begin to hope for England when saw her united and fraternised against the common foe. If the objects of reformers were alike, why quarrel about the means? why throw an additional weight into the scale of the enemy. He did hope that at the great banquet of Monday, in commemoration of the French revolution, that Socialists would show their comprehensiveness of sympathy by their presence. He had heard with great pain and heaviness of heart, the expression from one of the speakers, that English sympathies and feelings were only to be reached through their stomachs. He thought this was to be attributed greatly to Socialist and Chartist leaders, who addressed the selfish interests and lower feelings in their popular appeals. They tell the people to get up and act for their individual interests—that they must strive for great political and social changes, for the sake of raising their wages, or the obtainment of similar advantages. What is the consequence? That if they do not get their wages raised—if they do not benefit at once and individually, they drop off and cease their efforts. They should be told that they would reap misery, and that they should expect to leave their noble work of melioration as a legacy to their children and those who should come after them. Those who undertake to teach the people should give loftier lessons—they should touch on nobler chords. Let them cease appealing to the selfish interests, and thus leaving the people as great brutes as they found them. The example of their noble friend and guest, Weitling, might be worthily followed, as well as those which have been set by other of his compatriots and continental co-reformers—that generous devotion to the cause of freedom regardless of personal consequences should be incalculated. There was no doubt than that which had been hitherto endured, it would be met with equal readiness and fortitude.

Mr. M. Q. RYALL[18] spoke as follows:—The value to be attached to this meeting—notwithstanding that we are prone to think too much of "present occasions"—can hardly be overestimated. We meet to welcome a man who has done much in the enunciation and promulgation of great communist principles, who has given power to the helpless by teaching them to think justly and organise efficiently, and who has moralised them by teaching each to think of the permanent welfare of all; —we meet to welcome a man whom poverty did not render suppliant or submissive, and whom power could only punish, not subdue, who has been foremost, in the teeth of the most arbitrary and even illegally-exercised power, to give a further impetus to the glorious progress of free discussion. We *may* speak thus of the man if we choose only to look on him as an instrument. We compromise no doctrinal point of Owenian Socialism by recording our approval—we press forward no objectionable competitive motive when we simply express approbation, and may look upon it as an allowable, an appropriate, and a consistent stimulus to similar conduct in others. The dangers of too much martyrdom are not of the kind which we, as a body, have to fear. Whether there have been other "Rationalists" who may have acted equally on the prudential system, we have not, perhaps, experience to determine. We modern Rationalists, as a body, have not hitherto shown ourselves the men, by indiscreet daring and superfluous valour, to evince a reckless indifference to the better-to-be-safe course. An infusion, then, of courage—moral or physical, or both— nay, even a little spice of the frequently reprehended dare-devilism, might be added, without turning us entirely away from the proprieties and respectabilities. All of us, at any rate, from the most sensitively cautious to the most self-sacrificing and chivalric, know and feel the effects of progress in the attainment of free discussion. The bulk of society experience its advantages, the pioneers its difficulties, dangers, and sufferings, in wresting it from unwilling and powerful authority. High and great effort, and self negation, which constitute the first and most difficult steps in extensive reforms or revolutions, are the work of individuals. Bodies, societies, organizations carry on and prosper, but do not perform the most difficult and dangerous labour, that of the pioneer. We must not, then, forget the functions of individualism, nor fail to encourage a beneficial development: there is an importance, in my opinion, to be attached to this assembly, if I may indulge the hope of its being only the first of a continuous series, which I scarcely can expect to be estimated as highly by the members of our Society generally. The very circumstance of his being the first meeting of extreme social and political reformers of the great and rival nations during the half-dozen years of our organization, sufficiently attests the small value that has been put upon this cosmopolitan intercourse. It is with such intercommunication as with education and political rights—the less they were demanded, the more need of them was demonstrated by the very indifference. There may be some who would say, let us push on with our own views and objects, not diverted by what others are thinking, or saying, or doing, and leave them to do the same. I deem this not only selfish in the objectionable sense, but unwise, and, on the narrowest consideration, impolitic. We cannot pretend to all the knowledge on the great Social Science. We should not press forward with less rapidity, nor the less make good each past step, by being helped to discover and cast aside our errors. We should be able to turn the world into a Paradise, or something much better, and obtain the promised millennium—or that which would be superior to anything undignified by a Jewish scripture name—in much shorter time, with the counsel and co-operation of our brethren from abroad. A too limited intellectual, is like a too limited physical intercourse, productive of stunted, puny, and impotent progeny. If we had Communities to-morrow studding the entire country—the Communists being confined to the limited sphere of their respective localities, we should possibly have a set of vegetating automata, instead of animated, thinking, suggestive, and energetic men and women. If there were no doctrinal or other differences we should be benefited by companionship and co-operation, by making us all the more powerful. If, on the other hand, differences of opinion are great, the sooner we know and discuss them the better for the interests of all. Unlike those who discuss but to confound and triumph, and whose interest lies in justifying, ours consist in complete mutual understanding. Through the friends to whom we are now introduced, a better knowledge may be obtained of some of those important bases of first principles and schemes for a republican constitution and political organization which were developed by the great French revolution. The severely rigorous and compromising principles of a Robespierre or others of that school may be examined. The French, German, and English Communists may compare notes. We may discuss the comparative merits of that set of Social principles which refuses to begin with the consideration of self, and of that which refuses to recognise any merit or demerit rightly attaching itself to the thoughts, words, and actions of men, and therefore any justly consequent reward or punishment. We might determine whether the self-interest so frequently urged as a stimulus to English, reformers, did not operate against progression as an obstacle, more than it gained as an incentive, whenever that self-interest happens to be endangered. An example of the utility of this intercourse has been only now given in the able address of our friend Chillman, and the excellent exposition we have had of his views and those of his brother Socialists, in opposition to the incentive of selfishness. Our continental friends might determine whether the discovery, acceptance of, and the acting upon our views of the formation of character would not induce on their part a gentler, an improved mode of regarding and dealing with their fellow-men. we have been kept apart too long by the fraud and force of the governing, who have enlisted the Priest, the soldier, the constable, and the lawyer to engender and perpetuate animosities and punish us for intercommunion. We know how this is effected in our country. The manner in which these inimical feelings are fostered abroad, the systematic way in which they are encouraged, though not differing in the leading features, surprise and shock us only from our being unused to that precise form of tyranny. The student-life of Germany affords an illustration of this conservative corruption. The drinking, fighting, and the ordinary university dissoluteness of the generality of German students during their college career is familiarised to most English readers through the narrative of Howitt[19]. There is no less a sober, reflective, and studious section of students who devote themselves to pursuits of a totally different character, whose investigations are carried on for the maturing and promulgation of the best ideas, and, if necessary, to energetic action, for political and social advancement. It is an established fact, that not only are the dissolute upheld, and the more moral portion frowned on by the constituted authorities, but gross injustice is perpetrated towards the latter. In the slightest differences that would occur between these parties, differences usually provoked by the insolent bearing of those who were addicted to vices instead of philosophy, authority would step in, and adjudge, not by justice, but favouritism, thus showing that the profligate are their special *protégés*, while the moralist and humanitarian must be discounanced [sic] and even crushed. We could not, if we were willing, make up for the want of personal intercourse with reformers by learning what they think and do from the public journals. The journals conceal through indifference or avarice, those movements and agitations most completely favourable to popular liberty. The instance of Sweden has been hardly touched upon in the journals; and where it was impossible to avoid mentioning the great organic change about taking place, and the great popular agitation preceding or consequent, it has been partially or imperfectly given, or grossly misrepresented. In this great revolution, while we must concede to a young, noble-hearted, and enthusiastic monarch, (Oscar of Sweden) high approval for his, not kingly, but manly conduct, and chivalric determination to support the people's interests and enlarge the popular liberties, we must not forget that the people themselves are not idly moved with the current—not mere spectators—but actors, and ready actors in the great change. From our foreign friends I learn—and from none of the sources of ordinary journalism should we learn it, or anything most vitally interesting to us—that the people are sufficiently prepared to appreciate the revelation, and press on for the highest and best reformation, let opposition start from whatever quarter it may. Then let us the more mingle, and be mutually warned by our common reverses, or mutually encouraged by our common triumphs. We have to do something more, and better, than giving liberty—we have to ascertain perfectly, and teach the people boldly, what it is—how to get it, and to keep it. Then, if we have been hitherto kept apart by others, let us not be kept apart by ourselves, but by mutual inquiry, discussion, forbearance, and thorough humanitarian feelings, meet to forward not merely our particular, but the universal liberty, security, happiness. (Cheering.)

Mr. SULLY[20] said, a few words commendatory of the exertions of Mr. Weitling, and explanatory of the reasons which have induced himself and friends to determine on emigrating to the far west for the purpose of working out the theory of democratic Communism.

Mr. Alexander CAMPBELL[21] said, his country's bard, some thirty years ago, had said,

> It's coming yet, for a' that,
> When man to man, the world o'er,
> Shall brothers be, an' a' that.[22]

And that meeting was, to a great extent, a fulfilment of that poetic prophecy. Divide and conquer had hitherto been the watchword of the tyrant. Unite and be free should be the motto of the friends of benevolence and humanity. After alluding to Mr.

Weitling's exertions, Mr. C. proceeded at some length to review the struggles which had been made during the present century for freedom of speech and printing—alluding to the loss of property and repeated imprisonments which had been submitted to by Carlile[23], Hetherington, &c. He himself had been a martyr in this cause, and hundreds of others had been in like manner ready to throw themselves into the breach. Let their foreign friends, therefore, not depart with the impression that this inestimable privilege was lightly won or lightly prized. If we were a little ahead of other nations it was the consequence of many a hard fought battle in former years, and he would tell them that they, in like manner, must be prepared to suffer imprisonment and persecution, to any extent, in order to gain, this the first step in real emancipation. Mr. C. alluded to several other important topics, but the space we have already alloted [sic] to the meeting will not permit us to report more fully—he retired amidst the most cordial demonstrations of satisfaction.

During the evening, and between the various orations, the choir and vocalists favoured the meeting with chorusses [sic] and songs from the best masters, which gave an additional charm to the party, and elicited unequivocal marks of approval. They concluded by again singing the "Marseillaise," and the chairman, in a few words, terminated this interesting reunion a little before eleven o'clock. The interest and enthusiasm of those present continued unabated to the close.

Notes

1 For instance, the League of the Just had opened a London branch in 1840, and their representatives had been invited to visit Owen's model community at Queenwood (Lattek 1988, 265).
2 The John Street Institute was inaugurated in April 1840 as the new headquarters of the Owenite London Branch A1.
3 Robert Clarke.
4 Samuel Alfred Warner (c. 1793–1853), English chemist who falsely claimed to have invented explosive naval weapons.
5 Oscar I (1799–1859), king of Sweden and Norway (1844–1859). A liberal monarch, he established freedom of the press shortly after his coronation on 28 September 1844.
6 George Alexander Fleming.
7 William Cowper (1731–1800), *The Task* (1785), book V, *The Winter Morning Walk*.
8 Friedrich Engels. See Chapter 60 above.
9 The Anti-Corn Law League was founded in 1838 and campaigned for the repeal of the Corn Laws, which were later abolished in 1846.
10 The Owenite Halls of Science.
11 George Jacob Holyoake (1817–1906), English Owenite, co-operator and freethinker. He co-edited the *Oracle of Reason* with Charles Southwell. In 1842, Holyoake was convicted for blasphemy following a public lecture given at the Cheltenham Mechanics' Institute. That same year, he and Emma Martin co-founded the Anti-Persecution Union to support freedom of speech.
12 Charles Southwell (1814–1860), anticlerical journalist and editor of the *Oracle of Reason* (1841–1843). He was imprisoned for blasphemy in January 1842 (see Part 7, Chapter 45).
13 Thomas Paterson took over as editor of the *Oracle of Reason* after both Charles Southwell and George Jacob Holyoake were imprisoned. Paterson was in turn jailed for blasphemy in January and November 1843.

14 Matilda Roalfe was an Edinburgh author, bookshop owner and secularist publisher. She was jailed for blasphemy in 1844. Following her release she co-wrote *Law Breaking Justified* with Thomas Paterson to support freedom of speech.
15 Henry Hetherington (1792–1849), bookseller, co-operator, Chartist leader and editor of the *Poor Man's Guardian* (1831–1835, see Part 6, Chapter 39). In 1833, 1836 and 1840, he was jailed for his campaign against the taxation of newspapers, and for selling Charles Junius Haslam's *Letters to the Clergy of All Denominations* (1840), a Deist pamphlet.
16 Karl Schapper (1812–1870), German socialist, union leader and associate of Wilhelm Weitling and Karl Marx. He moved to London in 1840, where he chaired the local branch of the League of the Just.
17 Jacques Chilmann (1814–1879?), a radical French exile in London, and co-founder of the Société Démocratique française in 1839.
18 Maltus Questell Ryall, Lambeth socialist, contributor to the *Oracle of Reason* and secretary of the Anti-Persecution Union.
19 William Howitt (1792–1879), English writer. In 1840, he and his wife, poet Mary Howitt (1799–1888) moved to Heidelberg, Germany. William Howitt wrote a satire of local customs, *The Student Life in Germany* (1841) under the pseudonym of "Dr. Cornelius".
20 Charles Sully, a French bookbinder and Icarian socialist. He joined the Democratic Friends of All Nations and introduced Étienne Cabet to Robert Owen in 1847. He later joined the Icarian community at Nauvoo, Texas, and presumably died in the United States.
21 Alexander Campbell, co-operator and former Social Missionary (see Part 3, Chapter 20).
22 From Robert Burns's *A Man's A Man for A' That* (1795).
23 Richard Carlile (1790–1843), radical publisher and campaigner for universal suffrage and freedom of the press. He was imprisoned for seditious libel multiple times throughout his career.

BIBLIOGRAPHY

Primary sources

Archives and manuscripts

Bray Papers. n.d. London: London School of Economics.
Correspondence of Alexander Campbell. 1828. Robert Owen Collection. Manchester: National Co-operative Archive.
Correspondence of Benjamin Scott Jones. 1835–1837. Robert Owen Collection. Manchester: National Co-operative Archive.
Correspondence of George Mudie. 1823–1848. Robert Owen Collection. Manchester: National Co-operative Archive.
Correspondence of John Gray. 1823. Robert Owen Collection. Manchester: National Co-operative Archive.
Fenwick Weavers' Society Records. 1761–1873. Edinburgh: National Library of Scotland.
Godwin, William. 1788–1836. William Godwin's Diary. Oxford: Bodleian Library.
Goldsmid Letters. 1830. University College London. MS MOCATTA 22.
Hamilton Papers. n.d. Motherwell Public Library.
Hansard. 1840. *Parliamentary Debates*. 3rd Series, LI (1840), cols 530, 1187.
Letters of Anne and Jane Owen to Mrs Anne Owen. 1820. Branigin-Owen Collection. New Harmony, Indiana: Workingmen's Institute.
Lovett Papers. n.d. Senate House Library, University of London.
Milam, Benjamin R. 30 August 1830. Letter to Robert Owen. Robert Owen Collection. Manchester: National Co-operative Archive.
Owen, Robert. 1821. The Social System. Aberystwyth: National Library of Wales. MS 23902E.
Rocafuerte, Vicente. 17 October 1828. Letter to Robert Owen. Robert Owen Collection. Manchester: National Co-operative Archive.

Periodicals

Advocate of the Working Classes (1826–1827)
Black Dwarf (1817–1834)
Carpenter's Political Letters and Pamphlets (1830–1831)
Carpenter's Political Magazine (1831–1832)
Co-operative Magazine and Monthly Herald (1826–1830)

Crisis (1832–1834)
Economist (1821–1822)
Gazette of the Exchange Bazaars (1832–1833)
London Phalanx (1841–1843)
New Moral World (1834–1845)
Political Economist and Universal Philanthropist (1823)
Poor Man's Guardian (1831–1833)
Star, 15 April 1819
Tribune des femmes (1832–1834)
Weekly Free Press (1825)
Working Bee, 28 September 1839

Books and pamphlets

Beatson, Jasper. 1823. *An Examination of Mr. Owen's Plans for Relieving Distress, Removing Discontent, and "Recreating the Character of Man"*. Glasgow: W. Turnbull.

Bellers, John. [1695] 1818. *Proposals for Raising a Colledge of Industry of All Useful Trades and Husbandry*. In *New View of Society: Tracts relative to this subject...* […]. London: published by Robert Owen, printed for Longman, Hurst, Rees, Orme and Brown.

Bray, John Francis. 1839. *Labour's Wrongs and Labour's Remedy; or, the Age of Might and the Age of Right*. Leeds: David Green.

Carpenter, William. 1832. *Proceedings of the Third Co-Operative Congress; Held in London, and Composed of Delegates from the Co-Operative Societies of Great Britain and Ireland, on the 23rd of April 1832*. London: William Strange.

Cobbett, William. 1817. "Mr. Owen". *Black Dwarf*, 20 August 1817.

Colquhoun, Patrick. 1806. *A Treatise on Indigence*. London: J. Hatchard.

Colquhoun, Patrick. 1814. *A Treatise on the Wealth, Power, and Resources, of the British Empire in Every Quarter of the World*. London: J. Mawman.

Combe, Abram. 1823. *An Address to the Conductors of the Periodical Press upon the Causes of Religious and Political Disputes*. Edinburgh: printed by James Auchie.

Craufurd, Lieutenant General (Charles Gregan). 1817. *Observations on the State of the Country since the Peace; with a Supplementary Section on the Poor Laws*. London: printed for William Stockdale.

Dale, David. [1792] 1831. "Letter to Dr. Currie". In James Currie, *Memoir of the Life, Writings and Correspondence of James Currie*. London: printed for Longman, Rees, Orme, Brown and Green.

Durant, Jenny [Désirée Véret]. 1834. "Correspondance, 25 Octobre 1831". *Tribune Des Femmes*, February 1834.

Engels, Friedrich. [1845] 1892. *The Condition of the Working Class in England in 1844*, translated by Florence Kelley Wischnewetzky. London: George Allen & Unwin.

———. [1880] 1970. "Socialism: Utopian and Scientific". In *The Selected Works of Karl Marx and Friedrich Engels*, translated by Paul Lafargue, 95–151. Moscow: Progress Publishers.

Godwin, William. [1793] 2013. *An Enquiry Concerning Political Justice*, edited by Mark Philp. Oxford: Oxford University Press.

Gray, John. 1825. *A Lecture on Human Happiness*. London: Sherwood, Jones & Co.

Hazlitt, William. [1816] 1819. *Political Essays, with Sketches of Public Characters*. London: William Hone.
Hodgskin, Thomas. 1827. *Popular Political Economy. Four Lectures Delivered at the London Mechanics' Institution*. London: Charles and William Tait.
Holyoake, George Jacob. 1844. *A Visit to Harmony Hall*. London: Henry Hetherington.
———. [1875] 1908. *The History of Co-Operation*. London: T. Fischer Unwin.
Hume, David. [1772] 1994. "Of National Characters". In *Political Essays*, edited by Knud Haakonssen, 78–92. Cambridge: Cambridge University Press.
Jones, Lloyd. 1890. *The Life, Times, and Labours of Robert Owen*. 2 vols. London: Sonnenschein & Co.
Lovett, William. [1876] 1967. *Life and Struggles of William Lovett in His Pursuit of Bread, Knowledge and Freedom*. London: McGibbon & Kee.
Malthus, Thomas. [1798] 1817. *An Essay on the Principle of Population*. London: John Murray.
Mandeville, Bernard. [1714] 1724. *The Fable of the Bees: or, Private Vices, Publick Benefits*. London: printed for J. Tonson.
Marx, Karl. [1862–1863] 2000. *Theories of Surplus Value*. Amherst: Prometheus Books.
Marx, Karl, and Friedrich Engels. [1848] 1992. *The Communist Manifesto*, edited by David McLellan. Oxford: Oxford University Press.
Mill, James. 1808. *Commerce Defended. An Answer to the Arguments by Which Mr. Spence, Mr. Cobbett, and Others, Have Attempted to Prove That Commerce Is Not a Source of National Wealth*. London: C. and R. Baldwin.
Mill, James. [1819] 1992. "Essay on Government". In *James Mill: Political Writings*, edited by Terence Ball, 1–42. Cambridge: Cambridge University Press.
More, Thomas. [1516] 2010. *Utopia*, edited by George M Logan, translated by Robert M Adams. New York: Norton.
Owen, Robert. 1813. "A New View of Society; or Essays on the Principle of the Formation of the Human Character, and the Application of the Principle to Practice". In *Robert Owen. A New View of Society and Other Writings*, edited by Gregory Claeys, 1–92. London: Penguin Classics.
———. [1815] 1858. *Observations on the Cotton Trade*. In *A Supplementary Appendix to the First Volume of The Life of Robert Owen. Containing a Series of Reports, Addresses, Memorials, and Other Documents, Referred to in That Volume. 1803–1820*. Vol. 1. A. London: Effingham Wilson.
———. 1816. "Vue nouvelle de la société, ou essais sur le principe de la formation du caractère dans l'homme, et sur l'application pratique de ce principe". In *Bibliothèque Universelle Des Sciences, Belles-Lettres, et Arts*, translated by Charles-Philibert de Lasteyrie 3: 49–235.
———. 1817. *Report to the Committee of the Association for the Relief of the Manufacturing and Labouring Poor, laid before the Committee of the House of Commons on the Poor Laws*. London: printed for the author.
———. [1817]1972. "A Catechism of the New View of Society and Three Addresses". In *A New View of Society and Other Writings*, 170–223. London: Dent.
———. [1820] 1991. "Report to the County of Lanark". In *Robert Owen. A New View of Society and Other Writings*, edited by Gregory Claeys, 250–308. London: Penguin Classics.
———. 1824. "New Lanark: Address to the Inhabitants". *Republican*, July 1824.
———. 1824. *An Outline of the System of Education at New Lanark*. Glasgow: Wardlaw & Cunninghame.

BIBLIOGRAPHY

———. 1826. "Oration Containing a Declaration of Mental Independence". *New Harmony Gazette*, 12 July 1826.

———. 1827. "The Social System, Chapter V [Continued], Constitutions, Laws and Regulations of a Community". *New Harmony Gazette*, 21 February 1827.

———. 1833. "Letter from Robert Owen". *Crisis*, 24 August 1833.

———. 1835. "Public Meeting at the London Labour Exchange, May 1st, 1835". *New Moral World*, 16 May 1835.

———.1839. "Plans for Community Building. Extracts from a Letter from Robert Owen". *New Moral World*, 21 December 1839.

———. 1857. *The Life of Robert Owen, Written by Himself*. Vol. 1. 2 vols. London: Effingham Wilson.

———. 1858. *A Supplementary Appendix to the First Volume of the Life of Robert Owen. Containing a Series of Reports, Addresses, Memorials, and Other Documents, Referred to in That Volume. 1803–1820.* Vol. 1. A. London: Effingham Wilson.

———. 1858. "Letter Published in the London Newspapers of September 10th, 1817. A Further Development of the Plan for the Relief of the Poor, and the Emancipation of Mankind". In *A Supplementary Appendix to the First Volume of The Life of Robert Owen*, 119–137. London: Effingham Wilson.

———. 1858. *Threading My Way: Twenty-Seven Years of Autobiography*. London: Trübner & Co.

———. 1874. "An Earnest Sowing of Wild Oats". *The Atlantic Monthly*, July 1874.

———. 1905. "Constitution of the Preliminary Society of New Harmony, 27 April 1825". In *The New Harmony Movement*, edited by George Browning Lockwood, 84–90. New York: D. Appleton & Co.

Owen, William. 1906. *Diary of William Owen from November 10, 1824 to April 20, 1825*, edited by Joel W. Hiatt. Indianapolis: The Bobbs-Merrill Company.

Potter Webb, Beatrice. 1899. *The Co-Operative Movement in Britain*. London: Sonnenschein & Co.

Smith, Adam. [1776] 2008. *An Inquiry into the Nature and Causes of the Wealth of Nations. A Selected Edition*, edited by Kathryn Sutherland. Oxford: Oxford University Press.

Smith, James Elishama. 1833. *Lecture on a Christian Community: Delivered by the Rev. J.E. Smith, M.A. at the Surry Institution*. London: J. Brooks.

Southey, Robert. [1819] 1929. *Journal of a Tour in Scotland in 1819*. London: John Murray.

Thompson, William. 1824. *An Inquiry into the Principles of the Distribution of Wealth Most Conducive to Human Happiness Applied to the Newly Proposed System of Voluntary Equality of Wealth*. London: printed for Longman, Hurst, Rees, Orme, Brown and Green.

———. 1830. *Practical Directions for the Speedy and Economical Establishment of Communities: On the Principles of Mutual Co-Operation, United Possessions and Equality of Exertions and of the Means of Enjoyments*. London: Strange.

Thompson, William, and Anna Doyle Wheeler. [1825] 1994. *Appeal of One Half of the Human Race, Women, against the Pretensions of the Other Half, Men, to Retain Them in Political, and Thence in Civil and Domestic, Slavery*, edited by Michael Foot and Marie Roberts Mulvey. Bristol: Thoemmes.

To Unionists. Abstracts of the Proceedings of a Special Meeting of Trades' Unions Delegates. 1834.

Torrens, Robert. 1817. *A Paper on the Means of Reducing the Poor Rates and of Affording Effectual and Permanent Relief to the Labouring Classes*. London.

Warder, William S. 1818. "A Brief Sketch of the Religious Society of People Called Shakers, Communicated to Mr. Owen by W.S. Warder of Philadelphia, one of the Society of Friends". In *New View of Society. Tracts relative to this Subject...* […]. London: published by Robert Owen, printed for Longman, Hurst, Rees, Orme and Brown.

Secondary sources

Allen, Caroline Dale Baldwin, ed. 1990. *Look to the Distaff. A Record of Nine Generations of a Family Line*. Washington, Connecticut: privately printed.

Anderson, Bonnie S. 2000. *Joyous Greetings: The First International Women's Movement, 1830–1860*. Oxford: Oxford University Press.

Armytage, W.H.G. 1971. "Owen and America". In *Robert Owen, Prophet of the Poor*, edited by Sidney Pollard and John Salt, 214–238. London: Palgrave Macmillan.

Bakken, Dawn E. 2011. "'A Full Supply of the Necessaries and Comforts of Life': The Owenite Community of Blue Spring, Indiana". *Indiana Magazine of History* 107 (3): 235–249.

Baroteaux, Valérie. 2019. "À l'aube Du XIXe Siècle, les débuts du mouvement coopératif". In *Les coopératives: quelles réalités? Produire, commercer, consommer autrement*, edited by Laëtitia Lethielleux and Magali Boespflug. Reims: Éditions et Presses universitaires de Reims.

Bederman, Gail. 2005. "Revisiting Nashoba: Slavery, Utopia and Frances Wright in America, 1818–1826". *American Literary History* 17 (3): 438–459.

Beecher, Jonathan. 1986. *Charles Fourier. The Visionary and His World*. Berkeley: Berkeley University Press.

———. 1990. *Charles Fourier: The Visionary and His World*. Berkeley, Los Angeles and London: University of California Press.

———. 2001. *Victor Considerant and the Rise and Fall of French Romantic Socialism*. Berkeley, Los Angeles and London: University of California Press.

Bennett, Andrew. 2016. *The Hidden Oak. The Life and Works of George Mudie, Pioneer Co-Operator*. London: Albion Press.

Bensimon, Fabrice, ed. 2018. *Friedrich Engels. Écrits de jeunesse*. Vol. 2, Manchester, 1842–1844. Paris: Éditions sociales.

Berg, Maxine. 1980. *The Machinery Question and the Making of Political Economy (1815–1848)*. Cambridge: Cambridge University Press.

Bestor, Arthur. [1950] 2018. *Backwoods Utopias: The Sectarian Origins and the Owenite Phase of Communitarian Socialism in America, 1663–1829*. Philadelphia: University of Pennsylvania Press.

Boulukos, George. 2008. *The Grateful Slave: The Emergence of Race in Eighteenth-Century British and American Culture*. Cambridge: Cambridge University Press.

Bray, Charles. 1879. *Phases of Opinion and Experience During a Long Life: An Autobiography*. London: Longmans & Green.

Caine, Barbara. 1997. *English Feminism, 1780–1980*. Oxford: Oxford University Press.

Chaloner, W.H. 1954. "Robert Owen, Peter Drinkwater and the Early Factory System in Manchester, 1788–1800". *Bulletin of the John Rylands Library* 37: 79–102.

Chase, Malcolm. 1988. *The People's Farm: English Radical Agrarianism 1775–1840*. Oxford: Oxford University Press.

———. 2007. *Chartism: A New History*. Manchester: Manchester University Press.

BIBLIOGRAPHY

———. 2011. "Exporting the Owenite Utopia: Thomas Powell and the Tropical Emigration Society". In *Robert Owen and His Legacy*, edited by Chris Williams and Noel Thompson, 198–217. Cardiff: University of Wales Press.

———. 2017. *Early Trade Unionism: Fraternity, Skill and the Politics of Labour*. London: Routledge.

Claeys, Gregory. 1981. "Notes and Queries: Benjamin Scott Jones, Alias 'Philadelphus': An Early Owenite Socialist". *Bulletin of the Society for the Study of Labour History* 43: 14–15.

———. 1982. "Notes on Labour Biography: George Mudie, Fragments of an Owenite Autobiography". *Labour History Review* 45: 15–17.

———. 1982. "Paternalism and Democracy in the Politics of Robert Owen". *International Review of Social History* 27 (2): 161–207.

———. 1985. "The Reaction to Political Radicalism and The Popularisation of Political Economy in Early Nineteenth Century Britain: The Case of Productive and Unproductive Labour". In *Expository Science, Forms and Function of Popularization*, edited by Terry Shinn and Richard Whitley, 119–136. Dordrecht: D. Reidel Publishing Company.

———. 1986. "'Individualism', 'Socialism' and 'Social Science': Further Notes on a Process of Conceptual Formation, 1800–1850". *Journal of the History of Ideas* 47 (1): 81–93.

———. 1986. "John Adolphus Etzler, Technological Utopianism and British Socialism: The Tropical Emigration Society's Venezuelan Mission and Its Social Context, 1833–1848". *English Historical Review* 101: 351–375.

———. 1987. *Machinery, Money and the Millennium: From Moral Economy to Socialism, 1815–1860*. Cambridge: Cambridge University Press.

———. 1988. "Reciprocal Dependence, Virtue and Progress: Some Sources of Early Socialist Cosmopolitanism and Internationalism in Britain, 1750–1850". In *Internationalism and the Labour Movement 1830–1840*, edited by Frits Van Holthoon and Marcel Van der Linden, 1: 235–282. Leiden: Brill.

———. 1989. *Citizens and Saints: Politics and Anti-Politics in the Early Socialist Movement*. Cambridge: Cambridge University Press.

———. 1991. "Introduction". In *A New View of Society and Other Writings*, by Robert Owen, vii–xxxv. London: Penguin Classics.

———, ed. 1991. *Robert Owen. A New View of Society and Other Writings*. London: Penguin Classics.

———, ed. 1993. *The Selected Works of Robert Owen*. 4 vols. London: Pickering and Chatto.

———, ed. 2005. *Owenite Socialism: Pamphlets and Correspondence*. Vol. 1. 10 vols. London: Routledge.

———. 2005. "The Revival of Robert Owen: Crafting a Victorian Reputation, c. 1865–1900". In *The Emergence of Global Citizenship: Utopian Ideas, Co-Operative Movements and the Third Sector*, edited by Chushichi Tsuzuki, Naobumi Hijikata and Akira Kurimoto, 13–28. Tokyo: Robert Owen Association of Japan.

———. 2008. "Wallace and Owenism". In *Natural Selection & Beyond. The Intellectual Legacy of Alfred Russell Wallace*, edited by Charles H. Smith and George Beccaloni, 229–256. Oxford: Oxford University Press.

———. 2011. *Searching for Utopia: The History of an Idea*. London: Thames & Hudson.

Cole, G.D.H. 1944. *A Century of Co-Operation*. London: Allen & Unwin.

Cole, G.D.H. 1965. *The Life of Robert Owen*. London: Frank Cass.

BIBLIOGRAPHY

Cole, G.D.H., and A.W. Filson. 1965. *British Working Class Movements: Select Documents, 1789–1875*. London: Palgrave Macmillan.

Cole, G.D.H., and Raymond Postgate. 1939. *The British Common People 1746–1938*. New York: Alfred A. Knopf.

Colville, Deborah. 2011. "Burton Street Hall". UCL Bloomsbury Project. 2011.

Cory, Abbie L. 2004. "Wheeler and Thompson's 'Appeal': The Rhetorical Re-Visioning of Gender". *New Hibernia Review/Iris Éireannach Nua* 8 (2): 106–120.

Crook, David. 1999. "L'éducation collective des jeunes enfants en Grande-Bretagne: une perspective historique". *Histoire de l'éducation* 82: 23–42.

Cunningham, Hugh. 2014. *Time, Work and Leisure: Life Changes in England since 1700*. Manchester: Manchester University Press.

Davis, J.C. 1983. *Utopia and the Ideal Society: A Study of English Utopian Writing 1516–1700*. Cambridge: Cambridge University Press.

Davis, Robert A., and Frank O'Hagan. 2014. *Robert Owen*. London: Bloomsbury.

Desroche, Henri. 1959. "Messianismes et utopies. Note sur les origines du socialisme occidental". *Archives de sciences sociales des religions* 8: 31–46.

———. 1971. "Images and Echoes of Owenism in Nineteenth-Century France". In *Robert Owen, Prophet of the Poor*, edited by Sidney Pollard and John Salt, 239–284. London: Palgrave Macmillan.

Donnachie, Ian. 1998. "Robert Owen's Welsh Childhood". *Montgomeryshire Collections* 86: 81–96.

———. 2004. "Historic Tourism to New Lanark and the Falls of Clyde 1795–1830. The Evidence of Contemporary Visiting Books and Related Sources". *Journal of Tourism and Cultural Change* 2 (3): 145–162.

———. 2011. "Robert Owen. Reputation and Burning Issues". In *Robert Owen and His Legacy*, edited by Noel Thompson and Chris Williams, 13–31. Cardiff: University of Wales Press.

———. 2019. "'We Must Give Them an Education, Large, Liberal and Comprehensive'. Catherine Vale Whitwell: Teacher, Artist, Author, Feminist and Owenite Communitarian". *Women's History Review* 28 (4): 552–565.

Donnachie, Ian, and George Hewitt. 1993. *Historic New Lanark: The Dale and Owen Industrial Community since 1785*. Edinburgh: Edinburgh University Press.

Dooley, Dolores. 1995. "Anna Doyle Wheeler". In *Women, Power and Consciousness in Nineteenth-Century Ireland*, edited by Mary Cullen and Maria Luddy, 19–53. Dublin: Attic.

———. 1996. *Equality in Community: Sexual Equality in the Writings of William Thompson and Anna Doyle Wheeler*. Cork: Cork University Press.

Durieux, Catherine. 2005. "Marriage as Seen by Robert Owen and the Owenites". In *The Emergence of Global Citizenship: Utopian Ideas, Co-Operative Movements and the Third Sector*, edited by Chushichi Tsuzuki and et al., 95–110. Tokyo: Robert Owen Association of Japan.

Elliott, Josephine Mirabella. 1964. "The Owen Family Papers". *Indiana Magazine of History* 60 (4): 331–352.

Escott, Margaret. 2011. "Robert Owen as a British Politician and Parliamentarian". In *Robert Owen and His Legacy*, edited by Noel Thompson and Chris Williams, 129–154. Cardiff: University of Wales Press.

Fraser, E.M. 1937–38. "Robert Owen in Manchester". *Memoirs and Proceedings of the Manchester Literary and Philosophical Society* 82: 29–41.

Gans, Jacques. 1957. "L'origine du mot 'socialiste' et ses emplois les plus anciens". *Revue d'histoire économique et sociale* 30: 79–83.

———. 1962. "Robert Owen à Paris En 1837 (Coup d'œil sur le groupe des Owénistes parisiens)". *Le Mouvement social* 41: 35–45.

———. 1964. "Les relations entre socialistes de France et d'Angleterre au début du XIXe siècle". *Le Mouvement social* 46: 105–118.

Garnett, Ronald G. 1971. "Robert Owen and the Community Experiments". In *Robert Owen, Prophet of the Poor: Essays in the Honour of the Two Hundredth Anniversary of His Birth*, edited by Sidney Pollard and John Salt, 39–64. London: Palgrave Macmillan.

———. 1972. *Co-Operation and the Owenite Socialist Communities in Britain, 1825–45*. Manchester: Manchester University Press.

———. 1973. *William Pare, Co-Operator and Social Reformer*. Loughborough: Co-operative Union.

Geoghegan, Vince. 1991. "Ralahine: An Irish Owenite Community 1831–1833". *International Review of Social History* XXXVI: 377–411.

Gijwijt-Hofstra, Marijke. 2017. "Dutch Approaches to Problems of Illness and Poverty between the Golden Age and the *Fin de Siècle*". In *Health Care and Poor Relief in 18th and 19th-Century Northern Europe*, edited by Ole Peter Grell, Andrew Cunningham, and Robert Jütte, 259–269. London and New York: Routledge.

Gleadle, Kathryn. 1995. *The Early Feminists: Radical Unitarians and the Emergence of the Women's Rights Movement, 1831–51*. New York: St. Martin's Press.

Gough, Hugh. 2016. *The Newspaper Press in the French Revolution*. London: Routledge.

Grandjonc, Jacques. 1989. *Communisme/Kommunismus/Communism. Origine et développement international de la terminologie communautaire prémarxiste des utopistes aux néo-babouvistes*. Trier: Karl Marx Haus.

Gunn, Simon, and Robert J. Morris. 2001. *Identities in Space: Contested Terrain in the Western City since 1850*. Farnham: Ashgate.

Gurney, Peter. 1988. "'A Higher State of Co-Operation and Happiness': Internationalism in the British Co-Operative Movement". In *Internationalism and the Labour Movement 1830-1840*, edited by Frits Van Holthoon and Marcel Van der Linden, 2: 543–564. Leiden: Brill.

Gurney, Peter. 2017. *The Making of Consumer Culture in Modern Britain*. London: Bloomsbury.

Hardy, Dennis. 1979. *Alternative Communities in Nineteenth-Century England*. London and New York: Longman.

Harris, José. 1983. "Nature's Chastity". *London Review of Books*, 15 September 1983.

Harrison, J.F.C. 1967. "'The Steam Engine of the New Moral World': Owenism and Education, 1817–1829". *Journal of British Studies* 6 (2): 76–98.

———. 1969. *Owen and the Owenites in Britain and America: The Quest for the New Moral World*. London: Routledge.

———. 1971. "A New View of Mr. Owen". In Pollard and Salt 1971, 1–13.

Hasselmann, E. 1971. "The Impact of Owen's Ideas on German Social and Co-Operative Thought during the Nineteenth Century". In *Robert Owen, Prophet of the Poor: Essays in Honour of the Two Hundredth Anniversary of His Birth*, edited by Sidney Pollard and John Salt, 285–305. London: Macmillan.

Hayes, David. 2001. "'Without Parallel in the Known World': The Chequered Past of 277 Gray's Inn Road". *Camden History Review* 25: 5–9.

Hilton, Boyd. 1977. *Corn, Cash, Commerce: the Economic Policies of the Tory Governments, 1815–1830*. Oxford: Oxford University Press.
Himes, Norman E. 1930. "Robert Dale Owen, The Pioneer of American Neo-Malthusianism". *American Journal of Sociology* 35 (4): 529–547.
Hollis, Patricia. ed. 1969. *The Poor Man's Guardian 1831–1835*. 4 vols. London: Merlin Press.
———, 1970. *The Pauper Press: A Study in Working-Class Radicalism of the 1830s*. Oxford: Oxford University Press.
———, ed. 1973. *Class and Conflict in Nineteenth-Century England 1815–1850*. London: Routledge.
Holyoake, George Jacob. 1851. *The Last Days of Emma Martin: Advocate of Free Thought*. London: J. Watson.
———. [1875] 1908. *The History of Co-Operation*. London: T. Fischer Unwin.
Innes, Joanna. 2002. "Origins of the Factory Acts: The Health and Morals of Apprentices Act, 1802". In *Law, Crime and English Society, 1660–1830*, edited by Norma Landau, 230–255. Cambridge: Cambridge University Press.
Jones, Gareth Stedman. 1981. "Utopian Socialism Reconsidered. Science and Religion in the Early Socialist Movement". In *People's History and Socialist Theory*, edited by Raphael Samuel, 138–44. London: Taylor & Francis.
———. 1983. "Rethinking Chartism". In *Languages of Class: Studies in English Working-Class History 1832–1982*, 90–178. Cambridge: Cambridge University Press.
Jones, Lloyd. 1890. *The Life, Times and Labour of Robert Owen*. Vol. 1. 2 vols. London: Sonnenschein & Co.
Kay, Alison. 2012. *The Foundations of Female Entrepreneurship: Enterprise, Home and Household in London, c. 1800–1870*. London: Routledge.
Kirby, R.G., and A.E. Musson. 1975. *The Voice of the People: John Doherty, 1798–1854, Trade Unionist, Radical and Factory Reformer*. Manchester: Manchester University Press.
Kolmerten, Carol A. 1981. "Egalitarian Promises and Inegalitarian Practices Women's Roles in the American Owenite Communities, 1824–1828". *The Journal of General Education* 33: 31–44.
———. 1998. *Women in Utopia: The Ideology of Gender in the American Owenite Communities*. Syracuse: Syracuse University Press.
Kumar, Krishan. 1990. "Utopian Thought and Communal Practice. Robert Owen and the Owenite Communities". *Theory and Society* 19: 1–35.
Lambert, Cornelia C. 2011. "'Living Machines': Performance and Pedagogy at Robert Owen's Institute for the Formation of Character, New Lanark, 1816–1828". *The Journal of the History of Childhood and Youth* 4 (3): 419–433.
Lane, Fintan. 1997. *The Origins of Modern Irish Socialism, 1781–1896*. Cork: Cork University Press.
Lane, Margaret. 1972. *Frances Wright and the 'Great Experiment'*. Manchester: Manchester University Press.
Langdon, John. 2000. "Pocket Editions of the New Jerusalem: Owenite Communitarianism in Britain 1825–1855". DPhil, Department of History: University of York.
Latham, Jackie E.M. 1994. "Emma Martin and Sacred Socialism: The Correspondence of James Pierrepont Greaves". *History Workshop Journal* 38: 215–217.
Lattek, Christine. 1988. "The Beginnings of Socialist Internationalism in the 1840s: The 'Democratic Friends of All Nations' in London". In *Internationalism and the Labour Movement 1830–1840*, edited by Frits Van Holthoon and Marcel Van der Linden, 1: 259–282. Leiden: Brill.

BIBLIOGRAPHY

LeGates, Marlene. 2001. *In Their Time: A History of Feminism in Western Society*. London and New York: Routledge.

Levitas, Ruth. 2013. *Utopia as Method*. London: Palgrave Macmillan.

Macfarlane, Leslie J. 2016. *Socialism, Social Ownership and Social Justice*. Cham: Springer.

Mallet, Sylvie. 1980. "*Tribune des femmes*: Une éducation à l'indépendance économique'". *Romantisme* 28–29 (212): 203–212.

Marsh, Joss. 1998. *Word Crimes: Blasphemy, Culture, and Literature in Nineteenth-Century England*. Chicago: University of Chicago Press.

Marx, Karl, and Friedrich Engels. [1848] 1992. *The Communist Manifesto*, edited by David McLellan. Oxford: Oxford University Press.

McFadden, Margaret. 1989. "Anna Doyle Wheeler (1785–1848): Philosopher, Socialist, Feminist". *Hypatia* 4 (1): 91–101.

———. 2015. *Golden Cables of Sympathy: The Transatlantic Sources of Nineteenth-Century Feminism*. Lexington: The University Press of Kentucky.

Mercklé, Pierre. 2001. "Le socialisme, l'utopie ou la science? – La 'science sociale' de Charles Fourier et les expérimentations sociales de l'École sociétaire au 19e siècle". Doctoral Thesis in Sociology, Lyon: University Lumière Lyon 2.

Morgan, John Minter. 2010. In *Le Maitron. Dictionnaire biographique du mouvement ouvrier et du mouvement social*. Paris: Éditions sociales.

Moriarty, Theresa. 2012. "'One Darling Though Terrific Theme'. Anna Wheeler and the Rights of Women". In *The Politics of the (Im)Possible: Utopia and Dystopia Reconsidered*, edited by Bamita Bagchi, 109–122. New Delhi: SAGE Publications India.

Morris, Michael. 2018. "The Problem of Slavery in the Age of Improvement. David Dale, Robert Owen and the New Lanark Cotton". In *Cultures of Improvement in Scottish Romanticism, 1707–1840*, edited by Alex Benchimol and Gerard Lee McKeever, 111–131. New York: Routledge.

Moses, Claire G. 1982. "Saint-Simonian Men/Saint-Simonian Women: The Transformation of Feminist Thought in 1830s France". *Journal of Modern History* 54 (2): 240–267.

Navickas, Katrina. 2016. *Protest and the Politics of Space and Place 1789–1848*. Manchester: Manchester University Press.

Nyland, Chris, and Tom Heenan. 2003. "William Thompson and Anna Doyle Wheeler: A Marriage of Minds on Jeremy Bentham's Doorstep". In *The Status of Women in Classical Economic Thought*, edited by Chris Nyland and R.W. Dimand, 241–260. Cheltenham: Elgar.

O'Brien, Patrick K., and Roland Quinault. 1993. *The Industrial Revolution and British Society*. Cambridge: Cambridge University Press.

O'Hagan, Francis J. 2011. "Robert Owen and Education". In *Robert Owen and His Legacy*, edited by Chris Williams and Noel Thompson, 71–90. Cardiff: University of Wales Press.

Oliver, W.H. 1971. "Owen in 1817: The Millennialist Moment". In *Robert Owen, Prophet of the Poor. Essays in the Honour of the Two Hundredth Anniversary of His Birth*, edited by Sidney Pollard and John Salt, 166–187. London: Palgrave Macmillan.

Pankhurst, Richard. 1954. *William Thompson (1775–1833): Britain's Pioneer Socialist, Feminist and Co-Operator*. London: Watts & Co.

Parssinen, T.M., and Iorwerth Prothero. 1977. "The London Tailors' Strike and the Collapse of the Grand National Consolidated Trades' Union: A Police Spy's Report". *International Review of Social History* 22 (1): 65–107.

BIBLIOGRAPHY

Pilbeam, Pamela. 2013. *Saint-Simonians in Nineteenth-Century France. From Free Love to Algeria*. London: Palgrave Macmillan.

Pitzer, Donald E. 1997. "The New Moral World of Robert Owen and New Harmony". In *America's Communal Utopias*, edited by Donald E. Pitzer, 88–134. Charlotte: University of North Carolina Press.

Podmore, Frank. 1906. *Robert Owen. A Biography*. London: Allen & Unwin.

Polanyi, Karl. 1944. *Origins of Our Time. The Great Transformation*. New York: Farrar & Rinehart.

———. 1957. "The Machine and the Discovery of Society". Unpublished lecture. Karl Polanyi Papers. New York: Columbia University Library.

Pollard, Sidney. 1967. "Nineteenth-Century Co-Operation: From Community Building to Shopkeeping". In *Essays in Labour History*, edited by Asa Briggs and John Saville, 74–112. London: Macmillan.

Pollard, Sidney, and John Salt, eds. 1971. *Robert Owen, Prophet of the Poor: Essays in the Honour of the Two Hundredth Anniversary of His Birth*. London: Macmillan.

Poynter, John Riddoch. 1969. *Society and Pauperism: English Ideas on Poor Relief*. London: Routledge & Kegan Paul.

Prothero, Iorwerth. 1979. *Artisans and Politics in Early Nineteenth-Century London: John Gast and His Times*. London: Methuen.

Prum, Michel. 1993. "Capital Pre-Visited". *History of Economics Review* 19: 55–71.

———. 1994. "Skill Defended: Le concept de qualification chez Thomas Hodgskin". *Nouveaux Cahiers d'encrage*, May, 1–8.

———. 2012. "Hodgskin, Thomas". In *Le Maitron: dictionnaire biographique du mouvement ouvrier et du mouvement social*. Paris: Éditions sociales.

Purvis, Martin. 1987. "Nineteenth-Century Co-Operative Retailing in England and Wales: A Geographical Approach". DPhil, St. John's College: Oxford University.

Ricœur, Paul. 1985. *Lectures on Ideology and Utopia*, edited and translated by George H. Taylor. New York: Columbia University Press.

Rilliet, Jean, and Jean Cassaigneau. 1995. *Marc-Auguste Pictet ou le rendez-vous de l'Europe universelle, 1752–1825*. Geneva: Slatkine.

Robertson, A.J. 1969. "Robert Owen and the Campbell Debt 1810–1822". *Business History* 11: 23–30.

Rose, R.B. 1958. "John Finch, 1784–1857: A Liverpool Disciple of Robert Owen". *Transactions of the Historic Society of Lancashire and Cheshire* 109: 159–184.

Royle, Edward. 1974. *Victorian Infidels: The Origins of the British Secularist Movement, 1791–1866*. Manchester: Manchester University Press.

———, ed. 1976. *The Infidel Tradition. From Paine to Bradlaugh*. Basingstoke: Macmillan.

———. 1998. *Robert Owen and the Commencement of the Millennium: The Harmony Community at Queenwood Farm, 1839–1845*. Manchester: Manchester University Press.

Schlereth, Thomas. 1977. *The Cosmopolitan Ideal in Enlightenment Thought. Its Form and Function in the Ideas of Franklin, Hume, and Voltaire, 1694–1790*. Notre Dame: University of Notre Dame Press.

Schwartz, Laura. 2013. *Infidel Feminism: Secularism, Religion and Women's Emancipation, England 1830–1914*. Manchester: Manchester University Press.

Seed, John. 1982. "Unitarianism, Political Economy and the Antinomies of Liberal Culture in Manchester, 1830–50". *Social History* 7 (1): 1–25.

Silver, Harold. 1965. *The Concept of Popular Education*. London: McGibbon & Kee.

BIBLIOGRAPHY

Siméon, Ophélie. 2013. "De l'usine à l'utopie: New Lanark 1785–1825. Histoire d'un village ouvrier 'modèle'". PhD, Department of British Studies: University of Lyon.

———. 2014. "Entre 'Utopie' et 'Père du socialisme': Réceptions de Robert Owen en Grande-Bretagne". *Lien Social et Politiques* 72 (Autumn): 19–37.

———. 2017. *Robert Owen's Experiment at New Lanark. From Paternalism to Socialism*. London: Palgrave Macmillan.

———. 2018. "The Grand National Consolidated Trades' Union, 1833–34: Class and Conflict in the Early British Labour Movement". In *Labour United and Divided from the 1830s to the Present*, edited by Emmanuelle Avril and Yann Béliard, 21–32. Manchester: Manchester University Press.

———. 2020. "'Goddess of Reason': Anna Doyle Wheeler, Owenism and the Rights of Women". *History of European Ideas*.

Sraffa, Piero, ed. 1952. *The Works and Correspondence of David Ricardo*. Vol. 8, Letters 1819–June 1821. Cambridge: Cambridge University Press.

Stack, David. 1998. *Nature and Artifice: The Life and Thought of Thomas Hodgskin (1787–1869)*. London: Royal Historical Society.

Stenhouse, John. 2005. "Imperialism, Atheism and Race: Charles Southwell, Old Corruption, and the Maori". *Journal of British Studies* 44 (4): 754–774.

Stowitzky, Renee M. 2004. "Searching for Freedom through Utopia: Revisiting Frances Wright's Nashoba". History Thesis, Nashville: Vanderbilt University.

Taylor, Barbara. 1983. *Eve and the New Jerusalem: Socialism and Feminism in the Nineteenth Century*. London: Virago.

Thomas, Wynn. 2007. *A Bibliography of Robert Owen, 1771–1858*. Aberystwyth: National Library of Wales.

Thompson, E.P. 1963. *The Making of the English Working Class*. London: Victor Gollancz.

Thompson, Noel. 1984. *The People's Science. The Popular Political Economy of Exploitation and Crisis 1816–34*. Cambridge: Cambridge University Press.

———. 1988. *The Market and Its Critics. Socialist Political Economy in Nineteenth-Century Britain*. London: Routledge.

Timmons, Wilbert H. 1949. "Robert Owen's Texas Project". *The Southwestern Historical Quarterly* 52 (3): 286–293.

Tsuzuki, Chushichi. 1971. "Robert Owen and Revolutionary Politics". In *Robert Owen, Prophet of the Poor: Essays in the Honour of the Two Hundredth Anniversary of His Birth*, edited by Sidney Pollard and John Salt, 13–38. London: Palgrave Macmillan.

Tuck, Patrick N.J., ed. 1998. *The East India Company: 1600-1858*. London: Taylor & Francis.

Volwiler, Albert Tangeman. 1922. "Robert Owen and the Congress of Aix-La-Chapelle". *The Scottish Historical Review* 19 (74): 96–105.

Wardlaugh, Benjamin, ed. 2012. *A Wealth of Numbers. An Anthology of 500 Years of Popular Writing on Mathematics*. Princeton: Princeton University Press.

Weaver, S.A. 1987. *John Fielden and the Politics of Popular Radicalism, 1832–1847*. Oxford: Clarendon Press.

Weisser, Henry. 1975. *British Working Class Movements and Europe, 1815–48*. Manchester: Manchester University Press.

Whitbread, Nanette. 1972. *The Evolution of the Nursery-Infant School: A History of Infant and Nursery Education in Britain, 1800–1970*. London: Routledge.

Whitfield, Roy. 1988. *Frederick Engels in Manchester: The Search for a Shadow*. Manchester: Working Class Movement Library.

Yeo, Eileen. 1971. "Robert Owen and Radical Culture". In *Robert Owen, Prophet of the Poor: Essays in the Honour of the Two Hundredth Anniversary of His Birth*, edited by Sidney Pollard and John Salt, 84–114. London: Macmillan.